Stories OF Faith
AND Courage from
# THE REVOLUTIONARY WAR

# Battlefields
## *&*
# BLESSINGS

Stories OF Faith
AND **Courage from**

# THE REVOLUTIONARY WAR

# Battlefields

# BLESSINGS

## JANE HAMPTON COOK

LIVING
INK
BOOKS
*Writing Worth Reading*

**Battlefields and Blessings: Stories of Faith and Courage from the Revolutionary War**
Copyright © 2007 by Jane Hampton Cook
Published by Living Ink Books, an imprint of AMG Publishers
6815 Shallowford Rd.
Chattanooga, Tennessee 37421

Unless otherwise indicated, all Scripture quotations are taken from the Holy Bible, New International Version®. NIV®. Copyright ©1973, 1978, 1984 by International Bible Society. Used by permission of Zondervan Publishing House. All rights reserved.

All Scripture marked KJV are taken from the Holy Bible, King James Version, which is in the public domain.

Published in association with the literary agency of Nashville Agency, PO Box 110909, Nashville, TN 37222

ISBN 13: 978-089957042-6
ISBN 10: 0-89957-042-9

First printing—August 2007

Cover designed by Meyers Design, Houston, Texas
Interior design and typesetting by Reider Publishing Services,
    West Hollywood, California
Edited and Proofread by Rich Cairnes, Dan Penwell, Sharon Neal,
    and Rick Steele

Printed in Canada
13 12 11 10 09 08 07 –T– 7 6 5 4 3 2 1

# DEDICATION

In memory of U.S. Army Captain Shane Mahaffee, who in May 2006 surrendered his life in service to his country and the cause of freedom in Iraq.

And to my family: My husband, John Kim Cook
My sons, Austin and Zachary
My father, Larry Hampton
My brother, Steve Hampton

And to my nephews:

Jason
Jeffrey
Joel
Andrew
Samuel
Timothy
Joshua
Daniel

# CONTENTS

# CONTENTS

# CONTENTS

# CONTENTS

# CONTENTS

# CONTENTS

# CONTENTS

CONTENTS

# CONTENTS

# CONTENTS

# CONTENTS

# ACKNOWLEDGMENTS

HISTORY PROVIDES hindsight. Before writing this book, I didn't realize how many miracles molded America's quest for independence. One leading character stood out as I researched these stories from the Revolutionary War. He continued to show his hand over and over again in the preservation of the army, the personal lives of the patriots, and the rise of the United States. Many colonists called him Providence. They also saluted him as Captain and called on him as Lord. I want to thank God for the opportunity to write this book and for showing his marvelous deeds among history's pages, both in America's story and in Scripture.

I also want to thank my family, particularly my husband, Dr. John Kim Cook, who patiently listened for nine months as I talked about my double labor pains: my work on this book and pregnancy. About the time I began writing *Battlefields and Blessings: Stories of Faith and Courage from the Revolutionary War*, I found out I was expecting my second child. Six months into both incubations, I went into preterm labor with my son, which landed me on bed rest. Going from seventy-five miles an hour to zero in less than a minute usually means you have crashed a car. The result in this case, however, was the opportunity to delay my son's premature arrival through God's miracle of medicine. Thanks belongs to my doctors— Glen Silas, Anne Dobrzynski, David Berry, John Maddox, and my retired doctor, Melinda Kelly—for your healing hands and wise decision making during my high-risk pregnancy.

In between occasional contractions, bed rest allowed me to complete this book while also receiving the blessing of service from those who pitched in to help. I want to specifically thank my nephew, Joel Parker, who flew from Texas to Virginia to take care of my two-year-old son. I also want to thank my many friends from McLean Bible Church, Mothers of Preschoolers at Immanuel Bible Church, and others who provided meals, brought groceries, and gave us much-needed support. Thanks as well to friends Ben and Ashley Cannatti, whose loan of a laptop allowed me to finish this book while my computer was being repaired and I worked from bed. My gratitude also belongs to my parents, Larry and Judy Hampton, whose hearts were with me during bed rest even though their hands could not be.

# ACKNOWLEDGMENTS

Thank you to those of you who shared your stories with me: John and Heather Anderson, Betty Bryant, Mark Bryant, Justin Grove, Jennifer Massengale, Brad Randall, Bonnie and Vic Reid, and Ralph Weitz. Thank you as well to historians David Barton and Mary Thompson and author Joel Rosenberg for inspiring me with your writings.

I especially want to thank Dan Penwell and the hardworking folks at AMG Publishers for making this book and series possible. Your love for books and hearts for service are a blessing to authors, readers, and the industry. I also want to thank Jonathan Clements and the Nashville Agency for your professionalism and personal approach to business. Both have inspired me throughout the years as an author and speaker. Also, a special thank-you to Rich Cairnes who worked beyond the call of duty in researching and questioning me as he edited my manuscript. And a word of warm appreciation for Sharon Neal, the ultimate professional when it comes to proofreading. Thank you also to Rick Steele for his eye for detail and his prepress prowess. And thank you, as well, to Michele Buc, whose eye for the market and media has motivated me to try new things.

And thank you for reading this book. May *Battlefields and Blessings: Stories of Faith and Courage from the Revolutionary War* bless you.

# INTRODUCTION

WELCOME TO America's quest for independence. I hope these stories of courage and faith will fire up your patriotism and ignite your soul. The Revolution, however, was more than just a war. It was a turning of hearts and minds. Although this book takes you from the starting point to the finishing line in the overall race for independence, it also reveals the individual stories behind the Revolution. The people who lived through this difficult time faced choices and challenges that honed their characters and shaped their view of each other and of God. Their stories are as fascinating as the war itself. To keep their thoughts authentic, the book incorporates their original spellings from their written correspondence. To make the text flow more easily and without distractions, the term *sic* was not used after each misspelling.

Sprinkled throughout this book, usually once in each week, are two features: "Sabbath Rest" and "The Revolution Today." Because the Hebrew word *shabbath* means "to rest from labor," "Sabbath Rest" provides a time to rest and take a break from the story of the war, and to discover a preacher, his perspective, and a sermon from the era. The issues people of faith struggled with during the Revolution are often similar to modern-day struggles of the meaning of life, the desire for integrity in leadership, and the hope for peace from war. "The Revolution Today" highlights an idea, such as contentment, that is just as real today as it was back then. Fashion changes. Technology changes. Communication improves. The human heart, however, will always wrestle with despair, discouragement, and dishonesty while seeking to embrace peace, joy, and love. Micro-changes of the heart, mind, and soul continue the Revolution today.

These short stories and devotions are designed for the time-deprived modern-day reader. You can read them however you choose, as a daily dose of inspiration, an insightful weekly read, or a cover-to-cover download. You can start on January 1st or anytime during the year. If you enjoy daily readings, you may want to start on a Sunday or Saturday—whenever you take time for rest and worship. Regardless, I hope you enjoy the Revolution, one page-turn at a time.

Jane Hampton Cook

# 1. Prologue: What Is a Revolution?

What is a revolution?

Is it a year, the earth's 365-day orbital jig around the sun? Every time it passes through four seasons, the earth comes back altered, aged—changed. Is a revolution a day? Can a revolution take place with a simple rotation? Ancient astronomers considered a rotation a revolution. Each time the earth rotates on its axis it makes a mini-revolution.

The *Random House Unabridged Dictionary* defines revolution as "a sudden, complete or marked change in something." Whether you measure a revolution by a day or a year, something happens during a revolution—a revolution means change.

One of the America's most esteemed patriots asked a similar question. *"What do we mean by the American Revolution? Do we mean the American war?"* John Adams asked in a letter to a friend nearly forty years after the war's final shot was fired.

Adams knew the answer. He was an eyewitness to it. He understood that the American Revolution was not merely overthrowing the king's government by force. The American Revolution began long before the first musket flared. *"The Revolution was in the minds and hearts of the people; a change in their religious sentiments, of their duties and obligations,"* Adams explained.

The American Revolution was not simply a war. It was a transformation of the colonists' hearts and souls. For a few, the change was instant, a twenty-four-hour transformation. For most, the change came more slowly, after a longtime wrestling in their hearts over their allegiances, beliefs, and capabilities. Those who couldn't change their allegiance emigrated to England. But those who could change were forever transformed.

*"This radical change in the principles, opinions, sentiments, and affections of the people was the real American Revolution,"* Adams wrote.

To skeptics this radical change was merely a rebellion. Those who would rebel against one government would always rebel, no matter who was in charge. But to true believers, this was not a *rebellion*. It was a *revolution*, one that would transform a monarchy into a republic, colonies into states, Englishmen and Englishwomen into American patriots. A nation ruled by a king emerged as a nation governed by a constitution of the people.

"Generations come and generations go, but the earth remains forever. The sun rises and the sun sets, and hurries back to where it rises" (ECCLESIASTES 1:4, 5).

What does revolution mean to you? Perhaps it's a sudden change. Maybe it's a simple but noticeable change. Perhaps it's a more complete change, an obvious overthrow. As you discover the stories, sparks, and spirit of the American Revolution in this book, perhaps they will ignite a revolution in your heart, one that inspires your patriotism and nurtures your soul, one rotation at a time.[1]

**PRAYER**

*God, revolutionize my heart as you desire, one day at a time.*

## 2. Angels Watching Over Me

The news was false. He was not dead.

"*Dear Jack,*" he began his urgent letter, dated July 18, 1755, to his brother.

Fatigue swept over this English soldier, but rumors of his death drove him to write no matter how weary his hand or heavy his heart. Explaining the truth was the only way to prevent the smoke of misinformation from needlessly suffocating his family.

"*I take this early opportunity of contradicting both [my death and final words] and of assuring you that I now exist and appear in the land of the living by the miraculous care of Providence, that protected me beyond all human expectation,*" he explained.

After the indescribable battle in the Ohio Valley, this young colonel fell into the warm embrace of Maryland's Fort Cumberland. The terror he had just experienced plagued him worse than any nightmare. He couldn't shake the sight of his bullet-pierced coat. "*I had 4 Bullets through my Coat, and two Horses shot under me, and yet escaped unhurt,*" he recounted to Jack of how Providence had protected him.

Although he felt no physical injuries, the battle left his heart wounded. This new war was partially his responsibility. His earlier expedition for the British had resulted in the death of a French diplomat. The incident caused England's problems with the French and Indians to escalate faster than a ship could carry British soldiers to the American colonies. When the war came, he dutifully joined General Edward Braddock and his Virginia regiment. Their mission was to protect America's boundaries against the trespassing French and Indians in the Ohio Valley. But they failed.

*"We have been most scandalously beaten by a trifling body of men; but fatigue and want of time prevents me from giving any of the details till I have the happiness of seeing you at home; which I now most ardently wish for,"* he penned, knowing he would need a few days to regain his strength before traveling again.

Fort Cumberland's position along the Potomac River likely reminded him of another estate, a place he considered home. Located one hundred and fifty miles down the same river in Virginia was the house and farm of his deceased brother Lawrence. He had no idea how important that place would one day become to him.

*"I may thereby be enabled to proceed homewards with more ease; You may expect to see me there on Saturday or Sunday,"* he wrote.

*"I am Dr. Jack, y'r most Affect. Broth'r."*

And with that, twenty-two-year-old George Washington closed his letter. The awe of Providence's protection had sparked something inside him. Why had he survived? What was the meaning behind the four bullet holes in his coat and the horses shot from under him? While he recovered, he reveled in the mystery and meaning behind the miracle, evidence of the fingerprints of angels.[2]

> "The angel of the LORD encamps around those who fear him, and he delivers them" (PSALM 34:7).

**PRAYER**

*Lord, be my shield and protector. May I live today knowing you have given my life purpose and meaning.*

## 3. Let Down

Panic. They had panicked.

Not only was George Washington shocked over his own miraculous preservation after General Braddock's defeat, but he was also disappointed in the British regular soldiers who fought alongside him. Washington couldn't have felt more let down had his fellow soldiers committed treason.

*"We were attacked by a party of French and Indians, whose number, I am persuaded, did not exceed three hundred men; while ours consisted of about one thousand three hundred well-armed troops, chiefly regular soldiers, who were struck with such a panic that they behaved with more cowardice than it is possible to conceive,"* Washington related to his mother shortly after the battle.

The failure and flight of the regular British fighters was a sight he would never forget. *"In short, the dastardly behavior of those they call regulars exposed all others . . . they ran, as sheep pursued by dogs, and it was impossible to rally them,"* he wrote.

The warfare Washington had witnessed was far from the traditional forms of fighting practiced by regular British soldiers and their American militia. Braddock's European-style firing lines were no match for the French and Indians' tactics of shooting from behind trees.

In his letter to his mother, Washington explained his role in the battle: When General Braddock fell mortally wounded on the field, Washington had stepped up to direct the retreat. *"I was the only person then left to distribute the General's orders, which I was scarcely able to do, as I was not half recovered from a violent illness, that had confined me to my bed and a wagon for above ten days,"* he wrote, noting only thirty in Virginia's regiment survived.

Washington's statement revealed that he questioned his own leadership abilities. Could he have done more? But he was angrier at the behavior of his fellow Englishmen. He may not have been sure which was more revealing, the failure of the British regulars to fight or the successful surprise tactics of the enemy. Both were lessons he would not forget.

Although Washington was discouraged, others were encouraged. News of his bravery spread throughout the colonies and to England as well. The Reverend Samuel Davies spoke about Washington in a sermon he gave a month after Braddock's defeat. *"As a remarkable instance of this, I may point out to the public that heroic youth, Colonel Washington, whom I cannot but hope Providence has hitherto preserved in so signal a manner for some important service to his country,"* Davies proclaimed prophetically.

Like many great sermons of the era, Davies' message was published and distributed in a pamphlet in America and in England. Through Davies, many heard of the miraculous preservation of young Washington.

George Washington may have been down when he wrote his mother that day in 1755, but he was not out. His life had purpose. He had hope.[3]

> "Contend, O LORD, with those who contend with me; fight against those who fight against me" (PSALM 35:1).

*Grant me courage to persevere when I am down. Be my Strength when I am weak, fight against those who contend with me.*

# 4. There's Something about George . . .

There's something about George, James, the second Earl Waldegrave, may have thought as he began his memoirs one day in 1758.

James, once a prime minister of England, probably hesitated to put his concerns into writing. But something in his princely pupil's behavior perturbed him. Perhaps writing about it would clarify what it was about Prince George that bothered him.

"The Prince of Wales is entering into his twenty-first year, and it would be unfair to decide upon his character in the early stages of life, when there is so much time for improvement. His parts, though not excellent, will be found very tolerable, if ever they are properly exercised," James began.

And while George's character was tolerable, neither good nor bad, James doubted his protégé had the motivation to attempt greatness. He knew the next king of England would need to soar above mediocrity to end wars and make peace.

James may have stopped writing at that moment to reflect. He had treasured his friendship with George's grandfather, King George II, and respected him. James also knew the workings of the British government. When the king asked him to be the governor of his grandson George III, James dutifully accepted the mentoring assignment.

*Perhaps I should reflect on the prince's good points,* James may have thought as he penned the next line. *"He is strictly honest, but wants that frank and open behaviour which makes honesty appear amiable."*

James thought about young George's handling of money, which was inferior to his grandfather's business savvy. *"It was one of his favorite maxims that men should be just before they are generous: his income is now very considerably augmented, but his generosity has not increased in equal proportion,"* wrote James.

James probably put down his pen in frustration. The truth was harder to chew than month-old bread. Unless something changed, George's character would not make him a great king. The reason? George lacked the motivation to improve.

The mathematics of the situation was also troubling. George's father was dead, and his grandfather the king was seventy-five. It wouldn't be long before this uninspiring young man would become King George III. The thought of George the Mediocre as king was a constant source of concern.

> "By justice a king gives a country stability, but one who is greedy for bribes tears it down"
> (PROVERBS 29:4).

The words and tune of a new song, introduced to the court a few years earlier, may have surfaced in the mind of James, the second Earl Waldegrave, at that moment: *God Save the King.*

Indeed. God save us, everyone.⁴

**PRAYER**

*Father, examine my heart today. Remove any mediocrity that prohibits me from seeing and understanding you and the areas you want to change in my life.*

# 5. The Pigheaded Pupil

Certain human qualities sour the soul. When James, the second Earl Waldegrave, penned his analysis of his pupil, Prince George, in 1758, he described one of those costly characteristics.

"*He has spirit, but not of the active kind; and does not want resolution, but it is mixed with too much obstinacy,*" observed James. "*His religion is free from all hypocrisy, but is not of the most charitable sort; he has rather too much attention to the sins of his neighbor.*"

James knew the truth. Twenty-one-year-old George was pigheaded. He could smell the muck on those around him but couldn't detect when he needed to bathe in his own royal tub. Not only did James view George's stubbornness as a problem, but he also thought the prince lacked the temperament to overcome his obstinacy.

"*He has a kind of unhappiness in his temper, which, if it be not conquered before it has taken too deep a root, will be a source of frequent anxiety,*" fretted James. "*Whenever he is displeased, his anger does not break out with heat and violence; but he becomes sullen and silent, and retires to his closet; not to compose his mind by study or contemplation, but merely to indulge the melancholy enjoyment of his own ill humor.*"

Humility is one way to overcome pigheadedness. Unfortunately, George often looked inward, but only to sulk. When someone angered him, he went into his chamber in the castle, closed the door, and pouted. Rarely did a change in attitude emerge at the same time the prince did.

James turned to an old remedy for his pigheaded pupil. He hoped time would salvage George's character and remove his stubbornness before he became king. *"Though I have mentioned his good and bad qualities, without flattery, and without aggravation, allowances should still be made, on account of his youth, and his bad education,"* he wrote, chiding the nursery nannies who had spoiled young George.

*"During the course of the last year, there has, indeed, been some alteration . . . But whether this change will be greatly to his Royal Highness's advantage, is a nice question, which cannot hitherto be determined with any certainty,"* he concluded.

Perhaps James hoped a few more years would be enough time to prepare George for kingship. However, two years after his analysis, King George II died and Prince George became King George III. Time would do more to prove James, the second Earl Waldegrave, a political prophet than to improve George's pigheadedness.[5]

> "A man who remains stiff-necked after many rebukes will suddenly be destroyed— without remedy" (PROVERBS 29:1).

**PRAYER**

*Oh, Lord, help me listen to your voice. Allow humility to replace stubbornness in my heart.*

# 6. Two Georges, Two Hats

Both wore wigs. Both bore tails on their coats. Both wore riding boots. Such was the wardrobe of the two most influential men of the 1700s. The colonial George Washington was only six years older than his king, George III. Because both were raised to be English gentlemen, they were quite similar. Yet they emerged as far apart in sentiment as their birthplaces were in physical distance.

The difference was as simple as their headwear. One wore a tricorn, a three-sided farmer's hat. The other inherited a crown. And on the day of his coronation, King George III lost a diamond from that crown.

The ceremony was awkward from the start. After the bishop placed the crown on George's head, the king asked if he could place it on the altar as a gesture to the Almighty. The bishops agreed hesitantly, not because they objected to such a display of piety but because the move was a break with tradition. After placing his crown on the altar, George turned to his wife, Charlotte, and asked her to do the same thing. Her tiara, however, was stuck so firmly to her head that she could not remove it without much embarrassment to her vanity. He did not press the issue. At the end of the ceremony, with the new monarch's crown returned to his head, King George III and Queen Charlotte departed as regally as they had arrived.

*"On the return of the procession, an incident occurred, which, had it happened among the nations of antiquity, would have been considered an omen of evil portent, which could only have been averted by a whole hecatomb of sacrifices,"* British historian E. H. Nolan recorded. *"The most valuable diamond in his majesty's diadem fell from it, and was for some time lost, but it was afterwards found, and restored to his crown."*

It was not a sign of a moral lapse. *"From the beginning to the close of his long reign, George III manifested a decent, moral, and religious life, which doubtless had very beneficial effects upon society at large,"* Nolan wrote. *"One of the first acts of George III was a proclamation 'for the encouragement of piety and virtue, and for preventing and punishing of vice, profaneness, and immorality.'"*

The loss of the diamond indicated the trouble with royalty. Few hats come with such valuable jewels as a crown. Few jobs come with such distractions and temptations for pride and power as kingships. Leaders lose their focus when they hold on too tightly to their acquisitions. Whether in the form of a cap or a crown, the garland of wisdom is the most splendid piece of headgear. Perhaps it was wisdom and justice, not a diamond that King George III lost that day.[6]

> "Wisdom is supreme; therefore get wisdom. Though it cost all you have, get understanding. Esteem her, and she will exalt you; embrace her, and she will honor you. She will set a garland of grace on your head and present you with a crown of splendor" (PROVERBS 4:7–9).

**PRAYER**

*Set a garland of grace on my head and let wisdom rule my decision making today.*

# 7. The Revolution Today: Banner

On June 5, 1738, the day after the birth of King George III, Boston held a celebration, complete with unfurling banners. But the parade was not for the infant prince. The colonists would not learn the news of their future king's birth for several more weeks. Instead Bostonians celebrated the 100th anniversary of Boston's Ancient and Honorable Artillery

Company. Think about it. Something was old enough in the colonies in 1738 to celebrate a "centennial."

Lacking a military force, the early colonists organized an artillery company for their protection. The company received its charter in 1638 from the British governor. Each year since then, the Ancient and Honorable Artillery Company celebrates its beginnings with flags leading the way.

On the first Monday of June, members hold an election for their officers and sergeants. They celebrate with a parade that connects the past with the present. First they march from the Government Center to the Granary Burial Ground on Tremont Street to lay a wreath at the original commander's gravesite. Then they hold a memorial service for recently deceased members at the Cathedral Church of St. Paul on Tremont Street. The company reconvenes and concludes their parade by marching to Boston Common, where they collect the ballots and place them on the drumhead in front of the company, a reenactment of the first election in 1638. Four presidents have participated as company members over the years: James Monroe, Chester Arthur, Calvin Coolidge, and John F. Kennedy.

What is remarkable is that this ceremony has continued uninterrupted since it began. Nothing, not even the chaos of war, has stopped it. What has changed, however, are the colors, the banners. The original colonists hailed the British flag. But the Revolution would force them to question their allegiance. They would soon have to decide which banner they would salute.

Perhaps it was fitting, then, that on the 100th anniversary of the Ancient and Honorable Artillery Company, the Reverend Benjamin Colman preached on the everlasting banner, the one that transcends generations and spans continents.

*"And in that day there shall be a root of Jesse, which shall stand for an ensign of the people; to it shall the Gentiles seek: and his rest shall be glorious,"* the reverend read, quoting Isaiah 11:10 from the *King James Version* of the Bible.

> "In that day the Root of Jesse will stand as a banner for the peoples; the nations will rally to him, and his place of rest will be glorious" (ISAIAH 11:10).

Colman called on this group tasked with protecting Boston to turn to the Almighty as their protector and defender. *"He is our King and shall save us. His name is Jehovah-nissi, the 'Lord our Banner'!"* he proclaimed.

Colman understood that banners are symbols of allegiance, colors of protection no matter the century.[7]

**PRAYER**

*You are* Jehovah-nissi, *the Lord my banner. You are my true colors. I turn to you for salvation and protection.*

# 8. Sabbath Rest:
# A Not-So-Divine Sermon

The choice this pastor made was about as acceptable in the 1750s as women wearing pants.

Thirty-year-old Jonathan Mayhew, pastor of Boston's West Church, took a risk on January 30, 1750. The Church of England required ministers in both England and her American colonies to preach a constructive sermon on the 100th anniversary of the death of King Charles I. But instead of praising this dead king, Mayhew decided to preach against him.

King Charles I had believed in the "divine right of kings." As king he thought he was near deity, an extension of God. Not only that, he also had imposed his brand of religion on all of England. Charles I disbanded Parliament, stifled Puritans, and imposed taxes. The people fought back by trying and executing him in 1650 and replacing him with Oliver Cromwell. When Cromwell's term ended, the English reinstated the monarchy. King Charles II made his father's death a sacred holiday.

But Mayhew believed this "divine king" was far from a martyr. Charles I was closer to being a tyrant than a tiger is to its stripes.

The irony galled Mayhew. For years, ministers had been forced to infuse politics into their sermons by preaching an anniversary message heralding Charles I.

"*Tyranny brings ignorance and brutality with it. It degrades men from their just rank into the class of brutes; it damps their spirits,*" Mayhew wrote of this ecclesiastical tyranny, "*the most cruel, intolerable, and impious of any.*"

Mayhew knew his decision to mix colonial politics with religion from his Boston pulpit might be controversial to both the bishops and his congregation. He made it clear, however, he was not "*preaching politics, instead of Christ.*" He defended his decision by citing 2 Timothy 3:16, "*All scripture . . . is profitable for doctrine, for reproof, for correction, for instruction in righteousness*" (KJV).

"*Why, then, should not those parts of Scripture which relate to civil government be examined and explained from the desk, as well as others?*

*Obedience to the civil magistrate is a Christian duty,"* Mayhew told his parishioners.

Mayhew believed government was a moral and religious issue. After all, if private persons were required to yield to authority, then he could preach against tyranny from the pulpit.

> "He has made everything beautiful in its time. He has also set eternity in the hearts of men; yet they cannot fathom what God has done from beginning to end" (ECCLESIASTES 3:11).

This change in sentiment sparked something inside him; a change that followed Mayhew the rest of his life. Indeed, a similar revolution awaited his fellow colonists. And while Jonathan Mayhew began to preach radical ideas from the pulpit, another man left Boston to embrace the quiet life in Philadelphia.[8]

**PRAYER**

*Lord, thank you for reigning as the King of kings.*

# 9. Let Me Die Unlamented

Years before George III wore the king's crown and George Washington wore a soldier's hat, another man searched for just the right hat, one that would bring him contentment. *"Happy the man whose wish and care, a few paternal acres bound, content to breathe his native air, in his own ground,"* the poet wrote.

This man's philosophy of life was carefree. He believed time passed more easily when a man or woman found contentment in life's simple pleasures. *"Whose herds with milk, whose fields with bread, whose flocks supply him with attire, whose trees in summer yield him shade, in winter fire,"* he continued. *"In health of body, peace of mind, quiet by day, sound sleep by night; study and ease together mixt."*

All these, along with sweet recreation and meditation, were the poet's recipe for tranquility. This author exalted one of humanity's deepest desires—the pursuit of happiness. He believed the best reward for a quiet life was an even quieter death.

*"Thus let me live, unseen, unknown, thus unlamented let me die, steal from the world, and not a stone tell where I lie,"* he concluded.

Alexander Pope penned this poem. When this literary English giant died in 1744, another author paid him homage. The editor of America's best-selling almanac chose to print this poem as a eulogy to Pope. By omitting Pope's name and titling it "The Countryman," he gave Pope the gift of dying "unlamented," as he wished.

But the editor's connection to Pope was more than a mutual love of the smell of a book's binding or a whiff of ink from a freshly printed page. This man identified with Pope's desire for contentment. He also dreamed of living such a tranquil life that he could die *"unlamented"* with *"no stone to mark his grave."*

However, when this editor died decades later, he hardly left earth unnoticed. More than twenty thousand attended his funeral. Today, thousands throw pennies on his grave every year. The stone marking this "countryman's" life bears the name of Benjamin Franklin.

Franklin employed his pen and press to publish *Poor Richard's Almanac* from 1732 to 1758. Using the pseudonym of Richard Saunders, Franklin published pithy sayings, poetry (such as "The Countryman"), prose, weather predictions, a calendar, and other useful information. Franklin's almanac was second only to the Bible in many households for its authority on practical matters.

*Poor Richard's* sold ten thousand copies annually, which made Franklin an unparalleled celebrity. It was unclear who loved him more, the lords of London or his fellow American colonists.

Benjamin Franklin would have been content to die unlamented. Living a life of hard work mixed with good health was the perfect menu for his Quaker palate. But as sometimes happens in life, this countryman's country called him into a different pursuit. His purpose in life became not to die happy, but to live loudly for liberty.[9]

> "A man can do nothing better than to eat and drink and find satisfaction in his work. This too, I see, is from the hand of God, for without him, who can eat or find enjoyment?" (ECCLESIASTES 2:24, 25).

**PRAYER**

*Father, I thank you for the basics in life. Through you I can find satisfaction in my work and my recreation.*

# 10. Diligence

When the young Quaker businessman rolled his wheelbarrow through the streets of colonial Philadelphia in the 1730s, he hoped people would take notice. Benjamin Franklin wasn't merely showing off his wheels. He wanted his neighbors to observe his hands on the handles. They were symbols of something close to his heart: his diligence. After all, if people saw him working hard, then they might trust him with their business. Here's how Franklin described it:

*"To show that I was not above my business I sometimes brought home the paper I purchas'd at the stores thro' the streets on a wheelbarrow. Thus being esteem'd an industrious, thriving young man, and paying duly for what I bought, the merchants who imported stationery solicited my custom; others proposed supplying me with books, and I went on swimmingly,"* he reflected years later.

Franklin learned his diligent work ethic from his father, who frequently cited Proverbs 22:29 (KJV): "Seest thou a man diligent in his business? he shall stand before kings; he shall not stand before mean men."

Franklin took his father's philosophy to heart and turned it into a motto. *"I from thence considered industry as a means of obtaining wealth and distinction, which encourag'd me, tho' I did not think that I should ever literally stand before kings, which, however, has since happened; for I have stood before five, and even had the honor of sitting down with one, the King of Denmark, to dinner,"* Franklin wrote in his memoirs.

With his conscientious compass set, Franklin became a printmaker and a postmaster. In addition, this entrepreneur was always tinkering with new inventions. He was so mindful about paying off his debts, especially his printing house mortgage, he wore the wardrobe of a saver, not a spender. *"In order to secure my credit and character as a tradesman, I took care not only to be in reality industrious and frugal, but to avoid all appearances to the contrary. I drest plainly,"* he wrote.

Franklin also avoided any appearance of laziness. *"I was seen at no places of idle diversion. I never went out a fishing or shooting; a book, indeed, sometimes debauch'd me from my work, but that was seldom, snug, and gave no scandal,"* he jested.

His hard work and reading made him a renaissance man, accomplished in science, literature, business, politics, and diplomacy. Diligence was possibly Benjamin Franklin's strongest character trait throughout his eighty-four years. And while not every hardworking person meets five kings, diligence and conscientiousness are still valued today by the King of kings.[10]

> "Do you see a man skilled in his work? He will serve before kings; he will not serve before obscure men" (PROVERBS 22:29).

**PRAYER**

*Give me the strength today to work diligently as if for a king. And although my labor may not bring me recognition by others, help me take satisfaction in knowing that you value hard work.*

# 11. Thrift and Luxury

One morning meal took the frugal Franklin by surprise.

*"My breakfast was a long time bread and milk (no tea), and I ate it out of a two-penny earthen porringer, with a pewter spoon,"* Benjamin Franklin wrote of his humble dinnerware, a badge of his thrift. *"But mark how luxury will enter families, and make a progress, in spite of principle: being call'd one morning to breakfast, I found it in a China bowl, with a spoon of silver!"* he stated incredulously.

This luxurious upgrade in tableware shocked his fingers as much as any electricity he would ever feel from his kite string. If diligence dictated his business, frugality framed Franklin's home. Like many young couples, Benjamin and Deborah Franklin had started their life together on a meager income in 1730. But as his printing press and other businesses prospered, Franklin continued to live more like a pauper than a prince. One day his wife splurged by purchasing a china bowl and silver spoon for twenty-three shillings. She had no excuse, except she thought her husband deserved a silver spoon and china bowl after spending years of saving more pennies than he spent.

Frugality was as essential to Franklin's religion as paper was to his press. Quakers at that time often expelled members if their businesses went bankrupt or if they fell into debt. Franklin embraced tightly the value of economy. Thrift kept Franklin's pocketbook zipped.

*"We have an English proverb that says, 'He that would thrive, must ask his wife.' It was lucky for me that I had one as much dispos'd to industry and frugality as myself. She assisted me cheerfully in my business, folding and stitching pamphlets, tending shop, purchasing old linen rags for the paper-makers, etc., etc. We kept no idle servants, our table was plain and simple, our furniture of the cheapest,"* Franklin reflected.

Franklin shared his philosophy with the public. He often included pithy sayings about thrift and diligence in his annual almanac. *"When you are inclined to buy chinaware, chintzes, India silks, or any other of their flimsy, slight manufactures . . . all I advise is to put it off till another year, and this, in some respects, may prevent an occasion of repentance."*

Franklin believed frugality applied to both time and money. *"He that idly loses five shillings' worth of time loses five shillings, and might as prudently throw five shillings into the sea,"* he warned.

Franklin did not chase after money or time like the wind. He preferred to let his kite follow the wind in hopes of catching electricity. Benjamin

Franklin proved that industry and productivity are worth far more than material extravagances. He loved life more than money and thrift more than time.[11]

**PRAYER**

*May I find my contentment in you and not in my income. Keep me from the trap of thinking the money I have is never enough.*

> "Whoever loves money never has money enough; whoever loves wealth is never satisfied with his income. This too is meaningless" (ECCLESIASTES 5:10).

# 12. Franklin's Failure

Benjamin Franklin's plan failed. For perhaps the first time in his life, Franklin experienced an embarrassing public failure.

Representatives from seven of England's American colonies gathered in Albany, New York, in 1754. These delegates, however, brought with them more apathy than enthusiasm. The British government ordered these American colonists to meet. It was not their choice. The crown wanted them to unite against their common enemies and support the king's effort to win the war. The French and Indian War, known as the Seven Years' War in Europe, was the focal point of their discussions.

The Albany Congress was a one-time colonial version of the United Nations. The delegates thought of themselves as separate royal kingdoms. Although they all saluted the same king, their custom charters and constitutions made them as distinct as Spain was from Denmark. Their customs, manners, and modes of commerce gave them individuality. When the Albany Congress considered Franklin's Plan of Union, they saw little need to create a more united government among them. They were happy with the status quo.

*"IT IS proposed, that humble application be made for an act of Parliament of Great Britain, by virtue of which one general government may be formed in America,"* Franklin's plan began.

The plan was as simple as Franklin's tableware. Each colony would retain its individual constitution. The crown would choose a president-general, and the people would choose representatives for a grand council.

Franklin's plan was also quite Franklin—thriftiness and industry filled its pages. Representatives to the grand council would be allowed some wages *"lest the expense might deter some suitable persons from the service."* But the representatives would not earn *"too great wages, lest unsuitable persons should be tempted to cabal for the employment, for the sake of gain."*

Almost no one in either the colonies or England wanted to implement the plan. The Plan of Union was about as appealing as Dr. Franklin's urinary catheter invention.

Franklin decided the plan failed in the colonies because *"there was too much prerogative in it."* People were not ready to consider privileges and choices in a confederation of colonies. Franklin believed the plan failed in England because *"it was thought to have too much of the democratic."*

Franklin later conceded that the plan didn't satisfy him either, *"but it is [as good] as I could get it."*

The plan may have failed, but failure often produces future success. The Plan of Union presented in Albany planted a seed in the minds of

"You know, brothers, that our visit to you was not a failure" (1THESSALONIANS 2:1).

these disconnected colonies. It made them wonder what would happen if they formed a common government. They would one day reap the harvest of Benjamin Franklin's failure.[12]

**PRAYER**

*Thank you for your grace during life's failures and letdowns. And although they may not bear fruit today, may I learn in time the valuable lessons they may bring.*

# 13. Naked Truth

Benjamin Franklin revealed the naked truth in his almanac in 1744.

*"Courteous Reader,"* Franklin began the introduction to that year's issue of *Poor Richard's*. *"THIS is the Twelfth Year that I have in this Way laboured for the Benefit—of Whom? of the Publick, if you'll be so good-natured as to believe it,"* he wrote, possibly pausing before baring his soul. *"if not, e'en [then] take the naked Truth, 'twas for the Benefit of my own dear self,"* he added, perhaps with a cheeky grin.

Ever conscious of his reputation as a frugal Quaker and a diligent publisher, Franklin built his almanac readership through honesty and accuracy. He knew he provided the public with a service. His calendars and weather predictions were as precise as the bifocals he would one day invent. But he also valued his relationship with his readers, enough to admit the truth of his heart for business.

And so on that anniversary day in 1744, Franklin decided to have some fun in his introduction. He confessed his true intentions. The almanac was as much for him as it was for his audience. He admitted the almanac had brought him intellectual stimulation. It also bore him financial fruit. Such was Franklin's naked truth as an editor.

In that same publication, Franklin pointed out the folly and naked truth of one of his competitors, who carelessly predicted an eclipse that never took place. *"There is no manner of Truth in this Prediction,"* Franklin pointed out.

He then assured his readers he had not changed his ways or tried any wild new prediction processes. *"I have made no Alteration in my usual Method."*

Franklin closed his introduction with his usual warm greeting: *"I am, dear Reader, Thy obliged Friend."*

As often as the earth orbited the sun, Franklin sought to deliver an accurate and truthful almanac to his dear readers and friends, both in the colonies and England. His reputation resulted in many other successes. He was elected to the Pennsylvania Assembly and later appointed to the post of deputy postmaster of North America. His status and skills enabled him to write the Plan of Union.

Franklin's due diligence, thrift, and honesty also brought him more recognition by the king, who named Franklin as trade representative for the colonies. This post brought Franklin an opportunity more electrifying than his kite: a chance to move to London, which proved to be one of his favorite places.

> "Surely you desire truth in the inner parts; you teach me wisdom in the inmost place"
> (PSALM 51:6).

While Franklin enjoyed the fruit of his naked-truth approach to business in England, he had no idea just how much naked truth his friends in Boston would face in the next two decades. Their honest assessment would force Benjamin Franklin to make difficult choices about the truth of his loyalties in the years ahead.[13]

**PRAYER**

*Father, teach me your honesty and wisdom that I may see the naked truth in my life.*

## 14. The Revolution Today: A Blogger's Contentment

Benjamin Franklin would have been a great blogger.

If Franklin were alive today, there is no doubt he would be blogging. He would not be able to resist the ability to instantly express his opinion or post a new witty saying on the Internet through electronic commentaries or diaries known as blogs. Blogging would thrill a man with his writing ability and wit.

Franklin spent his building years doing just that, building his business and pursuing happiness. Franklin lived the American dream, and if he could have invented that idea, he would have. What drove him still drives us today: the pursuit for contentment, that desire to find meaning and happiness in life.

And just as Franklin took a moment to reflect on his life when he celebrated the twelfth anniversary of his almanac, so we often look at birthdays or anniversaries as moments to check our contentment scale.

"It's almost birthday time for me—42 years old—and as I was taking stock of my life, I couldn't help but compare myself with some of my Baylor [University] college roommates and the successes they've had," Brad Randall wrote on his blog.

This Dallas attorney then turned his attention to those college roommates as they pursued life, liberty, and happiness. "One such roommate is an official in the [George W.] Bush administration, married to an accomplished author. Another is a justice on the Texas Supreme Court—wow!! (though he might be praying each night that I've forgotten some things from those college days). Still another roommate, a native of Nigeria, is now a doctor who travels from his home in California each year at his own expense to provide free medical care to residents of his home village," Randall continued.

Comparisons are just that—comparisons. They often lead us to examine our own lives, but they aren't the leading markers on the contentment scale. External indicators often fall far short. Contentment comes from within.

"Successes all, for sure, and enough to make me wonder what I could have accomplished if I had chosen different paths. But hey, along with a job which I can tolerate and occasionally enjoy (and that pays the bills, kinda-sorta), I have a loving wife, two incredible boys, close family, and good friends. It's more than just 'being content where I am,' like the Apostle Paul. It's realizing that God is very good, and He has really blessed me. That's plenty of success for me," Randall concluded.

"I also picked some pretty awesome roommates," he added.

Just as the Revolutionary War began within the hearts of the colonists, so contentment begins with a heart focused on the things that truly matter in life.[14]

> "For we brought nothing into the world, and we can take nothing out of it. But if we have food and clothing, we will be content with that"
> (1 TIMOTHY 6:7, 8).

**PRAYER**

*God, I rest in you in this moment, in a posture of contentment. Naked you brought me in the world, and naked I will leave. Place the seed of contentment in me and allow it to blossom this week.*

# 15. Sabbath Rest: Commotions

K*ings and kingdoms are the most majestic sounds in the language of mortals,"* Samuel Davies began in a sermon to a congregation in Hanover County, Virginia, in 1756, *"and have filled the world with noise, confusions, and blood, since mankind first left the state of nature, and formed themselves into societies."* But as majestic as kings were, they were also a primary source of commotion.

A Delaware native, Davies had settled in Virginia to live as a circuit-riding preacher serving seven churches in five counties. As a result he knew men who had fought and died for King George II in General Edward Braddock's fatal battle. He saw the suffering of war from the tears of Virginians. The king's war with France and the Indians had struck Davies with tomahawk-like force. *"The disputes of kingdoms for superiority have set the world in arms from age to age, and destroyed or enslaved a considerable part of the human race,"* he lamented.

Davies questioned why war had come to the American colonies. *"Our country has been a region of peace and tranquility for a long time, but it has not been because the lust of power and riches is extinct in the world, but because we had no near neighbours, whose interest might clash with ours, or who were able to disturb us. The absence of an enemy was our sole defence,"* he told his listeners.

He concluded that the fading boundaries of colonization had drawn the lines of war. *"But now, when the colonies of the sundry European nations on this continent begin to enlarge, and approach towards each other, the scene is changed: now encroachments, depredations, barbarities, and all the terrors of war begin to surround and alarm us. Now our country is invaded and ravaged, and bleeds in a thousand veins,"* he continued.

And Davies, who would one day become the president of Princeton University, used his own testimony to comfort his congregation. *"These commotions and perturbations have had one good effect upon me, and that is, they have carried away my thoughts of late into a serene and peaceful region, a region beyond the reach of confusion and violence,"* he shared.

His was not a physical peace among the arrows of aggression. It was a determination of the mind, a strengthening of the spine. *"I mean the kingdom of the Prince of Peace. And thither, my brethren, I would also transport your minds this day, as the best refuge from this boisterous world, and the most agreeable mansion for the lovers of peace and tranquility,"* he said, painting a picture of heaven.

*"The kingdoms of Great-Britain, France, China, Persia, are but little spots of the globe,"* Davies concluded. *"Other kings have their soldiers; so all the legions of the elect angels, the armies of heaven, are the soldiers of Jesus Christ, and under his command."*

Samuel Davies found peace from the world's commotions in his faith.[15]

> "Jesus said, 'My kingdom is not of this world'" (JOHN 18:36).

**PRAYER**

*Thank you for the promise of eternity.*

# 16. The Passover

The news shocked James Otis. He couldn't believe it. The cap of contentment had fallen from his head. The new governor had appointed Thomas Hutchinson instead of James's father, Col. James Otis, as chief justice. For years the Otis family had expected the post to fall to Colonel Otis in the event of the presiding chief justice's death. The decision against his father shocked Otis's heart as if he had been struck by lightning.

*"Hasn't my family carried the banner of the crown? Aren't they among the most loyal subjects in Massachusetts?"* Such questions may have charged Otis's mind as he considered the impact of this bolt from the blue. Before the autumn of 1760, life had been especially good to thirty-five-year-old Otis. Not only was he the son of a prominent political figure, but he also had earned a reputation as one of the top attorneys in Massachusetts. He was second only to his law mentor, Jeremiah Gridley.

Otis was thrilled when his own loyalty and competency were rewarded in 1756. He received a promotion with a purse-bursting salary he couldn't refuse. Otis became advocate general in the vice admiralty court. This job allowed him to bring his gift of oratory to the courtroom's forefront. He filled his duties as chief prosecutor with devotion and passion, willingly prosecuting smugglers who evaded taxes supposed to be collected by the British customs officers.

But his father's failed promotion troubled him. *"Will I ever be able to make a case before Chief Justice Hutchinson without wondering how my father would have decided the case?"* he may have wondered a thousand times.

Otis knew the recent death of King George II would result in change. But he didn't expect the new court management to affect him so personally. It began when King George III appointed a new governor of Massachusetts. The previous governor had promised Otis's father the job of chief justice. The new governor had no loyalties or promises to keep to the Otis family.

Otis may have wondered if he would ever get over the bitterness he felt. Perhaps he would always think of his father in the courtroom, but he could only press on, hoping that one day he could make some sense of the disappointment.

Life's lightning strikes can have many effects. They leave some paralyzed. They polarize others. And they propel some to their knees before the Creator of the heavens and earth. Although we don't know for sure how this bolt affected James Otis's faith, we do know it fired a spark and ignited a flame of justice in his heart.[16]

> "Cast your cares on the LORD and he will sustain you; he will never let the righteous fall" (PSALM 55:22).

**PRAYER**

*Father, I thank you that you care about all my circumstances, including the ones beyond my control. Bring healing and understanding. May the seeds that have fallen in my life bring a great harvest.*

# 17. Resignation

Resign. That was his decision.

As soon as the customs officials left his office that winter day in 1761, James Otis knew what he had to do. He could no longer serve as advocate general for the Royal Colony of Massachusetts. He had to resign.

*"How could the king impose something so unconstitutional?"* he may have wondered as he sat at his desk contemplating his decision. The question of legality had rolled over and over in the sea of Otis's mind for weeks. But finding a solution to the problem was like a ship trying to sail without wind.

When King George III assumed the throne in October 1760, he began to enforce the Navigation Acts, which included Writs of Assistance. These impractical laws had been ignored by the colonists and their royal governors for years. Because Otis prosecuted smugglers as Boston's advocate general, he had spent many hours studying the legality of these writs. When he heard of the king's decision to enforce the Writs of Assistance in Boston, Otis was skeptical.

The writs allowed customs officials, or anyone they designated, to enter businesses and homes to search for smuggled goods. These writs were too vague. Contraband could be anything, including a sack of flour purchased legally from a merchant. Otis had concluded that narrow and specific writs, like those issued by kings centuries ago, were legal. If a customs official held evidence of tax evasion and was willing to take an oath over it, then a writ was legal. But these writs were too general. They did not require customs officials to take oaths. Otis feared that if the superior court upheld their legality, then customs officials could appoint anyone to search any person's home for any reason.

The writs thrust a dagger at the heart of British law, and Otis had to submit to his conscience that winter day in 1761. When several customs officials came to his home to ask him to represent them and the writs before the superior court, he had no other choice but to resign.

Not long after his resignation, Otis heard another knock on his door. He felt relieved when he opened it to find a group of merchants standing before him. They asked Otis to defend them in court.

"*Yes,*" he said eagerly. Here was his chance to oppose the writs. "*In such a cause as this I despise a fee.*"

Otis may have suspected some would think he was turning his resignation into revenge. But he couldn't contain the revolution rising inside him. James Otis had found his sea legs in the turbulence blowing across Boston. A lightning storm was brewing over Massachusetts Bay.[17]

> "Therefore, since we are surrounded by such a great cloud of witnesses, let us throw off everything that hinders and the sin that so easily entangles, and let us run with perseverance the race marked out for us" (HEBREWS 12:1).

**PRAYER**

*Lord, I resign the burdens weighing on my heart. May I run the race of life with perseverance and integrity.*

## 18. Home Invasion

The Boston Town Hall was packed with spectators. It seemed the whole city had come to watch James Otis oppose the Writs of Assistance in court that February day in 1761.

*"I will to my dying day oppose with all the powers and faculties God has given me, all such instruments of slavery on the one hand, and villainy on the other, as this Writ of Assistance is,"* Otis declared in his opening statement.

Otis knew his position was bold, but his passion was deep. He believed the Writs of Assistance were the worst instrument of arbitrary power ever found in an English law book. *"I was solicited to argue this cause as Advocate-General; and because I would not, I have been charged with desertion from my office. To this charge I can give a very sufficient answer. I renounced that office, and I argue this cause, from the same principle,"* he continued boldly.

Chief Justice Hutchinson, the man who received the position of chief justice instead of Otis's father, presided. Perhaps for the first time Otis understood Providence's hand in that seemingly unjust passing over. Otis might not have had the courage to oppose the king's writs in a court presided over by his own father.

*"And I argue it with the greater pleasure, as it is in favor of British liberty,"* he said.

Because Otis's presentation followed that of Jeremiah Gridley, his former law mentor who now held Otis's job as advocate general, he decided to use his familiarity with Gridley's tactics to his advantage. Otis deftly agreed with Gridley's assertion that certain writs were legal, ones that were specific and based on sworn testimony. Otis then argued that these newly enforced writs were too general and perpetual. Legal writs were specific and temporary. These writs were neither.

*"A man's house is his castle; and whilst he is quiet, he is as well guarded as a prince in his castle,"* Otis declared famously, not knowing he had just coined a new phrase. *"This writ, if it should be declared legal, would totally annihilate this privilege."* These writs put every man's castle at risk for an arbitrary invasion by the government. Otis objected to the fact that these writs allowed customs officers to designate anyone to search anyone else's home for any reason.

Otis's fiery oration continued for nearly five hours. At the end his transformation from a loyal crown advocate to a rebel with a cause was complete. The judges upheld the British government's position, but James Otis won the hearts of Bostonians. He had sparked cloud-to-cloud lightning in the skies over Boston. His argument was so compelling that most customs officers were

"When you make a loan of any kind to your neighbor, do not go into his house to get what he is offering as a pledge. Stay outside and let the man to whom you are making the loan bring the pledge out to you" (DEUTERONOMY 24:10, 11).

afraid to issue Writs of Assistance. The reason? They feared rebellion in Boston.[18]

**PRAYER**

*Thank you for the castle you have given me. Allow me to build a strong home, one protected from intruders such as envy, strife, or discontentment. Likewise, prevent me from intruding upon the castles of others.*

# 19. The Spark

But Otis was a flame of fire," reported the twenty-five-year-old Boston lawyer. As he listened to Jeremiah Gridley and James Otis present their cases before the superior court in February 1761, he feverishly scribbled his notes of the proceedings. His notes are the best existing record of James Otis's plea against the Writs of Assistance.

*"With a promptitude of classical allusions, a depth of research, a rapid summary of historical events and dates, a profusion of legal authorities, a prophetic glance of his eyes into futurity, and a rapid torrent of impetuous eloquence, he hurried away all before him,"* the young lawyer gushed over Otis's defense.

Otis knew many of the bystanders who came to the courtroom that day. He was especially familiar with the note-taker. Both Otis and Jeremiah Gridley had mentored this Harvard graduate. Like everyone else, Otis had noticed this man's slightness of stature. But he knew his height of intellect overcame any physical shortcoming. Otis saw great promise in the spirited John Adams. He had no idea how much his courtroom defense would ultimately affect Adams and the rest of Massachusetts.

*"American independence was then and there born. The seeds of patriots and heroes were then and there sown, to defend the vigorous youth, the* Non sine diis animosus infans," Adams wrote as he reflected on the courtroom scene. *"Every man . . . appeared to me to go away, as I did, ready to take arms against Writs of Assistance,"* Adams observed with a patriot's enthusiasm and a historian's accuracy.

*"Then and there was the first scene of the first act of opposition to the arbitrary claims of Great Britain. Then and there the child Independence was born. In fifteen years, that is in 1776, he grew up to manhood, and declared himself free,"* Adams later wrote.

Adams knew Otis's life mattered. Nothing could change that—not the king's decision to appoint a new governor, not the decision to name

Thomas Hutchinson as chief justice instead of Otis's father, and not Otis's decision to resign his crown appointment. In Otis's life, these things worked together to lead him to a critical time of decision.

> "If I have raised my hand against the fatherless, knowing that I had influence in court, then let my arm fall from the shoulder, let it be broken off at the joint" (JOB 31:21, 22).

Despite the obstacles in his path, James Otis used his God-given gift of oratory to speak against injustice and stand for liberty. Perhaps most of all, his words influenced the young John Adams. If the fire in one man could spark a revolution in another through one speech, think of how God can use you at the dinner table or in the boardroom or wherever life takes you.[19]

**PRAYER**

*God, I take seriously the people you have placed in my life. May I use opportunities you have given me to bring purpose and meaning to the lives of others.*

# 20. Peace with Sugar on Top

The celebrations on both continents were so loud, the cheering could be heard like thunder over the Atlantic.

Because he was living in London at the time, Benjamin Franklin was probably among the first Americans to hear the news. But it wasn't long before George Washington heard it in Virginia, and John Adams learned of it in Boston. All the colonies sighed in great relief and celebrated with even greater joy. The French and Indian War was over. Known as the Seven Years' War in Europe, the conflict ended when the British government signed the Treaty of Paris in 1763.

France had failed. As a result, Canada was now firmly in the hands of England. And Great Britain, though financially weakened, emerged as a superpower in the New World.

Boston turned to one of her favorite sons to celebrate the treaty: James Otis. After his stirring opposition to the Writs of Assistance two years earlier, Otis had become extremely popular. Bostonians rewarded him by electing him to the legislature. He represented them with passion, and poured his fervor into the town's celebration of the war's end.

The sweet peace propelled Otis to express strong affection for Great Britain. *"The true interests of Great Britain and her plantations are mutual, and what God in his providence united, let no man dare attempt to pull asunder,"* he declared. *"Their [the colonists'] loyalty has been abundantly proved, especially in the late war. Their affection and reverence for their mother country are unquestionable. They yield the most cheerful and ready obedience to her laws, particularly to the power of that august body, the Parliament of Great Britain, the supreme legislature of the kingdom and its dominions. These, I declare, are my own sentiments of duty and loyalty."*

His speech was like the phenomenon of ground-to-cloud lightning. His declaration of loyalty fired an upward charge into the sky.

But the celebrations weren't sweet for long. Within a year, the British government was starving because of its empty coffers. Parliament needed a way to pay for the French and Indian War. They passed the Sugar Act in 1764 to raise revenue in the colonies as payment for the war. The act required enforcement of a thirty-year-old law that had been ignored by both the crown and the colonies. Each gallon of sugar required a three-pence tax.

The decision was disturbing. When peace is superficially sweet, it is not serious or secure.[20]

> "They dress the wound of my people as though it were not serious. 'Peace, peace,' they say, when there is no peace"
> (JEREMIAH 6:14).

**PRAYER**

*God, give me that abiding peace, the serious kind that cannot melt when circumstances bring hot water in my life, the kind of peace that is as substantive as it is sweet.*

# 21. The Revolution Today: Treasure

Life for James Otis in the 1760s certainly did not turn out the way he planned. The new royal governor slighted his father. Otis was a great crown prosecutor but the king's new policies were too much for him to bear. These setbacks, however, led to a great moment in his life. He stood up for justice when he spoke against the Writs of Assistance in court and declared that a man's home was his own castle. Otis impacted the entire city of Boston as a result, including John Adams. And, as many patriots discovered in the Revolution, doing what is right in a respectful way does not often result in instant rewards.

Time and history, whether it is our own personal story or the story of America or stories in the Bible, give us an opportunity to reflect. We can't always see a purpose in everything that happens to us day to day. And it is easy to overanalyze. Sometimes we search for sand dollars or starfish only to find a bunch of sand. But the sand dollars of life, the starfish, and other treasures are there. Sometimes we just have to dig a little deeper.

After murdering a man in anger, Moses fled Egypt for the desert. This Hebrew, the adopted son of Pharaoh's daughter, had lived as a prince for years. He had as much education, wealth, and job security as any male living in Pharaoh's palace. Even though it certainly was wrong for him to murder a man for abusing Hebrew slaves, the Lord forgave Moses and gave him direction in the desert.

God allowed Moses to become a husband. He also led him into husbandry, turning him into a shepherd. Time spent herding and shearing sheep matured him. It helped him see the important things in life. Then God used a burning bush to catch Moses' attention. He sent Moses back to Egypt to stand up to Pharaoh for a grand purpose.

Had God not made the desert Moses' castle, Moses wouldn't have been prepared for his ultimate purpose on earth: to free the Hebrews from Pharaoh's slavery. Moses changed. He moved from living the good life in the king's court to petitioning the court for the Hebrews' release. Although Moses' purpose brought the wrath of an earthly king, it brought honor to an eternal king.

> "But store up for yourselves treasures in heaven, where moth and rust do not destroy, and where thieves do not break in and steal" (MATTHEW 6:20).

Heavenly treasure cannot be corrupted. No one can steal the credit or the joy. When life on earth seems thankless or stuck in neutral, looking heavenward brings a new perspective and hope for a better reward.[21]

**PRAYER**

*God, thank you for reminding me that fulfilling my purpose does not always bring earthly rewards. I seek to honor you with my decisions today.*

# 22. Sabbath Rest: Abiding in God

Samuel Dunbar was not only a seasoned pastor by the 1760s, but he was also an experienced military chaplain. Dunbar had accompanied British troops in a French and Indian War battle in 1755. He knew what it was like to abide in the trenches. So it is no wonder that he chose the topic of abiding in God when he preached before the royal governor of Massachusetts and the Massachusetts House of Representatives. Although Dunbar wrote eight thousand sermons during his long career, only nine of them, including this one, were published. Pastors published only their best work.

Reflecting on the British capture of Fort Ticonderoga, located in upper New York, from the French during the war, Dunbar chose the story of King Asa for his text to lead his congregation in celebration.

*"Before the battle, he [King Asa] led them to the throne of grace to pray, to obtain mercy, and find grace to help them, in this time of need and danger,"* Dunbar explained. *"Asa cried unto the Lord his God: It was a cry of faith, rather than of fear. His prayer was short, but fervent; a prayer of faith."*

The blessing that resulted from Asa's abiding was the defeat of his enemies. *"Something similar have been the exercise, the practice, and the experience of the people of God in these British American provinces and colonies."* In this comparison, Dunbar reminded his audience how the colonists had mustered both their forces and hearts before God.

*"But we, not trusting to an arm of flesh, not to our numbers nor strength, not to our sword nor bow, like godly Asa, cried to the Lord our God; we fasted and wept, and made supplication to him,"* Dunbar reminded the officials, crediting God for their recent successes.

But the story wasn't over. When Asa's army returned from battle, God sent a plain-spoken prophet named Azariah to meet them. *"The Lord is with you, while ye be with him, and if ye seek him, he will be found of you; but if ye forsake him, he will forsake you,"* Dunbar quoted from 2 Chronicles 15:2 (KJV).

Dunbar believed the prophet's message was relevant to his audience. *"The presence of God is equally necessary and beneficial, for the governour, as the general; for the court, as the camp; for the field of husbandry, as the field of battle; in peace, as in war; and for the wise and successful management of affairs at home, as abroad: and our enjoyment of it turns upon our being with God,"* Samuel Dunbar eloquently concluded.

God's desire to hear from his people is as relevant today as it was in the 1760s and as it was with King Asa. God wants us to abide in him, stay away from sin, and seek him.[22]

> "[Azariah] went out to meet Asa and said to him, 'Listen to me, Asa and all Judah and Benjamin. The LORD is with you when you are with him. If you seek him, he will be found by you, but if you forsake him, he will forsake you'"
> (2 CHRONICLES 15:2).

**PRAYER**

*Help me always remember I need your help. Abiding in you and staying away from sin is your desire for me, regardless of my circumstances.*

# 23. Stamp Act

A *stamp duty is confessedly the most reasonable and equitable that can be devised,"* Rhode Island attorney Martin Howard wrote of Parliament's decision to pass the Stamp Act in March 1765.

Perhaps he had heard of James Otis and the Bostonians who opposed the Writs of Assistance. Maybe he suspected that not everyone would share his opinion. For whatever reason, he adopted the pen name "The Farmer" to express his views in his pamphlet. The Stamp Act required the colonists to pay for a stamp for almost every paper transaction. By October 1765, playing cards, marriage licenses, legal documents, newspapers, and pamphlets, such as the one Howard published, would require a stamp.

This Rhode Islander's reasons for supporting the Stamp Act were personal and professional. Not only was he as loyal to the crown as a prince, but he was also frustrated by the prevalence of smuggling. He had witnessed it repeatedly. He was so tired of smuggling in the ports of Rhode Island and Boston that he didn't care if Parliament taxed the whole continent of North America.

*"It is notorious, that smuggling, which an eminent writer calls a crime against the law of nature, had well nigh become established in some of the colonies . . . corruption, raised upon the ruins of duty and virtue, had almost grown into a system,"* wrote Howard.

Howard supported Parliament's right to tax the colonists no matter how much it offended them. Unlike many colonists, he was not bothered by a glaring fact. The Stamp Act was the first time Parliament had taxed all the colonies. If smuggling was really the target, the tax was akin to a teacher punishing the whole class for the disobedience of a couple of students.

*"The jurisdiction of parliament . . . is transcendent and entire, and may levy internal taxes as well as regulate trade; there is no essential difference in the rights,"* he stated.

Howard understood the government's need for revenue. When the French and Indian War ended, King George III looked into the royal coffers and found them as dry as a well in a desert. Thanks to James Otis, enforcing the Navigation Acts and the Writs of Assistance had failed to produce sufficient income. *"Every Englishman, therefore, is subject to this jurisdiction, and it follows him wherever he goes. It is of the essence of government, that there should be a supreme head, and it would be a solecism [mistake] in politicks to talk of members independent of it,"* Howard insisted.

> "Submit yourselves for the Lord's sake to every authority instituted among men: whether to the king, as the supreme authority, or to governors, who are sent by him to punish those who do wrong and to commend those who do right"
> (1 PETER 2:13, 14).

Howard responded to the Stamp Act and British authority with unquestioned acceptance. His allegiance to England never wavered and only increased over time. Martin Howard paid a high price for his submission. As the conflict simmered, robbers ransacked his Rhode Island home, causing him to flee to England.[23]

**PRAYER**

*No matter what I think of the decisions of those in authority over me, may I show them respect as you have called me to do, knowing you are the Supreme Authority in my life.*

# 24. The Bystander

John Burke passed the gallows, which held two victims, on his way to the meeting. The site was a reminder that this was the seat of government, a place that stood for justice.

Burke arrived just as the debates began on May 30, 1765. This bystander probably wiped the sweat off his brow as he took a seat to watch Virginia's distinguished House of Burgesses discuss the day's burning issue. The temperature inside was hotter than the temperature outside. *"I was entertained with very strong debates concerning duties that the Parliament wants to lay on the American colonies, which they call or style stamp duties,"* he reported.

As the debates progressed, Burke watched the thermometer rise when attorney Patrick Henry rose to speak.

*"[Henry] stood up and said he had read that in former times Tarquin and Julius had each his Brutus, Charles had his Cromwell, and he did not doubt but some good American would stand up in favor of his country,"* recorded Burke.

Henry's shocking statement nearly caused the thermometer to explode in the House of Burgesses that day. Burke, the bystander, watched as the speaker of the house stood in response. He claimed Henry *"had spoken treason, and was sorry to see that not one of the members of the House was loyal enough to stop him before he had gone so far."*

Burke listened as the room fell silent, suffocated by the tension. Henry stood again and said, *"if he had affronted the Speaker or the House, he was ready to ask pardon, and he would show his loyalty to His Majesty, King George the Third, at the expense of the last drop of his blood."*

Henry explained he only had his country's dying liberty at heart and the heat of passion may have led him to say *"something more than he intended."* He begged the speaker's pardon.

What happened next was the most awesome sight of the day. This bystander watched as other members stood and backed Henry, which cooled the room faster than a summer rain ever could.

Henry's heat produced almost an overnight outcome. The next day the assembly passed resolutions opposing the Stamp Act. These resolves claimed the same rights for Virginians as possessed by those born in England. These peaceful proclamations purported that taxation through representation was the only *"security against a burdensome taxation, and the distinguishing characteristic of British freedom."*

As the bystander had recorded, Patrick Henry opposed the Stamp Act using strong but respectful rhetoric. He demonstrated the value of facing the heat and standing in protest while wearing a crown of respect for authority.[24]

> "So they shook the dust from their feet in protest against them" (ACTS 13:51).

**PRAYER**

*God, show me how to present in a respectful way my disagreements with authority.*

32

# 25. Flagrant Fire

The Boston attorney's account of the chilling fire flowed fervently from his pen.

*"The destructions, demolitions, and ruins caused by the rage of the Colonies . . . at that singular and ever-memorable statute called the Stamp Act, will make the present year one of the most remarkable eras in the annals of North America,"* Josiah Quincy wrote the morning after the triple fires.

Quincy reported the mob had assembled on King Street the night before, August 26, 1765. Their fury over the Stamp Act equaled the summer heat. The gang kindled a fire, lit torches, split into two groups, and marched to separate houses to punish two *"gentlemen of distinction"* who *"were accessories to the present [burdens]"* of the Stamp Act. In their fever they set fire to the men's homes, destroying the houses and furniture beyond repair. But the twin terror groups weren't finished. They had yet to start their most flagrant fire.

The two groups came back together for a single march to the house of Chief Justice Thomas Hutchinson. Hutchinson, however, had already learned of the other fires and managed to convince his entire family, except his oldest daughter, to leave. Hutchinson begged her over and over to depart. She was determined *"to stay and share his fate."* Fearing for her safety, Hutchinson finally swept her into his arms and fled his home, just before the incensed mob bolted through his front door.

Quincy wrote that this *"rage-intoxicated rabble beset the house on all sides, and soon destroyed every thing of value . . . The destruction was really amazing; for it was equal to the fury of the onset."*

Quincy noted the fire not only destroyed all of Hutchinson's belongings, but it also consumed many of the royal colony's most valuable documents. As a longtime servant of Massachusetts, Hutchinson kept many valuable records and ancient papers in his house. One raging flame destroyed both a family's home and records of a people's heritage.

By morning news of the Hutchinson fire and the losses spread more quickly than the three nighttime fires themselves. Quincy, who was sympathetic to the patriot cause, wrote that the fire in the breast of New Englanders would *"always distinguish them as the warmest lovers of liberty."* However, he also recognized the fire was a red alert. Anger over the Stamp Act spewed hot coals into the community. Some had gone too far. Their brazen acts of arson shook Boston's sense of justice and propriety.

*"Though undoubtedly, in the fury of revenge . . . for that of enslavers and oppressive tax-masters of their native country, they committed acts totally unjustifiable,"* Josiah Quincy concluded.

Daylight showed the mob's work for what it was: flagrancy out of control.[25]

**PRAYER**

*Search my heart today for any anger that needs to be tamed. And although the idea of setting a fire seems unthinkable to me, keep me from committing smaller but also unjustifiable acts today.*

> "His work will be shown for what it is, because the Day will bring it to light" (1 CORINTHIANS 3:13).

# 26. God, Give Us Better Hearts

How should a man have reacted, especially in public, after men burned his home, nearly killing him and his daughter? Boston attorney Josiah Quincy attended court the day after the flagrant fire at Thomas Hutchinson's house. With the precision of a clerk, Quincy recorded the moment when Hutchinson came into court.

*"The distress a man must feel on such an occasion can only be conceived by those who the next day saw his Honor the Chief-Justice come into court,"* Quincy recorded in his diary.

Quincy described Hutchinson as having tears in his eyes. His countenance *"strongly told the inward anguish of his soul."* Quincy wondered, *"What must an audience have felt, whose compassion had before been moved by what they knew he had suffered, when they heard him pronounce the following words in a manner which the agitations of his mind dictated?"*

The most obvious change in Hutchinson was his apparel. Gone were his court robes. His borrowed clothing, however, was nothing compared with his emphatic declaration of innocence. *"Yet I call God to witness,—and I would not, for a thousand worlds, call my Maker to witness to falsehood . . . that I never, in New England or Old, in Great Britain or America, neither directly nor indirectly, was aiding, assisting, or supporting—in the least promoting or encouraging—what is commonly called the Stamp Act; but, on the contrary, did all in my power, and strove as much as in me lay, to prevent it,"* Hutchinson claimed.

He then stated he had nothing to fear but his life, which was *"of but little value when deprived of all its comforts, all that was dear to me, and nothing surrounding me but the most piercing distress. I hope the eyes of the people will be opened, that they will see how easy it is for some designing, wicked man to spread false reports, to raise suspicions and jealousies in the minds of the populace, and enrage them against the innocent,"* Hutchinson warned.

The chief justice reminded the audience that the courts were designed to prosecute the guilty. *"This destroying all peace and order of the community,—all will feel its effects; and I hope all will see how easily the people may be deluded, inflamed, and carried away with madness against an innocent man,"* Hutchinson continued.

He concluded with a plea more feverish than the mob who had burned his home the night before. *"I pray God give us better hearts!"* he cried.

> "The Pharisee stood up and prayed about himself: 'God, I thank you that I am not like other men—robbers, evildoers, adulterers—or even like this tax collector" (LUKE 18:11).

Many may have wondered if his call for better hearts was a Pharisee-like prayer or an example of genuine humility. Only time would reveal Thomas Hutchinson's own heart. But in that moment all who heard him considered his plea.[26]

**PRAYER**

*Oh, Chief Justice of my soul, whether I find myself falsely accused or in a position to judge someone else, give me a better heart.*

# 27. A Spirited Protest

The odor of the fire at Thomas Hutchinson's home lingered in the air, drifting to nearby Cambridge, Massachusetts. Although the people did not forget the smell of burnt stamps, the fire left them with a burning question. How do you protest the injustice of the Stamp Act? If the Boston fires were an extreme smoke signal, the people of Cambridge set a more fitting example, but one still filled with a fiery spirit. They put their protest in writing.

The Cambridge residents held a legal meeting in October 1765, two weeks before the Stamp Act was to go into effect. *"It is the opinion of the Town that the Inhabitants of this Province have a Legal Claim to all the natural Inherent Constitutional Rights of Englishmen notwithstanding their distance from Great Britain,"* their proclamation began.

The power of the person in charge of distributing the stamps instilled Herod-like fear in the people of Cambridge. This judge had the authority to arbitrarily call people to court to any place he chose, forcing the colonists to bear an unreasonable travel burden. *"The Distributor of Stamps will have a Soveranity over Every thing, but the lives of the People, since it is in his Power to Summon Every one he pleases to Qebeck,*

*Montreal, or New found land, to answer for the pretended or Real Breaches of this Act,"* the proclamation continued.

The judicial process for prosecuting Stamp Act violators also angered them. Gone was a jury of peers. Enter a single Pilate-like judge. *"And when the faithfull Subject arrives there; By whom is he to be Tryed, not by his Peers (the Birth Right of Every English man). No but by the [judge] of Admiralty without a [jury], and it is possible without Law."* The residents also feared the stamp master would fine violators merely to pocket the earnings.

One more question also burned in their breasts: *"Why are not His Majesties' Subjects in Great Britain Treated in this manner, Why must we in America who have in Every Instance discovered as much Loyalty for His Majesty & Obedience to His Laws as any of His British Subjects?"*

The inhabitants pointed out they had already paid their French and Indian War debts with the blood of the colonists who had fought for the crown in the conflict. To keep their pocketbooks solvent and their liberty from languishing, the inhabitants of Cambridge used the proclamation to direct their representatives in the Massachusetts Assembly to call for the act's repeal.

Then they added this fiery prophecy: *"Let this Act but take place, Liberty will be no more, Trade will Languish & dye."*

Such was the attitude in this respectful protest. It was an example of respecting authority with a bold spirit.[27]

> "For God did not give us a spirit of timidity, but a spirit of power, of love and of self-discipline" (2 TIMOTHY 1:7).

**PRAYER**

*Father, may my responses today reflect spirit and enthusiasm while maintaining a code of respect for those around me.*

# 28. The Revolution Today: Anger

The way in which the colonists responded to the Stamp Act gives a lesson in anger management on a group scale. Patrick Henry constructively handled his anger by outlining his grievances. The town of Cambridge put their anger into a respectful resolution against the Stamp Act. But the Boston mob who burned Thomas Hutchinson's home obviously chose a different and nearly deadly path.

Anger is usually the result of a perceived injustice. Effectively managing anger is almost as critical to the mind as drinking water is to the body.

Because anger can be mismanaged, it's easy to equate anger with sin. "Anger is not evil; anger is not sinful; anger is not part of our fallen nature; anger is not Satan at work in our lives. Quite the contrary. Anger is evidence that we are made in God's image; it demonstrates that we still have some concern for justice and righteousness despite our fallen estate," counselor Gary Chapman wrote in his book *The Other Side of Love*, as reviewed in the Spring 2000 issue of *Marriage Partnership*.

Countless Biblical examples tell of God's anger against sin. Jesus became angry at those who used the temple as part of a moneymaking scheme. Anger is not sin, but mismanaged anger can lead to sin. Ephesians 4:26 puts it this way: "'In your anger do not sin': Do not let the sun go down while you are still angry."

Ignoring anger can lead to bitterness and unexpected outbursts. Constructively managing anger can alleviate pain and, in some circumstances, result in justice. "We've all seen the destructive forces of anger in our society, but that's not God's intention. I really believe that God wants anger to be used to correct wrongs and to bring about good, not destruction," stated Chapman in an interview. "God also intends anger to be a visitor, not a resident. If we can learn how to make it a visitor that comes and goes, and not let it live in our hearts, we'll create a climate in our marriages and families where we can deal in a positive way with things that go wrong."

> "My dear brothers, take note of this: Everyone should be quick to listen, slow to speak and slow to become angry"
> (JAMES 1:19).

Gary Chapman's prescription for anger management includes five steps: Acknowledge your anger, restrain your immediate response, determine the object of your anger, analyze your options, and then take constructive action.

Much of what led to America's Revolutionary War was a tug-of-war between constructive and destructive responses to anger. God gave us anger because he knows the value it can bring to life when we handle the objects of our anger with respect, truth, and love.[28]

### PRAYER

*Father, forgive me when I have misplaced or hidden my anger. Give me the courage to constructively manage it.*

# 29. Sabbath Rest: Natural Blessings

It seemed colonial opinion makers were always extolling the virtues of "natural rights." *Natural* meant foundational and intrinsic. And because natural rights were "God-given," the phrase became part of the vocabulary of the pulpit.

The idea of natural rights was frequently on the mind of Rev. Simeon Howard, pastor of Boston's West Church. Forty-year-old Howard was a respected minister and a graduate of Harvard. As the trouble with England increased, Howard chose natural liberty as the sermon topic for the Ancient and Honorable Artillery Company of Boston's annual election ceremony.

*"This liberty has always been accounted one of the greatest natural blessings which mankind can enjoy,"* Howard told his listeners. *"Accordingly, the benevolent and impartial Father of the human race, has given to all men a right, and to all naturally an equal right to this blessing."*

Galatians 5:1 was his main text: "Stand fast therefore in the liberty wherewith Christ hath made us free" (KJV).

Howard explained the verse's context. In the church's early days, a conflict between Jewish and Gentile Christians emerged over whether they should follow Jewish ceremonial laws. Paul explained that Christ had given them liberty by setting them free from the law. Howard believed that same principle applied to *"any other real and valuable liberty which men have a right to."*

Howard believed Christ's freedom placed all humanity in a natural state, equal in the pursuit of happiness. He defined these natural rights as *"everything that is opposed to temporal slavery."* Or *"all those advantages which are liable to be destroyed by the art or power of men."*

But Howard also believed natural liberty had limits. *"This however is not a state of licentiousness, for the law of nature which bounds this liberty, forbids all injustice and wickedness; allows no man to injure another in his person or property, or to destroy his own life,"* Howard said. Government's responsibility was to respect and protect those God-given rights and freedoms.

He also believed natural blessings came from God and were governed by him. *"And whatever share men enjoy of this liberty, we may properly say in the words of the text, that Christ has made them free with it,"* Simeon Howard said, praising the resurrected Christ as *"the head of God's providential government."*

And while humanity often uses measuring tapes of money, intellect, and status to quantify a person's worth, God looks to the heart. By creating men and women in his image, he gave them the natural blessing of intrinsic worth. He is the source of real value. He has released humanity from the tangle of legalism and the chain of sin.[29]

> "So God created man in his own image, in the image of God he created him; male and female he created them" (GENESIS 1:27).

**PRAYER**

*Thank you for creating me in your image and for blessing me with natural rights.*

# 30. Our Humble Opinion

The men who attended the historic meeting brought an attitude of humility in their hearts. *"The members of this Congress, sincerely devoted, with the warmest sentiments of affection and duty to his majesty's person and government,"* began the joint declaration. The gesture was so humble, it was as if they had tipped their tricorns to the king in unison.

Representatives from nine of the thirteen colonies attended the Stamp Act Congress in New York City in October 1765. Unlike the Albany Congress of 1754, this congress realized the value of forming a union, if only to address one issue, the Stamp Act. Also unlike the Albany Congress, which the crown had coerced colonial leaders into attending, this congress was the first time the colonies assembled on their own initiative. However, they still proudly unfurled the king's banner.

They chose to write a declaration of their rights, but they did so with the utmost humility. After all, submitting a formal supplication to the king was risky. *"In our humble opinion,"* the declaration proclaimed.

With their tone established, they then proclaimed to his majesty their allegiance, which was as dear to them as if they had been born in England. They also proclaimed *"all due subordination to that august body, the parliament of Great Britain."*

The declaration continued in this way, citing the natural rights of the colonists to be taxed but only with representation, which seemed unlikely. They acknowledged that traveling across the Atlantic Ocean was the biggest barrier to ensuring their natural rights through delegates to Parliament.

They also brought up the subject of the courts. Because Parliament established an admiralty court of judges to prosecute Stamp Act violators, the humble delegates identified trial by jury as an inherent right. They also noted that the Stamp Act imposed an undue financial burden on them.

Before ending their grievances, the representatives made one more point as clear as a trumpet call in the king's court. In their humble opinion, they had the right to express their views to the king.

*"That it is the right of the British subjects in these colonies to petition the king or either house of parliament,"* they added. The Stamp Act Congress concluded their petition with *"humble application to both houses of parliament, to procure the repeal of the act for granting and applying certain stamp duties."*

Thus, through humility and first-time unity, the colonists requested action by the king and Parliament. Thomas Hutchinson had prayed for better hearts, and this congress demonstrated just that.[30]

> "Before his downfall a man's heart is proud, but humility comes before honor"
> (PROVERBS 18:12).

**PRAYER**

*Cleanse me with humility, Lord. May I approach those around me as if they are kings, knowing I honor you when I treat others with a humble posture.*

# 31. Crashing the Courts

When the British government decided to disband the Massachusetts court system after the fallout over the Stamp Act in 1765, James Otis was as outraged as he was over the Writs of Assistance in 1761. The courts were as essential to justice as rain is to crops. This lightning luminary knew it was time to strike once again. Otis chose to give another speech. He hoped it would result in a positive change.

*"It is with great grief that I appear before your Excellency [Governor Hutchinson] and Honours [of the City Council] on this occasion,"* Otis proclaimed in front of the council on December 20, 1765.

Otis requested that *"all his Majesty's most loyal and affectionate British-American subjects"* receive ample redress of their grievances. He went so far as to call their enemies, both at home and abroad, *"cruel and insidious,"* and wished they would be *"put to shame and confusion."* His fire was so hot he accused Parliament of ignoring the first principles of liberty. *"It was once a fundamental maxim that every subject had the same right to his life, liberty, property, and the law that the King had to his crown; and 'tis yet, I venture to say, as much as a crown is worth, to deny the subject his law, which is his birthright,"* Otis said accusingly.

Otis asserted that the only time courts should be closed was during a war or an insurrection. In his opinion, the colonists' reaction to the Stamp Act was far from either. *"The shutting up of the courts is an abdication, a total dissolution of government. Whoever takes from the king his executive power, takes from the king his kingship,"* he insisted.

Otis knew the people of Massachusetts had succeeded in preventing the implementation of the Stamp Act by ignoring it. He also knew enforcing the Stamp Act was impractical, bordering on insane. He reminded his audience that the *"very people of England"* had risen in opposition to another bill and Parliament had repealed it.

Otis explained that the law books cried out against delaying justice. Closing the courts denied the colonists their rights. Worse, the action turned their *"divine"* king into a dictator. *"The king is always presumed to be present in his courts, holding out the law to his subjects; and when he shuts his courts, he unkings himself in the most essential point,"* Otis continued.

What James Otis was defending was not just the rights of the colonists. The courts are not a system originally created by humanity. God required the Israelites to establish a judicial system. Justice is a God-given principle. It is a value he takes seriously in the affairs of men and women.[31]

> "When men have a dispute, they are to take it to court and the judges will decide the case, acquitting the innocent and condemning the guilty" (DEUTERONOMY 25:1).

**PRAYER**

*Thank you for giving us a government that provides a judicial system. Renew in me a commitment to living a life that is just and righteous before your courts.*

# 32. The Case of External versus Internal

Parliament's inquisition of the American seated in front of them in February 1766 was more secret than the location of the key to the crown jewels. *"Was it an opinion in America before 1763 that the Parliament had no right to lay taxes and duties there?"* one of the questioners asked.

*"I never heard an objection to the right of laying duties to regulate commerce; but a right to lay internal taxes was never supposed to be in Parliament, as we are not represented there,"* the colonial defendant replied.

With the expertise of a man schooled in commerce, he then explained the difference between trade taxes and those prescribed by the Stamp Act. Because trade taxes were external taxes, their impact was limited to a segment of the colonists. The Stamp Act imposed internal taxes, which affected everyone.

Thus, the inquiry progressed one unknown day in February 1766. The most powerful players in Parliament participated as questioners. Their aim was to figure out what to do with the Stamp Act and the sticky residue it had left on the American colonies.

*"You say the Colonies have always submitted to external taxes, and object to the right of Parliament only in laying internal taxes; now can you show that there is any kind of difference between the two taxes to the Colony on which they may be laid?"* a questioner asked.

*"I think the difference is very great. An external tax is a duty laid on commodities imported,"* the American replied, explaining that external taxes are absorbed in the prices of sugar, wool, or other imports.

*"If the people do not like it at that price, they refuse it; they are not obliged to pay it. But an internal tax is forced from the people without their consent if not laid by their own representatives,"* the colonist continued.

Once again the American answered their questions with as much grace and ease as the best attorney in London. He was not a lawyer, but a businessman schooled in the practical art of life and the pursuit of happiness. Often called a doctor, he was the printer and scientist who had moved to England nearly ten years earlier to serve as Pennsylvania's colonial agent. And although the most distinguished men in Parliament served as inquisitors at this secret interrogation, they were no match for Franklin and his apt replies.

Benjamin Franklin's frankness came from his simple approach to life. His understanding of the difference between the two types of taxes was as clear to him as a glass of water. External taxes were more easily absorbed into the economy and less devastating to individuals. But the Stamp Act's internal taxes affected everyone's pocketbook each time they merely processed a piece of paper.

> "My flesh and my heart may fail, but God is the strength of my heart and my portion forever"
> (PSALM 73:26).

So it is with life. What affects the external is often temporary, but what affects the internal, the heart, can last an eternity.[32]

**PRAYER**

*Father, may I let go of the external, temporary things in life. Be the strength of my heart and my portion forever.*

# 33. Worn Pride

Parliament was tangled in more yarn than a thousand flocks of sheep could ever produce. They had to knit a solution to the Stamp Act. If internal taxes were as objectionable as Benjamin Franklin suggested, then perhaps the solution was to increase external taxes on imports such as wool. However, when one Member of Parliament asked Franklin this question in the secret inquiry of February 1766, the yarn he received nearly choked him.

*"I do not know a single article imported into the northern Colonies but what they can either do without or make themselves,"* the thrifty Franklin replied.

*"Do you not think cloth from England absolutely necessary to them?"* the questioner asked with astonishment.

Although Franklin was from Philadelphia, he had grown up in Boston. He understood Yankee ingenuity, Puritan plainness, and Quaker quietness better than any lord of London.

*"No, by no means absolutely necessary; with industry and good management, they may very well supply themselves with all they want,"* Franklin replied.

*"Will it not take a long time to establish that manufacture among them; and must they not, in the meanwhile, suffer greatly?"* the questioner continued.

*"I think not. They have made a surprising progress already. And I am of the opinion that before their old clothes are worn out they will have new ones of their own making."*

Franklin explained that many colonists had taken steps to increase wool production by refusing to eat lamb. Franklin also knew wearing fine clothing was as much a source of pride among England's upper crust as wearing plain black drab was to Puritans. *"The people will all spin and work for themselves in their own houses,"* Franklin said.

Another topic briefly replaced this thread of questioning, but the subject was hardly buttoned up. Another parliamentary questioner returned to the issue later in the inquiry. *"If the Stamp Act should be repealed, would it induce the assemblies of America to acknowledge the rights of Parliament to tax them, and would they erase their resolutions?"* the questioner asked.

*"No, never!"* Franklin answered emphatically.

*"Are there no means of obliging them to erase those resolutions?"*

*"None that I know of; they will never do it, unless compelled by force of arms."*

*"Is there a power on earth that can force them to erase them?"*

*"No power, how great soever, can force men to change their opinions."*

*"What used to be the pride of the Americans?"*

*"To indulge in the fashions and manufactures of Great Britain,"* Franklin answered.

This Member of Parliament then asked the most revealing question of this frank secret inquiry. *"What is now their pride?"*

Franklin answered with the naked truth. *"To wear their old clothes over again till they can make new ones,"* he replied. Benjamin Franklin believed Americans were more interested in wearing worn clothing stitched with justice than accepting the Stamp Act's tyranny in exchange for the benefit of fine British garb.[33]

> "I put on righteousness as my clothing; justice was my robe and my turban"
> (JOB 29:14).

**PRAYER**

*Show me the source of my pride today. Allow me to take pride in what glorifies you and to wear the clothing of justice and righteousness.*

# 34. Pitt in the Pit

*"Can anything less than a military force carry the Stamp Act into execution?"* Benjamin Franklin had been asked when some members of Parliament secretly questioned him about the Stamp Act.

*"I do not see how a military force can be applied to that purpose,"* Franklin replied.

*"Why may it not?"*

*"Suppose a military force sent into America: they will find nobody in arms; what are they then to do? They can not force a man to take stamps who chooses to do without them. They will not find a rebellion; they may, indeed, make one,"* Franklin responded.

Franklin may have been insulted at the dressing-down, but it likely led to one of the most extraordinary moments in Parliament in 1766. Franklin's defense—along with Patrick Henry's resolves, Cambridge's petition, and Thomas Hutchinson's fire—made obvious the need for Parliament to reconsider the Stamp Act.

It was Sir William Pitt who led Parliament out of the pit in which they found themselves. This former prime minister stood with the bravery of the fiercest redcoat when he called for repeal of the Stamp Act. *"I have been charged with giving birth to sedition in America,"* he began. Then he defended the right to speak freely, including his own. *"America is almost in open rebellion. I rejoice that America has resisted. Three millions of people so dead to all the feelings of liberty, as voluntarily to submit to be slaves, would have been fit instruments to make slaves of the rest."*

Pitt told his audience he did not want to bore them with cases from his dog-eared law books. Instead he rebutted the critics with more logic than the best Greek philosopher could ever have mustered. *"The gentleman asks, 'when were the colonies emancipated?' But I desire to know, when they were made slaves?"* Pitt asked, responding to an opponent.

After a few more statements, he arrived at his main point. *"It is, that the Stamp Act be repealed absolutely, totally, and immediately,"* he said, adding, *"because it was founded on an erroneous principle."*

But as much as Pitt believed in the repeal, he also concluded that the colonists needed to be censured for their noncompliance. *"At the same time, let the sovereign authority of this country over the colonies be asserted in as strong terms as can be devised, and be made to extend to every point of legislation whatsoever,"* he said.

> "Do not rule over them ruthlessly, but fear your God" (LEVITICUS 25:43).

From the pit of Parliament, Pitt led the way to resolution. The gents and lords of London changed their minds. They repealed the Stamp Act and attached a strong rebuke of the colonists' rebellion. William Pitt proved that ruthlessness was not a way to rule.[34]

**PRAYER**

*Give me the courage today to repeal the stamps of rebellion on my heart, that ruthlessness may not take root.*

# 35. The Revolution Today: Property Buzz

Property and taxes. Americans still love the one and despise the other. The most unpopular taxes are usually the most obvious taxes, especially when they directly affect people's property. The Stamp Act was atrocious in many ways because it was highly visible. By placing a stamp on people's possessions, the Stamp Act stung as strongly as a scarlet letter. From legal papers to playing cards, that stamp in the corner stood out more than the ace of spades in a handful of hearts.

Although state and local governments collect more in sales taxes than in property taxes, the property tax is still the most detested. "Polls show the property tax is the most unpopular tax," *USA Today* reported in August 2006. "A 2006 survey by the Tax Foundation, a non-partisan tax research group, found 39% considered it 'the worst' state or local tax, about twice as many as thought that of the state income or sales tax."

"People hate the property tax because it's visible," Tax Foundation economist Andrew Chamberlain explained. "One of the great ironies of tax policies is that people hate the tax that's easiest to see, not necessarily the one that costs them most."

Perhaps the reason property taxes continue to irritate Americans is an innate desire for ownership, whether it's land, clothing, or homes. Genesis 13 tells us that Abraham and his nephew Lot had so many "flocks, herds, and tents" the land couldn't sustain both of them. They decided to split up. Abraham gave Lot the first choice of land.

"Lot looked up and saw that the whole plain of the Jordan was well watered, like the garden of the LORD, like the land of Egypt, toward Zoar" (Genesis 13:10). Lot selfishly took the best property for himself.

But God rewarded Abraham's selflessness with a promise for posterity and property. After Lot left, God spoke to Abraham: "Lift up your eyes from where you are and look north and south, east and west. All the land that you see I will give to you and your offspring forever. I will make your offspring like the dust of the earth, so that if anyone could count the dust, then your offspring could be counted. Go, walk through the length and breadth of the land, for I am giving it to you" (Genesis 13:14–17).

> "And if you have not been trustworthy with someone else's property, who will give you property of your own?"
> (LUKE 16:12).

Abraham responded by building an altar to mark God's promise and praise him for his gifts of prosperity, progeny, and property. And while death and taxes are among life's most unwelcome certainties, God most certainly deserves *our* praise and thanks for his provisions.[35]

**PRAYER**

*Thank you for the tangible gifts you have given me, for the possessions I own. May I share them with a giving heart.*

# 36. Sabbath Rest: Springs of Joy

The governor of the royal colony of Massachusetts Bay declared July 24, 1766, as a day of thanksgiving throughout the province. When Parliament's decision to repeal the Stamp Act reached America's shores, it was the most refreshing news the parched Americans, particularly those in Massachusetts, could have tasted.

Charles Chauncy, pastor of Boston's First Church, chose to preach on this day of thanksgiving a message of celebration, joy, and praise. He compared the news of the Stamp Act's end to a satisfying drink. The decision had quenched the colonists' thirst for freedom from taxation without representation.

*"There is scarce a keener perception of pleasure . . . than 'being satisfied with agreeable drink,'"* he said. Refreshment, whether from good news or a cup of water, was nourishment. *"We are so formed by the God of nature, doubtless for wise and good ends,"* he said of thirst's ability to throw someone into a tormented state. *"The application of cooling drink is fitted, by an established law of heaven, not only to remove away this uneasiness, but to give pleasure in the doing of it, by its manner of acting upon the organs of taste,"* Chauncy continued.

The repeal of the Stamp Act had flowed like springs of joy throughout the colonies. *"No news handed to us from Great Britain ever gave us a quicker sense, or higher degree, of pleasure,"* stated Chauncy. *"Not merely the repeal, but that benevolent, righteous regard to the public good which gave it birth, is an important ingredient in the news that has made us glad."*

Chauncy explained that the news had reinvigorated commerce. It also refreshed the economy because it dried up the financial burden required to implement the act. But Chauncy took the opportunity to use the invigorating news to remind his parishioners of the power of a different kind of thirst. Thirst was not only physical, but it was also spiritual. Quenching the first was essential to humanity's tongue, the second to humanity's soul.

Thirst was God's way of showing humanity the need for spiritual refreshment. Parched emotions and deprived circumstances led hearts to

God. Chauncy reminded his audience that when David longed to *"appear before God in his sanctuary"* it resembled a *"panting of hart after the water brooks."*

We often find ourselves physically thirsty throughout the day. We drink to keep ourselves from dehydration. But, as Charles Chauncy understood, there are times in life when we are just as dry spiritually. God allows these moments to draw us closer to him, to his springs of joy.[36]

> "Like cold water to a weary soul is good news from a distant land"
> (PROVERBS 25:25).

**PRAYER**

*Quench my thirst, O Lord. Show me today why I am thirsty and lead me to look to you for refreshment.*

# 37. Don't Send the Bishops

Charles Chauncy, pastor of Boston's First Church, was so enthusiastic when he heard about the repeal of the Stamp Act that he would have rung the bells in heaven if he could have. But his enthusiasm was short-lived. He soon took an unusual stand for a clergyman. Chauncy opposed the Church of England's efforts to send more bishops to the colonies.

*"These Bishops should make use of their SUPERIORITY, as most probably they would, sooner or later, to influence our great men here . . . to carry into execution, measures to force the growth of the Church,"* he wrote in a letter to a friend in 1767.

Chauncy did not fear the spread of the gospel—far from it. And he fully supported freedom of religion. The colonists were not *"rest[r]ained in the exercise of that 'liberty wherewith Christ has made them free,'"* he said. Chauncy believed the Church of England's efforts to send more bishops to America was a way to make the Anglican Church the dominant church in the colonies, and thus establish a state religion. He was concerned about the church's political influence, not its spiritual impact.

Reverend Chauncy also feared that other denominations—who were *"far more numerous than the Episcopalians"*—would complain if the Church of England sent more bishops to the colonies. Chauncy felt more kinship to Americans from different denominations than he did to Anglicans in England.

*"For they [Americans of other denominations] are the descendants from ancestors, who subdued & cultivated this rude wilderness, amidst a thousand difficulties & hazards, so as to make it the pleasant fruitful land*

*we now behold it; hereby adding to the extent, strength and glory of the British Crown,"* he wrote.

Chauncy possessed a passion for freedom of religion. It was an integral part of his heritage. Chauncy was the great-grandson of a minister who fled religious persecution in England. Grandfather Chauncy arrived at Plymouth, Massachusetts, in 1638 and served as president of Harvard. The younger Chauncy alluded to his ancestry in his letter: *"They [the colonists] would hazard every thing dear to them, their estates, their very lives, rather than suffer their necks to be put under that yoke of bondage, which was so sadly galling to their fathers, and occasioned their retreat into this distant land, that they might enjoy the freedom of men and Christians."*

Charles Chauncy's stand revealed an unusual paradox for a pastor, but a key principle for an American undergoing a revolution of the heart and mind. By opposing the Church of England's efforts to send more bishops to the colonies in the 1760s, he stood firm for the freedom Christ has given to humanity.[37]

> "It is for freedom that Christ has set us free. Stand firm, then, and do not let yourselves be burdened again by a yoke of slavery" (GALATIANS 5:1).

**PRAYER**

*Thank you for setting me free in Christ. Thank you for the heritage of religious freedom in America, and for those who suffered so much for that freedom.*

# 38. Pseudonyms

First name. Last name. Given name. Christian name. Family name. Nickname. Pseudonyms. Name-calling. What's in a name? It's as simple as identity.

Probably no one was happier about the Stamp Act's repeal than the man many in Boston knew only as "the Puritan." His letters to the *Boston Gazette* championed his opinions on a wide variety of issues. He used different monikers to reinforce his positions. "Puritan" was his pseudonym for letters clamoring for religious liberty. He wrote this ditty nearly a decade before the Stamp Act: *"While it is grown fashionable for men of ingenuity and public spirit, with a noble ardour, to warn us against a tame submission to the iron rods; and LIBERTY, LIBERTY, is the Cry, I confess I am surprised to find, that so little attention is given to the danger we are in, of the utter loss of those religious Rights, the enjoyment of which our good forefathers had more especially in their intention, when they explored and settled this new world.*" The Puritan's letter to the *Gazette* appeared in 1758.

This Puritan feared the rise of "Popery" if the French won the French and Indian War. Today's culture cringes at such name-calling, but the anti-French sentiment in America and England was as much a clash against Catholicism, France's official state religion at the time, as it was against customs. Differences in religion were at the core of the friction between the British and the French, both in Europe and in the New World.

But this Puritan wasn't only concerned about religious rights and freedom. He was also an ardent supporter of civil rights. He used different names when addressing different issues. Depending on his mood and his views, sometimes this Puritan was *"Determinatus"* and other times he was *"Vindex."* Many times he was *"Candidus,"* but he was quite candid no matter what name he used.

By the early 1770s, his identity became clear, especially to the Sons of Liberty—an umbrella name for men who resisted the new taxes. They recognized him as one of their own and knew his writings. To others in Boston, he was the failed brewery house owner known for a decade as their tax collector. Then he earned the title "clerk" for the Massachusetts Lower House of Representatives, where he opposed the Stamp Act.

No matter what name he used on any given day, his identity was always known to the One who is neither Protestant nor Catholic. The father of liberty never forgot his name. Regardless of this man's pseudonym or his role in life, he was first and foremost Samuel Adams. His Father in heaven called him by name and does the same today.[38]

> "And the LORD said to Moses, 'I will do the very thing you have asked, because I am pleased with you and I know you by name'" (EXODUS 33:17).

**PRAYER**

*Whatever roles I take on today or titles I may be labeled, Lord, thank you for your promise to call me by name.*

# 39. The Circular

What's the point of writing a letter? To get someone to listen to what you have to say.

"*A man should have the free use and sole disposal of the fruit of his honest industry, subject to no control,*" Samuel Adams penned in a letter about a law of nature.

As clerk for the lower house of the Massachusetts Assembly, Adams found himself once again lifting his pen to protest a British tax. He sent copies of this official letter, known as the circular, to other colonial legislatures, members of Parliament, and the royal governor in February 1768. The letters he received in return were his ears.

The controversy was the Townshend Acts, Parliament's external taxes on imports such as paints, lead, glass, and tea. The question was "taxation without representation." Although Adams didn't use this exact phrase in his circular, he argued the point. "*What a man has honestly acquired is absoluetely his own, which he may freely give, but cannot be taken from him without his consent.*" He called representation an "*unalterable Right in nature, ingrafted in the British Constitution, as a fundamental Law.*" This right was "*sacred and irrevocable.*"

Although the Atlantic Ocean was a practical obstacle to direct colonial representation in Parliament, Adams believed the government had already created a system for the remedy. He explained that Britain established local, subordinate legislatures, such as the Massachusetts House, so "*that their subjects might enjoy the unalienable Right of a Representation.*" These legislatures were listening devices, hearing aids.

But the louder these legislatures cried, the more selective Parliament's hearing became. Adams believed the best way to catch the king's attention was to whisper sweetness. Thus his circular letters included embellishments such as calling the king "*our common head & Father.*"

Three months after Clerk Adams distributed copies of his circular letter on behalf of the Massachusetts House, he learned that many were listening to him. The assemblies of New Hampshire, Connecticut, and New Jersey endorsed Adams's letter. However, Britain's secretary of state ordered the governors of the colonies to stop their assemblies from endorsing Adams's circular. The royal governor of Massachusetts responded by dissolving the legislature when it refused to revoke the circular.

These events did not prevent Adams from writing letters. "*A man's property is his industry; and if it may be taken from him under any pretense whatsoever, at the will of another, he cannot be said to be free, for*" *he labors like a bond slave, not for himself but for another,"* he wrote to the *Boston Gazette* a year later.

And with every letter he wrote, Samuel Adams searched for listeners. His revolution had begun.[39]

> "Hear my prayer, O God; listen to the words of my mouth"
> (PSALM 54:2).

**PRAYER**

*Even when no one else listens, thank you for hearing me when I call.*

# 40. Commanding Officer

Who can unite soldiers and civilians? A heavenly commanding officer.

Two months after the royal governor dissolved the Massachusetts House, ships arrived in Boston Harbor that the colonists had hoped to never see: English warships. Two regiments of English infantry landed and took up quarters in Boston. But instead of resting their heads at the castle barracks outside town, they established residence in the middle of town. Their commanding officer ordered them to keep order.

Samuel Adams's pen flew. Principus Obsta wrote a letter to the *Boston Gazette* October 17, 1768, in response to the arrival of the troops. *"'Where Law ends, [says Mr. Locke] Tyranny begins,"* Mr. Obsta began of the failure in common sense. The truth was obvious—martial law and civilian law do not mix. Martial law occurs when a military force takes over a civil authority.

*"No man can pretend to say that the peace and good order of the community is so secure with soldiers quartered in the body of a city as without them. Besides, where military power is introduced, military maxims are propagated and adopted, which are inconsistent with and must soon eradicate every idea of civil government,"* he wrote.

Adams explained the difference between military and civilian law. Under martial law soldiers have one aim: to please their commanding officers. Adams believed commanding officers held an even more powerful grip on their soldiers' loyalty than the lawfulness of their commands. Civilians, on the other hand, were subject to the laws of the government. They called their commanding officer by a different name: conscience.

*"It is moreover to be observ'd that military government and civil, are so different from each other, if not opposite, that they cannot long subsist together,"* he concluded.

The presence of troops in Boston increased the protests against the Townshend Acts throughout the colonies. Virginian George Mason wrote resolutions protesting both the Townshend Acts and British opposition to Adams's circular letters. George Washington presented these resolutions to the Virginia House of Burgesses.

"*They [Virginia] put on the appearance of the Sons of Liberty,*" Adams later commented. However, when another commanding officer, the royal governor of Virginia, dissolved the House of Burgesses as a consequence, many more Virginians began to protest.

Adams knew military and civilian law blended together about as well as rocks and water. The presence of soldiers in Boston was a direct violation of Samuel Adams's views on property and the natural laws of men. He believed in separation of military and civilian affairs. He knew there was only one commanding officer who could regulate the hearts of both soldiers and civilians, and that was his heavenly Captain.[40]

> "No one serving as a soldier gets involved in civilian affairs—he wants to please his commanding officer"
> (2 TIMOTHY 2:4).

**PRAYER**

*Father, may I look to you and you alone as my commanding officer whether I live in the civilian or military world you have given me.*

# 41. By Me Kings Reign

H*ot, rash, disorderly proceedings, injure the reputation of a people as to wisdom, valour and virtue, without procuring them the least benefit,*" John Dickinson wrote in one of his dozen letters on the subject of authoritarian British rule.

This Pennsylvanian also opposed the Townshend Acts, but was suspicious of Samuel Adams, the Sons of Liberty, and their tactics. He preferred to use his pen to pitch his opposition without stirring people to disorder.

He called his writings, which were first published in the *Pennsylvania Chronicle*, "Letters from a Farmer in Pennsylvania." Dickinson recognized that governments make mistakes. It was the people's responsibility, however, to forgive and not antagonize.

"*Every government, at some time or other, falls into wrong measures; these may proceed from mistake or passion,*" he stated. "*But every such measure does not dissolve the obligation between the governors and the governed; the mistake may be corrected; the passion may pass over.*"

Dickinson had not lost faith in the king and Parliament. If the colonies responded with respect, he believed the British government would respond with more tenderness than a parent. *"Let us behave like dutiful children, who have received unmerited blows from a beloved parent. Let us complain to our parents; but let our complaints speak at the same time, the language of affliction and veneration,"* he pointed out in this same letter.

Dickinson cultivated respect for authority by sowing respectful suggestions throughout his letters. He believed a protest, such as boycotting British trade ships, could be accomplished without violence or destruction and wrote, *"If . . . our applications to his Majesty and the parliament for the redress, prove ineffectual, let us then take another step, by withholding from Great-Britain, all the advantages she has been used to receive from us."*

This farmer considered that not every tactic would work, but believed variety over time was the key to tilling, nourishing, and harvesting reconciliation. *"Then let us try, if our ingenuity, industry, and frugality, will not give weight to our remonstrances. Let us all be united with one spirit in one cause. Let us invent; let us work; let us save; let us at the same time, keep up our claims, and unceasingly repeat our complaints,"* he asked of his readers.

Recognizing God's supreme authority, Dickinson included a prayer in his letter. *"But above all, let us implore the protection of that infinite good and gracious Being, by whom 'kings reign and princes decree justice.'"*

John Dickinson's twelve respectful letters from "a Farmer in Pennsylvania" later earned him the name, "Penman of the Revolution."[41]

> "By me kings reign, and princes decree justice" (PROVERBS 8:15 KJV).

**PRAYER**

*Thank you for being the Supreme Authority in my life and for reminding me to respect the authorities you have placed over me.*

# 42. The Revolution Today: What's in a Name?

The Puritan. The Sons of Liberty. The troublemaker. Samuel Adams assumed many names and received many unfavorable labels throughout his protests of Britain's changing policies.

Our modern culture is no different. We smack labels on people without thinking. From bumper stickers to billboards, society is full of labels, both helpful and harmful. And sometimes a simple title change can have devastating effects. Such was the case in August 2006.

The news of the demotion was dreadful. The demoted one had been doted on, holding its esteemed label for seventy-six years.

The International Astronomical Union was the culprit. They shook up the solar system in August 2006 by stripping Pluto of its treasured title, "planet." But they didn't leave it title-less. Pluto became a "dwarf planet" instead. Its small size and failure to stay out of neighbor Neptune's orbit stripped it of its planetary power.

Pluto fans did what earthlings do. They protested by coming up with their own labels, their own slogans for the planet named after the Roman god of the underworld. One entrepreneur began selling "Pluto is a Planet" T-shirts on the Internet to express her opposition. Another protested with bumper stickers. "I'm not burning with anger about the Pluto decision, but it has touched a nerve with a lot of people," Chris Spurgeon said. This Los Angeles–based Web programmer sold "Honk if Pluto is still a planet" bumper stickers to raise funds for his favorite space-advocacy group.

Within twenty-four hours of the announcement, a San Francisco Internet company began selling more than one thousand products, from mugs to mouse pads. Fretting over the demise of Pluto, these slogans were as lively as the most heated political mottos.

"Pluto is in the Doghouse—Save Pluto"

"Pluto 2006: Running as an Independent Candidate"

"Pluto: One day you're in, the next day you're out"

For years children learned how to remember the names of planets through this clever slogan: My very excellent mother just served us nine pizzas. The first letter of each word is the first letter of a planet's name— Mercury, Venus, Earth, Mars, Jupiter, Saturn, Uranus, Neptune, and Pluto.

Just as God created Pluto as an icy mass of gases that sweats when it gets closer to the sun, so he created us even more unique and wonderful. Both favorable and unfavorable labels may have defined Samuel Adams and a moniker may have mattered to Pluto fans, but no title or slogan can change the essence of who God created us to be, earthlings in his image.[42]

> "I praise you because I am fearfully and wonderfully made; your works are wonderful, I know that full well" (PSALM 139:14).

**PRAYER**

*Thank you for creating me in your image. Thank you for my name and the unique qualities you have given me.*

# 43. Sabbath Rest:
# A Pastor's Redemption

While tensions with England brewed, a pastor who had once taken a huge risk by preaching politics from the pulpit learned a lesson in humility. *"I now partake no less in your common joy, on account of the repeal of that act; whereby these colonies are emancipated from a slavish, inglorious bondage,"* Jonathan Mayhew preached after the repeal of the Stamp Act.

When the colonists' rage over the Stamp Act peaked in August 1765, Mayhew had preached a sermon on liberty, calling on his parishioners to cut off those who would ensnare them. His words may have gone too far. Some believed Mayhew's sermon incited the mob that later burned Thomas Hutchinson's home. One of the arsonists claimed he "was excited to the idea" by a sermon.

After the fire, Mayhew wrote Hutchinson a sympathy letter. But regret weighed on his conscience with the weight of an anchor. And although he was thrilled to learn of the Stamp Act's repeal less than a year later, he preached hesitantly and more carefully on the subject.

*"But when you requested me to preach a sermon on this joyful occasion, I conclude it was neither your expectation nor desire, that I should enter very particularly into a political consideration of the affair,"* he explained.

But Mayhew did not grovel in his mistake in calling for "cutting off" those responsible for the Stamp Act. He had experienced forgiveness.

*"Thus 'our soul is escaped as a bird from the snare of the fowlers; the snare is broken, and we are escaped'; tho' not without much struggling in the snare, before it gave way, and set us at liberty again,"* he said.

This time Mayhew measured his words as carefully as an apothecary measured powder. He dared not imply guilt on the part of the king or Parliament. Instead he blamed some anonymous evil-minded individuals in Britain as the cunning fowlers.

Thus this humbled pastor praised the Lord. *"May that God, in whom our help has been, continue to protect us, our rights and privileges!"* he heralded.

Mayhew's enthusiasm continued to mount as he praised God's forgiveness and peace. *"And, of his infinite mercy in Jesus Christ, finally bring us all to those peaceful and glorious regions, where no evil spirits, no wicked fowlers will come; where no snares will be spread for us; no proud waters to go over our soul!"* he said, pointing his parishioners to their future in eternity.

> "We have escaped like a bird out of the fowler's snare; the snare has been broken, and we have escaped. Our help is in the name of the LORD, the Maker of heaven and earth" (PSALM 124:7, 8).

Although he couldn't undo the damage his first sermon may have inflicted on Thomas Hutchinson's home, he received a second chance to preach in a more responsible way on the same subject. God's redemption continues today, giving us opportunities to release us from both the fowler's snare and the chains of our own making.[43]

**PRAYER**

*Thank you for redeeming me from the fowler's snare through your Son, Jesus Christ. I confess my sins today and ask for a second chance.*

# 44. Insanity

James Otis had become a colonial celebrity by 1769. His opposition to the Writs of Assistance and then to the Stamp Act, along with his mentorship of Samuel Adams and John Adams, had forever changed Boston. *"[James] Otis' power was so magnetic that a Boston town meeting, upon his mere entering, would break out into shouts and clapping,"* a friend wrote about Otis's magnetism.

Although always fiery, Otis's temper became less controlled over time. His friends noticed that his eccentric ways became more exaggerated. The patriot was paranoid. One day in September 1769 Otis placed an advertisement in the *Boston Gazette*. In it he protested four customs commissioners. Otis believed they had *"assailed his character"* and *"formed a confederacy of villainy."* The advertisement was a public sign of his weakness. It seemed the great opponent of the Writs of Assistance was losing his mind.

*"On the evening of the following day, Mr. Otis went into a coffeehouse where John Robinson, one of the commissioners whom he had lampooned, was sitting. On entering the room, Mr. Otis was attacked by Robinson who struck him with his cane. Otis struck back. There was a battle. Those who were present were Robinson's friends. The fight became a melee,"* recounted Otis historian John Ridpath.

The fight left Otis bleeding, exhausted, and critically wounded in the head. *"On the morrow, Boston was aflame with excitement. Otis was seriously injured; in fact he never recovered from the effects of the assault,"* Ridpath wrote.

*"During the sessions of the Assembly, in the years 1770 and 1771, James Otis retained his membership, but the mental disease which afflicted him began to grow worse, and he participated only at intervals (and eccentrically) in the business of legislation,"* noted Ridpath.

Although Otis had been showing signs of mental illness, his head injury exaggerated his condition. The people of Boston honored Otis at a town meeting, expressing their "ardent wishes" for his recovery. But it was not meant to be.

*"From this time forth the usefulness of James Otis was virtually at an end. In the immortal drama on which the curtain was rising—the drama of Liberty and Independence—he was destined to take no part. The pre-revolutionist in eclipse must give place to the Revolutionaries,"* Ridpath wrote.

But Ridpath was wrong. Even the insane Otis would prove his life still had purpose. Although his flame had dwindled to a flicker, he would do something he had never done before. Thanks to those who bore his weakness by sheltering him, James Otis would soon fire a musket in battle to protect his homeland.[44]

> "We who are strong ought to bear with the failings of the weak and not to please ourselves"
> (ROMANS 15:1).

**PRAYER**

*Give me grace for those who are weak around me. Thank you for reminding me that purpose does not end with illness or even insanity.*

# 45. Securing Dependence

As Chief Justice Thomas Hutchinson watched tensions building and boycotts burgeoning in 1769, he secretly banged a gavel in his heart. He chose sides.

The raging fire that had destroyed his home may have motivated Hutchinson to call for *"God to give us better hearts"* in 1765, but its cinders left a permanent scar. The mark either sealed the sentiment he already held, or his troubles led him to abandon the colonies. Whichever the case, he revealed his choice to support the British in a private letter to a friend on January 20, 1769.

*"Because I think it ought to be so, that those [in Parliament] who have been most steady in preserving the constitution and opposing the licen-ciousness of such as call themselves sons of liberty will certainly meet with favor and encouragement,"* Hutchinson wrote of his hopes for Parliament's success in suppressing the colonies.

Hutchinson embraced his job as chief justice (and later lieutenant governor and governor) with the rigidity of a schoolmaster. He believed Massachusetts must be dependent on the parent country, an opinion opposite that of Samuel Adams and Patrick Henry.

If measures were not taken to secure this dependence, then *"it is all over with us. The friends of government will be utterly disheartened, and the friends of anarchy will be afraid of nothing, be it ever so extravagant,"* he continued.

After the patriots boycotted the Townshend Acts, Hutchinson's supreme aim was to secure dependence on England from the colonies. Issuing claims of independence was as outrageous to this colonial British official as moving to France. *"There must be an abridgment of what are called English liberties . . . there must be a great restraint of natural liberty,"* he wrote, expressing his belief that government must limit liberty.

But practicality also led him to believe that Americans must submit to more limits than their fellow citizens in England. *"I doubt whether it is possible to project a system of government in which a colony 3,000 miles distant from the parent state shall enjoy all the liberty of the parent state,"* he opined.

Then this schoolmaster made his most striking statement, one which made his choice crystal clear. *"I wish the good of the colony when I wish to see some further restraint of liberty rather than the connexion with the parent state should be broken,"* he wrote to his friend.

And with that stroke, Hutchinson privately proved he was loyal to the British. He continued his public image of impartiality, but his true sentiment was to secure dependence on England in the colonies. This letter would later become his Achilles' heel. Thomas Hutchinson depended on tyrannical as a solution to the conflict with the colonies.[45]

> "You say you have strategy and military strength—but you speak only empty words. On whom are you depending, that you rebel against me?" (2 KINGS 18:20).

**PRAYER**

*God, show me where my dependence lies and where my loyalties stand. Bring me into your strategy and purpose for my life.*

# 46. Witnesses to the Massacre

Mass murder forever stained Boston on March 5, 1770.

*"ON Monday Evening the 5th current a few Minutes after 9 O'Clock a most horrid murder was committed in King Street before the Customhouse Door by 8 or 9 Soldiers under the Command of Capt Tho Preston,"* John Tudor recorded in his diary.

This Boston merchant was an eyewitness to the event known today as the Boston Massacre. The massacre left behind a mystery that has intrigued the most curious of historical sleuths for more than two centuries. The question is this: Who started the massacre, the British soldiers or the colonists? Here is how Tudor saw it: *"This unhappy affair began by Some Boys & young fellows throwing Snow Balls at the sentry placed at the Customhouse Door."* Tudor noted that the soldiers came to assist the sentry, not to provoke the boys.

*"Soon after a Number of people collected, when the Cap^t commanded the Soldiers to fire, which they did and 3 Men were Kil'd on the Spot & several Wounded, one of which died next morning,"* Tudor reported.

Tudor explained that Captain Preston withdrew his soldiers immediately after the firing. Had he failed to do so, *"the Consequencis mite have been terable."* Alarm bells in town began to ring faster than the snowballs could fly. News of the killings turned Boston into a court of public opinion, leaving behind permanent stains of distrust and anguish.

A week after this "event of consequence," a committee of men, including Samuel Adams and Boston rich man John Hancock, issued a report. Here is how they saw it: *"On Friday the 2d instant, a quarrel arose between some soldiers of the 29th, and the rope-maker's journeymen and apprentices."* The report explained that the tensions between the soldiers and boys lasted all weekend and resulted in injuries on both sides.

*"This contentious disposition continued until the Monday evening following, when a party of seven or eight soldiers were detached from the main guard under the command of Captain Preston, and by his orders fired upon the inhabitants promiscuously in King street, without the least warning of their intention,"* the report continued.

Claiming *"strict truth"* this report complained that the soldiers had treated the colonists with the same prejudice, rudeness, and audacity as an enemy army. *"They landed in the town with all the appearance of hostility! They marched through the town with all the ensigns of triumph! and evidently designed to subject the inhabitants to the severe discipline of a garrison!"*

Was the massacre an accidental shooting or a deliberate act? Disagreement was the final verdict in the court of history. The confusion matched the condition of the colonies. As the committee reported, *"Such has been the general state of the town."*[46]

> "Ruthless witnesses come forward; they question me on things I know nothing about"
> (PSALM 35:11).

**PRAYER**

*When confusion is the final verdict of my day, help me to look to you for the truth and guidance to wash away any unwanted stains.*

# 47. Moving Day

Moving day came to Boston. The massacre moved the hearts and minds of many but divided a leader from his people.

Upon hearing the news that night, Thomas Hutchinson, now the lieutenant governor, called the magistrates into an emergency session to try to restore order. Hutchinson arranged for Captain Preston's arrest and dispersed the multitude gathered in the streets by 4:00 a.m.

While the law moved Hutchinson to prudence, that night brought Boston's residents more anguish and confusion than they had ever experienced as a community. Many were so affected by the violence that they met the next morning at Boston's Faneuil Hall to mourn. Several gave speeches, which brought more and more people, including merchant John Tudor, to the hall. They appointed a committee to prepare a message for Hutchinson.

*"That it is the unanimous opinion of this Meeting, that the inhabitants & soldiery can no longer live together in safety,"* Tudor wrote, adding that he had recorded the petition *"word for word."*

*"That nothing can Rationally be expected to restore the peace of the Town & prevent Blood & Carnage, but the removal of the Troops: and that we most fervently pray his Honor that his power & influance may be exerted for their instant removal,"* he continued.

Claiming he did not have the authority to remove the troops, Hutchinson declined the petition. His position seemed unwavering.

But Hutchinson's rejection merely motivated more residents to gather at Faneuil Hall. By noon the group had reached four thousand, forcing them to adjourn to a larger meetinghouse. Once again they petitioned Hutchinson to remove the soldiers.

Hutchinson brought this second request to the magistrates. For "the good order of the Town" they voted to send the soldiers to the castle barracks outside town. Although the soldiers did not return to Britain, the decision started bells ringing in the hearts of the residents. *"Mr Hancock . . . Read their Report as above, which was Received with a shoute & clap of hands, which made the Meetinghouse Ring,"* Tudor reported.

Two days later, the residents made one final move. While the bells pealed, they closed all the town's stores and buried the massacre victims in one grave. *"The several Hearses forming a junction in King Street, the Theatre of that inhuman Tragedy, proceeded from thence thro' the main street, lengthened by an immence Concourse of people . . . The sorrow Visible in the Countenances, together with the peculiar solemnity, Surpass description,"* John Tudor wrote, reporting that as many as twenty thousand followed the hearses on Boston's most sorrowful moving day.

> "I have not dwelt in a house from the day I brought the Israelites up out of Egypt to this day. I have been moving from place to place with a tent as my dwelling" (2 SAMUEL 7:6).

The massacre moved Bostonians to many places: prudence, petition, and pacification, but sadly, not peace.[47]

**PRAYER**

*Father, move me to your doorstep today. May I dwell in your tent, wrapped in peace.*

# 48. Trial of the Century

The people of Boston did not forget the Boston Massacre; neither did the patriot lawyer who defended the British soldiers in the most watched trial of the eighteenth century.

*"That large Church was filled and crowded in every Pew, Seat, Alley, and Gallery, by an Audience of several Thousands of People of all Ages and Characters and of both Sexes,"* John Adams wrote in his diary on March 5, 1773, three years after the massacre.

Adams had *"reason to remember that fatal Night."* Although he did not witness it, he was on the scene as soon as he heard the clanging alarm bells. Because his wife Abigail was *"in Circumstance,"* Adams returned to their house once he heard what had happened. The news did not send the pregnant Abigail into labor that night, but it did bring many labor pains to Adams.

Before the bells could strike noon the next day, a man knocked on Adams's door. Adams was shocked to learn Captain Preston had requested him as his defense attorney. He knew defending a British soldier in such a high profile would give him about as much popularity as Thomas Hutchinson had among Adams's patriot friends. But for Adams, this was not about pining for popularity but upholding a principle.

Believing the *"bar"* and the law *"ought in my opinion to be independent and impartial at all Times,"* Adams accepted the job of defense attorney, despite the strain it might put on his relationship with his cousin Sam.

Adams also made a pledge. He would not engage in *"Art or Address, No Sophistry or Prevarication in such a Cause."* To Adams, upholding the law required honesty and nothing *"more than Fact, Evidence and Law would justify."* He would not use the opportunity to gain publicity for himself.

By accepting the job, Adams proved his patriotism was more than a protest against stamps or a boycott against the Townshend Acts. The right to a fair trial was the soul of liberty, and he did his part to make sure the rights of the accused were upheld.

Although he faced *"Anxiety, and Obloquy [humiliation] enough"* for his decision, time proved Adams made a wise choice. *"It was, however, one of the most gallant, generous, manly and disinterested Actions of my whole Life, and one of the best Pieces of Service I ever rendered my Country,"* Adams reflected in his autobiography.

The verdict resulted in the acquittal of Captain Preston and six soldiers. Two other soldiers were convicted of manslaughter.

*"Judgment of Death . . . against those Soldiers would have been as foul a Stain upon this Country as the Executions of the Quakers or Witches, anciently. As the Evidence was, the Verdict of the jury was exactly right,"* Adams wrote.

The Boston Massacre bolstered the revolution going on in John Adams's mind and heart. It strengthened his commitment to justice.[48]

"Do not pervert justice; do not show partiality to the poor or favoritism to the great, but judge your neighbor fairly" (LEVITICUS 19:15).

**PRAYER**

*God, you are the Supreme Judge, the One who forgives sin and grants pardons. Grant me the grace to uphold justice.*

# 49. The Revolution Today: Sensational Coverage

If the Boston Massacre took place today, can you imagine the media coverage? All the media outlets and their gazillion satellite trucks would fill Boston's streets.

John Tudor's colorful testimony would come alive on TV, complete with his thick Boston accent and dramatic descriptions. The TV play-by-play would announce the shocking choice of John Adams as the defense attorney. Unlike some, Adams would avoid the cameras until after the trial. He loathed "art and address" by showboating attorneys. He would, however, make his views known after the verdict in a sit-down television interview.

Reporters would camp outside Thomas Hutchinson's office, trying to snag an interview with him. He would shun them. Instead, the TV cameras would show the same video of Hutchinson getting into his carriage and riding away.

Expert analysis would fill the airwaves with more predictions than the beginning of a season of Red Sox baseball. Reporters would ask experts endless questions such as:

"Why did it take Hutchinson until four o'clock in the morning to clear the streets?"

"Was there evidence tampering? After all, the snowballs melted before DNA could be gathered."

"Was the massacre a conspiracy by Samuel Adams to jump-start a revolution?"

"Are the Sons of Liberty a gang?"

"Why hasn't the jury delivered a verdict? It's been three hours already since they convened."

The sensationalist nature of our media today is not drastically different from colonial times. The technology and scope have changed, but not necessarily the dramatization. Silversmith Paul Revere engraved a drawing of the massacre. His single image depicted a line of British soldiers shooting the colonists as if firing on sitting ducks. When the colonists saw the picture in newspapers, they couldn't help but blame the soldiers. They were so hungry for an answer to "Why did it happen?" that many found the soldiers guilty before the trial began.

Sensationalism can color our understanding of truth, whether it's a political cartoon or continual footage of a person getting in and out of their car without talking to a reporter. Sensationalism can also color the truth of our own circumstances.

Sometimes we need to take a moment to think about our lives through a truth detector. Fortune-telling distorts our decisions. Life is too short to live it based on what we think will happen. The terms *always* and *never* can be misleading when we use them against loved ones or coworkers. Truth is a gift wrapped in the ribbons of God's promise to love and forgive.[49]

**PRAYER**

*I give you my mind. May I dwell on truthful thoughts and accept the times when I can't have instant answers to life's most confusing questions.*

> "Finally, brothers, whatever is true, whatever is noble, whatever is right, whatever is pure, whatever is lovely, whatever is admirable—if anything is excellent or praiseworthy—think about such things" (PHILIPPIANS 4:8).

# 50. Sabbath Rest: A Blueprint for Leadership

The Reverend Samuel Cooke knew how to embrace opportunity. When he spoke before Thomas Hutchinson and other Boston leaders on May 30, 1770, Cooke wasted no time in trying to abate the growing tension. But instead of taking direct aim at the political situation with a fiery sermon, he opted for a more subdued approach. He used the opportunity to draw a picture of leadership.

Cooke reminded his audience that the Supreme Ruler *"allows and approves of the establishment of [government] among men."*

But also he prodded these leaders to remember the people they led. They were to be as faithful to the law bench as pastors were to the pulpit. *"The first attention of the faithful ruler will be to the subjects of government in their specific nature,"* Cooke explained. He wanted the governor and legislators to remember they were not ruling over ants, but humans.

*"He will not forget that he rulest over men,—men who are of the same species of himself, and by nature equal,—men who are the offspring of God, and alike formed after his glorious image—men of like passions and feelings with himself, and, as men, in the sight of their common Creator of equal importance,"* Cooke reminded the leaders.

Cooke told them they also had a responsibility to make understandable laws. Purposefully confusing the uneducated man was immoral. It was as deceitful as a lie. *"Fidelity to the public requires that the laws be as plain and explicit as possible, that the less knowing may understand, and not be ensnared by them, while the artful evade their force,"* he said.

Government was not for the elite alone, but for the protection of the weak as well. *"The benefits of the constitution and of the laws must extend to every branch and each individual in society, of whatever degree, that every man may enjoy his property, and pursue his honest course of life with security."*

Cooke also urged this audience of magistrates to lead by example. *"Rulers are appointed guardians of the constitution in their respective stations, and must confine themselves within the limits by which their authority is circumscribed,"* he said.

Cooke reminded the leaders to admit when they were wrong. *"Justice also requires of rulers, in their legislative capacity, that they attend to the operation of their own acts and repeal whatever laws, upon an impartial review, they find to be inconsistent with the laws of God, the rights of men, and the general benefit of society,"* the Reverend Samuel Cooke taught.

The same can be said of leadership today. Leaders are most successful when they respect those in their care, make reasonable rules, lead by example, and admit their mistakes.[50]

> "The God of Israel spoke, the Rock of Israel said to me: 'When one rules over men in righteousness, when he rules in the fear of God, he is like the light of morning at sunrise on a cloudless morning, like the brightness after rain that brings the grass from the earth'"
> (2 SAMUEL 23:3, 4).

**PRAYER**

*God, enable me to lead with integrity in the roles you have given.*

# 51. When the Teakettle Boils

On the day of the Boston Massacre in 1770, Parliament, unaware of the event, made a critical decision. They repealed the Townshend Acts, but retained one tiny tax—the one on tea. By doing so, they struck a match and lit a fire under a kettle of water that boiled over three years later.

King George III then kindled New England's fires of rebellion when he appointed Thomas Hutchinson royal governor of Massachusetts. Because the colonists no longer paid his salary, Hutchinson was now completely indebted to the crown.

Selectman John Andrews felt the heat as the smoldering kindling grew into a fire that skipped across the ocean. Because he was elected by his fellow Bostonians to look after town affairs, Andrews attended many meetings. He heard the fireplace sizzle when Samuel Adams threw a pot of cold water on the British government's fire in 1772. Adams established Committees of Correspondence, which gave the Sons of Liberty a pot to clang for alerting their friends, citizens, and countrymen of any rights violations by the British. These committees formed throughout the colonies.

Andrews was a typical Bostonian. He enjoyed his fish, ale, and a good cup of tea, but only when he didn't have to pay a tax for it. Hence, when ships carrying tea entered Boston Harbor on November 29, 1773, Andrews knew boiling bubbles would follow in their wake.

*"Hall and Bruce [captains of the ships carrying the tea] arriv'd Saturday evening with each an hundred and odd chests of the detested Tea. What will be done with it, can't say: but I tremble for y<sup>e</sup> consequences,"* Andrews wrote to his brother.

Parliament had contributed to the simmering earlier that year when it ceased all import taxes on tea except for the three-pence-per-pound tax. Andrews heard the Boston merchants curse over the decision. The tax gave the British East India Company an unfair advantage over the Boston merchants because a surplus allowed this London company to sell tea at a lower price.

But what made the tiny bubbles float to the top of the kettle was the benefit the tea tax gave to Hutchinson's sons. As customs collectors they were allowed to keep a percentage of the tea taxes. And their pockets burst while the water boiled.

*"But am persuaded, from the present dispositions of y<sup>e</sup> people, that no other alternative will do, than to have it [the tea] immediately sent back to London again,"* Andrews explained to his brother. But before he could finish his letter, a commotion interrupted him.

*"Y<sup>e</sup> bells are ringing for a general muster, and a third vessel is now arriv'd in Nantasket Road. Handbills are stuck up, calling upon Friends! Citizens! and Countrymen!"* he ended his letter for the moment.

What John Andrews didn't know as he heard those bells the night of November 29, 1773, was that the boiling teakettle would soon overflow.[51]

> "Smoke pours from his nostrils as from a boiling pot over a fire of reeds"
> (JOB 41:20).

**PRAYER**

*Whatever may be boiling in my life today, help me overflow with grace and forgiveness to diffuse any anger, resentment, or malice in my heart.*

# 52. Tea-Stained Harbor

John Andrews nearly spilled his tea over the commotion outside his Boston home.

*"Such prodigious shouts were made, that induc'd me, while drinking tea at home, to go out and know the cause of it,"* Selectman Andrews wrote his brother about the night of December 16, 1773. The shouts stoked his fears that the kettle had boiled over.

Andrews had kept his eye on the brewing situation since ten o'clock that morning, when five thousand Bostonians assembled at the Old South Meeting House. They unanimously demanded the ships carrying the tea should immediately leave Boston Harbor. Until the shipowners paid the tea tax, the customs officers refused to give the ships a pass to leave. The assembly waited all day to hear from the governor.

When Andrews heard those loud shouts that evening, he raced to the meetinghouse. There he learned that Hutchinson had rejected the town's request to get the ships (and their cargo of tea) out of the harbor.

*"The house was so crouded I could get no farther than y^e porch, when I found the moderator was just declaring the meeting to be dissolv'd, which caused another general shout . . . you'd thought that the inhabitants of the infernal regions had broke loose,"* Andrews penned, explaining he went home and finished drinking his own tea.

Then he heard a rumor. Some men were planning to dump the ships' tea into the harbor. He had to see it for himself. The situation called for *"ocular demonstration,"* as Andrews described it.

*"They muster'd . . . to the number of about two hundred, and proceeded, two by two, to Griffin's wharf, where Hall, Bruce, and Coffin [the ship's captains] lay, each with 114 chests of the ill fated article on board . . . and before nine o'clock in y^e evening, every chest from on board the three vessels was knock'd to pieces and flung over y^e sides,"* he wrote of the overflow.

*"They say the actors were Indians from Narragansett. Whether they were or not, to a transient observer they appear'd as such, being cloath'd in Blankets with the heads muffled, and copper color'd countenances, being each arm'd with a hatchet or axe, and pair pistols,"* reported Andrews.

Andrews's *"ocular demonstration"* left behind a firsthand account of the Boston Tea Party, as it was called years later. When it was all over that night, the "Indians" dumped nearly 350 chests of tea. One question remains, however: Was Andrews an interested observer of the action, or more? As is often the case, only God and John Andrews know whether Andrews was merely a witness to the event, or a participant in the crime.[52]

> "You know we never used flattery, nor did we put on a mask to cover up greed—God is our witness" (1 THESSALONIANS 2:5).

**PRAYER**

*God, help me to remember that you are the Great Witness, the One who knows when I wear a mask, the One who is aware of all I do.*

# 53. Ministerial Vengeance

The Boston Tea Party left behind an aftertaste that affected all of Massachusetts. *"Boston will feel the whole weight of ministerial vengeance,"* Boston Selectman John Andrews accurately predicted. He rightly feared royal repercussions for the high crimes against tea.

King George III, Prime Minister North, and Parliament were so furious over the Tea Party that they used their pens to let out some steam and passed the Coercive Acts.

All Massachusetts tasted the over-brewed legislation. The Acts closed Boston's port, revoked the eighty-year-old Massachusetts royal charter, and sent three thousand British soldiers to Massachusetts. Worse, the acts quartered those soldiers in the homes of private citizens. And, worst of all, the legislation abolished town meetings. No longer could the people legally assemble. Gone was a fundamental right. Chaos was left to fill its place.

*"This was the boldest stroke, which had yet been struck in America,"* Gov. Thomas Hutchinson wrote. He believed no measure was too strong to put a stop to the raging patriots, who *"had nothing to fear for themselves. If the colonies were subject to the supreme authority and laws of Great Britain, their offences, long since, had been of the highest nature."* Hutchinson's letter was one of the last he wrote as governor.

*"And it is certain . . . that the body of the people had also gone too far to recede, and that an open and general revolt must be the consequence; and it was not long before actual preparations were visibly making for it in most parts of the province,"* Hutchinson observed.

But the Coercive Acts also left an aftertaste in Hutchinson's mouth, one that would burn him forever and take him away from his homeland. His failure to *"secure dependency"* in the colonies resulted in his resignation, or more likely, his firing. Hutchinson and his family fled Boston for England. They never returned to America.

King George III sent four British regiments to Boston and replaced Thomas Hutchinson with Gen. Thomas Gage. The change was more coercive than any other action by the king. Gage was not only the new governor, but he was also the commander-in-chief of the British armies. Martial law had fully come to Massachusetts.

> "'Although you wash yourself with soda and use an abundance of soap, the stain of your guilt is still before me,' declares the Sovereign LORD" (JEREMIAH 2:22).

Nothing, not soap, soda, or any other substance, could wash the tea stains from Massachusetts. Military rule was the king's solution there. And soon the aftertaste would spread to the other colonies.[53]

**PRAYER**

*Soap and detergent may wash the outside, but you, O Lord, are the only one who can remove the stains from my heart. Forgive me of my sins today.*

# 54. Life in the Wilderness

The lure of the wilderness. The pursuit of tranquility. The tenets of faith. The hope for peace. The American dream. Such were the forces that drove European colonists to come to America in the 1600s and 1700s.

Those same dreams led Daniel Boone to leave his North Carolina home on the first day of May in 1769. He had heard about the unsettled land west of the thirteen colonies from a friend who had traded with the Indians there. The tapestry his friend wove was too beautiful for Boone to merely envision. He had to go exploring and touch nature's threads with his own fingers.

Within forty days Boone and his company reached their destination. The sight was as magnificent to Boone as the moment Noah's bird returned with a branch. He had reached the top of the mountain, literally and figuratively.

*"From the top of an eminence, [we] saw with pleasure the beautiful level of Kentucky. We found everywhere abundance of wild beasts of all sorts, through this vast forest,"* Boone chronicled. What stood out to him the most were the buffalo by the hundreds that grazed on the *"herbage."* Boone described them as unafraid of the *"violence of man."*

But a valley usually follows a mountaintop. No sooner had Boone and his party descended the eminence than Indians captured them.

Boone and his companions endured life in a cane cage for a week. They used their time wisely by watching their captors closely. They earned the Indians' trust by showing no inclination to escape. But on the seventh night, Boone waited for his captors to go to sleep. Then he and his company broke their cages and escaped into the forest.

Captivity by Indians would have chased most men directly back to North Carolina. But not Boone. Once again the wilderness lured him. The magnificence of freedom erased any fear of captivity or anxiety about the unknown. *"The diversity and beauties of nature I met with in this charming season expelled every gloomy and vexatious thought,"* he recorded.

Boone returned to North Carolina, then struck out on his own revolution in 1773, leading five families and forty men into the wilderness. They became Kentucky's first English settlers.

> "The desert and the parched land will be glad; the wilderness will rejoice and blossom"
> (ISAIAH 35:1).

Daniel Boone embodied the American dream. The lure of liberty led him into the wilderness. Like his fellow Americans back east, he would face many more wildernesses before he could drink from tranquility's cup and rest from a revolution.[54]

**PRAYER**

*God, thank you for the mountaintop moments and for your promise to make my deserts bloom. You are my compass today.*

# 55. Sylvan Shade in the Wilderness

When Daniel Boone led settlers from the comforts of North Carolina into the Kentucky forest in 1773, he expected hardship. He also expected danger, especially from the Indians. He encountered both.

The residue of Britain's war with the French and Indians resulted in a deep mistrust between those who chattered with a British accent and those who conversed in native tongues. Boone and his settlers frequently faced tension and threats from the Indians. With problems ranging from horse stealing to massacres with tomahawks, the lure of liberty had yet to produce lasting peace.

In one episode, a tribe kidnapped Boone's daughters. Although he rescued them, he could not stop the conflict between the settlers and the natives. Boone and his settlers longed for the coolness that comes from the shade of a tree. That protection came, but not as a result of Boone's heroics. An unlikely source brought the sylvan shade they had pursued for so long.

One day a party of Indians stormed the house of a free African settler and his family. The Indian leading the attack *"attempted to captivate the negro, who happily proved an overmatch for him, threw him on the ground, and, in the struggle,"* Boone wrote, *"the mother of the children drew an ax from a corner of the cottage and cut his head off, while her little daughter shut the door."*

The mother then put an old rusty gun barrel through a small crevice in the door, which frightened the others away. After four years of hostility, the episode finally ended tensions with the local Indians.

*"Thus Providence, by the means of this negro, saved the whole of the poor family from destruction. From that time until the happy return of peace between the United States and Great Britain the Indians did us no mischief,"* Boone wrote.

*"Many dark and sleepless nights have I been a companion for owls, separated from the cheerful society of men, scorched by the summer's sun, and pinched by the winter's cold, an instrument ordained to settle the wilderness. But now the scene is changed: peace crowns the sylvan shade,"* he concluded.

And so Boone rested in the sylvan shade God provided through the bravery of the African settlers. By following liberty into the wilderness, Daniel Boone prepared the way for the Lord to touch his heart and make his paths straight.[55]

> "A voice of one calling: 'In the desert prepare the way for the LORD; make straight in the wilderness a highway for our God'"
>
> (ISAIAH 40:3).

**PRAYER**

*Thank you for clearing the wilderness. Make a straight highway for you in my heart.*

# 56. The Revolution Today: John Adams's Pen

The most flamboyant weapon in America's quest for independence was not a bayonet, musket, or cannon. It was a pen.

Boston attorney John Adams took up his pen nearly every day of his life. He wrote in his diary. He penned letters. He took notes at meetings. He wrote volumes. Through his pen Adams expressed his opinions, observations, and optimism. One day he dipped his pen into the well and wrote this in his diary: *"A pen is certainly an excellent instrument to fix a man's attention and to inflame his ambition."*

So with a pen Adams and other revolutionaries fanned the flames of their ambition. Images of some patriots are as familiar as the money in our pockets, such as George Washington and Thomas Jefferson. Adams once wrote, *"Mr. Jefferson had the Reputation of a masterly Pen."* The faces of Patrick Henry, John Hancock, and Samuel Adams are not as imprinted in our minds, but their names are familiar for their slogans, signatures, and speeches.

Sparks flew around the known and unknown, the seen and unseen. Many of these revolutionaries developed their philosophies about government, liberty, freedom, justice, humanity, and respect using their pens. Adams's pen was his instrument of diligence, his ability to manage his time, to fulfill his work—his pen was his computer.

*"I was born for Business; for both Activity and Study. I have little Appetite, or Relish for any Thing else. I must double and redouble my Diligence. I must be more constant to my office and my Pen. Constancy accomplishes more than Rapidity,"* Adams wrote in his diary on May 24, 1773.

Adams's pen revealed his purpose. *"Continual Attention will do great Things. The Frugality, of Time, is the greatest Art as well as Virtue. This Economy will produce Knowledge as well as Wealth,"* he continued.

Adams's pen made his joy complete because it enabled him to manage his work. God's purpose in the life of John Adams and others was in part made possible by their willingness to take up their pens and write.

And whatever tool God has given to fulfill his purpose in your life, whether it's a pen, a computer, a BlackBerry, a scalpel, a hammer, or a highchair, he wants to make your joy complete through the work of your hands and the habits of your heart.[56]

> "We write this to make our joy complete" (1 JOHN 1:4).

**PRAYER**

*Thank you for the instruments, the tools of work you have placed in my hands. May I use the material things you have given me to make your work and joy complete in me.*

# 57. Sabbath Rest: Refuge and Strength

Samuel Langdon was a preacher's preacher. This Boston-born Harvard graduate served as a chaplain for the British army. He later led a church in Portsmouth, New Hampshire, before Harvard made him their president in 1774.

And while Daniel Boone explored the wilderness and the king revoked the Massachusetts charter, Langdon contemplated God's power over chaos. As a former chaplain he understood the need to summon strength in the face of immense danger and overwhelming odds.

*"If God be for us, who can be against us? The enemy has reproached us for calling on his name, and professing our trust in him,"* he preached in a sermon to a congregation facing the anarchy in Massachusetts.

Langdon knew bitterness was brewing on both sides of the ocean. The source of this tension was more than geopolitical. In many ways, the friction between the average New Englander and the average Londoner was the same as the issue that divided their forefathers: religion. The English held contempt for the "saints" in America. Political cartoons provided proof of their disdain for these Puritan descendants. Many in England had not forgotten the Puritan protests of the previous century that led them to colonize America in the first place.

*"They have made a mock of our solemn fasts, and every appearance of serious Christianity in the land,"* preached Langdon. As a comfort for this ridicule, he reminded his listeners of God's supreme position in the universe. He was above religious snobbery. After all, he had the power to move mountains and create galaxies.

*"Then the Lord will be our refuge and strength, a very present help in trouble, and we shall have no reason to be afraid though thousands of enemies set themselves against us round about, —though all nature should be thrown into tumults and convulsions. He can command the stars in their course to fight his battles, and all the elements to wage war with his enemies,"* Langdon said.

The reverend reminded his audience that God had set the Israelites free from Pharaoh's hand. *"He can destroy them with innumerable plagues, or send faintness into their heart, so that the men of might shall not find their hands. In a variety of methods he can work salvation for us, as he did for his people in ancient days, and according to the many remarkable deliverances granted in former times to Great Britain and New England,"* he concluded.

Samuel Langdon knew the God he worshipped. He had confidence in the God he served. He believed God's power could restore the colonies. God was a refuge in the wilderness, a respite from a tea-stained harbor and a sea of political cartoons. God was above any revoked charter. He was mightier than a million muskets. He could change a king's heart. And he could make a people free.[57]

> "I will restore your judges as in days of old, your counselors as at the beginning. Afterward you will be called the City of Righteousness, the Faithful City"
> (ISAIAH 1:26).

**PRAYER**

*Thank you for reminding me of your great power, the work of your mighty hand. Thank you for giving me a purpose in life.*

# 58. Silent Ben

The abuse had gone on for more than an hour. This Philadelphian printer known for his pithy sayings remained speechless while his London accusers berated him in the most abusive language. Unlike the friendly but frank questioning he received from members of Parliament over the Stamp Act in 1766, this inquiry would forever injure Benjamin Franklin. Only a hangman's noose was worse than this execution of verbal abuse.

*"Spy, traitor, would-be assassin, rebel"* were among the many accusations hurled against Franklin that day, January 29, 1774.

Franklin was quite familiar with the three dozen men surrounding him at London's Cockpit Tavern. After all, they had been his friends. Together they had shared many glorious moments, such as cheering the king at his coronation fourteen years earlier. Franklin later reflected that his time in London was the happiest in his life. He loved the crown, the king, and the colonies. The rising conflict, however, had tormented his loyalties. When his friends, the distinguished advisors to the king called the Privy Council, encircled him that day at the tavern, he realized he had to make a choice.

Their verbal abuse and accusations were so grave Franklin might as well have been a prisoner in the Tower of London. Franklin chose the most appropriate response possible in this fake trial: silence.

Franklin historian Stacy Schiff described the moment in an interview for *The History Channel Presents: The American Revolution, 2006*. She said that Franklin was *"dressed down"* and *"humiliated,"* that he didn't say a word. While wearing his old clothes, a blue velvet suit, he stood with his *"head erect."* He stood *"stock still."*

Franklin's "crime" was sending to patriot leaders in Massachusetts letters written by Gov. Thomas Hutchinson five years earlier. The letters revealed that Hutchinson supported further restraint of liberty in the colonies. The king, Parliament, and Privy Council were so angry at Franklin he might as well have spied for France. The prime minister refused to give Franklin a hearing. He received no justice, just the mock trial at the tavern.

The clock tick-tocked for more than an hour, until the final accuser finished hurling insults at Franklin. When it was over, Franklin shook hands with "the last of his friends" and left the tavern in the same way he had stood: in silence. Within two days, the king withdrew Franklin's appointment as postmaster general. He packed his bags, boarded a ship, and returned to Philadelphia.

*"Many people have dated that as the moment Franklin becomes a revolutionary,"* commented Schiff.

*"Spots of Dirt thrown upon my Character, I suffered while fresh remain; I . . . rely'd on the vulgar Adage, that they would all rub off when they were dry,"* Franklin later wrote. And when they were dry, Franklin wore the tattoo of independence.

If pithy sayings made Benjamin Franklin a public celebrity, silence turned him into a revolutionary.[58]

> "Even a fool is thought wise if he keeps silent, and discerning if he holds his tongue" (PROVERBS 17:28).

**PRAYER**

*Father, I pray for discernment today, to know when to hold my tongue, and when to speak.*

# 59. An Apt Reply

Reality was not completely apparent to the delegates when the meeting began. Many were still squinting. But one man's apt comment would open their eyes, forcing them to see the naked truth. *"I hope future ages will quote our proceedings with applause,"* Patrick Henry said during the first meeting of the Continental Congress.

Representing Virginia, Henry was one of more than fifty delegates who had come to Philadelphia in September 1774. Their opinions were as different as their dialects and the twelve colonies they represented. (The colony of Georgia's remoteness and mixed political sentiments kept it from sending representatives.)

The delegates' enthusiasm may have been as fresh as their newly purchased suits, but these travelers were also nervous. Philadelphia was as foreign to them as France or Spain. Most had never placed their heels beyond their colony's boundaries.

John Adams's pen captured their emotions as well as their blindness. He loosely recorded his observations of the proceedings. He noted how easily they agreed on the first few housekeeping items. They met at the city tavern and then walked over to Carpenter's Hall, the location of which, near the state house and library, pleased them. With little opposition, they agreed to meet there. Then they elected a president and a secretary for their proceedings.

But their next decision—how to count their votes—led to a debate that would spark controversy for decades. Should the delegates from smaller colonies have the same voting power as delegates from larger colonies? Or should wealth, not population, determine the weight of their votes? Should each colony receive one vote based on the majority opinion among that colony's delegates? Should they send the matter to a committee?

Hence, Patrick Henry stood to help his fellow congressmen remember why they were there in the first place. "*Government is dissolved. Fleets and armies and the present state of things show that government is dissolved,*" he said, reminding them of the urgent matters behind their meeting. The men had decided to convene after the crown dissolved the government of Massachusetts Bay.

"*Where are your landmarks, your boundaries of Colonies? We are in a state of nature, sir,*" Henry cried out in an effort to splash water on their faces. Henry's speech allowed them to regain their focus. Even though he opposed weighting delegate votes based on colonial wealth or population, the issue seemed trivial to him when compared with the grave issues facing the group. Unity mattered more than form and function.

"*The distinctions between Virginians, Pennsylvanians, New Yorkers, and New Englanders, are no more. I am not a Virginian, but an American,*" he said. And with that blunt statement, Patrick Henry voiced a timely phrase that has sounded for centuries.[59]

> "A man finds joy in giving an apt reply—and how good is a timely word!" (PROVERBS 15:23).

*May my words be timely and encouraging today. Corral my tongue to give apt replies, fitting for your purpose.*

# 60. No Bigotry in Prayer

Samuel Adams declared he was not a bigot. This "Puritan" could hear a prayer from any gentleman of piety.

And with that, the Continental Congress decided to open their proceedings the next day with prayer. A few opposed the motion, citing the members' religious diversity. After all, could a Baptist and an Anglican hear the same prayer? Samuel Adams's words settled the issue. Just as church bells sounded the same no matter who rang them, so the members of the Congress could listen to a prayer pleading for wisdom.

The gentleman of virtue who opened the Continental Congress's deliberations on September 7, 1774, was the Reverend Jacob Duché. Wearing his full pontificals, or robes, this Anglican read from Psalm 35, part of the predetermined *"collections of the day": "Plead my cause, O LORD, with them that strive with me: fight against them that fight against me"* (Psalm 35:1 KJV).

The readings seemed ordained by God just for the Congress that day. Because the lion was a symbol for England and the Congress was an assembly, verses seventeen and eighteen seemed perfect for their proceedings: *"Lord, how long wilt thou look on? rescue my soul from their destructions, my darling from the lions. I will give thee thanks in the great congregation: I will praise thee among much people"* (Psalm 35:17, 18 KJV).

After the readings, Duché prayed for a trio of needs no one could object to: mercy, protection, and righteousness. *"Look down in mercy we beseech Thee, on these American States, who have fled to Thee from the rod of the oppressor, and thrown themselves on Thy gracious protection, desiring henceforth to be dependent only on Thee; to Thee they have appealed for the righteousness of their cause."*

Duché understood his audience's need to work in harmony. *"Be Thou present, O God of wisdom, and direct the counsels of this honorable assembly,"* he continued.

Duché also asked for a trinity of unity: wisdom, valor, and peace. *"[E]nable them to settle things on the best and surest foundation, that the scene of blood may be speedily closed, that order, harmony and peace may be effectually restored, and truth and justice, religion and piety prevail and flourish among Thy people,"* Jacob Duché prayed, concluding in the name of *"Jesus Christ, Thy Son, Our Savior. Amen."*

> "I will give you thanks in the great assembly; among throngs of people I will praise you"
> (PSALM 35:18).

Prayer made a difference to the Continental Congress. It lightened their load. Nothing has changed today. God still inhabits the prayers of his people, especially when they assemble to pray and jointly worship him.[60]

**PRAYER**

*Remind me of this story the next time I have an opportunity for prayer with others. May I praise you and honor you in public, whether the assembly be large or small.*

# 61. Good Days

There is such a quick and constant succession of new scenes, characters, persons, and events, turning up before me, that I can't keep any
regular account,"* John Adams recorded of the excitement during the first Continental Congress.

The delegates may have represented different colonies, but they shared something in common: sacrifice. Most left their professions at home, thus forfeiting significant income in order to find a solution for their problems with England.

Adams's sacrifice was no different from his colleagues. To attend the Congress, he gave up his law practice and transferred the management of his farm to his wife. Although his sacrifice was similar, his passion was more personal than that of most of the delegates. His beloved Boston was disappearing with each rising British tide.

Thus, Adams was as passionate about winning support for Massachusetts Bay from the other delegates as a captain trying to save his sinking ship. No other colony suffered from martial law at the dictates of a British military general. No other colony quartered soldiers in the homes of its citizens.

Adams soon realized, however, that the meetings of the Congress would ebb and flow with tedious debate. He would have to be patient to find a lifesaver for Massachusetts. His journal described both the good and bad days. Duché's first reading was one of those good days. Adams was so thrilled with the reading from Psalm 35 that he wrote Abigail and asked her to read it and share it with her father, a clergyman.

The reading *"was most admirably adapted, though this was accidental, or rather providential,"* Adams explained. *"A prayer which he gave us of his own composition was as pertinent, as affectionate, as sublime, as devout, as I ever heard offered up to Heaven. He filled every bosom present."*

Adams was not the only one nurtured by the prayer. A few days later, Adams dined with several of the delegates. Joseph Reed of Philadelphia talked about the *"masterly stroke of policy"* in moving that *"Mr. Duché might read prayers; it has had a very good effect, &c. He says the sentiments of people here are growing more and more favorable every day."*

Within a week, Adams experienced an even better day. With the fervor of a fiery sermon, the deliberations and debates stirred his patriotic soul. The colonies, which were as different from each other as separate nations, were coming together.

*"This was one of the happiest days of my life. In Congress we had generous, noble sentiments, and manly eloquence. This day convinced me that America will support Massachusetts or perish with her,"* John Adams wrote.

This gentleman attorney and farmer delighted in the good days of the Continental Congress. As every planter knows, a good day sprinkled with the right nourishment yields a fine harvest.[61]

> "Others went out on the sea in ships; they were merchants on the mighty waters. They saw the works of the LORD, his wonderful deeds in the deep" (PSALM 107:23, 24).

**PRAYER**

*Your deeds are marvelous, whether I view them from the top of a mountain or the deck of a ship. Thank you for the days of refreshment and nourishment for my heart and life's purpose.*

# 62. Not-So-Good Days

*"The deliberations of the Congress are spun out to an immeasurable length,"* John Adams penned. October 10, 1774, was not a good day for the Continental Congress. *"There is so much wit, sense, learning, acuteness, subtlety, eloquence, &c. among fifty gentlemen, each of whom has been habituated to lead and guide in his own Province, that an immensity of time is spent unnecessarily,"* he reported.

As an attorney, Adams valued persuasive oration as an art form. This critic of rhetoric grew impatient with his fellow delegates when their speeches were lengthy and/or pointless. Sometimes the speeches were more boring than a wooden box. The next couple of weeks continued this way.

*"In Congress, nibbling and quibbling as usual. There is no greater mortification than to sit with half a dozen wits, deliberating upon a petition, address, or memorial. These great wits, these subtle critics, these refined geniuses, these learned lawyers, these wise statesmen, are so fond of showing their parts and powers, as to make their consultations very tedious,"* opined Adams.

But in the middle of all these "not-so-good days," Adams also saw a growing unity among the group. Pennsylvania's House of Representatives invited the Continental Congress to dine with them at the city tavern. Adams described the event as *"a most elegant entertainment"* for the near one hundred men. He remembered one toast in particular for its potency. The moment left Adams intoxicated with liberty.

*"A sentiment was given: 'May the sword of the parent never be stained with the blood of her children.' Two or three broadbrims over against me at table; one of them said, this is not a toast, but a prayer; come, let us join in it. And they took their glasses accordingly,"* Adams recalled.

Congress adjourned at the end of October. Its mixture of good and not-so-good days ended in harmony and hope for resolving their conflict with England. Their most significant decision stirred Adams's soul with hopes for salvation from the anarchy in Massachusetts.

The Congress decided to organize a colony-wide boycott against British goods. By ceasing trade with Britain, they hoped to convince Parliament to repeal the Coercive Acts. The boycott just might cast the lifesaver Massachusetts needed.

John Adams was so hopeful as he left Philadelphia that he didn't expect to return for a reconvening of the Congress, which was tentatively scheduled for May 1775, but only as a backup plan.

> "As long as the earth endures, seedtime and harvest, cold and heat, summer and winter, day and night will never cease" (GENESIS 8:22).

*"Took our departure, in a very great rain, from the happy, the peaceful, the elegant, the hospitable, and polite city of Philadelphia. It is not very likely that I shall ever see this part of the world again, but I shall ever retain a most grateful, pleasing sense of the many civilities I have received in it."*[62]

**PRAYER**

*I thank you for the good days, the days of harvest, the days of plenty, the days when the sun shines.*

# 63. The Revolution Today: What Was an American?

What was an American in 1774? The colonists weren't Americans as we think of them today. They didn't identify with each other based on the name of their continent. They were from Boston or Richmond or Philadelphia. They weren't Americans. They were Englishmen and Englishwomen. They were the crown's subjects who happened to live in the king's colonies.

Patrick Henry provided the first definition when he hailed, *"I am not a Virginian, but an American."* In that moment, Henry expressed the essence of American patriotism. In that moment, he voiced a sentiment for the ages.

America is still the most patriotic nation in the world. According to a report released in June 2006 by the National Opinion Research Center at the University of Chicago, Americans ranked number one for patriotism among thirty-four nations surveyed.

"Americans ranked highest in the survey in pride for their democratic system, their political influence in the world, their economy, their achievements in science and technology and their military," read a press release detailing the results.

"Patriotism is mostly a New World concept, the researchers said. Former colonies and newer nations were more likely to rank high on the list, while Western European, East Asian and former socialist countries usually ranked near the middle or bottom," an Associated Press report explained in an article about the survey.

Today, American pride emerges routinely. Americans cheer for their Olympic hopefuls. On Memorial Day and Veterans Day, they honor the sacrifices of their military. They eat hot dogs, attend parades, and watch fireworks on the Fourth of July. They take pride in their home teams. They buy the latest technological wonders. They support and oppose political candidates. They buy and sell goods on eBay.

How does patriotism affect you? It's such a natural part of life in America that you may not notice it. When you speak, pray, and purchase, you show patriotism. As you pursue life, liberty, and happiness this week, you are fulfilling the patriotic creed.

Pride is often equated with boasting and self-importance. The Bible, however, encourages patriotic pride. Psalm 47 was an anthem of patriotism, a song of saluting: "He subdued nations under us, peoples under our feet. He chose our inheritance for us, the pride of Jacob, whom he loved" (Psalm 47:3, 4).

When we remember the Author of patriotism, we keep our patriotism from turning into selfish pride. When God is the Source of our pride, patriotism bursts forth with the most harmonious notes in the land of the free and the home of the brave.[63]

> "God has ascended amid shouts of joy, the LORD amid the sounding of trumpets" (PSALM 47:5).

**PRAYER**

*Thank you, Lord, for giving me freedom, for choosing patriotism as my inheritance. Be the Author of my anthem today.*

# 64. Sabbath Rest: Pillars

Even though the earth is round, it stands on pillars.

*"The Great God has made the governments and rulers of the earth its pillars, and has set the world upon them,"* the Reverend Benjamin Colman declared to his Boston congregation on August 14, 1730. Although he preached years before anyone ever thought about a Continental Congress, Colman expressed a core belief held by many of the colonists that continued beyond the 1770s.

The messages of Colman and other prerevolutionary preachers led to a religious revival the vibrations of which extended from New England to Georgia. This Great Awakening took place between 1739 and 1742, but its ripples continued for generations. Historians have designated this awakening as the beginning of a new era, not just for the colonial faith but for the colonial mind.

Colman believed God ordained kings and their governments. His metaphor for the earth's pillars came from Psalm 75:3: "When the earth and all its people quake, it is I who hold its pillars firm."

A building's pillars are functional. Sometimes, they are a structure's showpiece. *"The pillar is a part of great use and honour in the building: So is magistracy in the world . . . Kings bear up and support the inferior pillars of government, and a righteous administration restores a dissolving state,"* Colman said.

If God brings order to the world by ordaining governments and kings, then he also brings structure to his church. *"In like manner, wise and faithful ministers are pillars in the Church: Which is built on the Prophets and Apostles, Jesus Christ being the chief Corner-stone, Eph. ii. 20,"* Colman explained, adding that Christ told Peter he was the rock on which he would build his church.

Benjamin Colman's sermon defines the way many colonists viewed both the government and the church. Earlier generations of Britons believed the king was appointed by God. English kings, such as Charles I a century earlier, believed in their own deity. But the colonists, particularly the direct descendants of the Puritans, rejected the divine rights of kings. However, they still embraced the belief that government was a pillar of the earth, established by God. As a result they elevated the king to the highest place of respect and obedience. They did not equate him with God, but to rebel against the king was to shake one of the pillars God had put in place.

For many, the Revolution was a wrestling of the heart and mind. Was it acceptable to push on the pillars God had established? Was there ever a justification for it? Would it result in an earthquake extending across the Atlantic Ocean? Many concluded that government was one of God's pillars, but so was freedom from tyranny. Christ had set them free and they must stand firm for liberty.[64]

> "He raises the poor from the dust and lifts the needy from the ash heap; he seats them with princes and has them inherit a throne of honor. 'For the foundations of the earth are the LORD's; upon them he has set the world'"
> (1 SAMUEL 2:8).

**PRAYER**

*You, O Lord, are my cornerstone. Be the architect of my life. Give me structure and strength that I may house a life that honors you.*

# 65. Shoot the Scoundrels

N*othing remains but to conquer or to yield; to allow their claim of independence, or to reduce them by force to submission and allegiance."* The doctor of words penned his prescription for the Americans.

This Englishman had a cynical cure for the colonies. To him they had overdosed and were intoxicated with natural rights and liberty. If they would not submit, it was time to shoot the scoundrels. Such was his sarcasm.

If anyone could rival Benjamin Franklin for his sardonic sayings, it was England's Dr. Samuel Johnson. He wrote the dictionary, literally. This doctor of law was *"the most eminent man of letters then living in the English-speaking world."* The most profound difference between these two men was in their viewpoints. To Johnson, Franklin was a patriot. To Franklin, Johnson was an ardent ultra-Tory. And when Johnson dipped his pen into his well in 1775, he inked a diatribe of derisiveness strong enough to be felt across the ocean.

*"Men of the pen have seldom any great skill in conquering kingdoms, but they have strong inclination to give advice,"* he wrote, knowing that his words influenced many in England, and perhaps the king.

Continuing his prescription for the colonies, he cited the Continental Congress as the primary reason for England to use military force in America. *"THE Congress of Philadelphia"* ailed Johnson because it had *"convened by its own authority"* and not by royal authority. To Johnson the Continental Congress was illegal, defiant, audacious, and acrimonious. Their boycott of English goods was near treason.

Although he advocated military force, he qualified his argument by making it clear he was not a war hound, thirsty for blood. *"FAR be it from any Englishman to thirst for the blood of his fellow-subjects,"* he declared.

But he hoped the threat of force would be enough to cure the colonies. Johnson thought *"the rebels may be subdued by terrour rather than by violence"* and recommended the king implement *"such a force as may take away, not only the power, but the hope of resistance, and by conquering without a battle, save many from the sword."*

Although Johnson hoped his diatribe would lead to a full recovery, he became famous for one particular anti-American, sarcastic phrase. *"Patriotism is the last refuge of a scoundrel,"* Johnson told his biographer on April 7, 1775.

More than a century later, another lexicographer copied Johnson's definition of patriotism. In his *Devil's Dictionary*, Ambrose Bierce wrote: *"In Dr. Johnson's famous dictionary, patriotism is defined as the last resort of a scoundrel. With all due respect to an enlightened but inferior lexicographer I beg to submit that it is the first."*

By defining them as scoundrels, Samuel Johnson labeled all colonists crooks. That was his belief. The truth, however, was far different and much more complicated. Each side, like each generation, included those who were honest and those who were rogues.[65]

> "No longer will the fool be called noble nor the scoundrel be highly respected"
> (ISAIAH 32:5).

**PRAYER**

*May I select my words carefully today and show respect for others in what I say.*

# 66. The Die Is Cast

"T*he colonies are in open and avowed rebellion. The die is now cast. The colonies must either submit or triumph,"* King George III declared after learning of the Continental Congress's decision to boycott trade with Britain. To him, their decision was the final gamble.

The king, however, failed to recognize that many of his choices—such as revoking charters and supporting impractical legislation—had caused the conflict to escalate. He couldn't acknowledge his role in forcing the gamble. The die was cast, and he had painted many of the black dots on the white cubes with his own royal paintbrush.

The Continental Congress, however, did not haphazardly throw the die. They cast their lots with precision by establishing the Articles of Association. These articles created local committees, to be chosen throughout the colonies. Their job was to communicate with each other, enforce the trade boycott, and organize local militia. They were instrumental in launching the authority of the Congress and helping establish the Congress as the leaders of the colonists.

These associations did not escape the notice of the king's most loyal appointees.

*"A Committee has been chosen in every County, whose business it is to carry the Association of the Congress into execution,"* the Earl of Dunmore, the royal governor of Virginia, wrote of his observations. He noted that these committees had assumed authority to inspect merchants' books, invoices, and other secrets of the trade.

Dunmore watched in amazement as the committees convened *"with the greatest rigour. Every County, besides, is now arming a Company of men, whom they call an Independent Company, for the avowed purpose of protecting their Committees, and to be employed against Government, if occasion require,"* he continued.

Dunmore wrote that the committees *"have set themselves up superiour to all other authority, under the auspices of their Congress."* He noted that the committee members respected this new Congress more than they ever did their own legal government. Dunmore tried to appear unbothered by the committees. He predicted they would self-destruct. To him the committees were playing with gaffed dice or a stacked deck.

*"The arbitrary proceedings of these Committees, likewise, cannot fail of producing quarrels and dissensions, which will raise partisans of Government; and I am firmly persuaded that the Colony, even by their own acts and deeds, must be brought to see the necessity of depending on its mother country, and of embracing its authority,"* wrote Dunmore.

He also thought the boycott couldn't last because *"the people of Virginia are very far from being naturally industrious."* He assumed that once the resources dried up, so would the Continental Congress, their committees, and their militias.

But it was those same committees who would soon stand up against another governor, General Gage in Massachusetts. As 1774 drew to a close, the die was cast. The lots were drawn. Both sides had made their roll.[66]

> "The lot is cast into the lap, but its every decision is from the LORD"
> (PROVERBS 16:33).

**PRAYER**

*As easily as I can roll the dice, I cast my cares and concerns on you, knowing that you love me more than I can ever imagine.*

# 67. Give Me Liberty or Give Me Death

Besides, sir, we shall not fight our battles alone. There is a just God who presides over the destinies of nations, and who will raise up friends to fight our battles for us," Patrick Henry proclaimed as he continued his speech in the old church in Richmond on March 20, 1775.

Although Henry had not trained for the ministry, he was as skilled in rhetoric and zeal as the purest of Puritan preachers from of old. *"The battle, sir, is not to the strong alone; it is to the vigilant, the active, the brave,"* he cried.

The listeners that day were not merely members of the same congregation who met weekly for worship. They were parishioners of patriotism, members of associations representing their counties. Through the Continental Congress's encouragement, they had come together to proclaim their constitutional rights while asserting their allegiance to King George III.

Many who had come that day were instrumental in spreading and enforcing the boycott against Britain. The boycott seemed to be failing. As a result some may have walked into the church wondering if the effort was as dead as the wood that made up the pews.

*"There is no retreat but in submission and slavery! Our chains are forged. Their clanking may be heard on the plains of Boston! The war is inevitable—and let it come! I repeat it, sir, let it come!"* Henry called.

Many in the audience may have clung to hope that life would return again to the peaceful days, when the ties between country and colony were wrapped in mother-and-infant tenderness. But as in such relationships, the child grows up and must decide whether to embrace adulthood or pine for the innocent past.

*"It is vain, sir, to extenuate the matter. Gentlemen may cry, peace, peace—but there is no peace. The war is actually begun! The next gale*

*that sweeps from the north will bring to our ears the clash of resounding arms! Our brethren are already in the field!"*

*"Why stand we here idle? What is it that gentlemen wish? What would they have? Is life so dear, or peace so sweet, as to be purchased at the price of chains and slavery? Forbid it, Almighty God—I know not what course others may take; but as for me, . . . ,"* Henry cried.

Then he lifted his arms upward. His eyebrows tightened. His countenance bore the conviction of his soul. With his voice swelling to his loudest pitch, he cried out, *". . . give me liberty or give me death!"*

Patrick Henry took his seat. No one applauded, no one said a word. *"The effect was too deep"* as a witness later reported. When the *"trance of a moment"* was lifted, the members one by one began to stand and cry *"To arms!"* They left changed. A revolution had begun in the hearts and minds of these Virginians.[67]

> "Brandish spear and javelin against those who pursue me. Say to my soul, 'I am your salvation'"
> (PSALM 35:3).

**PRAYER**

*God, thank you that I do not have to fight my battles alone. You hear my cry, my call to arms.*

# 68. Revere's Ride

Paul Revere of Boston in the Colony of Massachusetts Bay in New England of lawful age doth testify and say that I was in Boston on the evening of the 18th of April, 1775,"* Paul Revere began his testimony about the night when speed became his sword and shield.

Revere explained that Dr. Joseph Warren had given him a special assignment. *"[Warren] desired me 'to go to Lexington, and inform Mr. Samuel Adams, and the Honorable John Hancock. Esq. that there was a number of Soldiers . . . marching to the bottom of the Common, where was a number of boats to receive them. It was supposed that they were going to Lexington, by the way of Cambridge River, to take them [Adams and Hancock] or go to Concord, to destroy the Colony stores [of ammunition].'"*

Messaging missions were nothing new for the silversmith. He had ridden great distances many times. The selectmen of Boston had called on him in 1773 to spread the news of the Boston Tea Party to New Yorkers. He had also carried messages calling for a meeting of a Continental Congress to New York and Philadelphia in 1774. The mission of April 18, 1775, however, required supernatural speed.

*"I proceeded immediately, and was put across Charles River, in a boat and landed near Charlestown Battery, went in to the town, and there got a horse,"* Revere testified, explaining he rode much of the way in a full gallop under a bright moon.

After alarming Adams and Hancock that British soldiers were traveling to Lexington, Revere headed for Concord to catch up with the other messengers who were also spreading the news. *"In an instant I saw four officers who rode up to me, with their pistols in their hands,"* Revere reported. These British regulars threatened his life if he did not stop. Racing into the nearby woods, Revere tried to escape to an adjacent pasture.

*"Just as I reached it, out started six officers, [seized] my bridle; put their pistols to my breast, ordered me to dismount, which I did. One of them, who appeared to have the command there; and much of a gentleman, asked me where I came from. I told him. He asked what time I left it. I told him [10:00 p.m.]. He seemed surprised,"* Revere reported of how impressed the officer was with his (Revere's) speed that night.

Revere described how the soldiers threatened his life if he did not tell the truth. Making him a prisoner, they led him back to Lexington and let him go. He then speedily returned to the meetinghouse to warn Hancock and Adams that the British weren't merely coming, they had come.

Paul Revere waved the warning flag that night. And he did it with all deliberate speed.[68]

> "He lifts up a banner for the distant nations, he whistles for those at the ends of the earth. Here they come, swiftly and speedily!"
>
> (ISAIAH 5:26).

**PRAYER**

*God, become my banner today. I know you do not delay, you come swiftly to answer my cries.*

# 69. The First Defensive

After the British soldiers released him, Paul Revere swiftly returned to the Lexington tavern where John Hancock and Samuel Adams were hiding. When Revere told them how the British had captured him and held him prisoner for a time, the trio decided to leave. They headed down the road a couple of miles. But Revere soon found himself on another mission. He returned to the tavern to retrieve the papers Colonel Hancock had left behind.

*"I sett off with another man to go back to the tavern to enquire the news. When we got there, we were told the troops were within two miles. We went into the tavern to git a trunk of papers belonging to Colonel Hancock. Before we left the house I saw the Ministerial Troops from the Chamber window coming up the road,"* Revere recounted.

*"We made haste and had to pass thro' our militia, who were on a green behind the meetinghouse to the number as I supposed about fifty or sixty. It was then daylight,"* said Revere.

The stage was set for more drama than Shakespeare could have ever penned. The colonial militia stood on Lexington's green and waited to defend their stores of ammunitions, while the British marched toward them. As he crossed the green and passed through the militia, Revere heard the commanding officer speak to his men. *"Lett the troops pass by, and don't molest them, without they [the British soldiers] begin first,"* Revere testified, repeating the officer's orders.

Revere crossed the road and watched the British troops as they appeared behind the meetinghouse. *"They made a short halt, when a gun was fired. I heard the report, turned my head, and saw the smoake in front of the troops. They imeaditly gave a great shout, ran a few paces, and then the whole fired,"* Revere reported.

*"I could first distinguish iregular fireing, which I suppose was the advance guard, and then platoons, At the time I could not see our militia, for they were covered from me by a house at the bottom of the road,"* he noted.

And thus Paul Revere heard the first shots fired in America's Revolutionary War. Because he wasn't on the green, he didn't see who was responsible for the hostile fire. After the abuse and threats he received that night from those British soldiers, there was no doubt to him who initiated the shots. The militia merely defended themselves against the hostile British advance.[69]

> "With bitterness archers attacked him [Joseph]; they shot at him with hostility" (GENESIS 49:23).

**PRAYER**

*Father, give me the courage to defend against the hostile advances that life sometimes brings.*

# 70. The Revolution Today: Riding for a Cause

Paul Revere rode for a cause that bright moonlit night in 1775. And Americans still ride, or walk, or jog for causes. These rides are not to warn of an invasion by a government enemy, but to sound the alarm about diseases that intrude on life just as suddenly.

Most of the time, these rides or races are Olympic-size group events. Races in the form of jogging, walking, or cycling attract millions to city streets every year. Washington, DC, has its Marine Corps Marathon. San Diego has its Rock and Roll Marathon. And of course, Boston has its marathon. Foundations for research on arthritis, breast cancer, leukemia, and diabetes, to name a few, often sponsor these races. Riders, runners, and walkers have raised millions of dollars, including $656 million in 2005, according to USA Track & Field's annual survey of more than two hundred charities. These big events result in big bucks while also providing publicity and awareness for the causes they champion.

Occasionally, however, the chance to ride for a reason comes in a one-on-one opportunity with a person of influence.

Such was the moment one hot August day in 2005. Seven-time Tour de France winner Lance Armstrong received an invitation from President George W. Bush that he could not refuse. The president asked Armstrong to take a bike ride through his ranch in Crawford, Texas. "The leader of the free world and the world's biking master rode for 17 miles on Bush's ranch for about two hours at midmorning. Bush showed Armstrong the sites of the ranch that he calls 'a little slice of heaven,' including a stop at a waterfall midway through the ride," the Associated Press reported.

The president presented Armstrong with a red, white, and blue shirt, a contrast from the athlete's famous yellow jersey symbolic of his winning rides. The shirt came with a slogan: "Tour de Crawford."

Armstrong took advantage of the opportunity and turned it into a ride for a cause. "Lance Armstrong said he set a one-day record during his bike ride with President Bush—not for cycling but for lobbying," the AP noted in another article. "During their two-hour ride on Bush's ranch Saturday, Armstrong pushed the president to spend more federal money on cancer research."

"I've never asked someone for so much money before," Armstrong, a cancer survivor, later told a television anchor.

Whether it's Paul Revere or Lance Armstrong, Americans understand the value of riding a race to win. Riding for a cause is more than just a ride. Speed is essential, but so is endurance. The aim is to finish. The apostle Paul understood this when he encouraged the Corinthians to live out their Christianity in a way that kept their eye on the prize, knowing their cause was heavenward.[70]

**PRAYER**

*Tie my running shoes, Lord. Turn me away from what distracts me from the finish line in the race you have arranged for me.*

"Do you not know that in a race all the runners run, but only one gets the prize? Run in such a way as to get the prize" (1 CORINTHIANS 9:24).

# 71. Sabbath Rest: All Is at Stake

A*ll is at stake—we can appeal to GOD, that we believe our cause is just and good,"* Pastor David Jones proclaimed enthusiastically in July 1775.

A crowd of three thousand soldiers, church members, and spectators gathered at the Baptist Church of the Great Valley in response to the Continental Congress's call for a day of prayer and fasting. Echoing Nehemiah 4:14, Jones asked his Pennsylvania audience to fight for their brothers, sons, daughters, wives, and homes.

*"Remember our Congress is in imminent danger. It is composed of men of equal characters and fortunes of most, if not superior to any in North-America. These worthy gentlemen have ventured all in the cause of liberty for our sakes,"* he said.

Jones believed failure to support the Continental Congress as brothers would bring the stain of infamy upon them. *"How could we bear to see these worthy patriots hanged as criminals of the deepest dye? This, my countrymen, must be the case, if you will not now as men fight for your brethren: Therefore if we do not stand by them, even unto death, we should be guilty of the basest ingratitude,"* he stated.

To speak openly and passionately for the cause of patriotism in front of this "Sermon-on-the-Mount-type crowd" was a redeeming moment for Jones. This patriot fled to Pennsylvania from his New Jersey church because too many loyalists there opposed his views.

*"If the groans and cries of posterity in oppression can be any argument, come now, my noble countrymen, fight for your sons and daughters,"* he continued. *"But if this will not alarm you, consider what will be the case of your wives, if a noble resistance is not made: all your estates confiscated, and distributed to the favourites of arbitrary power, your wives must be left to distress and poverty."*

Jones acknowledged the call to arms was alarming, but even the most tender of mercies from the British were cruel. He saw no alternative. *"Come then, my countrymen, we have no other remedy, but, under GOD, to fight for our brethren, our sons and daughters, our wives and our houses,"* he urged.

Again reminding his audience their cause was just, he made his loudest plea. *"If God be with us, who can be against us?"* he asked.

Jones's message was so powerful and poignant it echoed throughout the great valley, later known as Valley Forge. Booksellers sold copies of his message. The *Pennsylvania Gazette* advertised it.

> "What, then, shall we say in response to this? If God is for us, who can be against us?"
> (ROMANS 8:31).

And just as it was in David Jones's day, the truth of God's presence is real today. If God is with us, no one can be against us.[71]

**PRAYER**

*You are my Banner, Lord. You are the Great Presence in my life and nothing can stand against you.*

# 72. The Truth about Truth

What happened at Lexington and Concord? It depends on which version of the "truth" you believe.

The *London Gazette* and the *Salem* (Mass.) *Gazette* agreed on fewer facts than the king had friends in Boston. They agreed General Gage ordered British soldiers to travel by boat to Boston's countryside and destroy the militia's ammunitions. Messengers, such as Paul Revere, alerted the militia in Concord and Lexington. What happened next is where the two accounts split at the fork in truth's road.

*"Upon the King's Troops marching up to them [the militia],"* the London Gazette described, noting the troops marched to find out why the militia had assembled on the green, *"[the militia] went off in great confusion, and several guns were fired upon the King's Troops from behind a stone wall, and also from the meeting-house and other houses,"* the *London Gazette* printed, adding that the troops returned the militia fire.

The *Salem Gazette*'s explanation was as different in flavor as Samuel Adams's ale was from the king's tea. The troop's commanding officer *"accosted the Militia in words to this effect: 'Disperse, you rebels . . . throw down your arms and disperse'; . . . immediately one or two officers discharged their pistols . . . then there seemed to be a general discharge from the whole body,"* the *Salem Gazette* reported.

The troops then marched to Concord *"without any thing further happening"* according to the *London Gazette*, which noted the troops fulfilled their mission by burning gun carriages and throwing flour, gunpowder, and musket balls into the river.

But according to the *Salem Gazette* the truth was quite the opposite of *"without anything further happening."*

*"They [the troops] pillaged almost every house they passed by, breaking and destroying doors, windows, glasses, &c., and carrying off clothing and other valuable effects. It appeared to be their design to burn and destroy all before them; and nothing but our vigorous pursuit prevented their infernal purposes from being put in execution,"* Salem reported.

The Massachusetts paper also described the actions of the British as *"savage barbarity"* and accused them of *"shooting down the unarmed, aged, and infirm."*

*Salem* saw the militia's actions differently than those of the British troops. *"Not one instance of cruelty, that we have heard of, was committed by our victorious Militia; but, listening to the merciful dictates of the Christian religion, they 'breathed higher sentiments of humanity.'"*

*London* defined these *"higher sentiments of humanity"* as guerilla warfare. *"On the return of the Troops from Concord [to Boston], they were very much annoyed, and had several men killed and wounded by the rebels firing from behind walls, ditches, trees, and other ambushes,"* the English paper reported.

> "I do not write to you because you do not know the truth, but because you do know it and because no lie comes from the truth" (1 JOHN 2:21).

What was the truth? Where *Salem* exaggerated, *London* understated, and vice versa. The aftermath of these opposing "truths," this mystery in history, was war.[72]

**PRAYER**

*God, guard my tongue against wild exaggeration and misleading understatement. Your Word reminds me that "no lie comes from the truth."*

# 73. "In the Name of the Great Jehovah"

*D*eliver me this fort instantly," the colonial mountain man demanded of the British captain, who had hurried to the fort's entrance in his sleepwear.

Although the mountaineer was well over six feet tall, he was David fighting Goliath. Under the grey predawn skies of May 10, 1775, he and his band of colonists surrounded the unsuspecting sleeping giant. Surprise was their sling.

*"By what authority do you make this claim?"* the British captain asked. He couldn't have been more surprised at the demand than had an angel appeared on his doorstep.

*"In the name of the great Jehovah, and the Continental Congress,"* the colonist cried of his timeless God and the year-old Congress.

The British captain began to protest, but before he could finish speaking, the mountain man demanded an immediate surrender and drew his sword over the captain's head. The captain acquiesced.

And with that, the British handed Fort Ticonderoga over to Ethan Allen and more than eighty of his Green Mountain men and colonial militia. Together they captured one of the crown's finest military treasures. *"People refer to it [Fort Ticonderoga] as the Gibraltar of North America. It was by all standards the most spectacular fortress in North America,"* West Point military historian John Hall said in an interview for *The History Channel Presents: The American Revolution, 2006.*

Fort Ticonderoga was the most colossal and strategic British post in the colonies. Located in upper New York along Lake George, the fort was nestled in the Lake Champlain valley. As a gatekeeper between America and British-held Canada, Ticonderoga housed armaments more valuable in a war than gold.

The Green Mountain boys captured *"about one hundred pieces of cannon, one thirteen inch mortar, and a number of swivels,* [small, swiveling cannons],*"* Allen wrote in his report.

Although Allen and his men had been fighting New York colonists over land grants in Vermont, this battle required a new kind of courage. Land disputes were as easy as throwing pebbles into the lake, compared with freeing themselves of the human boulders surrounding the British fort. On the morning of the attack, Allen gave his men a pep talk.

*"Your valor has been famed abroad . . . I now propose to advance before you . . . for we must this morning either quit our pretensions to valor, or possess ourselves of this fortress in a few minutes, . . . ,"* he prodded, *"and, inasmuch as it is a desperate attempt, which none but the bravest of men dare undertake, I do not urge it on any contrary to his will. You that will undertake voluntarily, poise your firelocks."*

And so with their firelocks cocked in their arms and David's sling of courage in their hearts, Ethan Allen and his men captured the grandest of British forts and secured America's first military coup in the Revolution.[73]

> "David said to the Philistine, 'You come against me with sword and spear and javelin, but I come against you in the name of the LORD Almighty, the God of the armies of Israel, whom you have defied'"
> (1 SAMUEL 17:45).

*Cover me with your name as I go into battle today and give me the courage of David's sling in whatever I may face.*

# 74. Sharing Liberty's Luster

E*ver since I arrived at the state of manhood, and acquainted myself with the general history of mankind, I have felt a sincere passion for liberty,"* Vermont mountaineer Ethan Allen wrote of his reasons for risking his life to take Fort Ticonderoga.

Allen wrote a report of the battle. His audience was likely the Connecticut men who had financed his mission and the Continental Congress, who had not authorized it. *"The sun seemed to rise that morning with a superior luster,"* he wrote.

And although he correctly noted that *"Ticonderoga . . . smiled on its conquerors, who . . . wished success to Congress, and the liberty and freedom of America,"* he wrote with as much flamboyance as fact.

Allen may have explained in detail how his men captured the fort, but he failed to mention his co-conqueror. Joining him in the mission was a man from Connecticut, a militia captain and veteran of the French and Indian War. This man's posture was so erect, especially when riding a horse, that his very bearing was one of grandeur and leadership to most men—but not to Allen.

This Connecticut native received his commission from leaders in Massachusetts. Thus he and Allen were equals in purpose and rank. But they argued from the moment they met and joined forces en route to the fort. Allen assumed the senior leadership role and, in so doing, left Benedict Arnold second in command.

Both may have wanted to capture Fort Ticonderoga in the name of liberty, but personal glory overshadowed that noble goal, evidenced by Allen's failure to mention Arnold's name in his report. Allen may have arrived at manhood, but he held on to childish selfishness.

*"For an officer's honor, public recognition was key. If you played an important role and you weren't mentioned, that was very disrespectful. So Arnold was justifiably offended,"* said Caroline Cox, a historian at the University of the Pacific, in an interview for *The History Channel Presents: The American Revolution, 2006.*

And Arnold's troubles didn't end with Allen's slight. In fact, Allen's failure to share liberty's luster continued to frown on Arnold.

Fort Ticonderoga's capture forced the Continental Congress into a difficult position. They hadn't authorized either Allen, who soon returned to Vermont, or Arnold, who stayed at the fort. Some in Congress were not ready to make an offensive move against the British, but it was too late. They also didn't want to denounce such an important strategic victory. The capture squeezed congressional hesitation into hurried handshaking. They had to nominate men, form an army, and prepare for a military response by the British.

The Continental Congress later sent another man to command Fort Ticonderoga, leaving Arnold second in command once again. If Ethan Allen had given Arnold the credit he deserved, Congress may have given Arnold command of Fort Ticonderoga. Frustrated and hurt over the dishonors, Benedict Arnold resigned his position at the fort and headed for Massachusetts.[74]

> "Said Jesus, 'but I honor my Father and you dishonor me. I am not seeking glory for myself; but there is one who seeks it, and he is the judge'"
> (JOHN 8:49, 50).

**PRAYER**

*No matter how much I may seek recognition, Lord, you are the One who knows the motives of hearts and the motions of hands. May I honor you by sharing credit with those around me.*

# 75. Continental Burdens

Not only did the delegates to the second Continental Congress carry their knapsacks and trunks with them to Philadelphia in May 1775, but they brought another, heavier burden also as well.

At their meeting the previous autumn, they had put their hopes in a trade boycott against Britain. But the smoke from musket fire at Lexington and Concord had forced them to reconvene. They were no longer running a colony-wide boycott. They were running a war. They had to raise an army to support the colonial militia that had haphazardly surrounded British General Gage and his troops in Boston.

The newest member of the Congress perhaps carried the worst burden. Benjamin Franklin joined the deliberations with a heart heavier than anyone else. Forced out of England after a humiliating tongue-lashing by his so-called friends, Franklin returned home only to face another betrayal. The load he carried was the most intimate, personal burden possible.

*"Nothing has ever hurt me so much and affected me with such keen sensation as to find myself deserted in my old age by my only son. Not only deserted, but to find him taking up arms against me in a cause wherein in my good fame and fortune and my life were all at stake,"* Franklin later said.

Franklin spent his first few days in Congress quiet and withdrawn. Shortly after arriving in Philadelphia, he visited his son William Franklin. The pair had been as close as a father and son could be. Their loyalty to the crown over the years was unparalleled. Because of his father's influence with Parliament, William had served as New Jersey's royal governor. William had also been with Franklin when he conducted his famous kite experiment.

Franklin was shocked at William's deafness to the cause of the Revolution. Franklin tried everything. But nothing, not sentiment, rationality, or the humiliation Franklin endured that led to his ejection from England would change William's mind. Neither man would bend. They never reconciled.

Historians have noted the irony of their relationship. "Seems very strange to me that the old man should be the radical and the young man should be the conservative," observed historian Willard Sterne Randall in an interview for *The History Channel Presents: The American Revolution, 2006.*

The burden for both Benjamin Franklin and the second Continental Congress was now clear. They were launching a civil war. It was a weight too heavy for any of them to carry on his own. Distributing their load was as much a part of their unity as was their anger against Great Britain. They knew the only way to survive was to share the weight among them.[75]

> "[Moses prayed to God,] 'I cannot carry all these people by myself; the burden is too heavy for me'" (NUMBERS 11:14).

**PRAYER**

*Father, I give you my burdens today, knowing the load is too heavy for me to bear on my own.*

# 76. Adams's Southern Strategy

The news of the capture of Fort Ticonderoga shocked the Continental Congress with the force of one of the fort's cannons. The reason? They had not authorized Ethan Allen's mission. Congress's strategy had been defense, not offense.

But as the conflict became a war, their main concern was expelling General Gage and his army from Boston. To do so would require raising an army and appointing a commander-in-chief. They needed a new strategy. John Adams had just the plan they needed.

*"I had made no secret in or out of Congress of my Opinion that Independence was become indispensable; and I was perfectly sure, that in a little time the whole Continent would be of my Mind,"* Adams reported.

When he attended the first Congress in 1774, Adams employed the Massachusetts Bay strategy. He concluded that as long as Congress viewed the situation as merely a New England problem, they would not succeed. The colony-wide boycott proved to Adams that the delegates in 1774 had embraced the peril of his colony. Now it was time to overcome their regional differences and raise an army.

*"We were embarrassed with more than one Difficulty,"* he wrote of the second Congress. Rancor emerged between the northern colonies and the southern colonies as they debated war plans and peace petitions.

Adams described the conflict as a *"jealousy against a New England Army under the Command of a New England General."*

Hence, this man from Boston crafted a new strategy: independence by a southern route. One southerner had caught his attention. He had served in the Virginia House of Burgesses. Like Adams, this man was a gentleman planter. Unlike Adams, he was a veteran of the French and Indian War. But the man's most obvious quality was his appearance. This colonel wore his military uniform to the meetings of Congress. Without saying a word, George Washington made his qualifications for military leadership known. He looked and acted like a commander-in-chief.

*"But the Intention was very visible to me, that Colonel Washington was their Object [of the southern party],"* Adams recorded.

As impressed as he was with Washington, Adams had a problem. His friend and fellow Massachusetts delegate, Col. John Hancock, wanted the job. Although Hancock had been elected president of the Congress, he was counting on his fellow New England delegates, including Adams, to nominate him for the job of commander-in-chief.

John Adams, however, was independent. His ability to stand on his own became an instrument for the purposes of Providence.[76]

> "But the plans of the LORD stand firm forever, the purposes of his heart through all generations" (PSALM 33:11).

**PRAYER**

*Lord, I thank you that no matter the plans of humanity or the obstacles that block my path, your plans stand firm forever.*

# 77. The Revolution Today: Southern Strategy

Many have used the phrase "southern strategy" to describe Richard Nixon's run for the White House. Some claim Nixon originated the phrase. And indeed, his advisers did call their long-range campaign plans by that name. But the southern strategy of 1968 was far from John Adams's southern strategy of 1775. The difference was in the goal.

"It was called 'the southern strategy,' started under Richard M. Nixon in 1968, and described Republican efforts to use race as a wedge issue—on matters such as desegregation and busing—to appeal to white southern voters," *Washington Post* reporter Mike Allen explained in a 2005 article.

Allen's article was reporting the news of the day. Ken Mehlman, the Republican National Committee chairman at the time, told attendees at the 2005 NAACP national convention in Milwaukee the southern strategy of 1968 was "wrong."

"Some Republicans gave up on winning the African American vote, looking the other way or trying to benefit politically from racial polarization. I am here today as the Republican chairman to tell you we were wrong," Mehlman's prepared remarks confessed. He called the situation "not healthy for the country for our political parties to be so racially polarized."

Mehlman was right. Strategies that divide needlessly do not survive. John Adams's southern strategy, however, was not aimed at polarizing people by race. It was designed to bring a group of regional leaders together behind a common cause. His was an effort to unite the colonies of New England with the colonies of the South. Adams needed a long-term plan. He needed a respected Virginian to lead the effort to drive the British from Boston.

Strategies abound today. There are strategies for weight loss, for business growth, for economic success, and for football games. *Strategy* is often defined as "a plan of action" or "maneuvers designed to reach a desired goal." Strategies, however, are not the same as tactics. Strategies are long-term. The military distinguishes strategy from tactics this way: "In military usage, a distinction is made between strategy and tactics. Strategy is the utilization, during both peace and war, of all of a nation's forces, through large-scale, long-range planning and development, to ensure security or victory. Tactics deal with the use and deployment of troops in actual combat."

The word *strategy* appears only three times in the *New International Version* of the Bible. In each of these instances, strategy is a long-range plan that is useless unless God is in it. As the southern strategy of the 1960s died, so others like it will suffer the same fate. Strategies serve the most useful purpose when the goal honors God and the tactics used to reach that goal are just as honorable.[77]

> "Devise your strategy, but it will be thwarted; propose your plan, but it will not stand, for God is with us" (ISAIAH 8:10).

**PRAYER**

*God, I look to you as the source of the long-term plan for my life.*

# 78. Sabbath Rest: Subjects and Authorities

When Jonathan Mayhew preached on civil government to his parishioners at Boston's West Church, he spoke about their responsibility to submit to authorities. His principles were foundational. To Mayhew, it was proper for *"all who acknowledge the authority of Jesus Christ"* to understand Christ's doctrine relating to civil government.

Although Christ's kingdom is not of this world, Mayhew said, *"his inspired apostles have, nevertheless, laid down some general principle concerning the office of civil rulers, and the duty of subjects."* Obligation to authority was as fundamental as gravity's pull.

Mayhew explained that many early Christians did not believe they were subject to civil authority of any kind. As a result, these Christians spoke disrespectfully of their rulers and refused to pay taxes. This view came from both Jewish Christians and Gentile Christians. The Jewish Christians believed they were free from civil authority because they were God's chosen people. Likewise, Gentile Christians believed Christ had set them free from any other subjection.

Paul responded to both viewpoints in a letter to the Romans: *"Let every soul be subject unto the higher powers. For there is no power but of God: the powers that be are ordained of God"* (Romans 13:1, KJV).

Thus, Mayhew concluded, regardless of the form of government, God had put civil authority in place. Just as he had put the sun in the sky to govern the day and the moon to light the night, God organized societies through governments. *"There should be some persons vested with authority in society, and for the well-being of it,"* he said.

Mayhew concluded that the happiness of society depended on its members' willingness to submit to governmental authority. Respecting authority was a responsibility to God. *"Disobedience to civil rulers in the due exercise of their authority is not merely a political sin, but a heinous offence against God and religion,"* he said.

But Mayhew just as passionately believed that obedience to authority was not as unlimited as the sky. Those in authority also had a responsibility to obey God. He cited Scriptures, such as *"Love not the world, neither the things that are in the world. If any man love the world, the love of the Father is not in him"* (1 John 2:15 KJV) to show that man was to honor God first.

Jonathan Mayhew made his point that God has ordained authority. We are to obey our rulers and leaders with respect. But our love for God and obedience to him supersedes the laws of man. In a world where the king reigned supreme, that belief made Mayhew a revolutionary.[78]

> "Everyone must submit himself to the governing authorities, for there is no authority except that which God has established. The authorities that exist have been established by God" (ROMANS 13:1).

**PRAYER**

*Teach me to love your Word. May my obedience to civil authority reflect my love for you.*

# 79. Countenance

*I had no hesitation to declare that I had but one Gentleman in my Mind for that important command,"* John Adams wrote in his reflections on that June day in 1775 when he made the most important nomination of his life.

Before arriving at his announcement, Adams described the uncertain state of the colonies, the people's anxiety, and Congress's expectations. He also discussed *"the probability that the British Army would take Advantage of our delays, march out of Boston and spread desolation as far as they could go."*

Adams then moved that Congress appoint a general to assume command over the regional militias gathered at Cambridge, Massachusetts. *"And that was a Gentleman from Virginia who was among Us and very well known to all of Us, a Gentleman whose Skill and Experience as an Officer, whose independent fortune, great Talents and excellent universal Character, would command the Approbation of all America, and unite the cordial Exertions of all the Colonies better than any other Person in the Union,"* Adams proclaimed.

Not only did he keep his eyes focused on George Washington, but Adams also watched the reaction of John Hancock, president of the Congress. With the skill of a hunter, Adams made his best observation as soon as he fired his shot and nominated Washington.

Washington immediately darted from the room, a gesture that enabled Congress to debate his nomination with as much freedom as possible.

Adams saw a sudden change in Hancock's expression. When he described the circumstances that had brought Congress to the crossroads of choosing a general, Adams noted Hancock *"heard me with visible pleasure."*

*"But when I came to describe Washington for the Commander, I never remarked a more sudden and sinking Change of Countenance. Mortification and resentment were expressed as forcibly as his Face could exhibit them. Mr. Samuel Adams Seconded the Motion, and that did not soften the Presidents Physiognomy at all,"* Adams observed.

The debate over whether to appoint Washington for the post centered on whether a general from the South could command New England militia. The formal debate ended with no conclusion. The delegates decided to discuss the subject of Washington's nomination informally during breaks and dinners.

*"Pains were taken out of doors to obtain a Unanimity, and the Voices were generally so clearly in favour of Washington that the dissentient Members were persuaded to withdraw their Opposition, and Mr. Washington was nominated,"* Adams reflected.

Adams never knew whether Hancock truly wanted the job or merely hoped to be nominated just to have the honor of "declining" it. Adams respected Hancock's contribution to the cause through his leadership in the Sons of Liberty, but Adams knew Hancock had no battle experience.

Hancock's reaction to the nomination of George Washington confirmed John Adams's choice. John Hancock's countenance could not conceal his conceit.[79]

> "You overpower him once for all, and he is gone; you change his countenance and send him away"
> (JOB 14:20).

**PRAYER**

*Lord, shine your countenance on me. May I reflect your character and not my own vanity today.*

# 80. Modest Acceptance

Where John Hancock was vain, George Washington was modest.

*"Though I am truly sensible of the high honor done me, in this appointment, yet I feel great distress, from a consciousness that my abilities and military experience may not be equal to the extensive and impor-*

*tant trust,"* Washington began his acceptance speech to Congress as commander-in-chief.

Such considerate language was typical for this English gentleman. His passion for politeness began when he was a teenager. Through a tutor's encouragement, Washington copied *110 Rules of Civility and Decent Behaviour in Company and Conversation* into his schoolbook. He committed many if not all these rules to memory. These sayings molded Washington into a man of courtesy. The first rule—*"Every Action done in Company, ought to be with Some Sign of Respect, to those that are Present"*—may explain Washington's deference to his audience that day.

His assessment of his military experience was as understated as possible. Twenty years earlier, in 1755, following General Braddock's defeat during the French and Indian War, Washington became the commander of all of Virginia's colonial forces. For three years he led numerous men to defend Virginia's mountainous western frontier. He had seen frequent combat engagements with Indians.

*"However, as the Congress desire it, I will enter upon the momentous duty, and exert every power I possess in their service, and for the support of the glorious cause,"* Washington promised. *"I beg they will accept my most cordial thanks for this distinguished testimony of their approbation."*

Washington's experience was not limited to the battlefield. After resigning his position as commander of Virginia's forces in 1758, he was elected to Virginia's House of Burgesses. His eligibility came from his landholdings at Mount Vernon, the Potomac River estate he inherited from his half-brother Lawrence. For sixteen years he lived as a gentleman planter there, a role suited to one with his name—*Washington* means "farmer."

Thus, this man schooled in the military, government, business, and agriculture concluded his remarks as quickly as he began them, with a tip of his tricorn hat to courtesy.

*"But, lest some unlucky event should happen, unfavorable to my reputation, I beg it may be remembered by every gentleman in the room, that I, this day, declare with the utmost sincerity, I do not think myself equal to the command I am honored with,"* he said, accepting the position without pay except expenses.

Washington's acceptance speech comprised fewer than two hundred words. Perhaps his decision to embrace brevity came from this rule in his

> "For by the grace given me I say to every one of you: Do not think of yourself more highly than you ought, but rather think of yourself with sober judgment, in accordance with the measure of faith God has given you" (ROMANS 12:3).

schoolbook of manners: *"Let your discourse with men of business be short and comprehensive."*

George Washington did not think of himself more highly than others. Indeed, his sober judgment was one of the traits that led to his nomination.[80]

**PRAYER**

*Remind me today, Lord, not to think of myself more highly than I ought, and to be polite out of respect for you.*

# 81. Predicting the Future

M Y DEAREST: *I am now set down to write to you on a subject, which fills me with inexpressible concern, and this concern is greatly aggravated and increased, when I reflect upon the uneasiness I know it will give you,"* George Washington began his most famous letter to his wife, Martha, on June 18, 1775.

With the straightforwardness of a reporter and the drama of a novelist, Washington shared his news. Congress had placed *"the whole army raised for the defense of the American cause"* under his care. He told her it was necessary for him *"to proceed immediately to Boston to take upon me the command of it."* He expressed his hesitancy to part from her and their family. Spending a day with Martha had brought him more than *"seven times seven"* years of happiness, far, far more than one day on the field could ever bring.

*"But as it has been a kind of destiny, that has thrown me upon this service, I shall hope that my undertaking is designed to answer some good purpose,"* he continued, adding that refusing Congress's request would have brought dishonor on their family.

Washington also held the poet's penchant for pithiness in his pen. He believed the conflict would be over within a few verses. He certainly did not expect a Homer-like epic. *"I shall rely, therefore, confidently on that Providence, which has heretofore preserved and been bountiful to me, not doubting but that I shall return safe to you in the fall, . . . ,"* he wrote. *"I therefore beg, that you will summon your whole fortitude, and pass your time as agreeably as possible."*

Washington also possessed the realism of a biographer. Because *"life is always uncertain"* he enclosed a copy of his will, recently drawn up, to provide for Martha in case of his death.

*"I shall add nothing more, as I have several letters to write, but to desire that you will remember me to your friends, and to assure you*

*that I am, with the most unfeigned regard, my dear Patsy, your affectionate, &c."*

With the control of a playwright, Washington sought to draft his own destiny. His desire to compose the four acts of his life was no different from anyone else's. But George Washington acknowledged that the God who had preserved his life during the French and Indian War ultimately held his destiny. He could not predict the future. He didn't know how this revolution would change him, but he was certain of one fact. Providence was the great author.[81]

> "Many are the plans in a man's heart, but it is the LORD's purpose that prevails" (PROVERBS 19:21).

**PRAYER**

*Help me accept the truth that I cannot predict my future. Instead allow me to trust you today and tomorrow, knowing that you promise to be with me wherever I go.*

# 82. Confirming a Life Purpose

The pamphlet accused Martha Washington of loyalty to the crown. But the scandal was as false as General Washington's wooden teeth. People who knew Martha saw the publication for what it was: propaganda to discourage the patriots.

Col. Edmund Pendleton, who accompanied Washington as he left Mount Vernon to attend the Continental Congress in 1774, was among the first to witness Martha's resoluteness to the patriot cause: *"I was much pleased with Mrs. Washington and her spirit. She seemed ready to make any sacrifice and was cheerful though I knew she felt anxious. She talked like a Spartan mother to her son on going to battle. 'I hope you will stand firm—I know George will,' she said. When we set off in the morning, she stood in the door and cheered us with the good words, 'God be with you gentlemen.'"*

Hence, the propaganda pamphlet probably shocked Martha, who understood the meaning of loyalty better than many. If the authors had known her story, they might not have had the gall to write such lies. When a person has loved and lost and loved again, life takes on a new meaning. Love is too short to destroy it with disloyalty.

Eighteen-year-old Martha had married Daniel Custis, a farmer twenty years her senior, in 1749. Death, however, had embraced them more than had happiness. Two of their four children died before the age of five, and Custis died less than eight years after their marriage.

But life changed when the widow Custis met Colonel Washington. After a short courtship, the pair married in 1759. When God brought her a second chance, she embraced it with warmth and commitment. *"She [Martha] reminded me of the Roman matrons of whom I had read so much, I thought that she well deserved to be the companion and friend of the greatest man of the age,"* an aide to an American general later reflected.

The Washingtons spent sixteen years together, until the Continental Congress called him into military service in 1775. Although it was something he had longed for, marrying Martha had given him a new life purpose: domestic tranquility. Washington embraced Martha's children with the tenderness of a father and moved them to Mount Vernon, his inherited estate.

And so this Spartan of an American knew what she had to do when she learned of Washington's role as commander-in-chief. No longer was she a British subject and the wife of a Virginia farmer. She was the wife of a revolutionary, one who could be tried for treason and hanged if the British won the war. Just as he had confirmed her life purpose by embracing her family when they married, Martha Washington knew it was time for her to sacrifice. She became a patriot, determined to face whatever this new road would bring. Failure to do so might just cost the colonies their liberty.[82]

> "The man said, 'This is now bone of my bones and flesh of my flesh; she shall be called "woman," for she was taken out of man'" (GENESIS 2:23).

**PRAYER**

*Give me the courage to change with the seasons of life.*

# 83. Be Strong and Courageous

The congratulatory letters poured into Gen. George Washington's mailbox in the summer of 1775. As commander-in-chief, Washington was the man of the patriot hour. It didn't take an astute politician to know that Washington could bestow favor, or he could take it away. He could make men's military careers, and he could break them.

The letters he received had about as much in common as the men who wrote them. They came from governors, friends, military officers, colonial leaders, and others of General Washington's social stature. Most were pledges of support and best wishes for victory. These men uniformly addressed Washington as *"your Excellency"* and concluded with the common colonial salutation, *"Your most obedient and humble servant."*

One letter stands out for its message.

*"SIR, Suffer me to join in congratulating you, on your appointment to be General and Commander-in-Chief of the troops raised, or to be raised, for the defence of American liberty,"* Jonathan Trumbull began his letter to Washington. *"Men, who have tasted freedom, and who have felt their personal rights, are not easily taught to bear with encroachments on either, or brought to submit to oppression. Virtue ought always to be made the object of government. Justice is firm and permanent."*

Trumbull then described the *"rigor and military force"* artfully imposed by *"His Majesty's ministers."* He believed the colonies were *"driven to an absolute necessity"* to defend their rights militarily.

This letter next demonstrated such spiritual strength it could have been written by the most eloquent preacher in Boston. But it was a political leader, the governor of Connecticut, who penned this courageous prose.

He explained why he was writing. Congress had proclaimed a fast throughout the colonies. They were *"to stand before the Lord in one day, with public humiliation, fasting, and prayer, to deplore our many sins, to offer up our joint supplications to God, for forgiveness, and for his merciful interposition for us in this day of unnatural darkness and distress."*

Trumbull noted that God had directed a wonderful union among them. Then he made his strongest point: *"Only be thou strong and very courageous (Joshua 1:7 KJV),"* he wrote, seeking to encourage Washington through the blessing Joshua received when God made him commander of the Israelite army.

*"May the God of the armies of Israel shower down the blessings of his Divine Providence on you, give you wisdom and fortitude, cover your head in the day of battle and danger, add success, convince our enemies of their mistaken measures, and that all their attempts to deprive these Colonies of their inestimable constitutional rights and liberties are injurious and vain,"* Trumbull concluded prayerfully.

Jonathan Trumbull knew that George Washington would need Joshua's blessing to make an impossible mission possible. He understood the value of strength and courage.[83]

**PRAYER**

*Lord, may I remember to be strong and courageous today, knowing you have promised to be with me.*

> "Have I not commanded you? Be strong and courageous. Do not be terrified; do not be discouraged, for the LORD your God will be with you wherever you go" (JOSHUA 1:9).

# 84. The Revolution Today: Specialties

Specialties. When we think of specialists, we often think of doctors. The human body is so complex that we have developed a medical system based on specialties.

Even children are aware of these specialties. During the descent on an airplane, a mother encouraged her three-year-old son to swallow several times to keep his ears from hurting. After Rik ignored her suggestions, she decided to put on her other hat, her medical cap. She reminded Rik she was also a doctor. "Doctor Mommy says to swallow," she said.

Now, like some young children, Rik had visited several different doctors in his young life. He had seen his regular doctor, the pediatrician. He had also visited the bone doctor who treated his arm when he broke it. His mom, a radiologist, had looked at his X-ray, but the bone doctor checked his cast. Then he had met the nose doctor who surgically removed a few English peas from his nostrils. With his familiarity with specialists, Rik's answer to Doctor Mommy's orders to swallow made complete sense. "No, Mommy. I need to know what the ear doctor says," he replied.

We all have different abilities. Some of us are destined to become doctors, others of us faint at the sight of blood. And like George Washington, some of us are destined to be generals. Others of us are happy to serve in the ranks. John Hancock found himself accepting the title of president of a political body and relinquishing his hopes for military leadership and glory.

And although Hancock had his flaws, he fully embraced his role. He became a very effective leader of the Continental Congress. Perhaps he believed that too much was at stake to bear a grudge over a missed promotion. Maybe he decided the Revolution, and hence life, works best when we accept our gifts and use them to fulfill our responsibilities.

Scripture reminds us there is one body but many parts. First Corinthians 12:4–6 states: "There are different kinds of gifts, but the same Spirit. There are different kinds of service, but the same Lord. There are different kinds of working, but the same God works all of them in all men."

God has given us specialties. We can't all be hands or feet. We can't all be ligaments or bones. These specialties contribute to the complex func-

> "As it is, there are many parts, but one body. . . . Now you are the body of Christ, and each one of you is a part of it" (1 CORINTHIANS 12:20, 27).

tioning of God's body. And just as the human body is multifaceted, so are the people who make up God's body of believers in him. Each has an important function.[84]

**PRAYER**

*Thank you for giving me a special role in your body. Put blinders on me to keep me from jealousy and allow me to fully embrace my gifts and responsibilities.*

# 85. Sabbath Rest: Standing Firm for Liberty

The tensions in the colonies, particularly in Boston, brought many men of faith to their knees. It also forced many pastors to open their Bibles in search of clarity as the curtain went up on the war and conflict escalated. While Scripture clearly acknowledges government and authority as established by God, it also requires humanity to stand firm for liberty and cast off the yoke of slavery. It is this concept that led many ministers, including Simeon Howard, to preach on Galatians 5 as they searched for answers to the drama playing before their eyes.

*"It is the duty of all men to stand fast in such valuable liberty, as providence has conferred upon them,"* the Reverend Howard proclaimed.

In the first part of his sermon, Howard told his parishioners that Christ was the Author of liberty, the Source of the natural rights of man. *"Stand fast therefore in the liberty wherewith Christ hath made us free,"* begins Galatians 5:1 (KJV).

In the next part of Howard's message, he focused on the second half of the verse, humanity's responsibility to stand firm for that freedom: *"And be not entangled again with the yoke of bondage."*

*"Let me now offer a few considerations to shew the obligations men are under to defend that liberty which providence has conferred upon them. This is a trust committed to us by heaven: we are accountable for the use we make of it, and ought therefore, to the best of our power defend it,"* he said.

He reminded his audience of the parable of the servant. The servant received a talent from the Lord but failed to invest it, allowing it to go to waste, dishonoring God as a result. *"Out of faithfulness then, to God and in order to escape the doom of slothful servants, we should endeavour to defend our rights and liberties,"* he cried, noting that nature required man to provide for the temporal happiness of his family.

*"But in what way can a man be more justly chargeable with this neglect, than by suffering himself to be deprived of his life, liberty or property, when he might lawfully have preserved them?"* he asked.

From Howard's perspective, standing firm for liberty was a God-given responsibility. This principle was foundational for those who embraced the patriot cause. It provided justification for a war of defense against the British. It gave the patriots an explanation for the times in life when it was appropriate to shake God's pillar of government. Standing firm for liberty was a responsibility.

Simeon Howard also believed standing firm for liberty took the form of putting bread on a family's table, working industriously, paying the bills, and living an honest life. Standing firm for liberty by embracing life's basic responsibilities is a concept that transcends generations.[85]

> "His master replied, 'Well done, good and faithful servant! You have been faithful with a few things; I will put you in charge of many things. Come and share your master's happiness!'"
> (MATTHEW 25:23).

**PRAYER**

*Thank you for reminding me to invest the talents you have given me and to embrace the responsibility to care for myself and my family as an obligation of liberty.*

# 86. The Newlyweds

Although Henry and Lucy Knox had married a year earlier, it was time to elope in June 1775. Martial law imposed by the British in Boston left them no choice. Against her family's wishes they had to choose which coat to wear.

To stay in Boston or to sneak into Cambridge to join the patriots was a decision more difficult than the one to marry. Leaving meant losing their home, family, and Knox's beloved bookstore, their primary source of income.

Twenty-five-year-old Knox had worn the colonial coat with dignity in Boston's Grenadier Corps. When General Gage first saw the corps perform, he was impressed with their *"martial bearing."* The athletic Knox stood above the rest. The British regular army had tried to recruit Knox on many occasions. They couldn't understand why he sympathized with the *"provincial patriots." "His patriotism was as sincere as it was ardent, and he did not for a moment hesitate, but embarked heart and hand in the patriot cause,"* Knox historian Francis Drake reflected on Knox's sympathies. Drake compiled a collection of Knox's correspondence for publication in 1873.

Gage interdicted the departure of men like Knox. As a result, choosing to flee Boston was dangerous that June of 1775. But Knox's heart was in Cambridge with the patriots. Knox's wife also complicated their decision. Lucy Flucker Knox was the daughter of a high-ranking loyalist. *"Miss Flucker was distinguished as a young lady of high intellectual endowments, very fond of books, and especially the books sold by Knox, to whose shelves she had frequent recourse,"* wrote Drake.

*"I am in a state of anxiety heretofore unknown,"* Knox had written three months before their marriage in 1774. Knox was confident in Lucy but anguished over her father's disapproval.

However, it was Knox's very resoluteness that first captivated her. From the moment Lucy saw him marching in a summer parade, she was smitten. *"While on a gunning excursion among the islands in Boston Harbor, he lost, by the bursting of his fowling-piece, the smaller two fingers on his left hand,"* Drake explained. *"At the next parade of the corps Lieutenant Knox appeared with his wound handsomely bandaged with a scarf, which of course excited the sympathy of the ladies."*

Hence, the worst part of Knox's desire to go to Cambridge was its effect on Lucy. He may have asked these questions: Should she stay with her family? If she joined him, would she see her family again? Lucy, however, gave Knox the relief he needed. No matter where she would lay her head in the future, Lucy was as determined to stay with Knox as he was to join the patriots.

> "The LORD God made garments of skin for Adam and his wife and clothed them" (GENESIS 3:21).

They sealed their choice with stitches one June night in 1775. When Lucy sewed Knox's sword into the lining of her cloak, they were ready. The pair, disguised in modest coats, escaped from Boston into Cambridge. Lucy took refuge in a nearby town while he built fortifications with the patriots. Henry Knox had said good-bye to the redcoats and embraced the motley attire of a patriot.[86]

**PRAYER**

*Just as you have provided clothing for my body, clothe my heart in humility and give me grace for those who find themselves making difficult choices.*

# 87. The Race for Bunker Hill

"T HE day,—perhaps, the decisive day,—is come, on which the fate of America depends. My bursting heart must find vent at my pen," Abigail Adams wrote on Sunday, June 18, 1775, in a letter to her husband, John. How she longed for his comforting embrace. But Philadelphia might as well have been half a world away. Alone again, she turned to her faith as her compass. Her pen was her therapy.

Abigail could see flames flying into the sky from Breed's Hill on the Charlestown peninsula. The site overlooked the harbor and the British troops in Boston proper. Ever since Lexington and Concord, she had lived in a state of uncertainty, along with her fellow Bostonians. She had seen men, such as Dr. Joseph Warren, leave their families to join the thousands of militiamen surrounding British General Gage's thousand troops in Boston. Warren had given Paul Revere his instructions to go to Lexington in April of that year. Abigail had lived in the shadow of a siege for two months. By June, the day of decision had finally arrived.

What she didn't know as she wrote were the facts leading to the battle. Two days earlier, leaders of the Massachusetts Committee of Safety decided to preempt a British strike. They secretly ordered twelve hundred men to build fortifications and trenches on Bunker Hill. The militia decided instead to fortify Breed's Hill because it was closer to Boston Harbor. Four thousand men led by General Putnam and Doctor Warren prepared the breastworks.

On the morning of June 17th, the British awoke to see the hill's fortifications, which were one hundred and sixty feet long and eighty feet wide. They responded by attacking. The British advanced three times before taking the hill.

Although Abigail didn't have all of the facts at that moment, what she did know grieved her. "*I have just heard, that our dear friend, Dr. Warren, is no more, but fell gloriously fighting for his country; saying, better to die honorably in the field, than ignominiously hang upon the gallows,*" she wrote to John. "*Great is our loss. He has distinguished himself in every engagement, by his courage and fortitude, by animating the soldiers, and leading them on by his own example.*"

Abigail turned to her faith as she struggled with the loss of her friend and the battle of

> "I have seen something else under the sun: The race is not to the swift or the battle to the strong, nor does food come to the wise or wealth to the brilliant or favor to the learned; but time and chance happen to them all" (ECCLESIASTES 9:11).

Bunker Hill, as it came to be called. *"The race is not to the swift, nor the battle to the strong; but the God of Israel is he, that giveth strength and power unto his people. Trust in him at all times, ye people, pour out your hearts before him; God is a refuge for us,"* she quoted, combining Ecclesiastes 9:11 and Psalm 68:35 (KJV).

And with her compass set and her pen flowing, Abigail Adams poured out her heart to God and her husband.[87]

**PRAYER**

*Father, sometimes life seems all about chance and luck. But I know you supplant luck. You are my refuge when I am not swift or strong.*

# 88. Sanctuary in the Shadow of Ashes

Abigail Adams continued her letter to her husband on the afternoon of June 18, 1775. After sharing with him the loss of their friend Joseph Warren, she revealed the fiery outcome of the battle of Bunker Hill. *"Charlestown is laid ill ashes,"* she wrote.

The British had burned the peninsula city. Three hundred buildings were destroyed. Abigail could still see smoke billowing into the air from Charlestown. This colossal sight gave rise to something else in Abigail: terror. The horror that struck her was stronger than her fear of sea travel. She realized the battle might come her way.

*"It is expected they will come out over the Neck to-night, and a dreadful battle must ensue. Almighty God, cover the heads of our countrymen, and be a shield to our dear friends,"* she wrote.

*"How many have fallen, we know not. The constant roar of the cannon is so distressing, that we cannot eat, drink, or sleep. May we be supported and sustained in the dreadful conflict."*

Abigail knew it was important to share with John her plans in case the battle came to their home called Quincy, which was south of Boston. *"I shall tarry here till it is thought unsafe by my friends, and then I have secured myself a retreat at your brother's, who has kindly offered me part of his house. I cannot compose myself to write any further at present. I will add more as I hear further."*

Within a few days Abigail learned the militia retreated north, not south. As British munitions ran out, so did Abigail's fear. To her and her fellow Bostonians, Bunker Hill appeared to be a formidable victory for the British. But as time went by, their perspective changed.

The British may have taken the hill, but their victory came at a cost far larger than their prize. Their bright red coats had made them easy targets, and the patriots conserved their musket balls by firing at the British only when they could see the "whites of their eyes." More than two hundred redcoats perished. Nearly nine hundred were wounded. These casualties totaled 40 percent of General Gage's forces. The colonists, however, lost only one hundred forty men to death's volley. Another three hundred were wounded.

Bunker Hill bolstered the colonists' confidence. It gave them hope of beating the British. Once the smoke cleared, Abigail Adams and her fellow Bostonians were able to see how God had given them a sanctuary in the shadow of ashes. His power was as clear to them as the whites of the redcoats' eyes.[88]

> "You are awesome, O God, in your sanctuary; the God of Israel gives power and strength to his people. Praise be to God!" (PSALM 68:35).

**PRAYER**

*Thank you for giving me a sanctuary of strength and power. I praise you, God, for your might and glory.*

# 89. Lightning Strike on Bunker Hill

Bunker Hill proved that Boston's great lightning bolt had not lost his charge.

*"Women & Children flying into the Country, armed Men Going to the field, and wounded Men returning from there fill the Streets. I shan't Attempt a description,"* James Warren wrote to his wife, Mercy Otis Warren, on June 18, 1775. Unlike Doctor Joseph Warren, James had survived.

Warren was so worried about his wife's safety that he encouraged her to retreat into the countryside with their sons. Never before had he seen his fellow countrymen and women fleeing in such chaos. It was as if a volcano had erupted on Bunker Hill followed by a thousand lightning strikes.

Then Warren shared with Mercy a most interesting detail about the battle. The fray had fired up an old family flame. *"Your Brother borrowed a Gun, &c., & went among the flying Bullets at Charlestown retd. last Evening 10 o'Clock,"* he wrote of James Otis, Mercy's brother who had been living with them off and on since the assault that left him acutely insane. Otis had vacillated between the Warrens' house and a caretaker in the country. Because his condition was not harmful to others, he didn't need someone to watch him continuously.

Moments of sanity seized Otis occasionally. John Hancock once observed a flicker of the old Otis at a dinner he hosted. Although it was clear Otis's intellectual courtroom prowess had faded, his passion had not. Hence, when the minutemen passed by the Warren house on their way to Bunker Hill in June 1775, Otis was stirred by news of the impending battle. *"He was suddenly seized with a martial spirit. Without saying a word to a single soul, he slipped away unobserved and hurried on towards Boston,"* Otis historian John Ridpath described.

*"On the roadside he stopped at a farmhouse and borrowed a musket, there being nothing seemingly in his manner to suggest mental derangement. Throwing the musket upon his shoulder he hastened on, and was soon joined by the minutemen coming from various directions. 'Falling in' with them, he took an active part in that eventful contest until darkness closed in upon the combatants,"* Ridpath wrote.

In his letter to his wife, Warren also explained that Otis's insanity returned after the battle. *"Your Brother Jem dined with us yesterday behaved well till dinner was almost done. & then in the old way got up went off where I know not. has been about at Cambridge & Roxbury several days."*

Hence, a man suffering from insanity found a way to make sense of all the chaos. By joining the fight, James Otis contributed what he could to the cause he had ignited a decade earlier. In that moment, his weakness emerged as strength.[89]

> "But he said to me, 'My grace is sufficient for you, for my power is made perfect in weakness.' Therefore I will boast all the more gladly about my weaknesses, so that Christ's power may rest on me" (2 CORINTHIANS 12:9).

**PRAYER**

*Lord, thank you for making your power known in weakness, for your care of the lowliest bird and the most fragile flower. May your strength rest on me today.*

# 90. Scarcity

*I was struck with General Washington. You had prepared me to entertain a favorable opinion of him, but I thought the half was not told me,"* Abigail Adams wrote to her husband shortly after Washington arrived at Cambridge. *"Dignity with ease and complacency, the gentle-*

*man and soldier, look agreeably blended in him. Modesty marks every line and feature of his face,"* she continued, her heart overflowing with hope for military salvation.

Abigail was so impressed that she turned to poetry to describe Washington: *"Those lines of Dryden instantly occurred to me. Mark his Majestick fabrick! He's a temple Sacred by birth, and built by hands divine. His Souls the Deity that lodges there. Nor is the pile unworthy of the God."*

And while Abigail and others in Boston took stock of Washington, he took stock of his situation. Washington assessed the facts on the ground by visiting the militias and determining the enemy's position.

*"The bulk of their army commanded by General Howe [who had replaced Gage], lays on Bunker's Hill,"* Washington reported in a letter to John Hancock. Although the militia surrounded the British regulars by land, they could not stop the British navy from supplying General Howe and his army from the harbor.

What Washington discovered about his own army's stock could be summed up in one word: scarcity. Where Washington gushed with competence in Abigail Adam's eyes, he saw that the army lacked the basics. They did not know how to take a simple count of their men. They were as inexperienced as day-old eagles. "How could such an army ever defeat the redcoats and drive them from Boston?" he likely wondered.

*"We labor under great disadvantages for want of tents, for though they have been helped out by a collection of now useless sails from the seaport towns, the number is yet far short of our necessities,"* Washington wrote, detailing the scarcity of resources, such as tents, shirts, ammunition, and money.

The gunpowder supply had dwindled to only nine rounds per man. When Washington learned this, he was unable to speak for more than an hour. *"But I most sincerely wish the whole army was properly provided to take the field, as I am well assured, that besides greater expedition and activity in case of alarm, it would highly conduce to health and discipline,"* he explained.

Although his army lacked resources and knowledge, they were rich in enthusiasm. *"The deficiency of numbers, discipline and stores can only lead to this conclusion, that their spirit has exceeded their strength,"* he concluded.

> "A little sleep, a little slumber, a little folding of the hands to rest–and poverty will come on you like a bandit and scarcity like an armed man" (PROVERBS 24:33, 34).

George Washington's job was to turn scarcity into plenty before the poverty of war broke his army's bank of patriotism.[90]

PRAYER

*Lord, grant me the eagerness to work hard when the going is tough and my motivation is weak.*

## 91. The Revolution Today: Scarce Belongings

We were denied visas (again!)," a friend e-mailed.

The Andersons (name changed) had been living in Central Asia, where they ran a nonprofit organization that provided job training. John and Heather Anderson were people of faith who built relationships and shared their experience and beliefs in a friendship-like way. They returned to the States in the spring of 2006 so Heather could give birth to their third child in America.

Before leaving Central Asia, they received a visit from a government official. The inspection went well and the Andersons hoped they would finally receive long-term visas to continue living in their host country.

But they received the bad news during their stay in the States. Not only were they denied long-term visas, but they were also denied short-term visas. As a result, they could not return, even to collect their belongings. "Now, we are faced with the reality that our family will not be able to get back into Central Asia to get our stuff . . . We were denied entry to the country, even for one month," they wrote.

The Andersons took comfort by honestly confessing their disappointment and looking to the promises of Scripture. They didn't try to hide behind a façade of fake faith. Their hearts were genuinely broken over their loss of friendships and possessions. "I would love to say that we 'joyfully accepted' all of this, but that's probably not entirely accurate. But we can truthfully say that through all of this we are beginning to see the true value of focusing on our 'better and enduring possessions' (Hebrews 10:34) in heaven," John wrote.

But their story did not end in homelessness. Their nonprofit organization found another place for them to live. "Once I learned we'd be moving to Turkey, I e-mailed a guy who works there, just to say we would be living close to him. He replied and said they were actually moving to the States for at least a year and wanted to know if I would be interested in using their furniture and stuff (including bikes and toys for the boys) so that he can avoid paying for a storage unit," Mr. Anderson wrote.

At the time of their e-mail exchange, the Andersons didn't know they wouldn't be able to retrieve their belongings. But God knew what they needed. After losing almost all of what they owned, they were able to move into a completely furnished house.

Whether we lose a single piece of jewelry on a vacation or all our belongings in a fire, loss is extremely difficult. It is hard to imagine the scarcity George Washington and his army faced. There are times in life, even in the midst of plenty, when God reminds us to hold our possessions loosely and to concern ourselves with more lasting valuables.[91]

"You sympathized with those in prison and joyfully accepted the confiscation of your property, because you knew that you yourselves had better and lasting possessions" (HEBREWS 10:34).

**PRAYER**

*God, I thank you for the gift of material goods, knowing you provide more lasting possessions for me in heaven.*

# 92. Sabbath Rest: Should Christians Take Up Arms?

One of the religious questions facing the colonists was whether Christianity allowed men to take up arms and shed blood. Rev. Simeon Howard approached this difficult issue in a sermon to a Boston congregation before the war began.

Howard pointed to a moment in Pilate's trial of Jesus. Christ was accused of trying to establish a "temporal kingdom" against the Roman Empire. *"If my kingdom were of this world, then would my servants fight, that I should not be delivered to the Jews: But now is my kingdom not from hence,"* Christ replied (John 18:36 KJV).

*"Our Lord here, plainly allows that it is fit and proper for temporal kingdoms to fight in defence of their liberty,"* Howard said, noting that Christ did not need to take up arms to defend a spiritual kingdom.

Howard also told the account of Cornelius, a centurion who came to Peter. When Peter shared Christ's salvation with Cornelius, Peter told him to turn from sin, not his profession. *"We do not find that the apostle directed him to quit his military profession, or intimated that it was inconsistent with the spirit of Christianity; which he certainly would have done, had the character of a soldier and a good Christian been incompatible,"* Howard explained.

Baptist preacher David Jones gave a similar viewpoint in a sermon he preached: *"The reason why a defensive war seems so awful to good people is, they esteem it to be some kind of murder: but this is a very great mistake; for it is no more murder than a legal process against a criminal,"* he said.

Jones explained the colonists prosecuted public offenders, such as robbers and murderers, allowing for the death penalty. *"He that is not clear in conscience to gird his sword, if he would act consistently, must never sit on a jury to condemn a criminal,"* Jones said.

Although many pastors concluded Christianity was compatible with taking up arms, force was not their first line of defense. Such a decision was a last resort, a fourth act in an unresolved drama. If the climax led to continued slavery, taking up arms was necessary in their view.

*"We have no choice left to us, but to submit to absolute slavery and despotism, or as free-men to stand in our own defence, and endeavor a noble resistance . . . every reasonable method of reconciliation has been tried in vain;—our addresses to our king have been treated with neglect or contempt,"* David Jones implored, citing Romans 8:31: *"'If God is for us, who can be against us?'"*

"It is for freedom that Christ has set us free. Stand firm, then, and do not let yourselves be burdened again by a yoke of slavery" (GALATIANS 5:1).

And just as these pastors looked to Scripture for answers, praying and studying God's Word continues to provide direction today for such difficult issues.[92]

**PRAYER**

*Show me what it means to stand firm for liberty in my life today.*

# 93. Speaking the Same Language

*George Washington] really has a task that is absolutely mind-boggling. We say that there was an army around Boston. There wasn't an army around Boston, there was a gaggle,"* explained University of the Pacific historian Caroline Cox.

Washington's gaggle at Cambridge suffered from more than just scarcity. *"These men are ragged, disheveled, getting drunk on duty, no knowledge of how to handle a musket efficiently. There was no discipline; there was certainly no hygiene, very little structure. It was a mess,"* Cox said.

In many ways the militias who came from neighboring towns and colonies to rescue Bostonians were as different from each other as the Spaniards and French. One of Washington's greatest tasks was turning these separate militias into a united Continental army.

*"I am of the opinion that a number of hunting shirts not less than 10,000, would in a great degree remove this difficulty in the cheapest and quickest manner,"* Washington wrote to John Hancock. He hoped that uniforms would *"unite the men, and abolish those provincial distinctions which lead to jealousy and dissatisfaction."*

But uniforms could not teach conduct on the field. To do this required teaching them a language beyond the King's English. They needed a common military code. Washington's job was to create it. His code would also require translators, experienced officers, or "engineers," to show the militia how to fight as one.

*"In a former part of this letter I mentioned the want of engineers; I can hardly express the disappointment I have experienced on this subject,"* Washington wrote of one of his worst military headaches.

*"The skill of those we have, being very imperfect and confined to the mere manual exercise of cannon: Whereas—the war in which we are engaged requires a knowledge comprehending the duties of the field and fortifications,"* Washington continued, asking Hancock to find men with such skills.

Another key to Washington's new code was discipline. Without it, he had no hope of pushing the British from Boston. *"It requires no military skill to judge of the difficulty of introducing proper discipline and subordination into an army while we have the enemy in view,"* he wrote.

Although his army faced more problems than he could have imagined when he accepted the position, George Washington had faith. Whether his men were from Massachusetts, Rhode Island, or Connecticut, they all spelled liberty the same way. *"I have a sincere pleasure in observing that there are materials for a good army, a great number of able-bodied men, active zealous in the cause and of unquestionable courage,"* he concluded hopefully.

Indeed freedom hung on the success of a military code.[93]

> "The LORD said, 'If as one people speaking the same language they have begun to do this, then nothing they plan to do will be impossible for them'" (GENESIS 11:6).

**PRAYER**

*May I speak your love language today, Lord. Thank you for giving me your code through your Son, Jesus Christ.*

# 94. Olive Branch Petition

*"O that peace would once more extend her olive Branch,"* Abigail Adams wrote to John Adams on July 15, 1775, after telling him their farm crops looked *"blooming."* She then quoted famed English poet Alexander Pope: *"This Day be Bread and peace my lot."*

An olive branch of peace was indeed on the minds of many delegates to the Continental Congress that July. Led by John Dickinson, a group of moderate voices petitioned King George III and asked him to address their grievances to prevent more bloodshed. Congress passed the measure, dated July 8, 1775.

*"To the King's Most Excellent Majesty, Most Gracious Sovereign,"* Dickinson began this humble petition. He avoided writing detailed accounts of the colonies' past grievances. Instead his olive branch was flowery. It employed euphemisms and compliments as often as possible: *"The union between our Mother Country and these Colonies . . . produce[s] benefits so remarkably important."* And the colonies *"beheld Great Britain rising to a power the most extra-ordinary the world had ever known."*

But the desperate thrust of this petition was to stop the war. Dickinson believed he and his fellow colonists were obligated to *"Almighty God, to your Majesty, to our fellow-subjects, and to ourselves, immediately to use all the means . . . for stopping the further effusion of blood."*

Dickinson used every dovish phrase he could muster to receive a touch from the king's scepter of peace. *"We solemnly assure your Majesty, that we not only most ardently desire the former harmony between her and these Colonies may be restored, but that a concord may be established between them,"* he wrote.

Over and over again Dickinson used the olive branch petition to seek resolution. *"We therefore beseech your Majesty . . . to settle peace through every part of our Dominions."* The petition asked for some mode of permanent reconciliation, and repeal of the statutes that distressed the colonies, to prevent *"the further destruction of the lives of your Majesty's subjects."*

John Dickinson assured the king peace would bring a *"united sense of your American people."* He concluded, *"That your Majesty may enjoy long and prosperous reign . . . is our sincere prayer."*[94]

**PRAYER**

*Father, you are the God of peace. May I make peace in my heart with you and those around me, knowing that your peace is full of hope and promise for the future.*

> "Make peace with me and come out to me. Then every one of you will eat from his own vine and fig tree and drink water from his own cistern" (ISAIAH 36:16).

# 95. Liberty's Birthmark

Liberty was born with a birthmark. And as much as the Revolution changed the hearts and minds of the people, there was one change that was too much for too many to make: an end to ownership of African slaves. The issue rose and receded with the regularity of waves crashing against the shore.

One distasteful moment took place when South Carolina's Edward Rutledge motioned for General Washington to *"discharge all the Negroes, Slaves as well as Freemen in his Army."* Slaveholder Washington complied, but only for a time. After a shortage of men, he reinstated them.

This issue was complex. Because slavery was prevalent in the South, it was the northern members of Congress who opposed counting slaves as part of the population, out of fear of giving southern delegates more power. The tide rose even higher when the royal governor of Virginia issued an edict from his hiding place on a boat off the coast of Norfolk. *"And I do hereby further declare all indented Servants, Negroes, or others, (appertaining to Rebels,) free that are able and willing to bear Arms,"* Lord Dunmore wrote in a proclamation. He hoped to convince slaves and free Africans to join the British army.

Dunmore went into hiding about the time George Washington assumed command of the Continental army. He fled Virginia's capital and took refuge in a country hunting lodge and then a ship. His power to make such a promise came from his decision *"to execute Martial Law."* His purpose was to *"restore his MAJESTY'S STANDARD"* and recruit slaves for speedily *"joining His MAJESTY'S Troops."*

Many slaves took the risk and escaped their plantations to join the British. *"If you have the opportunity to throw in your lot with people who are promising you a much better situation than you have had, you'd be silly not to take that promise seriously,"* George Washington University historian James O. Horton observed in an interview for *The History Channel Presents: The American Revolution, 2006.*

Lord Dunmore's proclamation and others like it left behind a beach of confusion, filled with seaweed, rocks, debris, and disappointment. Many slaves answered the call to serve the British, but few received freedom as a reward. Those who survived the war and fought for the British were either recaptured or sent to Canada or the Caribbean. The Africans who fought for the patriots did receive their freedom, but their sacrifices were not considered enough to free their families and friends still enslaved.

> "So also, when we were children, we were in slavery under the basic principles of the world" (GALATIANS 4:3).

History would rightfully brand slavery as the birthmark of the Revolution. But the basic principles of the Revolution would give rise to another tide, one that would eventually wash away the mark of slavery.[95]

*I thank you that you are the Great Liberator of souls, that your ways are higher than those of humanity. Free me from the chains that enslave me.*

# 96. The Refugees

I heartily wish every Tory was extirpated from America; they are con-tinually, by secret means, undermining and injuring our cause," Abi-gail Adams privately confessed to her husband in 1775.

Abigail was happy to see liberty wash away as many loyalists from America's shores as possible. Although hundreds took comfort in the motherland they supported, many concluded England was no more their home than Iceland. Their mother country embraced them with open mouths but closed palms. Forced to leave their land and labor behind, these immigrants often arrived and remained in poverty.

*"In plain English, my purse is nearly empty,"* Judge Samuel Curwen wrote. This native of Salem, Massachusetts, arrived in London on July 4, 1775.

Six months later, Curwen was in no better financial shape than when he arrived. *"May the afflictions I have suffered the past year, in an unhappy banishment from my family, friends and country, be the means of increasing my reliance on, and submission to the all-disposing hand of the wise and righteous Governor of the universe,"* Curwen wrote as 1775 closed. England was a friendless place to an American pauper.

Colonists, particularly New Englanders, who were loyal to the crown found themselves facing difficult choices. Staying in America subjected them to danger and ridicule, such as tarring and feathering. Many lost their homes to fire and vandalism. Many who fled to England were once the wealthiest of colonists, but their exile thrust them into deep poverty. England was a more expensive place than America.

*"I find my finances so visibly lessening, that I wish I could remove from this expensive country . . . To beg is a meanness I wish never to be reduced to, and to starve is stupid; one comfort, as I am fast declining into the vale of life, my miseries cannot probably be of long continuance,"* Cur-wen wrote as he waited to receive a check from the British government to compensate him for his losses.

Curwen's poverty went beyond his pocketbook. He had left his fam-ily behind in Salem. *"I received a letter from London informing me of my wife's health and welfare in November last, and that she had been obliged to pay ten pounds sterling to find a man for the American army in my stead,"* he wrote.

Two years after his arrival, Curwen finally received money from the British government. He accepted the one hundred pounds as a gift from God and left the bank *"very joyous and I hope grateful to that Being who has, my friends, been pleased in the midst of gloomy prospects to set my feet on firm ground and establish my goings: may I wisely improve this gracious indulgence."*

Samuel Curwen's memoirs serve as a reminder of the inhumanity behind war's harshness, of the refugee suffocated by the rubble.[96]

> "Hide the fugitives, do not betray the refugees"
> (ISAIAH 16:3).

**PRAYER**

*Thank you for the home you have given me, for my place of dwelling. As I take refuge in you, give me compassion for those who are suffering a poverty deeper than I will ever know.*

# 97. Liberty's Tree

Not all migrants moved from the colonies to England. Just as the political climate boiled into a war, a young man with the gift of language emigrated from England to America. Thomas Paine was a thinker, a poet, and a philosopher who would soon impact all the colonies with the flourish of his pen and the power of the press.

Paine first received admiration for his work as an editor for the *Pennsylvania Magazine*. And while the Continental Congress met in Philadelphia in 1775, this immigrant published a poem called the "Liberty Tree."

Paine's fanciful tree was the child of the "Goddess of Liberty" who came to earth in a chariot, cheered by ten thousand celestials. Her mission was to plant the "Liberty Tree." His poem explained how the roots of this liberty tree grew deep. Its branches flourished, bearing fruit and drawing immigrants, like him, from all around.

*"Unmindful of names or distinctions they came, for freemen like brothers agree, with one spirit endued, they one friendship pursued, and their temple was Liberty Tree,"* Paine wrote, painting a picture with a portrait artist's skill.

Paine was one of those who came without *"distinction."* He held no glorious English title such as duke or earl. Most of his business attempts in England had failed. But after meeting Benjamin Franklin in 1774, Paine was inspired. America would welcome his ideas and ingenuity.

In his poem, Paine's Liberty Tree continued to grow. Its worshippers lived in harmony and contentment. They even willingly fought the battles for Old England, such as the French and Indian War, for *the honour of Liberty Tree.*

Paine's poem flourished with the freedom of the press and freedom of speech. He felt free to express his true fears about the king and Parliament, especially the House of Lords.

*"But hear, O ye swains, ('tis a tale most profane,) how all the tyrannical powers? King, Commons, and Lords, are uniting amain, to cut down this guardian of ours,"* he wrote.

He used his poem as a call to arms. *"From the east to the west, blow the trumpet to arms, thro' the land let the sound of it flee, let the far and the near,—all unite with a cheer, in defence of our Liberty Tree,"* Paine concluded, signing his name *"Atlanticus."*

> "The righteous will flourish like a palm tree, they will grow like a cedar of Lebanon; planted in the house of the LORD, they will flourish in the courts of our God" (PSALM 92:12, 13).

Although Paine's fanciful poem reflected the idealism of an immigrant, he won the hearts of his fellow patriots. Thomas Paine and his poem flourished at the hand of the Master Gardener. And soon his common sense would take root throughout the land of the "Liberty Tree."[97]

**PRAYER**

*Lord, you are the Master Gardener, who makes my life flourish, who waters and nourishes me so I might grow in you.*

# 98. The Revolution Today: Interpreting

What is the difference between a translator and an interpreter? "Translation is written, interpreting is spoken," the American Translators Association (ATA) explains in a guide for hiring translators and interpreters.

George Washington needed both to enforce his military code for the fledgling Continental army. These men spoke English, but, not unlike today, their common language was not enough to unite them. They needed written orders from their commander-in-chief. They also needed guides—other generals and officers—to explain Washington's written orders and interpret his instructions for establishing order.

Translators are "effective bridges between the languages they work in," the ATA notes, adding that style and terminology are essential. Translation is more than just spitting out text in another language. Subtleties such as tone and style are just as important. They are the body language of translating. Communication depends on technique, too.

A true translator or interpreter is not merely someone who is bilingual. Just because someone can speak two languages does not mean they can effectively switch back and forth between the two. They have to be able to compensate for clichés or cultural quirks. "Bilingualism is something else. Bilinguals speak two languages fluently, but are not necessarily good at moving between the two, especially in writing. And experience shows that many people described as bilingual overestimate their communication skills all together," the guide explains.

Immigrant Samuel Curwen and emigrant Thomas Paine recognized life in England was different from life in the American colonies despite their common language. The gap between the people of the two continents was indeed as wide as the Atlantic.

The Bible includes an interesting verse about interpreting. Left for dead by his brothers after he dreamed they would one day bow to him as a king, Joseph was captured and spent years in an Egyptian prison. His ability to interpret Pharaoh's dreams freed him, ultimately leading him to assume the most powerful leadership position in Egypt. Years later when a famine drove his brothers to Egypt to beg for food, Joseph met with these "strangers" but kept his identity a secret at first.

And although he could understand the language of his brothers, Joseph still used an interpreter to communicate with them. What he learned caused him to wail. "He turned away from them and began to weep, but then turned back and spoke to them again" (Genesis 42:23). The fact that Joseph, the man who could interpret Pharaoh's dreams, needed an interpreter is insightful. In the most emotional hour of his life, Joseph relied on someone to not merely translate words but to help him make sense of them.

> "They did not realize that Joseph could understand them, since he was using an interpreter"
> (GENESIS 42:23).

Some days are like that. We need wise counselors to interpret the chaos around us. We need the Lord's Scriptures, reliable ministers, and trustworthy friends to support us. And we need to be interpreters when others struggle.[98]

**PRAYER**

*May I choose wise interpreters for my life and may I be a wise interpreter for someone else today.*

# 99. Sabbath Rest: Shackles of Slavery

Slavery was a common theme for politicians and pastors in the 1770s. Slavery would have made a top ten list of metaphors used in the Revolution because it defined America's bondage to England.

Rhode Islander Nathaniel Niles, a graduate of both Princeton and Harvard, was no stranger to this subject. He addressed slavery using 1 Corinthians 7:21 (KJV) as his text: *"Art thou called being a servant? care not for it: but if thou mayest be made free, use it rather."*

*"At first glance, it is certain, this text refers to a state of personal servitude,"* Niles emphasized.

*"Now, if Paul esteemed personal liberty a valuable inheritance, he certainly esteemed the liberty of a community a far richer inheritance . . . Hence, we may observe from the text, that CIVIL LIBERTY IS A GREAT GOOD."*

Although he believed freedom from slavery was a great good, Niles was hesitant to take up arms against England. He turned to the Bible's most courageous slave, Daniel, who lived in slavery in Babylon, as a model. *"Let us all, like Daniel of old, piously pour out our hearts before God, acknowledging our own sins, and those of our people. Meanwhile, let us encourage no practice, in ourselves or others, that tends to enslave our country,"* he urged his congregation.

Unlike some, Niles believed the colonies had no grounds to complain about England's oppression as long as they enslaved Africans. *"God gave us liberty, and we have enslaved our fellow-men. May we not fear that the law of retaliation is about to be executed on us? What can we object against it? What excuse can we make for our conduct?"* he asked.

*"Would we enjoy liberty? Then we must grant it to others. For shame, let us either cease to enslave our fellow-men, or else let us cease to complain of those that would enslave us,"* reasoned Niles.

Hindsight shows us that slavery was indeed hypocrisy in America's first civil war. Niles saw the contradiction and spoke out against it. But how often are we slaves to our own blindness, unable to see our own sin so plainly before us? It took courage for Niles to speak out against slavery, just like it takes courage for us to search our own souls and ask God to forgive us for the sins that cloud our own lives. Indeed, freedom is more than just a physical condition; it's also a spiritual one.

*"To be freemen of Jesus Christ will exceedingly sweeten the enjoyment of civil liberty if we can obtain it, or soften the fetters of slavery if we shall be forced to wear them,"* Nathaniel Niles predicted.[99]

> "Were you a slave when you were called? Don't let it trouble you— although if you can gain your freedom, do so"
>
> (1 CORINTHIANS 7:21).

**PRAYER**

*Give me the courage to search my heart for the sin that enslaves me. May I have the strength to admit my wrongdoing and weaknesses to you. Forgive me and lead me to healing.*

# 100. The King's Declaration

The Continental Congress's olive branch petition reached London five weeks after John Dickinson led the effort to draft it. But George III refused to receive it, much less read it. Ignoring the petition was the king's way of whacking their olive branch into pieces with his scepter. In fact he responded with more fury than a storm can sink a ship. With Poseidon-like vengeance, he thrust his trident spear into the colonies by issuing his own declaration.

*"Whereas many of our subjects in divers parts of our Colonies and Plantations in North America, misled by dangerous and ill designing men, and forgetting the allegiance which they owe to the power that has protected and supported them,"* he began in his Declaration of Rebellion.

The sins of the colonists were as endless as the sea in the king's eyes. Disorderly acts that were disturbing the public peace, obstructing lawful commerce, and oppressing loyal subjects *"have at length proceeded to open and avowed rebellion,"* the petition boomed.

No matter the assurances of loyalty he had received from the petitions of the Stamp Act Congress and the Continental Congress. The king believed the colonists were long *"preparing, ordering and levying war against us"* through their *"traitorous correspondence."*

George III was blind to the patriots' point of view. Dictionaries define obstinate as *"adhering to an opinion, purpose, or course in spite of reason, arguments, or persuasion."* Failing to listen is a characteristic of obstinacy. Insulated in his castle, this king, who had never visited his American colonies, refused once again to hear their side. America was an important marker on the map of his kingdom. Her ships were his spoils. Holding on to power was more important than reading a petition.

In the fifteen years of his reign, time had changed the colonies but not the king. The obstinate pupil of James, the second Earl Waldegrave, had grown more, not less, pigheaded with time. His own thunder had deafened his ears.

The king used his Declaration of Rebellion to intimidate his other subjects. It proclaimed the obligation of civil and military Englishmen *"to suppress such rebellion, and to bring the traitors to justice"* and *"make known all traitorous conspiracies and attempts against us, our crown and dignity."*

Thus the king made it a punishable crime for anyone to aid and abet the traitorous, rebellious colonies. The petition was *"Given at our Court at St. James"* on August 23, 1775, and concluded with the epithet *"God save the King."* While King George III refused to read the Continental Congress's olive branch petition, he hoped God would listen to him and honor his own petition against the colonists.[100]

> "O LORD, save the king! Answer us when we call!"
> (PSALM 20:9).

**PRAYER**

*You are the Great Petition-Answerer. Thank you for hearing me when I call and listening to my petitions and cries.*

# 101. May It Please Your Excellency

"MAY IT PLEASE YOUR EXCELLENCY," Benedict Arnold wrote to George Washington from Maine's Kennebec River on October 13, 1775. He explained that he and his men had experienced a very *"fatiguing time"* since leaving on their mission the previous month.

As much as he longed for liberty's triumph, Arnold also passionately hoped to earn his commander-in-chief's respect. And he was on his way to succeeding. Arnold may have been slighted at Fort Ticonderoga in May 1775, but his role in capturing the fort had caught the attention of General Schuyler, commander of the Continental army's northern department.

Schuyler recommended Arnold for a mission into Canada. Washington approved, and Congress commissioned Arnold a colonel. His goal was to capture Quebec by following the rivers that led there. He had procured plenty of French riverboats, but his men had trouble maneuvering them, as he explained to Washington in his letter.

*"The men in general not understanding bateaux, have been obliged to wade, and haul them more than half way up the river,"* he wrote, noting his men were in high spirits despite their waterlogged fatigue.

Although his men were jubilant, Arnold bore a heavy personal grief that autumn. Shortly before leaving for Maine, he learned his wife had died. They had built a life together with their three sons in Connecticut. Their domesticity had given Arnold confidence to overcome his father's ghosts.

His father's bad business decisions and alcohol abuse had thrown his family into debt, forcing Arnold to leave school at age fourteen. Because his father had disgraced and dishonored the Arnold family, Arnold was driven to restore his family name. And he was on his way. By 1775, this thirty-four-year-old had become a pharmacist, bookseller, ship trader, and real estate proprietor. A successful military mission could add medals to complement his mettle. He was desperate to prove his ability to Washington.

*"We have been obliged to force up against a very rapid stream, where you would have taken the men for amphibious animals, as they were a great part of the time under water,"* Arnold wrote boastfully. He continued to highlight the obstacles they had faced, and praise his men for overcoming them. *"Add to this the great fatigue in portage; you will think I have pushed the men as fast as they could possibly bear. The officers, volunteers, and privates in general, have acted with the greatest spirit and industry,"* wrote the colonel.

And as anyone who desired to please their commander, Arnold concluded his letter by sealing it with respect and humility: *"I am, with the greatest respect, your Excellency's Most obedient humble servant."*

And with that, Benedict Arnold sought his commander's approval.[101]

> "Then they said to him, 'Please inquire of God to learn whether our journey will be successful.' The priest answered them, 'Go in peace. Your journey has the LORD's approval'"
>
> (JUDGES 18:5, 6).

**PRAYER**

*I seek your approval as I navigate the path I find myself on today.*

# 102. John Hancock, the Preacher?

Samuel Adams may have written letters to newspaper editors, but it was his friend John Hancock who paid the bills.

Shipowner. Merchant trader. Financier. Militia colonel. Captain of Liberty. Just as he owned many ships, John Hancock wore many titles. He was as prominent as any businessman in Boston. As a wealthy man he had the leisure to organize the Sons of Liberty and finance their committees of correspondence. In addition to being elected president of the Continental Congress, he also served as president of the provincial congress of Massachusetts, which assembled in the fall of 1775.

In this role, Hancock became a preacher of sorts. He did not deliver a sermon in a house of worship, but one of his messages was so powerful for its spiritual message that it could have been written by a "man of God." If Rev. Jonathan Mayhew could mix a little politics into his sermons, then Hancock could put a little preaching in his proclamations. He used the pulpit of politics to encourage his depressed Bostonians to look to God as their solution to the siege of Boston by the redcoats.

*"From a consideration of the continuance of the gospel among us, and the smiles of Divine Providence upon us with regard to the seasons of the year, and the general health which has been enjoyed . . . ,"* Hancock began, explaining his reasons for issuing this proclamation.

Although 1775 had begun with shouts of a boycott, it had led to the beating of war drums at Lexington, Concord, and Bunker Hill. With Boston surrounded by militia, Hancock realized one voice had emerged from the clamoring: the voice of unity. *"From a consideration of the union which so remarkable prevails, not only in this province but throughout the continent, at this alarming crisis, it is resolved . . . that it is highly proper that a day of public thanksgiving should be observed throughout this province,"* his pronouncement read.

John Hancock asked the people of Massachusetts to assemble on December 15, 1775, to thank God for the *"blessings we enjoy."* He also called on the *"people to humble themselves before God, on account of their sins for which he hath been pleased, in his righteous judgment, to suffer so great a calamity to befall us as the present controversy between Great Britain and the colonies."*

Thus, this political preacher looked to houses of worship and prayer as a solution to the perils of his colony.

Government leaders continue to issue such proclamations. Often they call for reflection, thanksgiving, and prayer. Sometimes these calls come on Thanksgiving Day, Christmas Day, or national days of prayer. Sometimes they are responses to national tragedies, such as September 11, 2001. Regardless of when they occur,

> "For my house will be called a house of prayer for all nations" (ISAIAH 56:7).

God's house is a dwelling place of prayer for all the nations who will call on his name.[102]

**PRAYER**

*God, thank you for reminding me to seek you and to pray for my community, nation, and world.*

# 103. Home on the Road

I*now sit down to tell you that I arrived hear safe, and our party all well,"* Martha Washington wrote from Cambridge to her friend Elizabeth Ramsey in Alexandria on December 30, 1775.

Martha was as out of place in a military camp as a cow in a castle, but she dared not be anywhere else. When George Washington accepted his command in June, he promised he would return home by autumn. But by the time the leaves abandoned Mount Vernon's oak trees, Martha knew that their comfortable house was no longer her home. Her husband was her home, and he was in Cambridge.

A general once described Martha as *"a modest and respectable person, who loves her husband madly."* That love translated into loyalty. Cambridge was the first stop on Martha's road to her new life purpose as the commander-in-chief's wife. She traveled nearly five hundred miles with her son and daughter-in-law over crude roads in a carriage pulled by four horses to get there.

It was her path through Philadelphia that shocked her more than any road rut. The greeting she received in the patriots' capital surprised her more than had she suddenly become queen. In a way, she had. *"I don't doubt but you have seen the Figure our arrival made in the Philadelphia paper and I left it in as great pomp as if I had been a very great somebody,"* Martha wrote to her friend.

The war forced many couples to make difficult decisions and undergo personal revolutions. While Abigail Adams endured the hardships of running a farm by herself to support her family, Martha endured the trials of travel. Change required Martha to take new risks, and in 1775, travel was sometimes risky. The destination was clear, but not always the outcome.

*"What doesn't really strike home is the impact of this travel and these events on her life,"* Mount Vernon historian Mary Thompson related in a talk she gave on Martha and the Revolution at the 2002 Annual George Washington Symposium, held at Mount Vernon, Virginia. Threats to personal safety were a part of life on the road.

*"Now, when a person can, in theory, given the traffic conditions, drive from Mount Vernon to Boston in eight hours or less—or even fly there in an hour—there is no way to understand the physical punishment of several weeks to a month of travel, one way, in order to go the same distance,"* Thompson said.

Martha endured the journey by counting her blessings along the way: *"We were fortunate in our time of setting out as the weather proved fine all the time we were on the road,"* she assured Elizabeth. Safely arrived, Martha Washington undoubtedly wondered what else this new life on the road would bring as she joined her husband at their new headquarters.[103]

> "Where you go I will go, and where you stay I will stay. Your people will be my people and your God my God" (RUTH 1:16).

**PRAYER**

*Thank you for the safe travels you have given me. You are my God and I will follow where you lead me today.*

# 104. Fear and Affability

I confess I shudder every time I hear the sound of a gun,"* Martha Washington reported in a letter to her friend Elizabeth Ramsey on December 30, 1775.

George Washington had turned the abandoned home of a wealthy Tory into his headquarters at Cambridge. Although its sturdy walls created a secure atmosphere, the occasional cannon blast reminded Martha of the reality she faced. Military custom may have suspended combat for the winter, but all she could hear were the sounds of war.

*"I have waited some days to collect something to tell, but alas there is nothing but what you will find in the papers—every person seems to be cheerful and happy hear,—some days we have a number of cannon and shells from Boston and Bunker's Hill, but it does not seem to surprise anyone but me,"* continued Martha.

She may not have been as well educated as she wished, but Martha didn't let her embarrassment over spelling errors stop her from using one of her best weapons against fear: writing to friends like Elizabeth. Her second-best weapon was pouring her heart and hands into hospitality. *"I have been to dinner with two of the generals, Lee and Putnam,"* she wrote.

Martha had entertained hundreds at Mount Vernon over the years. She probably missed her kitchen and its ability to cure savory salty Virginia ham to her culinary perfection. But she accepted her new table, and those of others, which were seasoned more with company than spices. Her role as hostess was one of the best gifts she gave her husband on the road. She used her charm to soften the troubled hearts of the officers. *"Mrs. Washington combines in an uncommon degree great dignity of manner with the most pleasing affability,"* an impressed soldier later wrote, describing Martha and her social graces.

If cannon fire reminded Martha of the need to nurture relationships for her husband, the rubble reinforced it. *"I just took a look at pore Boston and Charlestown—from prospect Hill Charlestown has only a few chimneys standing in it,"* she wrote Elizabeth.

*"There seems to be a number of very fine buildings in Boston that God knows how long they will stand; they are pulling up all the wharfs for firewood—to me that never see anything of war, the preparations are very terable indeed, but I endeavor to keep my fears to myself as well I can,"* she added.

Martha tasted both the tartness of terror and the sweetness of society in Cambridge. Both were genuine. But Martha Washington had long ago built her home on wisdom's pillars. And at Cambridge, she chose to set her table in wisdom's kitchen.[104]

> "Wisdom has built her house; she has hewn out its seven pillars. She has prepared her meat and mixed her wine; she has also set her table"
> (PROVERBS 9:1, 2).

**PRAYER**

*Show me how to set my table in wisdom's house. Give me the insight I need to prepare a feast for those around me today.*

# 105. The Revolution Today: Soldier's Inbox

Mail in the mailbox. The need is as real today for military families as it was during the Revolution.

"Since the earliest days of combat, one of the greatest morale boosters for a soldier is when the mail comes in. With access to the Internet, written mail has taken a back seat, but it's not so much the letter that is important, it's the communication with the family," U.S. Army Captain Dan Sukman explained on August 10, 2006. Sukman wrote a series called

*Soldier's Diary* for the FOX News Web site (www.foxnews.com) during his one-year deployment to Iraq.

Although today's mail arrives with the regularity of a sunrise and e-mail is instant, mail delivery during the Revolutionary War was unreliable. The system of horseback riders carrying letters from post to post often failed. Hence, if a soldier met a stranger who would be traveling near his home, he would ask him to deliver a letter to his family. If a wife learned neighbors were traveling in the direction of the army, she would send her letter with them. Such was the situation facing Joseph and Sarah Hodgkins as 1776 began.

*"My dear I take this opportunity to write a line or two to inform you that we are all in a Comfortable State of Health through the goodness of God, and I hope these lines will find you posest of the Same Blessing,"* Sarah wrote to her husband, Joseph, who joined the Continental army in Cambridge in January 1776, from their home in Ipswich, Massachusetts. *"I received yours by Mr Smith and I rejoice to hear that you are well,"* she continued, noting she had received one of Joseph's letters.

The modes of communication are different today, but the emotions haven't changed. Words from home can soothe souls on the front lines. A line from a soldier can also bring reassurance to a father, mother, wife, or child.

Captain Sukman noted that his inspiration for writing about military families came from his fellow soldiers. "The first [inspiration] is having seen my roommate wear Superman pajama pants to bed. I made fun of him until he explained how they were a gift sent over from his son. I still make fun of him for it, but it shows how his family at home can keep his morale high while deployed in Iraq," Sukman wrote.

The Stryker Brigade was Sukman's second inspiration. Their stay in Iraq had been extended four months when he wrote his article in August 2006. "When we sign up for this job, we know and understand the hardships that come with it. Frequent combat tours are a possibility, spending time overseas is expected—it's what we volunteered for. Family members don't volunteer, they don't sign a contract, but their sacrifice is just as great," Dan Sukman wrote.

Whether the year is 1776 or 2006, hope from home is the blessing of the battlefield.[105]

> "Then all the people left, each for his own home, and David returned home to bless his family"
> (1 CHRONICLES 16:43).

**PRAYER**

*Father, may I be a blessing to my family in what I say and how I say it.*

# 106. Sabbath Rest: Getting Real

In his Thanksgiving sermon on December 15, 1775, William Gordon encouraged his congregation in Roxbury, Massachusetts, to get real. Gordon's message was a response to the proclamation issued by John Hancock and the Massachusetts provincial congress to pray and give thanks as the year concluded. His sermon was so well received that he presented it again for the prestigious Boston Lecture.

Gordon, who was also a chaplain to the Massachusetts provincial congress, was concerned about the odor of his flock. He feared some of them smelled of pretension. He wanted to make sure they wielded authenticity as conscientiously as they employed their pens and muskets. *"What is religion, with the generality, more than being baptized, attending public worship stately on the Lord's day, owning the covenant, coming to the Lord's table, and then being orderly in the outward deportment?"* he asked.

He cited Matthew 15:8 to make his case for getting real before God. *"'This people draweth nigh unto me with their mouth, and honoureth me with their lips; but their heart is far from me.' . . . Though the appearances of religion among this people are great and many, yet it is to be feared that real religion is scarce, that the power of godliness is rare, and that while there is much outward show of respect to the Deity, there is but little inward heart of conformity to him,"* Gordon declared.

The preacher feared that religious activities could easily become nothing more than healthy habits and rituals of appearances. Getting real meant believing in the divinity of God, who abhors sin. Getting real included appreciating the *"beauty"* of holiness. Getting real resulted in a desire to love God and the Lord Jesus through words and action.

And although Gordon called upon his parishioners to repent of their sins and open their hearts before God, he just as often reminded them of God's goodness. *"We adore the goodness of God, which has kept us from being consumed by the ravages of war. It is of the Lord's mercies that we are not consumed, because his compassions fail not,"* he said, reflecting on Lexington, Concord, Bunker Hill, and the siege of Boston.

Gordon also sought to encourage his audiences to find the flowers among the thorns of the Revolution, to smell sweetness when they could. *"And much more so that, in the distressing and alarming situation of our public affairs, there have been so many favorable circumstances to preserve us from fainting, to hearten us up, and to encourage our hopes in expecting that we shall*

> "Because of the LORD's great love we are not consumed, for his compassions never fail"
> (LAMENTATIONS 3:22).

*at length, in the exercise of prudence, fortitude, and piety, get well through our difficulties."*

Although 1775 had brought more hardship than any other year seen by Massachusetts since its founding, William Gordon knew there were a thousand reasons to thank God, get real before him, and reflect on his goodness. After all, a new year was coming, and 1776 would prove to be a banner year.[106]

**PRAYER**

*Thank you for the blessings you have given me. I choose to count them and turn my inward heart to you in thanksgiving and praise.*

# 107. Favor over Failure

Benedict Arnold had failed. *"I make no doubt you will soon hear of our misfortune on the 31st ultimo [December 31, 1775],"* Arnold wrote to General Washington on January 14, 1776, two weeks after his army failed to capture Quebec.

Several weeks earlier, Arnold had written Washington of the strong prospects for victory over the motley Quebec garrison. Gen. Richard Montgomery, who had successfully captured Montreal, arrived at Quebec with reinforcements. But Arnold and Montgomery's combined forces of thirteen hundred proved no match for British Gen. Guy Carleton and his trained forces.

Arnold now told Washington that he had tried to *"put the best face on matters, and betrayed no marks of fear"* before his men. He also attempted to wear his *"best face"* in his letter to Washington. *"My detachment had carried the first battery. My being wounded, and the loss of their guides, retarded them much. After the death of the General, they sustained the force of the whole garrison for a considerable time, who fired from under cover, and had every advantage of situation,"* Arnold wrote, grimacing with each stroke of his pen. General Montgomery's death was the most serious setback of the battle.

Arnold, who received a leg wound, explained that his men had been overpowered and forced to retreat. Arnold lost half his men to death, wounds, or capture.

There was one outcome, however, that could have been worse. *"Governor Carleton treats them with humanity,"* Arnold wrote, referring to those taken prisoner, *"and has given leave for their baggage to be sent in to them."*

Arnold was very grateful to Carleton for humanely treating his men. Arnold had seen the worst of humanity in Canada during the French and Indian War. As a fifteen-year-old, he joined the Connecticut militia and marched with the British to oppose a French invasion from Canada. The worst part was not the failed battle but the captivity. The Indians were so angry at the surrender terms arranged by the French that they massacred nearly two hundred British and colonial prisoners. The slaughter permanently turned Arnold's heart against the French.

But as he wrote his letter to Washington in 1776, he received just the encouragement he needed to lighten his heart at that moment. One of Washington's letters had finally reached him. Arnold wrote, *"Your favor of the 5th ultimo is just come to hand. It gives me a most sensible pleasure, to have your approbation of my conduct."*

Arnold had lost the battle for Quebec, but he had not lost his commander-in-chief's approval, which mattered almost as much as victory. Though wounded and defeated, Benedict Arnold's honor was still intact.[107]

> "Good understanding wins favor, but the way of the unfaithful is hard"
> (PROVERBS 13:15).

**PRAYER**

*Grant me favor with you and others. Also, may I develop a habit of seeking to understand those around me.*

# 108. Anonymous Pain

As the year 1776 began, choosing anonymity was merely common sense.

It seemed the young man had failed each time he wore employment's apron. He had worked unsuccessfully as a house servant, merchant mariner, and corset maker. Now he walked the road of publishing, wondering whether it would lead to success or another dead end.

Although he had been slaving over his writing for what seemed like a century, the timing of his publication was the most powerful of medicines. This anonymous author published the first edition of his fifty-page pamphlet on the same January day in 1776 when he and his fellow Philadelphians learned the news. King George had declared war. This author's words would prove to be the perfect antidote for this royal infliction.

"*Perhaps the sentiments contained in the following pages, are not yet sufficiently fashionable to procure them general favor,*" the author wrote in his introduction, justifying his anonymity. He knew his radical views were as unfashionable in England as a French wig. He hoped Americans would welcome his writings, which he considered as sensible as they were accurate.

"*A long habit of not thinking a thing wrong, gives it a superficial appearance of being right,*" he continued, noting that opposition to new ideas is often born from custom. "*But the tumult soon subsides. Time makes more converts than reason.*" Central to his pamphlet was this statement: "*The cause of America is in a great measure the cause of all mankind.*"

The patriots were hungry for his words. They were thrilled to see their principles in print. The young man wrote with such poignancy and simplicity that his audience begged for more copies of this document. This failed businessman's first edition was such a success, he found himself sleeping in his printing apron more often than his nightshirt. Questions as to his identity quickly emerged. He responded through the following note on February 14, 1776.

"*Who the Author of this Production is, is wholly unnecessary to the Public, as the Object for Attention is the Doctrine itself, not the Man. Yet it may not be unnecessary to say, That he is unconnected with any Party, and under no sort of Influence public or private, but the influence of reason and principle,*" the writer explained.

Some thought he was John Adams; others, Samuel Adams. The author who proclaimed these great thoughts and the others outlined in his pamphlet wisely hid behind anonymity as the war began in 1776. After all, this man was young but not stupid. He was a radical with common sense. And so, Thomas Paine named his document, *Common Sense*.[108]

> "Even as he walks along the road, the fool lacks sense and shows everyone how stupid he is" (ECCLESIASTES 10:3).

**PRAYER**

*God, give me your clarity today to use my common sense to discern the complex circumstances surrounding me.*

# 109. Sickly Constitution

"My, is the constitution of England sickly," Thomas Paine wrote in *Common Sense*, which he first published in January 1776.

Using such radical statements, Paine unlocked the English constitution with the skill of a locksmith and the grace of a wordsmith. He believed tradition had closed the doors on reason. *"The prejudice of Englishmen, in favor of their own government by king, lords, and commons, arises as much or more from national pride than reason,"* Paine wrote.

One of the keys to truly understanding the Revolutionary War is understanding the structure of the English government of the 1700s. In the second section of *Common Sense*, Paine explained the flaws of England's three-door constitutional system.

The first door was the king, who inherited his power. The second door included the members of the upper class and peers to the king who made up the House of Lords. The third door opened to the common men, who were elected to make law in the House of Commons. *"The two first [the king and House of Lords], by being hereditary, are independent of the people; wherefore in a constitutional sense they contribute nothing towards the freedom of the state,"* stated Paine.

To this young (and as yet anonymous) author, the monarchy was a ridiculous contradiction, a castle sealed against entry by those affected by its decisions. *"The state of a king shuts him from the world, yet the business of a king requires him to know it thoroughly,"* he wrote.

In Paine's view, the moat surrounding the monarchy was a river muddied by absolute power. And although the House of Commons could check the power of the king through legislation, the king held the stronger position. His ability to veto and reign until death gave him absolute power. *"Though we have been wise enough to shut and lock a door against absolute monarchy, we at the same time have been foolish enough to put the crown in possession of the key,"* he pointed out.

The English constitution created a three-legged stool in which one leg was stronger, taller, and wider than the others, throwing liberty off balance. Such uneven pillars cannot support even the strongest of fortresses.

*"Some writers have explained the English constitution thus; the king, say they, is one, the people another; the peers are an house in behalf of the king; the commons in behalf of the people; but this hath all the distinctions of an house*

> "Jesus knew their thoughts and said to them: 'Any kingdom divided against itself will be ruined, and a house divided against itself will fall'" (LUKE 11:17).

*divided against itself,"* Thomas Paine wrote, proposing it was time to make some changes. The English constitution had pitted the House of Commons against the absolute rule of the king.

And indeed, the sand had shifted under the castle housing the English constitution. The English government was sickly because it was divided against itself.[109]

**PRAYER**

*Make me watchful today for fissures in my own home. Give me the wisdom to make any changes I need to bring unity to my family.*

# 110. Sickly Monarchy

M*ale and female are the distinctions of nature,"* Thomas Paine wrote in *Common Sense.* *"But there is another and greater distinction for which no truly natural or religious reason can be assigned, and that is, the distinction of men into KINGS and SUBJECTS,"* he concluded. And just as Paine unlocked the English constitution, so he also diagnosed the sickness of the monarchy.

Because the monarchy promoted idolatry Paine described kings *"as the most prosperous invention [of] the Devil."* Paine's *Common Sense* was radical but not irrational. He turned to history and Scripture to show just how sick the institution of the monarchy really was.

*"According to the scripture chronology,"* Paine wrote, pointing out there were no kings in humanity's early stages, *"the Heathens paid divine honors to their deceased kings, and the Christian world hath improved on the plan by doing the same to their living ones."*

Paine reminded his readers that for three thousand years after Moses' death, the Israelites lived under *"a kind of republic"* administered by judges. *"Kings they had none, and it was held sinful to acknowledge any being under that title but the Lord of Hosts,"* Paine wrote. He believed exalting one man over the rest was a violation of nature and Scripture, explaining how Gideon and Samuel both opposed establishing a monarchy.

When Gideon marched victoriously against the Midianites, the Jews wanted to make him king. He responded by saying, "The Lord shall rule over you." Likewise Samuel opposed choosing a king. He only did so after the Lord gave him permission because the nation of Israel had rejected his original system. Samuel warned the people that one day they would "cry out for relief from the king you have chosen, and the LORD will not answer you in that day" (1 Samuel 8:18).

Paine deftly interpreted a verse commonly used as a reason favoring rule by kings: *"Render to Caesar the things that are Caesar's, and to God the things that are God's"* (Mark 12:17 KJV). Paine didn't believe the verse applied to the patriots because the Israelites were not ruled by a monarchy at that time. Instead, they were *"in a state of vassalage to the Romans."*

Paine believed the monarchy's *"hereditary succession"* was evil. *"For all men being originally equals, no one by birth could have a right to set up his own family in perpetual preference to all others for ever, and though himself might deserve some decent degree of honors of his contemporaries, yet his descendants might be far too unworthy to inherit them,"* he wrote.

After a long discussion of the tempestuous history of the English monarchy, Paine wrote, *"The nearer any government approaches to a republic the less business there is for a king."*

Through Scripture, Thomas Paine used examples from the King of kings to show the fallacy of a system based on earthly kings.[110]

> "But Gideon told them, 'I will not rule over you, nor will my son rule over you. The LORD will rule over you'" (JUDGES 8:23).

**PRAYER**

*You are my King of kings, the only Ruler of my heart. Keep me from elevating one person over another, because your love extends to everyone.*

# 111. The Remedy: 'Tis Time to Part

Thomas Paine had a remedy for the pain he outlined in *Common Sense*. He called it independence. *"The sun never shined on a cause of greater worth,"* he gushed.

After diagnosing the sickliness of the English constitution and its monarchy, Paine prescribed a remedy. *"We have it in our power to begin the world over again,"* he wrote. *"Every thing that is right or natural pleads for separation. The blood of the slain, the weeping voice of nature cries, 'TIS TIME TO PART."*

Paine challenged even *"the warmest advocate for reconciliation"* to show a single advantage in remaining connected to Britain. He argued that America's goods would continue to fetch market prices in Europe. Staying connected to Britain would forever involve America in England's wars with other nations—nations that America had no quarrels with. Not only that, Paine went as far to assert that the Almighty never intended for England to have authority over America. After all, he placed an ocean between them.

"*O ye that love mankind! Ye that dare oppose, not only the tyranny, but the tyrant, stand forth!*" he cried. "*Now is the seed time of continental union, faith and honor.*"

Paine also outlined a practical plan for a new government in America, one that established effective checks and balances among executive, legislative, and judicial branches. His plan abolished the monarchy and restored the divided houses of the English constitution.

Paine's pamphlet became a best seller because it offered the cure Americans had been too afraid to taste, much less digest. "*Some say 100,000 copies were published. Translate that into population rates today, that would be like selling twenty million books through Amazon and Barnes and Noble. That's an awful lot of communicating,*" said historian Gary B. Nash in an interview for *The History Channel Presents: The American Revolution*, 2006.

"*We don't have a statue of Paine. He's got to be the only founding father who has not been commemorated in marble and bronze because he was too radical,*" contends Nash.

When Abigail Adams read Paine's work she was as joyful as a patient fully recovered from an illness. Abigail wrote John in March 1776 about the potency of Paine's prescription. "*I am charmed with the sentiments of 'Common Sense,' and wonder how an honest heart, one who wishes the welfare of his country and the happiness of posterity, can hesitate one moment at adopting them,*" Abigail wrote.

*Common Sense* charmed the nation and gave them the remedy they needed. Hundreds were ready to stand with Paine as a "*good citizen, an open and resolute friend, and a virtuous supporter of the RIGHTS of MANKIND and of the FREE AND INDEPENDENT STATES OF AMERICA.*"

> "For the LORD is our judge, the LORD is our lawgiver, the LORD is our king; it is he who will save us" (ISAIAH 33:22).

Thomas Paine's writing sparked a revolution of the minds and hearts in some. For others, *Common Sense* simply stoked the revolution already taking place.[111]

**PRAYER**

*Thank you for the freedom you have given our nation. Thank you for being my King, my Savior, my Lawmaker, and my Lord.*

# 112. The Revolution Today: Common Colds

Just as Americans began to make sense of Thomas Paine's *Common Sense*, the infections of separation and fear plagued Sarah Hodgkins. While her husband Joseph served in the Continental army at Cambridge, she anguished over his absence from their home in Ipswich, Massachusetts.

*"I want to See you very much[.] I think you told me that you intended to See me once a month,"* Sarah Hodgkins wrote on February 20, 1776.

Unlike today, soldiers joining Washington's army expected to be home or at least be able to visit in a month or so. They left their firesides for a temporary fight. Sarah had noticed that Joseph's initial promises of returning within a month faded with each letter he sent her. *"& I don' hear as you talk of coming but I must confess I dont think it is for want of a good will that you dont come home,"* she wrote astutely.

Boston was still barricaded. She knew spring might bring a major battle to rattle the British loose. *"It is generally thoght that there will be something done amongst you very Soon,"* she wrote, *"but what will be the event of it God only knows."*

The common cold infecting military families today is the same. Regardless of the century, war's deployments and extensions flow from war's uncertainties. It is impossible for families to know what is truly going on in a war zone or how long it will take for a homecoming.

In an entry for his FOX News blog from Baghdad, Iraq, in 2006, U.S. Army Captain Dan Sukman explained the plague of information and misinformation that infects families at home.

"As a soldier, we understand the intricacies of what is going on over here; our families when watching the news, be it FOX News or CNN, only get vague generalities of the situation. A nightly news report on a helicopter going down in Iraq can cause undue stress on thousands of families, all of whom may wonder if that is their loved one's area. (This is not a criticism of the press, rather a comment on what our families can go through)," Sukman wrote.

"Over here we know what is happening to us, and to our comrades. Family members can go weeks on end without hearing from a loved one. They live with the potential of a soldier walking up to their door in a Class A uniform with the worst possible news."

Fear is the source of this infection. Faith is a prescription. Sarah Hodgkins put it this way in her letter to her husband in February 1776:

*"I am distressed about you my Dear but I desire to commit you to God who alone is able to preserve us through all the deficulty we have to pass through[.] May he Strengthen your hands & incorage your heart to carry you through all you may be called in the way of your duty."* [112]

**PRAYER**

*I commit my fears to you, the God I trust over humanity's inflictions.*

"When I am afraid, I will trust in you. In God, whose word I praise, in God I trust; I will not be afraid. What can mortal man do to me?" (PSALM 56:3, 4).

# 113. Sabbath Rest: Convulsions

"*C*onvulsions and commotions." That is how Connecticut Rev. Samuel Sherwood described America's earthquake-like rupture with England. To Sherwood and many other pastors, the rumbling chaos seemed ripped from the pages of Revelation. Sherwood concluded that tyranny was not the nature of the beast . . . it *was* the beast.

"*It has, from the beginning, been the constant aim and design of the dragon, sometimes called the beast, and the serpent, satan, and the devil, to erect a scheme of absolute despotism and tyranny on earth, and involve all mankind in slavery and bondage,*" Sherwood proclaimed in a sermon he delivered to his church in Weston, Connecticut, in January 1776.

Tyranny's scheme was simple. If Satan could keep humanity in a state of "*servile subjection*" through institutions of political, emotional, and religious slavery, then he could topple the liberty and freedom "*the Son of God came from heaven to procure.*" Sherwood, however, did not leave his congregation hopeless. He reminded them of God's power to transcend this earthquake of evil.

God promises to give power to his faithful witnesses and servants: "*And if any man will hurt them, fire proceedeth out of their mouth, and devoureth their enemies. And if any man will hurt them, he must in this manner be killed*" (Revelation 11:5 KJV).

Sherwood believed the colonies were in the infancy of freedom, the perfect place to overcome tyranny. "*Liberty has been planted here; and the more it is attacked, the more it grows and flourishes. The time is coming and hastening on, when Babylon the great shall fall to rise no more; when all wicked tyrants and oppressors shall be destroyed for ever,*" he said.

Sherwood believed that if America became the birthplace for liberty, the message of the gospel would more easily spread throughout the world. Such freedom of religion would prosper the church. "*These commotions and convulsions in the British empire, may be leading to the fulfillment of such prophecies as relate to the downfall and overthrow, and to the future glory and prosperity of Christ's church,*" he said.

And so this fiery preacher from Connecticut saw hope for both the colonies and the church beyond the chaos. Samuel Sherwood believed the King of kings would overcome both political and religious tyranny. And if the Lord of lords can overthrow oppression, he can surely overthrow the micro- and macro-commotions and convulsions of life today.[113]

> "Then they heard a loud voice from heaven saying to them, 'Come up here.' And they went up to heaven in a cloud, while their enemies looked on" (REVELATION 11:12).

**PRAYER**

*Thank you for bringing peace to the commotions and convulsions of life.*

# 114. Knox Knocks

Henry Knox knocked on the doors of Fort Ticonderoga. For a bookseller his was an unusual mission. The fierce weather made it dangerous, but Knox's determination to carry out his mission was unbendable. He desperately wanted the British out of his beloved Boston. Knox knew that Washington didn't have the artillery to do it.

So he volunteered to retrieve the cannons and ammunition from Fort Ticonderoga and transport them to camp, a five-hundred-mile round-trip. Unlike fleeing to Cambridge with his wife Lucy six months earlier, this bookworm would soon learn whether he had the ability to turn knowledge into know-how. The outcome would show whether his past had prepared him for the patriot cause or merely propelled him to imprudence.

*"The garrison at Ticonderoga is so weak, the conveyance from the fort to the landing is so difficult, the passage across the Lake so precarious, that I am afraid it will be ten days, at least, before I can get them on this side,"* Knox wrote Washington on December 17, 1775.

Knox, however, accurately predicted the time it would take to load the sixty tons of artillery onto the sleds. *"It is not easy to conceive the difficulties we have had in getting them over the Lake, owing to the advanced season of the year, and contrary winds; three days ago it was very uncertain whether we could have gotten them over until next spring; but now, please God, they shall go,"* Knox continued. He also noted he had made *"forty-two exceedingly strong sleds"* and acquired *"eighty yoke of oxen, to drag them."*

How did this Boston bookstore owner become an authority on conveying artillery? Books. Knox had read volumes of military hardbacks, which gave him familiarity with weapons. Knox also had something in common with cataloguing cannons. A bookseller knew how to keep inventory.

*"I hope in sixteen or seventeen days to be able to present to your Excellency a noble train of artillery, the inventory of which I have inclosed,"* Knox continued. He had meticulously documented the dimensions and quality of each piece.

Through icy, rutted roads and snowy hills, Knox and his men pulled the artillery from upper New York to Cambridge. Each cannon weighed between one hundred and five hundred pounds. Knox's arrival on January 24, 1776, was the best New Year's greeting Washington could have received. And for Knox's knocking and know-how, Washington promoted him to colonel of the artillery.

Henry Knox's accomplished mission revealed his capabilities. His past exertions advanced his future efforts.[114]

> "For we are God's workmanship, created in Christ Jesus to do good works, which God prepared in advance for us to do" (EPHESIANS 2:10).

**PRAYER**

*Thank you for the work you have given me to do, both in the past and today. Use my work to your glory in the future.*

# 115. Chance Meeting?

Some moments in life appear trivial when they happen. Only time reveals their significance. Such was the meeting between Henry Knox and John André during Knox's trip to Fort Ticonderoga. *"Chance made them one stormy winter night inmates of the same cabin on the border of Lake George,"* Knox historian Francis Drake explained.

Just as Knox's choice to travel tested his capabilities, it also revealed his character and personality. Shortages of accommodations often required traveling strangers to share sleeping quarters, which was a common practice in the 1770s. Although Knox was not far from Fort Ticonderoga, the weather forced him and his party to take shelter in a lakeside cabin. The storm had also led a group of American soldiers to spend the night there.

Knox's party, which included his brother, likely arrived last. Perhaps Knox's *"pleasing manner,"* as John Adams once described it, led him to give the men in his group first choice on beds. Generosity proved as essential to his character as athleticism was to his frame.

Hence, Knox found himself sharing quarters with a stranger named John André. Careful to follow the unwritten code of war, they both concealed the purpose of their travels. The pair confined their conversation to their personal interests, likes, and dislikes. *"Their ages were alike; each had given up the pursuits of trade for the military profession, of which each had made a study; and their tastes and aims were similar,"* Drake noted.

Knox and André discovered they had so much in common that they could have been brothers. *"They parted on the morrow with strong mutual sentiments of regard and good-will, and their interview left an indelible impression on the mind of Knox. The respective condition of the two was not mutually made known until just as they were about to part,"* Drake wrote.

Knox was unaware that André was a British sympathizer and a prisoner of war until their departure. He discovered that the other party of Americans had captured the gallant André. They were taking him to Lancaster, Pennsylvania, where he would stay unless released through a prisoner exchange.

> "There is a time for everything, and a season for every activity under heaven: . . . a time to kill and a time to heal, a time to tear down and a time to build"
> (ECCLESIASTES 3:1, 3).

Once again Knox faced the irony of war. Just as his marriage to Lucy and his relationship to her loyalist father had shown, this was a civil war. It wasn't merely a war between two powers. It was a brawl between brothers, a sibling rivalry for control of the family homestead. Choices were tests of character and capabilities.

Giving others preference in sleeping quarters showed Henry Knox's generosity. But he had no idea how his amiable conversation with John André would later test his character in one of the most painful episodes of the war.[115]

**PRAYER**

*God, I trust you with my time today, knowing you are the Author of the seasons of life and Guardian of my time.*

# 116. The Hills Are Alive with the Sound of Cannon

I wish we could sell them another hill at the same price," Rhode Island Gen. Nathanael Greene later reflected about Bunker Hill.

After watching the stagnant British army for nine months, Greene and other officers in General Washington's army had come to a key conclusion in the spring of 1776: Bunker Hill had weakened the enemy. The British may have won that battle, but the number of casualties had diluted their abilities.

British General Howe had maintained his position in Boston since the summer of 1775. Washington's ragtag army had surrounded Howe's army by land. The sea blocked the backs of the redcoats. Neither side had made any significant moves. But the New Year had brought Henry Knox and Fort Ticonderoga's artillery to General Washington.

The commander-in-chief then employed a strategy he had used as a young man when he took the job of surveyor in Virginia: observation. As soon as he saw a break in the wintry weather, Washington decided he would take action.

The opportunity came after dark on March 4, 1776. The general ordered companies of men to fire on the British from three separate locations. This decoy allowed two thousand other soldiers and four hundred oxen to haul the Fort Ticonderoga artillery. They took these weapons to the most commanding views of Boston Harbor, the twin hills of Dorchester Heights. The men set up the cannons and built earthen forts to protect them.

In a letter to Continental Congress President John Hancock, Washington reported the operation occurred *"without the least interruption or annoyance from the enemy."*

Washington also called on others to observe for him. Through one of his spies, he quickly learned that when General Howe awoke the next morning, he was shocked to see the cannons on the heights. *"That early on Tuesday morning [British] Admiral Shuldham discovering the works our people were throwing up on Dorchester Heights, immediately sent an express to General Howe to inform him,"* Washington told Hancock. Shuldham told Howe they would be attacked or forced to withdraw their ships from the harbor.

Washington also learned that three thousand British soldiers embarked on boats later that day with plans to land at the base of the heights and launch an assault. But they didn't make it. The weather set them back. *"It was generally believed the attempt would have been made,*

had it not been for the violent storm which happened that night," Washington wrote. His spy
also overheard several of the soldiers say a battle at Dorchester would be *"another Bunker Hill
affair."*

George Washington's strategy of *"ocular
demonstration"* was working. He was content to
wait and watch for what the British would do
next. Boston would not be won by leaps and
bounds but by incremental observations.[116]

> "The watchman
> went and told the
> king, 'I see men in
> the direction of
> Horonaim, on the
> side of the hill'"
> (2 SAMUEL 13:34).

**PRAYER**

*Thank you for the gift of observation. Make me a watchman today. Keep
my eyes open to see what you would have me see.*

# 117. 'Tis a Sweet Retreat

Watching a retreat is sweet.

*"IT IS with the greatest pleasure I inform you that on Sunday last
[March 17, 1776], the instant, about nine o'clock in the forenoon, the
ministerial army evacuated the town of Boston, and that the forces of the
United Colonies are now in actual possession thereof,"* Gen. George
Washington wrote joyfully to John Hancock.

Watching a peaceful, orderly retreat, however, is even sweeter, as
Washington conveyed. *"I beg leave to congratulate you, Sir, and the honorable Congress, on this happy event, and particularly as it was effected
without endangering the lives and property of the remaining unhappy
inhabitants,"* he continued.

For months the sea had provided an escape and supply route for General Howe's Royal Army and Navy. But when Washington placed the cannons from Fort Ticonderoga on Dorchester Heights, General Howe
realized his sea route was in danger. He ended his occupation of Boston.
As Washington watched the remaining British ships leave Boston's harbor, he sent men to survey the damage from the nearly yearlong siege. He
reported his observations to Hancock. *"The town, although it has suffered greatly, is not in so bad a state as I expected to find it,"* Washington
wrote of Boston's general condition.

The commander-in-chief then turned to another matter, one that was
personal to Hancock. *"[A]nd I have a particular pleasure in being able to
inform you, Sir, that your house has received no damage worth mentioning.*

*Your furniture is in tolerable order, and the family pictures are all left entire and untouched. Captain Cazneau takes charge of the whole, until he shall receive further orders from you,"* Washington reported.

Washington's observations proved to be as keen as an eagle's. *"The situation in which I found their works evidently discovered that their retreat was made with the greatest precipitation. They have left their barracks and other works of wood at Bunker's Hill all standing, and have destroyed but a small part of their lines,"* he added.

Washington's watchfulness went beyond inventories and housekeeping items. He drew conclusions about the conditions of the enemy based on what they left behind. Their retreat was hastier than burglars fleeing a house as the homeowner arrived.

*"They have also left a number of fine pieces of cannon, which they first spiked up, also a very large iron mortar; and, (as I am informed,) they have thrown another over the end of your wharf,"* George Washington wrote, explaining his plans for incorporating the British weapons into his army. *"I have employed proper persons to drill the cannon, and doubt not I shall save the most of them . . . From an estimate of what the quartermaster-general has already discovered, the amount will be twenty-five or thirty thousand pounds."*

> "A longing fulfilled is sweet to the soul, but fools detest turning from evil" (PROVERBS 13:19).

Thus the British retreat was a sweet treat for the continentals. Boston was free at last.[117]

**PRAYER**

*Thank you for providing for my needs and satisfying my soul with sweetness.*

## 118. Before the Ink Dries

John Hancock punctuated his praise to Providence with capital letters. The British evacuation of Boston was indeed a capital victory.

*"The same Providence that has baffled their attempt against the Province of Massachusetts Bay will, I trust, defeat the deep-laid scheme they are now meditating against some other part of our country,"* John Hancock began a letter to General Washington shortly after the triumph. *"This success of our arms naturally calls on me to congratulate you, Sir, to whose wisdom and conduct it has been owing,"* he wrote, adding he hoped Washington experienced *"genuine satisfaction"* over the victory.

*"The pleasure you feel must be the most rational and exalted,"* Hancock penned.

With pauper-like humility, the wealthy Hancock also took a moment to thank Washington for *"the attention you have showed to my property in that town."* If Hancock had once coveted Washington's role, he now embraced his former rival as a friend. If he had doubts of Washington's abilities, Hancock realized this Virginian was the right man at the right time for Boston.

Before the ink of Hancock's congratulatory sentences could dry, he outlined his concerns about the next front in the war. The destination of Howe's army was a mystery. As if he was firing rounds from a musket, Hancock briskly addressed several urgent issues concerning preparations for the next campaign. He asked Washington for an update on the number of troops in camp. Congress needed the count so they could request arms from state assemblies.

Hancock next took aim at the problem with Canada. The British stronghold in Canada greatly concerned Hancock and Congress. The effort by Benedict Arnold to secure an American foothold in Canada had recently failed. With the British out of Boston, General Howe was likely to turn to Canada for assistance. Reinforcements would allow him to easily attack New York or Pennsylvania. *"I am commanded to direct that you detach four battalions into Canada from the army under your command, as soon as you shall be of opinion, that the safety of New York and the Eastern service will permit,"* Hancock wrote, swiftly ending his letter with a promise of more directions and information to come.

> "Even the stork in the sky knows her appointed seasons, and the dove, the swift and the thrush observe the time of their migration. But my people do not know the requirements of the LORD" (JEREMIAH 8:7).

Although celebrations often follow victory, rest after battle is a semicolon in war, not a concluding period. Hancock's letter showed he was confident in Washington and in his own role as Congress's president. John Hancock approached his job at a no-time-to-waste pace. And indeed, some seasons in life require such swift velocity. The Lord, however, conducts the tempo.[118]

**PRAYER**

*Lord, you are the Grand Creator of time. Hasten or slow my pace today, whatever is required to do the work for which you have created me. I embrace you and your timetable for my life.*

# 119. The Revolution Today: Service

"Capt. Daniel P. Sukman has wanted to be a soldier his whole life," FOX News reported on the U.S. Army captain who wrote *Soldier's Diary*, a series for the network's Web site. Sukman's Internet entries chronicled his service in Baghdad in 2006. This captain, who grew up on Long Island, New York, had attended Norwich University, a private military college in Vermont, before entering the army.

"Like most real soldiers—as opposed to many of those portrayed on the screen—Dan takes a serious-minded, workaday approach to his occupation. One does not get the sense of brashness or youthful arrogance from meeting him; ditto any tendency toward exaggeration or self-importance," the article continued about Sukman.

After his commissioning as a second lieutenant in 2000, Sukman served as a platoon leader in South Korea. He was serving as a deputy provost marshal for Army Central Command in Kuwait when the Iraq War began in March 2003. Three months later, Sukman attended an Army Captains Career Course in the States and earned a master's degree in business and security management at the same time. He returned to Iraq in 2006 for a yearlong deployment.

"Dan says that being a soldier is more than a job; it is who he is. After all, he didn't just fall into this life," the FOX News article went on.

Today's military is a volunteer force, filled with career-minded soldiers such as Sukman. But intentional soldiering is not how America's army began.

The voice that led Sukman to the U.S. Army in 2000 was the same cry heard by soldiers of the Revolution, such as Joseph Hodgkins. This shoemaker from Ipswich, Massachusetts, did not grow up aspiring to be a soldier. But when the British assaulted his homeland, he fought alongside his neighbors at Bunker Hill. Service then called him into the Continental army, where he fought as one of Washington's soldiers.

In 1776, no one forgot the colonies were in chaos because the war was on their shores. The circumstances and locations of war have changed, but the Revolution continues today in the attitude of service.

"For readers who don't live near a U.S. military base or personally know anyone serving abroad, it can be difficult to remember this nation is waging a war. Maybe it's that we have trifles like 'American Idol' or 'Dancing With the Stars' to distract us. Or maybe it's because the lives lost or forever changed by this war are so often drowned out by partisan politics," the FOX News article on Sukman continued.

"Dan Sukman will tell you that none of that stuff matters when you are patrolling a hostile neighborhood in Baghdad or trying to train Iraqi police officers in the hope that they will one day relieve you of your duties. His favorite line from 'The Shawshank Redemption' says it all: 'Get busy living, or get busy dying.'"

"If a man dies, will he live again? All the days of my hard service I will wait for my renewal to come" (JOB 14:14).

From its founding soldiers like Joseph Hodgkins to its twenty-first-century career makers like Dan Sukman, service is the hallmark and heritage of the American military.[119]

**PRAYER**

*God, renew my appreciation for those who have served and are serving for freedom.*

# 120. Sabbath Rest: A Pastor Digresses

Preacher Samuel West took a break from soldiering under the command of George Washington to speak to the Massachusetts House of Representatives on May 29, 1776. His message was on the topic of submitting to God. And as sometimes happens in pulpit proclamations and public speeches, he digressed.

*"I cannot but take notice how wonderfully Providence has smiled upon us by causing the several colonies to unite so firmly together against the tyranny of Great Britain,"* West said, referring to the recent reconvening of the Continental Congress.

It is difficult to grasp the emotions that captivated the colonists as they put their hope in the men gathering in Philadelphia to discuss their fate. Most had never traveled beyond the boundaries of their colony. To see the colonies come together through the Congress was a miracle, one that brought the same nerves and excitement as a new romance. West embraced it this way: *"Though differing from each other in their particular interest, forms of government, modes of worship, and particular customs and manners, besides several animosities that had subsisted among them, that, under these circumstances, such a union should take place as we now behold, was a thing that might rather have been wished than hoped for."*

And although the colonies were distinct, with unique customs, climate, and charters, they came together because they suffered from a common cold. The conflict that started between Massachusetts and England had spread throughout the colonies like a virus. The land of different accents shared the same affliction.

Calling the Continental Congress *"the Lord's doing,"* West returned to his sermon's central message. God was their Supreme Authority. *"They [the English government] are robbing us of the inalienable rights that the God of nature has given us . . . and has confirmed to us in his written word as Christians and disciples of that Jesus who came to redeem us from the bondage of sin and the tyranny of Satan, and to grant us the most perfect freedom,"* he told the listening legislators.

West encouraged them to put their faith in God. *"But we have this for our consolation: the Lord reigneth; he governs the world in righteousness, and will avenge the cause of the oppressed when they cry unto him. We have made our appeal to Heaven, and we cannot doubt but that the Judge of all the earth will do right,"* Samuel West concluded.

> "He will judge the world in righteousness; he will govern the peoples with justice" (PSALM 9:8).

Digressions are as common in life as they are in public speeches. Sometimes they are insightful. Other times they are silly. God, however, cannot digress from his righteousness, because his righteousness is his nature.[120]

**PRAYER**

*God, you are the One who reigns supreme. Nothing can change your righteousness. Thank you for offering me hope through your Son, Jesus Christ.*

# 121. Problems with Promotions

Gen. George Washington may have driven the British out of Boston in March, but one victory does not a revolution make. There was a need to expand the army, while trying to anticipate the next British move. Washington found himself faced with many difficult decisions, including which officers to recommend to the Continental Congress for promotion.

*"From the last accounts from Great Britain, it appears absolutely necessary that there should be an augmentation of the American forces, in consequence of which I suppose there will be several promotions,"* Brig. Gen. Nathanael Greene began his letter to Washington from his Long Island post in May 1776.

The subject of promotions was a delicate one. Greene knew it was best to handle his request with care. While he knew it could be counterproductive to push too hard, Greene felt the need to state his own case for advancement. He had to make his plans, hopes, and concerns known to the commander-in-chief.

*"As I have no desire of quitting the service, I hope the Congress will take no measure that will lay me under the disagreeable necessity of doing it,"* Greene wrote on. *"Every man feels himself wounded, where he finds himself neglected, and that in proportion as he is conscious of endeavouring to merit attention."*

Greene had entered the army as a brigadier general. Although at age thirty-three he was Washington's youngest general, he knew promotions were based on capability and service, not age. If Washington and Congress, however, made their selections based on favoritism rather than merit, they would insult Greene's honor. Promotions based on favors might be taken to mean that Greene, and others, had failed in their command.

*"I shall be satisfied with any measure that the Congress shall take, that has not a direct tendency to degrade me in the public estimation. A measure of that sort would sink me in my own esteem, and render me spiritless and uneasy in my situation, and consequently unfit for the service,"* Greene warned.

After revealing his fears, Greene expressed his loyalty. He had to make sure Washington did not mistake his ambition for self-importance. *"I have ever found myself exceeding happy under your Excellency's command. I wish my ability to deserve [a promotion] was equal to my inclination to merit. How far I have succeeded in my endeavours, I submit to your Excellency's better judgment,"* he concluded.

By raising the subject of promotions with George Washington, Nathanael Greene took a risk. But he knew that if he didn't sow the seed, he could never reap the harvest of a promotion.[121]

> "Remember this: Whoever sows sparingly will also reap sparingly, and whoever sows generously will also reap generously"
> (2 CORINTHIANS 9:6).

**PRAYER**

*God, may I use my gifts to sow generously for you this week.*

# 122. Mold Maker and Mold Breaker

As an iron foundry owner, Nathanael Greene was a mold maker. And as a Quaker who supported the war, he was a mold breaker. But when this brigadier general approached the subject of promotions with General Washington, he conformed to the most appropriate pattern possible: the mold of modesty.

*"I consider myself immediately under your Excellency's protection, and look up to you for justice,"* he implored Washington in a letter he wrote from Long Island in May 1776. He hoped Congress would award him the rank of major general for the next campaign against the British.

Greene's desire for a promotion was as much a reflection of his commitment to serve as it was his ambition. After all, he knew his family and friends in Rhode Island had cast their hopes for security on him. Their future weighed on him like one of the thousands of anchors his foundry had turned out over the years.

*"I hope I shall never be more fond of promotion than studious to merit it. Modesty will ever forbid me to apply to that House for any favors,"* he wrote of his desire for justice, not favoritism.

Greene was one of the first brigadier generals to report for duty in Cambridge. After the Battle of Bunker Hill in June 1775, the Rhode Island assembly decided to send troops to Boston and turned to their most capable legislator for leadership. Greene came from a respected family of blacksmiths and skilled laborers. No matter his Quaker upbringing. As he had done on many occasions, Greene had broken the mold of pacifism and forged his own path. He answered his fellow legislators' call and led a brigade of three regiments to Cambridge. There he was one of the first to welcome the commander-in-chief when Washington assumed command.

Greene hoped his efforts to lead his Rhode Islanders in the overnight effort to fortify Boston's Dorchester Heights had proved to Washington both his capabilities and his commitment to serve.

*"I wish for nothing more than justice, either upon principle of merit or rank,"* he explained. Greene then made a pledge of loyalty. *"I feel myself strongly attached to the cause, to the Continental Congress, and to your Excellency's person."*

Although his promotion was uncertain, Greene knew one thing for sure: The risk to his revered Rhode Island would continue until the redcoats sailed home. *"But should any thing take place contrary to my wishes, which might furnish me with sufficient reason of quitting the service, yet I will not do it, until the danger and difficulties appear less than at present,"* he promised, referring to his response should Washington or Congress pass him over for promotion.

Within a few weeks of molding this letter with modesty, Greene received his promotion. But as the battle of New York would show, forging a revolution could be hotter than working in a foundry. Only time and challenges would prove whether Nathanael Greene's character was cast in the mold of service or self-importance.[122]

> "He mocks proud mockers but gives grace to the humble" (PROVERBS 3:34).

**PRAYER**

*Mold my heart in modesty today and cast my character in a pattern that conforms to your will for my life.*

# 123. Bricks and Bushes

When John Adams considered the momentous idea of independence in May 1776, he found fresh inspiration from a sermon. This message gave him insight into his own purpose in the chaos.

"*I have this Morning heard Mr. Duffil [Duffield] upon the Signs of the Times. He run a Parrallell between the Case of Israel and that of America, and between the Conduct of Pharaoh and that of [King] George,*" Adams wrote to his wife, Abigail, on May 17, 1776.

Adams had heard George Duffield preach many times during Adams's participation in the Continental Congress. In an earlier letter, he told Abigail that Duffield was a preacher "*whose Principles, Prayers and Sermons more nearly resemble, those of our New England Clergy than any that I have heard.*"

Duffield's comparison between Pharaoh and King George tasted sweeter than manna to Adams. The reason? It made sense of the madness. "*Jealousy that the Israelites would throw off the Government of Egypt made him issue his Edict that the Midwives should cast the Children into the River, and the other Edict that the Men should make a large Revenue of Brick without Straw,*" Adams reminded her of the account. Then he explained Duffield's analogy.

"*He concluded that the Course of Events, indicated strongly the Design of Providence that We should be separated from G. Britain, &c,*" continued Adams.

Indeed. The decisions of King George III were Pharaoh-like in their end result: oppression. "*Is it not a Saying of Moses, who am I, that I should go in and out before this great People?*" Adams noted.

What also pressed on Adams's mind was his own call, his own burning bush triggered by musket fire. "*When I consider the great Events which are passed, and those greater which are rapidly advancing, and that I may have been instrumental of touching some Springs, and turning some small Wheels . . . I feel an Awe upon my Mind, which is not easily described,*" he told Abigail as he tried to grasp the gravity of the situation in one hand and hope for liberty in the other.

"*[Great Britain] has at last driven America, to the last Step, a compleat Separation from her, a total absolute Independence, not only of her Parliament but of her Crown,*" he wrote. Adams added that there was something very "*unnatural and odious*" in a government that was "*1000 leagues*" away.

Whatever role he would play in this separation operation—whether he would speak with the eloquence of Aaron or muster the courage of

Moses to face Pharaoh—Adams knew one thing was certain. *"Confederation will be necessary for our internal Concord, and Alliances may be so for our external Defence,"* John Adams concluded.

America would need many bricks of colonial unity sealed by the mortar of foreign alliances to construct a new nation.[123]

> "The bricks have fallen down, but we will rebuild with dressed stone; the fig trees have been felled, but we will replace them with cedars" (ISAIAH 9:10).

**PRAYER**

*Restore a fresh sense of purpose in my life.*
*Replace any bricks that have fallen into disrepair and rebuild my foundation, with you as my cornerstone.*

# 124. The New Guy in Town

He was the new guy in town. No one who met him failed to notice his youth. When this tall, slender, thirty-three-year-old redhead joined the Continental Congress in Philadelphia in June 1776, he brought with him newness and *"a reputation for literature, science, and a happy talent for composition,"* as John Adams later reflected.

Thomas Jefferson arrived at the most pivotal point in Congress's deliberations. Thomas Paine's *Common Sense* had moved many colonists to action, ready to crush the English constitution with the club of independence.

*"The delegates from Virginia moved in obedience to instructions from their constituents that the Congress should declare that these United colonies . . . be free & independent states,"* Jefferson recorded of the actions of Virginia's elder statesman, Richard Henry Lee.

Lee submitted three resolutions, including one for independence in June 1776. Congress responded by appointing three committees, one to draft a declaration of independence, one to draft a treaty with France, and one to draft a new constitution.

Without experience in diplomacy, Jefferson joined the declaration committee, along with John Adams and Benjamin Franklin. *"The committee for drawing the declaration of Independence desired me to do it,"* Jefferson explained of his assignment to draft the document.

John Adams later explained how the youngest member of the committee came to craft the declaration: *"YOU inquire why so young a man as Mr. Jefferson was placed at the head of the Committee for preparing a Declaration of Independence? I answer: It was the Frankfort advice* [referring to an earlier meeting of some colonial leaders in Frankfort, New York], *to place Virginia at the head of everything."*

Jefferson was chosen partially because he was from Virginia. Just as Adams nominated Virginian George Washington for the post of commander-in-chief, so he also named Jefferson to write the declaration. He believed the stronger the bonds were between New England and the South, the more likely independence would succeed.

One question remained. Why didn't forty-six-year-old Richard Henry Lee write the declaration? It was his resolution that first led Congress to consider independence. Adams explained that Lee served on the committee to draft the more lengthy constitution. He didn't have time to write the shorter declaration.

Although he was the newest delegate, Jefferson impressed his colleagues, especially Adams, with his pen as much as Washington did with his military leadership. *"Writings of his [Jefferson's] were handed about, remarkable for the peculiar felicity of expression,"* Adams later recounted. *"Though a silent member in Congress, he was so prompt, frank, explicit, and decisive upon committees and in conversation . . . that he soon seized upon my heart."*

And that is how the newbie in Congress came to write one of the most significant political documents ever drafted. Thomas Jefferson wrote it simply because he was chosen. He put on paper the changes in sentiment stirring in the hearts of his countrymen and countrywomen.[124]

> "For many are invited, but few are chosen"
> (MATTHEW 22:14).

**PRAYER**

*Father, thank you for choosing me. Thank you for the work you have given my hands to do today.*

## 125. Breathless Debate

After emptying what seemed like a thousand bottles of ink, Thomas Jefferson completed the Declaration of Independence in late June 1776. For two weeks, consumed with the concept of independence, he had scratched and smoothed words into a flowing form. But the clock was ticking. It was time for Congress to unite behind their declaration.

Jefferson first turned to the two men he most trusted. *"Before I reported it to the committee, I communicated it separately to Dr. Franklin and Mr. Adams, requesting their corrections, because they were the two members of whose judgments and amendments I wished most to have the benefit,"* Jefferson reflected.

Adams later wrote, *"I was delighted with its high tone and the flights of oratory with which it abounded, especially that concerning* [abolishing] *negro slavery, which, though I knew his southern brethren would never suffer to pass in Congress, I certainly never would oppose."*

Congress was in such a hurry to see the declaration, Adams noted, that Jefferson presented the document in his handwriting, not in printed form. Congress received it on June 28, 1776, but then tabled it for future discussion.

Jefferson knew his task of convincing Congress to vote for the declaration was a formidable one. Although they had appointed a committee on the subject, adopting a declaration of independence would require more courage than they had yet to muster. If any decision led to General Howe's gallows, it was this one. Hence, Jefferson knew the document needed Congress's wholehearted approval for its success. Unity would take a little time.

The delegates decided to first review Richard Henry Lee's resolution for independence. Then they debated whether to adopt Jefferson's declaration.

The debate centered on two major points of conflict: criticism of the common people in England and slavery. Several members wanted to distinguish the British government from the English people. *"For this reason those passages which conveyed censures on the people of England were struck out, lest they should give them offence,"* Jefferson wrote. *"The clause too, reprobating the enslaving the inhabitants of Africa, was struck out in complaisance to South Carolina and Georgia."*

Throughout the debate, Jefferson tried to be *"a passive auditor of the opinions of others, more impartial judges than I could be, of its merits or demerits."*

Elder statesman Benjamin Franklin sat next to Jefferson during the discussions. Franklin tried to cure Jefferson's despondency with funny stories and *"observed that I was writhing a little under the acrimonious criticisms on some of its parts,"* remembered Thomas Jefferson.

The clock kept ticking, as the debate would not abate for another three days. As often happens, achieving unity required both time and endurance.[125]

> "How good and pleasant it is when brothers live together in unity!"
> (PSALM 133:1).

**PRAYER**

*Thank you for the pleasantness of unity and harmony in life. I pray for patience when life does not bring immediate gratification to my heart.*

# 126. The Revolution Today: Vocations

*There is a time to pray and a time to fight, and that time has now come!"* Rev. John Peter Muhlenberg proclaimed to his congregation as he removed his clerical robes to reveal his military uniform. So goes the story of how Muhlenberg said good-bye to the flock he had shepherded in Woodstock, a town in Virginia's Shenandoah Valley.

Like Nathanael Greene, Muhlenberg had broken the mold of expectations. He initially pursued commerce and joined the British army before returning to America and becoming a preacher, as his father had planned for him. His mold-breaking continued while a pastor. Muhlenberg started out leading Swedish-German Lutheran congregations in Philadelphia but willingly became an Anglican pastor and served in the House of Burgesses when he moved to Virginia.

Unlike Muhlenberg, who traded his clerical robes for a soldier's garb, military chaplains today wear both. Justin Grove was serving as associate director of comments in the White House Office of Presidential Correspondence when he answered a different calling.

"After the terrorist attacks on 9-11, I was so inspired by our Armed Services and their families that I wanted to do my part to serve them," Grove remembered. "The choice to specifically serve as a Chaplain came after much prayer and guidance from several Active Duty chaplains who were serving in the area. They spent time to discuss and pray with me about serving in this way. The Lord eventually confirmed this calling on my life. I am very grateful for this opportunity because as a Chaplain there are many opportunities to have a widespread and positive impact throughout the Navy."

While continuing to work in the federal government, Grove completed Officer Indoctrination School and Chaplain School in Newport, Rhode Island, where he learned the basics of being a U.S. Navy officer and a chaplain in a pluralistic military.

"Since Navy Chaplains are often stationed with the Marine Corps, we also received Amphibious Marine Expeditionary Training, which prepared us to be deployed with a Marine unit. This training included spending a week in the woods: bivouacking, marches with full gear, obstacle courses, etc.," Grove told of his chaplain candidacy, which also included seminary and ordination requirements. He is now a commissioned officer in the reserves.

The duties of today's military chaplains may vary from conducting worship services to counseling, but they serve a united force. "Navy Chaplains play a vital role in helping their fellow sea-service personnel negotiate the crucial moments in their lives. They provide moral support for young people away from home for the first time, lend advice to individuals facing personal or emotional difficulties, and provide spiritual assistance to people from all walks of life," Justin Grove stated.

> "The purposes of a man's heart are deep waters, but a man of understanding draws them out"
> (PROVERBS 20:5).

Breaking molds by changing vocations is more common today than ever. Part of the Revolution's legacy of liberty is the freedom to pursue new interests and jobs.[126]

**PRAYER**

*God, you know the depths of my heart better than I do. Fulfill your purpose in me in the coming week.*

# 127. Sabbath Rest:
# John Witherspoon's Providence

*Providence*. Our modern-day dictionaries define this word as "fate," "luck," or "destiny." Today, its use seems very formal, but references to Providence appear over and over again in the colonial vernacular. Providence obviously meant much more to the sons and daughters of Puritans than our modern-day definitions. Providence was a name for God, not a flippant reference to good fortune. George Washington used the term many times to explain seemingly unexplainable circumstances. One of the rules of civility taught Washington to speak of God in only the most respectful terms. Providence was a term of respect.

And unlike the deist belief that God created the earth and then washed his hands of any involvement in humanity, the colonists looked for examples of Providence's intervention in their lives.

*"There is not a greater evidence either of the reality or the power of religion, than a firm belief of God's universal presence, and a constant attention to the influence and operation of his providence,"* Presbyterian minister John Witherspoon stated from his Princeton, New Jersey, pulpit. *"It is by this means [Providence] that the Christian may be said, in the emphatical scripture language, 'to walk with God, and to endure as seeing him who is invisible,'"* he explained.

Witherspoon was one of the greatest ministers of the revolutionary age. He held a strong belief in the intervention of Providence. After all, Providence had led this Scottish immigrant to America to accept the position of president of Princeton College (now University). Witherspoon had long abhorred mixing the sacred with the secular, but by 1774, he concluded liberty was a spiritual matter, not just a political one. Providence had led him into politics.

Witherspoon delivered his first sermon with political overtones in May 1776. *"The doctrine of divine providence is very full and complete in the sacred oracles. It extends not only to things which we may think of great moment, and therefore worthy of notice, but to things the most indifferent and inconsiderable,"* he said.

Witherspoon turned to Jesus' words in Matthew 10:29, 30 (KJV): *"Are not two sparrows sold for a farthing? and one of them shall not fall on the ground without your Father. But the very hairs of your head are all numbered."*

> "So don't be afraid; you are worth more than many sparrows" (MATTHEW 10:31).

Thus, Witherspoon believed Providence ruled over all his creatures. God had allowed the crisis with England to take place. Providence was guiding the colonies. And in Witherspoon's own life, Providence guided his path. A month after delivering this message, John Witherspoon was elected to the Continental Congress, just in time to address the issue of independence.[127]

**PRAYER**

*God, I praise you for your providential hand. Thank you for caring about the tiniest details of my life.*

# 128. Full-Grown Patriots

*The second day of July 1776, will be the most memorable epoch in the history of America. I am apt to believe that it will be celebrated by succeeding generations as the great anniversary festival,"* John Adams wrote to his wife on July 3, 1776.

Congress's decision to adopt Richard Henry Lee's resolution for independence on July 2, 1776, set off fireworks in Adams's patriotic soul. *"It ought to be commemorated, as the day of deliverance, by solemn acts of devotion to God Almighty. It ought to be solemnized with pomp and parade, with shows, games, sports, guns, bells, bonfires and illuminations, from one end of this continent to the other, from this time forward forever more,"* proclaimed Adams. But July 4, the day Congress adopted Jefferson's Declaration of Independence, not Lee's resolution, became the holiday known as Independence Day.

Both the resolution and the Declaration were important for another reason. They marked maturity in the Congress. They graduated from fledgling flag-wavers to full-grown patriots. *"This, however, I will say for Mr. Adams, that he supported the Declaration with zeal and ability, fighting fearlessly for every word of it,"* Thomas Jefferson later wrote.

Jefferson graciously honored Adams for advocating the rights of the Revolution. *"For no man's confident and fervid addresses, more than Mr. Adams', encouraged and supported us through the difficulties surrounding*

175

*us, which, like the ceaseless action of gravity, weighed on us by night and by day."*

With great discipline and respect, Congress had debated the Declaration for three days. On July 4th, every member who was present, except for one, voted for the Declaration. John Dickinson of Delaware was the exception. *"The sentiments of men are known not only by what they receive, but what they reject also,"* Jefferson wrote about Dickinson.

Perhaps Dickinson still put his hope in the olive branch petition he had drafted a year earlier. Or perhaps the seeds of independence fell on rocky soil in his heart. Whatever the reason, Dickinson could not support the Declaration of Independence.

The seeds of patriotism, however, fell on the most fertile soil in John Hancock's soul. He is the primary reason why history remembers July 4th more fondly than July 2nd. As president of the Congress, Hancock bravely and boldly signed the Declaration on July 4th. The remaining members signed it on August 2nd. Each signature was a symbol of maturity and courage. The reason? Each "John Hancock" provided tangible proof of treason in the eyes of the British.

> "When I was a child, I talked like a child, I thought like a child, I reasoned like a child. When I became a man, I put childish ways behind me"
> (1 CORINTHIANS 13:11).

Congress also graduated to full-grown patriots by distributing the Declaration throughout the colonies. They sent copies to assemblies, public safety committees, and the Continental troops. They hoped it would light a fire among the people. And indeed it did. The Declaration of Independence turned a rebellion into a revolution. The child Independence became a young adult.[128]

**PRAYER**

*God, cast off the things within me that keep me from maturity, that keep me from becoming an independent adult who is mature in you.*

# 129. The Declaration

The Declaration of Independence gave the United States of America a Genesis-like foundation. Its bullet-point complaints about the king may have been relevant to 1776, but its themes are as universal as the land under humanity's feet.

First, the Declaration was unanimous. Although John Dickinson voted against it, he was overruled by his fellow delegates from

Delaware. Hence, the Declaration derived its power from its one-state, one-vote unanimity. This single voice of separation soared throughout America's skies, seas, and soil. *"THE UNANIMOUS DECLARATION OF THE THIRTEEN UNITED STATES OF AMERICA,"* the document began.

Second, the Declaration was respectful of those most affected by the separation. *"WHEN in the Course of human events, it becomes necessary for one people to dissolve the political bands which have connected them with another . . . a decent respect to the opinions of mankind requires that they should declare the causes which impel them to the separation,"* the Declaration stated before outlining the details of their grievances.

Third, the Declaration was rooted in the belief that God valued life and liberty. *"We hold these truths to be self-evident, that all men are created equal, that they are endowed by their Creator with certain unalienable Rights, that among these are Life, Liberty and the pursuit of Happiness."*

Fourth, the Declaration was secure against an avalanche of abuse by authority. It called for claiming those God-given rights through government. Humanity had a right to disband government if that government abolished those rights. *"That to secure these rights, Governments are instituted among Men, deriving their just powers from the consent of the governed, That whenever any Form of Government becomes destructive of these ends, it is the Right of the People to alter or to abolish it, and to institute new Government,"* the document asserted.

Fifth, the Declaration was sensible. Although its ideas were radical, it was not impractical. What kept the Declaration from justifying the continuous overthrow of governments was this statement: *"Prudence, indeed, will dictate that Governments long established should not be changed for light and transient causes."*

Sixth, the Declaration was justifiable. After presenting these universal ideas, the Declaration presented twenty-seven "bullet points," or facts, to candidly prove the king's *"absolute Tyranny over these States."*

Seventh, the Declaration appealed *"to the Supreme Judge of the world"* and declared, *"That these United Colonies are, and of Right ought to be Free and Independent States; that they are Absolved from all Allegiance to the British Crown, and that all political connection between them and the State of Great Britain, is and ought to be totally dissolved."*

Through these universal themes, the Declaration championed human life. The founders

> "So God created man in his own image, in the image of God he created him; male and female he created them" (GENESIS 1:27).

sought to restore order out of chaos by seeking to protect the rights of those created in the image of God.[129]

**PRAYER**

*Thank you for declaring your love for me, for creating me in your image, for endowing me with life and liberty.*

# 130. Needling Martha

The doctor's office was possibly the last place Martha Washington wanted to visit as her road of loyalty continued into the summer of 1776. *"Not just capture and wayward artillery, but illness, as well, threatened Martha Washington's safety during the war,"* related Mount Vernon historian Mary Thompson.

But if Martha wanted to survive life on the road with her husband, she had to endure the needle and its dangerous effects. To do so required her to travel to Philadelphia. Just as the Continental Congress closed their doors to contemplate independence in 1776, Martha Washington contemplated the results of her smallpox inoculation.

*"The military camps brought together men from different parts of the country, from relatively isolated farms and small communities into crowded conditions, where they came into contact with disease-causing agents from other areas, to which they had no immunity,"* Thompson said. She noted that inadequate food and poor hygiene lowered immunity to rampant diseases, especially smallpox. Such diseases could be as fatal as a cannon blast.

*"Mrs. Washington would have been introduced to these conditions,"* Thompson explained, *"and especially the danger of smallpox, during the first winter of the war in Cambridge and it was sometime during that first stay in camp that she made the decision to be inoculated herself, a choice which would have an impact on her health and future ability to come to headquarters."*

Martha had two cheerleaders in her camp. General Washington knew how much she feared the smallpox inoculation. Her fear was so strong no one told her that her son Jack Custis had received the inoculation while a teenager away at school; she learned the news after his recovery. Washington privately doubted her "resolution" but praised her courage.

But it was her second cheerleader, Jack, who was perhaps proudest of her decision. *"My dear Mama,"* Jack began in his letter dated June 9, 1776. *"The receipt of your kind letter . . . gave Me the sincerest plea-*

*sure to hear You were in so fair a way of getting faverably through the Smallpox."*

Unlike most vaccinations today, inoculation back then used a live virus. Doctors took a small secretion from a blister of an infected patient and transferred it to the patient receiving the inoculation. The hope was that only a mild case of smallpox would emerge. If patients survived the inoculation, they enjoyed a life-long immunity.

*"The smal Danger attending that Disorder by Inoculation when the patients follow the Directions of their Physician, has releived Me from much Anxiety,"* Jack wrote. *"I do with the truest affection congratulate you on and thank God for your recovery."*

Not only do illnesses, especially serious ones, require top medical care, they also require cheer-leaders to encourage and embrace the afflicted. Martha Washington was blessed with both.[130]

> "Even though my ill-ness was a trial to you, you did not treat me with contempt or scorn. Instead, you welcomed me as if I were an angel of God, as if I were Christ Jesus himself"
> (GALATIANS 4:14).

**PRAYER**

*God, I pray for grace and sensitivity to those who face serious illnesses.*

# 131. Defining a Tyrant

How do you define an obstinate tyrant? You do what he has refused to do. You outline his transgressions for him.

A characteristic of obstinacy is a refusal to admit your own mistakes, sins, and failures. One purpose of the Declaration of Independence was to indict King George III and identify his *"history of repeated injuries and usurpations."* To the patriots, the king's sins were as numerous as the jewels in his crown.

*"He has refused his Assent to Laws, the most wholesome and necessary for the public good,"* the Declaration of Independence claimed, citing George III's refusal to allow his governors to enact laws without his permission.

The king had also fatigued the colonists by requiring them to attend courts miles away from their homes. He had refused to create laws for *"establishing judiciary powers"* and made judges dependent on him for salaries. The king had dissolved local assemblies. Worst of all, he had established martial law in Massachusetts.

*"He has kept among us, in times of peace, Standing Armies without the Consent of our legislature,"* the Declaration continued. The king had sent *"large bodies of armed men"* to the colonies and then protected those soldiers through mock trials.

He was a tyrant for *"cutting off our Trade with all parts of the world: For imposing taxes on us without our Consent."* He took away *"our Charters, abolishing our most valuable Laws, and altering fundamentally the Forms of our Governments."*

The king had *"abdicated Government here, by declaring us out of his Protection and waging War against us"* and then plundering America's seas and coasts. He had hired foreign mercenaries to fight against the colonists. He had also kidnapped Americans *"on the high Seas to bear Arms against their Country, to become the executioners of their friends and Brethren."*

Thus were the multitude of sins committed by His Royal Obstinacy. *"A Prince, whose character is thus marked by every act which may define a Tyrant, is unfit to be the ruler of a free People,"* the Declaration concluded.

As King George III's teacher, James, noted in 1758, *"[George] has rather too much attention to the sins of his neighbor."* James, the second Earl Waldegrave, saw that King George III lacked the discipline to look inward. It would prove to be one of his great follies.[131]

> "He will die for lack of discipline, led astray by his own great folly"
> (PROVERBS 5:23).

**PRAYER**

*Show me my stubborn ways. Do not let me be led astray by my own follies, failures, or faults. Instill in me the discipline I need to overcome weaknesses.*

# 132. British Fleet

The British were coming. The British were coming. But where were they coming to? To New York, of course.

*"Flushed with the idea of superiority after the evacuation of Boston, the Americans desire decisive action. Nothing is more sought for by us,"* Gen. William Howe proclaimed, describing his emboldened determination.

When Howe left Boston in March 1776, he was down but not out. After taking refuge in Nova Scotia, he chose New York as his aim that summer. And just as the Continental Congress finalized the Declaration of Independence, General Howe arrived on Staten Island. *"General Howe, as you have heard, is arrivd at New York [July 4th]. He has brought with him from 8 to 10,000 troops,"* Samuel Adams chronicled in a letter to a friend on July 12th. *"Lord Howe [the general's brother] arrivd the last Week, and the whole Fleet is hourly expected. The Enemy landed on Staten Island."*

Local residents watched in both awe and horror as the British military filled New York's waters with endless white sails. When would the ships stop coming? And how many would there be when the last ship arrived? The British fleet was a show of force unlike anything Americans had ever seen. *"When the British come in the summer of 1776 it's like Star Wars. It's the Empire Strikes Back. It's the Death Star,"* described author and historian Evan Thomas in an interview for *The History Channel Presents: The American Revolution, 2006.*

Both sides understood New York's strategic significance. New York's islands were America's geographical fulcrum. If the British controlled New York, they could push the patriots off balance and barricade the Revolution. If the Continental army secured New York, America might win the war by autumn.

For many on Staten Island and Long Island, the emotional impact of seeing endless white sails was more powerful than any Declaration of Independence. They were ready to declare their allegiance to the side that was most likely to manage the gallows. With the king's authority behind him, Howe tapped this fountain of fear. He offered pardons to anyone who would take an oath to the crown. Thus, many New York loyalists received British troops with *"great demonstrations of joy."*

For George Washington and his army of ten thousand, the arrival of the British was an unfolding reality in the summer of 1776. They had no idea how many British were coming or how long it would take before they all arrived. The process was so incremental that the Continentals could not understand the size or scope of what they were facing. Each day brought more anxiety than the day before. They had no idea when the battle would come.

> "There are three things that are too amazing for me, four that I do not understand: the way of an eagle in the sky, the way of a snake on a rock, the way of a ship on the high seas, and the way of a man with a maiden" (PROVERBS 30:18, 19).

Sometimes great fleets sail into life slowly, bringing anxiety, fear, and apprehension. It's often hard to comprehend the size of an incremental giant.[132]

PRAYER

*Father, give me insight to comprehend the colossal fleets that sail into my life or the lives of others. Help me to have faith to face these giants.*

# 133. The Revolution Today: Hooah!

H*ooah!*

Perhaps you've heard this loud outburst. When the president of the United States speaks to members of the U.S. Army, many don't merely applaud. Instead they shout *hooah!* when they like what they hear. For some it's an airborne burst. They shout it when they jump out of an airplane.

"You can hear it echoing from the hallowed halls of Fort Benning, Georgia's Infantry Center to the ranges at Fort Lewis, Washington. It is uttered at award ceremonies, bellowed from formations, and repeated before, during, and after training missions," wrote twenty-two-year-career Air Force veteran Rod Powers.

"No matter how one might spell the word—with or without a hyphen, a U instead of two Os, and so on—the word is still an expression of high morale, strength and confidence. And, when powered by an overwhelmingly proud, and usually loud, tone of voice, *hooah* seems to stomp out any possibility of being bound by the written word," Powers continued.

What does *hooah* mean? It means several things. It means "yes, I agree." It means "hurray." It means "here we go."

"It means we have broken the mold. We are battle focused. *Hooah* says 'Look at me. I'm a warrior. I'm ready. Sergeants trained me to standard. I serve America every day, all the way,'" boasted former Army Chief of Staff Gen. Gordon R. Sullivan.

The Revolution had its own *hooah*. When something extraordinary excited the redcoats or the Americans, they shouted out *huzzah!* An old English expression of joy, *huzzah* is the likely predecessor of *hooah*.

And when horseback riders delivered copies of the Declaration of Independence throughout the colonies, you can believe that the Americans shouted *huzzah*. "*In the town squares all over the country, church bells were ringing, people were huzzahing, crowds were applauding, people really did believe the birthday of a new world was at hand,*" UCLA historian Gary B. Nash explained.

Samuel Adams described the outburst of enthusiasm this way: *"Our Declaration of Independency has given Vigor to the Spirits of the People."* What excited the vigor of the colonists was the explosion of the monarchy on America's shores. What excites the military today are those mold-breaking moments, those opportunities to shout with enthusiasm for their nation.

> "Come, let us sing for joy to the LORD; let us shout aloud to the Rock of our salvation" (PSALM 95:1).

Was your week a *hooah* week, or a *ho-hum* one? Sometimes a way to ease the ho-hums is to thank God for the good things in life and shout *hooah* or *huzzah*.[133]

**PRAYER**

*Thanks for giving me so much in life to shout about. I shout for joy to you, Lord, for your mercy, salvation, and grace.*

# 134. Sabbath Rest: Ripe and Rotting

When John Witherspoon broke with his *"no politics from the pulpit"* policy in May 1776 and delivered his first sermon on the subject, he chose an unusual Scripture for his text. He believed a psalm nobly expressed Providence's role in America's conflict with Britain: "Surely the wrath of man shall praise thee: the remainder of wrath shalt thou restrain" (Psalm 76:10 KJV).

Witherspoon's controversial choice matched his controversial conclusion. *"I am sensible, my brethren, that the time and occasion of this psalm, may seem to be in one respect ill suited to the interesting circumstances of this country at present,"* Witherspoon said, noting that the phrase described the end of a war, not the beginning of one.

But he told his congregation that even the *"most impetuous and disorderly passions of men"* were *"subject to the dominion of Jehovah . . . The truth, then, asserted in this text . . . is, That all the disorderly passions of men, whether exposing the innocent to private injury, or whether they are the arrows of divine judgment in public calamity, shall, in the end, be to the praise of God,"* Witherspoon proclaimed.

Witherspoon saw the tumultuous times as paths leading to God's glory and the raising of a nation. *"Or, to apply it more particularly to the present state of the American colonies, and the plague of war. The ambition of mistaken princes, the cunning and cruelty of oppressive and corrupt ministers, and even the inhumanity of brutal soldiers, however dreadful, shall finally promote the glory of God, and in the mean time, while the storm continues, his mercy and kindness shall appear in prescribing bounds to their rage and fury,"* he concluded.

Two months after Witherspoon delivered this provocative message, he made another provocative decision. He signed the Declaration of Independence, becoming the only member of the clergy to do so. When someone questioned his decision and whether the colonies were ripe for independence, Witherspoon replied, *"In my judgment, sir, we are not only ripe, but rotting."*

Witherspoon would go on to play a prominent role in the Continental Congress. He served on the committee to set peace terms.

His role as a professor at Princeton was just as influential. His pupils included a future president, James Madison, who studied under him for a year before the war began. He also tutored twenty-one future senators, twenty-nine representatives, fifty-six state legislators, and thirty-three judges, three of whom were appointed to the Supreme Court.

> "Surely your wrath against men brings you praise, and the survivors of your wrath are restrained"
> (PSALM 76:10).

Witherspoon saw a great purpose in the struggles of 1776. Indeed, through John Witherspoon and other leaders, Providence ripened a nation and harvested independence, all to his glory.[134]

**PRAYER**

*God, you use circumstances for your glory. I praise you, the Mighty God, the Ruler of all, the Lord of purpose.*

# 135. Too Close to Home

M*y Lucy and her babe are at Stamford or Fairfield [Connecticut], where she writes me she is very unhappy, and wants to return here again,"* Henry Knox wrote to his brother William from the Continental camp on Manhattan in July 1776.

Knox and his wife had taken up quarters near the city's batteries. The presence of women at camp was not uncommon. Many took on essential domestic responsibilities, such as cooking and first aid. Lucy's situation was a bit different, however. Because her parents' loyalties to the crown were completely sealed, they fled Boston with the British army after Washington's victory there in March. Lucy and her infant had nowhere to go. They stayed with Knox.

However, when British sails appeared in New York Harbor, Knox couldn't bear for Lucy to remain with him any longer. He feared an imminent attack. The sails were too close to Knox's growing family. *"Indeed, the circumstances of our parting were extremely disagreeable. She had, contrary to my opinion, stayed too long,"* he told William.

The movements of the British unlocked the deepest of feelings between the lovebirds, which erupted into a quarrel over where Lucy and their child should reside. *"From the hall window, where we usually breakfasted, we saw the ships coming through the Narrows, with a fair wind and rapid tide, which would have brought them up to the city in about half an hour. You can scarcely conceive the distress and anxiety that she then had. The city in an uproar, the alarm guns firing, the troops repairing to their posts, and every thing in the [height] of bustle,"* Knox continued.

Although he wanted Lucy closer to his side than his sword, he knew she needed to leave. *"I am not at liberty to attend her, as my country calls loudest. My God, may I never experience the like feelings again! They were too much; but I found a way to disguise them,"* he wrote.

Anguished over the ships within their window's view, Knox convinced Lucy to take refuge in Connecticut. It wasn't long before circumstances confirmed their choice. *"I thank heaven you were not here yesterday,"* Knox wrote Lucy on July 13, 1776. *"Two ships and three tenders of the enemy about twenty minutes past three weighed anchor, and in twenty-five minutes were before the town. We had a loud cannonade, but could not stop them, though I believe we damaged them much. They kept over on the Jersey side too far from our batteries . . . I was so unfortunate as to lose six men by accidents, and a number wounded. This affair will be of service to my people: it will teach them to moderate their fiery courage."*

> "When you enter a house, first say, 'Peace to this house'" (LUKE 10:5).

While the British showed their superiority, Knox proved his character. He had the courage to protect his home and the selflessness to think of his wife and child's safety over his comfort. No matter how ferocious the war, Henry Knox was determined to let peace reign over his home.[135]

**PRAYER**

*Wherever my house may be, however often it moves or wherever my family is scattered, bring peace to my home and let it begin with me.*

# 136. Howe to Snub Washington

Gen. William Howe did not want to battle the Americans anymore than he wanted to fight his brother. After all, the general had fought alongside the colonials during the French and Indian War. And while the Howe brothers prepared for all-out war, their first strategy in New York was diplomacy. General Howe ordered several ships to sail past Manhattan's batteries and fire across the waters on July 12th. The firing didn't last long. Similar to a lion's first growl, it was a show of force. Its goal was to sever the Continentals' communication by water with Fort Ticonderoga. As Henry Knox related to Lucy, *"We had a loud cannonade."*

Historian Caroline Cox of the University of the Pacific explained, *"In fact Howe's goal was not to win, it was to force the Americans to a conference table."*

Lord Howe followed his brother's barrage by sending a letter, under flag protection, to George Washington. Howe, however, made one of the worst mistakes he could in writing to the etiquette aficionado. Instead of addressing Washington as "Your Excellency," as military protocol dictated for the commander-in-chief of an army, Howe merely called him *"George Washington, esquire."* Thus, Howe gave Washington no higher status than a private citizen. Whether his snub was purposeful or accidental, Howe failed to acknowledge Washington as an equal leader of a legitimate army. By doing so, he ridiculed the Revolution.

Washington refused the letter. Politeness and respect were his badges of honor. Independence could not last without recognition by the British.

Howe sent an officer, Colonel Patterson, to meet with Washington on July 20th. Bringing Washington a mouthful of compliments, Patterson referred to him as *"His Excellency."* He explained *"that General Howe much regretted the difficulties which had arisen respecting the address of the letters; that the mode adopted was deemed consistent with propriety, and was founded on precedent, in cases of ambassadors and plenipotentiaries, where disputes or difficulties had arisen."*

Patterson reminded Washington that he (Washington) had addressed a letter to *"the honourable William Howe"* a year earlier. Washington explained that his letter to Howe the previous summer was a response to a letter Howe had sent him using the same form of address. Because an officer on duty accepted the letter, Washington was unable to decline it. There was also a significant difference between the summer of 1775 and the summer of 1776—its name was the Declaration of Independence.

The colonel made one last effort to convince the American commander to accept Howe's most recent letter. He reminded Washington that King George III had given the Howe brothers the power to issue pardons. Washington replied with polite firmness *"that those who had committed no fault, wanted no pardon; and that the Americans were only defending what they deemed their indubitable rights."* Patterson called Washington's position *"debatable"* and left.

> "Surely mockers surround me; my eyes must dwell on their hostility" (JOB 17:2).

Washington knew independence required legitimate recognition by Britain. On this point, this man of manners would not be mocked. Congress agreed and passed a resolution supporting George Washington's decision.[136]

*Give me discernment to recognize legitimate insults, those that require a response and those that don't. Help me to know if, when, and how to respond when people insult or mock me.*

# 137. The Time Is Now at Hand

The time is now near at hand, which must determine whether Americans are to be freemen or slaves,"* George Washington declared to his troops. While he had worked endlessly to prepare their arms for battle in New York, Washington knew he had another task that was just as important. He had to prepare their hearts.

*"Whether they [Americans] are to have any property they can call their own; whether their houses and farms are to be pillaged and destroyed, and themselves consigned to a state of wretchedness from which no human efforts will deliver them. The fate of unborn millions will now depend, under God, on the courage and conduct of this army,"* stressed Washington.

The commander-in-chief knew what it was like to be young and fight. This was the former twenty-two-year-old colonel who saw his then-fellow redcoats flee during General Braddock's failed battle with the French and Indians in 1755. As commander of the Virginia forces, he had witnessed frontiersmen fight for their homesteads against pillaging Indians. He knew a savage enemy's nationality was irrelevant. The enemy, whether British, French, or Indian, was just that—the enemy.

*"Our cruel and unrelenting enemy leaves us only the choice of a brave resistance, or the most abject submission. We have therefore to resolve to conquer or to die,"* he thus declared.

This man of manners, who would not be mocked, called upon his army's sense of duty and personal integrity for motivation to stand by their arms. *"Our own, our country's honour, call upon us for a vigorous and manly exertion; and if we now shamefully fail, we shall become infamous to the whole world,"* he warned his men.

Washington also knew from experience that Providence intervened in the affairs of man. His own miraculous survival of four bullets through his coat had confirmed it. *"Let us then rely on the goodness of our cause, and the aid of the Supreme Being, in whose hands victory is, to animate and encourage us to great and noble actions,"* he said with the same muscle of faith flexed by his friend Jonathan Trumbull, who had encouraged Washington to be strong and courageous in a letter the year before.

The general, this former land surveyor who had employed his powers of observation to defeat the British in Boston, also reminded his men that America was watching and waiting. *"The eyes of all our countrymen are now upon us, and we shall have their blessings and praises, if happily we are the instruments of saving them from the tyranny meditated against them. Let us therefore animate and encourage each other, and show the whole world that a freeman contending for liberty, on his own ground, is superior to any slavish mercenary on earth."*

And while they watched the incremental arrival of the British fleet, George Washington encouraged his men with these and other such statements in the summer of 1776.[137]

> "Now go out and encourage your men" (2 SAMUEL 19:7).

**PRAYER**

*Put words of encouragement in my mouth today. May I give those around me a gift by what I say, when I say it, and how I say it.*

# 138. Melting a Monarchy

People I am told, recognize the Resolution [of independence] as though it were a Decree promulgated from Heaven," Samuel Adams wrote to a friend on July 27, 1776.

Indeed the change seemed as swift as the day the Lord blew the locusts out of Egypt to give Pharaoh yet another chance to set the Israelites free. As Adams continued writing his letter, he habitually chose the word *colonies* to describe his fellow patriots. But then he realized he needed to make a change. *"Or as I must now call them STATES,"* he corrected himself.

Adams, however, knew the Declaration was more than a change in vocabulary. This Continental Congress member recognized that not only had the Declaration of Independence turned the colonies into states, but it had also changed the war's purpose as well.

Before the Declaration, the British strategy was to scare the colonists into submission. Hence, the conflicts at Lexington, Concord, Bunker Hill, and Boston were largely scare tactics and showcases of power, rather than a carefully planned military strategy. The British wanted to spank the colonists and then go home.

Likewise, before the Declaration the patriots sought solutions to their grievances. They wanted representation before taxation. They wanted the Massachusetts charter reinstated. They wanted trial by juries. They wanted negotiation. But now they wanted something else. The revolution stirring in their hearts prevented them from turning back. Independence was now the only thing that would quench their fiery thirst.

Samuel Adams described this change of purpose in a colorful way. *"Monarchy seems to be generally exploded,"* he wrote.

And indeed, it was—literally. Patriots in New York decided to melt the monarchy after they heard the news of the Declaration of Independence. John Hancock sent a broadside to George Washington, who had made his headquarters on Manhattan Island. Washington ordered the Declaration to be read aloud to his army on July 9th. The huzzahing of soldiers thundered up the Hudson River and high into heaven.

That same night, a group of Americans walked to the place where the Broadway intersected with the Bowling Green. With the flames of the Revolution inspiring them, this group pulled down a bronze and lead statue of King George III. They then melted his likeness, and used the melted mass to make forty-two thousand musket balls.

And like Samuel Adams, the troops had, along with new ammunition for their muskets, a new purpose in their hearts.[138]

> "And the LORD changed the wind to a very strong west wind, which caught up the locusts and carried them into the Red Sea. Not a locust was left anywhere in Egypt"
> (EXODUS 10:19).

**PRAYER**

*God, open my heart to embrace the changes you place in my life. As you give me new gifts and opportunities, may I embrace your plans for me with zeal.*

# 139. Sizing Up a Giant

Fee . . . fi . . . fo . . . fum . . . A giant rose with the August sun. The redcoats may have landed on Staten Island with only ten thousand men on July 4, 1776, but within a month their camp had more than doubled in size. Their numbers swelled to twenty-four thousand by the time General Howe's final reinforcements arrived from England and Charleston, South Carolina, in August. Not only that, but their fleet included one hundred and thirty ships. The shadow of the British giant fell over the isles of New York, and he smelled the blood of American Englishmen.

The odds facing Washington's patriots were indeed David-versus-Goliath-like. The British outnumbered them two to one based on the number of capable fighting men. Historian (as well as a U.S. Supreme Court chief justice, a former Continental army officer, and U.S. secretary of state) John Marshall, who published a collection of George Washington's papers, described the Continental army as *"unstable in its nature,—incapable, from its structure, of receiving discipline,—and inferior to its enemy, in numbers, in arms, and in every military equipment."*

Marshall also explained that the Continentals' inadequate shelter led to an invisible invader: Disease plagued Washington's forces as much as the fear of the colossal British presence.

*"For the several posts on New York, Long, and Governor's Island, and Paulus Hook, the army consisted of only seventeen thousand two hundred and twenty-five men, of whom three thousand six hundred and sixty-eight were sick,"* Washington reported in a letter to Congress on August 8th. He lamented that his only hope for reinforcements was from a Maryland battalion that had yet to arrive.

*"These things are melancholy, but they are nevertheless true. I hope for better,"* Washington continued in his letter. As difficult as the situation was, this commander-in-chief was determined not to lose hope. *"Under every disadvantage, my utmost exertions shall be employed to bring about the great end we have in view; and, so far as I can judge from the professions and apparent dispositions of my troops, I shall have their support."*

The number of able fighting men was not the only problem. The situation in New York was further complicated by another number—distance. The scope of New York's islands forced Washington to scatter his forces. Some posts were as far apart as fifteen miles with *"navigable waters"* separating them. Washington also responded to the giant of distance with optimism.

> "The least of you will become a thousand, the smallest a mighty nation. I am the LORD; in its time I will do this swiftly" (ISAIAH 60:22).

*"The superiority of the enemy, and the expected attack, do not seem to have depressed their [his army's] spirits . . . ,"* he wrote. *"The enemy will not succeed in their views without considerable loss. Any advantage they may gain, I trust will cost them dear."*

Washington did receive a boost, however, shortly after writing this letter. The Maryland men arrived, along with Pennsylvania regiments, and New England and New York militias. Even though a fourth of George Washington's army was ill, his numbers increased to twenty-seven thousand men. With each new arrival, the size of the British giant diminished.[139]

PRAYER

*God, I praise you for strengthening the weak, for boosting the weary, and for making the least mighty. Thank you for giving me courage to face life's greatest giants.*

# 140. The Revolution Today: Preparation

If one word summarized the summer of 1776 for the army, it was *preparation*. The more experienced British knew how to prepare for battle. Their ships carried the resources they needed: men, tents, equipment, armaments, and food. General Howe waited patiently until these necessities were in place. Perhaps his show of force in mid-July was merely an effort to buy time until his army was fully prepared.

Washington prepared his men too, as best he could. Where they lacked supplies, he tried to make up for it by preparing their minds for action. He used written orders, speeches, and the Declaration of Independence to stoke the fires of their patriotic souls. Henry Knox prepared by sending his wife and child to a safer location.

Today, military preparedness is different in scope but not in meaning. The army of 1776 would not recognize the sophistication of America's modern army. But they would understand the sentiment behind the supplies. They would recognize the spirit of preparation, the "operating tempo."

"We're prepared to execute any mission we're assigned as the theater reserve," Col. Brian Beaudreault said of the 15th Marine Expeditionary Unit's (MEU) preparations for deployment in the Middle East in August 2006.

For six months the members of this MEU underwent intensive training at Camp Pendleton, California. Their assignment was to serve six months as U.S. Central Command's theater reserve force for operations in Iraq. "We're ready for everything from sustained combat operations ashore to humanitarian relief operations and everything in between," Beaudreault told the Armed Forces Press Service.

In the final days leading up to their deployment, these 2,300 Marines wrapped up last-minute details at the base and at home. The purchasing chief processed last-minute orders for gear. Another checked travel vouchers. Mechanics turned wrenches and checked transmission fluid. Medics packed their life-saving equipment. Others tested a new tactical water purification system to ensure its operation during deployment.

These Marines also prepared by spending time with their families and getting their personal affairs in order. From setting up automatic bill payments to wrapping Christmas presents, they understood the power of tangibly preparing their families for their absence.

No matter what, preparation has a bonus—the more it's done, the better you get at it. "We've done this before," Staff Sergeant Dwayne Benjamin explained. "When you do this over and over, things tend to get—not easier, but simpler . . . You have a job to do . . . My head is always in the game."

Chief Warrant Officer Mike Chaney said, "You do all this training, so you just want to get out there and get the deployment going. We're Marines, and we're just ready to go."

The words *prepare* and *preparation* appear a total of 176 times in the *New International Version* of the Bible. Preparation has a purpose in life. It not only makes us ready. It keeps our minds alert. It leads us to action.[140]

> "Therefore, prepare your minds for action; be self-controlled; set your hope fully on the grace to be given you when Jesus Christ is revealed" (1 PETER 1:13).

**PRAYER**

*Use the coming week, Lord, to prepare my mind for action.*

# 141. Sabbath Rest: Which Side Was God On?

W*hich side then is Providence likely to favour?"* Methodist preacher John Fletcher asked in a sermon he gave in England in 1776. *"In America we see a number of rising states in the vigour of youth, and animated by piety. Here we see an old state, inflated and irreligious, enervated by luxury, and hanging by a thread. Can we look without pain on the issue?"*

Fletcher was so well respected that his friend, Methodist founder John Wesley, called him superior *"in holy tempers and holiness of conversation."* It was this temperament that gave him the credibility to openly question the behavior of his fellow English subjects.

*"In this hour of tremendous danger, it would become us to turn our thoughts to heaven. This is what our brethren in the colonies are doing. From one end of North America to the other, they are fasting and praying. But what are we doing? Shocking thought! We are ridiculing them as fanatics, and scoffing at religion,"* Fletcher declared of English snobbery.

He did not, however, support the revolutionaries. *"To disregard the king's righteous commands, as the colonists do, is bad: But to despise the first-table commandments of the King of kings, as we do, is still worse,"* the preacher admonished.

Fletcher also saw a lack of humility among his fellow Englishmen and Englishwomen. He feared they were trusting too much in their redcoats and not enough in God. *"If the colonists throng the houses of God, while we throng play-houses, or houses of ill fame; if they croud their communion-tables, while we croud the gaming table or the festal board; if they pray, while we curse; if they fast, while we get drunk; and keep the sabbath, while we pollute it; if they shelter under the protection of heaven, while our chief attention is turned to our troops; we are in danger—in great danger,"* he warned.

Fletcher feared that no matter how formidable their British forces, their integrity was poor, making their success doubtful. *"A youth that believes and prays as David, is a match for a giant that swaggers and curses as Goliath,"* he pointed out.

> "Some trust in chariots and some in horses, but we trust in the name of the LORD our God"
> (PSALM 20:7).

More than anything, Fletcher longed for his fellow English subjects to put their trust in God. *"Save us, O king of heaven, when we call upon thee. Some put their trust in chariots, and some in horses: But we will remember the name of the Lord our God,"* he prayed.

John Fletcher's theology said God was concerned about the hearts of men and women regardless of which side of the Atlantic they inhabited. But out of his national pride he hoped Providence would favor England in the war.[141]

**PRAYER**

*God, show me where I am putting my trust in other things and not you today. Enable me to trust you and not in my own strength or the strength of others.*

# 142. Barricading Brooklyn

Some of history's best leaders were masters of pragmatism. Such was the case with George Washington as he prepared for battle in New York. Common sense guided his hands as much as etiquette ruled his tongue.

*"As the defence of Long Island was intimately connected with that of New York, a brigade had been stationed at Brooklyn, a post capable of being maintained for a considerable time,"* historian John Marshall wrote of the Continentals' fortifications.

Throughout the summer, Washington had ordered his officers to prepare for an attack. One of his most practical decisions was to build the strongest post possible on Long Island. He ordered General Sullivan and his brigades to construct an extensive camp at Brooklyn Heights, which Marshall described as *"a village on a small peninsula made by East river, the Bay, and Gowan's Cove."* The reasons for selecting Brooklyn Heights were practical. The camp faced the island's mainland. Its hilly, wooded terrain also provided a natural barrier.

*"In front of the camp was a range of hills covered with thick woods, which extended from east to west nearly the length of the island, and*

*across which were three different roads leading to Brooklyn Ferry. These hills, though steep, are every where passable by infantry,"* described Marshall.

But the soldiers did not rely on nature's barricades alone for protection. They built earthen works across the entire peninsula. With a muddy shield protecting them from the front, common sense led them to also protect their backs from the sea.

*"The rear was covered and defended against an attack from the ships, by strong batteries on Red Hook and on Governor's Island, which in a great measure commanded that part of the bay, and by other batteries on East river, which kept open the communication with York Island,"* Marshall detailed.

With Brooklyn barricaded, Washington also paid close attention to his army's other posts. Common sense had led him to survey key positions and place men at pivotal points. *"The residue occupied different stations on York Island,"* Marshall recorded, noting that many posts were designed to cut off British communication.

Common sense came to George Washington as regularly as the breeze from the harbor. While he lived each day in the shadow of the British giant, he anticipated an attack on any of his posts. *"Expecting daily to be attacked, and believing that the influence of the first battle would be considerable, the Commander-in-chief employed every expedient which might act upon that enthusiastic love of liberty,"* praised John Marshall.

> "When my heart was grieved and my spirit embittered, I was senseless and ignorant; I was a brute beast before you. Yet I am always with you; you hold me by my right hand" (PSALM 73:21–23).

And common sense is often God's right hand.[142]

**PRAYER**

*Sharpen my senses, renew my mind. You uphold me and are always with me.*

# 143. Ready at a Moment's Call

*The enemy's whole reinforcement is now arrived,"* George Washington warned in orders to his men, *"so that an attack must, and will soon be made."*

The commander-in-chief repeated his order that every officer and soldier *"have his arms and ammunition in good order; keep within his quar-*

*ters and encampments as far as possible; be ready for action at a moment's call."*

Washington knew it was time. The size of the British giant was as clear to him as the horizon over New York's waters. He had prudently barricaded Brooklyn and placed men in strategic places on Long Island and nearby sites. But he also knew his resources were scarce. A quarter of his men were sick. And those who were well were about as orderly as a gaggle of geese. Even though victory seemed questionable at best, Washington tried to compensate by giving his troops a commissioning.

*"And when called to it [action], remember, that liberty, property, life, and honour, are all at stake; that upon [your] courage and conduct rest the hopes of [our] bleeding and insulted country; that [your] wives, children, and parents, expect safety from [you] only; and that we have every reason to believe, that heaven will crown with success so just a cause,"* he exhorted the men.

Washington looked hopefully to the righteousness of the cause on which they stood. Justice could deliver a victorious verdict. *"The enemy will endeavour to intimidate by show and appearance; but remember, they have been repulsed on various occasions by a few brave Americans; their cause is bad; and if opposed with firmness and coolness on their first onset, with our advantage of works, and knowledge of the ground, the victory is most assuredly ours,"* he predicted confidently.

In his call for readiness at a moment's notice, Washington also reminded his soldiers of the consequences for disobedience. *"Every good soldier will be silent and attentive, wait for orders, and reserve his fire until he is sure of doing execution; of this the officers are to be particularly careful,"* he ordered.

Washington's discipline was strict. He ordered that any soldier who retreated without orders should be shot. He also promised recognition and rewards for those who distinguished themselves in service. He knew that unless his army would *"acquit"* themselves as *"men,"* slavery would continue to strangle independence.

> "But commission Joshua, and encourage and strengthen him, for he will lead this people across and will cause them to inherit the land that you will see" (DEUTERONOMY 3:28).

*"Thus did he, by infusing those sentiments which would stimulate to the greatest individual exertion, into every bosom, endeavour to compensate for the want of arms, of discipline, and of numbers,"* John Marshall described George Washington's commissioning of his troops.

Power comes from a commissioning. Its strength is in the hearts of those who receive it.[143]

**PRAYER**

*God, I pray for those who are leaders in my life. Give them wisdom, especially when faced with tough choices and extraordinary circumstances.*

# 144. Losing Long Island

W E HAVE *had a glorious day against the rebels,"* a British field officer wrote in jubilation. No longer stuck on Staten Island, this officer, along with four thousand other British soldiers, crossed the narrows and took their first giant steps onto the long island.

"*We landed on this island the 22d [of August], and that day marched toward Brookland Ferry, opposite New York, where this island is separated from the town by the East River,*" he wrote to a friend about the battle.

This advance army landed under the cover of British ships, which protected them from the sea. The redcoats marched toward the Continental army's earthen works with confidence and eagerness in their ranks. "*We took post within musket shot of their un-finished works. The troops were all on fire to force their lines, but General Howe, in whose conduct the utmost prudence and vigilance have been united, would not permit it,*" recounted the British field officer. Howe waited for four days for the rest of the redcoats to land and take their positions. By this time the British numbers exceeded twenty-four thousand.

"*It was not till eight o'clock at night on the 26th that we received our orders to attack, and at eleven the whole army was in motion. The reserve, commanded by Lord Cornwallis, the first brigade of which our regiment makes a part, and the light infantry of the army, the whole under the command of General [Henry] Clinton, marched by the right,*" the officer reported of their night march through Long Island's Jamaica Pass.

"*The road to the right, after a march of about seven miles, brought us to an easy and undefended ascent of the hills, which we possessed at daybreak [August 27th], and continued our rout, gained the rear of the rebels,*" the officer recorded in his memoirs.

And while his regiment came upon the American defenses from the right and rear, it was a foreign force that defeated the Americans from the left and front. The British had not only come to Long Island, but they had also brought paid German fighters, the Hessians, with them. These military men were known more for their might than their sense of right.

"*By this masterly maneuver the rebels were immediately thrown into general confusion, and behaved most shamefully. The numbers killed, wounded, and taken you will see in the [London] Gazette. Some of the Hessians told me they had buried between 400 and 500 in one pit,"* he journaled.

This British officer was a callous witness in liberty's Long Island nightmare. George Washington's gaggle of geese had panicked and turned into a fleeing flock at the first sounds of fire.[144]

> "Doom has come upon you—you who dwell in the land. The time has come, the day is near; there is panic, not joy, upon the mountains" (EZEKIEL 7:7).

**PRAYER**

*God, it seems every day I learn of tragedy from the news media. People panic when bad things happen. Keep me from the callousness that comes from regular doses of tragic news.*

# 145. Preservation by Choice

As the action became warm, General Washington passed over to the camp at Brooklyn, where he saw, with inexpressible anguish, the destruction in which his best troops were involved, and from which it was impossible to extricate them."* This is how historian John Marshall described Washington's distress over the Battle of Brooklyn.

Washington watched his world fall apart on Long Island. Weeks of fortifications and thousands of prayers did not seem to make a difference. Indeed, General Sullivan could not even muster his troops long enough to sustain the first shots fired by the Hessians on the road to the Americans' Brooklyn camp. After several skirmishes in the woods, the Americans were able to regain some of their lines but lost most of their detachments in the process, forcing them to retreat behind the earthen works to their camp.

Washington estimated he lost about a thousand of the nearly ten thousand men who were positioned on Long Island. The numbers, however, were difficult to obtain. Many men were buried in creek beds and marshes. Others who were missing merely escaped and fled for their homes. General Howe estimated the American losses at nearly two thousand, which included valuable prisoners of war. Regardless of the discrepancies, the formula equaled loss.

The Continental army had failed. All the factors against them—their scarce resources, lack of discipline, and inexperience—had proved to be stronger than their zeal. By the morning of August 28th, Washington's arsenal of strategic options was depleted. His hour of need was an hour of contemplation and decision.

*"Should he [Washington] attempt any thing in their favour with the men remaining within the lines, it was probable the camp itself would be lost, and that whole division of his army destroyed,"* Marshall wrote of the precarious position of the Brooklyn Heights camp.

The prospects of bolstering his numbers were even more remote. *"Should he bring over the remaining battalions from New York, he would still be inferior in point of numbers; and his whole army, perhaps the fate of his country, might be staked on the issue of a single battle thus inauspiciously commenced,"* continued Marshall.

Washington was forced to rely on his practical side once again. Victory was no longer his goal; survival took its place. The preservation of his army became paramount.

*"Compelled to behold the carnage of his troops, without being able to assist them, his efforts were directed to the preservation of those which remained,"* historian William Jackman wrote in *History of the American Nation,* published in 1911.

> "But God sent me ahead of you to preserve for you a remnant on earth and to save your lives by a great deliverance"
> (GENESIS 45:7).

As night fell, George Washington searched for a way to rescue his remnant.[145]

**PRAYER**

*Father, thank you for abiding in the remnants of life. When prayer seems to go unanswered, thank you for your deliverance by a different route.*

# 146. Howe to Lose by Winning

It was General Howe who gave George Washington the gift he needed to escape Long Island. Howe mistakenly believed the Americans were in better shape than they were. After his initial attacks and counterattacks, he ordered his troops to camp within six hundred yards of the Americans' outermost redoubt at their Brooklyn Heights camp on the night of August 28, 1776.

*"Believing the Americans to be much stronger than they were in reality, and unwilling to commit any thing to hazard, General Howe made no immediate attempt to force their lines,"* outlined historian John Marshall.

Washington took advantage of Howe's hesitancy as fast as he could mount his favorite horse. He chose to lead his troops in an overnight escape. Using as many fishing boats and ferries as they could find, the remaining nine thousand or so Continentals passed over a narrow point in the river between Long Island and Manhattan. They nearly ran out of time. But an early morning fog protected them, blocking them from the view of the British. The fog was providential, as if God cupped his hands and blew a cloud to earth to surround them in mist.

Marshall wrote that *"all the troops and military stores, with the greater part of the provisions, and all the artillery, except such heavy pieces . . . were carried over in safety."*

The next morning the British found a multitude of empty tents at the Continental camp. The British field officer, however, continued to boast of their Brooklyn success. He described the moment as *"leaving us in possession of this island, which entirely commands New York."*

Hindsight showed the British may have won Long Island but they suffered an even greater defeat—a lost opportunity. *"The failure to capture them [the Continentals] and to really put a stop to the war by rounding up the rebel forces really was perhaps one of the greatest blunders of the war. Because it was in New York with the greatest armada, the greatest number of men that they had at anytime in those eight years, the British lost their best opportunity to win the war at a stroke,"* speculated historian Barney Schecter in an interview for *The History Channel Presents: The American Revolution, 2006.*

Although Washington's decisions were criticized and second-guessed, Marshall praised the commander-in-chief for his practical decision-making and his ability to accept defeat and move on quickly. *"To withdraw, without loss, a defeated, dispirited, and undisciplined army from the view of an experienced and able officer, and to transport them in safety across a large river, while watched by a numerous and vigilant fleet, require talents of no ordinary kind,"* stated Marshall.

> "Though I walk in the midst of trouble, you preserve my life; you stretch out your hand against the anger of my foes, with your right hand you save me" (PSALM 138:7).

*"The retreat from Long Island may justly be ranked among those skilful manoeuvres which distinguish a master in the art of war,"* he concluded.

George Washington proved he was a wise warrior who knew how to navigate troubled waters.[146]

**PRAYER**

*God, thank you for the times in my life and in the lives of others when you provide a cloud, a fog, to protect us from the lion who does not retreat.*

# 147. The Revolution Today: Language Barriers

The story of the Revolutionary War is full of tales that reveal God's guiding hand, even in the midst of defeat.

One such story took place on the night of General Washington's retreat from Long Island. A woman, the wife of a British loyalist, lived near the ferry where Washington's army was escaping over to Manhattan Island. When she saw what was happening, she sent her African servant to alert British soldiers about the Continentals' evacuation. The servant got as far as a British outpost, but the men who guarded it were Hessians, German troops hired by the British. These German-speaking soldiers could not understand the servant's English.

They detained him as a prisoner until morning, when a British officer arrived to interpret. As soon as he heard the news, he sent soldiers to the shore. But it was too late. When they reached the dock, they watched as the last boat ferried the final patriot soldiers across the water, beyond the range of a musket. Not only had a fog protected the Continentals, but so had a language barrier. If the Hessians had been able to understand the servant, or if British soldiers had guarded the outpost instead, the war might have been lost on the spot for the patriots.

"The safe retreat of the patriot army was by many attributed to a peculiar Providence. It was a trust in this Providence, a calm assurance of ultimate success under its guiding care that strengthened the hearts of the patriots in their darkest hour of trial," historian William Jackman concluded.

The Bible shows several instances where God used language for his purpose. Genesis tells us God confused the languages of those who built the tower of Babel to prevent further disobedience by conspiracy. Yet in the book of Acts, God performs a miracle by allowing the people on the day of Pentecost to hear his message in their own language.

Translating is as essential a part of today's world as ever. Language barriers sometimes pose problems for medical personnel and patients. Businesses must bridge language barriers to make their commerce global. The deaf community relies on interpreters as their ears in the hearing world. Language can both confuse and unite people.

The American Translators Association has published a guide for such circumstances. They understand what it takes to hire a translator or an interpreter. One of their suggestions is simple: "Take the burden off words," the guide advises, recommending pictures and diagrams as ways to bridge language barriers.

And pictures are one way God has translated his glory regardless of any human language. Perhaps that's why he chose both a fog and a language barrier to disguise the Continental army that night on Long Island. The skies proclaim God's handiwork in language understood by those who simply choose to look heavenward.[147]

**PRAYER**

*Lift my eyes to your skies at least once today, that I may reflect on your glory.*

"The heavens declare the glory of God; the skies proclaim the work of his hands. Day after day they pour forth speech; night after night they display knowledge. There is no speech or language where their voice is not heard" (PSALM 19:1–3).

# 148. Sabbath Rest: Homeland Security

How did the average New Yorker respond to the British success on Long Island in 1776? The loyalists were overjoyed, but the patriots feared for their lives. One such New York patriot was Presbyterian minister Abraham Keteltas. When the British occupied Long Island, Keteltas fled his home and settled in Newburyport, Massachusetts, where he supplied the pulpit of the First Presbyterian Church. It was there under the candlelight of an evening lecture that he delivered one of his most memorable sermons, called "God Arising and Pleading His People's Cause."

Keteltas turned to the Psalms for comfort in this public response to his personal loss. He analyzed an incident in David's life when the king feared for his own viability. David was greatly distressed over his failed homeland security policy. An army had invaded, spoiled, and burned a town. Most sickening of all, these enemies carried away local women. David's life was threatened by the people, who wanted to stone him for his failure to prevent the invasion and protect them and their families.

"[W]e read, that under these afflicting circumstances, 'he [David] encouraged himself in the LORD his God,'" preached Keteltas, quoting 1 Samuel 30:6 (KJV). "In this respect, the royal Psalmist exemplified in his conduct, the exercise of every believer. They all fly to God for refuge in time of trouble, and expect comfort and relief from his power and grace, from his glorious perfections and precious promises," he told his congregation.

He reminded them of Asaph, author of Psalm 73. "'Whom have I in heaven but thee? and there is none upon earth that I desire besides thee. My flesh and my heart faileth: but God is the strength of my heart and my portion for ever,'" he quoted (vv. 25, 26 KJV).

Not only was this preacher looking to God to lift his spirits, but he was also counting on God even if independence died on the vine. "Although the Fig tree should not blossom, though there should be no fruit on the Vine, though the labor of the Olive should fail, though the field should yield no meat, though the flock should be cut off from the fold, and though there should be no herd in the stall, the believer will rejoice in the Lord, and joy in the God of his salvation," Keteltas continued, paraphrasing Habakkuk 3:17, 18 (KJV).

He encouraged his audience that nothing, not even an invasion by the enemy, was too difficult for God. *"If prospects should look dark, earth should shudder on her basis, and no light nor relief should appear to the eye of sense, yet the believing heart will trust in the name of the Lord, and stay itself upon its God,"* he instructed.

And indeed the blackest cloud had rolled through this preacher's life. New York held the fragments of bullets and bones while redcoats lived on top of its ashes. But Abraham Keteltas was determined to trust in God. It was time to go on with life.[148]

> "David was greatly distressed because the men were talking of stoning him; each one was bitter in spirit because of his sons and daughters. But David found strength in the LORD his God" (1 SAMUEL 30:6).

**PRAYER**

*I look to you when the darkest clouds cover my life or the life of someone I care about. Be my strength when I can't see sunlight.*

# 149. New Life

While the Continentals retreated from Long Island, Martha Washington waited in Philadelphia for word from two fronts. *"The general myself and Jack are very well[.] Nelly Custis is I hope getting well again, and I believe is with child. I hope no accident will happen to her in going back,"* Martha Washington had written her sister earlier in 1776.

Martha's son Jack and his wife, Nelly, had accompanied her to Cambridge the previous year. But they didn't stay long. Even though they had passed the time as pleasantly as possible, they were *"often alarmed with fears of the British, whose bombs burst frequently over the place of their residence,"* a relative later confided.

Martha's suspicions were true. Nelly was pregnant when she and Jack left Cambridge for their Maryland home. Martha's compassion for Nelly, however, was born as much from experience as it was kinship. Nelly had earlier given birth to a stillborn child, and Martha understood her grief. Martha had witnessed the death of three of her four children by 1776. Jack was her last living child. Two died as young children and her seventeen-year-old daughter Patsy died of a seizure.

Hence, Martha labored over twin burdens during her stay in Philadelphia in August 1776. Both had the possibility of bringing news of a birth, one of a child and the other a nation. She welcomed prescriptions for both.

By the end of August, Martha learned of the defeat on Long Island and her husband's retreat to Manhattan. When she received Jack's letter dated August 31st, her hands must have trembled. Now, more than ever, she needed the cure of good news.

*"I have the extreme Happiness at last to inform you, that Nelly was safely delivered this Morning about five oClock of a fine Daughter, . . . ,"* Jack wrote his mother, *"and It affords Me much Pleasure that I have an opportunity of transmitting this agreeable News so early, I make not the least Doubt but you will heartily join us in the Pleasure We feel on this Happy event."*

Jack told his mother he wished she could be there with him to *"see this strapping Huzze."* He noted the clothes they had waiting for her were too small. *"She is in short as fine a healthy, fat baby as ever was born,"* he proclaimed proudly.

Because his mother couldn't be there, Jack attempted to paint a word picture of his new daughter, noting with humor that she looked more like the plump doctor who delivered her than anybody else. *"She has a double Chinn something like His, in Point of Fatness with fine black Hair, and Eyes, upon the whole I think It is as pretty and fine a Baby as ever I saw. This is not my opinion alone, but the Opinion of all who have seen Her—I hope she will be preserv'd as a Comfort, and Happiness to us all,"* he wrote.

> "A cheerful look brings joy to the heart, and good news gives health to the bones" (PROVERBS 15:30).

The news was just the medicine Martha Washington needed. Nothing, not even war, could stop the cycle of life.[149]

**PRAYER**

*Thank you for the gift of smiles and laughter and for providing good news for my heart.*

# 150. A Fruitless Meeting

Parliament had decided to try negotiation in 1776. They put their conditions in writing and sent one of their senior army officers, General Sullivan, to America. He arrived on General Howe's doorstep after the Battle of Long Island.

*"That, in conjunction with General Howe, he [Sullivan] had full powers to compromise the dispute between Great Britain and America, on terms advantageous to both,"* historian John Marshall wrote.

Because Sullivan received his mission before Parliament learned of the Declaration of Independence, he could only address members of Congress as private citizens, not as government leaders.

Sullivan's inability to recognize their public function put Congress in a difficult position, with two equally unattractive options. Rejecting his offer to negotiate could rattle the public. But accepting the offer could indicate Congress was not serious about independence.

Congress compromised and sent a committee of three to meet with Sullivan. The elder statesman, Benjamin Franklin, possessed wisdom and industriousness. John Adams bore passion for the cause. And twenty-seven-year-old Edward Rutledge was fresh with spirit. The trio arrived at Staten Island on September 11, 1776, to meet with Sullivan and Howe.

With *"great politeness"* Howe began by saying Parliament's orders prevented him from treating them as a committee of Congress. He could only confer with them as private citizens. The committee responded politely; they came mostly to listen.

*"He [Howe] offered peace only on the condition that the colonies should return to their allegiance and obedience to the British crown,"* wrote Marshall.

The reply was blunt: *"A return to the domination of Great Britain was not now to be expected."*

The three Americans cited as one of their reasons the king's refusal to listen to their humble petitions. They also explained the people had called for the Declaration. As a result, they were independent states. They could not rescind their independence.

*"So that it was not in the power of congress to agree for them that they should return to their former dependent state; that there was no doubt of their inclination for peace, and their willingness to enter into a treaty with Britain, that might be advantageous to both countries,"* Marshall reported.

The committee indicated it would be easier for Howe to obtain *"fresh powers"* from Britain to negotiate with them as independent states than it would be for the colonies to submit to his terms.

> "How useless to spread a net in full view of all the birds!"
> (PROVERBS 1:17).

*"His Lordship then expressed his regret that no accommodation was like to take place, and put an end to the conference,"* recorded Marshall.

Thus, like many moments in life, this meeting proved fruitless. But Benjamin Franklin earned a new job as a result. Congress soon sent him to France as America's diplomat there.[150]

PRAYER

*God, I know sometimes life brings useless results. Give me wisdom on how to spend my time today and also the grace to not let fruitlessness frustrate me.*

# 151. Reaching Harlem's Heights

There were two Clintons warring in the battles of New York. George Clinton fought for the Americans, and Henry Clinton fought for the British.

"*ABOUT the middle of last week it was determined, for many reasons, to evacuate the City of New York,*" George Clinton wrote about General Washington's orders to leave the island of Manhattan.

After losing Long Island and learning of the fruitless peace negotiations, which were as much a fraud as anything else, Washington had few options. Calling the situation "*distressing,*" he decided to evacuate Manhattan. He had heard the humming. The British swarmed around the island like buzzing bees waiting to strike at any moment. If they stung at the right time, they could forever paralyze the Continental army, and thus the Revolution.

"*And from the movements of the enemy on Long Island, and the small Islands in the East River, we had great reason to apprehend they intended to make a landing, and attack our lines somewhere near the city,*" General Clinton wrote, describing how the Continentals steadily crept up the island and reached Harlem Heights.

Clinton looked for good news wherever he could find it. The British miscalculated their Manhattan arrival. "*The enemy, on landing, immediately formed a line across the island. Most of our people were luckily north of it, and joined the army,*" Clinton said, noting that even though the Continentals were retreating, their losses were few.

A four-hour skirmish ensued September 16, 1776, at Harlem Heights. The effort was enough to keep the British from completely overtaking the Continental army. The bees could fly but they were unable to fatally sting.

"*They were opposed with spirit,*" Clinton wrote of his men's efforts. Even though the redcoats outnumbered them two to one, the Continentals pushed back the British swarm three times. The Americans lost thirty soldiers. The British lost ninety. "*I consider our success in this small affair, [at Harlem] at this time, almost equal to a victory. It has animated our troops, gave them new spirits, and erased every bad impression the retreat from Long Island, &c., had left on their minds. They find they are able,*" with inferior numbers, to drive their enemy, and think of nothing now but conquest."

But from the heights of Harlem, Clinton could smell the smoke and see the flames in lower Manhattan. This taste of destruction was enough to make a patriot ill. More than three hundred buildings burned after the British buzzed their way through and up the island. Nonetheless, Clinton continued to look for hope wherever he could find it.

> "But as for you, be strong and do not give up, for your work will be rewarded"
> (2 CHRONICLES 15:7).

George Clinton's optimistic description of the evacuation of New York can be explained by his personal connection to the place. New York was his home. Just as Henry Knox had proved in Boston, these Continentals did not give up their hometowns without a fight.[151]

**PRAYER**

*Father, thank you for never giving up on me. Provide me with opportunities to encourage others not to give up when I am strong, and send others to encourage me when I feel like giving up.*

# 152. Discipline and Diligence

Discipline and diligence are companions as close as a sword and a shield. The battles of Brooklyn Heights and Harlem Heights revealed the value of both in the form of Henry Knox.

*"You wish to know how I pass my time. I generally rise with or a little before the sun and immediately with a part of the regiment attend prayers, sing a psalm, and read a chapter [in the Bible at] the Grand Battery,"* Knox wrote to his wife Lucy two weeks before the Battle of Long Island.

Reading the Bible and praying gave Knox strength as he oversaw fortification-building. The disciplines of his faith encouraged his diligence. *"I dispatch a considerable deal of business before breakfast. From breakfast to dinner I am broiling in a sun hot enough to roast an egg. Sometimes I dine with the generals, Washington, Putnam, Stirling, &c; but I am mortified that I haven't had them to dine with me in return. However, that cannot be. I go to bed at nine o'clock or before, every night,"* he wrote of his daily routine. He was so busy he didn't have time to return dinner favors commonly exchanged by officers.

Knox's discipline included crossing over to Long Island with Washington each day to evaluate the situation and the barricades at Brooklyn

Heights. When the British routed the Americans from Long Island at the end of August, Knox was forced to abandon valuable ammunition. But he did not leave behind his diligence or sense of duty.

*"I met with some loss in my regiment: they behaved like heroes, and are gone to glory. I was not on the island myself, being obliged to wait on my Lord Howe and the navy gentry who threatened to pay us a visit,"* he wrote to Lucy in a brief note on August 27, 1776.

The evacuation of Manhattan provided further heartbreak for Knox. Artillery is very precious to an army. Like a parent protecting his children, Knox was determined to save as many cannons and arms from capture as possible. His diligence turned into round-the-clock discipline.

*"Constant fatigue and application to the business of my extensive department has been such that I have not had my clothes off once o' nights for more than forty days,"* he wrote to his brother about the retreat.

Just as he had worried in July that Lucy had stayed too long in New York, Knox found himself facing the consequences of the same dilemma. He was so diligent in removing artillery from Manhattan that the British nearly captured him. He seized a boat at the last moment and slipped into Harlem. No one was more relieved to see Knox than Washington. He was so happy that he gave Knox a fatherly embrace.

> "Be diligent in these matters; give yourself wholly to them, so that everyone may see your progress"
> (1 TIMOTHY 4:15).

Discipline and diligence revealed Henry Knox's wholehearted devotion.[152]

**PRAYER**

*Thank you for the twin gifts of discipline and diligence. May I exercise both today in a fresh new way.*

# 153. Hanging Hale

I *only regret that I have but one life to lose for my country"* are among the American Revolution's most famous words.

The story leading up to this passionate cry is murky at best. After the disaster of Long Island, George Washington desperately needed intelligence on where the British planned to attack Manhattan Island. Hence, he employed a network of spies.

A twenty-one-year-old captain volunteered for the mission. A graduate of Yale, Nathan Hale had spent time teaching before joining Washington's army. Thus, he naturally employed the cover of a schoolteacher when he arrived at Long Island as a spy.

What happened next is not clear. Hale was captured, but how is a mystery. Some historians claim Maj. Robert Rogers of the Queen's Rangers met Hale in a tavern and befriended him. Rogers pretended to be a patriot. When Hale confessed his true intentions, he blew his cover. Rogers arrested him.

Historian William Jackman had a different explanation for how Hale was taken: *"He [Hale] passed to the island, obtained the knowledge desired, notes of which he took in Latin. As he was returning he fell in with a party of the enemy, [and] was recognized by a Tory relative,"* Jackman wrote.

However they caught him, the British then took Hale to General Howe. After questioning him, Howe ordered Hale hanged the next morning, September 22, 1776.

Historians describe Hale's experience the night before his death as cruel. Caught in a shark's grip, he received no mercy. The British denied Hale access to a clergyman. They ignored his request for a Bible. They ripped his letter to his mother into pieces. The reason for these denials was to prevent the patriots from rallying behind a martyr. One historian quoted the officer in charge of Hale as saying, *"The rebels should never know they had a man who could die with such firmness."*

But the Continentals did learn of Hale's brave steps up to the gallows. Hale's resoluteness could not be kept secret. A British soldier reported his story to William Hull, an American officer. The intellectual Hale took his final phrase from a play called *Cato*: *"How beautiful is death, when earn'd by virtue! Who would not be that youth? What pity is it That we can die but once to serve our country."* Hull publicized Hale's bravery and honored him as America's first spy.

> "Be strong and let us fight bravely for our people and the cities of our God. The LORD will do what is good in his sight" (2 SAMUEL 10:12).

Today, the Central Intelligence Agency's Langley, Virginia, headquarters features a statue of Hale. He is also remembered in stone at Yale University and at the Tribune Tower in Chicago. Nathan Hale's bravery continues to remind others of the value of service, sacrifice, and strength.[153]

**PRAYER**

*Lord, thank you for the bravery of those who have gone before me and have sacrificed their lives for my freedom.*

# 154. The Revolution Today: September 11th's Sanctuary

How does Providence work today? He still moves in mysterious, even revolutionary, ways.

"My first return to St. Paul's Chapel was the day after [September 11, 2001]," Rector Lyndon Harris explained. He put on his boots and hiked down Broadway, "hoping that I could get in, hoping that the building is still standing."

Harris had no idea what he would find. The oldest church in continuous operation on Manhattan, St. Paul's, had been located on Church Street for more than two centuries. But because it faced the World Trade Center, Harris knew its survival was unlikely. When terrorists flew jetliners into the World Trade Center on September 11th, the towers collapsed, raining debris and dust everywhere, especially on adjacent properties. Other nearby buildings were destroyed.

"Every step of the way my heartbeat was just pounding because I fully expected everything to be demolished. When I got here, it was a very emotional moment to see this church standing, very powerful," Harris said.

The rector wasn't the only one who found the church's survival a miracle. "I was looking around, I had to go to the bathroom," related Tim O'Neill of the New York Police Department. He had been working on the recovery at the World Trade Center site. "And I saw footprints going into St. Paul's front door," he said of his decision to enter the chapel. O'Neill felt an eerie silence as he looked around. "Look at that, not even a window is broken in here, I can't believe that. It's right behind a grave yard, but it's intact,'" he said in awe.

The rubble was less than thirty feet away, yet the church looked as pristine inside as it had the previous Sunday. No broken windows, no debris. O'Neill described the scene as unbelievable. "It added a little spirituality, and a little reminder, to me at least anyway, that it [St. Paul's] was protected. It was immediately designated a sanctuary by a higher power," O'Neill said.

St. Paul's miracle has its critics. A physicist, who had developed theories about how the tower's fall created air pockets of protection in random places, shrugged off a miraculous intervention for the church. September 11, 2001, however, was not the first time the Creator of physics had turned St. Paul's into a sanctuary of miracles.

When fire broke out after the American army evacuated New York in 1776, local residents created a bucket brigade to transport river water and put out the fire in an effort to save St. Paul's. Every other building in the Wall Street district was left in ruins except for this brownstone chapel. The church was only ten years old at the time. God has used St. Paul's to stand the test of time as a testimony to his miraculous power. He still moves and provides sanctuaries.[154]

> "A glorious throne, exalted from the beginning, is the place of our sanctuary" (JEREMIAH 17:12).

**PRAYER**

*Lord, as you have from the beginning of the earth, be thou my sanctuary today.*

# 155. Sabbath Rest: God's Cause

A*rise, O God, plead thine own cause,"* Abraham Keteltas said, quoting Psalm 74:22 (KJV) as his sermon text. The purpose of this exiled Long Islander's message was to help his audience in Newburyport, Massachusetts, understand God's purposes. His first point concerned truth.

*"By the cause of God we are to understand the whole system of divine truth. Our blessed Lord, when he was arraigned before Pilate, declar'd, 'for this end was I born, and for this end came I into the world, that I might bear witness to the truth'"* (John 18:37 KJV). This also was *"the grand design of all the dispensations of God to men,"* he declared.

Keteltas told the congregation that the preservation of the Bible's texts revealed God's plan for humanity's redemption. After Adam and Eve's fall, God's truth was completed through our redemption by Jesus Christ. *"This cause, Christ, his apostles, martyrs, and confessors, have held so dear, that they have seal'd them with their blood. This is a cause that God loves and upholds, he has styl'd himself the God of truth,"* he said.

Keteltas then explained the second cause of God: *"universal righteousness."*

*"The moral law, or the ten commandments is the rule of this righteousness, and besides the moral law, all those duties which are incumbent upon us, as fallen creatures; such as the great duties of faith, repentance and conversion, which imply the forsaking of every sin, and the practice of every virtue,"* he said.

But Keteltas also believed God had a third purpose: *"the welfare of his people."*

*"I add the welfare of the people, who believe and profess the above mentioned system of divine truths, and practice the righteousness just now describ'd, is the cause of God. They are a society of holy and regenerate souls; trusting in the mercy of God through Christ."*

Keteltas understood that God's people transcended cultures and languages. He was a true New York original. Because he was bilingual, this minister of Dutch ancestry was able to preach in both Presbyterian and Dutch and French Reformed churches. He understood that God loved his people, regardless of their origins. *"Christ loved the church, and gave him-*

self for it, gave himself to a life of sorrows, to inexpressible agonies, and to the accursed death of the cross," he continued. "Thus you see my brethren, that the cause of truth, the cause of religion, the cause of righteousness, the cause of his church and people, is the cause of God. It is, as the psalmist expresses it, his own cause."

> "Rise up, O God, and defend your cause; remember how fools mock you all day long" (PSALM 74:22).

In the middle of the cause called the Revolution, this minister reminded his new congregation of God's everlasting causes. The Lord's truth, righteousness, and love for the church haven't changed. They are just as real today as they were to Abraham Keteltas. For this Dutchman the Revolution was a revelation of the purposes of God.[155]

**PRAYER**

*Thank you, God, for showing me the simplicity of your causes. Thank you for your truth, your righteousness, and your love.*

# 156. The Hired Help

B RAVE Germans, what a brand of shame you allow to be marked on your noble brows!" the French count began his protest in his pamphlet.

Just as expediency led Judah's King Amaziah in the Bible to hire Israelites to fight for him, so England employed the practice of hiring mercenaries. They leased from Germany soldiers known as Hessians. To many Frenchmen, including the Count de Riquetti, the practice was akin to enslaving Africans. Money mattered more than emancipation; profit trumped honor.

"Huddled together like flocks of sheep in the ships of foreigners, you cross the seas; you hasten through reefs and storms, to attack a people who have done you no harm, who are defending the most just of causes, who are setting you the noblest of examples," the count continued in his written flogging.

The battles of Long Island and Harlem Heights introduced Americans to these German fighters, whose fierceness was as apparent as their medieval gold helmets. To the patriots, the Hessians were hired help. Mercenaries had no place in a war against brothers. Worst of all, the Hessians had a reputation for pillaging and raping.

This French count gave the Hessians a warning. He understood the potency of justice and freedom. "Do you know what nation you are going *to attack? Do you realize the power of the fanaticism of liberty? It is the only fanaticism which is not odious, it is the only one which is worthy; but it is also the most powerful of all,"* he wrote in his publication.

The count also had a remedy for the Hessians. With the earnestness of a doctor, he prescribed an about-face. *"Leave this ground sullied by despotism; cross the seas, hasten to America,"* he said. *"But embrace there your brothers; defend this noble people against the haughty rapacity of their persecutors; share their happiness; double their strength; assist them with your industry; make their riches your own, by increasing them,"* he prompted.

Many Hessians were unhappy serving the British army in America. One soldier complained, *"All the officers have to add money of their own, or else live poorly."* He couldn't even buy a bottle of wine with the amount of money the British paid him.

And in many cases, the English soldiers got along with the Germans about as well as they did with the French. *"The Devil of Jealousy has been aroused because the English see that my men drill quicker and more promptly . . . Hence, instead of the former friendship between us, there is now enmity,"* this same Hessian complained.

King Amaziah had about as much satisfaction with the mercenaries he had hired to fight as the English did with their German warriors. God's provision proved better than hiring those whose only motive is monetary gain.[156]

> "Amaziah asked the man of God, 'But what about the hundred talents I paid for these Israelite troops?' The man of God replied, 'The LORD can give you much more than that'"
> (2 CHRONICLES 25:9).

**PRAYER**

*Remove any mercenary motives from my heart. Although money is a valuable necessity, keep me from being addicted to it.*

# 157. Defending White Plains

*The war should be defensive . . . we should, on all occasions, avoid a general action, nor put any thing to the risk, unless compelled by necessity, into which we ought never to be drawn,"* George Washington concluded.

The loss of Long Island had sealed a determination in Washington, one he had long been mulling over in his mind. This was primarily a defensive war. His army was not strong enough to play offense. Defense and preservation were their best chance for survival, and thus to secure independence. Offense must be saved for only the most extreme situations.

Following Harlem Heights, Washington held a war council with his officers. By this time, the popular Gen. Charles Lee had returned from his successful southern command. South Carolina patriots had defeated some British soldiers at a skirmish at Fort Moultrie, the fort guarding Charleston. Several other officers had also returned through prisoner exchanges. These and other advisers recommended every American post in New York be abandoned.

Nathanael Greene, however, convinced Washington that Fort Washington could be defended with the three thousand men who were there. Washington agreed with Greene. The rest of the army made their way to the town of White Plains, where they built a camp.

And just as Washington had determined, the action at White Plains was defensive. *"No general action was designed on our part, and I believe one thousand men were never, at one time, engaged with the enemy,"* recorded American Gen. William Heath of the October 16th battle at White Plains.

Heath described how the British made the first attack. They took one hill south of the Continental camp. Rather than continuing their assault, they delayed their offense as if to play out their cards. The British erected five batteries on high ground, creating their own version of "Dorchester Heights." The presence of these cannons made the American camp virtually indefensible.

*"The scene was grand and solemn; all the adjacent hills smoked as though on fire, and bellowed and trembled with a perpetual cannonade and fire of fieldpieces, hobits, [small mortars on gun carriages, in use before the howitzer] and mortars. The air groaned with streams of cannon and musket shot; the hills smoked and echoed terribly with the bursting of shells,"* Heath wrote of the scene.

> "Brothers and fathers, listen now to my defense"
> (ACTS 22:1).

George Washington then played his most powerful defensive card. He ordered a retreat. *"The general last night [October 31st] drew off most of the troops from the lines there, and this morning the guards and sentries burned the town and forage all around it,"* William Heath wrote. He explained how the army carried away all their stores and planted artillery on the hills back of town to trump the British advance.

This defensive measure delayed the British from proceeding further, allowing the American army to successfully retreat once again. Defense bought another day for both preservation and independence.[157]

PRAYER

*Help me play defense without being defensive. Allow me to respect government actions and decisions.*

# 158. A Good Man Groans

The loss of New York's Fort Washington on November 16, 1776, anguished Maj. Gen. Nathanael Greene more than any setback since the war's beginning. The reason? He had convinced George Washington the fort was defendable. Because this five-sided earthwork reached into the sky at two hundred and thirty feet above tidewater, it seemed impenetrable.

*"The misfortune of losing Fort Washington, with between two and three thousand men, will reach you before this, if it has not already,"* Greene wrote. Greene sought comfort from his friend Henry Knox, who had retreated with the rest of the army after the battle of White Plains.

Greene knew he could confide in Knox. These New England officers shared a love for books, which had made them fast friends. Like Knox, Greene's knowledge of warfare came from hours of study. Unlike Knox, whose family supported his education, Greene had to fight for his schooling. Greene's Quaker father believed a skill, such as blacksmithing, was far more important than any learning a book could bring.

Greene, however, broke with his father's pattern and studied under a Scottish teacher. The books he read led him to embrace the principles of the Revolution. From natural law to natural rights, Greene's military service was hardly a natural outcome from his upbringing. As was his personal pattern, he cut his own mold while casting iron in his father's foundry.

Greene wrote Knox that General Washington had been with him for several days at Fort Lee, across the North River, prior to the battle. They along with other officers had been discussing what to do next about Fort Washington. Once again Greene broke the mold of conventional wisdom. While the others encouraged Washington to abandon the fort, Greene argued that the army could continue to defend it. Unfortunately this iron forger misfired in his new role as a major general.

Greene explained that he joined Washington with two other generals to scout for a new position, which led them to cross the river. Just as they stepped into the boat, the British appeared on a nearby hill and began to fire. *"There we all stood in a very awkward situation. As the disposition [outlook] was made, and the enemy advancing, we durst not attempt to make any new disposition,"* Greene recalled, adding they urged Washington to get to safety while they stayed behind. *"But his Excellency thought it best for us all to come off together, which we did, about half an hour before the enemy surrounded the fort."*

> "I am feeble and utterly crushed; I groan in anguish of heart" (PSALM 38:8).

The events leading to the fort's complete capture left Greene utterly crushed. By sharing his anguish with Henry Knox in this letter, Nathanael Greene sought relief. He knew sharing a burden can go a long way to lightening it.[158]

**PRAYER**

*Send me encouragement when my heart groans in anguish and give me a tender heart for those who are groaning around me.*

# 159. Iron Sharpens Iron

Before the battle began, the Americans had refused to surrender Fort Washington.

*"Howe's adjutant-general made a demand of the surrender of the garrison in the general's name but was answered by the [American] commanding officer that he should defend it to the last extremity,"* Nathanael Greene continued in his letter to Henry Knox about the battle of Fort Washington.

Greene described how the British came back down the river from their victory at White Plains. They landed a party at the fort's headquarters. On the morning of November 16, 1776, they demanded quarter, but the three thousand Americans fought instead. The British and Hessian forces totaled eight thousand. The loss brought tears to General Washington's eyes as he learned his youngest soldiers were stabbed to death with British bayonets. More than fifty Americans were killed, nearly a hundred wounded, and close to three thousand American soldiers were captured.

The failure of Fort Washington grieved Greene to the point of near suffocation. The emotional debris covered him. Although the British arrived on the river sooner than the Continentals had hoped, Greene knew the real reason for the fort's failure: the fortifications were incomplete.

Greene and Knox had worked together to plan the fort. They combined their knowledge of artillery to craft its defenses. Greene understood the importance of fortifications more than most. The process for casting iron depended on strong fortifications. Greene knew every aspect of his father's iron business, which was a complex process.

Workers collected and stored raw iron ore. To turn it into usable iron, they placed the ore in furnaces fired by charcoal and wood. The process depended on a precise amount of air in the furnaces. Too much air consumed the wood, resulting in a misfire of the ore. Workers spent hours patching holes in the furnaces to keep the air out and fortify the process. Success would allow them to cast the iron into molds for anchors and other forms made by die casters. Failure to fortify the process wasted valuable resources. Catastrophic failure would result in an explosion and the death of a coal worker.

Likewise, the failure to completely fortify Fort Washington led to its demise. Time was likely the greatest enemy at the fort. The men ran out of time before they could finish Knox and Greene's fortification plan. *"Had that been complete, I think the garrison might have defended themselves a long while, or been brought off. I feel made vexed, sick and sorry. Never did I need the consoling voice of a friend more than now. Happy should I be to see you. This is a most terrible event: its consequences are justly to be dreaded,"* Greene groaned, asking Knox to send him any encouraging word.

Nathanael Greene knew that Henry Knox, better than anyone, would understand his grief over the failure to patch the "air pockets" of the fort. He looked to his friend to comfort his soul as he grieved the loss of his men.[159]

> "As iron sharpens iron, so one man sharpens another"
> (PROVERBS 27:17).

**PRAYER**

*Use me to fortify and encourage a friend today.*

# 160. Taking Cover

*Sir: I have this Moment arrived at this Place,"* George Washington wrote from New York's Aquackinack bridge on November 21, 1776. Washington was in a place he never wanted to be. Once again, he was on the run with an army. Where he would lead them was about as clear as the smoke that encircled Fort Washington six days earlier.

Washington's immediate purpose, however, was clear. He had to inform the governor of New York of his most recent decision. *"After the unfortunate Loss of Fort Washington, it was determined to evacuate Fort Lee, in a great Measure; as it was in a Manner useless in obstructing the*

*Passage of the North River, without the assistance of Fort Washington,"* he explained to the governor.

Fort Lee, named after Gen. Charles Lee and located on the North River, was the last Continental post in New York.

*"The Ammunition and some other Stores were accordingly removed,"* Washington wrote.

The British had thwarted their efforts, however. *"But, before we could effect our purpose, the Enemy landed yesterday Morning, in very considerable numbers, about Six Miles above the Fort; Their intent evidently was to form a line across, from the place of their landing to Hackensack Bridge, and thereby hem in the whole Garrison between the North and Hackensack Rivers,"* explained Washington.

Washington's men were desperate for another Long Island miracle, but this time there was no fog to mask their steps. They needed a bridge to preservation, and that is exactly what they found. *"However, we were lucky enough to gain the Bridge before them; by which means we saved all our men, but were obliged to leave some hundred Barrels of Flour, most of our Cannon, and a considerable parcel of Tents and Baggage,"* Washington wrote of their retreat.

Upon reaching the bridge Washington tapped his surveyor skills. After quickly evaluating the terrain, he realized his army was in danger of *"being pent up"* between two rivers. Likewise, the open and level countryside made the area *"unfit for making a stand."* No matter how much his military reputation may have suffered over the loss of New York, he would not put his army in a position to be annihilated for the sake of a glorious last stand. Once again this commander-in-chief embraced pragmatism and preservation over his own status.

> "All who handle the oars will abandon their ships; the mariners and all the seamen will stand on the shore"
> (EZEKIEL 27:29).

*"It was determined to draw the whole of our Force over this side of the River, where we can watch the operations of the Enemy, without danger of their surrounding us, or making a Lodgement in our Rear,"* he wrote.

George Washington also asked the governor for militia reinforcements to cover the rear of the army, allowing them to continue their retreat into New Jersey. Even though he had to abandon ship, this captain found safety in a bridge that led to Providence's shore.[160]

**PRAYER**

*Thank you for providing bridges in life. Thank you for the firmness of land and the strength and security your escape routes bring.*

# 161. The Revolution Today: Dusty Bells

"Dust. Dust was everywhere," Rev. Daniel P. Matthews proclaimed in his first sermon following the attacks of September 11, 2001. The rector of Wall Street's Trinity Church described the plague of dust on New York as unbelievable. But he also reminded his congregation that dust had another purpose. It served as a symbol: They were not alone in their tragedy.

"Dust did not just fall in southern Manhattan. Dust fell over all the world on September 11," Matthews stated dramatically. He reminded his congregation that people throughout the world were mourning with them. "Everybody is covered with the dust of the World Trade Center of September 11. None is without dust."

Matthews also encouraged his audience to take comfort in the story of the bells. Through a presidential proclamation, President George W. Bush called on Americans to come together in a day of prayer and remembrance on September 14, 2001. The president's proclamation encouraged people to pray and churches to ring their bells at noon.

Dr. Matthews called one of the church's engineers and asked if they could ring the bells of St. Paul's Chapel, which is a part of Trinity's parish, and next to the site of the World Trade Center.

"No," was his reply. They couldn't do it. The church had no electricity, and the bells were electric. By this time New York's governing authorities had also restricted access to the entire Wall Street district.

An hour later the engineer called Matthews back. They had done it. Mike and Jim, the two engineers, and Lyndon Harris, the chapel's rector had risked their lives by carefully climbing St. Paul's dark wooden bell tower to ring the bells at noon.

"While Jim held a flashlight, Mike found a steel pipe and 'whacked' the bell 12 times. Rescuers at Ground Zero removed their hats and stood in silence," the chapel's Web site later reported.

The bells gave the firefighters, police officers, and other rescue workers on the scene a chance to attend "church."

"The workers stood in silence as if to say, 'The Lord God reigns, even in this hell,'" related Daniel Matthews in his sermon. "Sometimes in the midst of the most horrible tragedies, we see with eyes with which we haven't seen before, at times like this a bell becomes more than just a bell; it becomes a sacrament."

And in that sermon, dust became a symbol of comfort. Bells bore the people's atonement. God still reigned.[161]

**PRAYER**

*Father, thank you for your compassion in grief, for the encouragement of bells buried in dust that lead hearts to look to heaven evermore.*

"Let him bury his face in the dust—there may yet be hope . . . Though he brings grief, he will show compassion, so great is his unfailing love" (LAMENTATIONS 3:29, 32).

# 162. Sabbath Rest: God's Pleading Our Cause

*The phrase of God's pleading his people's cause, frequently occurs in scripture,"* Abraham Keteltas proclaimed to his congregation in Newburyport, Massachusetts.

Keteltas defined *pleading* as a term often connected with a lawyer who supplicates on behalf of a client. In the same way God has pleaded for his people's cause throughout time. His methods are his Word, Spirit, and providence.

God uses his Word to implore against *"injustice, oppression, tyranny, murder, theft, plunder, adultery, slander, false witness, unjustly coveting our neighbour's property,"* enumerated Keteltas.

The Lord commanded the Israelites not to oppress one another. He also used his Word to encourage *"love, benevolence, compassion, humanity, peace, and righteousness."*

*"God pleads his own and his people's cause, by his omnipotent, omniscient, and omnipresent spirit,"* Keteltas said, adding that God's Spirit fills the souls of his people with faith and courage. His spirit can change the hardest of hearts, even the obstinacy of an earthly king.

*"Lastly: God pleads his own, and his people's cause by his providence. The whole history of it, from the creation of the world, is a series of wonderful interpositions in behalf of his elect."*

Keteltas cited several examples in the Bible where God's providence intervened, such as when *"the stars in their courses fought against Sisera."* *"For them [the Israelites], he dried up the red sea, to make them a passage, and drowned Pharaoh and his host in a watery grave: he went before them with a pillar of cloud by day, and a pillar of fire by night."*

But this Dutch minister also pointed out a more contemporary parallel, one the patriots would have understood. When Philip II, the King of Spain, oppressed the Dutch and their religious liberties, God's providence intervened. *"[W]hereupon, relying on God, they, although but a handful of men, against a mighty monarchy, rebelled against Spain . . . and at length, after a long, and arduous struggle, were acknowledged by their tyrants, to be free and independent states!"* he reminded his listeners.

*"The cause of this American continent, against the measures of a cruel, bloody, and vindictive ministry, is the cause of God . . . Liberty is the grand fountain, under God, of every temporal blessing . . . it is favorable to the propagation of unadulterated Christianity. Liberty is the parent of truth, justice, virtue, patriotism, benevolence, and every generous and noble purpose of the soul."*

> "Whom have I in heaven but you? And earth has nothing I desire besides you. My flesh and my heart may fail, but God is the strength of my heart and my portion forever" (PSALM 73:25, 26).

With the skill of an attorney, Abraham Keteltas pleaded his case before his congregation. God continues to use his Word, Spirit, and providence to advocate on behalf of those who believe in him.[162]

**PRAYER**

*Thank you for being my Advocate, for pleading the case of truth and righteousness and for giving me liberty.*

# 163. Wanted: A Few Good Men

What good were ten thousand cannons without courage and capability behind them?

General Washington was not alone in his anguish after losing Long Island, Manhattan, and White Plains. His officers were just as frustrated as he was over the militia, who fled faster than a flock of birds at the sound of the redcoats' muskets on Long Island. These losses in New York disturbed Henry Knox's diligent soul.

*"The militia get sick, or think themselves so, and run home; and wherever they go, they spread a panic,"* Knox wrote to his wife, Lucy, in the autumn of 1776. *"It is, as I always said, misfortunes that must raise us to the character of a great people,"* he continued hopefully. *"One or two drubbings will be of service to us; and one severe defeat [by] the enemy, ruin. We must have a standing army."*

The militia was not the only problem. Knox concluded Washington needed better officers. *"The general is as worthy a man as breathes, but he cannot do every thing nor be everywhere. He wants good assistants. There is a radical evil in our army—the lack of officers. We ought to have men of merit in the most extensive and unlimited sense of the word,"* Knox wrote in a letter to his brother William.

Without naming names, Knox continued to express his disappointment in the army's officers. *"Instead of which, the bulk of the officers of the army are a parcel of ignorant, stupid men, who might make tolerable soldiers, but [are] bad officers; and until Congress forms an establishment to induce men proper for the purpose to leave their usual employments and enter the service, it is ten to one they will be beat till they are heartily tired of it."*

Knox knew it was possible to teach military preparedness. After all, he had learned the arts of artillery from two sources: his bookstore's military books and his practical service in Boston's Grenadier Corps before the war. *"We ought to have academies, in which the whole theory of the art of war shall be taught, and every other encouragement possible given to draw persons into the army that may give a luster to our arms. As the army now stands, it is only a receptacle of ragamuffins,"* he wrote.

Knox had dissected the problem with a biology teacher's skill. To win the war, the army needed men who wore the banners of capability and discipline. But Knox's own discipline protected him from utter despair. He found hope in faith.

> "He chose capable men from all Israel and made them leaders of the people, officials over thousands, hundreds, fifties and tens" (EXODUS 18:25).

*"We want great men, who when fortune frowns will not be discouraged. God will I trust in time give us these men,"* Henry Knox concluded.[163]

**PRAYER**

*Whether it's voting in an election or choosing friends, may capability be my watchword and guide my heart.*

# 164. Unpardonably Lonely

Americans were always thirsty for war news. Their sense of separation fell, then rose again with the arrival and departure of each horseback rider who came into town.

*"I am told that Lord Howe has lately issued a Proclamation offering a general Pardon with the Exception of only four Persons viz Dr Franklin, Col Richard Henry Lee Mr John Adams & myself,"* Samuel Adams wrote to his wife, Betsy, on November 29, 1776.

And although the pace of communication was slow, rumors managed to make their way through the colonies. As always, some were true, others were not. *"I am not certain of the Truth of this Report,"* Adams added.

The first part of the news later proved true. Howe had issued a proclamation offering leniency to those who pledged allegiance to the king. This declaration coaxed turtles out of their shells by forcing everyone to make a choice.

*"If it be a Fact I am greatly obligd to his Lordship for the flattering opinion he has given me of my self as being a Person obnoxious to those who are desolating a once happy Country for the sake of extinguishing the remaining Lamp of Liberty,"* Adams wrote. *"And for the singular Honor he does me in ranking me with Men so eminently patriotick."*

Adams enjoyed being included in the company of Franklin, his friend Richard Lee, and his cousin. He was proud to make the short list of unpardonable traitors. But Adams was not so brash as to ignore the gravity of his circumstances. America was losing the war. Less than six months after the Declaration of Independence, Washington had been forced to abandon New York.

His own actions and letters were particularly galling to the British, Adams knew. After all, not only was he a signer of the Declaration of Independence but he was also a leader of the Sons of Liberty. Like a spy, his life was in jeopardy if the British ever caught him. A common belief among the band of traitors known as the Continental Congress was this: if they didn't hang together, they'd all hang separately.

Adams took the unpardonable rumor seriously enough to alert his wife. But he also tried to comfort her by questioning its truthfulness. He longed to hear how she was doing. He craved a touch of Boston in Philadelphia. *"I hope you will write to me by every opportunity. Pay my due Respects to my Family and Friends and be assured that I am most affectionately, yours,"* he concluded.

> "Turn to me and be gracious to me, for I am lonely and afflicted"
> (PSALM 25:16).

With such flying rumors and bad news from the front, Samuel Adams and the other members of Congress could not help but feel lonely in their Philadelphia boardinghouses. Loneliness had crept into their midst, along with apprehension and a longing for good news.[164]

**PRAYER**

*God, I look to you to cheer me when I am lonely. You are the Great Humorist, the Great Comforter. Allow me to be a breath of fresh air, a blast of good news to others who may be lonely.*

# 165. When Losing a General Is Good News

I am going into the Jerseys for the salvation of America," American Gen. Charles Lee proclaimed rashly. In truth, Lee sought military salvation for his own glory.

After New York's fall, Lee was thrilled when General Washington made his next major decision. He prudently split the army into two and gave Lee the responsibility of leading half the army across New Jersey. By taking separate routes, the army had a greater chance of surviving the journey through largely loyalist territory. But when Washington arrived near Philadelphia, he found himself waiting on Lee. The rash Lee had stalled fifty miles north. Without directly ordering him, Washington implored Lee to come to Philadelphia. Lee ignored him. The reason? Lee coveted Washington's job. New York's fall had emboldened Lee's efforts to convince Congress to make him commander-in-chief.

"*Lee is arguably the most qualified general officer in the American army in a strictly military sense,*" military historian John Hall said, noting that Lee had fought in wars in the colonies and in Europe.

Lee's very strength—his experience—was not enough to overcome the obvious differences between the two men. Where Washington was graceful, Lee was coarse. Washington behaved like a gentleman; Lee caroused with women.

Washington was neat. Lee was messy, paying little attention to hygiene and traveling around with a pack of even smellier dogs. Washington and Lee had one common denominator—ambition. But there was a difference in how far their drive would take them. Unlike Washington, Lee put personal glory above the cause.

While stalling in Morristown, New Jersey, Lee made an imprudent decision. He left his troops on the morning of December 13, 1776, and traveled three miles to a tavern to enjoy a relaxing breakfast. But a local Tory had tipped off the enemy to Lee's plans. British scouts tracked, surprised, and captured him.

"*General Lee without a hat, clad in a blanket-coat and slippers, was mounted on a horse that stood at the door, and borne off in triumph to the British army,*" historian William Jackman relayed.

Washington described Lee's capture as "*an additional misfortune, and the more vexatious, as it was by his own folly and Imprudence.*" But Lee's imprisonment proved to be fortunate. Many historians believe Lee would have made even more rash and fatal decisions as commander-in-chief.

*"Lee's success [in overthrowing Washington] would have proved most unfortunate for the country, for he had neither the judgment nor the principle necessary to guide it safely through the approaching crisis,"* Jackman concluded.

Hence, Charles Lee, the man who sought military salvation in New Jersey, lost it to his own folly.[165]

> "A prudent man keeps his knowledge to himself, but the heart of fools blurts out folly" (PROVERBS 12:23).

**PRAYER**

*Your Word warns me against imprudence. Keep my heart from folly and my decisions from rashness.*

# 166. Washington Discouraged

The Jerseys; it was really in the hands of the enemy before my arrival," Gen. Charles Lee later said about his march through New Jersey and his capture. And although folly was his downfall, Lee was right on this point. After the fall of New York, the colony of New Jersey fell into the chaos of a civil war. Locals fought each other with vengeance.

*"As Washington flees across New Jersey and people are unwilling to help them, he fully realizes that this revolution might be over. He's the commander-in-chief of an army that has shrunk drastically. He's on the run with the enemy on his heels,"* historian Bruce Chadwick explained in an interview for *The History Channel Presents: The American Revolution, 2006.*

The state of New Jersey brought a black cloud of discouragement over Washington.

*"This being perfectly well known [New Jersey loyalty] to the Enemy, they threw over a large body of Troops, which pushed us from place to place till we were obliged to cross the Delaware with less than 3000 Men fit for duty, owing to the dissolution of our force by short Inlistments; the Enemy's numbers, from the best Accts. exceeding Ten and by some 12,000 Men,"* General Washington wrote from Trenton in a letter to his brother on December 18, 1776.

Rain fell from Washington's dark cloud as he considered the approaching deadline. Many of his men's enlistment terms would expire at the end of the year, just days away.

*"We are in a very disaffected part of the Province; and, between you and me, I think our affairs are in a very bad situation,"* General Washington

told his brother. He had no doubt General Howe wanted to take Philadelphia. But he also knew his men were too weak to stop Howe. *"In a word, my dear Sir, if every nerve is not strained to recruit the new army with all possible expedition, I think the game is pretty near up."*

Washington sprinkled his letter with further evidence that the contest seemed over for the Americans. The colonies were losing their resolve. Congress was relying too much on inexperienced militia. *"You can form no idea of the perplexity of my situation. No man, I believe, ever had a greater choice of difficulties, and less means to extricate himself from them."*

The commander-in-chief may have been discouraged, but he was also a sunny optimist. *"However, under a full persuasion of the justice of our cause, I cannot entertain an Idea, that it will finally sink, tho' it may remain for some time under a cloud,"* George Washington concluded.

Righteousness of the cause gave him hope for a rainbow.[166]

> "Whenever the rainbow appears in the clouds, I will see it and remember the everlasting covenant between God and all living creatures of every kind on the earth" (GENESIS 9:16).

**PRAYER**

*Thank you for your promise of the rainbow, the covenant of encouragement you have made with us.*

# 167. Tired Faces

"T*hese are the times that try men's souls,"* Common Sense author Thomas Paine wrote in December 1776. Paine had witnessed the trials of the army firsthand as a soldier in Washington's army. When the year drew to a close, he took up his pen once again and published *American Crisis* to encourage his dispirited fellow patriots.

While Paine's words brought the army intellectual encouragement, General Sullivan brought reinforcements. After Lee's capture in mid-December, Sullivan marched Lee's troops to Washington's camp near Philadelphia, giving the commander-in-chief six thousand more men.

Even with this numerical boost, Washington grew more anxious with each sunset. Most of his troops' enlistments expired on December 31st. If independence was to be won, Washington knew he needed to do something to convince these men to stay in the army. He had fought too hard to let the mere ticking of a clock complete the British goal of Continental capitulation. He also needed a slice of victory to regain the confidence of the members of Congress who had supported Lee's coup for commander-in-chief.

*"He [Washington] was anxious to strike a blow that should revive the courage of the army and the people before the disbandment of those troops whose terms of enlistment were about to expire,"* historian William Jackman wrote.

Washington and the rest of the army were not the only ones fatigued—General Howe was just as weary of this war in which he never wanted to lead. His own soul was being tried by the times. The daggers of his detractors pierced him with Lee-like underhandedness. Howe's critics wanted to know why he had not won the war by now. What Parliament didn't realize was that Howe's army was as thinly spread across New Jersey as jam on bread. Howe compensated by placing units of Hessians at various points along the Delaware River.

*"The American soldiers hated them [the Hessians] intensely for their savage bayoneting on the battlefield,"* Jackman wrote, calling the Hessians *"terrorists"* who *"plundered indiscriminately."*

Howe chose Colonel Rahl, a German commander who distinguished himself at White Plains and Fort Washington, to guard the river at Trenton, New Jersey. But by Christmas, Rahl and his fifteen hundred troops were also tired. He was ready to enjoy some good wine and relax.

*"This brave but careless commander took his ease, enjoyed his music and bath, and when it was proposed to throw up works upon which to mount cannon in readiness against an assault, said merrily: 'Pooh pooh! an assault by the rebels! Let them come; we'll at them with the bayonet,'"* Jackman wrote. One account says Colonel Rahl was playing cards when the order to fortify his position arrived.

Such were the tired faces facing the final days of 1776.[167]

> "Even youths grow tired and weary, and young men stumble and fall" (ISAIAH 40:30).

**PRAYER**

*Father, when I am weary, I pray for your deep and abiding rest to bring a smile to my face and encouragement to my soul.*

# 168. The Revolution Today: A Maize Maze

One damp fall Saturday morning, my family visited a corn maze west of Washington, DC. We city slickers were ready for some amazing country fun. And that is what we found.

I had never been inside a cornfield, much less one turned into a maze. To play the game we had to successfully pass through eight stations in the maze. At each stop we answered a multiple choice question about the habits and characteristics of bats. Each answer corresponded with a separate direction on our map: right, left, or behind. Whether we were wrong or right, our answers dictated our direction.

Without knowledge of bats, we mostly guessed. Sometimes we easily arrived at the next station. Just as often, we followed a circle or hit a dead end.

When you're in a maze, you can't see the big picture. Ten-foot-high cornstalks surround you, preventing you from knowing where you are going or where you've come from. You can only see the path in front of you.

"Everywhere you turn, it's a sea of green and gold and downright corn-fusing! That's the idea behind the corn maze craze that's stalking the country," is the way an article in *Family Circle* described the dizzying sensation of a maze.

We were not without help, however. We carried a tall pole with us. If we raised our pole, a guide watching from a bridge that overlooked the maze came to our rescue. An hour into the confusing fun we lifted our flag. The guide gave us a clue. To exit the maze, all we needed was to take the left path at each fork.

The guide's left-handed advice proved to be right, and we exited the maze. Because mazes only make sense from an aerial view, the guide in the sky was in the best position to show us the way out.

The MAiZE, the world's largest cornfield maze company, noted that mazes have been used for centuries for different purposes, including teaching us about life. "Some ancient mazes were used as a form of art work in gardens, some were for entertainment, and others were constructed to symbolically portray the journey of life," the MAiZE explained.

Life is often like a maze. When the Israelites fled Egypt to wander in the desert's maze, God provided a cloud by day and a pillar of fire by night to guide them. The questions George Washington and the Continental Congress faced as 1776 came to a close required them to look to the Guide in the Sky for the big picture.

The Guide in the Sky still leads us today. God uses his Word and his hand to show us the way out of life's many mazes.[168]

**PRAYER**

*God, show me the pillars of cloud and fire to help me find my way out of the mazes I am facing today or will face in the future.*

"By day you led them with a pillar of cloud, and by night with a pillar of fire to give them light on the way they were to take" (NEHEMIAH 9:12).

# 169. Sabbath Rest: The Mayhew Dilemma

What do patriots do when their religion requires them to pray blessings for the king and acknowledge him as gracious? Such was the Mayhew-like dilemma facing many congregations and churches throughout the colonies after the war began.

*"The American Revolution inflicted deeper wounds on the Church of England in America than on any other denomination because the King of England was the head of the church. Anglican priests, at their ordination, swore allegiance to the King,"* related a historian for the Library of Congress on the library's Web site (www.loc.gov).

The issue not only affected priests in the pulpit but also the prayer book in patriots' pockets. *"The Book of Common Prayer offered prayers for the monarch, beseeching God 'to be his defender and keeper, giving him victory over all his enemies,' who in 1776 were American soldiers as well as friends and neighbors of American Anglicans."*

Another prayer called on men and women to bless *"our most gracious sovereign Lord King George."* And although Christians are to pray for their enemies, the intent of these prayer book blessings was to honor authority, not tyranny.

And just as Jonathan Mayhew broke with the Church of England in 1750 to preach against Charles I as a tyrant instead of a martyr, many other revolutionary Anglicans made the same decision. They maintained their loyalty to the King of kings, but replaced references to their earthly king in their prayer books.

A convention of Maryland Anglicans voted in 1776 *"that every Prayer and Petition for the King's Majesty, in the book of Common Prayer . . . be henceforth omitted in all Churches and Chapels in this Province."* One minister there covered the passages with pieces of paper.

The prayer that God strengthen *"'thy servant GEORGE, our most gracious King and Governour' was changed to a plea that 'it might please thee to bless the honorable Congress with Wisdom to discern and Integrity* to pursue the true Interest of the United States,'" noted a Library of Congress historian.

Jacob Duché, who had encouraged the Continental Congress with his prayers, called a meeting to decide what to do. The problem was so great the vestry considered closing Christ Church to avoid praying for the king. Worshipping God, however, prevailed over reverence for King George III. As the Anglicans in Maryland had done, this Philadelphia church chose to pray for Congress instead. They continued to honor God by praying for those in authority.

"That it may please thee to endue the Congress of the United States & all others in Authority, legislative, executive, & judicial with grace, wisdom & understanding, to execute Justice and to maintain Truth," the wardens of Christ Church wrote. These revolutionaries sought to honor the King of kings by praying for their new authority figures.[169]

> "Listen to my cry for help, my King and my God, for to you I pray" (PSALM 5:2).

**PRAYER**

Listen to my prayer, O King of kings. You are my God and Supreme Authority.

# 170. The Crossing

The strategic fork in the road George Washington faced at the end of December 1776 was more than the intersection of defense and offense. The choice he made could affect the "fate of unborn millions," as he had reminded his troops before the battles of New York. God had preserved the army with a fog, a bridge, and a general's blunder. Each was as amazing as a heat wave in a northeastern winter.

And so it is no wonder Washington turned to the unexpected for his last attempt to regain the confidence of Congress and convince his men to stay in the army past their December 31st enlistment expiration. In a tactical about-face, Washington switched his troops' direction from defense to offense.

"The evening of the twenty-fifth I ordered the troops intended for this service to parade back to McKonkey's Ferry, that they might begin to pass [over the Delaware River] as soon as it grew dark, imagining we should be able to throw them all over, with the necessary artillery, by twelve *o'clock, and that we might easily arrive at Trenton by five in the morning, the distance being about nine miles,"* recorded Washington.

The commander-in-chief knew the Germans held hearty celebrations. Feast days such as Christmas were no exception. A night of wine might decrease the resistance of Colonel Rahl and his nearly two thousand soldiers. The strategy of surprise had served Washington well before. After all, it was the sudden appearance of Fort Ticonderoga's cannons on Dorchester Heights that drove the British from Boston.

There were, however, numerous icy kinks, clinks, and chunks obstructing his December surprise. The river was more solid than his timetable.

*"But the quantity of ice, made that night, impeded the passage of the boats so much, that it was three o'clock before the artillery could all be got over; and near four before the troops took up their line of march,"* Washington wrote in anguish.

The crossing was to begin at nightfall, with hopes of forging the Delaware River before midnight. Washington wanted to have plenty of time to march the nine miles by land under the cover of darkness. The four-hour delay put the army in great danger of someone seeing them in the sunrise and alerting Rahl. *"This made me despair of surprising the town, as I well knew we could not reach it before the day was fairly broke,"* he wrote of their tardiness.

As much as he hoped to surprise the Hessians, the delay forced George Washington to another crossroad. Should he abandon his plans and retreat to safety by recrossing the river? Or should he press on to Trenton with the knowledge that a loyalist might alert the Germans? The decision could prove as treacherous as crossing the Delaware.[170]

> "When you pass through the waters, I will be with you; and when you pass through the rivers, they will not sweep over you. When you walk through the fire, you will not be burned; the flames will not set you ablaze" (ISAIAH 43:2).

**PRAYER**

*God, send your angels to surround me when life takes me through treacherous waters and consuming fire.*

# 171. Raging River

The storm continued to rage while George Washington contemplated whether to recross the Delaware River or attack Trenton on the morning of December 26, 1776. Perhaps no one felt the chill of the icy river and the scourge of the night crossing more than the man in charge of the artillery. The responsibility of ferrying the men and ammunitions across the river fell to the meticulous mind and attentive arms of Henry Knox.

*"A hardy design was formed of attacking the town by storm,"* Knox wrote, describing the plan in a letter to his wife, Lucy. Knox explained his perspective behind Washington's decision to cross in the first place. The enemy *"had obliged us to retire on the Pennsylvania side of the Delaware, by which means we were obliged to evacuate or give up nearly all the Jerseys."*

Not long after the Continentals formed their camp, they discovered *"the preservation of Philadelphia was a matter exceedingly precarious,— the force of the enemy three or four times as large as ours."*

Knox was often the first to analyze the strength of the enemy, based on their arms. He noted the British army had scattered their troops at *"distant places in New Jersey,"* but Trenton's *"cantonments"* were the largest. *"Trenton is an open town, situated nearly on the banks of the Delaware, accessible on all sides. Our army was scattered along the river for nearly 25 miles. Our intelligence agreed that the force of the enemy in Trenton was from two to three thousand, with about six field cannon, and that they were pretty secure in their situation,"* he wrote of the Hessian regiment based there.

Knox then used matter-of-fact terms to tell Lucy about the coldest and most challenging night of 1776. *"Accordingly a part of the army, consisting of about 2,500 or 3,000 passed the River on Christmas night, with almost infinite difficulty, with 18 field-pieces. The floating ice in the River made the labor almost incredible,"* he wrote, not even mentioning the challenge of finding enough boats to carry the men and ammunitions across and conducting the affair in silence. Two men died of frostbite after crossing the river. The army also left bloody footprints behind in the ice and snow. *"The night was cold and stormy; it hailed with great violence; the troops marched with the most profound silence and good order,"* he reported.

But the sleet did not subside after they arrived on the New Jersey side. The approach of daylight did not dissipate the hail or the storm. *"The storm continued with great violence, but was in our backs, and consequently in the faces of our enemy,"* he wrote. Knox then made an important conclusion after the crossing. Diligence had overcome the raging river.

*"However, perseverance accomplished what at first seemed impossible,"* Henry Knox concluded of the Delaware crossing.[171]

**PRAYER**

*Father, thank you for the gift of faith that secures raging rivers and allows me to cross onto unknown shores.*

> "When the river rages, he is not alarmed; he is secure, though the Jordan should surge against his mouth"
> (JOB 40:23).

# 172. The Decision

B ut as I was certain there was no making a retreat without being discovered and harassed on repassing the river, I determined to push on at all events," George Washington wrote of his decision to press ahead on the morning of December 26, 1776. The risk of detection was just as great in the sunlight, whether his army recrossed the Delaware River or attacked Trenton. Following pragmatism and courage, Washington nimbly chose offense.

With his decision made, the commander-in-chief turned his attention to the battle plan. He divided his nearly three thousand men into two divisions. One approached the Hessian position from the north. The other approached from the south. *"They marched in two divisions, one led by Washington (with whom were Generals Greene, Stirling, Mercer and Stephen), by a circuitous route to the north of the town, while the other, under Sullivan . . . was to advance by a direct road along the river to the west and south side. Sullivan was to halt at a certain point to allow time for the main division to make the circuit,"* described historian William Jackman.

Jackman noted Washington's division did not arrive in the *"immediate neighborhood of Trenton"* until eight in the morning, well past daylight. The hailstorm may have slowed their march, but it also had an unexpected benefit. *"It [the storm] had also aided to conceal their movements from the enemy,"* Jackman wrote.

However, a man by the roadside saw Washington's division as they arrived. The advance party had no idea if this farmer-type was someone they could trust or if he was a loyalist like many of those who had tried to block their flight from New York through New Jersey the previous month.

*"Washington, who had pushed on with the advance, asked of a man who was chopping wood by the roadside the way to the Hessian picket,"* Jackman told the story.

*"He answered gruffly, 'I don't know,' and went on with his work. 'You may tell,' said Captain Forrest of the artillery, 'for that is General Washington.' 'God bless and prosper you,' exclaimed the man, raising his hands to heaven, 'the picket is in that house, and the sentry stands near that tree,' "* Jackman chronicled.

Within minutes, Washington's advance party overtook the Hessian's picket-guards.

*"Late as it was, the Hessians were completely surprised. According to their custom, they had indulged freely in the festivities of Christmas, and were resting thoughtless of danger, when the drums suddenly beat to arms. All was confusion,"* Jackman wrote.

And that is how the battle of Trenton began. George Washington made his choice, and the river gates to the palace were thrown open.[172]

> "The river gates are thrown open and the palace collapses"
> (NAHUM 2:6).

**PRAYER**

*Thank you, God, for showing your hand in the unlikeliest places, from a storm in the sky to a woodsman by the roadside.*

# 173. The Enterprise

W e] *entered the town with them pell-mell,"* Henry Knox wrote to Lucy about the army's headlong rush to take down the Hessians' pickets, or advanced guards, at Trenton.

The surprise attack began about 8:00 a.m. on December 26, 1776. The enterprise was more incredible than anything Knox had ever before seen. After a series of disasters in New York, Knox was hungry to see success. To this man of artillery, this revolutionary battle seemed stripped from the pages of Revelation.

*"Here succeeded a scene of war of which I had often conceived, but never saw before. The hurry, fright and confusion of the enemy was [not] unlike that which will be when the last trump shall sound,"* Knox described the chaos.

The Germans fighting for the British could not have been more surprised at the Continentals' attack had the heavens cracked and burst forth with the army of God. *"They endeavored to form in the streets,"* Knox described of the Hessians' hasty attempt to form their lines along the town's cobblestones. He noted the Continentals had placed cannons at the heads of the streets to prevent the Hessians from such boulevard maneuvers. *"These, in the twinkling of an eye cleared the streets,"* he wrote of his artillery's success in stopping the street activity.

Although the Hessians tried to take shelter behind houses, the Continentals' *"musketry soon dislodged them,"* Knox wrote. He had observed that Trenton was an open town, accessible from all sides. The Hessians tried to take advantage of the terrain by moving the battle away from the settlement.

*"Finally they were driven through the town into an open plain beyond. Here they formed [their lines] in an instant,"* Knox wrote of their professionalism and ability to quickly get into place. *"Measures were taken for putting an entire stop to their retreat by posting troops and cannon in such passes and roads as it was possible for them to get away by. The poor fellows after they were formed on the plain saw themselves completely surrounded, the only resource left was to force their way through numbers unknown to them,"* reported Knox.

And as was typical of Knox, he not only counted the Americans' cannons, but also the enemy's. His account of the enterprise would not have been complete without his assessment of the Hessians' artillery power. *"The Hessians lost part of their cannon in the town: they did not relish the project of forcing, and were obliged to surrender upon the spot, with all their artillery, six brass pieces, army colors &c.,"* he wrote of the surrender.

The crossing of the Delaware River led to victory in the city. As a result, Henry Knox, a man of faith, would soon see Providence shine on him in a whole new light.[173]

> "There is a river whose streams make glad the city of God, the holy place where the Most High dwells" (PSALM 46:4).

**PRAYER**

*God, you are the Great Creator, the One whose rivers lead to your dwelling place in a city on high.*

# 174. The Triumph

I HAVE *the pleasure of congratulating you upon the success of an enterprise, which I had formed against a detachment of the enemy lying at Trenton, and which was executed yesterday morning,"* General Washington wrote jubilantly in a letter to the Continental Congress on December 27, 1776.

Washington had not felt so much joy since the British left Boston the previous March. Indeed, it was his first solid victory in nine months. A fog, a bridge, and a general's blunder had preserved the army during their losses. And it was a river crossing that led them to an offensive enterprise, which resulted in triumph at Trenton.

*"As the divisions had nearly the same distance to march, I ordered each of them, immediately upon forcing the out-guards, to push directly into the town, that they might charge the enemy before they had time to form,"* Washington explained of his strategy to divide his army and attack Trenton from both the north and the south.

*"Finding from our disposition, that they were surrounded, and that they must inevitably be cut to pieces if they made any further resistance, they agreed to lay down their arms. The number that submitted in this manner was twenty-three officers and eight hundred and eighty six men,"* Washington reported.

The most significant casualty of the battle was the Hessian's commander. Colonel Rahl escaped from his headquarters and retreated into the street. When Washington's men saw him, they opened fire. Rahl fell wounded. Surrounded, he surrendered. He later died from his wounds.

*"Colonel Rahl, the commanding officer, and seven others were found wounded in the town. I do not exactly know how many were killed; but I fancy twenty or thirty, as they never made any regular stand. Our loss is very trifling indeed, only two officers and one or two privates wounded,"* Washington wrote.

This commander could not have been prouder of his men's behavior. They had not panicked like a gaggle of geese, as they had at Long Island. Instead they had soared. They had answered the trumpet call of duty, and they had triumphed. *"In justice to the officers and men, I must add, that their behavior upon this occasion reflects the highest honor upon them,"* continued Washington.

Even though his men were indescribably exhausted from their overnight crossing of the Delaware River, they gave this enterprise their all. *"The difficulty of passing the river in a very severe night, and their march through a violent storm of snow and hail, did not in the least abate their ardor; but, when they came to the charge, each seemed to vie with the other in pressing forward;*

> "But let justice roll on like a river, righteousness like a never-failing stream!" (AMOS 5:24).

*and were I to give a preference to any particular corps, I should do great injustice to the others,"* praised George Washington.

Justice rolled like a river. Liberty had crossed the stream.[174]

**PRAYER**

*Thank you for your righteousness, for your never-ending commitment to justice and your never-failing stream of blessings.*

# 175. The Revolution Today: Crossings

If you walk into the lobby of the White House's West Wing or through the halls of New York's Metropolitan Museum of Art, you might notice they have something in common. Both display the famous painting called *Washington Crossing the Delaware*. New York's is an artist's original. The White House version is a copy. *Washington Crossing the Delaware* is one of the most recognizable paintings of the American Revolution. It is known, however, for its errors as much as it is for its portrayal of Washington as a strong leader.

"Details such as the American flag—not adopted until six months after Washington's crossing—and the type of boat are inaccurate. The painting's efficiency as national myth is easy to see: the flag, set off by a searing silvery sky, towers over the scene, its shaft soaring heavenward, Washington a figure of invincible resolution," art critic Jonathan Jones explained.

But there is an irony. This painting showing Washington on his way to defeat German soldiers, the Hessians, was painted by a German. Emanuel Leutz had migrated to America with his parents but returned to Germany. Perhaps Leutz painted the picture in 1851 to symbolize the determination that motivates people to make difficult journeys, such as emigrating to America.

"It might also be read as a painting about migration. Just like Washington crossing the Delaware, German migrants fleeing political oppression and poverty were making the long, cold Atlantic crossing," Jones noted.

Crossing the Delaware has become an American metaphor, a symbol for overcoming obstacles. U.S. Defense Secretary Donald Rumsfeld recalled the moment in his 2005 Christmas message to U.S. troops: "By serving our country this season, whether you are stationed at home or abroad, you are part of an American tradition as old as the struggle for our nation's independence, when Washington crossed the Delaware River on Christmas night. And like that of those who fought before you, the work you do will be remembered, and recounted, many Christmases from now," Rumsfeld wrote.

The defense secretary was no stranger to obstacles in life, especially those that come with service. "During World War II, my father spent more than one Christmas thousands of miles from home on an aircraft carrier in the Pacific theater. My family and I missed him, but we took comfort in the knowledge that his service was important and that he was fighting for us and for our country," he remembered.

> "They feast on the abundance of your house; you give them drink from your river of delights"
> (PSALM 36:8).

"And even though there may be no place you would rather be this season than home with them, know that what you are doing—wherever you are—protects them and provides them with a truly special gift. You are defending their freedom. And they are safer because of your service," Donald Rumsfeld concluded.

As difficult as crossings are, they are often a gift of sacrifice.[175]

**PRAYER**

*God, you are the Creator of rivers, the Carver of streams, the Great Painter of life's most beautiful and challenging landscapes.*

# 176. Sabbath Rest: River of Rejoicing

George Whitefield did not live long enough to learn of George Washington's Delaware River crossing on Christmas night in 1776. But there's no doubt Whitefield would have preached in celebration. It wouldn't have been hard for him to muster up a message. He could have resurrected a sermon he gave in Philadelphia in 1746. Whitefield, along with many others, believed God had used a storm at sea to prevent the French from recapturing Cape Breton and Nova Scotia. And like Washington's river crossing, it was a moment to celebrate.

*"And shall we not rejoice and give thanks? Should we refuse, would not the stones cry out against us? Rejoice then we may and ought: But, Oh! let our rejoicing be in the LORD, and run in a religious channel,"* Whitefield proclaimed over the sea victory.

Whitefield knew what it was like to have the stones cry out against him. He had experienced an impoverished childhood in England. But Whitefield overcame his lot. He graduated from Oxford, made friends with John and Charles Wesley, and began a ministry that spanned two continents. Preaching forty hours a week, this evangelist became one of America's most influential itinerants. His oration was so powerful, Benjamin Franklin once responded by giving money to Whitefield's orphanage in Savannah. Regardless of the situation, Whitefield praised God.

*"This we find has been the practice of GOD's people in all ages. When he was pleased with a mighty hand and outstretched arm to lead the Israelites through the Red Sea as on dry ground,"* he proclaimed in this message celebrating God's hand.

Whitefield supported the American Revolution long before it began. After traveling to nearly every major seaport in the colonies, Whitefield had come to love America. In a meeting with other clergy in Portsmouth, New Hampshire, in 1764, he shared secret plans of the British government to end colonial self-government and establish the Anglican Church. Whitefield told the ministers, *"I can't in conscience leave the town without acquainting you with a secret. My heart bleeds for America. O poor New England! There is a deep laid plot against your civil and religious liberties, and they will be lost. Your golden days are at an end. You have nothing but trouble before you . . . Your liberties will be lost."*

Whitefield died of an asthma attack in 1770 in Massachusetts. He lived long enough to see trouble brewing with England. No matter the problem or the celebration, George Whitefield gave God the glory. He continuously waded into the channel of rejoicing.[176]

> "Let them give thanks to the LORD for his unfailing love and his wonderful deeds for men" (PSALM 107:31).

**PRAYER**

*May I wade deeply into your river with rejoicing today over the marvelous works you have shown me.*

# 177. Service Rewarded

"Providence seemed to have smiled upon every part of this enterprise," Henry Knox wrote triumphantly to Lucy, two days after the army successfully crossed the Delaware River and beat the Hessians at Trenton.

It was Knox who had orchestrated the miraculous feat of acquiring boats and loading and boarding them under weather conditions as treacherous as his journey from Fort Ticonderoga. Through icy waters in the darkest of night he enforced General Washington's orders to hurry the men across the Delaware River in the wee hours of December 26, 1776. Not only did Providence smile on the army's efforts, but he also sprinkled some sunlight on Knox's service.

"His Excellency the General has done me the unmerited great honor of thanking me in public orders in terms strong and polite. This I should blush to mention to any other than to you, my dear Lucy; and I am fearful that even my Lucy may think her Harry possesses a species of little vanity in doing [it] all," Knox shared sheepishly.

A few days later, Knox had even more exciting news to report. "Will it give you satisfaction or pleasure in being informed that the Congress have created me a general officer—a brigadier—with the entire command of the artillery?" he wrote with more excitement than a schoolboy at graduation. "If so, I shall be happy. It was unsolicited on my part, though I cannot say unexpected. People are more lavish in their praises of my poor endeavors than they deserve."

Knox had received many informal words of encouragement and praise for his efforts. However, he knew the promotion to brigadier general was the result of nothing more than hard work. "All the merit I can claim is *industry. I wish to render my devoted country every service in my power; and the only alloy I have in my little exertions is, that it separates me from thee—the dearest object of all my earthly happiness. May Heaven give us a speedy and happy meeting,"* he wrote hopefully.

Before he found a messenger to carry his letter to Lucy, Knox further reflected on Trenton and added a postscript. He knew the battle had been hard on the local residents. *"The attack of Trenton was a most horrid scene to the poor inhabitants. War, my Lucy, is not a humane trade, and the man who follows [it] as such will meet with his proper demerits in another world,"* he added.

> "He is like a well-watered plant in the sunshine, spreading its shoots over the garden" (JOB 8:16).

Although the war separated Henry and Lucy, crisis could not kill their companionship or celebration. By sharing his joy with his wife, Henry Knox embraced the warmth of God's sunlight. His promotion revealed the value of hard work and difficult choices, and the prudence of rewarding them.[177]

**PRAYER**

*Thank you for providing sunshine, for its warm embrace. May I be a light for others by thanking them for their work on my behalf today.*

# 178. Strategy: Offense or Defense?

What strategy did General Washington choose after his triumph at Trenton? Offense? Or defense? He offered a ten-dollar bounty to men whose enlistments expired December 31. Enough responded to save the army from capitulating to contract expiration. Washington also had dispatched recruiters to find more soldiers for his army. He had already written what seemed like a thousand letters to leaders of the individual states for reinforcements.

Washington, however, was in desperate need of intelligence to *"ascertain the movements and designs of the enemy"* after Trenton. He sent Colonel Joseph Reed, a somewhat ironic choice, to reconnoiter the New Jersey countryside. Washington knew Reed had been a confidant of Gen. Charles Lee, but Reed was also a native of Pennsylvania and quite familiar with the neighboring New Jersey territory. The colonel set out on horseback toward nearby Princeton to seek information on the enemy's movements.

*"With Reed were six young horsemen, members of the 'Philadelphia City Troop,' full of fire and zeal, but who had never seen active service,"* historian William Jackman wrote about their spy mission.

They found the residents of Princeton tight-lipped and unwilling to cooperate. *"No reward could induce the terror-stricken people to approach Princeton and bring them information,"* Jackman explained.

Reed and his men then rode toward the town's college. On their way, they saw a British dragoon or cavalryman moving from a barn to a farmhouse. But before they could snap their horses' reins and gallop toward the man, they saw another soldier riding to the same farmhouse. Soon a dozen dragoons were within their view.

*"They [Reed's men] charged at once and surrounded the house, 'and twelve dragoons, well armed, with their pieces loaded, and having the advantage of the house, surrendered to seven horsemen, six of whom had never seen an enemy before, and, almost in sight of the British army, were brought into the American camp at Trenton, on the same evening,'"* Jackman recorded, quoting Washington.

The information they gained from these soldiers was invaluable. Reed and his men learned that General Howe had sent General Cornwallis to Princeton. Cornwallis was planning to march his force of more than seven thousand to Trenton the next day.

Reed and his men rushed the momentous news to Washington, who responded by writing Congress that the British were *"assembling their whole force at Princeton. Their great preparations and some intelligence I had received . . . gave me the strongest reasons to conclude, that an attack upon us was meditating,"* George Washington predicted.[178]

> "For lack of guidance a nation falls, but many advisers make victory sure" (PROVERBS 11:14).

**PRAYER**

*Father, thank you for providing guidance in my life. Lead me to choose my advisers carefully, and may I provide wise advice to those you have placed in my circle of influence.*

# 179. Escape

Never had the prospect of the Americans been so gloomy," historian William Jackman wrote about the situation facing General Washington at Trenton on January 2, 1777.

Through Colonel Reed's spying, Washington knew Cornwallis planned to attack him. Indeed, Cornwallis was eager to *"bag the fox."* Washington held a war council with his officers. What should they do? A retreat seemed impossible. The Delaware River was filled with huge chunks of floating ice. Washington asked his men to develop *"an expedient"* maneuver to relieve them of their chilling dilemma.

It was Washington, however, who found a way to beat Cornwallis's plans. He concluded Cornwallis would need a large division to attack the Continentals at Trenton. But the British stored supplies at Princeton and Brunswick, and Cornwallis would be forced to leave those places poorly guarded if he attacked Trenton.

*"Washington proposed to march by a circuitous and obscure road round the left flank of the enemy to Princeton, capture the forces there, and then push on and seize the stores at Brunswick. The plan was accepted at once, and the officers entered into it with alacrity,"* Jackman wrote, calling the maneuver *"one of the boldest and best conceived of the whole war."*

By four in the afternoon on January 2nd, Cornwallis's men arrived and formed a camp outside Trenton. Washington employed several decoys to deceive the crafty Cornwallis. These subterfuges included leaving behind small parties of men to noisily dig trenches, replenish campfires, and guard bridges. Through these tactics, Washington gave Cornwallis the appearance of a *"regular encampment."* He also hoped these maneuvers would *"avoid the appearance of a retreat."* At midnight, Washington and his men silently stole out of their camp and took a roundabout route to Princeton. *"The difficulty of crossing the Delaware, on account of the ice, made our passage over it tedious,"* the commander-in-chief later wrote.

But recrossing the Delaware and traveling to Princeton brought greater results than he could have imagined. *"Happily we succeeded. We found Princeton about sunrise, with only three regiments,"* Washington reported, noting the remnant of redcoats made a gallant resistance but lost.

The general took time to praise his troops. *"I must do them the justice however to add, that they have undergone more fatigue and hardship, than I expected militia, especially citizens, would have done at this inclement season,"* he wrote to Congress.

After the twin successes of Trenton and Princeton, George Washington decided to encamp his troops for the winter. *"I am just moving to Morristown [New Jersey], where I shall endeavor to put them under the best cover I can. Hitherto*

"But you give us victory over our enemies, you put our adversaries to shame" (PSALM 44:7).

*we have been without any; and many of our poor soldiers quite barefoot and ill clad in other respects.*"[179]

**PRAYER**

*Father, you are the Great Warrior, the Victorious Commander who loves righteousness and preserves justice. Thank you for your gift of peace.*

# 180. Repose

"*Sir, . . . no event of an important and interesting Nature has occurred,*" General Washington wrote to the Continental Congress on February 14, 1777. The inactivity of the past month had made Washington nearly as happy as his successes at Trenton and Princeton.

"*Unless the Successes of our parties in foraging, and bringing off Several Horses, Wagons and some fat Cattle and Sheep, which were contiguous to and around the Enemy's Lines are considered as such,*" he continued with a humorous flair.

The twin victories of Trenton and Princeton had not only brought cheer to the Continental army, but they had also renewed Congress's confidence in Washington. As a reward, Congress bestowed Washington all authority over military matters. Historian John Marshall described these "*bold, judicious, and unexpected attacks*" as saving Philadelphia and recovering the state of New Jersey. The successes also "*revived the drooping spirits*" of the people.

Washington hoped to revive his own army's sagging spirits by moving them to Morristown, New Jersey, for the winter. This location proved to be strategic. Except for a few skirmishes, his army found much rest and repose there. The region's natural resources provided food. Morristown allowed Washington's men to relish the victories of Trenton and Princeton and also to recover from the disappointments of 1776.

Washington wasted no time. This shepherd had a vision for how to rebuild the meager flock of fifteen hundred in his care. He appointed a "*clothier general*" to develop a plan for acquiring clothing and shoes for the army. He also made secret arrangements for doctors to set up hospitals at Morristown's churches to inoculate his army against smallpox. Inoculation was a rare practice in America, frequently viewed with suspicion. But the disease had so impaired his troops in 1776 that inoculation was a risk worth taking.

"*It is with much concern, that the situation of our Affairs obliges me to mention so frequently the want of Money,*" Washington wrote. A revolution could not be won on zeal alone. It required cash. Washington addressed this issue repeatedly in his letters to Congress. *"Our distress on this Account is great indeed and the injury the Service receives almost inconceivable. Not a day, an Hour, or scarcely a Minute passes without complaints and applications on this Head. The recruiting of the Regiments is most materially retarded by it,"* he continued.

But he also gave Congress good news in this letter. General Knox had learned that Springfield, Connecticut, was ripe with quantities of copper, tin, and other materials needed to make cannons. The location was out of reach by ships, making it secure from the enemy. Washington ordered Henry Knox to establish a foundry there.

For George Washington, the winter was not a time of inactivity. If December 1776 was a time to fight, the winter of 1777 was a time to rebuild. Wisdom knows her seasons.[180]

> "Wisdom reposes in the heart of the discerning and even among fools she lets herself be known" (PROVERBS 14:33).

**PRAYER**

*Lord, I pray for your wisdom and discernment today as you guide my activities, whether it's time to rebuild or rest.*

# 181. Pattern of Industry

When Morristown's ladies received an invitation to call upon her ladyship, they couldn't have been more thrilled had the invitation come from a queen in her castle.

Martha Washington had returned to her husband's camp just as the last snow melted that winter. The general's wife was the fresh air and morale boost this New Jersey town needed. For weeks the soldiers had ravished the area's food sources. They also brought diseases, turning two of Morristown's three churches into infirmaries.

On the day of the appointment, the local ladies dressed in their finest. *"As she was said to be so grand a lady, we thought we must put on our best bibs and bands. So we dressed ourselves in our most elegant ruffles and silks and were introduced to her ladyship,"* a Mrs. Troupe wrote, describing their preparations.

But the women were surprised when they found that the short, slightly plump woman who greeted them was dressed more like a servant than a queen. *"We had expected to find the wealthy wife of the great general elegantly dressed, for the time of our visit had been fixed: but instead she was neatly attired in the plainness of her habits,"* another woman exclaimed at the sight of Martha's homespun dress, a contrast to their extravagant, likely European clothes. *"We felt rebuked by the plainness,"* she added.

Martha's attire was not the only sight that shocked them. While she talked with them, she was knitting wool socks at a feverish pace. *"There we were without a stitch of work . . . and the general Washington's lady with her own hands was knitting stockings,"* recorded Mrs. Troupe, embarrassed at her own idle hands.

But Martha's busy hands had a purpose. She believed American ladies should be patterns of industry because *"separation from the mother country"* would dry up resources and conveniences.

*"She seems very wise in experience, kind hearted and winning in all her ways. She talked much of the suffering of the poor soldiers especially the sick ones. Her heart seems to be full of compassion for them,"* Mrs. Troupe commented.

Martha was taking a new step on her journey of loyalty to her husband, his troops, and their new country. She had decided it was time for the female patriots to make a contribution. She not only brought the sample pattern to Morristown in 1777, she *was* the sample pattern. Martha Washington became a leader of the petticoats.[181]

> "In her hand she holds the distaff and grasps the spindle with her fingers"
> (PROVERBS 31:19).

**PRAYER**

*Father, enable me to lead by example. Rip out the stitches of hypocrisy in me so I may lead others as much by what I do as what I say.*

# 182. The Revolution Today: Sewn Pride

What is your pride? To Benjamin Franklin, his pride was wearing his old clothing. He wasn't the only American to take pride in a fabric. To the Ross family, their pride was their grandmother's role in creating the flag. And they used an affidavit to sew the final stitches in her legacy.

"While there is no doubt that the real Betsy Ross was worthy of interest in her own right, it is the legend of Betsy sewing the first stars and stripes that has made her an unforgettable historical figure," proclaims the Web site for the Betsy Ross House (www.betsyrosshouse.org).

Although it is certain Betsy Ross worked as an upholsterer in Philadelphia, her role in sewing the first American flag is supported by swearing, not her signature.

"The Betsy Ross story was brought to public attention in 1870 by her grandson, William Canby, in a speech he made to the Historical Society of Pennsylvania. Canby and other members of Betsy's family signed sworn affidavits stating that they heard the story of the making of the first flag from Betsy's own mouth," the Web site continues.

This oral history relays that three men—George Washington, Robert Morris, and George Ross—visited Ross at her upholstery shop. They asked if she could make a flag from a sketch someone had drawn on a piece of paper. Ross's family members communicated what happened next in their sworn testimonies.

*"Washington asked if Betsy could make a flag from the design. Betsy responded, 'I do not know, but I will try.'"* She may have changed the design from six-pointed stars to five-pointed stars.

Unfortunately, neither Ross nor Washington left a record of the appointment. There is no correspondence to prove the story. The story is plausible for several reasons, however. George Ross, one of the flag committee members, was the uncle of Ross's deceased husband. Betsy Ross was also paid a large sum of money from the Pennsylvania State Navy Board for making flags in May 1777, a month before the Continental Congress issued a resolution proclaiming the thirteen stars and stripes as the nation's banner. Ross made flags throughout her life.

Perhaps the best proof is in the affidavit. Ross's family members were either glory seekers or truth tellers. Taking an oath is a serious gesture, a commitment of truth. The Bible uses the term *sworn* to mean an irrevocable oath, a pledge of the utmost truth. Isaiah 62:8 tells us, "The LORD has sworn by his right hand and by his mighty arm." Psalm 89:35 reveals, "Once for all, I have sworn by my holiness—and I will not lie to David."

Making a pledge to tell the truth is as important to history as it is to our lives today.[182]

> "The LORD has sworn by the Pride of Jacob: 'I will never forget anything they have done'" (AMOS 8:7).

**PRAYER**

*May I take pride in my words and pledge honesty in what I say and do.*

# 183. Sabbath Rest: Dignity Identified

*"Shew Thyself a Man"* was the theme of one of Nathanael Emmons's greatest sermons.

For nearly fifty-five years Emmons served as pastor of the Congregational Church in Franklin, Massachusetts, near the Rhode Island border. Most pastors began their messages with an introduction. In this sermon, Emmons used the foreword to identify the context of his theme before outlining his points.

*"David closed the scene of life, with that propriety of conduct, and that composure of mind, which at once displayed the beauty of religion, and the dignity of human nature,"* Emmons began. He stated that David's estate planning was intact. David had entrusted his son Solomon with the care of his family and government.

*"Accordingly he called him into his presence, and with equal solemnity and affection, addressed him in these memorable words, 'I go the way of all the earth: be thou strong therefore, and shew thyself a man,'"* Emmons continued (1 Kings 2:2 KJV).

Modern sensitivities keep "manhood" from making a top ten list of sermon topics. But the 1770s were different. Men were dying for a cause that sometimes seemed as unreachable as the bottom of the ocean. And the women they left behind shed enough tears to fill the sea. Emmons knew the war had raised questions about life and death. He developed this sermon to shed light on the value of human dignity. His message was as timely as Martha Washington's arrival at Morristown.

*"This appellation sometimes signifies the dignity, and sometimes the meanness of our nature. Job makes use of it to express our meanness and turpitude in the sight of God,"* continued Emmons.

Job called the "Son of Man" a worm and showed contempt for humanity's ineptness. Emmons pointed out that Isaiah took a different approach. *"But Isaiah employs this same appellative to represent the dignity of human nature, when he calls upon stupid idolaters to 'remember this, and shew themselves men.' So here, David in his dying address to Solomon, 'shew thyself a man,' evidently means to use the term in the best sense, and to urge him to act up to the dignity of his nature, and the end of his being,"* Emmons concluded.

> " 'I am about to go the way of all the earth,' he said. 'So be strong, show yourself a man' " (1 KINGS 2:2).

After introducing his theme, Emmons expressed his desire to properly develop his message. His goal was to lead his audience through a clear understanding of the meaning and application of *"shew yourself a man."*

His sensitivity to his sermon topic revealed his respect for his God and his responsibility to his congregation. Nathanael Emmons was every bit the man he sought to show.[183]

**PRAYER**

*Enable me to deeply understand the dignity you have bestowed on me, as your most cherished creature.*

# 184. The Winter Games

I *most sincerely wish, it were in my power to procure the immediate Release of all our Officers and Soldiers who have been so unfortunate as to fall into the hands of our Enemies,"* General Washington wrote to his friend Jonathan Trumbull on February 1, 1777.

Prisoner exchanges were among the most elusive games the Continentals played with the British. Washington continually called on General Howe to demonstrate evenhandedness in prisoner of war concessions. Equal rank trades proved next to impossible. Washington tried asking for those Americans who had been in captivity the longest, but the British did not always play the winter games fairly. Trading was closer to a sport than a negotiation.

*"That I might avoid any imputation of partiality, for the Officers of any particular State; I have in all my Letters to General Howe . . . directed an equal proportion of officers of the Eastern and Southern States, to be sent out,"* Washington reported.

*"But without paying any regard to my request, they have given Pennsylvania more than her proportion, having never discharged one of the Maryland Officers taken upon Long Island,"* he lamented to Trumbull.

Washington completed his letter to Trumbull. But before he could dispatch it, he received a written message from the imprisoned General Lee. *"Lord and General Howe have given me permission to send the inclosed to the Congress,"* Lee explained to Washington, imploring him to forward his letter.

Whether Lee was a pawn or a true broker, no one knew. He asked Congress to send two or three gentlemen to New York for negotiations. Congress refused. They were not going to play another game of tic-tac-toe diplomacy with the British.

John Adams described the request as *"artful stratagem of the two grateful [Howe] brothers to hold up to the public view the phantom of a negotiation, in order to give spirits and courage to the Tories."* Adams believed the maneuver was mostly an attempt by Howe to show the British government he had tried to end the war through conciliation.

*"I confess it is not without indignation that I see such a man as Lee suffer himself to be duped by their policy so far as to become the instrument of it,"* John Adams wrote. He noted that the failed Staten Island negotiations *"did us a great and essential injury at the French court, you may depend upon it. Lord Howe knows it, and wishes to repeat it."*

Indeed, consideration of France's possible response was behind Congress's maneuvers in the winter games. If America even gave the appearance of negotiating with the English, how could they win French support for independence? Congress was unwilling to participate in Britain's shell game.[184]

> "The lazy man does not roast his game, but the diligent man prizes his possessions" (PROVERBS 12:27).

**PRAYER**

*Father, give me the diligence to know which possessions to prize and which ones to let go. Reestablish my priorities and make me nimble to shift and adjust.*

# 185. More than Numbers

A temporary army was no match for a permanent one.

*"The problem, that a nation can be defended against a permanent force, by temporary armies, by occasional calls of the husbandman from his plough to the field, was completely disproved,"* historian John Marshall wrote of the militia system.

The idea behind militias was to call up men on short notice for short terms. This created an unstable force while preventing the army from building on experience. Marshall noted that in 1776 *"America had nearly perished in its cradle"* because of it.

As much as he recognized the flaws in the system, Gen. George Washington only had so much time to argue for a long-term solution. He needed more men for the summer campaign of 1777. He could not just hope that the British Parliament would grow tired of the war, or that France would send troops. He could not herd elephants with a fly swatter. Once again Washington approached the situation with practicality.

*"The utmost efforts were made by the Commander-in-chief to collect a sufficient number of troops to enable him to give a decisive blow to some one of the positions of his enemy,"* Marshall wrote.

Washington sent letters to state leaders asking them to fulfill their quotas and send recruits. The states were more interested in protecting their own borders than faraway colonies. Washington handled this challenge with the same practicality he showed in sending Joseph Reed to spy on Princeton. He asked state leaders to send their men to nearby locations. He knew they were more likely to defend their neighbors than travel cross-country.

*"I have wrote the Assembly of the Massachusetts State and the Convention of New Hampshire, requesting their good Offices and exertions, to promote the raising of their Regiments as expeditiously as possible,"* Washington told Congress.

Washington implored leaders in New Hampshire and Massachusetts to send their recruits to one of the most valuable catches of all: Fort Ticonderoga. Gen. Phillip Schuyler, who guarded the fort, had sent Washington an urgent request for reinforcements. The fort was a prime target.

Washington consequently asked state leaders from New Jersey to North Carolina to send troops to Morristown to defend Philadelphia. He relied on southern recruits to guard the south. But, according to Marshall, George Washington and Congress did not place their hope alone in numbers and new recruits.

*"The earnest desire of congress, [is] to make the army under the immediate command of General Washington sufficiently strong, not only to curb and confine the enemy within their present quarters . . . but, by the divine blessing, totally to subdue them before they can be reinforced,"* John Marshall wrote.

In trying to increase the size of their forces, these patriots did not put their hope in numbers alone. They also looked to the Great Mathematician to multiply their efforts.[185]

**PRAYER**

*God, I put my hope in you. You are my shield and my help, my strength and my song.*

> "No king is saved by the size of his army; no warrior escapes by his great strength. . . . We wait in hope for the LORD; he is our help and our shield"
> (PSALM 33:16, 20).

# 186. Honor and Honesty

Before Benedict Arnold received General Washington's most recent letter in March 1777, he had laid aside *"all thought of making a general attack on Rhode Island."*

While Washington and his men took respite in Morristown and General Schuyler worried about Fort Ticonderoga, Arnold embraced another mission. His job was to conduct reconnaissance on Rhode Island and determine whether the patriots could recapture Newport, which the British had seized in December 1776. After recovering from his leg wound and leaving Canada in mid-1776, Arnold had transferred from the army's northern department into the eastern department.

But Washington's letter put Arnold in a more difficult position. As much as he wanted to please him, Arnold decided to give Washington his honest opinion; even if it wasn't what the commander-in-chief wanted to hear.

*"When the attack was first proposed, we had reason to think your Excellency had a force superior to the enemy in the Jerseys. I am sorry to say, we now have reason to think the case is altered,"* Arnold began his analysis in the letter he wrote Washington on March 11, 1777, from Providence. Arnold was *"dubious of the propriety of the attack, as the enemy now rest secure and easy in their quarters."*

Mathematics was also a factor in Arnold's conclusion. *"I am fully of opinion it will be imprudent to force them to action, until our new levies are in a manner complete. From our strength and numbers, which do not exceed four thousand raw militia, we have no reasonable prospect of succeeding against four thousand well-disciplined troops."*

But Washington was not the only one anxious for a victory in Newport. The local Rhode Island militia was so ready to attack the British that they were blind to reality. *"Notwithstanding, the Assembly of this State have lately requested General Spencer to make an attack on the enemy on Rhode Island, which he seems inclined to do, and the militia are collecting for the purpose. It is proposed to attack the west end*

> "The prudent see danger and take refuge, but the simple keep going and suffer for it"
> (PROVERBS 27:12).

*of the Island, with three thousand men. I am much averse to this plan, as I am fearful it will bring on a general action, and end in our disgrace,"* Arnold warned Washington.

Disgrace is the opposite of honor. As much as Arnold longed for Washington's approval, he valued his honor and reputation above all else. His desire for valor motivated him to give Washington his truthful and honest opinion. And Benedict Arnold was right. The army was too weak at the time to fight the British in Rhode Island.[186]

**PRAYER**

*I pray for prudence today and for the insight to make decisions that are honest and honorable.*

# 187. Prickly Porcupine

"*Congress have doubtless a right of promoting those, whom, from their abilities, their long and arduous services, they esteem most deserving. Their promoting junior officers to the rank of Major-General, I view as a very civil way of requesting my resignation, as unqualified for the office I hold,*" Benedict Arnold wrote to General Washington on March 11, 1777, from Providence, Rhode Island.

After giving Washington his honest opinion about the unlikely prospects for victory in Rhode Island, Arnold put his pen to the issue of his failed promotion. He had been passed over by Congress. Worse, the men who were promoted to major general were all juniors compared with Arnold's rank of brigadier general. Arnold hadn't felt more slighted since Ethan Allen had failed to give him credit for his role capturing Fort Ticonderoga in 1775.

"*My commission was conferred unsolicited, received with pleasure only as a means of serving my country,*" he wrote, referring to his earlier commission as brigadier general. Others had witnessed Arnold's tendency to bristle, but this letter may have been the first time Arnold displayed his sharpness to Washington.

"*With equal pleasure I resign it, when I can no longer serve my country with honor. The person who, void of the nice feelings of honor, will tamely condescend to give up his rights, and hold a commission at the expense of his reputation, I hold as a disgrace to the army, and unworthy of the glorious cause in which we are engaged,*" he opined.

Arnold may have failed in Quebec in 1776, but he certainly did not behave dishonorably. His attention to detail and concern for the welfare of his men guided his decisions. He was no coward and considered himself a man of the highest character. But Arnold was covered with more quills than a porcupine, and he used them to protect himself from those he considered predators.

"*When I entered the service of my country, my character was unimpeached. I have sacrificed my interest, ease, and happiness in her cause.*

*It is rather a misfortune than a fault, that my exertions have not been crowned with success. I am conscious of the rectitude of my intentions,"* he continued.

Arnold was too quick to jump to conclusions. He assumed Congress's decision to pass him over for promotion was purposeful. He was so angry that he overreacted and requested a court of inquiry into his conduct. *"And, though I sensibly feel the ingratitude of my countrymen, every personal injury shall be buried in my zeal for the safety and happiness of my country, in whose cause I have repeatedly fought and bled, and am ready at all times to resign my life,"* he wrote.

Benedict Arnold may have pledged his all for the good of the cause, but his hyper-defensiveness was as evident as the quills flexing across his spine.[187]

> "He who speaks on his own does so to gain honor for himself, but he who works for the honor of the one who sent him is a man of truth; there is nothing false about him"
> (JOHN 7:18).

**PRAYER**

*Show me any areas in my life where my desire to gain honor for myself supersedes my desire to honor you.*

# 188. Lonely Lucy

Although she was happy for her husband when he received accolades from his fellow soldiers and a promotion by General Washington and the Continental Congress, Lucy Knox was very, very lonely.

When the war started in 1775, she had helped her husband, Henry, join the patriot cause and escape from Boston into Cambridge. After the British left Boston in March 1776, Lucy accompanied her beloved "Harry" to New York. Her stay was longer than he thought safe and shorter than she had hoped. She unwillingly fled to Connecticut after the British fleet arrived in New York Harbor.

By May 1777 she found herself caring for her child in Brookline, Massachusetts, where she had traveled to receive inoculation for smallpox. Her isolated recovery only increased her loneliness.

*"I have no company here but Madame Heath, who is so stiff it is impossible to be sociable with her, and Mr. Gardner the treasurer, so that you may well think what I feel under my present anxiety,"* Lucy wrote to Henry.

Lucy's misery was not the only result of her separation from Henry. Returning to Massachusetts revived memories of her family. When the

British evacuated Boston, they took as many loyalists—including her parents and siblings—with them as their ships could hold. These evacuees traveled to New York, Canada, and England. She had not seen her family. Worst of all, she had not heard from them. Lucy contemplated the probability that they had disowned her. Henry knew how much the possibility pained her.

*"Though your parents are on the opposite side from your Harry, yet it's very strange it should divest them of humanity. Not a line! My God! What stuff is the human heart made of? Although father, mother, sister, and brother have forgotten you, yet, my love, your Harry will ever esteem you the best boon of Heaven,"* Knox wrote encouragingly on May 20, 1777.

Lucy's anguish intensified when a startling piece of news reached her in Brookline. A Frenchman had arrived on America's shores. He claimed he was the new commander of the artillery, the job Henry held. *"A French general [Ducoudray], who styles himself commander-in-chief of the continental artillery, is now in town. He says his appointment is from Mr. Deane, that he is going immediately to headquarters to take command, that he is a major-general,"* Lucy wrote, adding wistfully, *"Who knows but I may have my Harry again?"*

Ducoudray's claims of knowing princes and holding high military titles were more boastful than believable. *"This I am sure of, he will never suffer anyone to command him in that department. If he does, he has not the soul which I now think him possessed of,"* Lucy wrote defensively.

Although she desperately wanted a cure for her loneliness and to be reunited with her husband, Lucy Knox didn't want Henry to lose his commission. He had sacrificed too much to leave in dishonor.[188]

> "God sets the lonely in families, he leads forth the prisoners with singing. . . . Praise be to the LORD, to God our Savior, who daily bears our burdens" (PSALM 68:6, 19).

**PRAYER**

*You are the Great Burden Bearer, who sees the lonely and hears the cry of the most despondent of hearts.*

# 189. The Revolution Today: Carrier Pigeons

Lucy Knox was not the only lady to experience the loneliness of war. Abigail Adams felt it, too. While men labored together on the field or in meeting rooms, women often labored by themselves at home with their children. Sometimes the weather made them even more isolated.

*"We have had very severe weather almost ever since you left us,"* Abigail wrote to John Adams on March 8, 1777. She had written him three letters but a heavy snowstorm had isolated her so much she had no idea if he had received any of them.

*"We know not what is passing with you nor with the Army, any more than if we lived with the Antipodes,"* Abigail wrote. Her loneliness was so great she might as well have been living in the Indian Ocean, the antipode, or region diametrically opposite America on the globe.

Abigail, however, had a solution to her problems. *"I want a Bird of passage,"* she wrote satirically. But a carrier pigeon could not cure an ailment as common to humanity as loneliness. Americans today have their carrier pigeons. They are cell phones, e-mail, instant messaging, and other technological wonders. Although Americans are more connected than ever, it is possible they are also lonelier than ever.

"The evidence shows that Americans have fewer confidants and those ties are also more family-based than they used to be," Lynn Smith-Lovin, a sociology professor, reported. She was one of the authors of a study on social isolation in America published in 2006. The study compared the same survey questions asked nineteen years apart, first in 1985 and then again in 2004.

"In 1985, the typical American named three people that he or she talked with about matters that were personally important. About half of the confidants mentioned in 1985 were family members—spouses, parents, children, brothers, sisters. The other half were people they met through the community—co-workers, neighbors, people they joined in voluntary associations," Smith-Lovin explained.

"By the time we asked the questions again in 2004, people's most common answer (25 percent of the sample) was that they didn't talk to anyone about things that were important to them," she wrote, adding that people had lost about one-third of their contacts.

"Networks are important to both individuals and to our larger social system. These kinds of close relationships offer all types of benefits, including social support, help in ordinary times and emergencies, information to help solve problems and values that shape our world view and politics."

Loneliness prevents people from talking to others about matters important to them. Isolation of this kind, whether it's from a war, a snowstorm, or the trap of technology, is not good.

> "Turn to me and be gracious to me, for I am lonely and afflicted"
> (PSALM 25:16).

God created humans as social beings and designed them for companion-ship, not disconnection.[189]

**PRAYER**

*Enhance my circle of influence that I may turn loneliness—mine or some-one else's—into companionship.*

# 190. Sabbath Rest: Dignity Defined

"The dignity of man appears from his bearing the image of his Maker," Nathanael Emmons declared in his sermon on the dignity of man to his Massachusetts congregation.

Emmons told his listeners that God formed *"a more noble and intelligent creature to bear his image."* Because God breathed life into their nostrils, men and women are the only creatures created in God's image.

*"This allows us to say, that man is the offspring of God, a ray from the fountain of light, a drop from the ocean of intelligence. Though, man, since the fall, comes into the world destitute of the moral image of God, yet . . . he still bears the natural image of his Maker. His soul is a transcript of the natural perfections of the Deity,"* Emmons continued.

The Lord gave man something he didn't give other creatures. He gave him a soul. *"God is a spirit, and so is the soul of man; God is intelligence and activity, and so is the soul of man. In a word, man is the living image of the living God."*

But the Lord did not confine man's dominion to the earth. *"God has, besides, instamped a dignity upon man by giving him not only a rational, but an immortal existence,"* asserted Emmons. *"The soul, which is properly the man, shall survive the body and live forever."*

Emmons pointed to the lifespan of God's lesser creatures to explain humanity's capacity for immortality. *"The creatures and objects, with which we are now surrounded, have but a short and momentary being. One species of insects, we are told, begin and end their existence in twenty-four hours,"* he said, noting that larger animals have longer life cycles than mere bugs.

Emmons shared that God cared for all his creations, but humanity was Providence's favorite, which is why he gave angels *"charge over"* men and women. God also gave humans a gift: a large world to inhabit and explore.

*"But, the most distinguishing and most astonishing display of the divine mercy, is the incarnation and death of the Son of God for the salvation of man. By the incarnation of Christ, our nature was united with*

the divine, and the dignity of man with the dignity of Christ," proclaimed Emmons.

> "Who knows if the spirit of man rises upward and if the spirit of the animal goes down into the earth?"
> (ECCLESIASTES 3:21).

He noted the eternity of Christ was God's ultimate gift to the souls of his most honored creatures. *"Hence all the sufferings, which Christ hath endured on earth, and all the honours, which he hath received in heaven, have displayed the dignity of man. And for the same reason, the dignity of man will be eternally rising, with the rising honour and dignity of Christ,"* Nathanael Emmons concluded.[190]

**PRAYER**

*Thank you for breathing life into me, for giving me a soul.*

# 191. Circumstances beyond Control

I am determined to contribute my mite to the defence of the country, in spite of every obstacle," Henry Knox wrote to Lucy in May 1777.

When Lucy alerted him about the rumors of Mr. Ducoudray's arrival from France, Knox hoped the news would prove false. But it was true. Once again Knox faced a test of his character and capabilities. Like the direction of the wind, the outcome was beyond his control.

Silas Deane, one of America's representatives in France, had given Ducoudray and other Frenchmen commissions in the army. Deane had promised Ducoudray the position of head of the artillery, which was Knox's job. Ducoudray's purported qualifications included the birthright of lordship, rank of brigadier general, and connections to many dukes and princes throughout Europe.

The slowness of communication prohibited Deane from knowing who held what position and who had been promoted. He was unaware of the facts on the ground in America, just as Congress and the army were unable to know the challenges their diplomats faced in France. Congress faced some difficult choices. Would they accept help from France, even if it cost them capable American officers such as Henry Knox?

*"The Congress have taken some precious steps with regard to Mr. Ducoudray. They have resolved that Mr. Deane has exceeded his commission, and that they cannot ratify his treaty with Mr. Ducoudray. Pretty this!—to bring a gentleman 1,200 leagues to affront him,"* Knox wrote Lucy with relief.

But Knox soon discovered the matter was not resolved. Congress changed its mind and began accepting some commissions. The news demoralized and threatened Washington's officers. Not all members of the Continental Congress were happy. Some believed that Deane, a businessman, was more motivated by imports than independence.

*"I am sorry to be obligd to think, that a Monopoly of Trade, and not the Liberty of their Country, is the sole Object of some Men's Views. This is the Cake which they hope shortly to slice and share among themselves,"* Samuel Adams snarled over Deane's decisions.

Generals Knox, Sullivan, and Greene wrote to Congress and expressed their outrage in polite terms. Their letters angered some, who demanded an apology. Believing an apology for expressing their opposition was unnecessary, the generals did not respond. With the matter firmly beyond their control, all they could do was wait.

Hope arrived from George Washington's pen. He wrote to Congress that Ducoudray's appointment would force Knox into retirement. He called Knox *"a man of great military reading, sound judgment, and clear conceptions."* Knox was *"one of the most valuable officers in the service,"* Washington told the lawmakers.

Congress listened to George Washington. Henry Knox kept his job. (And General Ducoudray's qualifications proved to be fraudulent.)[191]

> "We wait in hope for the LORD; he is our help and our shield" (PSALM 33:20).

**PRAYER**

*I wait on you today for the circumstances beyond my control. You are my help and hope.*

# 192. A Soldier's Love Letter

Love kept liberty alive in the hearts of many soldiers.

*"AFTER a very severe march one hundred miles of the way on foot, through the woods in an excessive miry Road, wet, rainy weather accompanied with Snow and Hail, I arrived the 20th of May at Ticonderoga,"* Col. Alexander Scammell wrote to his *"dearest Nabby"* on June 8, 1777.

*"And if they [the British] make an attempt upon us in the same place [Fort Ticonderoga] I nothing doubt we shall be able by the smiles of superintendent Providence to give them as fatal an overthrow,"* he wrote optimistically.

Even though Scammell was well supplied, he couldn't escape the drought in his heart. He missed his love. *"Tho I should much rather be able to retire to enjoy the sweets of Liberty and domestick happiness, but more especially the pleasing Charms of your dear Company. But so long as my Country demands my utmost Exertions, I must devote myself entirely to its Service."*

Scammell tried to encourage his betrothed by telling her his present situation was *"very agreeable,"* adding he hoped autumn would bring him the pleasure of seeing her in Boston. *"The tender moments which we have spent together still, and ever will, remain fresh in my memory—You are ever present in my enraptur'd heart—& a mutual return of Affection from you, I find more and more necessary to my Happiness."*

Distance could not squelch Scammell's love. It served to strengthen it. *"Altho I am far distant from you, still remember that I am your constant, and most affectionate admirer."*

He also explained he would have written sooner, but another duty called him—court. He sat on a court-martial to try soldiers who attempted to spread smallpox. The proceeding had worried Scammell more than any other duty he had undertaken. *"I hope therefore that you will not impute any neglect to me But ever consider me unalterably thine—My Lovely Girl, write every Opportunity,"* he concluded.

Unable to send his letter right away, Scammell added this postscript two weeks later: *"PS—I long for the time when through you I can send my dutiful Regards to your Hon'd Parents by the tender Name of Father & Mother—June 23d 1777. I congratulate you upon the Cause of your Fear being remov'd as Burgoyne is going to attack Ticonderoga & not Boston. I hope we shall be able to keep him off."*

Scammell's love kept his hopes alive. The thought of seeing Nabby kept him motivated. It was for love he was willing to give up his life. Alexander Scammell was a true soldier of the heart.[192]

> "Above all, love each other deeply, because love covers over a multitude of sins" (1 PETER 4:8).

**PRAYER**

*God, thank you for the capacity to love and for its power to motivate us to sacrifice for each other. Thank you for loving me so much that you gave up your Son for my redemption.*

# 193. A Double Dose of Rivalry

R ivalry is bad enough, but sometimes it comes in double doses. Both sides saw its effects in the campaign of 1777.

The Americans guarding Fort Ticonderoga awoke on July 6, 1777, to the presence of British cannons mounted across the way on Mount Defiance. General Schuyler faced a force of eight thousand British soldiers—more than three times the size of his force. What could he do? His choices were fight, flight, or capture. He fled. For the sake of preservation, Schuyler led his men in a retreat.

The British commander responsible for recapturing Fort Ticonderoga was Gen. John Burgoyne. Arriving in Canada in the spring of 1777, he vowed to take the Hudson River. Fort Ticonderoga was the first step to prove his superiority among his band of British brothers.

But as often happens, a rivalry of sorts emerged. *"[In late July 1777] Washington learned from spies in New York that Howe was preparing for an expedition by water, but its destination was a profound secret. Burgoyne was evidently pressing on toward the South, to obtain possession of the Hudson,"* historian William Jackman recorded.

*"Did Howe intend to move up that river to cooperate with him, and thus cut off the communication between New England and the other States; to make an attack on Boston . . . or to endeavor to reach Philadelphia by water?"* Jackman wrote of Washington's questions.

Washington learned the answer in August. Howe had abandoned Burgoyne. Seeking revenge for Trenton, Howe couldn't keep his eyes off Philadelphia, the Continental capital.

But Washington was not without his own rivalry challenges. General Gates and General Schuyler had fought the previous year over who was the ranking general of the northern division of the American forces posted along the Canadian border. Gates became an even greater problem for Washington in the spring of 1777. He began to send his requests directly to Congress, without going through his commander-in-chief.

> "It is true that some preach Christ out of envy and rivalry, but others out of goodwill"
> (PHILIPPIANS 1:15).

*"Congress directed Washington to 'forward two troops of horse to General Gates.' Washington thought that the requisitions of Gates should be made directly to himself, or that at least he should receive a duplicate of them; but Gates insisted on dealing directly with congress, as 'the common parent of all the American armies,'"* Jackman explained.

Once again, rivalry threatened the American cause. But this time it also threatened the British.[193]

**PRAYER**

*Examine my motives, Lord. Search my heart for anything that rivals you or that produces envy in me.*

# 194. Honor Restored

I have the Honour to inclose you an Extract of a Letter from Genl. Washington from which you will perceive the General is of Opinion [that you are] 'a brave, active and judicious officer,'" Continental Congress President John Hancock wrote to Benedict Arnold on July 12, 1777.

Although he had been passed over for promotion earlier in the winter, the spring and summer of 1777 smiled on Arnold. With thoughts of resigning after his failed promotion, he returned to his Connecticut home in April. But his homecoming was bittersweet and shorter than a snowstorm in spring. Arnold had scarcely embraced his three sons when he learned the British had invaded his beloved Connecticut. He could not let his personal demons keep him from fighting for his sons or his home state.

Arnold learned that the British had landed a force of two thousand on the coast and marched to Danbury, a supply depot for the Continental army. With thoughts of home burning in his breast, Arnold mustered a hundred volunteers and joined Gen. David Wooster's five hundred Connecticut militia. Together they harassed the British as they retreated from Danbury to Ridgefield in April 1777. Wooster was killed in the skirmishes, and Arnold injured his leg when his horse was shot and fell on him. But their mission succeeded.

For his valor and ingenuity in Connecticut, Arnold finally received the promotion he had long wanted. Congress commissioned him a major general. Not only that, but by the summer, Washington had an important assignment for him.

Hancock informed Arnold he *"should be immediately employed in collecting the Militia to check the Progress of Genl. Burgoyne, as very disagreeable Consequences may be apprehended if the most vigorous Measures are not taken to oppose him."* Washington wanted to send Arnold to the northern department to block Gen. John Burgoyne after his capture of Fort Ticonderoga.

*"The Congress therefore concurring in opinion with General Washington who has strongly recommended you for this Purpose, have directed*

*You to repair immediately to Head Quarters to follow such Orders as you may receive from him on the Subject,"* Hancock concluded.

But it was Washington's oral recommendation to Hancock that probably stirred Arnold's heart. *"His [Arnold's] presence and activity,"* Washington told Hancock, *"will animate the Militia greatly, and spur them on to a becoming conduct."*

> "At the same time that my sanity was restored, my honor and splendor were returned to me for the glory of my kingdom" (DANIEL 4:36).

With his homeland protected and his honor restored, Benedict Arnold headed north to join Horatio Gates and check John Burgoyne's movements.[194]

**PRAYER**

*Thank you for those times in life when you restore honor and reward hard work for your glory.*

# 195. A Star Appears from the East

Would the British take him before he had a chance to kiss America's shores? Such was the question facing the French musketeer as he sailed toward South Carolina's sand in the summer of 1777.

From the moment he first learned about America's revolt at a party hosted by King George III's brother in 1775, he was secretly smitten with the patriot cause. After hiring his own ship, this nineteen-year-old slipped out of France against the expressed will of his own king. The reason? The Marquis de Lafayette was in love with liberty enough to leave behind his daughter and pregnant wife. Lafayette wrote to his wife, Adrienne, that he, along with the ten other French adventurers aboard his ship, sailed several days along the coast *"which swarmed with hostile vessels."*

*"When I arrived, everybody said that my vessel must inevitably be taken, since two British frigates blockaded the harbor,"* Lafayette told her. The wind, however, rescued this wistful Frenchman. *"By a most wonderful good fortune, a gale obliged the frigates to stand out to sea for a short time. My vessel came in at noon-day, without meeting friend or foe,"* Lafayette proclaimed joyfully.

He then rode on horseback nine hundred miles to Philadelphia to present his credentials to the Continental Congress for a command in the army. *"I have such confidence in my lucky star, however, that I hope it will reach you. This same star has befriended me, to the astonishment of everybody here. Trust to it yourself, and be assured that it ought to calm all your fears,"* he urged her.

This French star's timing was less than stellar, however. Many Americans were as fearful of formal French adventurers as they were of their Catholic religion. Not only that, but Lafayette also had received his commission from Silas Deane. Congress was so disgusted with Deane's first round of recruits, led by the odious Ducoudray, they rejected Lafayette's request for a meeting. Undaunted, Lafayette responded with a note.

*"After the sacrifices I have made, I have the right to exact two favors: one is, to serve at my own expense; the other is, to serve at first as a volunteer,"* he told the Congress.

Hence, the Marquis de Lafayette's humility and zeal shone brighter than his ambition. This lover of liberty convinced Congress of his sincerity. After reviewing his letters of introduction, Congress granted him the rank of major general but on one condition. He was not to hold a command. His title was merely honorary.

And with that, this French volunteer with a meaningless rank hurried to join General Washington's army. It was time for France's twinkling star to meet America's shining star. Both, however, had yet to burn their brightest and fulfill their highest purpose.[195]

> "There are also heavenly bodies and there are earthly bodies; but the splendor of the heavenly bodies is one kind, and the splendor of the earthly bodies is another. The sun has one kind of splendor, the moon another and the stars another; and star differs from star in splendor" (1 CORINTHIANS 15:40, 41).

**PRAYER**

*Lord, thank you for the splendor of your creation. And just as you give nature purpose, how much more have you given me purpose today.*

# 196. The Revolution Today: Love and War

"*Marry my love"* topped the to-do list of an officer from the 611th Air Intelligence Squadron (AIS) after he learned the news. His deployment came a year earlier than his expected rotation. Because this career field was undermanned, the air force decided to send him to Iraq at the end of January 2007.

Maj. Greg Soukup and his fiancée, Kristen Owens, had planned a large out-of-town wedding in February 2007. But the sped-up deployment notice nearly crushed their wedding cake. They called their loved ones and the businesses they had hired and cancelled their plans. To their surprise the hotel and airlines refunded all of their deposits after learning of Soukup's deployment.

The call to duty, however, did not silence their wedding bells. The 611th Air Operations Group and the 611th AIS threw the couple a wedding at Elmendorf Air Force Base in Alaska. Although the bride walked down a hallway and not an aisle to meet her groom, the wedding was complete with a cake, decorations, flowers, champagne, ring, and air force family members in dress blues. The 611th AIS's commander officiated at their marriage ceremony.

The couple's sacrifice did not go unnoticed by the highest sources. "We are very proud of them both and thank them for their dedication to our nation and our Air Force. I'm grateful that our nation is blessed with men and women willing to make these types of sacrifices to defend our freedom," Lt. Gen. Douglas Fraser, head of the Alaskan Command, commented.

Service often requires sacrifices from matrimony. Sometimes it speeds up a wedding, sometimes it delays. Sometimes it stretches matrimony's existing bonds.

Although such sacrifices of love for country did not begin with the Revolutionary War, they are certainly a legacy of it. Liberty, a cause greater than himself, lured Alexander Scammell away from his fiancée. His love letters were the best record she had of him after his death near the end of the war.

Lafayette called parting from his wife of two years, Adrienne, a *"sorrow."* They had married at age seventeen. Only one thing could lure Lafayette away from his wife and that was liberty. He later reflected on this grand passion: *"When I first learnt the subject of this quarrel [in America], my heart espoused warmly the cause of liberty, and I thought of nothing but of adding also the aid of my banner."*

Pennsylvania pastor David Jones described such sacrifices as essential to a life of liberty. *"Come then, my countrymen, we have no other remedy, but, under GOD, to fight for our brethren, our sons, and daughters, our wives and our houses,"* Jones cried.

Love shines its brightest when it reflects the sunlight of service and sacrifice.[196]

> "And live a life of love, just as Christ loved us and gave himself up for us as a fragrant offering and sacrifice to God" (EPHESIANS 5:2).

**PRAYER**

*Father, thank you for the sacrifice of love you have given me through Christ.*

# 197. Sabbath Rest: Dignity's Quartet

Nathanael Emmons wanted to articulate his sermon on the dignity of man in the clearest of terms. He turned to a straightforward technique as understandable today as it was in the late 1700s—Emmons numbered the points of his message. As a result, his message rang true with the clarity of a string quartet.

*"First, man hath a capacity for constant and perpetual progression in knowledge,"* Emmons declared. He also noted that animals have a degree of knowledge. The ox may know his owner, but such creatures are incapable of expanding their knowledge through the study of books. *"The bee cannot improve her skill, nor the ant her prudence, by observation or study . . . But, man is capable of improving in knowledge as long as he enjoys the means or materials of improvement,"* continued Emmons, referring to Solomon as an example of someone whose wisdom increased and surpassed all others.

*"Secondly, man hath a capacity for holiness as well as knowledge. The horse and mule which have no understanding, and indeed all the lower animals, are utterly incapable of holiness . . . But man is capable of holiness. His rational and moral faculties both capacitate and oblige him to be holy."*

Humans are able to discern right from wrong. They have a conscience. They are capable of justice, mercy, and humility.

*"Thirdly, that man hath a capacity for happiness, equal to his capacity for holiness and knowledge. Knowledge and holiness are the grand pillars which support all true and substantial happiness,"* Emmons proclaimed, describing how Solomon fell to his knees at the dedication of the temple because he was so full of joy.

*"Fourthly, that man hath a capacity for great and noble actions,"* stated Emmons. He cited the Middle East's pyramids, tombs, and temples and pointed to Greece and Rome as examples of humanity's ability to build great things. He also praised Newton for his material discoveries and Locke for his intellect. Emmons proclaimed that greater things, such as the spread of the gospel, were yet to be completed.

"*Thus the image, which man bears of his Maker, the immortal spirit which resides with him, the distinguishing favours, which he has received from the Father of mercies, and all his noble powers and faculties, unite to stamp a dignity upon his nature, and raise him high in the scale of being,*" Emmons concluded.

> "The ox knows his master, the donkey his owner's manger, but Israel does not know, my people do not understand"
> (ISAIAH 1:3).

In this sermon, Nathanael Emmons fine-tuned dignity's quartet of knowledge, holiness, happiness, and action. He wanted his congregation to understand they were more than mere beasts burdened by life's labors. Because of God's gift of dignity, they had great potential.[197]

**PRAYER**

*God, I pray for the ability to fully understand, appreciate, and use the capacity you have given me for knowledge, holiness, happiness, and action.*

# 198. Learn or Teach?

If I did not misunderstand, what you, or some other Member of Congress said to me, respecting the appointment of the Marquis De la Fayette, he has misconceived the design of his appointment," George Washington wrote to Benjamin Harrison, a member of Congress, on August 19, 1777.

The young French musketeer perplexed Washington more than any other foreigner he knew. Lafayette and Washington had met at a dinner party on July 31st, the day Lafayette received his commission from Congress. The commander-in-chief was so touched by the volunteer's personal sacrifices to join the army that he likened him to family and suggested he take up quarters in his household. Washington, however, also asked Lafayette to submit to the army's customs and manners.

The next day Washington took Lafayette to the Delaware River's banks to review the troops. Knowing his experience as a French musketeer and dragoon, Washington watched with some embarrassment at the paradox. Dressed in his fancy and flawless French uniform, Lafayette watched an army whose hunting shirts and pants were as mismatched as they were modest. When Washington commented on the disparity between the American and French armies, Lafayette responded humbly, "*I am here to learn, not to teach.*"

The reply surprised Washington, who had nearly lost one of his best generals, Henry Knox, to a boastful Frenchman. To Washington, haughtiness, not humility, seemed to reign in the hearts of most of the French officers who wanted to join the army. Lafayette's zeal, however, soon overtook his humility. Since reviewing the troops, Lafayette had repeatedly expressed his desire to command a division. His behavior left Washington confused.

*"If I understand him, that he does not conceive his Commission is merely honorary; but given with a view to Command a division of this Army,"* Washington continued in his letter to Harrison. *"True, he has said that he is young, and inexperienced, but at the same time has always accompanied it with a hint, that so soon as I shall think fit for the Command of a division, he shall be ready to enter upon the duties of it; and in the mean time, has offered his service for a Smaller Command."*

Washington concluded his letter by asking Harrison to clarify Congress's intentions. Harrison wrote Washington the next day. Lafayette's commission was merely honorary. He was to fight, not lead.

Washington's confusion was not the result of miscommunication. Lafayette knew his position was honorary from the moment he received it. In fact, he had promised Congress he would not ask for a command. Lafayette merely showed the paradox of youth. He had zeal for the patriot

> "It is not good to have zeal without knowledge, nor to be hasty and miss the way" (PROVERBS 19:2).

cause, but lacked knowledge of American ways. Time would prove whether the Marquis de Lafayette would be true to his words. Had he come to learn or teach? Would his knowledge measure up to his zeal?[198]

**PRAYER**

*Open my heart to your teaching today. May I not let zeal overtake my need to learn from you or those around me.*

# 199. September 11th

I shall begin by telling you that I am well, because I must end by telling you that we fought in earnest yesterday, and we were not the victors," the Marquis de Lafayette wrote to his wife from a makeshift infirmary on September 12, 1777.

When Washington learned that General Howe had landed his army in Maryland and was marching to Philadelphia, he moved his army south.

Because the main road from Maryland crossed the Brandywine River at Chad's Ford, the site was an ideal location for stopping the British.

On the morning of September 11th, the British began firing cannons from the river, leading Washington to move the bulk of his forces on the left toward the river.

The British river maneuvers, however, proved to be nothing more than a hunter's ruse. By 2 p.m., it was clear Howe had divided his army. The smoke coming from the river was a decoy from his first division. A second larger division had marched seventeen miles up the river, where they crossed it, came back down, and attacked the Americans from the right. The British huntsmen had trapped their ducks.

The deception left the Americans scrambling across the hills faster than frantic fowl. Although forced to adjust their lines, they did not give up without a fight. The right wing fought the attacking British and Hessians for more than an hour, which gave the rest of the army time to regroup behind the Birmingham Meeting House.

The dismal situation stirred Lafayette's patriotic soul. Then this honorary general who longed for a command asked Washington if he could join the ranks and fight. Washington agreed. Lafayette rode over to a hill behind the meetinghouse and found a group of men who were struggling to get into formation. Lafayette dismounted, helped them to adjust their lines, and fought alongside them as if he had always been part of their flock. The flurry came to a swift end when a huntsman struck this most exotic French bird.

> "Greater love has no one than this, that he lay down his life for his friends" (JOHN 15:13).

*"The English honored me with a musket shot, which wounded me slightly in the leg,"* Lafayette told his wife. He didn't notice his injury until blood began oozing from his boot. *"But the wound is nothing, dear heart; the ball hit neither bone nor nerve, and all I have to do for it to heal is to lie on my back for a while—which puts me in very bad humor,"* Lafayette wrote from his sickbed.

*"This battle will, I fear have unpleasant consequences for America; we must try to repair the damage, if we can,"* he concluded.

As he contemplated the future of the war, this French star, the Marquis de Lafayette, had fired a flare of friendship at Brandywine that would not go unnoticed.[199]

**PRAYER**

*Thank you for the gift of friendship. Show me how to be a better friend, one who shows love with sacrifice.*

# 200. Unwavering Faith

Brandywine was bad, but it was not a disaster. One patriot's unwavering strength after the disaster revealed a faith that burned brightly. *"I trust the same Divine Being who brought us together will support us,"* Henry Knox wrote to his beloved wife in mid-October 1777. Although his letter was partly a response to her concerns over food shortages, Knox also revealed his conclusions about Brandywine.

Knox told Lucy he believed the British were not as strong as they seemed. The reason? The American army had continued to use the Delaware River after the battle of Brandywine. A more powerful British army would have stopped them. *"If the enemy cannot get their shipping up, Philadelphia is one of the most ineligible places in the world for an army surrounded by rivers which are impassable, and an army above them,"* Knox continued hopefully.

Knox knew, however, that the American army was in no shape to attack *"ineligible"* Philadelphia. The *"entire want of clothing"* and shortages of armaments for such a large-scale attack were among his reasons. He thought the army should go into winter quarters in a nearby location. Knox considered their setbacks as *"exceedingly heavy, but it must stimulate us to make greater exertions."*

*"I have sanguine hopes of being able to live this winter in sweet fellowship with the dearest friend of my heart . . . Observe my dear girl, how providence supports us. The advantages gained by our Northern army give almost a decisive turn to the contest,"* he wrote of his hopes to see her.

It might be easy to assume that Knox's faith was merely an inheritance. After all, his Presbyterian ancestors came from Scotland's lowlands, home of the great religious reformer, John Knox. Henry's family may have passed on their beliefs to him, but by this time in his life, he had embraced them as his own.

*"For my own part, I have not yet seen so bright a dawn as the prospect, and I am perfectly convinced in my own mind of the kindness of Providence towards us as I am of my own existence,"* Knox concluded his letter.

> "The God of Israel spoke, the Rock of Israel said to me: 'When one rules over men in righteousness, when he rules in the fear of God, he is like the light of morning at sunrise on a cloudless morning, like the brightness after rain that brings the grass from the earth'"
> (2 SAMUEL 23:3, 4).

Knox's ability to look at the sunrise side of the mountain, not the sunset side, was a reflection of his faith and respect for God. Within weeks of his letter, Henry Knox received a *"kindness from Providence"* in the form of a leave of absence. He returned to Boston to visit Lucy. She later joined him at Valley Forge in the spring.[200]

**PRAYER**

*Thank you for the ray of hope faith provides. Your righteousness shines more brightly than a sunrise on a cloudless day.*

# 201. Double Standoff

I *will fly to your assistance,"* Maj. Gen. Benedict Arnold promised Gen. Horatio Gates in August 1777.

After receiving his promotion and Washington's orders, Arnold proceeded with all possible speed to the northern department in New York. Congress had appointed General Gates as the top commander there. Together the pair stopped General Burgoyne's southward advance down the Hudson River. By October they faced a standoff near Saratoga, a town west of the river. *"The advanced sentries of my pickets are posted within shot, and opposite the enemy's. Neither side have given ground an inch,"* Gates wrote to Washington on October 5th.

For two weeks the Americans and British had camped within cannon fire of each other. Their position was about six miles from Saratoga. Neither side had moved. But Gates was content to wait. He had the manpower he needed. After Burgoyne aligned himself with the Iroquois, New England militia had flocked to Gates. Their anger against the Indians, who had recently scalped a white woman, was as great as their rage against the redcoats. Burgoyne, however, had yet to receive his promised reinforcements.

*"From the best intelligence, he [Burgoyne] has not more than three weeks' provision in store; it will take him at least eight days to get back to Ticonderoga; so that, in a fortnight at farthest, he must decide whether he will rashly risk, at infinite disadvantage, to force my camp, or retreat to his den,"* Gates predicted in his letter to Washington.

But Gates found himself in another standstill, and this one was with Arnold. Although he had flown to Gates's side, Arnold found the old general to be a poor listener. Like a fox scraping his claws on the door of the chicken coop, Arnold was ready to attack Burgoyne. This internal American standoff had started when Gates failed to send Arnold reinforcements at the battle of Bemis Heights three weeks earlier. The move had angered Arnold and left his men to repulse the entire British left wing. Arnold's men credited him with the victory.

*"The soldiers attributed the success of the late battle to the generalship of Arnold. But for some reason, jealousy perhaps, Gates removed him from his command,"* wrote historian William Jackman.

By October the standoff with the British had intensified, and so had Gates and Arnold's polar positions. Where Arnold employed persistence, Gates preferred passivity. They were as far apart on strategy as Maine was from Georgia. Ignoring Arnold in all his letters to Washington, Gates predicted victory.

*"I must have the fairest prospect to be able to reënforce your Excellency, in a more considerable manner than by a single regiment,"* he wrote of the prospects.

And with a double standoff at hand, Horatio Gates and Benedict Arnold waited for the British to attack.[201]

**PRAYER**

*Lord, you are the Great Reviver, the One who redeems my life when I am surrounded, who brings me up from the pit.*

> "The engulfing waters threatened me, the deep surrounded me . . . But you brought my life up from the pit, O LORD my God" (JONAH 2:5, 6).

## 202. Saratoga

The final battle of the Saratoga standoff began two days later on October 7, 1777. Under the command of German Baron von Riedesel, the British began their assault with the skill of hunters. Burgoyne had given up on receiving reinforcements. He chose to attack, not retreat.

*"Arnold was in his tent, brooding over the treatment he had received [from Gates], and had almost resolved to leave the army. Suddenly he heard the noise of battle; his ruling passion was instantly on fire,"* historian William Jackman wrote of Arnold's decision to defy Gates and join the battle. *"Mounting his horse, he rode with all speed to the scene of conflict. Gates, who saw him as he dashed away, exclaimed: 'He will do some rash thing,' and sent after him orders, by Major Wilkinson, to return; but in vain,—Arnold heard only the roar of battle."*

With the abandon of a deer, Arnold rode into the fray. *"He rushed into the thickest of the fight, cheered on the men, who answered him with shouts of recognition,"* Jackman wrote. *"To those looking on, he seemed insane. By his exertions the British lines were broken again and again."*

But when a British general fell, the whole British line gave way. They abandoned their cannon and rushed to their camp. *"In spite of a shower of grape [clusters of small iron balls fired from a cannon] and musketry, the Americans rushed headlong to the assault,"* described Jackman. *"Arnold rode directly into a sally-port, where his horse was shot under him, and he himself was severely wounded—a ball had shattered his leg. His men now fell back."*

The Americans returned to their camp. They slept with their muskets in anticipation of a renewed attack. But sunrise brought a surprise. The gravely weakened British hunters had begun a retreat to Saratoga, six miles away. They left behind their prey.

Jackman noted that after the battle, General Gates sent his report to Congress, not to Washington *"as was his duty."* He also slighted Arnold in his report, but the soldiers who fought that day did not forget Arnold's valor. *"The soldiers in the army attributed the success of the battles at Saratoga to the skilful management of Arnold and Morgan,"* stressed Jackman. *"Gates did not even mention their names in his full dispatches to Congress."*

For his courage and injuries, Arnold received acclaim from an important source. *"Permit me to assure you Sir I respect your Character as a Citizen & Soldier of the United States of America, that I rejoice at your recovery from the dangerous Wounds which you lately received in the defence of your Country, that I wish you perfect health & a continued Succession of honour, that I am with very great respect & Esteem,"* John Hancock later wrote to Benedict Arnold.[202]

> "The lion perishes for lack of prey, and the cubs of the lioness are scattered" (JOB 4:11).

**PRAYER**

*Thank you for the times in life when you give victory to the hunted. I praise you for your might.*

# 203. The Revolution Today: Unknown Soldiers

I *have spent an Hour, this Morning, in the Congregation of the dead,"* John Adams wrote to his wife, Abigail, of the memorable site.

*"I took a Walk into the Potters Field, a burying Ground between the new stone Prison, and the Hospital, and I never in my whole Life was affected with so much Melancholy,"* he lamented of the trenches' stench in Philadelphia's center square. *"The Graves of the soldiers, who have been buried, in this Ground, are enough to make the Heart of stone to melt away."*

Stones mark the place Adams walked that day. But they do not herald Adams, they cry out for those unknown soldiers. Today, this memorial is known as Washington Square. A plaque marks the tomb of the Unknown Soldier of the American Revolution: "Beneath this stone rests a soldier of Washington's army who died to give you liberty."

Such markers of brotherhood transcend generations. While leaving Iraq for Kuwait in December 2006 with a FOX News crew aboard a U.S. Marine C-130 aircraft, Lt. Col. Oliver North had an Adams-like moment.

"Today's flight, call sign 'Midas 10,' is designated as an 'Angel Flight.' It carries the flag-draped metal coffin containing the body of a young Marine captain, killed yesterday by enemy fire . . . Everyone is painfully aware that back home, an American family is going to grieve for Christmas," North wrote of the somber flight.

After describing some of his observations over Iraq, North concluded with their arrival in Kuwait. "The sun was setting as six camouflage-clad pall bearers reverently carried the flag-draped coffin down the ramp of the C-130. At the command of the pilot who had flown the 'Angel Flight,' an honor guard of soldiers, sailors, airmen, Guardsmen and Marines drawn up in two ranks on either side of the ramp saluted the fallen Marine captain," North reported.

"Where did this detail come from?" North asked a staff sergeant.

The soldiers had come from all over the base. "We do it for every Angel Flight. The same thing will happen when he arrives in the states— even if it's Christmas. He's our brother," the sergeant replied.

" 'He's our brother.' What an eloquent statement about those who have fallen in this war. No press; no cameras—just a simple, moving ceremony honoring one of America's fallen heroes. As Americans celebrate the birth of the son of God this week, they should pause to thank Him for giving us men and women willing to make such sacrifices. They are America's greatest Christmas gift," concluded North.

And whether it's John Adams walking past a mass grave in 1777 or Oliver North watching soldiers salute the fallen in 2006, the inscription of the Revolution's unknown soldier memorial applies: "Freedom is a light for which many men have died in darkness."[203]

> "Over her tomb Jacob set up a pillar, and to this day that pillar marks Rachel's tomb" (GENESIS 35:20).

**PRAYER**

*Father, thank you for the men and women, the unknown heroes, who have been willing to make such sacrifices for my freedom.*

# 204. Sabbath Rest: Dignity Applied

In one of Nathanael Emmons's greatest sermons, he outlined the dignity of man. He began by showing how God distinguished men and women among all his creation by giving them a soul.

Then he explained the heart of his message. As a result of being created in God's image, humans were free to pursue knowledge, holiness, and happiness. They also had the capacity to act and do great things.

Then, after identifying and explaining humanity's dignity, this Massachusetts preacher provided an application. Humanity had a responsibility to respond to the dignity bestowed on them by God. Service through worship was the best place to begin. *"Our minds are so framed, that we are capable of knowing, of loving, and of serving our Creator; and this lays us under moral obligation to worship and obey him,"* Emmons told the worshippers.

Humanity was free to respond to God, whether they lived during war or peace. Emmons believed that embracing faith and its tenets, such as worshipping God, was the highest response humanity could give the dignified role God had given them. *"Happy is the man who findeth religion: For the merchandise of it is better than the merchandise of silver, and the gain thereof than fine gold. She is more precious than rubies. . . . Let us all then put on this rich and beautiful ornament, and shew ourselves men,"* he said, paraphrasing his primary text, 1 Kings 2:2, along with Proverbs 3:14, 15.

Emmons also believed that another response was to pursue knowledge and explore God's gift of rationality. *"What has been said concerning the nature and dignity of man, shows us, that we are under indispensable obligations to cultivate and improve our minds in all the branches of human knowledge,"* he said, encouraging his congregation to study all sorts of topics, such as nature, and to read all sorts of books with sound judgment and prayer.

*"Liberty, which is the birth-right of man, and congenial with his nature, ennobles and exalts the mind,"* he said. *"For, in free republics, where liberty is equally enjoyed, every man has weight and influence in proportion to his abilities, and a fair opportunity of rising, by the dint of*

merit, to the first offices and honours of the state."

To Nathanael Emmons, pursuing knowledge was a freedom resulting from God's twin gifts of independence and dignity. *"In this respect, how wonderful the smiles of Providence upon you! Whose heart doth not glow with gratitude for the auspicious occasion which hath now brought us together!"* he exulted.[204]

> "How much better to get wisdom than gold, to choose understanding rather than silver!"
> (PROVERBS 16:16).

**PRAYER**

*Your wisdom, your knowledge, is so much more valuable than an earthly treasure chest of a million gold and silver coins! Thank you for the gift of faith.*

# 205. Marching into the Unknown

The military march brought the baroness more despondency than she had felt since arriving in America. Far from a parade of pomp, the British and Hessians began a stuttered procession into the unknown on October 9, 1777.

*"WE were halted at six o'clock in the morning to our general amazement. General Burgoyne ordered the artillery to be drawn up in a line, and to have it counted. This gave much dissatisfaction, as a few marches more would have ensured our safety,"* Baroness von Riedesel wrote hopelessly.

While her husband served as a Hessian commander under Burgoyne, the baroness's job was to care for their young children. Although she was far from the comforts of a German castle, she smiled at their family togetherness. But Burgoyne's decision to halt the retreat confused her. *"On the 9th, it rained terribly the whole day; nevertheless we kept ourselves ready to march,"* she said, noting their Iroquois co-fighters had lost their courage and fled. *"My chamber-maid exclaimed the whole day against her fate, and seemed mad with despair."*

The baroness thought Burgoyne had lost his mind when she learned he had stopped the march to count his men to surrender. *"We reached Saratoga about dark, which was but half an hour's march from the place where we had spent the day. I was quite wet, and was obliged to remain in that condition, for want of a place to change my apparel. I seated myself near the fire, and undressed the children, and we then laid ourselves upon some straw,"* she described.

*"I asked General Phillips, who came to see how I was, why we did not continue our retreat, my husband having pledged himself to cover the movement, and to bring off the army in safety,"* recorded the baroness.

*"'My poor lady,' General Phillips replied. '[Y]ou astonish me. Though quite wet, you have so much courage as to wish to go farther in this weather. What a pity it is that you are not our commanding general! He complains of fatigue, and has determined upon spending the night here, and giving us a supper,"* the baroness quoted, adding that Burgoyne spent half his nights singing and drinking.

But the baroness was not singing on this retreat into the unknown. John Burgoyne had refused to accept Horatio Gates's demand for an unconditional surrender. Their failure to come to terms resulted in a stop-start retreat by the British on October 9th. As the baroness awoke the next morning, she expected the lines to continue marching. But as sometimes happens in life, the next day brought an unexpected turn of events. Baroness von Riedesel and the British continued their journey into the unknown.[205]

> "They charge like warriors; they scale walls like soldiers. They all march in line, not swerving from their course"
> (JOEL 2:7).

**PRAYER**

*Lord, the next time I find myself in a stop-start march into the unknown, remind me that you have promised to be with me wherever I may go.*

# 206. Thirsty for Surrender

The Baroness von Riedesel woke up the morning of October 10, 1777, only to realize her nightmare was true. Even though she had spent the entire previous day in the rain, she was parched. And her desire to reach safety with her children and her husband, General von Riedesel, became more elusive as the day progressed. Musket and cannon fire began again that afternoon. The reason? General Burgoyne and General Gates could not agree on surrender terms.

*"My husband sent me word that I should immediately retire into a house which was not far off,"* she wrote, explaining that she and her children got into her carriage and rode to the house. *"I saw, on the opposite bank of the Hudson, five or six men, who aimed at us with their guns. Without knowing what I did, I threw my children into the back part of the vehicle, and laid myself upon them. At the same moment the fellow fired, and broke the arm of a poor English soldier,"* her tale continued.

No sooner had she rushed her children into the house than the Americans began firing on it. The baroness concluded the other side thought a general was with them. *"[W]hile, in reality, none were there except women and crippled soldiers. We were at last obliged to descend into the cellar, where I laid myself in a corner near the door. My children put their heads upon my knees. An abominable smell, the cries of the children, and my own anguish of mind, did not permit me to close my eyes, during the whole night,"* she complained.

The next morning found her counting chaos. Eleven cannonballs passed through the house. *"A poor soldier, who was about to have a leg amputated, lost the other by one of these balls . . . I was myself in the deepest distress, not so much on account of my own dangers, as of those to which my husband was exposed,"* she wrote.

But as thirsty as she was for safety, the need for nourishment overtook her and those with her. *"The want of water continuing to distress us, we could not but be extremely glad to find a soldier's wife so spirited as to fetch some from the river, an occupation from which the boldest might have shrunk, as the Americans shot every one who approached it. They told us afterwards that they spared her on account of her sex,"* the baroness added.

Although she thought she needed food and safety, what Baroness von Riedesel, and the British army, really needed was surrender. It was time for John Burgoyne to yield to life's circumstances and surrender.[206]

> "I spread out my hands to you; my soul thirsts for you like a parched land"
> (PSALM 143:6).

**PRAYER**

*Many things in life make me thirsty, Lord. Use these moments to lead me to you and may I drink from your fountain and taste your springs of joy.*

# 207. Capitulation

"*The troops surrendered themselves prisoners of war and laid down their arms,"* the Baroness von Riedesel wrote about General Burgoyne's capitulation to General Gates on October 17, 1777. Although the war was not over, surrender brought an unexpected peace, which continued throughout her surprisingly lengthy stay in North America.

After receiving a note from her husband, the baroness and the others in the cannon-worn house paid the woman who had risked her life to bring them water. The baroness then put their children in a carriage and became a prisoner of war.

She learned Gates and Burgoyne had agreed to a *"treaty of convention."* Under these terms, Burgoyne agreed to be a captive along with his flock of five thousand. The prisoners were to return to England and never come back to America as fighters.

*"[I] was gratified to observe that no body looked at us with disrespect, but, on the contrary, greeted us, and seemed touched at the sight of a captive mother with three children,"* the baroness wrote of her ride into the American camp.

When she approached some tents, a handsome man came toward her. He offered her his arm, helped her children from the carriage, and escorted them to a tent. *"You tremble,"* American General Schuyler said tearfully. *"[D]o not be alarmed, I pray you."*

*"Sir,"* she cried, *"a countenance so expressive of benevolence, and the kindness which you have evinced towards my children, are sufficient to dispel all apprehension."*

General Schuyler also made her a kind offer. *"You may find it embarrassing to be the only lady in such a large company of gentlemen; will you come with your children to my tent, and partake of a frugal dinner, offered with the best will?"* he asked. She agreed.

*"He regaled me with smoked tongues, which were excellent, with beefsteaks, potatoes, fresh butter, and bread. Never did a dinner give me so much pleasure as this. I was easy, after many months of anxiety, and I read the same happy change in the countenances of those around me,"* she remembered.

After such turmoil the baroness found rest in capitulation's arms. Although the Continental Congress rejected the terms, the baroness and other prisoners continued to find peace through unexpected hospitality. They became known as the Convention army and traveled throughout New England, Virginia, and Philadelphia until the war's end. The Baroness von Riedesel wrote of the hospitality and many kindnesses she experienced during her travels. Although the war was not over, with each drink of wine and crust of bread she tasted in America, she found peace.[207]

> "You have filled my heart with greater joy than when their grain and new wine abound. I will lie down and sleep in peace, for you alone, O LORD, make me dwell in safety" (PSALM 4:7, 8).

**PRAYER**

*You alone are safety. You alone are peace. You alone fill my heart with joy and my mouth with sustenance.*

# 208. **Rules of Engagement**

The rules of engagement in the 1700s were as closely linked to a code of honor as a book is to its spine. That code affected the outcomes of Brandywine and Saratoga, and the ultimate fate of America.

Because General Burgoyne had allied his army with the Iroquois, the Americans believed they were justified in using Indian techniques at Saratoga. Hence, Colonel Morgan and his sharpshooters hid behind trees and fired their rifles at the British. Whereas cannons spread smoke and balls on the field like wind scatters leaves, rifles gave soldiers the precision of a hawk.

During the battle one of Morgan's men spotted an officer within range of his rifle. He faced a critical decision. Should he shoot or not? Pinpointing an officer was like ripping the cover off the honor codebook. It was not a gentlemanly act, but neither was scalping an innocent woman, an atrocity the Iroquois had recently committed. The American shot the officer. British General Frazer's death became the turning point in Saratoga's last battle. *"The whole [British] line gave way, abandoning their cannon, and with the greatest effort regained their camp,"* wrote historian William Jackman.

A month earlier, a similar question had presented itself at Brandywine. But this time, the situation was reversed. Captain Ferguson, a British officer, had developed a lighter weight rifle with a longer range. In the midst of the Battle of Brandywine, Ferguson saw an American general within range of his deadly accurate weapon. He hesitated. Should he shoot or not? Ferguson's hand revealed the heart of a gentleman soldier. He held his trigger and didn't shoot.

*"The American Revolution occurs during what some historians term the age of limited warfare. These professional military officers, who deem themselves professionals, did not think it was gentlemanly or honorable to intentionally lay low an enemy officer,"* West Point historian John Hall explained.

Both sides made on-the-spot decisions about whether or not to adhere to the code of honor in 1777. Both decisions profoundly affected the war. The death of General Frazer was the turning point of Saratoga and led to the first significant American victory that year.

Had Britain's Captain Ferguson shot the American officer at Brandywine, the war might have turned out very differently. Many historians

> "Give everyone what you owe him: If you owe taxes, pay taxes; if revenue, then revenue; if respect, then respect; if honor, then honor"
> (ROMANS 13:7).

believe that the officer within Captain Ferguson's range was General Washington. Once again, Providence's hand protected George Washington. Respect for respect and honor for honor ruled the day.[208]

**PRAYER**

*God, may I follow your code by showing those around me both respect and honor.*

# 209.  A Discerning Ear

Saratoga may have given Americans a victory, but Brandywine handed Philadelphia to General Howe, who turned a house on Second Street into his headquarters.

Howe soon learned Washington's army was camped fourteen miles away at White Marsh. Although winter was approaching, this scavenger was not quite ready to rest in his nest. With the instincts of a vulture, Howe planned a surprise strike on Washington's weary army.

Under Howe's orders, a British officer walked across Second Street to the home of the Darrahs, known Quakers, on December 2, 1776. When Lydia Darrah answered the door, the officer asked if he could use her house that evening. Seeing no alternative, Lydia submitted. The British likely trusted the Darrahs because their Quaker religion *"forbade them to practice the arts of war."* The *American Quarterly Review* published Lydia's account years later.

*"'And be sure, Lydia,' the officer concluded, 'that your family are all in bed at an early hour. I shall expect you to attend to this request. When our guests are ready to leave the house, I will myself give you notice, that you may let us out,'"* the *Review* reported.

Lydia felt an unexplained uneasiness when she escorted British officers to a parlor in her house that night. Like prey in the claws of a predator, she obeyed the officer's order by closing the door, and retiring to her chamber down the hall. But she found it impossible to sleep.

*"She became more and more uneasy, till her nervous restlessness amounted to absolute terror. Unable longer to resist the impulse—not of curiosity, but surely of a far higher feeling—she slid from the bed, and taking off her shoes, passed noiselessly from her chamber and along the entry."*

Emboldened with unexplained courage and discretion, Lydia approached the meeting room, put her ear up to the keyhole, and listened. *"A voice was heard reading a paper aloud. It was an order for the troops to quit the city on the night of the fourth, and march out to a secret attack upon the American army, then encamped at White Marsh."*

She couldn't have been more shocked had lightning struck her. Lydia crept back to her room and threw herself on her bed. Thousands of thoughts pulsed through her mind as she contemplated what she had heard. A few minutes later, the British officer knocked on her chamber door.

*"She knew well what the signal meant, but took no heed. It was repeated, and more loudly; still she gave no answer. Again, and yet more loudly, the knocks were repeated; and then she rose quickly, and opened the door,"* the article recounted.

The officer ordered Lydia Darrah to escort them out of her house. After locking the door, the only sound this discreet Quaker could hear was the beating of her own heart.[209]

> "Discretion will protect you, and understanding will guard you" (PROVERBS 2:11).

**PRAYER**

*Lord, allow discretion to guide me today, to guard my heart and my tongue.*

# 210. The Revolution Today: Columbia

The victory of Saratoga was so sweet to one Continental chaplain that he composed a song. Perhaps also inspired by Thomas Paine's call to create a new world, the Reverend Timothy Dwight saw visions of grandeur for the empire he and the other patriots hoped to establish. The name of Dwight's world was not America, however. It was "Columbia."

*"COLUMBIA, Columbia, to glory arise, The queen of the world, and the child of the skies!"* his song began.

"Columbia" derives its name from the Italian explorer Christopher Columbus. Pre-Columbian means "pre-Christopher Columbus." Before the Revolution, the colonists had given English explorers more credit than others for exploring the New World. But with the Revolution came a change in perception. Christopher Columbus grew more popular with the colonists for his 1492 ocean-blue voyage. As a result "Columbia" meant "new world." To Dwight, this new nation emerging from battles such as Saratoga would rise and rival the old world of Europe.

*"A world is thy realm: for a world be thy laws, Enlarged as thine empire, and just as thy cause; On freedom's broad basis, that empire shall rise,"* dreamed Dwight in his song.

Like many patriots, Dwight also hoped to create a world of learning. This future president of Yale included this line: *"Fair Science her gates to thy sons shall unbar."* But as the grandson of Jonathan Edwards, one of the leaders of the Great Awakening, Dwight also saw "Columbia" as the song of angels. *"Perfumes, as of Eden, flow'd sweetly along, and a voice, as of angels, enchantingly sung."*

*Columbia*'s word cousin, *Columba*, means "dove" or "peace." It is a Roman name that comes from a saint who converted much of Scotland to Christianity. To Dwight, "Columbia" would likewise be a place for the hopeless and the helpless, the immigrant and the rejected. *"To thee, the last refuge of virtue designed, Shall fly from all nations the best of mankind,"* he wrote.

As a result of such poems and other usages of the word, many patriots wanted to name their new country "Columbia" instead of the United States of America, which they thought was too long and not nearly as poetic.

Columbia did not die. Although the United States of America became the national name and a South American country (Colombia) took the title in Spanish, the Revolution's Columbia lives on in the United States. Millions of Americans in nearly thirty states live in a county or city bearing the name Columbia. Columbia is also a large river running through Canada, Washington, and Oregon. NASA chose Columbia as the name for one of its space shuttles. It is the name of a major university. The song "Hail, Columbia" is the vice president's anthem. And, of course, the District of Columbia is our nation's capital.

*Columbia* may be an outdated name for the United States, but its meaning hasn't changed. It is still a reminder of the unity that emerged from the new world created by revolutionaries.[210]

> "Undoubtedly there are all sorts of languages in the world, yet none of them is without meaning" (1 CORINTHIANS 14:10).

**PRAYER**

*Thank you for the blessing that the meaning of words can bring.*

# 211. Sabbath Rest: Wesley's Wheels within Wheels

Not long after General Burgoyne's troops circled their wagons in surrender to General Gates, John Wesley preached on the workings of wheels. He chose this mysterious passage as his text: *"Their appearance and their work was as it were a wheel in the middle of a wheel"* (Ezekiel 1:16 KJV).

Although Wesley, the great Methodist, supported his homeland and opposed America's war for independence, he saw God's hand moving with the steadiness of the cogs of a wheel in North America. The purpose of his sermon was to first *"trace each wheel"* and then analyze how the wheels related to each other.

*"It is by no means my design to give a particular detail of the late transactions in America; but barely to give a simple and naked deduction of a few well-known facts,"* he began, pointing out that he knew the subject of the war was delicate.

Wesley explained how the Great Awakening had swept from Georgia to New England and back again in the 1730s and 1740s. *"Many sinners were deeply convinced of sin, and many truly converted to God. I suppose there had been no instance in America of so swift and deep a work of grace, for an hundred years before; nay, nor perhaps since the English settled there,"* he said.

But Wesley believed that as America grew wealthier through trade, they traded this spirit of humility for a spirit of pride. *"Riches poured in upon them as a flood, and treasures were heaped up as the sand of the sea . . . The more riches they acquired, the more they were regarded by their neighbours as men of weight and importance,"* he said.

Wesley connected these wheels of wealth to the wheels of independence. He showed how the Continental Congress's decision to boycott British trade sent Americans into poverty. And he was right. By this point in the war, America's wheels of wealth had run off the road and into the ocean. In Wesley's mind, independence may have been the result of pride but it was also America's salvation, a path to return to God.

"*Who would have imagined that this evil disease would lay a foundation for the cure of all the rest?*" he asked. "*But liberty, real, legal liberty; which is an unspeakable blessing. He will superadd to Christian liberty, liberty from sin, true civil liberty; a liberty from oppression of every kind; from illegal violence; a liberty to enjoy their lives, their persons, and their property; in a word, a liberty to be governed in all things by the laws of their country.*"

John Wesley may have opposed America's war, but he believed it would result in "*the glorious liberty of the children of God!*" And indeed, the coming winter would bring many, including a doctor at Valley Forge, to their knees to contemplate true liberty.[211]

> "Each appeared to be made like a wheel intersecting a wheel" (EZEKIEL 1:16).

**PRAYER**

*Thank you for uncovering the mysteries of wheels in the middle of wheels, for the times in life when you make all the pieces of a puzzle into a sensible picture.*

# 212. The Warning

Sleep completely eluded Lydia Darrah that night. She was shocked at the conversation she had overheard among the British officers, who demanded to use her home and ordered her to leave them alone while they met. But Darrah had daringly eavesdropped on their closed-door meeting. What she learned terrified her. The British planned to march from Philadelphia and attack General Washington's army at White Marsh. No matter what this Quaker's religious beliefs about war, her country was in danger.

"*Should she awaken her husband and inform him? That would be to place him in special jeopardy . . . No, come what might, she would encounter the risk alone. After a petition for heavenly guidance, her resolution was formed,*" the American Quarterly Review stated.

The next morning Lydia told her husband she needed to obtain flour from a nearby mill. She acquired a pass to cross British lines, dropped her sack at the flour mill, and walked in the snow "*with all haste towards the outposts of the American army. Her determination was to apprise Washington of the danger.*"

On her way she saw Lieutenant Colonel Craig, an acquaintance. "*To him she disclosed the secret, after having obtained from him a solemn promise not to betray her individually, since the British might take vengeance on her and her family,"* the article explained.

Lydia retrieved her sack, filled it with flour, and returned home. The next day a knocking on her door drained all color from her face. She mustered her composure and once again welcomed the British officer into her home. *"With a pale cheek, but composed, for she placed her trust in a higher Power, Lydia obeyed the summons . . . 'Were any of your family up, Lydia, on the night when I received company in this house?'*

*"'No,' was the unhesitating reply. 'They all retired at eight o'clock.'*

*"'It is very strange,' the officer said, then mused a few minutes. 'You, I know, Lydia, were asleep; for I knocked at your door three times before you heard me—yet it is certain that we were betrayed. I am altogether at a loss to conceive who could have given the information of our intended attack to General Washington! On arriving near his encampment we found his cannon mounted, his troops under arms, and so prepared at every point to receive us, that we have been compelled to march back without injuring our enemy, like a parcel of fools.'"*

> "Like a gold ring in a pig's snout is a beautiful woman who shows no discretion"
> (PROVERBS 11:22).

The man left and a relieved Lydia closed the door behind him.

*"But the pious Quakeress blessed God for her preservation, and rejoiced that it was not necessary for her to utter an untruth in her own defence,"* the article concluded.

Lydia Darrah's daring and discretion kept Washington's army out of the vulture's beak. Once again God preserved the army. This time it was through a quiet Quaker pacifist.[212]

**PRAYER**

*Thank you for using discretion in a mighty way during the Revolution. Show me when I need to hold my tongue and when I need to speak.*

# 213. Stuck in the Marsh

Evidence from General Washington himself lends credibility to Lydia Darrah's story. According to Darrah's account, the British planned their sneak attack for December 4, 1777. That same day, Washington issued this order from his White Marsh headquarters:

*"The troops are constantly to have one day's provisions on hand, ready cooked. The officers are to pay particular attention to this, and consider it*

*as a standing rule, that if they are suddenly called to arms the men may not be distressed,"* the commander-in-chief wrote.

Washington clearly wanted his army to be able to fight or retreat at a moment's notice. By this time he also had concluded that White Marsh was not the best place to rebuild his army. A marsh was about as secure for an army as a rabbit trap was for a rabbit. Washington wanted something more strategic for his winter camp. He needed a place where his men could build shelter and find food. He sought a location with natural barriers. Washington was tired of being stuck in the marsh. Within days of Lydia Darrah's daring, the commander-in-chief began making plans to get out of the marsh. It was a process of pulling up his tent pegs and gathering his markers.

Washington first ordered his men to halt further investment in their camp.

*"[T]he General earnestly recommends that no more tents be pitched than are absolutely necessary to shelter the troops. Neither officers nor men are to be absent from camp upon any pretence whatever,"* Washington ordered on December 9th. He needed everyone to return to White Marsh.

The next step was to count heads. He wanted them to stop gathering stones, as Ecclesiastes puts it. He had to know how many men were stuck in the marsh. *"Each officer commanding [a] brigade is to make a return to morrow at orderly time of their killed, wounded and missing since General Howe's late march from Philadelphia, and if any during that time, lost to a sense of duty, have infamously deserted, their names are to be added to the same returns,"* the commander directed.

Washington also chose to gather the wounded and disabled. *"Brigade returns are to be made . . . of all the sick in camp, and in private houses, about the country, and of the number of wagons necessary to transport them to the hospitals,"* Washington ordered.

Because wagons were scarce, he asked that everyone who was able to march do so. He knew *"some of the sick will be left in camp."*

George Washington knew it was time to move on. He had gathered his stones, the markers of his camp. As sometimes happens in life, it was time to move out of the marsh and into the valley.[213]

> "There is a time for everything, and a season for every activity under heaven: . . . a time to scatter stones and a time to gather them" (ECCLESIASTES 3:1, 5).

**PRAYER**

*Father, I pray for discernment to know how to spend my time today and this week. Show me where I need to invest and where I need to let go.*

# 214. Giving Thanks

While General Washington gathered his stones and prepared to march his army to Valley Forge in December 1777, the Continental Congress also counted their markers of success. It was time to call on the patriots to give thanks for the blessings of 1777 and pray for *"the greatest of all human Blessings, INDEPENDENCE and PEACE."*

*"It is therefore recommended by congress, that Thursday the 18th. day of December next be set apart for Solemn Thanksgiving and Praise,"* the Continental Congress wrote in a Thanksgiving declaration. They believed it was *"the indispensable duty of all men, to adore the superintending providence of Almighty God."*

As the year drew to a close, Congress decided it was time to thank God, confess sins, and implore him for his further blessings. *"And it having pleased him in his abundant mercy, not only to continue to us the innumerable bounties of his common providence, but also, to smile upon us in the prosecution of a just and necessary war, for the defence of our unalienable rights and liberties,"* the proclamation reminded the citizens.

Congress sent their declaration through General Washington to the army. Washington included the announcement in his general orders. Congress's proclamation overflowed with a cornucopia of requests. It called on the patriots to give thanks for their harvest of victories while asking them to submit their hearts to God.

*"[T]hat at one time, and with one voice, the good people may express the grateful feelings of their hearts, and consecrate themselves to the service of their divine benefactor,"* the proclamation heralded.

*"And that, together with their sincere acknowledgements and offerings they may join the penitent confession of their manifold Sins, whereby they had forfeited every Favor; and their humble & earnest Supplication that it may please God through the Merits of Jesus Christ mercifully to forgive and blot them out of Remembrance,"* the resolution encouraged.

Congress also asked for guidance for America's sea captains, prosperity for traders, blessing on farmers, and wisdom for educators.

Saratoga likely topped their list of blessings. Brandywine, however, revealed this was an incremental war. It was not a neat chain of victories with each link leading directly to success. The Revolution was a tug-of-war, a pushing-and-pulling, progress and regression. To the patriots, victory sometimes seemed as unreachable as the clouds. This was not the quick and easy victory they had hoped for in 1775. This war was a slog.

Resolutions of thanks such as this one reminded the patriots to count their blessings and to pray for the ability to live another day in their efforts to secure liberty from the English lion's lair.[214]

**PRAYER**

*Dear Lord, thank you for the blessings you have given me. Thank you for the times of peace, the times for enjoying food and reflecting on your goodness.*

> "There is a time for everything, and a season for every activity under heaven: . . . a time to love and a time to hate, a time for war and a time for peace" (ECCLESIASTES 3:1, 8).

# 215. Marching from the Marsh to the Valley

Dr. Albigence Waldo was a surgeon in George Washington's army. He was one of the medics who complied with the general's order to gather the sick, march out of the marsh, and advance into the valley.

"*We are order'd to march over the River—It snows—I'm Sick—eat nothing—No Whiskey—No Baggage—Lord Lord—Lord. The Army were 'till Sun Rise crossing the River—some at the Waggon Bridge, & some at the Raft Bridge below. Cold & Uncomfortable,*" he wrote in his journal on December 12th.

"*Dec. 13th.— The Army march'd three miles from the West side the River and encamp'd near a place call'd the Gulph and not an improper name neither—For this Gulph seems well adapted by its situation to keep us from the pleasure & enjoyments of this World, or being conversant with any body in it,*" he recalled of his first impressions.

Valley Forge was a remote place. Waldo thought it was better suited to a retreat for philosophers than a camp for soldiers. He knew Washington had not brought them there to turn them into Epicureans. After a little thinking, Doctor Waldo decided to evaluate the place's merits.

"*No—it is, upon consideration, for many good purposes since we are to Winter here—1st There is plenty of Wood & Water. 2dly There are but few families for the soldiery to Steal from—tho' far be it from a Soldier to Steal,*" he wrote.

Valley Forge's velvety forests provided forage. The area's topography was more solid than the marsh, making it a better place to build shelters. "*4ly There are warm sides of Hills to erect huts on,*" Doctor Waldo wrote.

He also thought the place's isolation would turn some soldiers into saints. *"5ly They will be heavenly Minded like Jonah when in the belly of a great Fish,"* he wrote.

But Doctor Waldo also recognized the benefits of the valley's quietness. Twenty-three miles from Philadelphia, Valley Forge was an ideal place to watch the British movements. Its creeks and rivers provided the army with natural fortifications. He concluded that life in the valley might provide some inspiration.

*"6ly. They will not become home Sick as is sometimes the Case when Men live in the Open World—since the reflections which must naturally arise from their present habitation, will lead them to the more noble thoughts of employing their leizure hours in filling their knapsacks with such materials as may be necessary on the Journey to another Home,"* Albigence Waldo continued.

> "There is a time for everything, and a season for every activity under heaven: . . . a time to tear and a time to mend, a time to be silent and a time to speak" (ECCLESIASTES 3:1, 7).

More importantly Valley Forge's remoteness might just turn the army into a fighting force. And that was what George Washington had in mind when he selected Valley Forge.[215]

**PRAYER**

*God, I take a moment to quietly reflect before you and to count my blessings no matter where my life may be today.*

# 216. Building a City on Firecake

What was for dinner at Valley Forge? Smoked firecake.

Dr. Albigence Waldo probably wasn't sure which was more deplorable: firecake or campfire smoke. The soldiers had to build their own huts and roads at Valley Forge. As a result, the only way to keep warm in the camp's early days was to continually burn campfires. Waldo's skin was so sore from the smoke that he feared his eyes were *"spoiled."*

And while they labored on their huts, the men relied on firecake for sustenance. But this manna was far from heaven to Waldo. *"A general cry through the camp this evening among the soldiers—'No Meat!—No Meat!'—the distant vales echoed back the melancholy sound . . . What have you for our dinners, boys? 'Nothing but fire cake and water, Sir,' At night—'Gentle men, the supper is ready.' What is your supper, Lads? 'Fire cake and water, Sir,'"* Waldo wrote.

Firecake was a tasteless pancake, a mixture of a little flour and water cooked over a fire. Waldo preferred quail but he knew any kind of meat was as precious a commodity as money.

*"Our Division is under marching orders this morning. I am ashamed to say it, but I am tempted to steal fowls if I could find them—or even a whole hog—for I feel as if I could eat one. But the impoverished country about us, affords but little matter to employ a thief—or keep a clever fellow in good humor,"* Waldo wrote.

Even though he complained for the thousandth time about firecake and water, this doctor cheered himself with a common antidote. *"But why do I talk of hunger and hard usage, when so many in the world have not even firecake and water to eat,"* he wrote, counting his blessings as best he could.

*"Huts go on slowly—cold and smoke make us fret . . . But man kind are always fretting, even if they have more than their proportion of the blessings of life. We are never easy—always repining at the Providence of an All wise and Benevolent Being—blaming our country—or faulting our friends,"* he wrote, knowing that somewhere, somebody else lived under worse conditions.

Waldo spent Christmas in an uncompleted shelter and mourned the *"sweet felicities"* he had left at home. But he learned to survive by way of distractions. A friend taught him to darn socks. Another taught him how to lay bricks for a chimney. The doctor also treated the sick. The New Year brought him hope.

> "It is man's fuel for burning; some of it he takes and warms himself, he kindles a fire and bakes bread" (ISAIAH 44:15).

*"1778. January 1st.—New Year. I am alive. I am well. Huts go on briskly and our camp begins to appear like a spacious city,"* he wrote.

Valley Forge eventually reached one-third the size of Philadelphia. Through firecake and excessive cold, Albigence Waldo and the army built Washington a city.[216]

**PRAYER**

*God, thank you for providing the necessities in my life. Thank you that I am alive and have food to eat.*

# 217. The Revolution Today: Medics

Although most of Dr. Albigence Waldo's journal chronicles the hardships of soldiering at Valley Forge, Waldo's top job was doctoring. Duty called him to the worst scenes.

*"I was call'd to relieve a Soldier tho't to be dying—he expir'd before I reach'd the Hutt. He was an Indian—an excellent Soldier—and an obedient good natur'd fellow,"* Waldo wrote of his medical mission on January 4, 1778.

U.S. Army Sgt. Eric Hayes followed in the footsteps of Waldo and others when he embarked on a humanitarian mission to Kenya. "During my tour as a civil affairs specialist on a civic action team for Combined Joint Task Force—Horn of Africa, I worked on several Medical and Veterinary Civic Action Programs, better known as MEDCAPS and VET-CAPS," Hayes began his commentary.

And like Waldo, he couldn't help but notice the challenging landscape. "I shared the excitement of being a wandering explorer with a driving focus to accomplish a specific task. The brightly-colored kikois (rectangle-shaped wrap cloths) and collared shirts contrasted with a landscape alien to me. The smell of roasted curried goat, unfamiliar to me, permeated the air," he noted, explaining that their plan was to help as many people as possible.

"The first barriers for us to cross were language and culture. It was difficult at first, but by learning a few words and using an interpreter, we were able to build a relationship unlike any I've experienced before. This was the connection between two cultures that makes civil affairs successful and awe-inspiring."

Respect for family was one of the qualities that stood out among the Kenyans. "When people were too sick to travel to the MEDCAP, they would often send their children in their place, walking barefoot for miles on wild dirt paths hoping to pick up some medicine to treat their family members," Hayes recounted.

"One of the greatest challenges we faced during the MEDCAP was getting medical treatment to the most people in an effective manner. When villagers heard that a MEDCAP was taking place nearby, they showed up expecting some form of treatment for their ailments," detailed Hayes.

These expectations sparked the medics to work as tirelessly as possible. In some ways, they were building Valley Forge–like huts of protection for the Kenyans. The treatments they provided built walls of support against disease and served a longer-term national security interest for the United States by building stronger bonds with African nations. These medics would never witness the long-term payoff, but the short term brought indescribable satisfaction.

"However, through the long hours of toil, the rewards were priceless. Watching complete strangers leave your sight smiling, walking down a dusty path with an arm full of medicine and vitamins, sure that the treatments would make their families healthier and happier, made our efforts worthwhile," Sgt. Eric Hayes reported proudly.[217]

**PRAYER**

*Give me a heart to serve those in the greatest need. I know that when I serve others, I also serve you.*

> "He who is kind to the poor lends to the LORD, and he will reward him for what he has done" (PROVERBS 19:17).

# 218. Sabbath Rest: War Weary

When Phillips Payson gave the 1778 annual election sermon in Boston, he knew his audience of legislators were as weary of war as if they had been fighting for one hundred years. With no end to the conflict in sight, Payson stepped up to the pulpit with the dual messages of hope and perseverance. He also knew it was an honor to be chosen to preach this annual message to government leaders.

*"It seems as if a little more labor and exertion will bring us to reap the harvest of all our toils; and certainly we must esteem the freedom and independency of these states a most ample reward for all our sufferings,"* exhorted Payson.

Payson shared their suffering not as a pastor but as a compatriot. He had participated in the earliest stages of the war. When the British fled Lexington and Concord in April 1775, Payson led a group that captured eleven soldiers and killed one. He embraced the cause of freedom as his own. Thus, he used Galatians 4:31 (KJV) to remind his listeners they were *"not children of the bondwoman, but of the free."*

*"In this, the greatest of all human causes, numbers of the virtuous Americans have lost their all,"* he reminded the congregation reverently. But he corrected his choice of words, choosing to clarify the sacrifice of those who had fallen: *"I recall my words—they have not lost it; no, but, from the purest principles, have offered it up in sacrifice upon the golden altar of liberty. The sweet perfumes have ascended to heaven, and shall be had in everlasting remembrance,"* he continued.

Payson called upon his audience to use the *"blood of our friends and countrymen, still crying in our ears"* as motivation to keep going and to arouse the fire of their passion.

He decided to paint a motivational vision of what a free America would look like. He hoped by *"anticipating the future glory of America"* they would find courage to keep going. *"In this light we behold our country, beyond the reach of all oppressors, under the great charter of independence, enjoying the purest liberty; beautiful and strong in its union, the envy of tyrants and devils, but the delight of God and all good men,"* preached Payson.

He then turned his message into a patriotic prophesy. Their new country would be *"a refuge to the oppressed; the joy of the earth; each state happy in a wise model of government, and abounding with wise men, patriots, and heroes,"* he predicted.

"But the Jerusalem that is above is free, and she is our mother. . . . Therefore, brothers, we are not children of the slave woman, but of the free woman" (GALATIANS 4:26, 31).

*"Hail, my happy country, saved of the Lord! . . . Hail, happy posterity, that shall reap the peaceful fruits of our sufferings, fatigues, and wars!"* Payson joyfully proclaimed.

And like us today, Phillips Payson knew that one way to overcome difficulties was to focus on the end result: freedom for the oppressed.[218]

**PRAYER**

*Thank you for reminding me to look to your purpose in life for hope when times are hard. And although I may not see all the fruits of my labor, I trust you to reap a harvest in my life and legacy.*

# 219. The Micromanager

Preservation of the army proved to be more than just retreating, finding resources, and building a camp. If the Revolution was to be won, discipline had to reign supreme.

*"We might accuse him of being a micromanager. But in fact this was a situation that needed micromanaging,"* historian Caroline Cox said as she described George Washington's efforts to instill discipline and rebuild his force during the winter of 1778.

Week after week Washington found himself troubleshooting as the mayor of Valley Forge. Problems in camp arose frequently. Washington responded with vigor and a strong hand. He issued order after order to accomplish his goal of preparing his men to face General Howe in the upcoming summer campaign.

*"A strict Compliance with this order is expected from every Officer,"* Washington wrote after forbidding horses in the camp, except those that were necessary for the public good. Too many horses would quickly drain the food supplies. He also ordered the men to save the horns from slaughtered cows for tools and to take *"speedy measures to exchange raw-hides for shoes."* Unvaccinated soldiers were to report immediately to the surgeon's tent for smallpox inoculation.

But amusements were also keeping his men from becoming a united, dependable force. He therefore banned such distractions as *"spirits"* and gambling.

*"The Commander in Chief is informed that gaming is again creeping into the Army,"* Washington noted, promising to make an example of those who engaged in the practice, *"and to avoid discrimination between play and gaming forbids Cards and Dice under any pretence whatsoever."*

Desertion was perhaps the most serious threat. Because his utmost goal was to preserve the army, he couldn't afford to give up the cause of independence because of needless attrition. *"The most pernicious consequences having arisen from suffering persons, women in particular to pass and repass from Philadelphia to camp under Pretence of coming out to visit their Friends in the Army and returning with necessaries to their families, but really with an intent to intice the soldiers to desert,"* Washington dictated, forbidding such visitors.

Washington's management style was not all about "thou shalt not." He knew his men needed a schedule, a daily proactive plan to keep them from distractions, motivate them, and build trust. *"Reveille will beat at day-break; the troop at 8 in the morning; the retreat at sunset and taptoo at nine o'Clock in the evening,"* he ordered, establishing a uniform pattern for answering the drummer's call.

Washington the micromanager was instilling discipline in troops who badly needed boundaries. Discipline was the first step toward rebuilding his fighting force. Failing to enforce discipline was a gamble that George Washington was unwilling to take.[219]

> "Buy the truth and do not sell it; get wisdom, discipline and understanding"
> (PROVERBS 23:23).

**PRAYER**

*May I pursue your wisdom and accept your discipline with openness, knowing life offers many temptations to gamble away what is good and honorable to you.*

# 220. Crime and Punishment

Discipline in General Washington's army was more than just rules about gambling and answering reveille's morning call. Preserving the army and securing liberty forced Washington into the role of judge and jury. Practicality and urgency led him to enact and enforce a code of military justice and martial law. Enforcement was the most effective way to show the army that Washington meant what he said.

"*Lieutt. Grey . . . being guilty of theft and other behavior unbecoming the character of an officer and gentleman,*" Washington's secretary began to write one of what seemed like ten thousand reports of courts-martial that winter.

Grey was found guilty of "*ungentleman, unofficer like behavior in absenting himself from camp without leave; associating with a soldier, robbing and infamously stealing.*" He was discharged and rendered incapable of serving as an officer. It was to "*be esteem'd a crime of the blackest Dye, in an officer or even soldier to associate with him after the execution of this just, though mild punishment.*"

In order to secure the safety of his army, Washington also had to enact martial law among the locals. Several residents violated orders from the Continental Congress and sent cattle and other food to the enemy in Philadelphia. Washington was often the only one in a position to enforce these laws among civilians.

"*William Maddock an Inhabitant of the State of Pennsylvania tried for attempting to drive Cattle in to the Enemy, found guilty of the charge, being a breach of a resolution of Congress,*" Washington's papers recorded of the conviction and fine.

The more serious the crime, the more public was the punishment. Washington's officers chose a portion of the army—those who most needed a reminder—to gather on the grand parade and watch a guilty soldier receive his punishment. Sometimes it was lashings. Sometimes, as in the case of Lieutenant Grey, a sword was broken over his head. Discipline was occasionally a life-or-death matter.

"*A detachment of a Captain and forty men from each brigade are to attend the execution of John Reily on the grand parade at ten o'Clock tomorrow forenoon,*" began a death sentence recorded in Washington's papers. Not only did Reily try to desert, but he also freed two British prisoners of war in the process. Treason had sealed his fate.

Discipline was a serious business. Securing independence depended on discipline as much as it did on muskets and diplomacy. Washington could not afford to let folly lead his army astray. The cause would die if he did. George Washington understood that discipline keeps order and preserves the common good.[220]

**PRAYER**

*God, show me the areas where I need to listen to your guidelines for my life.*

> "Folly is bound up in the heart of a child, but the rod of discipline will drive it far from him"
> (PROVERBS 22:15).

# 221. Quartermaster Spoils

*D**ec. 28th.—Yesterday upwards of fifty Officers in General Green's Division resigned their Commissions . . . All this is occasion'd by Officers Families being so much neglected at home on account of Provisions. Their Wages will not considerable purchase a few trifling Comfortables here in Camp, & maintain their families at home,"* Dr. Albigence Waldo wrote of Greene's predicament and the army's financial conditions in early 1778.

The officers resigned because they could not support their families. Waldo wrote that enlisted men were better off financially than officers. States supplied the soldiers serving from their states. Because officers held more responsibility, the cost of providing for them was greater. As a result, many officers did not receive enough money to take care of their families. The problem was so severe some officers had resorted to begging.

Finances were not the only problem facing Greene or the army that year. The army's stores were as empty as a creek during a drought. A menu of problems contributed to the low food supplies. The quartermaster and the men in his department usually knocked on the doors of local farmers and others to find food for the army. Unfortunately, many people had succumbed to scams by other men who pretended to acquire food on behalf of the army. This deception, combined with soaring inflation, had led to the department's depletion.

*"Many difficulties had grown out of this neglect; the army was irregularly supplied with provisions and forage, while the country people suffered much on account of the demands made upon them for provisions by unauthorized foraging parties,"* historian William Jackman wrote.

Although the problems were numerous, the quartermaster department was primarily starved for leadership. As quartermaster, General Mifflin was disorganized. He lacked both the foresight of squirrels to store acorns for the winter and the craftiness of raccoons to scavenge when necessary.

*"We are still in danger of starving. Hundreds of our horses have already starved to death,"* Maj. Gen. Nathanael Greene wrote to his friend Henry Knox, who was away in Boston visiting his wife. The food shortages and the loss of many of his officers had put Greene in a difficult position.

*"The Committee of Congress have seen all these things with their own eyes. They have been urging me for several days to accept the quartermaster-general's appointment, his Excellency [Washington] also presses it upon me exceedingly,"* Greene wrote to Knox. *"I hate the place [the quartermaster department], but hardly know what to do."*

The lackluster job of quartermaster was as exciting to Greene as returning to the life of a blacksmith. He much preferred a battle command. But he chose an attitude of service over self-centeredness. Nathanael Greene became the quartermaster, and by doing so, this revolutionary showed he was working for the food that does not spoil. [221]

> "Do not work for food that spoils, but for food that endures to eternal life, which the Son of Man will give you. On him God the Father has placed his seal of approval"
> (JOHN 6:27).

**PRAYER**

*Thank you for your provisions, for the necessities in life. May I work for the food that doesn't spoil and taste the sweetness of service.*

# 222. Threats to the Wife

Kidnapping. Espionage. Such were some of the rumored threats against Martha Washington's security throughout the war.

Year after year, as she followed the road of loyalty by joining her husband in his winter camp, Martha heard the whispers of plots to kidnap her or attempts to steal her mail for information. The worst part for Martha was detecting the truth. It was impossible to know if these threats were as real as a snake in the river grass or as imaginary as a ghost in the attic. She relied on her family and friends for information.

*"I am sorry I have Nothing to inform you of, Every Thing being quiet (which is I think the best News) since is reported & sworn to by Two Deserters, that Dunmore is dead of the Flux (I wish it may be true),"* Martha's son Jack wrote to her in August 1776. He had heard that Lord Dunmore was dead.

Dunmore, the royal governor of Virginia, was at the center of kidnapping threats against Martha, which began in 1775. Before the war, the Washingtons and Dunmore had been on such friendly terms that they had shared a meal together. But Washington's decision to lead the Continental Army made him a traitor to Dunmore. Thus, rumors that Dunmore planned to sail up the Potomac, ransack Mount Vernon, and capture Martha spread throughout Virginia.

Washington asked his cousin Lund to manage Mount Vernon in his absence. Although he wrote Lund that he could *"hardly think that Lord Dunmore can act so low, so unmanly a part, as to think of seizing Mrs. Washington by way of revenge upon me,"* Washington couldn't take any chances. When the rumors reached their peak in the summer of 1775, Lund and others urged Martha to flee Mount Vernon. She did, but stayed away only a short time. She wasn't going to let a governor-turned-pirate frighten her. The end of 1776 brought relief from the Dunmore kidnapping rumors. He didn't die as Jack had heard, but instead had escaped to New York.

Martha also knew her correspondence could be used as intelligence if read by the wrong person. She usually limited her letters to known facts or family fare, such as the birth of Jack's children. Sometimes she was a propagandist. In a letter to Mercy Otis Warren, she deftly veiled the miserable conditions faced by the army at Valley Forge in 1778.

*"The General is in camped in what is called the great Valley on the Banks of the Schuykill officers and men are cheifly in Hutts, which they say is tolarable comfortable; the army are as healthy as can well be expected in general—the General's apartment is very small he has had a log cabben built to dine in which has made our quarter much more tolarable than they were first,"* she wrote.

Martha Washington knew that kisses from the enemy could be fatal. But she didn't let them keep her from living her life of loyalty to her family and friends. She simply was cautious.[222]

> "Faithful are the wounds of a friend; but the kisses of an enemy are deceitful." (PROVERBS 27:6 KJV)

**PRAYER**

*Father, may I not let the bad news I hear in the media or other sources trap me in a state of fear. Give me discernment for trusting others.*

# 223. Respect, the Result of Discipline

*He has always acted wisely hitherto. His conduct when closely scrutinized is uncensurable,"* Dr. Albigence Waldo described George Washington in his Valley Forge memoirs.

Washington earned the trust of his men because he demonstrated personal discipline. And with the wisdom of a father, Washington stretched this trust by giving the soldiers a gift they desperately required: drill tactics. As much as they needed the boundaries of discipline, Washington's Valley Forge army, particularly his new recruits, also needed to learn the skills of the military trade. Once again Washington employed the strategy of surprise. He turned to a European for help.

*"UPON my arrival at the army I was . . . received with more marks of distinction than I had expected. General Washington came some miles*

*to meet me and accompanied me to my quarters, where I found an offi-cer and 25 men on guard,"* recorded Gen. Frederick William, Baron von Steuben, as he later reflected on his arrival at Valley Forge.

*"On my remonstrating against this on the ground that I was simply to be regarded as a volunteer, he replied in the most courteous manner that the entire army took pleasure in protecting such volunteers,"* remem-bered von Steuben.

Von Steuben brought with him the hopes and dreams common to most immigrants to America. He wanted a fresh start. Where European armies had rejected him, Washington accepted him. The reason? More than any other goal, Washington wanted to turn his army into a fearless fighting force, ready to take on the British after the winter snow melted. He hoped von Steuben's knowledge of European war tactics would be just the medicine his army needed.

*"In a word, if Prince Ferdinand of Brunswick or the first field-marshal of Europe had arrived in my place he could not have been received with more marks of distinction than I was,"* von Steuben wrote in describing his first review of the army.

Von Steuben started by training a small, select group of men. He taught them how to form tight formations and proper ways to hold and use bayonets. When this unit proved proficient in the new drills, they taught other regiments. This unit-teaching-unit phenomenon multiplied until these techniques became second nature to each man in the army. Von Steuben gave the Continentals new tactical skills while boosting their morale and confidence.

> "Moreover, we have all had human fathers who disci-plined us and we respected them for it. How much more should we submit to the Father of our spirits and live!"
> (HEBREWS 12:9).

*"Baron von Steuben's genius was the ability to distill state-of-the-art European drill tactics to this raw material that was the American soldier,"* West Point historian John Hall concluded.

Because von Steuben earned the army's respect, Congress commissioned him a major general. *"Thank God that up to the present they have been [his talents] received with appreciation; and cheerfully will I die for a nation that has so highly honored me with its confidence,"* Baron von Steuben reflected.[223]

**PRAYER**

*Father, I thank you for those who molded me and disciplined me in the past. May I honor you by showing respect to the authorities you continue to put in my life.*

## 224. The Revolution Today: Discipline, a Compass

Discipline was George Washington's compass throughout the war. As a result of his training at Valley Forge, his forces became *"army strong."* Washington's desire for discipline has become a perpetual inheritance of the U.S. military.

Discipline proved to be the hallmark of the four thousand members of the 172nd Stryker Brigade Combat Team. Following an unexpected extension in 2006, they spent sixteen months in Iraq, one of the military's longest deployments. When it was over, these "Artic Wolves" returned to Fairbanks, Alaska, where they uncased their unit's colors and took time to mourn during a redeployment ceremony. Twenty-six members of the Artic Wolves had been killed and another three hundred and fifty had been injured during the deployment.

"You took on the mission, and you did what great American army units have done throughout our history. You accomplished that mission," Army Secretary Francis J. Harvey said of their service, which took place in the face of growing violence in Iraq. Strength was a result of their discipline.

"You have been strong on the outside, but also strong in mind. You never broke under pressure. You have been strong in spirit, by never accepting defeat. You have been strong in heart by never forgetting those for whom you fight. You have been strong in character by maintaining the highest ethical conduct while fighting the enemy . . . [who has] no moral compass," Harvey continued. "You are truly 'Army Strong.'"

These Artic Wolves had hunted terrorists and insurgents in the desert, patrolling northern and western Iraq and Baghdad's most dangerous places. "You are proven in combat and tested," Col. Michael Shields, the brigade commander, said. He talked about their professionalism, especially during the lowest points. One such moment took place when a unit carried a wounded soldier to a combat hospital only to return to their mission. They maintained "discipline despite the emotional load they were carrying."

The high points were also characterized by discipline. "And those are your high points, when you watch these soldiers perform, watch how they treat people with dignity and respect under some of the most demanding conditions on this planet, up against the most demanding threat that rarely comes out of the shadows . . . It is an incredible, humbling experience to watch them perform."

Then Col. Michael Shields added, "The strength of the wolf is the pack, and the strength of the pack is the wolf. Arctic Wolves."

Discipline is no stranger to the U.S. military, thanks to its Revolutionary War origins. Discipline is a compass in life, providing boundaries and giving direction. Discipline provides protection against laziness, gluttony, infidelity, and other such destroyers. Discipline points to hope. It allows us to unfurl its colors in celebration.[224]

"Discipline your son, for in that there is hope; do not be a willing party to his death"
(PROVERBS 19:18).

**PRAYER**

*Give me a heart for discipline and a willingness to follow it like a compass.*

# 225. Sabbath Rest: Devilish King

Did the devil make George III do it? An anonymous author thought so. He or she published a *"Dialogue between the Devil, and George III, Tyrant of Britain."* The piece featured a fictional conversation between the devil and King George III throughout the war. Although a satire and not a sermon, this dialogue showed the prowling nature of evil. Here is a sample of how the "dialogue" progressed in 1777:

*"Where is Burgoyne? Howe has taken Philadelphia, and is shut up in it. Clinton has, with great loss, taken a small fort and burnt a town up Hudson's river, and run back to New York,"* the devil cursed.

George's reply was blame, blame, blame. *"We are all in tears, but what can I do more; I sent fleets and armies, which all my ministers swore were more than sufficient to lay America prostrate at my feet,"* the king answered.

*"Instead of showing the spirit of a lion, you have the head of a goat and the heart of a sheep; and if you don't pursue your plan until the work is complete, by the ghost of Nero, I hope the English will play Charles with you,"* the devil said, implying that George might die at the hands of his own people as Charles I had more than a century earlier.

The devil then used shame to drive his point home. *"If you fail, what a deform'd mongrel puppy you will appear to all the world; neither generosity and benevolence to gratify your people, nor art and spirit enough to make yourself a tyrant—poor dog! you'll be the scorn of the world,"* he rebuked.

*"I wish I had not begun, but there is no retreat,"* the king replied. *"I'll move every wheel to increase my force by sea and land; I will send commissioners with great promises (which I can easily break when the business is done) and large bribes, and partly by art and partly by force, I may yet succeed."*

*"Do you see what the French are doing?"*

*"Yes, my liege; do help me curse them."*

*"Words are but wind, a million oaths won't sink a French ship, nor will ten thousand curses kill one rebel,"* the devil shot back.

In this pretend story, King George III promised to further the devil's kingdom and called himself a tyrant, something that pleased the devil, of course. *"You have a good heart, George, and I'll make something of you yet,"* the devil *"promised."*

Although this dialogue was the result of an imaginative patriot's mind and pen, its value is more than entertainment. When the lion seeks to devour, it is time to take cover, to be self-controlled and alert.[225]

> "Be self-controlled and alert. Your enemy the devil prowls around like a roaring lion looking for someone to devour" (1 PETER 5:8).

**PRAYER**

*God, make me alert to life's temptations. Strengthen my self-control that I may resist those who do not have my best interest at heart.*

## 226. King George's Gulf

*Independence can never be possible,"* King George III wrote confidentially to Lord North, his prime minister, on January 13, 1778. North was the king's right-hand man, his most trusted confidant.

The king started 1778 with his usual New Year's Resolution: no independence for the colonies. *"I do not think there is a man either bold or mad enough to presume to treat [negotiate] for the mother country on such a basis [as independence],"* he continued.

One characteristic of obstinacy is the inability to face reality, to accept the truth. The king still failed to recognize that no mother could nurture her children or understand their needs with an ocean separating them. The king ignored a basic fact of life: When children grow into adults, they want to lead independent lives.

The king also failed to accept the reality that his decisions and Parliament's tax policies had led to America's rebellion. If anything, he believed they had been too lenient and declared to North *that the too great lenity of this country encreased their pride and encouraged them to rebel."*

One reality King George embraced was his legitimate duty to England to win the war. It was his job to second-guess his generals. He analyzed the war with the skill of a chess champion. The king called Saratoga a *"disaster."* Numbers, not tactics, were to blame for the fall of his pawns. The king believed General Howe was so obsessed with capturing Philadelphia he failed to come to General Burgoyne's aid. Thus, the king decided to move his rook. He replaced General Howe with General Clinton in

1778. In his letter to Lord North, the king also revealed another shift in tactics. A land war alone was futile.

*"A sea war is the only wise plan,"* he wrote North. *"Preventing the arrival of military stores, cloathing, and the other articles necessary from Europe, must distress them, and make them come into what Britain may decently consent to."*

On the whole, the king was confident of his ability to achieve checkmate. He trusted his bishop Lord North to effectively manage the few members of Parliament who opposed the war when the next session began.

*"The accounts from America are most comfortable,"* he concluded.

Hence, as 1778 dawned, the gulf between America and King George III of England was even wider than the Atlantic Ocean itself and more complicated than a champion's chessboard.[226]

> "The LORD will dry up the gulf of the Egyptian sea; with a scorching wind he will sweep his hand over the Euphrates River. He will break it up into seven streams so that men can cross over in sandals" (ISAIAH 11:15).

**PRAYER**

*Thank you for your promise to dry up the gulf, to allow us to cross into heaven via the bridge of your Son.*

# 227. All the King's Spies

King George III's spies were watching Benjamin Franklin's every move in France. Espionage was as essential to winning the war as the king's sea strategy. The king's spies had been sending regular updates on Franklin's progress, or more accurately, his lack of progress.

*"It also appears . . . that Franklin and Deane . . . have no power of treating [securing a treaty with France],"* King George III wrote gleefully. The news was more amusing than the jokes of his court jesters.

By January 13, 1778, the king had received letters that had made him doubt Franklin and Deane's ability to secure a deal with France. He was confident in his sources. After all, one of his spies was as close to Franklin as Franklin's desk.

*"It turns out in retrospect that his [Franklin's] own secretary was a spy. And that anything that crossed Franklin's desk was sent back within the week via a little bottle sunk beneath a tree . . . and those dispatches arrived regularly [to the king in England] seventy-two hours later,"* told Benjamin Franklin historian Stacy Schiff.

Espionage, common sense, and, yet again, stubbornness, led King George III to bet on France. He doubted Franklin could get France's cooperation because of an obvious paradigm. No matter how much France disliked England, why would the king of France support the right of a people to rebel against royalty? Wouldn't his people rebel as a result?

*"It seems like a fool's error when you think about it. Franklin is sent to an absolute monarchy to ask them to fund a revolution against a king. But the truth is the animus on the French part against the English is so great that this is a very easy argument to make,"* Schiff explained.

King George III underestimated France's desire for revenge against England. He doubted the French king would do anything more than tacitly acknowledge Benjamin Franklin and the American diplomats. The king of France certainly would not provide the Americans with money, arms, troops, and naval support.

*"But Franklin is too deep to draw it up [a treaty with France] solely from malevolence; it occurs to me therefore that if he could obtain any answer it would be tacitly acknowledging him and his colleagues . . . and admitting the right of the rebel colonies . . . to be united states,"* King George III wrote.

> "We are all the sons of one man. Your servants are honest men, not spies"
> (GENESIS 42:11).

The king also underestimated Franklin, who was aware of the spies in his midst. *"Because of the espionage Franklin realized the only way to keep a secret was to keep it to himself. And he's very, very closed mouth, plays his cards very close to his chest,"* Schiff noted.

Benjamin Franklin was no king's fool. And February 1778 would prove it.[227]

**PRAYER**

*Allow me to see through the fraudulent ways of others and protect me from any temptation to deceive.*

# 228. Franklin's Joy

Benjamin Franklin was so thrilled when he finally learned the news of Saratoga that he sounded the French horn, at least the one in his heart. It didn't matter to Franklin that General Gates took all the credit and ignored Benedict Arnold's courage and sacrifice. America might win the war after all.

*"I RECEIVED . . . your most agreeable congratulations on the success of the American arms in the Northern Department,"* Franklin wrote to his friend Thomas Cushing on February 21, 1778.

The news had given Franklin just the *"event of consequence"* he needed to reach a deal with France. As soon as he could arrange it, he had secretly met with the King of France, Louis XVI. Perhaps as a symbol of his personal revolution, Franklin chose to wear his blue velvet suit to the meeting. It was the same suit he had worn that fateful day in January 1775, when the English king's Privy Council *"dressed him down"* over distributing Thomas Hutchinson's letters.

Franklin, however, knew his meeting with King Louis XVI could sew the most significant new stitches in America's pursuit of liberty. And as he had told members of Parliament during the Stamp Act inquiry in 1766, the pride of Americans was *"to wear their old clothes over again till they can make new ones."*

In his letter to Cushing, Franklin revealed his success. He celebrated the completion of *"two treaties with his most Christian Majesty: the one of amity and commerce, on the plan of that proposed by Congress."*

*"The great principle in both treaties is a perfect equality and reciprocity; no advantage to be demanded by France, or privileges in commerce, which the States may not grant to any and every other nation,"* Franklin wrote.

Franklin believed the French King had acted wisely in the name of long-lasting friendship. *"In short, the king has treated with us generously and magnanimously; taken no advantage of our present difficulties, to exact terms which we would not willingly grant, when established in prosperity and power,"* he wrote.

When England heard the news, they reached for more guns and ammunition, not trumpets of celebration. By recognizing American sovereignty, France had provided the starved American cause what it most needed abroad: legitimacy. By giving America a trading partner, France ensured America's economy. *"Several of the American ships, with stores for the Congress, are now about sailing under the convoy of a French squadron. England is in great consternation, and the minister,"* Franklin wrote with glee.

But while Benjamin Franklin sounded the figurative French horn, George Washington was

> "Sound the ram's horn at the New Moon, and when the moon is full, on the day of our Feast"
> (PSALM 81:3).

in a literal fight for his life. The outcome would determine whether or not his army would survive.[228]

**PRAYER**

*I today celebrate the life you have given me. Thank you for bringing us days of feasting, the times when we can dance in the moonlight.*

# 229. Articles

Our Business is to secure America against the Arts & the Arms of a treacherous Enemy," Samuel Adams wrote to a friend in early 1778.

Since Lexington and Concord in 1775, the Continental Congress had been consumed with the sudden responsibilities of making war and seeking peace. Like captains of a newly built ship, they found themselves overwhelmed by acquiring supplies, testing riggings, and plugging holes before they could sail without sinking. The Declaration had been their first successful test drive, but they had yet to finish the essential job of establishing a new government.

From the first day of boarding their new vessel, they had tried to launch a government. When Congress established a committee to draft a declaration of independence in June 1776, they also created a committee to craft a new constitution governing a confederation of the states. Adams was a strong supporter of this loose approach to government, but it took more than a year for Congress to ratify the new document. Congress passed the Articles of Confederation in November 1777, which also required ratification by the states. The ratification process kept the riggings loose on this new ship, *United States.*

Adams, however, was thrilled to report the good news of January 21, 1778. He was a proud son of Massachusetts that day. Boston had endorsed the Articles, an important step toward Massachusetts ratifying them. He returned to the role of clerk and wrote a proclamation for Boston's decision.

*"The Articles of confederation and perpetual Union between the several States now represented in the Continental Congress, having been laid before this Town, were distinctly and repeatedly read and maturely considerd,"* he wrote.

Adams then praised Boston's decision: *"The said Articles appear to be well adapted to cement the Union of the said States, to confirm their mutual Friendship, establish their Freedom and Independence, and promote their general Welfare."*

Adams was as supportive of states' rights as he was of Boston. He supported the articles in part because they did not give Congress the power to tax and gave each state one vote in Congress. Delegates could not serve more than three years in a six-year time period. As tight and restrictive as the Articles were, they were far

> "Your rigging hangs loose: The mast is not held secure, the sail is not spread"
> (ISAIAH 33:23).

from a secure mast fit for sailing a new ship. Samuel Adams was unable to accept the problems of these loose riggings. He also did not realize just how long it would take for all the states to ratify the articles. The process for launching a new government would not be completed until the mast was secure.[229]

**PRAYER**

*Lord, enable me to build strong foundations in all areas of my life, from my family to my work.*

# 230. Arachnophobia

After finally receiving the command he had longed for, the Marquis de Lafayette found himself caught like a fly in a spider's web. He was unwittingly tangled in a plot to overthrow George Washington as commander-in-chief.

*"I need not tell you how sorry I am at what has lately happened; it is a necessary result of my tender and respectful friendship for you, which is as true and candid as the other sentiments of my heart,"* Lafayette wrote to Washington from his new post in Albany, New York, in March 1778.

The links in the Frenchman's chain of respect for Washington had increased with each passing day. While Lafayette recovered from his wounds after Brandywine, Washington told the doctors to look after him as if he was his own son. The general also recommended that Congress give him a command. The only better news Lafayette received in 1777 was that his wife had given birth to another daughter.

Congress rewarded him for his service at Brandywine and named Lafayette commander of *"an irruption"* to be made into Canada. The plan made sense at first. After all, he was well qualified to invade Canada, where most of the residents spoke French. But when he arrived in Albany in January 1778, Lafayette learned his command was not all that it had seemed to be. He discovered that some in Congress had made other significant changes after Washington's defeat at Brandywine. They had named Gen. Horatio Gates as president of a new Board of War to oversee the Canadian expedition. Lafayette felt betrayed when he learned that Washington had not been consulted on creating this war board, implementing the Canadian expedition, or assigning Gates's role.

*"When I was in Europe, I thought that here almost every man was a lover of liberty, and would rather die free than live a slave . . . There are open dissensions in Congress; parties who hate one another as much as the common enemy; men who, without knowing anything about war, undertake to judge you, and to make ridiculous comparisons. They are infatuated with Gates, without thinking of the difference of circumstances, and believe that attacking is the only thing necessary to conquer,"* he wrote of his astonishment.

It seemed to Lafayette as if Gates had deceitful designs on Washington's position. Lafayette also discovered that the new war board had made promises it could not keep. When he arrived in Albany, Lafayette realized there were not enough men, money, or supplies to carry out the Canadian expedition.

*"These ideas are entertained by some jealous men, and perhaps secret friends of the British government, who want to push you, in a moment of ill humor, to some rash enterprise upon the lines,"* he warned Washington.

> "What he trusts in is fragile; what he relies on is a spider's web" (JOB 8:14).

The Marquis de Lafayette may not have been sure which was more fragile: George Washington's tenure as commander-in-chief or the Canadian expedition. No matter how much he wanted a command, he could not linger in a silk web.[230]

**PRAYER**

*Father, show me the spider webs in my life, the fragile places that have ensnared me. Release me from them and allow me to trust in your unbreakable chains of love and truth.*

# 231. The Revolution Today: Lies

Espionage. Deception. Lies. These were real threats to the American Revolution. The depravity of humanity could have ensnared Benjamin Franklin and led the Marquis de Lafayette astray. Franklin's secretary read his mail and secretly communicated its contents to King George III. Lafayette was deceived more by one-on-one conversations than promises made in letters. Because letters leave a paper trail, the weapons of deceit are more likely to be spoken words, not open written correspondence.

A 2004 study by Cornell University revealed that people are more likely to lie with their mouths than they are with their hands. Lies also hide behind the unseen.

"The weapon of choice, it turns out, is the telephone. People lie more often over the telephone than in any other form of communication, according to new research out of Cornell University. And if you fire off an e-mail to the boss, you're probably going to tell her you never wanted to go to that boring meeting anyway, because you're far more likely to tell the truth in an e-mail than in a face-to-face meeting, or over the phone, or through instant messaging," ABC News reported of the Cornell study.

The study set out to find out which type of communication most often led to lying. The researchers asked thirty students to track their social communication for a week and note when they lied and how they transmitted the lies. The students submitted their reports anonymously to reduce the chance they would lie about their lying. They confessed to lying approximately one-fourth of the time. Their primary method was the telephone.

"The clear winner in the tally was the telephone, which was involved in 37 percent of the deception. Face-to-face conversations included lies 27 percent of the time, and instant messages came in at 21 percent. But e-mail turned out to be a model of integrity, accounting for only 14 percent of the lies," the report explained.

> "God is not a man, that he should lie, nor a son of man, that he should change his mind" (NUMBERS 23:19).

Because e-mail leaves behind a record, people were less inclined to lie in an e-mail message than they were in face-to-face conversations or over the telephone.

"It's easier to lie over the telephone because the other person can't see our expressions, or know we are dressed for the beach instead of the office. And most importantly, the conversation is unlikely to be recorded," the report continued.

Satan used a spoken lie to deceive Eve in the Garden of Eden. He told her she would not die if she ate the forbidden fruit. Eve believed him and convinced Adam to eat the fruit with her. Hence, it was a lie, a spoken word, that led to humanity's downfall and separation from God. The remedy God has provided through his Son, however, has overcome deception and lies, no matter how they are transmitted. God's forgiveness is available to supersede the father of lies.[231]

**PRAYER**

*Father, protect my heart from lies. You are the God of truth.*

# 232. Sabbath Rest: Lexington Reflection

The upheaval and anarchy of the Revolution certainly made it seem as if the world were ending. When Congregationalist minister Jacob Cushing delivered a sermon on the third anniversary of the battle of Lexington in April 1778, he renewed a call to arms in an effort to encourage the disheartened.

*"You were spared, it may be, further to signalize yourselves, and to do yet greater service for GOD and your bleeding country,"* he said while standing on the same green grass where the first shots of the war were fired.

*"To arms! To action, and the battle of the warrior! is the language of divine providence; and you have every motive imaginable to awaken, and excite you to be up and doing the work of the Lord faithfully,"* he proclaimed.

Cushing asked his audience to reflect on both their duty and the honor of God. *"The honour and glory of GOD, and the salvation of your country under GOD, call aloud upon all. Duty, interest, liberty, religion and life, every thing worth enjoyment, demand speedy and the utmost exertions,"* he pleaded.

And although he knew it was time to *"excel in the art of war"* as a necessity in the evil world in which they lived, he also reminded them of God's eternal world. *"'All that cometh is vanity,'"* he said, quoting Ecclesiastes 11:8 (KJV). *"All things are liable to change, and in perpetual uncertainty. Every thing tends to dissolution, and GOD alone is invariable."*

Cushing held a temporal view of life. He believed the end of time would witness the end of *"jarring nations."* God's kingdom will be the only one left standing, and Cushing wanted to see his fellow patriots as part of God's heavenly army. He not only issued a call to arms to his congregation, but he also issued a call for them to secure peace with God.

*"We are all children of mortality—and must die out of this world,"* Cushing said, *"being called to glory by virtue, let us diligently and conscientiously perform all the duties of our holy religion; labour*

to secure our peace with GOD, through Jesus
Christ our only Saviour—that we may be perfect
and compleat in him, as our head," he told his
parishioners.

Americans witnessed so many tragedies and
terrorist acts during the Revolution it seemed as
if the world were coming to an end. The same
could be said of today. Jacob Cushing's call to
arms was temporal, something that applied to his
circumstances. But his call to making peace with
God through Christ transcends generations and
is as real in this century as it was on Lexington's
green in 1775 and 1778.[232]

> "But if a man live many years, and rejoice in them all; yet let him remember the days of darkness; for they shall be many. All that cometh is vanity" (ECCLESIASTES 11:8 KJV).

**PRAYER**

*Father, thank you for reminding me that life on earth is temporary, but you are eternal and sent your son, Jesus Christ, for my salvation.*

## 233. Conway Cabal

From his post in Albany, the Marquis de Lafayette also discovered that General Gates was not the only one weaving a web of silk threads around General Washington. General Conway, an Irishman who had served in the French army, was central to the cabal.

*"But the promotion of Conway is beyond all my expectations,"* Lafayette continued in his letter to George Washington from his post in Albany in March 1778. He noted that Conway's reputation for bravery and experience in thirty campaigns had impressed him at first. But he later learned the truth: The cabal was as cannibalistic as a black widow spider.

Lafayette realized that Conway had deceived him *"by entertaining my imagination with ideas of glory and shining projects."* Conway had been promoted to inspector general and then was assigned as second-in-command to Lafayette in the Canadian expedition.

*"I have inquired into [Conway's] character, and found that he is an ambitious and dangerous man. He has done all in his power to draw off my confidence and affection from you. His desire was to engage me to leave this country,"* Lafayette told Washington.

The plotters had tried to destroy confidence in Washington and elevate Gates through anonymous letters and underhanded appeals sent to members of Congress and men like Lafayette. *"Such disputes, if known* to the enemy, may be attended with the worst consequences," he wrote, noting that "slavery, dishonor, ruin, and the unhappiness of a whole nation" would result from the trifling wiles of a few men in Congress and the army. Lafayette was concerned that the web would not only destroy Washington, but also the Revolution. Lafayette knew the first way to strike the web was to reassure Washington of his loyalty.

"My desire of deserving your approbation is strong; and, whenever you shall employ me, you can be certain of my trying every exertion in my power to succeed. I am now bound to your fate, and I shall follow it and sustain it, as well by my sword as by all the means in my power," Lafayette promised Washington, adding that his youth may have made him too "warm" but his concern over the plot was great.

Lafayette struck another blow to shatter the web. He asked Congress to replace Conway with the Baron von Kalb as his second-in-command for the expedition. If the Marquis de Lafayette had his way, this plot would merely prove to be a vain conspiracy among men.

A shattered web, however, will merely return if you don't catch the spider.[233]

> "Why do the nations conspire and the peoples plot in vain?" (PSALM 2:1).

**PRAYER**

Protect me from conspiracy, from those people whose motives are vain, and from my own desire for self-glory.

# 234. Washington's Kibosh

George Washington put the kibosh on the Conway cabal by striking at the spider.

"General Conway's merit as an officer and his importance in this army exist more in his own imagination than in reality," Washington wrote to a member of Congress of his opposition to Conway's promotion.

Washington also calmly responded to the Marquis de Lafayette's letter of loyalty and Conway's attempt to overthrow him. "It will ever constitute part of my happiness to know that I stand well in your opinion," Washington wrote Lafayette from Valley Forge. He reassured the Frenchman of his friendship and praised his integrity for rejecting Conway's plot and its intrigues.

"But one gentleman, whose name you have mentioned, had, I am confident, far different views. His ambition and great desire of being *puffed off, as one of the first officers of the age, could only be equalled by the means which he used to obtain them,"* Washington wrote of his incorrigible enemy, who had *"I am persuaded, practised every art to do me an injury."*

Conway's motives galled Washington because they were opposite his own. Washington had not taken command for personal ambition or financial gain. He had learned long ago such motives cloud the cause. They can produce disastrous effects.

*"How far he may have accomplished his ends, I know not; and, except for considerations of a public nature, I care not,"* he explained, adding that steadiness was his weapon against such slander as Conway spewed.

Washington also agreed with Lafayette that the dissensions in Congress and the army were dangerous to the patriots' cause. But he warned the exuberant youth against worrying too much.

*"The fatal tendency of disunion is so obvious,"* he wrote, *"we must not, in so great a contest, expect to meet with nothing but sunshine. I have no doubt that everything happens for the best, that we shall triumph over all our misfortunes."*

Washington's steadiness led to his survival. His opposition to Conway's promotion, along with Lafayette's request for the Baron de Kalb to be his second-in-command instead of Conway, led Conway to resign. After his departure, the cabal ceased to exist.

> "And we know that in all things God works for the good of those who love him, who have been called according to his purpose" (ROMANS 8:28).

With the British occupation of Philadelphia and few resources, an invasion of Canada proved as foolish an idea as invading London. Congress cancelled the plan, which had strayed from their mission. The purpose of the war was not to acquire territory. It was to secure liberty and defend America's interests. Once again Providence had protected George Washington and, as Washington had suggested to the Marquis de Lafayette, worked all things for his good.[234]

**PRAYER**

*As I seek your purpose for me, I pray for the steadiness to remember that you work all things for my good.*

# 235. Bribing Conciliation

The minority in Parliament in 1778 couldn't have surprised King George III and Lord North more had they voted to make England an ally of France.

When Parliament convened in the spring of 1778, many members were outraged to learn of General Burgoyne's alliance with the Iroquois from the previous year. The news strengthened the moral arguments of those in Parliament who supported America. The king faced a new reality. The minority opposition in Parliament was growing.

*"They, from the first, had opposed the war as unjust, and had opposed the enlisting of Hessians; but more especially did they denounce the inhuman policy of employing savages to murder and scalp their brethren beyond the Atlantic,"* historian William Jackman wrote of Parliament's minority.

This group also had heard from their constituents, particularly the British merchant class, whose inability to trade with Americans had resulted in a loss of revenue. England was emptying the royal coffers only to lose thousands of men to death, disability, or desertion. The opposition had not peaked, but it was strong enough in 1778 to force Lord North to introduce legislation for reconciliation.

*"Lord North was constrained to bring in two bills, by which the king hoped to reconcile his American subjects,"* Jackman wrote. *"One of these bills exempted the Americans from taxation, the other appointed commissioners to negotiate with them, for the purpose of restoring the royal authority."*

Parliament authorized three men, including a former (and the first) governor of West Florida (a British colony that did not join in the Revolution), and the brother of a former Maryland governor, to travel to America as peace commissioners. They arrived in June 1778.

*"The commissioners sent their proposals to Congress, but that body refused to treat [negotiate] until the independence of the States was acknowledged and the British troops withdrawn,"* Jackman wrote.

Parliament had not authorized the commissioners to grant independence. When they realized conciliation had failed, the commissioners took extreme measures. They peddled peace with a price and a prize.

*"By . . . means of a loyalist lady of Philadelphia, [the commissioners] made propositions to General Joseph Reed, of ten thousand pounds and any office in the colonies he might choose if he would aid the object of the mission,"* Jackman wrote. *"To which offer he made this memorable reply: 'I am not worth purchasing, but such as I am, the king of England is not rich enough to buy me.'"*

Hence, the bribery failed. Once again the leaders of England attempted a "payoff" by trying to solve the crisis without granting independence.[235]

**PRAYER**

*God, open my eyes to the hidden bribes in life, the lures that degrade my identity as created in your image.*

> "Do not accept a bribe, for a bribe blinds those who see and twists the words of the righteous" (EXODUS 23:8).

# 236. Finishing a General

*I will finish the war here, or it will finish me,"* Baron von Steuben wrote. This man of military maneuvers had become one of George Washington's best generals.

The war would not finish von Steuben, but it would finish one of his most unreliable colleagues. *"When it was known that a French fleet was expected on the coast, the British hastened to evacuate Philadelphia and retreat to New York,"* historian William Jackman wrote, noting that Congress reoccupied Philadelphia.

Washington now had the opportunity he needed to show off his larger, stronger, and more disciplined army. His thirteen thousand men were emboldened by von Steuben's tactics. As General Clinton, who had replaced Howe at the king's request, and his army of ten thousand marched from Pennsylvania through New Jersey to New York, Washington waited for the right moment to strike. The heat was high both in Washington's heart and in the countryside.

*"Washington was soon in pursuit. The weather was excessively warm, and the heavily armed British moved very slowly. The Americans soon came up,"* Jackman wrote of the 104-degree heat.

Not only did June 1778 bring the worst heat wave to strike the colonies in decades, but it also fired tension between old rivalries. Gen. Charles Lee had recently returned to the army after a prisoner exchange. Washington held a war council to discuss whether to attack or merely harass Clinton's troops during their New Jersey march. Generals Greene and Lafayette favored attacking. Lee preferred harassment. With his disagreement well known, the rash Lee quickly gave up his seniority and allowed Washington to choose another general to lead the battle in his place.

*"Washington therefore sent Lafayette forward with two thousand men, to take position on the hills, and thus crowd Sir Henry Clinton off into the plain. The next morning Lee had changed his mind and asked to*

*be given a command. Washington sent him forward with two brigades,"* recounted Jackman.

Lee approached the British camp at Monmouth Courthouse on the morning of June 28, 1778. Claiming the thick woods obstructed his view, Lee retreated instead of attacking as Washington had ordered. Lee's men, not knowing what to do or where to go, fled in confusion.

Washington was angry. He confronted Lee and relieved him of his duty. Lee later received a court-martial, which resulted in his dismissal. Thus the war did not finish von Steuben, but it did Lee. Folly and imprudence had led to his complete downfall.

> "If you take your neighbor's cloak as a pledge, return it to him by sunset"
> (EXODUS 22:26).

Decades after the war, historians discovered Lee's letters in Britain's royal archives. During his captivity, Charles Lee had written plans showing the British how they could overtake the Americans. For whatever reason, the British ignored his plans. Perhaps they couldn't trust a chameleon.[236]

**PRAYER**

*Strengthen me that I may keep my word to those around me. Let discretion, not folly, govern my promises to others.*

# 237. Monmouth Matters

General Lee's insubordination literally thrust General Washington into the line of fire. At one o'clock in the afternoon on June 28, 1778, with less than half a mile separating the armies, Washington stepped in and personally commanded his troops in the battle of Monmouth.

*"Washington hastily formed the men on a rising ground. The enemy came up in force [within an hour], and other divisions of the Americans also mingled in the conflict,"* historian William Jackman described. Washington led with fierce determination. He had worked too hard rebuilding his army at Valley Forge to lose because of Lee's foolishness.

*"He then does something astounding. He rides back and forth in front of his lines to rally the troops, putting himself in the line of the fire, risking his life as he asked his own men to risk theirs,"* recounted historian Bruce Chadwick.

As a veteran of the French and Indian War, Washington knew what it was like to have four bullets go through his coat and two horses shot from beneath him. He had faced death before. *"People who know Wash-*

*ington in the war think that he has a feeling of invincibility because he puts himself in the line of fire so often,"* Chadwick added. *"The British open up on him and miraculously miss him."*

For five hours in unbearable heat the Americans successfully repelled assault after assault. Had General Howe been in charge of the British, he no doubt would have been shocked to see these Americans. This was not the frightened fleeing force of 1776 or the half-disciplined army of 1777. This was an army knitted together with skills, strength, and spirit.

Nightfall brought a temporary ceasefire. *"The Americans slept upon their arms, expecting to renew the contest in the morning. But Clinton skillfully drew off his army during the night, and at daylight was far on his way. Washington did not attempt to pursue, as the weather was intolerably warm, and the march through a sandy region, destitute of water,"* chronicled Jackman.

Washington gave his men time to recuperate. Then he marched them across New Jersey to White Plains, New York. There he waited for word of the French fleet's arrival.

*"The Americans lost altogether about two hundred, many of them on account of the extreme heat: the British lost three hundred in the battle, and on the march two thousand Hessians deserted,"* Jackman noted.

Some historians have concluded that Monmouth was a draw, others have credited the Americans. Regardless, for the first time, the Continentals proved their pluck through battlefield tactics, not surprise attacks or retreats. They held their own.

> "Behold, I have given him for a witness to the people, a leader and commander to the people" (ISAIAH 55:4 KJV).

Monmouth also mattered because it also showed the military mettle of the man of manners. This *"forever solidifies Washington's position as the unquestioned commander-in-chief,"* asserted Chadwick.[237]

**PRAYER**

*Thank you for the leaders you have placed in my life. Grant them wisdom.*

# 238. The Revolution Today: Numbers

"Miami, 2007: Coaches score a Super Bowl touchdown in black history," a headline could have read that year. Not only will Super Bowl XLI be remembered as the day the Colts beat the Bears, but it will also be remembered for its marker along history's timeline. For the first time, the Super Bowl's head coaches were African Americans. Appropriately, the game took place during February—Black History Month.

Unlike most of the Super Bowl's oddball-humored commercials, Coca-Cola heralded this historic milestone with a simple, poignant ad. The commercial featured dates and short sentences in plain letters against a simple background. Next to each statement was the outline of green-glassed Coca-Cola bottles, whose changing shapes and sizes reflected the corresponding year.

"North Pole, 1909: A black man is on top of the world," the first tribute flashed. The timeline began with a salute to Matthew Alexander Henson, the indispensable assistant to Robert Peary. Together, they reached the frozen wonder.

"Tuskegee, 1941: Pilots prove heroism has no color," the commercial continued, referring to World War II's first black fighter pilot unit.

"Brooklyn, 1947: Baseball shows us courage, it's #42," the ad flashed, applauding Jackie Robinson's accomplishment as the first black player of the modern major leagues.

"Montgomery, 1955: Woman remains seated. And stands for justice." The commercial praised Rosa Parks's unwillingness to give up her seat on a passenger bus to a white man.

"DC, 1963: A man inspires a nation to dream together." The ad reminded viewers of Dr. Martin Luther King's famous speech that defined the American civil rights movement.

The ad then switched to the modern day, exchanging its nostalgic green-glass Coca-Cola bottles for a red one. "Coca-Cola celebrates black history: Especially today," it concluded, saluting the Super Bowl's coaches.

Dates are important to history, but the significance of a timeline is not its numbers but the people behind them. If Coca-Cola had existed during the Revolutionary War, its commercial could have started with this line: "Monmouth, 1778: After freezing at the Forge, seven hundred black Continentals fired their heat in the heat." General George Washington approved the request by the leaders of Rhode Island to create an all-black regiment that first fought at Monmouth. This force of freemen and former slaves would become one of the army's finest.

> "Take a census of the whole Israelite community by their clans and families, listing every man by name, one by one" (NUMBERS 1:2).

The Bible's book of Numbers is a Super Bowl of statistics. The word *number* appears sixty-six times. Dates and numbers are sometimes boring, but they also give us a chance to take stock and count our blessings.

They can leave us with a "census" of our lives, of where we have been and where we need to go.[238]

**PRAYER**

*Father, allow me a moment today to take stock of my life and count the blessings you have given me.*

# 239. Sabbath Rest: Counting Deliverance

Nothing new therefore, can be suggested by me on this occasion," Jacob Cushing declared in his sermon. "*I have only to stir up your pure minds, by way of remembrance, of the transactions of that awful day; to excite your devotion, and to recommend a religious improvement of GOD's righteous dispensations then, and through three revolving years now completed.*"

Three years after the Revolutionary War's first shots rang out, Jacob Cushing stood on the green at Lexington, Massachusetts. His purpose on that Sunday, the 20th of April, 1778, was to deliver a fiery sermon. His goal was twofold: to encourage his audience to turn to God for salvation and to provide them with a remedy for their woes.

The memory of that night was as vivid to Cushing as the green grass he stood on. This preacher described the British as night-stalking cowards who "*attacked us altogether defenceless.*" But as others who had lived through the tragedy and grief of that moonlit night, he described God's mercy with even more brilliance. Cushing's therapeutic solution for the patients gathered around his pulpit was practical. He wanted them to count their blessings.

"*With astonishment and gratitude we recollect the kindness of our almighty Preserver, that no more were slain by the hand of violence; and that the people willingly offered themselves to 'the help of the Lord against the mighty [Judges 5:23 KJV],' who manfully opposed the efforts of British pride, power and barbarity,*" he said.

Cushing pointed out the positive. He described how "*the hand of GOD was visible in these things; and the power and goodness of GOD manifested in our deliverance.*" He realized how weak and unprepared the colonists were for "*such a sudden assault.*" He called on his congregation to adopt the words of the psalmist in Psalm 124:2–3 (KJV): "*If it had not been the Lord who was on our side, when men rose up against us: Then they had swallowed us up quick, when their wrath was kindled against us,*" he said. Although the war had brought the most terrible

plague on America's shores, the Lord had preserved them from annihilation.

*"But blessed be GOD, to whose infinite
mercy we ascribe our deliverance, who was then
a present help,"* praised Cushing. *"These bar-
barous savage enemies were put into fear; they
were made to flee before us, and hastily to retreat
(as wild beasts to their dens) before a few scattered, undisciplined freemen: Not to our courage
or conduct, but to GOD's name be all the praise
and glory."*

While counting blessings cannot reverse
tragedy, it can, as Jacob Cushing believed, ease a
burden and give hope for the future.[239]

> "If the LORD had
> not been on our
> side when men
> attacked us, when
> their anger flared
> against us, they
> would have swal-
> lowed us alive. . . .
> Praise be to the
> LORD, who has
> not let us be torn
> by their teeth"
> (PSALM 124:2, 6).

**PRAYER**

*Remind me to take time today to count the blessings you have given me.*

# 240. A Blue Greene

When Nathanael Greene became the army's chief food forager he did
not give up his major general responsibilities. For months he sin-
gle-handedly carried the twin burden.

And this double duty turned Greene blue in July 1778. The rebuke he
received from General Washington for not returning to headquarters after
a special assignment likely troubled him more than any criticism he had
ever received from his fellow Quakers for embracing a musket.

*"Your Excellency has made me very unhappy. I can submit very
patiently to deserved censure; but it wounds my feelings exceedingly to
meet with a rebuke for doing what I conceived to be a proper part of my
duty, and in the order of things,"* Greene wrote to Washington of his
anguish.

Greene refreshed Washington's memory. Washington had asked him
to survey New York's Croton River. Because Greene, a Rhode Islander,
was a stranger to the region, he believed the task required a thorough
examination.

With the skill of a lawyer, the unschooled Greene defended his
actions. Washington had rebuked him for not returning to headquarters
to report his survey in person. Greene reminded him that he (Greene) had
written Washington a report of his findings. He did not return to head-

quarters because of his quartermaster duties. He had more letters to return and matters to regulate than his clock had minutes.

Greene also told Washington it was impossible to serve as quartermaster if he spent too much time at headquarters. Constant attendance there was harmful. He needed time to ask farmers for food by knocking door-to-door. Headquarters was also a half day's ride from Greene's camp. The intense summer heat made the journey unbearable even to Greene, one of the most robust and athletic officers in the service. *"And here I must observe, that neither my constitution nor strength is equal to constant exercise,"* he wrote of the burden.

Greene also noted he did not foresee Washington's objection to the way he had handled his assignment. Why? Greene knew he had served with propriety. He had not wasted hours fishing or stargazing. More than any other watchword, diligence had guided his double duties.

*"If I had neglected my duty in pursuit of pleasure, or if I had been wanting in respect to your Excellency, I would have put my hand upon my mouth, and been silent upon the occasion; but, as I am not conscious of being chargeable with either the one or the other, I cannot help thinking I have been treated with a degree of severity that I am in no respect deserving,"* explained Greene.

Because Nathanael Greene had cast himself into a mold of service and not selfishness, he confidently approached George Washington with a clear conscience. By doing so, he brought his request for justice to Washington.[240]

> "O LORD, do not rebuke me in your anger or discipline me in your wrath. Be merciful to me, LORD, for I am faint; O LORD, heal me, for my bones are in agony" (PSALM 6:1, 2).

**PRAYER**

*I ask for your mercy today. May I end today with a clear conscience.*

# 241. Rebuke's Respect

I am glad to hear General Greene is Quartermaster-General; it is very interesting to have there an honest man and a friend of yours," the Marquis de Lafayette wrote to General Washington.

Lafayette had no idea just how anguished Greene was over a rebuke he had recently received from Washington. Because of the overwhelming demands of being quartermaster, Greene had reported the findings of a land survey in writing, not in person. Washington's rebuke of Greene's choice, however, forced Greene to explain his actions. Greene's response showed his clear conscience while also revealing his respect for his commander-in-chief.

*"Your Excellency well knows how I came into this department. It was by your special request, and you must be sensible there is no other man upon earth would have brought me into the business but you,"* Greene wrote in his July 21, 1778, letter to Washington. Greene explained why he accepted the quartermaster job.

*"The distress the department was in . . . and the difficulty of engaging a person capable of conducting the business, together with the hopes of meeting your approbation, and having your full aid and assistance, reconciled me to the undertaking."*

Greene also reminded Washington of the department's progress. The time to prepare for the summer campaign seemed shorter than a day. Yet Greene had found enough supplies for the army's journey from Valley Forge to New York, which resulted in the battle of Monmouth.

*"And reflect with what ease and facility you began your march from Valley Forge . . . you will do me the justice to say I have not been negligent or inattentive to my duty,"* Greene requested firmly.

This quartermaster then reaffirmed his commitments. *"I have, in every respect, since I had my appointment, strove to accommodate the business of the department to the plan of your Excellency's operations. And I can say, with great truth, that ever since I had the honor to serve under you, I have been more attentive to the public interest, and more engaged in the support of your Excellency's character, than ever I was to my own ease, interest, or reputation,"* he explained confidently.

Greene's devotion to a job he didn't want proved his loyalty. He had learned the art and science of management from his father's Quaker work ethic and his family's iron foundry. History reflected fondly on quartermaster Greene and this episode.

*"The system with which Greene performed all his duties was soon apparent; the army was regularly furnished with provisions and ammunition, so that it could be ready to march at a few minutes' notice,"* historian William Jackman wrote.

His response to George Washington's rebuke for not reporting his river survey in person reinforced his loyalty. Nathanael Greene's open rebuttal revealed his love for a cause and his respect for his commander.[241]

> "Better is open rebuke than hidden love" (PROVERBS 27:5).

*God, allow me to accept those moments of rebuke, regardless of whether they are justified. Use them to reveal my hidden love for you and those around me.*

# 242. The Rebuke's Revelation

Had General Washington rebuked a lesser man he would have endured unending attempts to undercut him that July of 1778. But when he unfairly censured Quartermaster Gen. Nathanael Greene for reporting a survey in writing instead of in person, Washington received a letter lavished in loyalty and not licentiousness.

"*I have never solicited you for a furlough to go home to indulge in pleasure, or to improve my interest, which, by the by, I have neglected, going on four years,*" Greene continued in the last half of his July 21, 1778, letter to Washington. He knew even his dear friend, Henry Knox, had received a leave of absence to visit his wife.

Unlike other generals such as Charles Lee or Horatio Gates, Greene had not sought public glory for his sacrifices. "*I have never confined myself to my particular line of duty only . . . I have never been troublesome to your Excellency, to publish any thing to my advantage, although I think myself as justly entitled as some others,*" he continued.

Greene's loyalty to Washington was unmistakable. Over and over again, he had protected Washington's interests. "*I have never suffered my pleasures to interfere with my duty; and I am persuaded I have given too many unequivocal proofs of my attachment to your person and interest, to leave a doubt upon your mind to the contrary.*"

Greene had also shown his loyalty with his lips by speaking honestly. "*I have always given you my opinion with great candor, and executed your orders with equal fidelity,*" he reminded Washington. "*I do not mean to arrogate to myself more merit than I deserve, or wish to exculpate myself from being chargeable with error, and in some instances negligence. However, I can speak, with a becoming pride, that I have always endeavoured to deserve the public esteem, and your Excellency's approbation.*"

Greene noted that he was aware of many problems in the quartermaster department, but none of them justified Washington's rebuke. "*It is almost impossible to get good men for the conducting of all parts of so complex a business. It may, therefore, naturally be expected that many things will wear an unfavorable complexion,*" he pointed out.

But his most revealing line of loyalty was this one: "*As I came into the Quarter-master's department with reluctance, so I shall leave it with pleasure. Your influence brought me in, and the want of your approbation will induce me to go out,*" Greene concluded.

> "Do not rebuke a mocker or he will hate you; rebuke a wise man and he will love you"
> (PROVERBS 9:8).

George Washington had unfairly rebuked a wise man. But the matter revealed a greater truth: Nathanael Greene's loyalty to Washington and love of his country were stronger than a mountain of iron.[242]

**PRAYER**

*God, build my character into such a strong fortress that an unfair rebuke or criticism will show my loyalty and love for you.*

# 243. Newport News

"I*N the year 1778, a plan was formed for the recovery of Rhode Island from the hands of the British,*" American colonel John Trumbull wrote of the war's strategy shift from land to sea, which threatened to overtake him.

By the time August arrived, both sides had shifted more positions and players than a court jester could juggle balls. After retreating from Monmouth, General Clinton's army arrived in New York City to reinforce the British occupation there. General Washington moved his army to West Point. Congress reoccupied Philadelphia, while the injured hero of Saratoga, General Benedict Arnold, became the military governor there. John Hancock left Congress to lead a Massachusetts militia. And General Sullivan became the American commander near Newport, Rhode Island.

But the change that most affected Trumbull, son of the Connecticut governor, was the British maneuverings in New York Harbor. They positioned their ships in a way that forced arriving ships to dock in more shallow water. Finding his warships too heavy for the remaining space, France's Count D'Estaing headed for Rhode Island. And so did Trumbull.

"*By the coöperation of a French fleet of twelve sail of the line, commanded by the Count D'Estaing, and a body of American troops, commanded by General Sullivan. The fleet arrived off New York early in July, and in August sailed for Rhode Island. I seized this occasion to gratify my slumbering love of military life, and offered my services to General Sullivan, as a volunteer aid-du-camp,*" Trumbull wrote of his decision to become a messenger in the war.

The combined plan excited Trumbull's hopes for victory. D'Estaing would fight Lord Howe and the British at sea while General Sullivan would attack Newport by land. But the plan soon shifted with the force of a hurricane.

*"The French fleet, which had passed Newport, and lay at anchor above the town, were drawn off from their well-selected station by a clever manœuvre of Lord Howe, the very day after the American army had landed on the island,"* Trumbull explained.

*"The two fleets came to a partial action off the capes of the Chesapeake, in which they were separated by a severe gale of wind; the French, more damaged by the tempest than by the enemy, put into Boston to refit, and General Sullivan was left to pursue the enterprise with the army alone,"* Col. John Trumbull wrote of the storm.

"Every good and perfect gift is from above, coming down from the Father of the heavenly lights, who does not change like shifting shadows" (JAMES 1:17).

The news from Newport was not good. And as sometimes happens, it was a shift in strategy that left Trumbull and the Americans shaking in the shadow of a storm.[243]

**PRAYER**

*Thank you for being a God who does not change like a shifting shadow. When life suddenly shifts underneath my feet, I look to you for strength and stamina.*

# 244. Headdress

I t soon became evident that the attempt was vain, so long as the enemy could receive supplies and reinforcements by water, unmolested," Col. John Trumbull wrote of the army's decision to retreat from Newport. The enemy, however, was not going to allow the Americans to leave without a fight.

*"Soon after daybreak the next morning [August 29th], the rear-guard, commanded by that excellent officer, Colonel Wigglesworth, was attacked on . . . Windmill Hill; and General Sullivan, wishing to avoid a serious action on that ground, sent me with orders to the commanding officer to withdraw the guard,"* Trumbull wrote.

Trumbull's mission proved to be one of the most dangerous moments in his life. The hill he faced was too steep for his horse to trot much less gallop. He was forced to ride at a leisurely pace, increasing his risk of being hit by flying bullets.

"*Nothing can be more trying to the nerves, than to advance thus deliberately and alone into danger. At first, I saw a round shot or two drop near me and pass bounding on,*" he recorded in his memoirs, noting that he also saw a man hit among the hailstorm of musket balls. Trumbull then relayed his conversation with Wigglesworth.

"*I know your errand, but don't speak; we will beat them in a moment,*" Wigglesworth said when Trumbull arrived.

"*Colonel Wigglesworth, do you see those troops crossing obliquely from the west road towards your rear?*" Trumbull said.

"*Yes, they are Americans, coming to our support,*" Wigglesworth answered.

"*No, sir, those are Germans; mark, their dress is blue and yellow, not buff; they are moving to fall into your rear, and intercept your retreat. Retire instantly—don't lose a moment, or you will be cut off.*"

Wigglesworth retreated. But Trumbull's mission was not over. He continued to deliver messages throughout the day, but with an inconvenience: a mark on his head.

"*Soon after this, as I was carrying an important order, the wind, which had risen with the sun, blew off my hat. It was not a time to dismount for a hat. I therefore tied a white handkerchief round my head . . . I formed, the rest of the day, the most conspicuous mark that ever was seen on the field,*" Trumbull wrote of the target that made him stand out like a lone cloud in an otherwise clear blue sky.

> "But not a hair of your head will perish. By standing firm you will gain life" (LUKE 21:18, 19).

"*For never was [an] aid-du-camp exposed to more danger than I was during that entire day, from daylight to dusk,*" he concluded.

Col. John Trumbull then praised God for his survival. "*With this headdress, duty led me to every point where danger was to be found, and I escaped without the slightest injury. It becomes me to say with the Psalmist, 'I thank thee, Oh thou Most High, for thou hast covered my head in the day of battle!'*" (140:7 KJV).[244]

**PRAYER**

*Thank you for caring so much for me that you know the number of hairs on my head at any given moment. I seek to stand firm for you under your head covering of protection.*

# 245. The Revolution Today: Survival

Colonel John Trumbull was amazed that his white *"headdress"* did not make him more of a target that bullet-ridden day at Newport in 1778. He experienced what many soldiers, mariners, and pilots have encountered ever since: the mystery of survival. Trumbull did not understand how he made it after being so exposed to danger and seeing bullets and cannon blasts blow off men's arms in his path. Like many before and after him, he turned to God for answers. Trumbull's story has been repeated throughout history. And during Vietnam, another young man encountered the same phenomenon of protection.

"Vic left for Vietnam on March 22, 1972, for a year tour as a crew member aboard an AC-130 gunship," his wife Bonnie Reid explained.

Their first child, Sherry, was only six and a half weeks old at the time. Less than three months later, on June 18th, Bonnie and Sherry went over to a friend's house for dinner. Vic's college roommate from Texas A&M University and his wife had invited them.

"We had finished dinner and I was sitting on the couch with Sherry when I had a strange feeling sweep over me. I excused myself and went home with Sherry. (It was already Sunday, June 19th in Vietnam)," Bonnie described of the prompting.

She didn't know until later why she had suddenly become so disturbed. "Unbeknownst to me, Vic had been on a mission and his plane was hit by a surface-to-air Missile, lost a wing, and was blown apart. There were fifteen crew members aboard the plane and only three got out alive—Vic being one of them."

The area, a remote spot at the time, was covered by the North Vietnamese army, who beat the trees to try to scare survivors out of their hiding places. The AC-130 flew its missions at night.

"Vic was not supposed to be on that flight since he had flown the night before. The guy that was supposed to fly took himself off flying status because a Buddhist Monk told him something was going to happen. The person they tried to get to replace him was downtown, so they went and got Vic out of bed to fly," Bonnie explained.

"Vic found a downed tree that had a hollow area beneath it. He crawled under it and covered himself with leaves, etc., to conceal himself. This was after he dug a hole and buried a picture of me and Sherry, and his Aggie ring, so if he was captured they would not find them on him."

Although one of his two radio transmitters did not work, Vic was able to use the other one to call the aircrews searching for him. He helped them to pinpoint his location, which was unmapped at the time. Eighteen hours after his plane went down, Vic Reid was rescued. And like John Trumbull two centuries earlier, he experienced two miracles beyond his understanding that night: surviving a plane crash and being rescued.[245]

"Trust in the LORD with all your heart and lean not on your own understanding" (PROVERBS 3:5).

**PRAYER**

*Your ways are mysterious, Lord, and beyond my understanding. I seek to trust you with life's mysteries.*

WEEK 36

# 246. Sabbath Rest: Departed Friends

Nathanael Greene was not the only Quaker to support the war. The Revolution sparked the same change of sentiment within many of the Society of Friends.

"*Some Quakers were conscientiously convinced that they could, despite the Friends' peace testimony, take up arms against the British. Calling themselves 'Free Quakers,' they organized in Philadelphia. The majority of Quakers adhered to the denomination's traditional position of pacifism and disowned their belligerent brethren,*" wrote a historian from the Library of Congress.

These Free Quakers made their own declaration of independence. They published a broadside or poster explaining their views.

"*Among the very great number of persons you have disowned for matters religious and civil, a number have felt a necessity for uniting together to discharge their religious duties which we undoubtedly owe to God and one another,*" the broadside began.

After being disowned by their friends for their support of the patriots, these Quakers believed it was their duty to God to continue in their worship of him. Even though this broadside was not a sermon, it reflects the beauty of trying to solve differences with humility.

"*And we rejoice in a firm hope, that as we humble ourselves before God, his presence will be found in them and his blessing descend and rest upon them,*" the broadside continued.

The "Free Quakers" declared their anguish over those who had disowned them and "*separated yourselves from us, and declared that you have no unity with us.*" The broadside had another purpose. The Free Quakers declared their rights to the property they had shared with the others for meetings and for burials. Before they tried to solve the dispute in a court of law, they wanted to resolve it in the court of cordial friendship.

"*It is very far from our wish to seclude you from a joint participation in the use of it; neither do we mean to solicit a decision in the law,*" the broadside continued.

The Free Quakers expressed their desire to speedily and amicably resolve the matter. They closed their broadside with the spirit of forgiveness. *"As Christians, laboring in some degree to forgive injuries, we salute you, and tho disowned and rejected by you, we are your friends and brethren."*

Their assertions are similar to the schisms that churches sometimes face today. The tone of this broadside was not contentious. They did not name-call. Instead these Free Quakers approached their brethren with humility.[246]

> "When men have a dispute, they are to take it to court and the judges will decide the case, acquitting the innocent and condemning the guilty" (DEUTERONOMY 25:1).

**PRAYER**

*God, thank you for desiring humanity to settle their disputes with each other. Grant me the spirit of humility when I try to resolve conflicts.*

# 247. Newport Native

Nathanael Greene was more despondent than most over Count d'Estaing's departure from Newport. The French flight wrecked the patriots' plans with as much force as the storm that had damaged the French fleet.

*"This disagreeable event has, as I apprehend, ruined all our operations,"* General Greene wrote to General Washington from the camp near Newport on August 28, 1778.

Greene described the American forces as respectable, numbering nearly nine thousand. But he had conceded that most had less than nine months' military experience. As a result the Americans relied on the French as if they were their own kin. When the French fleet fled, the reaction was brotherly bedlam.

*"It struck such a panic among the militia and volunteers, that they began to desert by shoals,"* reported Greene. *"The fleet no sooner set sail, than they began to be alarmed for their safety. This misfortune damped the hopes of our army, and gave new spirits to that of the enemy."*

Just as Benedict Arnold courageously defended Connecticut and Henry Knox knocked on doors for Boston, Greene asked to serve in the Newport campaign. The place was as close to his heart as his uniform. Newport was special to this native Rhode Islander because it was the site of his personal renaissance. It was in Newport that he studied under the tutelage of Ezra Stiles, a Congregationalist minister. Stiles introduced Greene to John Locke's political philosophy, Jonathan Swift's literature, and Isaac Watts's hymns. Greene had emerged as a patriot, a learned man, a more reverent soul, and an even more dedicated Rhode Islander.

But as much as Greene wanted to entirely blame the French, he knew the Americans were to blame as well. Some of the responsibility rested on General Sullivan and his soldiers. Sullivan's battlefield behavior was beyond reproach but his after-battle decisions were foolish.

*"General Sullivan very imprudently issued something like a censure in general orders,"* Greene wrote of Sullivan's absolute reprimand of the French. *"It opened the mouths of the army in very clamorous strains."*

Intelligence had also falsely raised their hopes. Spies had revealed the British were terrified of a combined French fleet and American land forces. *"Indeed, [British] General Pigot was heard to say, the garrison must fall, unless they were speedily relieved by a British fleet,"* Greene wrote.

*"The disappointment is vexatious and truly mortifying. The garrison was so important, and the reduction so certain, that I cannot with patience think of the event."*

For this native son, brotherly abandonment led to estrangement and despair in Newport.[247]

> "My kinsmen have gone away; my friends have forgotten me. My guests and my maidservants count me a stranger; they look upon me as an alien" (JOB 19:14, 15).

**PRAYER**

*God, I thank you that you will not abandon me. You are the ultimate Father, Brother, and Friend.*

# 248. Faulting the French

D*on't be surprised, my dear General; the generosity of your honest mind would be offended at the shocking sight I have under my eyes,"* the Marquis de Lafayette wrote to General Washington from camp near Providence on August 25, 1778.

This forlorn French star described his heart as *"injured"* after the Americans retreated from Rhode Island. Although Lafayette was devastated at the outcome, he was more upset at the blame game. The whispers among the soldiers shouted like cannons into Lafayette's ears. His beloved Americans faulted the French for the Rhode Island rout.

Unlike Greene, Lafayette decided the fault was less with the French and more with the Americans, whose land forces arrived a day earlier than

France's Count d'Estaing and America's General Sullivan had agreed to in their written plan.

*"The same day we landed, without his [d'Estaing's] knowledge, an English fleet appears in sight,"* Lafayette added, noting the situation was uneasy.

*"But, finding the next morning that the wind was northerly, being also convinced that it was his duty to prevent any reënforcement at Newport, he [d'Estaing] goes out, under the hottest fire of the British land-batteries; he puts the British navy to flight, and pursues them, and they were all in his hands when that horrid storm arrived to rain on all our hopes. Both fleets are divided, scattered,"* he continued.

Lafayette related that after the storm the French fleet met again. They soon discovered that their shattered boats and lack of food and water made them vulnerable. Intelligence from Sullivan also indicated the British were sending out another fleet. Lafayette and Greene sailed out to consult with d'Estaing. They learned the count was under orders from King Louis XVI to return to Boston in case of an accident.

*"He [d'Estaing] called a new Council of War, and, finding every body of the same opinion, he did not think himself justifiable in staying here [in Newport] any longer, and took leave of me with true affliction, not being able to assist America for some days; which has been rewarded with the most horrid ungratefulness,"* he wrote of the multitude of pointing fingers he had seen among American soldiers. Lafayette refused to sign the American petition against the French.

*"The Count said to me these last words: 'After many months of sufferings, my men will rest some days; I will man my ships, and, if I am assisted in getting masts, &c., three weeks after my arrival I shall go out again, and then we shall fight for the glory of the French name, and the interests of America,'"* wrote Lafayette, quoting Count d'Estaing.

> "Your servants are given no straw, yet we are told, 'Make bricks!' Your servants are being beaten, but the fault is with your own people" (EXODUS 5:16).

This French star, the Marquis de Lafayette, hoped to rise above the blame game by revealing the truth as he saw it.[248]

**PRAYER**

*Father, I cannot stand blameless before you. Forgive me for my sins and hold back my hand the next time I am tempted to point fingers.*

# 249. Freedom from Grumbling

As much as winning the war, the Marquis de Lafayette longed to see cooperation and mutual friendship develop between the nation of his birth and his adopted land. After the Rhode Island rout, the animosity between the two pained him as sibling rivalry does a father. The fury nearly knocked this French star from the skies.

*"Forgive me for it; it is not to the Commander-in-chief, it is to my most dearest friend, General Washington, that I am speaking, I want to lament with him the ungenerous sentiments I have been forced to see in many American breasts,"* Lafayette continued in his letter to George Washington on August 25, 1778, after the French fleet fled Rhode Island.

*"Could you believe that . . . instead of resenting their accidents as those of allies and brothers, the people [American militia] turned mad at their departure, and, wishing them all the evils in the world, did treat them as a generous one would be ashamed to treat the most inveterate enemies?"* Lafayette asked as the anguish poured from his pen.

Lafayette tried to show the positive outcomes of Count d'Estaing's arrival and the count's desire to contribute to the American cause. Despite the temporary failure in Rhode Island, the French fleet's appearance in America's waters caused the British to evacuate Philadelphia and opened up *"all the harbors."*

*"Frenchmen of the highest character have been exposed to the most disagreeable circumstances; and yet, myself the friend of America, the friend of General Washington, I am more upon a warlike footing in the American lines than when I came near the British lines at Newport,"* he wrote. *"Such is, my dear General, the true state of matters. I am sure it will infinitely displease and hurt your feelings."*

Reassuring his commitment to America's thirteen stars, Lafayette made it clear he did not blame anyone in particular. *"I have no complaints at all to make to you against any one; but I lament, with you, that I have had an occasion of seeing so ungenerous sentiments in American hearts,"* he wrote, adding his opinion on the true source of blame: desire for personal glory.

*"All that I know is, that I shall be very happy to see the fleet coöperating with General Washington himself."*

Lafayette wondered if he could do more to foster a better relationship between the awkward allies. He decided to return to France to serve as an intermediary between the Americans and the French. He also wanted to see the face of his second daughter and mourn the death of his first daughter. By year's end, Congress sent him home to consult with Benjamin Franklin.

Hence, the Marquis de Lafayette found a way to rise above the faultfinding. He was more determined than ever to forge friendship. Each hardship increased the luster of the luminary Lafayette.[249]

> "These men are grumblers and fault-finders; they follow their own evil desires; they boast about themselves and flatter others for their own advantage" (JUDE 16).

**PRAYER**

*God, show me the difference between grumbling and submitting my burdens before you. Free me from the temptation to find fault and replace it with the desire to serve.*

# 250. Kinsmen-Redeemers

Your Excellency may rest assured, that I have done every thing in my power to cultivate and promote a good understanding, both with the Count [d'Estaing] and the Marquis, and flatter myself that I am upon very good terms with them both," Nathanael Greene wrote to General Washington on August 28, 1778.

As abandoned as Greene felt following the French fleet's flight from Newport, he made an important decision. He could have ruined Lafayette's reputation. Instead this iron foundry owner cast a mold of friendship and forgiveness. Greene chose to shine a light of loyalty on this rising French star. He became Lafayette's closest "kinsman-redeemer."

"The Marquis's great thirst for glory, and national attachment, often run him into errors. However, he did every thing to prevail on the Admiral to coöperate with us, that man could do. People censure the Admiral with great freedom, and many are imprudent enough to reproach the nation through the Admiral," Greene wrote.

Greene's need to redeem didn't end with Lafayette. From his new position in Boston, he learned the British were trying to make the most of the strained French-American relationship.

"The secret enemies to our cause, and the British officers in the neighbourhood of this place, are endeavouring to sow the seeds of discord as much as possible between the inhabitants of the place [Boston] and the French belonging to the fleet," Greene wrote to Washington on September 16th.

Greene and John Hancock explained to the French officers that the British were behind the rumors, that their common enemy had been whipping up dissension. *"The French officers are well satisfied this is the state of the case, and it fills them with double resentment against the British,"* continued Greene. *"The Admiral and all the French officers are now upon an exceeding good footing with the gentlemen of the town. General Hancock takes unwearied pains to promote a good understanding with the French officers. His house is full from morning till night."*

*"All the French officers are extravagantly fond of your Excellency; but the Admiral more so than any of the rest. They all speak of you with the highest reverence and respect."*

Nathanael Greene then reported a gesture that sealed their efforts to redeem their *"kinsmen"* French. They cast another mold of redemption, one in the shape of a portrait. *"General Hancock made the Admiral a present of your picture. He was going to receive it on board the fleet by the firing of a royal salute,"* he wrote.

They used the power of gift-giving to soften the strained French-American relationship. This was one of many steps needed to build a successful working relationship between the two bands of brothers.[250]

> "Although it is true that I am near of kin, there is a kinsman-redeemer nearer than I" (RUTH 3:12).

**PRAYER**

*Thank you for the power of friendship and the joy that comes when strained relationships are redeemed through forgiveness and selfless giving.*

## 251. Reputations Threatened by Storm

Life for the Continental Congress wasn't easy in Philadelphia. They may not have suffered the severest elements of nature, as had the troops at Valley Forge, but they faced their own set of changing weather patterns. Sometimes their struggles were quite personal, worsened by rumors of more rain.

When John Hancock left the Continental Congress to return home to Boston, his townsfolk wildly speculated about his decision. Had he failed in Congress? Was there an argument? Why did he leave? The rumors reached the ears of Samuel Adams, who was still with the Continental Congress. He did his best to correct the record.

*"You ask me what occasiond the very sudden return of Mr H—,"* Adams responded to his friend's letter in August 1778. *"I answer in his own Word to me, His own Want of Health & the dangerous Illness of his Lady. You say he arrivd quite unexpected—you must surely be mistaken;*

*for he publickly said he had Leave of Absence from his Constituents,"* defended Adams, countering the conjectures and reporting on the illness of Hancock's wife. *"It is the Lot of a great Man to have every Movement he makes critically scanned, and the strangest Constructions are oftentimes put upon those parts of his Conduct which may be most easily explained."*

But Hancock was not the only one with a cloud hanging over his decisions. Adams himself was the target of falsehoods that hit him harder than hailstones.

*"My Boston Friends tell me with great Solicitude that I have Enemies there. I thank them for their Concern for me, and tell them I knew it before,"* Adams wrote to his wife. *"The Man who acts an honest Part in publick Life, must often counteract the Passions Inclinations or Humours of weak and wicked Men,"* he continued, *"and this must create him Enemies. I am therefore not disappointed or mortified."*

Adams believed these rumors were intentional untruths from his foes. He understood that his enemies wanted to remove him from the Massachusetts Assembly and the Continental Congress. He knew virtue would overpower forty days of rain with the beauty of a rainbow. *"I flatter my self that no virtuous Man who knows me will or can be my Enemy; because I think he can have no Suspicion of my Integrity,"* he told his wife confidently.

Adams's faith was also a lightning rod protecting him from sudden lethal surges. *"But they say my Enemies 'are plotting against me.' Neither does this discompose me, for what else can I expect from such kind of Men. If they mean to make me uneasy they miss their Aim; for I am happy and it is not in their Power to disturb my Peace,"* he wrote of the truth.

> "The righteous hate what is false, but the wicked bring shame and disgrace" (PROVERBS 13:5).

Righteousness was Samuel Adams's umbrella.[251]

**PRAYER**

*God, stir my heart. Be my umbrella today against the falsehoods of life.*

# 252. The Revolution Today: Not Knowing

"Not knowing. Not knowing how badly hurt he was, not knowing how he was doing, not knowing what the next step would be," is how Bonnie Reid described the hardest part of learning her husband's plane had been shot down in Vietnam in 1972.

"I wasn't notified when Vic was taken to the MASH unit in Da Nang until Vic called his father who was at Webb Air Force Base in West Texas. His dad called my dad and my dad told me," Bonnie recalled. She was told Vic had lost his leg.

And although the greatest miracle was Vic's survival, their ability to speak to each other while Vic was in the hospital at Clark Air Force Base in the Philippines was also remarkable.

"Unable to get a call through to him, I called a general at Hickam Air Force Base in Hawaii, who was the father of one of Vic's classmates. His daughter and I were also good friends. I explained the situation to General McNabb and he sent a priority message to the Clark Air Force Base hospital that Lieutenant Reid was to have an immediate line to call me stateside," Bonnie said.

Vic and Bonnie were then able to talk, which brought her great relief. It turned out Vic had not lost a leg. Instead, shrapnel had severed ligaments in his left foot.

"Fortunately, I never received a phone bill for all of my calls to the Philippines. Unbeknownst to me, someone who worked at the phone company knew my dad and took care of it for me. As you can imagine, the bill would have been huge," Bonnie said with relief.

Vic spent a month in the hospital and then went to Thailand to finish his required days in that country. "Once I was able to talk with him, it was better. I actually had a calm about me. I had total faith that God would not let anything else happen to him. It was clear to me that God had saved Vic for a reason. After all, out of fifteen crew members on that plane, only three got out alive. God had to have had a reason He kept Vic alive," she said.

"Over the years it has been made clear to me that that was correct. Vic has touched so many lives with his testimony. I remember vividly when we were stationed at Castle Air Force Base in Merced, California, and we had one of Vic's students over for dinner. This young man told us he was an atheist. I asked him why and his reply was simply that he did not believe in a God. I told him about Vic's experience and explained that there had to be a God and why I believed so. That young man became a Christian."

Like Col. John Trumbull after the battle of Newport in 1778, Vic and Bonnie Reid turned their worst "not knowing" moment into oppor-

> "In all your ways acknowledge him, and he will make your paths straight" (PROVERBS 3:6).

tunities to acknowledge God and the miracle he had worked in their lives.[252]

**PRAYER**

*I salute you today, Lord, and acknowledge your presence in my life and the lives of others.*

# 253. Sabbath Rest:
# Advantageous Connections

I t is certain, however, that we did not seek an independence; and it is
equally certain that Britain, though she meant to oppose it with all her
power, has by a strange infatuation, taken the most direct, and perhaps
the only methods that could have established it," Samuel Cooper said,
accepting the idea of war.

Cooper, the pastor of Brattle Street Church in Boston, began this sermon with a comparison of Israel's government to America's. Then he
swiftly entered the waters of recent history. Although America had not
sought war, the conflict had resulted in the unexpected blessing of liberty.
Becoming an independent nation was a better long-term solution than an
ineffective dependence on Britain.

Cooper also noted that America's quest for independence had begun to
ripple to foreign shores. Waves of respect began to form in other nations.
Cooper cheered these *"new, advantageous and honorable connections."* With
France as an ally, final victory might cast its anchor on America. This alliance
just might encourage other nations to recognize America's sovereignty.

*"Independence gives us a rank among the nations of the earth, which
no precept of our religion forbids us to understand and feel, and which
we should be ambitious to support in the most reputable manner,"* he told
his congregation.

*"It opens to us a free communication with all the world, not only for
the improvement of commerce, and the acquisition of wealth, but also for
the cultivation of the most useful knowledge. It naturally unfetters and
expands the human mind, and prepares it for the impression of the most
exalted virtues."*

Cooper believed that divine Providence had smiled on America as a
result of the Declaration of Independence. The alliance of the colonies,
now states, was evidence of Providence's rain of favor resulting from
their willingness to pursue justice. *"We have stood upon the ground of
justice, honor, and liberty, and acted merely a defensive part,"* observed
Cooper. In his view, war was necessary. Failure to fight would have been

the true act of rebellion, disobedience to the *"heavenly call."*

Indeed by entering into the conflict, America demonstrated a collective faith before Providence, and received the blessing of respect among nations. Samuel Cooper used this sermon to reflect upon the war and give thanks for France, America's most advantageous political connection. And by doing so he praised America's most advantageous spiritual connection.[253]

> "Open the gates that the righteous nation may enter, the nation that keeps faith"
> (ISAIAH 26:2).

**PRAYER**

*I pray for our nation. May people look to you and recognize that you are their most advantageous connection.*

# 254. Manifesto

The Continental Congress found itself facing a big problem in the fall of 1778.

*"The United States . . . having been at length forced to shake off a yoke which had grown too burdensome to bear, they declared themselves free and independent,"* Congress's manifesto began.

With no clear exit strategy and reports of British barbarity in the countryside, it was time to remind Americans what was manifestly obvious to Congress. When the members of Congress looked in the mirror, they saw men committed to independence. But many Americans saw Congress's intentions with the clarity of seeing through a foggy window. For the common good, Congress needed to rally the troops, stir the patriots, and fan the flames. They turned to Samuel Adams, the "Puritan" famous for his anonymous publications, to pen their manifesto.

*"Their virtuous citizens have borne . . . the loss of many things which make life desirable,"* the manifesto proclaimed in an effort to show Americans that Congress viewed their sacrifices with the closeness of a spyglass and the clarity of a crystal.

*"Their brave troops have patiently endured the hardships and dangers of the situation,"* the manifesto added, praising America's successful campaigns such as Boston, Trenton and Princeton, and Saratoga.

The document also reflected the faith of the members of Congress. Although their desire was *"to love their enemies as children of that Being who is equally the Father of all,"* they *"could not prevent"* the calamities of war.

The manifesto then outlined recent grievances against the king and his army. The British army had allowed prisoners of war to rot to death. They had tried to bribe American diplomats. They had burned *"defense-less villages"* and *"butchered"* Americans.

*"They have made a mock of religion by impious appeals to God,"* the manifesto continued, adding that Britain's failure to uphold virtue was shameful.

*"We, therefore, the Congress of the United States of America, do solemnly declare and proclaim that if our enemies presume to execute their threats, or persist in their present career of barbarity, we will take such exemplary vengeance as shall deter others from a like conduct,"* the manifesto committed.

The members of the Continental Congress were so determined to show the justice of their cause that they were willing to stand before God on the matter.

*"We appeal to the God who searcheth the hearts of men for the rectitude of our intentions,"* the manifesto concluded. And thus with the common good in mind, the Continental Congress issued a manifesto.[254]

> "Now to each one the manifestation of the Spirit is given for the common good"
> (1 CORINTHIANS 12:7).

**PRAYER**

*Reveal to me ways to show concern for the common good of those around me. May my life manifest your compassion for others.*

# 255. Martha's Loneliness

George Washington's decision to camp his army in Middlebrook, New Jersey, in 1779 increased the loneliness afflicting his wife. Letters from home were so scarce Martha wondered if her children and friends had forgotten her.

*"Not having received any letter from you, the two last posts—I have only to tell you, that the general & myself are well, all is quiet in this quarters; It is from the south ward that we expect to hear news,—we are very anxious to know how our affairs are going in that quarters,"* she wrote to Jack and Nelly in March 1779.

Loneliness brought a bit of paranoia to her pen. *"I hear so very seldom from you, that I don't know where you are . . . The last letter from*

*Nelly she now says Boath the children have been very ill, they were she hoped getting better—if you do not write to me—I will not write to you again or till I get letters from you,"* she stated, noting that some friends had forgotten to write to her.

Martha's anxiety mirrored her son's apprehension during the New York campaign in 1776. No news was not good news. Isolation was madness. *"I am kept in the cruelest State of Uncertainty. I have scarcely had a Letter from New York, the Gen has been much kinder than I expected, but the others have very seldom wrote,—I must beg of you to write me everything you can collect relative to the Army at New York &c in Canada, and all other News, by every Post,"* Jack had written his mother in August 1776.

Loneliness was the price of loyalty. Martha and Jack were primarily devoted to their immediate families. As Martha's last living child Jack had committed himself to his own growing clan. As much as Martha wanted to be with her grandchildren, her first priority was to care for her home on the road.

*"Mrs. Washington would remain loyal to the Revolution, but her devotion was to more than just an idea of what constituted a proper government. A large part of the faithfulness to 'the cause,' shown by her during the war, derived from the tremendous personal loyalty she felt toward her husband,"* expressed Mount Vernon historian Mary Thompson.

*"This comes through most strongly when the illnesses and deaths of various family members pulled her in several directions,"* Thompson said, noting that not even her sister's death or her mother's illness induced Martha to return to Virginia.

Although loneliness threatened her, it did not overtake her. Martha Washington understood the value and reward of caring for those in her immediate care, her husband and his army.[255]

> "Do not forsake your friend and the friend of your father, and do not go to your brother's house when disaster strikes you—better a neighbor nearby than a brother far away" (PROVERBS 27:10).

**PRAYER**

*God, may I reach out to those closest to me today, the ones I can touch and hear. May I be present for those around me.*

# 256. Southern Flood

On the banks of the Savannah River, Gen. Benjamin Lincoln picked up his pen and wrote a letter to George Washington. The news he had to share in early January 1779 drummed like a funeral dirge in his patriotic ears. The previous two weeks had nearly buried America's southern army.

*"I received information at Charleston, that the enemy had arrived, with upwards of twenty ships, at Tybee, near the mouth of the River Savannah, and in a harbour south of the river,"* he wrote.

As swiftly as they entered the harbor, the British had taken Savannah on December 28, 1778. America's five hundred men were trapped by three thousand enemy forces on one side and an impassable swamp on the other.

When this New Englander accepted the role of commander of the armies in the South, he hoped to find a multitude of militia and a brimming supply of meals and munitions. Instead, Lincoln found a region flooded with problems.

*"I have met with almost every disappointment since I came into this department [the army in Georgia]. After an encouragement to expect a force consisting of seven thousand men, besides the militia of South Carolina and Georgia, I have now only fourteen hundred,"* Lincoln revealed to Washington.

*"I was assured that there were a great plenty of supplies and military stores; instead of which, there were no field-pieces, arms, tents, camp utensils, lead (and very little powder), intrenching tools; and, in short, hardly all articles in the arsenal or Quartermaster-General's store . . . I forbear; the subject is disagreeable; for you to hear, will be painful,"* Lincoln told his superior.

The southern commander also described how the overflowing banks of the Savannah River prevented boats, and thus recruits, to easily pass through. The British commanded the region's other navigable rivers. Worst of all, Lincoln found a downpour of opposition from Georgians loyal to the crown.

But Lincoln did not end his letter without hope. *"As soon as a body of men, equal to covering the State of Georgia, can be collected, we shall recross the Savannah,"* he promised.

Whether or not he realized it, Benjamin Lincoln found himself in the middle of Britain's new

> "Rescue me from the mire, do not let me sink; deliver me from those who hate me, from the deep waters. Do not let the floodwaters engulf me or the depths swallow me up or the pit close its mouth over me" (PSALM 69:14, 15).

strategy. The British had decided the North was in a stalemate, and sent three thousand troops to Georgia. They hoped to win by taking the American colonies one by one. Beginning with Georgia, they planned to flood the far South and work their way north to Virginia.[256]

**PRAYER**

*Thank you for holding back the floodwaters. I look to you for those times in my life when I need rescuing.*

# 257. Southern Storms

I have daily the unhappiness to see families of affluence fleeing before the enemy, reduced in a few hours to a state of want," Gen. Benjamin Lincoln wrote to George Washington about the civil war he saw and heard about in Georgia. Although he had witnessed many terrors on the battlefield, these hostilities horrified Lincoln.

With a flood of British soldiers pouring into Georgia, loyalists emerged from the dark clouds to rain terror and ruthlessness on their neighbors. Many Georgia Tories attacked patriots with more surprise than a blue norther.

Georgia was unique among its sister states. The colony's remoteness, poverty, and mixed political sentiments prevented its leaders from sending representatives to the first meeting of the Continental Congress in 1774. And when Georgia's three delegates arrived in Congress in 1775, their manner of dressing was as unique to the other delegates as their manner of speaking.

*"Two of the Georgia Delegates are possessed of Homespun Suits of Cloaths, an Adornment few other Members can boast of,"* a delegate from New Jersey wrote.

Boston was probably the American town most dedicated to the Revolution. The further south one went, the more divided the people's politics.

*"Ever since hostilities had begun, in 1775, the revolutionary party had been dominant in the South. Yet now again in 1779 the British flag floated over the capital of Georgia. Some rejoiced and some mourned. Men do not change lightly their political allegiance,"* historian William Jackman told.

Jackman noted that loyalists began to assert themselves once British soldiers captured Savannah in December 1778. They rallied again when the redcoats took Augusta in February 1779. *"When the British seemed secure in Georgia,"* described Jackman, *"bands of Loyalists marched into the British camp in furious joy that now their day was come, and gave no gentle advice as to the crushing of rebellion."*

The conflict among loyalists and patriot neighbors became as ruthless as earlier conflicts between settlers and Indians. *"Many a patriot farmhouse was now destroyed and the hapless owner either killed or driven to the mountains to live as best he could by hunting. Sometimes even the children were shot down,"* Jackman wrote.

After the losses of Savannah and Augusta, farmer fought against farmer, neighbor against neighbor, and army against army. Such hostilities weakened the Americans while strengthening the British. By the spring of 1779, the British army was strong enough to synchronize a system of supply posts throughout Georgia. They had in place the resources they needed to march northward into the Carolinas.[257]

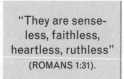

"They are senseless, faithless, heartless, ruthless" (ROMANS 1:31).

**PRAYER**

*When I hear of humanity's ruthlessness, use such news to draw me to you and seek your goodness.*

# 258. Honor Questioned

The prospects for victory in New England seemed reduced to rubble. George Washington found himself facing a military standstill in 1779. Although no major battles with the British ensued that year, Washington was not idle: Indian raids, scarcity of funds, and, worst of all, courts-martial, plagued the commander-in-chief.

One of the most serious blows came from Benedict Arnold's service as the military governor of Philadelphia. When the British departed the city and the patriots returned to power, Arnold became the military governor there. He closed all the stores to take an inventory, which was a common martial law practice. But Arnold's decisions, coupled with his prickly personality and temper, propelled many, including Joseph Reed, to action. The result was an avalanche.

Reed began a newspaper campaign to remove Arnold. Once again Arnold lost the respect he thought he deserved. Facing yet another assault on his honor, Arnold felt his only recourse was to resign from his Philadelphia command—but not until he cleared his name, as he explained to Washington.

*"When you were so kind as to permit me to resign my command of this city, and retire from the service until recovered of my wounds, I expected to have it done immediately,"* Arnold wrote to Washington on March 19, 1779, *"but the villainous attacks made on my character by the president and council of this state in their publications made it necessary for me to continue in my command until their charges were cleared up or resign under the idea of compulsion and disgrace."*

Arnold informed Washington that the Continental Congress had exonerated him. *"A committee of Congress having reported in my favor, that objection ceases, I have therefore in consequence of your Excellency's permission relinquished my command,"* Arnold wrote.

Philadelphia had been good for Arnold in one way. He had met a young woman, Peggy Shipman. Although rumors abounded that she was a loyalist, Peggy stole Arnold's heart. The pair married.

With his name seemingly cleared by Congress and his bride by his side, Arnold looked toward his future and hoped he could once again serve Washington in a field assignment. *"As long as my wounds will permit, I shall be happy to take a command in the line of the Army and at all times of rendering my Country every service in my power,"* he offered. But Benedict Arnold would soon stumble over his past. He would face a court-martial for his actions as Philadelphia's military governor.[258]

> "'A stone that causes men to stumble and a rock that makes them fall.' They stumble because they disobey the message— which is also what they were destined for" (1 PETER 2:8).

**PRAYER**

*Father, keep me from decisions that will make me stumble before you.*

# 259. The Revolution Today: Thanking Those Who Serve

Brother against brother. Neighbor against neighbor. It's hard to imagine life during the Revolutionary War, especially in 1779 when the South erupted into a civil war following British victories in Georgia. It's hard to imagine something you haven't seen or experienced. And although Americans have grown accustomed to watching tragedies unfold, television and the movies do not issue licenses of empathy or understanding.

Military families especially need support when the news is filled with war. It's easy to identify these families if they live on a military installation. "Most military communities are packed with a soldier's immediate family: wife, husband and kids. You can find them outside of our military bases in towns like Clarksville, Fayetteville and Killeen to name a few," Captain Dan Sukman explained in his diary for the FOX News Web site.

But many military families, particularly those whose family members serve in the National Guard and Reserves, blend into their hometowns.

"Family members are a little more difficult to recognize. They don't wear a uniform, no high and tights on the tops of their heads, but you can find them in almost any community. They attend and teach in our schools and coach and participate in local athletic teams. Often they do so without one of their parents attending a game, or meeting their teacher at the local school," Sukman wrote, noting that one of the best ways to help is to recognize the sacrifices they have made. A "thank you" goes a long way.

Often the worst words a military family member can hear are these: "I understand what you are going through," particularly from someone who has not been there. So what can you say to wartime military families who live in daily uncertainty or who have lost a loved one?

"I would thank them for being strong for their loved one and allowing them to go defend our country," suggested military wife Bonnie Reid. Her husband survived a plane crash in Vietnam.

In addition to saying "thanks," another way to express comfort and encouragement is through prayer. "I would let them know that there are many of us praying for them and their loved ones and how grateful we are that they are willing to go and defend our freedoms and help others gain theirs," Bonnie continued.

Love is also best expressed through action, not just words.

"Acknowledge the sacrifice they have made and assure them that there are many who are praying for them. Stay in touch with them if you are able and find ways to help. Help with the kids, chores, meals, dealing with settlement matters, etc.," shared Bonnie Reid.

> "Do not be wise in your own eyes; fear the LORD and shun evil. This will bring health to your body and nourishment to your bones" (PROVERBS 3:7, 8).

Thanksgiving, prayer, and practical help are wise ways to nourish the hearts of those who serve.[259]

**PRAYER**

*God, give me the opportunity to thank someone who has served our nation through the military.*

# 260. Sabbath Rest:
# Revolutionary Religion

The revolutionary religion of the patriots resulted in several changes of the mind and heart. They had decided that their king was completely human, devoid of any divinity. Many now equated the monarchy with evil. Preachers were no longer afraid to speak on the civic responsibility of citizens. Pastors wrestled openly from the pulpit about whether Christians could take up arms. The biblical principle of standing firm for liberty provided a standard for rejecting tyranny.

One minister, who had served on the bench and in the colonial halls of Connecticut's general assembly, asked a different question before the war. What was the government's role in religion? His answer explains why so many ministers delivered sermons explicitly proclaiming the religion of Christ to an audience of government leaders.

Elisha Williams's sermon on the essential rights of Protestants presented another colonial viewpoint: Government should not establish any religion. *"That the civil authority have no power to establish any religion (i.e., any professions of faith, modes of worship, or church government) of a human form and composition,"* he proclaimed.

Establishing religion meant interfering with church government or prescribing worship. Williams believed such matters were the dominion of God, not government.

*"It does, I think, from hence follow, that no order of men have any right to establish any mode of worship, &c. as a rule binding to particular Christians . . . ,"* he said. *"Religion must remain on that foot where Christ has placed it. He has fully declared his mind as to what Christians are to believe and do in all religious matters."*

Religion and government were as intertwined in the colonies as the threads of a seaman's rope. Because England had designated a state church, the colonists feared their new governments might impose church membership.

*"But to carry the notion of a religious establishment so far as to make it a rule binding to the subjects, or on any penalties whatsoever, seems to*

me to be oppressive of Christianity," stressed Williams, who opposed obliging "Christians to believe or practice any thing in religion not true or not agreeable to the word of God."

Elisha Williams simply believed "that a Christian is to receive his Christianity from Christ alone."[260]

**PRAYER**

Thank you for reminding me it is you alone who deserves to be called "Teacher" and "Father." You alone are the Author of faith.

> "And do not call anyone on earth 'father,' for you have one Father, and he is in heaven. Nor are you to be called 'teacher,' for you have one Teacher, the Christ"
>
> (MATTHEW 23:9, 10).

# 261. Impatient for Justice

Coordinating the trial of Benedict Arnold seemed as endless as the snow at Valley Forge. Although Congress had accepted Arnold's defense of his actions as military governor in Pennsylvania, they had referred the matter to a military court, adding yet another boulder on Washington's mountain of problems. On April 20, 1779, Washington wrote to Arnold that his trial was scheduled for May 1, 1779. But six days later, Washington wrote Arnold again.

"I found myself under necessity of postponing your trial to a later period, than that for which I notified your attendance. I send you this information in a hurry," Washington told him about the change. He also told Arnold that the council of Pennsylvania, Arnold's accusers, requested the trial delay. They needed more time to bring their witnesses from Virginia and the Carolinas to New York.

Arnold exploded. He considered producing witnesses a "pretence" and a "calculated" move to delay justice. Arnold believed three months was plenty of time to bring any evidence against him. He also called his opponents "cowards" and "villains." His language was hotter than a thousand campfires.

"I have been injustly accused and that I have been refused justice from Congress on the report of this committee," Arnold defended himself in writing to Washington. His anger then turned into irrational threats.

"For heavens sake let me be immediately tried and if found guilty, Executed. I want no favor. I ask only for Justice. It is denied me from your Excellency. I have no where to seek it but of the Candid Public before whom I shall be under the necessity of laying the whole matter," Arnold thundered.

The man who once pined for the commander-in-chief's respect now bad-mouthed him. *"Having made every sacrifice of my Fortune and my blood and become a Cripple on the Service of my Country, I little expected to meet the ungrateful Returns I have received of my Countryman,"* he responded.

Washington responded by giving Arnold a trial date in early June. Assuring him it would take place unless something extraordinary prevented it, Washington also reminded Arnold that he had to be fair to both sides. Although he held no unfavorable sentiments toward Arnold, the charges were serious.

By midsummer the trial was postponed indefinitely for the same reasons as the earlier delay. Arnold requested a leave of absence to tend to personal affairs. But he soon would write another letter, one that would forever change him and alter the course of the war. As much as Benedict Arnold wanted justice and fairness, he lacked the patience to wait for it. His overreaction and defensiveness would prove his downfall.[261]

> "Masters, provide your slaves with what is right and fair, because you know that you also have a Master in heaven" (COLOSSIANS 4:1).

**PRAYER**

*God, make me aware of the times when I needlessly put off or delay responsibilities you have given me. May I treat others fairly.*

# 262. Naval Novelty

The two enemy ships were stuck together like conjoined twins.

*"A novelty in naval combats was now presented to many witnesses, but to few admirers,"* Lt. Richard Dale wrote of the entangled ships who *"lay closely pressed against each other"* on their starboard sides.

Worse for Dale, he was on board the ship that was sinking. A crewman on America's forty-two-gun *Bonhomme Richard*, Dale witnessed one of the most desperate battles in naval history. He was also one of Captain John Paul Jones's most trusted officers.

Jones's mission was to cruise the British seas and harass English vessels. He departed with the *Richard* (named after Benjamin Franklin's almanac *Poor Richard's*) and four other American and French ships in late August 1779. They came upon a convoy of English merchant ships off the coast of Scotland on September 23rd. These British ships were protected by a forty-four gun ship called the *Serapis*. When the *Serapis* and the *Bonhomme Richard* came within range of each other, the *Serapis* crew demanded to know the name of the American ship. They threatened to fire if the *Bonhomme Richard* failed to answer.

*"At this moment I received orders from Commodore Jones to commence the action with a broadside, which indeed appeared to be simultaneous on board both ships,"* Dale reported of the double firing.

And with cannons blazing from both ships, the battle began. Dale explained how the ships passed each other a couple of times. Once when the captain of the *Serapis* steered ahead, he attempted to rake the *Bonhomme Richard* but discovered he didn't have enough space. Jones then obtained the headway and ran the *Bonhomme Richard*'s bow into the stern of the *Serapis*.

The ships separated, but not for long. In the time it takes for a fisherman to cast his net, the *Serapis* attempted to reel in her prey. *"The Serapis bore short round upon her heel, and her jib boom ran into the mizen rigging of the* Bonhomme Richard,*"* Dale wrote when the pole on the bow of the *Serapis* ran into the *Richard's* middle mast.

While Jones ordered his men to fasten the two ships together with a heavy towing rope, the *Serapis* tried to let go of her anchor and escape the entanglement. But Jones was faster and the naval novelty was sealed. The bow of the *Serapis* lay square along the *Bonhomme Richard*'s stern. *"The action recommenced from the starboard sides of the two ships,"* Dale wrote.

The fighting continued for another hour. Soon it was clear to John Paul Jones and Richard Dale that the *Bonhomme Richard* was sinking. They were dashed upon the rocks, caught in a fisherman's snare. It was time to pray.[262]

> "Fearing that we would be dashed against the rocks, they dropped four anchors from the stern and prayed for daylight" (ACTS 27:29).

**PRAYER**

*When life throws me against the rocks, remind me to pray. You are the Anchor of my life.*

# 263. Striking against a Strike

What motivated John Paul Jones to risk entangling his ship with the British? The answer was as simple as a flag. *"Has your ship struck [surrendered]?"* a *Serapis* crew member called shortly after the fighting began on September 23, 1779.

Captain Jones wondered why the British called for quarter so early in the battle. But the flagless mast of his ship, *Bonhomme Richard,* revealed the answer. Jones concluded that cannons had blown the flag away, or his crew had removed it. Regardless, the flag's absence was a sign of surrender.

The situation angered Jones more than being called a pirate, which the British called him repeatedly. He knew the source of the appellation. Years earlier, while leading a British trade ship in the Caribbean, Jones had ordered a man flogged for mutiny. But the crew went too far, and the man later died. Realizing he could not receive justice in a British court, Jones emigrated to his brother's Virginia plantation. Much like Moses fleeing Egypt for the desert, Jones found new life in America.

*"Surrender? I have not yet begun to fight!"* Jones replied, and then ordered his men to begin. Jones later modestly described his now-famous charge. *"The English commodore asked me if I demanded quarter, and I having answered him in the most determined negative, they renewed the battle with double fury,"* Jones wrote.

Shortly after his cry for justice, the two ships became entangled and the *Bonhomme Richard* began to sink. *"My situation was really deplorable; the* Bonhomme Richard *received various shot under water . . . the leak gained on the pumps, and the fire increased much on board both ships . . . My treacherous master-at-arms let loose all my prisoners without my knowledge, and my prospects became gloomy indeed,"* recalled the American captain.

Jones then ordered his sharpshooters to target the men on the deck of the *Serapis.* Their success enabled his men to board the enemy ship. *"I would not, however, give up the point. The enemy's mainmast began to shake, their firing decreased fast, ours rather increased, and the British colours were struck at half an hour past ten o'clock,"* Jones remembered.

The *Bonhomme Richard* sank, but the *Serapis* was Jones's prize and transport to safety. Jones later received three new names for his bravery. In France he earned the title *Chevalier,* or "knight." The Continental Congress made him a gold medalist. And although he remained a pirate to the British, John Paul Jones became the first American naval hero.[263]

> " 'A thousand will flee at the threat of one; at the threat of five you will all flee away, till you are left like a flagstaff on a mountaintop, like a banner on a hill.' Yet the LORD longs to be gracious to you; he rises to show you compassion" (ISAIAH 30:17–18).

PRAYER

*Thank you that you don't strike your colors. You are a God of justice and mercy.*

# 264. Of Food and Money

I find our prospects are infinitely worse than they have been at any period of the War," George Washington wrote to Congress from his winter headquarters in Morristown, New Jersey, in late 1779.

Once again scarcity threatened his army, and thus his plea for help. If the army dissolved over the lack of food, the Revolution would also starve to death. Washington begged, *"Unless some expedient can be instantly adopted a dissolution of the army for want of subsistence is unavoidable. A part of it has been again several days without Bread."*

Unfortunately, Washington's problems at Morristown were only just beginning as he penned his letter to Congress in December of 1779. The winter of 1779–80 proved to be colder than Valley Forge.

*"It was said to be the worst winter in the history of North America. There were twenty-six snow storms, six of blizzard proportions. It was so cold that in the month of January on all but two days the temperature was below freezing,"* historian Bruce Chadwick explained.

The extreme cold plagued the army well into the spring. May's flowers saw snow showers. The scarcity of food mirrored the shortages in the economy. The coffers were so empty that Congress was more than six months behind in paying Washington's army.

*"The Army never stood in greater need of them. On several days the Troops have been intirely destitute of provision of this kind, and at best they have only received for a considerable time past, but an Eighth, a Quarter, a Half allowance,"* Washington wrote of the back wages.

Washington may have been a micromanager, but he was also a middle manager. He was the midpoint in the army's train of resources. Washington begged for allowances and food from Congress while shouting the needs to state leaders, who were responsible for feeding the soldiers from their states.

*"It is with infinite pain I inform You, that we are reduced to a situation of extremity for want of meat. On several days of late the Troops have been entirely destitute of any,"* he wrote to his friend in Connecticut, Governor Jonathan Trumbull.

Washington praised his men for their handling of the situation. *"The men have borne their distress with a firmness and patience never exceeded, and every possible praise is due the Officers for encouraging them to it, by precept, by exhortation, by example,"* he told Trumbull.

> "Listen to my cry, for I am in desperate need; rescue me from those who pursue me, for they are too strong for me"
> (PSALM 142:6).

Washington knew, however, that the bounds of desperation could only go so far. Hunger pains and empty pockets might lead some to take desperate measures.

*"But there are certain bounds, beyond which it is impossible for Human nature to go. We are arrived at these,"* George Washington warned.[264]

**PRAYER**

*Thank you for being a God who sees our desperation and hears our cries.*

# 265. Charleston's Noose

As the British sought to capture Charleston, South Carolina, America's richest port, they employed a surefire strategy: the siege.

*"A siege is a very methodical and time-consuming reduction of a strategic place. The engineers will begin to dig what is called the first parallel. Parallel trenches are essentially concentric circles dug around the post. The siege is rather similar to an incremental tightening of a noose,"* West Point historian John Hall described.

The first concentric circle began in England as the year 1779 entered its final season. The British government was anxious to find a way to end the war. *"The question they're asking is why isn't the war over yet?"* historian Christopher Brown explained in an interview for *The History Channel Presents: The American Revolution, 2006.* The crown longed for checkmate over stalemate.

The British government drew their second concentric circle when they sent General Clinton to Charleston. He sailed from New York in December 1779 with one hundred ships and eight thousand men.

After conceding Georgia to the British the year before, Gen. Benjamin Lincoln kept an eye on their movements from Charleston, a strategic position at the junction of two rivers. He learned of Clinton's arrival in late January of 1780. But as closely as he kept his spyglass on the British, his search for reinforcements nearly made him myopic.

*"I hear, but have no official notice of it, that the Virginia line are ordered from the main army, to reenforce this department. If this should*

*prove true, it will be fortunate indeed for this country,"* Lincoln cautiously wrote General Washington on January 8, 1780.

Two weeks later Lincoln learned Clinton's ships had sailed south. The final grains of sand in the hourglass were sliding to its base. Lincoln knew it would take a miracle for three thousand troops to march five hundred miles from Virginia to Charleston in time to reinforce him.

Lincoln looked to other places for men. He asked leaders in Georgia to call up the militia. He implored South Carolina's government to arm the only other labor group available—slaves. And just as a South Carolina delegate had earlier called on Washington to dismiss free blacks from the army, so its leaders also declined Lincoln's request.

George Washington's army was in no position to send his men to Charleston. They were suffering miserably in Morristown, New Jersey, in the winter of 1780. Many did not have shoes, and they certainly could not travel the distance in time to rescue Benjamin Lincoln. As the siege began, Charleston was in the center of a noose of concentric circles. Time would prove whether enough men were available to rescue her.[265]

> "Draw water for the siege, strengthen your defenses! Work the clay, tread the mortar, repair the brickwork!"
> (NAHUM 3:14).

**PRAYER**

*Father, strengthen me during the times when life surrounds and squeezes, when work or stress lays siege to me. Bring people to my aid and inspire me to encourage others when I see them surrounded.*

# 266. The Revolution Today: A Jones-like Hero

It was an army colonel who showed John Paul Jones-like heroism on the sea that day.

Lt. Col. R. H. (Bill) Rogers was training Filipino soldiers at Cebu, Philippines, when he was forced to surrender the island to the Japanese on May 15, 1942. Imprisoned at Davao Penal Colony with survivors from the Bataan Death March, Rogers lived as a prisoner of war for two and a half years. His leadership continued even while he was a prisoner.

Because Rogers was forty years old and a reserve officer in the 368th Infantry Division when the military called him to active duty in 1941, he was a generation older than most American soldiers at the time. This high school vocational agriculture teacher from Del Rio, Texas, also had the leadership skills needed for the situation he faced.

Rogers became the senior officer in charge of seven hundred fifty fellow prisoners who, against the rules of the Geneva Convention, were forced to build an air strip at Lasang. "He continually interceded with cruel Japanese authorities to alleviate his men's suffering at the risk of his own life," Betty Rogers Bryant said of her father's leadership.

The Japanese transferred these men aboard a Japanese Hell ship, a freighter called the *Shinyo Maru*, in September 1944. A Hell ship was any ship used by the Japanese to transport prisoners.

"The terrible conditions in the bottom hold of this ship were unbearable. Men were dying and going crazy. The Japanese closed the hatch covers over the hold and the men were suffocating. There were only a few port holes and the men took turns trying to get air. Dad gave up his turn for his men in worse shape," described Bryant, noting that her father demanded the Japanese remove the hatch covers. He resorted to begging, a sight that spoke loudly of the anguish and suffering of the men. Rogers asked a fellow prisoner and seminary student, John Morrett, to hold a service for the men because the chaplain was too weak.

Rogers was in the middle of the ship when an American submarine, the *USS Paddle*, torpedoed the Japanese freighter. "They had no idea Americans were aboard and thought they were only torpedoing a Japanese freighter. Eighty-two of the 750 survived and swam to shore. They were hidden by the Filipinos until rescued later by the American submarine *USS Narwhal*," detailed Bryant.

Rogers did not survive. But the men who did, including Morrett, who later became an Episcopal priest, have heralded the heroism of the high school teacher from Del Rio. The man named Bill Rogers continued to lead men no matter the conditions. He led them through an island-surrender and a torpedoed torture chamber of a ship. His commitment and courage hail the heritage of John Paul Jones and others who have not yet begun to fight.[266]

> "In the day of great slaughter, when the towers fall, streams of water will flow on every high mountain and every lofty hill. The moon will shine like the sun, and the sunlight will be seven times brighter, like the light of seven full days, when the LORD binds up the bruises of his people and heals the wounds he inflicted" (ISAIAH 30:25, 26).

**PRAYER**

*Father, thank you for the gift of courage in the face of life's worst trials.*

# 267. Sabbath Rest: Civil Blessing

Although Massachusetts was the first colony to join in the Revolution, it was the last of the thirteen states to adopt a state constitution. Samuel Cooper, who had succeeded Benjamin Colman as senior pastor of Boston's Brattle Street Church, delivered his finest sermon after learning the news.

*"Their Congregation shall be established before me, . . . and their nobles shall be of themselves, and their Governor shall proceed from the midst of them,"* Cooper read with joy as he quoted Jeremiah 30:20, 21 (KJV).

Cooper had long believed that God would provide Massachusetts with a government. In fact, he believed so strongly in the cause that he considered Jeremiah 30:20 to be a Massachusetts-made prophesy.

*"The prophecy seems to have been made for ourselves, it is so exactly descriptive of that important, that comprehensive, that essential civil blessing,"* he explained of the joy that had spread throughout Boston in March 1780 over the constitution, drafted by John Adams.

Cooper had championed American freedom since 1754, when he published a pamphlet called "The Crisis." He also contributed to newspapers. His views were so well known by both Americans and the British that he was forced to flee for his life in April 1775, less than ten days before the skirmish at Lexington.

Cooper likened America's situation to that of Israel. *"Like that nation we rose from oppression, and emerged 'from the House of Bondage': Like that nation we were led into a wilderness, as a refuge from tyranny, and a preparation for the enjoyment of our civil and religious rights,"* compared Cooper.

Cooper believed the states had too *"lightly esteemed the Rock of their Salvation."* But the war had humbled America, and the Massachusetts Constitution gave him hope for final victory. *"This day, this memorable day, is a witness, that the Lord, he whose 'hand maketh great, and giveth strength unto all, hath not forsaken us, nor our God forgotten us.'"*

Indeed, the Massachusetts Constitution was tangible evidence that the days of anarchy resulting from the king's decision to revoke the province's charter were over. The rule of state law reigned once again.

> "Their leader will be one of their own; their ruler will arise from among them" (JEREMIAH 30:21).

"*This day, which forms a new era in our annals, exhibits a testimony to all the world, that contrary to our deserts, and amidst all our troubles, the blessing promised in our text to the afflicted seed of Abraham is come upon us: 'Their Nobles shall be of themselves, and their Governor shall proceed from the midst of them [Jeremiah 30:21 KJV],'*" quoted Cooper.

Samuel Cooper saw God's hand and it gave him hope.[267]

**PRAYER**

*Thank you for providing the gift of leadership.*

# 268. Surrender

The British drew their third concentric circle around Charleston, South Carolina, on February 1, 1780, when General Clinton and his formidable army landed twenty miles south of America's wealthiest port. They began their march toward the city, digging trenches, and taking positions as they inched their way toward the southern jewel.

General Benjamin Lincoln's agony alone nearly choked him as he anticipated how, when, and where the British would attack. He ordered his men to build trenches around Charleston, moving outward and farther away from the city with each new ring. At some point, he knew the trenches between the two armies would move within cannon range of each other.

"*It is, my dear Sir, among my first misfortunes, that I am not near enough to your Excellency to have the advantage of your advice and direction. But this I cannot enjoy. I feel my own insufficiency and want of experience. I can promise you nothing but a disposition to serve my country,*" Lincoln wrote Washington on January 23, 1780.

Indeed Lincoln needed Washington's nimble strategy of vacillating between offense and defense. Although he was undermanned and undersupplied, he decided to take a stand at Charleston when retreat was the more practical option. His sense of duty blinded him.

"*If this town should be attacked, as now threatened, I know my duty will call me to defend it as long as opposition can be of any avail. I hope my inclination will coincide with my duty,*" he explained to Washington of his decision.

Lincoln's men may have obstructed the rivers, but the British broke through and crossed the Ashley River on March 29th. This success further tightened the noose around Charleston.

*"Seven ships of war passed Fort Moultrie yesterday afternoon, and anchored near where Fort Johnson stood, with no other apparent injury than the loss of one topmast,"* Lincoln wrote Washington on April 9th.

Located six miles from the harbor, Fort Moultrie was built to protect Charleston by sea. By successfully passing through the American lines there, the British drew their tightest circle yet. Lincoln lost his seaside escape route.

Just as Fort Moultrie fell, Lincoln received land reinforcements from Virginia. These men had marched double time to reach Charleston. But their weak numbers cast a shadow over the miracle of their arrival. Instead of three thousand men, the Virginia regiment totaled fewer than eight hundred. Lincoln was outnumbered nearly two to one. His hopes sank deeper with each sunset. The multi-month siege ended on May 12, 1780, when Benjamin Lincoln surrendered the American army's entire southern division to the British.[268]

> "Then lay siege to it: Erect siege works against it, build a ramp up to it, set up camps against it and put battering rams around it"
> (EZEKIEL 4:2).

**PRAYER**

*Seize my heart today. Allow me to take joy in the knowledge that you are a personal God who loves me even when my defenses fail me.*

# 269. An American Mutiny

*The want of provision last night produced a mutiny in the Army of a very alarming kind,"* George Washington wrote to Connecticut Governor Jonathan Trumbull in May 1780.

As Washington had predicted months earlier, the lack of food and money drove some men to desperation. Congress had failed to significantly improve the situation. Scarcity caused anxiety to overflow into mutiny. *"Two Regiments of the Connecticut line got under Arms,"* he explained, noting they intended to convince the whole army to desert. Fortunately, the regiment's officers, along with help from soldiers from Pennsylvania, put down the resistance.

*"But this without relief can only be momentary. I will not dwell longer upon this melancholy subject, being fully convinced that Your Excellency will hasten to us every possible relief in your power,"* Washington pleaded.

Washington also tempered his account of the incident in a report to Congress. His moderate description of the mutiny was a sharp contrast to the drama he used to prevent such *"pernicious consequences"* in the future.

The punishment for mutiny was death. Washington ordered the mutineers to the gallows. He also directed the entire army to gather in front of the gallows to watch the executions. *"Washington wanted to use punishment, capital punishment in particular, sparingly. But he also knew it was great theater,"* historian Caroline Cox explained.

Washington was not about to let a mutiny mutilate his army. He had overcome too much by May of 1780 to let it all fall apart. To preserve the army, Washington had risked his reputation by changing his strategy, vacillating between retreat and attack. He had survived underhanded tactics from insubordinate generals. He had risked his life by riding through the lines at Monmouth. Hence Washington, who once had lines of the playwright Cato read to his audience, embraced the drama of theater and the grace of faith to subdue the mutiny.

*"All eight were put on top of the gallows, nooses were put around their heads,"* described historian Bruce Chadwick. *"Their graves had been dug in front of the gallows and their coffins, which he [Washington] had ordered manufactured, placed in front of their graves."*

But before the execution could take place, a soldier stepped forward and called out, *"Reprieve from the commander-in-chief."*

Relief swept over the mutineers and the soldiers who were watching. Seven of the eight were pardoned. One was hanged. George Washington used the theatrics as a warning against mutiny and to keep his army from dropping the curtain on the Revolution. The men didn't deserve the pardons, yet they received their commander's unmerited grace.[269]

> "Who is a God like you, who pardons sin and forgives the transgression of the remnant of his inheritance? You do not stay angry forever but delight to show mercy" (MICAH 7:18).

### PRAYER

*You are the Great Pardoner, the One who forgives my sin and offers me a reprieve through your Son.*

# 270. A Parliamentary Mutiny

It was unclear which was worse: the king's temper or his tendency to sulk like a captured pirate.

On the morning of June 13, 1781, King George III awoke with a troubled heart. At twenty-five minutes past seven he picked up his pen and put his worries on paper. *"IT is difficult to express which appears more strongly, the manly fortitude of the great majority last night in rejecting the hackneyed question of a Committee for considering the [end of the] American war, or the impudence of the minority in again bringing it forward,"* he wrote.

Parliament plagued him. Although he applauded the majority in Parliament for rejecting efforts to end the war, he was greatly concerned about the growing strength of the minority. They were near mutiny. And like George Washington, appearances also concerned this George. He worried that the minority's voices would be heard across the English Channel into France. *"For whoever the most ardently wishes for peace must feel that every repetition of this question in Parliament only makes the rebels and the Bourbon [French royal] family more desirous of continuing the war, from the hopes of tiring out this country,"* he mused.

Whether the mutiny was in Parliament or Morristown, an internal uprising could have devastating consequences if not quenched. In many ways the American war was a million leagues away, a sight unseen for an obstinate tyrant. But the rebellion in Parliament was beginning to splash saltwater on the king's face. If strong enough, the voices of the minority could turn the tide across the Atlantic.

King George did not understand the minority in Parliament or why they were gaining strength. His viewpoint blinded him. After all, how could any true Briton fail to see that the loss of America would reduce Britain's power in the world? Wasn't it his duty to hold on to Britain's power at all costs? In his eyes, the king steered his ship with steadiness, not stubbornness.

*"We have it not at this hour in our power to make peace; it is by steadiness and exertions that we are to get into a situation to effect it; and with the assistance of Divine Providence I am confident we shall soon find our enemies forced to look for that blessing,"* the king wrote hopefully.

And just as his mentor, James, the second Earl Waldegrave, had observed so many years ago, the king's melancholy temper was dangerous. Anger led him to go to his chamber, close the door, and sulk. Rarely did a solution emerge when he did.

*"For we are contending for our whole conse-quence, whether we are to rank among the great Powers of Europe, or be reduced to one of the least considerable,"* King George III lamented.[270]

> "A quick-tempered man does foolish things, and a crafty man is hated" (PROVERBS 14:17).

**PRAYER**

*Show me how to effectively manage my emo-tions, to face them and control them in ways that honor you.*

# 271. Alter Ego Returns

A*n old Correspondent begs room for a few Words,"* Samuel Adams wrote to the editors of the *Boston Gazette* in June 1780.

Nothing could quench the thirst for freedom in a true patriot. Noth-ing could mellow the passion of Adams. Service in government sometimes tempers even the most flamboyant politicians, but not Adams. His years in the Continental Congress and the Massachusetts provincial government had not tamed his spirit. Instead, they had refined his writing skills.

Adams had learned when to use the words of a diplomat and when to invoke the vocabulary of a radical. Although at one point he had been so sick in Philadelphia he thought he might die, Adams was determined to live to see a victorious end to the Revolution. He was just as resolute in his desire to encourage the people. So it is no surprise that Adams picked up his pen and returned to his alter ego as an anonymous editori-alist. His purpose was to fan the flames and encourage the people to stay strong until the end.

*"Formerly this great contest was carried on upon paper. The con-spirators against the rights and liberties of our country left no art untried, to induce the people to submit to their unrighteous claims. But they were circumvented by our watchful patriots. They were, if I may use the expres-sion, out-reasoned by some, and laughed off the stage by others,"* Adams wrote, reminding his readers that the war had started through protests of the pen, not the power of black powder.

He then reflected on how this war of words had moved into a war of arms. A change in the hearts of patriots motivated them to sacrifice life and limb for liberty. *"The people of this country were not driven to take up arms, they did it voluntarily in defence of their liberty. They properly considered themselves as called by GOD, and warranted by HIM, to encounter every hazard in the common cause of Man,"* Adams reminded the *Gazette's* readers.

He reminded the people of the army's resolution and praised General Washington. *"We have had for several years past a well-appointed Army.—An Army of which both Officers and Privates are daily increasing in discipline—An Army inferior perhaps to none at this time on the face of the earth and headed by a COMMANDER, who feels the Rights of the Citizens in his own breast, and experience has taught us, he knows full well how to defend them,"* Adams continued.

He then reminded people of the spiritual side of the struggle, and encouraged them to honor God through their resolution and determination: *"Them that honour me I will honour, and they that despise me shall be lightly esteemed,"* Samuel Adams wrote, quoting 1 Samuel 2:30 (KJV).[271]

> "Those who honor me I will honor, but those who despise me will be disdained" (1 SAMUEL 2:30).

**PRAYER**

*Father, I seek to honor you with my words and actions today. Embolden me where I need determination and humble me where I need to let go.*

# 272. Vindex

*O*ur affairs appear to be approaching to a great crisis,*" Samuel Adams continued in his June 1780 newspaper editorial.

Adams knew it was time to issue another call to arms. He informed them that France had promised strong naval support. Congress had asked states for additional men and arms. They hoped a final battle would lead to ultimate victory, vindicating their Declaration of Independence. It was time for the people to respond to their allies.

*"The PEOPLE, the PEOPLE must, under GOD, give energy to this all important call, and enable the combined Forces at once to put an end to the War. If the PEOPLE NOW exert themselves, one struggle more, by the blessing of Heaven, will rid us of all our Enemies,"* he wrote as forcefully as his pen would bleed.

Adams knew the expectations were growing more intense with each gallop of Washington's horse. King Louis XVI was as impatient for a final victory as was Congress, although for different reasons. All of Europe closely watched the events unfolding in America.

*"Our GENERAL, with his officers and army, are filled with ardor and generous ambition to signalize their valour in the SALVATION of*

*our country—SUPERIOR BEINGS would look down with the utmost astonishment, if we should let this GOLDEN OPPORTUNITY slip—It cannot be,"* Adams warned.

He knew a final battle would not be successful without a renewed vigor among the people. Liberty's vindication depended on more men taking up arms. *"Our young men, ambitious of laurels, will, at such a time, fly to their arms with the speed of the wind, and ALL will be engaged in furnishing them with necessary supplies, so shall this very campaign be DECISIVE and GLORIOUS,"* he predicted.

Adams—whose state was as dear to him as his own name—called on the people of Massachusetts to participate in this final vindication. *"This State began the noble contest; we will honor ourselves by our utmost exertions to put a glorious end to it: we will contend with our sister States in nothing, but who shall have the greatest share of honor in this last and crowning effort,"* he implored. *"Be assured, my dear countrymen, the liberty, the happiness of America, and its consequence in the eyes of the world, depend upon our PRESENT activity and spirit."*

Adams concluded his call for vindication by signing his pseudonym, Vindex, the name of the shrewd Roman governor whose passionate love of freedom led to the fall of the Emperor Nero. But Adams also included this line, his true source of vindication: *"We will not be wanting to ourselves, and the* LORD *do that which seemeth to him right."*[272]

> "'The LORD has vindicated us; come, let us tell in Zion what the LORD our God has done'" (JEREMIAH 51:10).

**PRAYER**

*You are the Great Vindicator. Thank you for preparing the paths of justice and righteousness.*

# 273. The Revolution Today: Comfort

"I have met 25 of these survivors and learned all about my Dad's command. These men had the highest respect for my Dad," Betty Rogers Bryant said.

Bryant's father, Lt. Col. Bill Rogers, died during World War II as a prisoner of war while aboard a Japanese freighter struck by a torpedo from an American submarine. Only eight-two of the seven hundred and fifty Allied prisoners on board survived.

A graduate of Texas A&M University, Rogers was serving as a reserve officer in the 368th Infantry Division when he received the call to active duty. Betty was only four years old when her father went off to war in 1941. When someone dies under such unimaginable circumstances, families are often left with many unanswered questions.

"My mother never used the word *died*, but always told us our Dad was lost in the war. She did not allow the family to have a memorial service. We had mothers, yet we were referred to as War Orphans and we are Gold Star Children," Bryant explained.

For Bryant one of the greatest comforts came decades later when she read an article in *The Dallas Morning News Scene Magazine* about a documentary highlighting Houston's Shoss brothers, who escaped from their captors within one day of each other.

"Morris Shoss escaped from a Japanese Hell ship on the day my Dad died on one. I obtained his phone number from the feature writer and when I called him, he said, 'Your Dad was my commanding officer,' and I just couldn't believe it," reported an amazed Bryant.

Morris sent Bryant a list of the survivors and then contacted them on her behalf. Bryant attended their reunions. "Locating these men opened up a whole new world for me," she said. "They described him as a strong leader and a strong Christian. I think his military training at A&M and strong faith carried him through and made him a successful leader."

Comfort most poignantly comes through memorials, which is why markers and gatherings on Memorial Day and other occasions are so important. "Attending the 50th Anniversary and Memorial Service of The Shinyo Maru Survivors on September 7, 1994, in Springfield, Missouri, was an unforgettable experience. I spoke on the significance of the occasion—that being the only service ever held for my Dad. Finding out about my Dad has been so rewarding and brought peace and closure for us. Documenting his heroism and supreme sacrifice for his country is comforting to us and all our family," Bryant said, noting that she quoted John 15:13, "Greater love hath no man than this, that a man lay down his life for his friends," at the event.

> "Blessed are those who mourn, for they will be comforted" (MATTHEW 5:4).

"This is very meaningful to me and describes my Dad and his men who paid the supreme sacrifice for this country," she said proudly. Betty Rogers Bryant found comfort in Scripture and in those who benefited from her father's heroism.[273]

**PRAYER**

*You are the God of comfort. Use me in the coming week to comfort someone in need.*

# 274. Sabbath Rest: Charter from Heaven

To Samuel Cooper, the new Massachusetts Constitution was a charter from heaven.

*"The form of government originally established in the Hebrew nation by a charter from heaven, was that of a free republic, over which God himself, in peculiar favour to that people, was pleased to preside,"* Cooper explained to his congregation upon learning that Massachusetts had adopted a state constitution.

Cooper's fellow Bostonian John Adams had drafted the Massachusetts Constitution. Adams devised a system of separate powers. The document established a two-house legislature combined with an executive with veto power. And unlike the days of Thomas Hutchinson, who served in both an executive and judicial role under the colony's royal charter, this constitution established an independent judiciary. Cooper saw parallels between the new governing document and the government God established among the Israelites.

*"It consisted of three parts; a chief magistrate who was called judge or leader, such as Joshua and others, a council of seventy chosen men, and the general assemblies of the people,"* he said of the Jewish government, noting that the fountain of civil power flowed from the people's assemblies.

*"Even the law of Moses, though framed by God himself, was not imposed upon that people against their will; it was laid open before the whole congregation of Israel; they freely adopted it, and it became their law, not only by divine appointment, but by their own voluntary and express consent. Upon this account it is called in the sacred writings a covenant, compact, or mutual stipulation,"* taught Cooper.

Cooper noted that Joshua's final public statement was to call the assemblies together to renew their covenant with the Ten Commandments. Describing the Israelite assembly as *"august,"* Cooper restated their commitment as if it were a new pledge for his congregation.

*"The people replied, the Lord our God we will serve; we consent, and are determined to be governed by the laws and the statutes he has been so*

*graciously pleased to afford us. 'And Joshua said unto the people, Ye are witnesses against yourselves that ye have chosen the* LORD, *to serve him. And they said, We are witnesses,'"* Cooper quoted from Joshua 24:22.

Cooper was so passionate about the Massachusetts Constitution he considered it a government established by God, one that should not be overturned. *"If ever we renounce the constitution and happy settlement granted to us by heaven; if ever we break the sacred compact; this day, and all the public and voluntary transactions of it, must be a witness against us,"* he warned his parishioners.

> "And the people said to Joshua, 'We will serve the LORD our God and obey him'" (JOSHUA 24:24).

Samuel Cooper was prophetic. And unlike the other twelve original state constitutions, the Massachusetts Constitution, though amended periodically, has never been rewritten.[274]

**PRAYER**

*God, you are the great Covenant Maker. I seek to serve you today in obedience.*

# 275. A Lady's Sentiments

Is it necessary to see something to believe it is true? When it comes to tragedy, merely hearing about something is usually enough to convince most people something horrific has happened. A lady from New Jersey in 1780 revealed the power of bad news. The atrocities by the British were so great that she said she would be appalled by them even if she weren't a patriot. The *"bare recital"* of their deeds, a mere mention, was enough to make a believer out of her. She expressed her sentiments in a New Jersey newspaper article.

*"Was I unconnected with America by ties of friendship or blood, was I not attached by the love of one's country which is inherent in some degree in every breast,"* the lady wrote, *"the bare recital of their unjust claims, their cruelty's and their crimes would fill my soul with horror, and I regard them not only as unprovoked aggressors, but as enemies by principle and example to mankind in general."*

The profaneness of battle sickened her, while the atrocities against the innocent caused her physical discomfort. The terrorism in the South was greater than a thousand nightmares.

*"But as if it were not enough unjustly to spill the blood of our country-men, to lay waste the fields, to destroy our dwellings and even the houses consecrated and set apart for the worship of the Supreme Being, they have desolated the aged and unprotected, and even waged war against our sex,"* she continued, lambasting the British.

Word of horrors traveled fast during the war. The result was a wake of terror. *"Who that has heard of the burning of Charleston . . . of the wanton destruction of Norfolk and Falmouth or their wasting the fine improvements in the environs of Philadelphia,—of the tragic death of Miss McCrea, torn from her house, murdered and scalped by a band of savages hired and set on by British emissaries,"* she began her question.

While the identity of this woman is lost to history, her reaction to terrorism is something people can still identify with today. *"These [atrocities] are truth sufficiently affecting to touch with pity and compassion even hearts hard as marble, and cannot fail to make a deep and lasting impression in the minds of us all,"* the writer concluded.

Hearing of a tragedy is often enough to believe it on faith, no matter how wild or horrible the account may be. But faith in God and the eternal sunshine of his Son is so much greater. Faith is being sure of hope and certain of what we cannot see.[275]

> "Be joyful in hope, patient in affliction, faithful in prayer" (ROMANS 12:12).

**PRAYER**

*God, guide my heart today. Keep me from misplacing my faith. Instead may I put my hope in you.*

# 276. A Purse Response

The sacrifices of the Continental army had not gone unnoticed. After expressing her horror over abuses by the British, a patriot lady in New Jersey rose to the defense of the Continentals. She did so by writing an article for the newspaper.

*"It is to this class of men we more immediately owe our defence and protection; they have borne the weight of the war, and met danger in every quarter; and what is higher praise?"* she asked, extolling them for their *"Roman courage."*

She had heard the bad news of the war, which prompted her to write about how the army's *"perseverance suffered the extremes of heat and* cold, *the attacks of hunger, and the pain of long and fatiguing marches through parts before unexplored by armies, in which had scarcely ever before born the print of human feet.*"

The change in the hearts and minds of Americans continued in 1780 through newspaper articles such as this one. Not only was it the arms of men that stood out to her, but it was also their attitudes. "*It wast enough for these brave men to reflect they were engaged in the best and most glorious of all causes, that of defending the rights and liberties of their country, to induce them to behave with so much resolution and fortitude,*" she continued. "*Their many sufferings so cheerfully undergone, highly merit our gratitude and sincere thanks, and claim all the assistance we can afford their distresses.*"

This woman could not fight with a musket, but she could fight with her pocketbook. She understood what many women had concluded. They must respond to the patriotic muster of the men in their lives. They must also give what they could, if only from their purses.

"*If we have it not in our power to do from the double motive of religion and a love of liberty, what some Ladies of the highest rank in the court of France every day perform for motives of religion only in the hospitals of the sick and diseased, let us animate one another to contribute from our purses in proportion to our circumstances towards the support and comfort of the brave men who are fighting and suffering for us in the field,*" she urged.

> "In everything I did, I showed you that by this kind of hard work we must help the weak, remembering the words the Lord Jesus himself said: 'It is more blessed to give than to receive'"
> (ACTS 20:35).

Battle lines would only go so far without the aid of pursestrings. This woman understood the power of giving over receiving, the power of doing what she could do. It was essential to give money to buy clothing and food to "*keep the enemy from our borders.*"

With her call to action completed, this patriot from New Jersey ended humbly: "*When I say this, I mean only to express the feelings of a woman, my sentiments being ever in favour of the spirit which my countrymen have so often manifested when their services have been required.*"[276]

**PRAYER**

*Thank you for reminding me of the power of giving as a response to a need.*

# 277. Working with Eager Hands

The New Jersey lady's newspaper article calling on her fellow patriots to give money to the Continental army was part of a larger campaign by women to do what they could for the cause. And although Martha Washington led by example, she also led with her voice. As she returned home to Mount Vernon in June 1780, Martha stopped in Philadelphia. The mission of this farmer's wife was to sow some seeds for the army. It was time for the ladies to work with eager hands.

"She, along with several other prominent ladies, including Benjamin Franklin's daughter, became involved in a campaign to enlist the help of America's women in providing aid to the soldiers in the Continental Army," Mount Vernon historian Mary Thompson reflected in a presentation she gave on Martha's involvement in the war.

Esther DeBerdt Reed led the women's effort in Philadelphia. She was the wife of Joseph Reed, who had served General Washington in earlier campaigns before returning to Pennsylvania to serve the government there through the governing council. "Given her husband's position, Mrs. Reed undoubtedly knew something about the problems, which had plagued the army at Morristown, however, it is impossible not to think that Mrs. Washington was the source, through personal conversation, for enough first-hand examples of suffering and need in camp to spur the other ladies into action," stressed Thompson.

"The basic idea, as outlined in The Pennsylvania Gazette, was for one lady to be chosen by the other women in each county, to act as a local treasurer, gather in funds, and keep a record of each donation in a little book. When the money had been collected, each county treasurer would send both the contributions and the registers to the first lady of her state, who would, in turn, send it along to Martha Washington."

The patriotism of the ladies and their project was a blessing to General Washington. He put together a plan for how the donations could be used. "I very much admire the patriotic spirit of the Ladies of Philada., and shall with great pleasure give them my advice, as to the application of their benevolent and generous donation to the soldiers of the Army," he wrote to Joseph Reed.

Washington concluded that one need in particular would best match the contributions. "I would, nevertheless, recommend a provision of shirts in preference to any thing else, in case the fund should amount to a sum equivalent to a supply of eight or ten thousand. The Soldiery are exceedingly in want of them, and the public have never, for several years past, *been able to procure a sufficient quantity to make them comfortable,"* George Washington noted.

The work of the ladies was sealed. It was time to stitch shirts and work with eager hands.[277]

> "She selects wool and flax and works with eager hands"
> (PROVERBS 31:13).

**PRAYER**

*I pray for a willingness to work with eager hands, no matter how meager the task today.*

## 278. Blessing of Work

Esther Reed had good news to report to George Washington. Her fund-raising for the soldiers through the ladies' "door-to-door" efforts had reaped a harvest.

*"THE subscription set on foot by the ladies of this City for the use of the soldiery, is so far completed as to induce me to transmit to your Excellency an account of the money I have received,"* she explained, noting the effort was not yet equal to their wishes. *"But I am persuaded [the money] will be received as a proof of our zeal for the great cause of America and our esteem and gratitude for those who so bravely defend it,"* Esther wrote.

The ladies of Philadelphia had received subscriptions or pledges for more than $200,000 and had 625 pounds on hand, *"for a total value, in paper money, of $300,634, or $7,500 specie [coin],"* outlined Mount Vernon historian Mary Thompson.

Esther had written ladies in other states to launch a campaign. Martha Washington called on Martha Jefferson, the wife of Thomas Jefferson, who was then governor of Virginia, to lead women in that state in a similar effort. Martha Jefferson received the suggestion with eagerness.

*"I undertake with chearfulness the duty of furnishing to my country women an opportunity of proving that they also participate of those virtuous feelings which gave birth to it,"* Mrs. Jefferson responded.

Contributions ranged from a widow's mite to a millionaire's pounds. *"More than 1,600 individuals in that city made donations to the cause, including a black woman named Phyllis, who gave seven shillings and six pence, the Countess de Luzerne, who provided $6,000 in paper money, and the wife of the Marquis de Lafayette, who sent one hundred guineas in specie,"* accounted Thompson.

Martha Washington donated $20,000, or 6,000 pounds, in *"bounty to the soldiers,"* a Mount Vernon account book recorded.

Esther Reed, however, did not live to see the completion of the project. She did not fully recover from giving birth in May 1780 and died during a dysentery epidemic in September. She was only thirty-four years old. Her work continued through the eager hands of another patriot, the daughter of Benjamin Franklin.

*"After Mrs. Reed's death, Sarah Franklin Bache headed the project in Pennsylvania, sending 2,200 shirts, each bearing 'the name of the married or unmarried lady who made it,' in December, when she wrote that she hoped they would 'be worn with as much pleasure as they were made,'"* reported Thompson.

Esther Reed's work resulted in a harvest of clothing and a bountiful legacy.[278]

> "For the LORD your God will bless you in all your harvest and in all the work of your hands, and your joy will be complete" (DEUTERONOMY 16:15).

**PRAYER**

*Thank you for the harvest that comes with hard work. Your blessings are greater than I can imagine.*

# 279. Yankee Doodle Dandy

One of the best medicines in the war was not a balm but a song.

*"The old woman . . . immediately fell singing and dancing 'Yankee Doodle' with the greatest air of good humour,"* Rhode Island surgeon Isaac Senter recorded in his diary about a merry old woman he met on a Canadian expedition early in the war.

*"Yankee Doodle went to town, A riding on a pony; Stuck a feather in his hat and called it macaroni,"* the most popular verse of the song goes.

The song was originally a satire, intended to make a laughingstock of the Americans. *Yankee* was a nickname for New Englanders but the term applied also to any colonist. *Doodle* meant a country bumpkin. *Macaroni* was a label for Britons who liked to show off by wearing pretentious clothing.

It was a British surgeon who invented the lyrics for "Yankee Doodle." Dr. Richard Schackburg wrote the song to tease the motley American colonists he and other British soldiers had fought with during the French and Indian War.

The British ridicule rose to a piercing crescendo when the Revolutionary War began. British Gen. Hugh Percy had his troops play "Yankee Doodle" to ridicule the Yankees as they marched to Lexington and Concord on April 19, 1775.

*"Yankee Doodle came to town, For to buy a firelock; We will tar and feather him, And so we will John Hancock,"* went the verse.

But it was the Americans who had the last laugh. They played the song as they forced the British back to Boston after Lexington. They also played the song at Bunker Hill.

After George Washington arrived at Cambridge in 1775, someone added this verse to the catchy tune: *"And there was Captain Washington upon a slapping stallion, A giving orders to his men; I guess there was a million."*

The Continentals knew how to mock a mockery.

*"The name [Yankee] has been more prevalent since the commencement of hostilities . . . The [British] soldiers at Boston used it as a term of reproach, but after the affair at Bunker's Hill, the Americans gloried in it,"* wrote a British officer at the battle of Saratoga. *"Yankee Doodle is now their paean, a favorite of favorites, played in their army, esteemed as warlike as the Grenadier's March—it is the lover's spell, the nurse's lullaby . . . it was not a little mortifying to hear them play this tune, when their army marched down to our surrender,"* the British officer continued.

> "Our mouths were filled with laughter, our tongues with songs of joy. Then it was said among the nations, "The LORD has done great things for them" (PSALM 126:2).

As they did during the Revolution, people have always turned to songs as one of the best reprieves from a dissonant day.[279]

**PRAYER**

*May I sing of joy to you today. Fill my heart with laughter and merriment.*

## 280. The Revolution Today: Yankee Doodle Balm

Although "Yankee Doodle" may not seem funny to modern-day ears, it certainly made for good humor in a very serious war. Perhaps it is fitting that a surgeon wrote the first lyrics for Yankee Doodle. Laughter is good medicine. Research is proving it.

"Using laughter-provoking movies to gauge the effect of emotions on cardiovascular health, researchers at the University of Maryland School of

Medicine in Baltimore have shown for the first time that laughter is linked to healthy function of blood vessels," a study revealed in March 2005.

"Laughter appears to cause the tissue that forms the inner lining of blood vessels, the endothelium, to dilate, or expand, in order to increase blood flow," the report continued.

The study included ten healthy men and ten healthy women with normal blood pressure, cholesterol, and blood glucose levels. Each watched a short segment of each of two movies, shown forty-eight hours apart. One movie was funny. The other was intense. The volunteers fasted before randomly seeing the movies. They also received a baseline blood vessel reactivity test. The study revealed striking contrasts.

"Overall, average blood flow increased 22 percent during laughter, and decreased 35 percent during mental stress," the study reported. The research evaluated the endothelium, which a dictionary defines as "a thin layer of flat epithelial cells that lines the lymph vessels, blood vessels, and the inner cavities of the heart." Blood vessel tone, blood flow regulation, blood thickening, and infection response are among its several powerful effects.

"The endothelium is the first line in the development of atherosclerosis or hardening of the arteries, so, given the results of our study, it is conceivable that laughing may be important to maintain a healthy endothelium, and reduce the risk of cardiovascular disease," Dr. Michael Miller, the principal researcher, suggested.

Mental stress harms the endothelium, and laughter reduces mental stress. "The magnitude of change we saw in the endothelium is similar to the benefit we might see with aerobic activity, but without the aches, pains and muscle tension associated with exercise," stated Miller. "We don't recommend that you laugh and not exercise, but we do recommend that you try to laugh on a regular basis. Thirty minutes of exercise three times a week, and 15 minutes of laughter on a daily basis is probably good for the vascular system."

> "A cheerful heart is good medicine, but a crushed spirit dries up the bones"
> (PROVERBS 17:22).

This twenty-first century study proves what humanity has known throughout time. It was true in the Revolution and it is true today. Laughter is good medicine. Abigail Adams put it this way in a letter she wrote to her husband after the war: *"I hope you will be in good Spirits all the Time I am gone, remembering Solomon's advice that a merry Heart was good like a medicine."*[280]

**PRAYER**

*Thank you for the healing power of laughter.*

# 281. Sabbath Rest: Overcoming Evil

Evil overcome by good. The topic appears in movies, books, and real life. This desire for the triumph of good was as real to the patriots as it is today. Henry Cummings, longtime pastor of the First Congregational Parish of Billerica, Massachusetts, preached on the topic during the war. People were hungry to hear that evil would not win in the end.

*"I doubt not, my hearers, but you can recollect instances . . . wherein the lusts of particular persons have been either remarkably restrained, or remarkably over-ruled, as occasions of good, where evil was designed and intended,"* Cummings reminded his congregation.

He believed these moments were opportunities to praise God. Whenever good thwarted evil, men and women were to look to God. *"Every instance of this kind, that comes within our view, should lead us to admire and adore the wisdom and goodness of God, who disappointeth the evil designs of sinners, and causeth even the operation of their lusts to be productive of events, in favour of those whom they meant to injure,"* preached Cummings.

He then gave his audience examples from the Bible to support his call to adoration. *"The story of Joseph, in the book of Genesis, affords one instance, to this purpose. Instigated by pride, envy, anger and unreasonable resentment, his brethren sold him into Egypt. They had nothing in view, in this base and unnatural action, but the gratification of their own unruly passions and corrupt lusts; but the wisdom of GOD over-ruled it for good, contrary to their expectation and design,"* Cummings reminded his listeners of Joseph's rise in the Egyptian court, which resulted in saving his family, and ultimately the nation of Israel, from a famine.

*"The wrath and madness of Pharaoh, and the cruelties which his haughty and savage temper prompted him to exercise upon the children of Israel, in order to check their growth, and secure them in a state of dependence and base servitude, prepared the way, under the government of Providence, for their remarkable deliverance,"* the preacher continued.

Cummings noted that these occasions were *"a series of such wonderful displays of the power of GOD, as could not but excite all pious observers, to pay him their devout honors and adorations."*

This pastor, who had served as a delegate to the convention in 1780 that passed the Massachusetts Constitution, fervently believed that God was in control. He was the one who overcame evil, no matter if malice, murder, or treason ruled in men's hearts. The patriots needed the message Henry Cummings and others preached to make it to the end of the war. Evil had not yet been conquered.[281]

> "Do not be overcome by evil, but overcome evil with good" (ROMANS 12:21).

**PRAYER**

*God, may your purpose prevail in my heart today. Overcome any evil there with your goodness and truth.*

# 282. Drafting

I t is an old maxim, that the surest way to make a good peace is to be *well prepared for war,"* George Washington wrote in August 1780. With the skill of an attorney, Washington picked up his pen and lobbied Congress in favor of a remedy he had long contemplated. The desperation of the times led him to make a case for a military draft.

One of the worst mistakes of the Revolutionary War was the system of relying on states to supply militias and men for the army. Militia contracts were short, sometimes as short as three months. The problem had plagued Washington from the beginning of the war, and by August 1780 he was more than ready to inoculate his army from further harm caused by this political disease.

*"If a draft for the war or three years can be effected, it ought to be made on every account. A shorter period than a year is inadmissible. To one who has been witness to the evils brought upon us by short enlistments, the system appears to have been pernicious beyond description,"* Washington wrote.

If one issue could be identified as the main cause of the army's misfortunes, it was short-term enlistments. Washington used his letter to review the war, pointing over and over again to the need for longer-term contracts. *"Had we formed a permanent army in the beginning, which, by the continuance of the same men in service, had been capable of discipline, we never should have had to retreat with a handful of men across the Delaware in '76, trembling for the fate of America,"* the commander-in-chief wrote.

Washington also believed short-term contracts had depleted the war chest. *"The derangement of our finances is essentially to be ascribed to it . . . We have had, a great part of the time, two sets of men to feed and pay, the discharged men going home and the Levies coming in,"* he explained.

Untrained troops led to the defeat at Brandywine and suffering at Valley Forge. Short-term contracts required Washington's officers to continually retrain soldiers. He continued, *"Our discipline also has been much injured, if not ruined, by such frequent changes."*

Washington also concluded that these brief enlistments had prolonged the war. *"There is every reason to believe, the War has been protracted on this account . . . Had we kept a permanent army on foot, the enemy could have had nothing to hope for, and would in all probability have listened to terms long since,"* he conjectured.

George Washington argued that recruiting men for three-year terms would show the enemy that America was as serious about independence in 1780 as it had been in 1776. This commander knew a glorious cause required a long-term commitment.[282]

> "You must have accurate and honest weights and measures, so that you may live long in the land the LORD your God is giving you" (DEUTERONOMY 25:15).

**PRAYER**

*Father, thank you for your long-term commitment to me.*

## 283. Gates Steps to the Plate

When General Lincoln's troops were captured at Charleston in May 1780, Washington turned to his most trusted general, Nathanael Greene, for redemption. Time and time again, Greene had proved his loyalty. His willingness to become quartermaster, his loyal response following Washington's unfair rebuke, and his efforts to redeem the strained relationships between the French and Americans revealed a pattern. Greene had cast himself in the mold of selflessness.

Washington wanted to place Greene in charge of the southern army. Instead, Congress commissioned the hero of Saratoga, Horatio Gates. The move angered Washington. Unlike Greene, Gates's pattern was cunning selfishness. Placing the southern forces on Gates's plate was as wise as slamming a china bowl with a hammer: Nothing but broken pieces would remain.

*"Horatio Gates wanted to be commander-in-chief of the American Army. It goes much beyond that,"* outlined historian Willard Sterne Ran-

dall. *"Whoever was the victorious leader of the revolutionaries would emerge as the leader of the new nation . . . I think he may have been that ambitious and that foolish."*

Washington decided to send another trusted general, Baron de Kalb, south with two thousand men from the Maryland lines to join Gates. But Gates's patience was as thin as a tin cup. He didn't take time to rebuild the army and assess the strength of his reinforcements. He was deaf to de Kalb's guidance.

*"Contrary to the advice of de Kalb and his officers, who recommended a circuitous route through the fertile and friendly county of Mecklenburg, Gates immediately gave orders to march direct on Camden [in South Carolina],"* detailed historian William Jackman.

Gates was in such a hurry he left his supply wagons behind to lighten his load. He decided to rely on the promise of new supplies from neighboring towns. But these provisions never caught up with Gates and the southern army.

*"They marched through a region of pine barrens interspersed with swamps, and almost destitute of inhabitants. Their only food was green corn, unripe apples and peaches, and such lean wild cattle as chance threw in their way. The wagons never overtook them, but disease did, and the suffering soldiers were greatly enfeebled,"* wrote Jackman.

For three weeks Gates prodded his hungry men. They arrived twelve miles from Camden and established a camp. Gates received fresh reinforcements from local militia, who were as anxious as Gates to fight. *"His army had increased almost daily, principally from North Carolina and Virginia, and now numbered nearly four thousand, of whom two-thirds were Continentals,"* Jackman wrote.

Because Horatio Gates had filled his own plate with ambition and failed to supply enough food for his soldiers' plates, only three thousand men were fit for battle. The rest were too fragile to fight.[283]

> "Like tying a stone in a sling is the giving of honor to a fool" (PROVERBS 26:8).

**PRAYER**

*Lord, thank you for honoring wisdom even when humanity honors those who make foolish choices.*

# 284. Hasty Gates

Haste makes waste. And too much of it can destroy an army.

When General Gates heard that British General Cornwallis, and his army of five thousand were near Camden, South Carolina, he decided he could no longer wait. No matter his men did not have enough food or that the freshest soldiers in his army were immature local militia. Gates was ready to step up to the plate at Camden.

His opponent was Britain's modern-day Hannibal. Less than a month after capturing Charleston, General Clinton decided to return to New York. He left the most capable general in the British army in charge. Lord Cornwallis pushed northward in an effort to follow the British strategy of capturing the South one state at a time.

Gates's battle plan was as hasty as his decision to fight. *"Certain of victory, Gates imprudently made no arrangements for a retreat, or the preservation of his stores,"* historian William Jackman wrote. *"Gates made a move the following night [August 15, 1780] to take a position nearer Camden, and Cornwallis made a similar move to surprise Gates. The advance guards met in the woods; after some skirmishing, both armies halted till morning. With the dawn, the battle commenced."*

Gates put de Kalb's regulars on the right and the eager local militia on the left, leaving his army unbalanced. *"The British army will put its best units at the right of its line, which is a place of honor. From the British perspective the British have their best regiments facing off against the weakest and most ill-prepared American regiments,"* described West Point military historian John Hall.

The outcome was never in question. *"The militia proved their inexperience and fled when Cornwallis's men attacked them. The flight opened the path to attack de Kalb's flank. [The] Continentals stood their ground firmly, until their brave commander, de Kalb, who had received eleven wounds, fell exhausted—then they also gave way,"* Jackman wrote of de Kalb's death.

Gates all at once realized the impact of his hasty decisions and panicked. He rode two hundred miles, hardly stopping, with fewer than two hundred men following him. His impatience resulted in the loss of half the southern army, which scattered throughout South Carolina after the battle. A thousand men, more than a fourth of

> "He shall say: 'Hear, O Israel, today you are going into battle against your enemies. Do not be fainthearted or afraid; do not be terrified or give way to panic before them'"
> (DEUTERONOMY 20:3).

the army, were killed or wounded. Another thousand were captured. The British suffered fewer than four hundred killed, wounded, and missing.

The southern department was again defeated, losing all their artillery and most of their supplies. Horatio Gates's haste had led to his own panic and a devastating loss.[284]

**PRAYER**

*I thank you that you are not a God of panic, but you are a God who leads with courage and strength.*

# 285. Fort Arnold

The spring of 1780 brought Benedict Arnold the news he had long waited to hear. He received a verdict in his court-martial. Acquitted of two charges and convicted of two, Arnold's punishment for his decisions as commander of Philadelphia was nothing more severe than a reprimand from George Washington for *"imprudent and improper"* actions.

A year earlier Arnold had told Washington of his desire to command a field position. With the court-martial over, Washington was prepared to do just that. To show his renewed confidence in Arnold, Washington called him to a face-to-face meeting on August 1, 1780. There he offered Arnold control of the army's entire left wing. But Arnold's reply stunned Washington. Claiming continued pain from his Saratoga wound, Arnold instead asked to command West Point, which was then called Fort Arnold. Located along the Hudson River sixty miles north of New York City, West Point was the American position most coveted by the British.

*"At West Point the river remains tidal, which is to say at some times of the day it flows south and at other times of the day it flows north. This made West Point an ideal place to mount cannons on both sides of the river as ships had to navigate this very tricky curve"* was how West Point historian John Hall described the Point's S-shaped curve.

Washington considered Arnold's request with the deliberation of a judge. Although Arnold was prickly and hot tempered, Washington admired Arnold's leadership qualities, his willingness to take risks, and his loyalty. From his headquarters at Peekskill, New York, Washington wrote Arnold a letter on August 3rd informing him of his decision. *"You are to proceed to West Point and take the command of that post and its dependencies,"* Washington ordered.

And in that moment, Washington unwittingly fell into Arnold's trap. Arnold had turned his coat from blue to red.

The delay of his court-martial the previous year led Arnold to over-react and make a crucial decision before a verdict was reached. In the spring of 1779, Arnold anonymously wrote a British major, a friend of Arnold's wife Peggy. Arnold promised the British he would deliver West Point to them in exchange for enough money to fill his pockets to over-flowing.

Washington may have been surprised at Arnold's "desk job" request, but he was not suspicious. He gave Arnold complete authority of West Point and requested that he build the fort into the strongest fortification possible. *"[A]nd you will endeavor to obtain every intelli-gence of the Enemy's Motions,"* Washington's order clearly stated.

Indeed, Benedict Arnold would do just that. George Washington, however, unbeknownst to him, was now the enemy.[285]

> "Brother will betray brother to death"
> (MATTHEW 10:21).

**PRAYER**

*Keep my heart from betraying those closest to me.*

# 286. Arnold's Betrayal

"*GENERAL ARNOLD is gone to the enemy,"* George Washington wrote to Nathaniel Wade on September 25, 1780. Washington told Wade he was temporarily in charge of West Point and asked him to be *"as vigilant as possible"* against an attack.

With as much urgency as Paul Revere's ride to Lexington, Washington sent several such short dispatches as soon as he discovered the horrible news. He informed his army of the treason so they could prepare their defenses.

Arnold's betrayal wounded Washington deeply, but it didn't keep him from losing his composure. Washington had what Arnold lacked: patience and the ability to clearly see reality. And just as he had as a young man with four bullets through his coat in the French and Indian War, Washington maintained his composure as he battled the treason's aftermath. Washington wrote Congress a complete account. *"I have the honor to inform Congress that I arrived here [West Point] yesterday about 12 o'clock on my return from Hartford,"* Washington explained of his planned meeting with Arnold. *"Some hours previous to my arrival Major General Arnold went from his quarters . . . as it was supposed over the river."*

Washington crossed the river only to discover Arnold was not there. After recrossing the river, Washington received a message that a handful of American militia had captured a spy, who concealed a detailed description of West Point in his boot. When Washington recognized Arnold's handwriting, he knew Arnold had betrayed the cause.

After questioning Arnold's staff, Washington concluded that Arnold had learned of the spy's captivity shortly before Washington's arrival and had fled. The commander-in-chief assured Congress that he took *"such measures as appeared the most probable to apprehend him."*

*"But he had embarked in a barge, and proceeded down the river under a flag to the vulture ship of war, which lay at some miles below . . . He wrote me after he got on board a letter, of which the inclosed is a copy,"* Washington explained. *"I have been and am taking proper precautions, which I trust will prove effectual, to prevent the important consequences which this conduct on the part of General Arnold was intended to produce."*

Washington also concluded that the members of Arnold's household, including his wife Peggy, were innocent of wrongdoing. But Washington was wrong about Peggy. British General Henry Clinton later paid Peggy for her services.

Benedict Arnold's betrayal was as much a personal betrayal against Washington as it was against his country. Yet Washington did not let his emotions affect his ability to make important decisions to secure his troops and communicate the facts to Congress. Nothing, not even betrayal, could rattle George Washington.[286]

> "And while they were eating, he said, 'I tell you the truth, one of you will betray me'"
> (MATTHEW 26:21).

**PRAYER**

*Father, I can't imagine the sting of betrayal. Thank you for the gift of repentance and mercy that is available through you.*

# 287. The Revolution Today: Supply Lines

Getting ahead of ourselves. Outrunning our supply lines. It happens when our speed exceeds our means. That is what happened to General Gates, and it cost him his job. The U.S. military found themselves faced with a similar challenge near the end of World War II. Failing to solve the problem could have cost them victory.

Gen. George S. Patton achieved a huge victory in August 1944. American, British, and other Allied forces had battled the Germans in France for two months following the D-Day invasion at Normandy. Finally, tanks from the U.S. 3rd Army broke past enemy lines. Suddenly what had been a slow progression turned into a speedy streak.

"Patton's forces, as well as other U.S. units, soon outran their supply lines. A method had to be found to provide food, fuel, ammunition and other supplies to the fast-moving U.S. Army as it pushed the Germans eastward," Gerry Gilmore explained in an article he wrote for the *Armed Forces Press Service*.

"The solution, the 'Red Ball Express,' was formed on August 25, 1944. The express was a truck convoy supply operation that ran 24 hours a day from the Normandy beaches to the front lines. The majority of the drivers who drove for the express were African-Americans."

These truck drivers and mechanics kept the trucks working, the infantry supplied, and the tankers full as Patton pushed toward Germany in the fall of 1944. *Red Ball* was an appropriate name for this operation because it was a term for priority freight used by the railroads. Drivers for the military's Red Ball Express transported more than four hundred thousand tons of supplies and used nearly six thousand vehicles in the process.

Supreme Allied Commander Gen. Dwight D. Eisenhower called the Red Ball Express a "lifeline." "To it falls the tremendous task of getting vital supplies from ports and depots to the combat troops, when and where such supplies are needed, material without which the armies might fail," he wrote in a message to the troops in the fall of 1944.

> "This service that you perform is not only supplying the needs of God's people but is also overflowing in many expressions of thanks to God"
> (2 CORINTHIANS 9:12).

The operation stopped when the need for supply speed ended. Patton's push slowed down in December as the Germans resisted and tried one last major offensive known as the "Battle of the Bulge." Spring brought the suicide of Adolf Hitler and the arrival of Soviet troops in Berlin, resulting in World War II's end.

Had Horatio Gates stopped and formed something akin to the Red Ball Express in 1780 rather than pressing ahead in foolish haste, he might have beaten the British at Camden.

We often get ahead of ourselves and overrun our supply lines. Sometimes we need to adjust our attitude or thinking and allow service, not selfishness, to guide our decisions.[287]

**PRAYER**

*Father, allow me to slow down today and evaluate the needs of those around me whom I may serve.*

## 288. Sabbath Rest: Choosing Leaders

Simeon Howard succeeded the deceased Jonathan Mayhew as pastor of Boston's West Church. And his sermons were so eloquent that he was chosen in 1780 to deliver Boston's annual election sermon. Appropriately, Howard's topic was choosing leaders, something he and his fellow Bostonians hoped they would soon do as part of a new nation.

Howard chose the story of Moses and Jethro as his leading example. After the Israelites escaped from Egypt, Moses took on the heavy burden of governing a wandering people. His father-in-law, Jethro, observed that the load of leadership was too great for Moses. He suggested Moses choose leaders over the people.

*"There can be no doubt but that God approved this measure,"* Howard explained, calling God the *"sole legislator. From then it appears that even in this government, which was so immediately the work of God, room was left for men to make such appointments."*

Howard then made a surprising observation. Moses may have appointed leaders but the people had a role in choosing them. *"This is . . . plainly intimated by Moses in his . . . discourse, recorded in the first chapter of Deuteronomy, where he says to the people, 'I spake unto you at that time, saying, I am not able to bear you myself alone: . . . Take ye wise men, and understanding, and known among your tribes, and I will make them rulers over you,'"* (vv. 9, 13 KJV).

By putting these two passages together, Howard concluded that Moses appointed men who were nominated by the people. *"So these officers were without a doubt elected by the people, though introduced by Moses into their office. And, indeed, the Jews always exercised this right of choosing their own rulers; even Saul and David, and all their successors in the throne, were made kings by the voice of the people. This natural and important right God never deprived them of,"* emphasized Howard.

Howard explained the division of the Israelite government. Moses managed the greater issues and controversies among the people. He left these appointed, local officials to handle smaller matters.

And just as in Moses' time, Howard did not believe a man was born into leadership. *"A man may be more qualified than others to lead, but*

*he is no magistrate or lawgiver till he is appointed*
*such by the people,"* he went on.

As Benedict Arnold's betrayal shows, choosing leaders is important. Leadership is not inherited, it is earned by qualifications and capabilities. It requires integrity.[288]

**PRAYER**

*Give me wisdom the next time I have the opportunity to choose a leader. Remind me of Moses and the importance you place on leadership.*

# 289. A Duty of Conscience

Benedict Arnold's betrayal stunned Henry Knox for many reasons. Knox had personally trusted Arnold. It was hard to believe the same man who had demonstrated such kindness by escorting Lucy to Valley Forge in 1778 could show such malevolence two years later. Knox was among the first to learn of the treason. He had traveled with Washington to West Point to meet Arnold. Knox, along with Lafayette, saw Washington's face grow whiter than his wig when he learned of the treason.

But it wasn't only Arnold's betrayal that unnerved the usually unwavering Knox. Knox's face turned almost as white when he learned Arnold's accomplice was an acquaintance. The war had brought Knox yet another test of character.

*"It is to vindicate my fame that I speak, and not to solicit security. The person in your possession is Major John André, adjutant-general to the British army,"* André wrote to Washington after his capture.

Because he was a general, Knox served on the board to try André. As he learned of André's role in the treason, Knox couldn't help but remember the amiable man he had met on his journey to Fort Ticonderoga in 1775. He had so much in common with André they could have been brothers.

Knox and the other generals on the trial board realized that André's circumstances were a cruel twist of fate. André had taken papers from Arnold on neutral territory. When Arnold learned André could not sail to British turf before daylight, he asked André to remove his uniform and to wait until the next day to depart for British territory. The British officer complied, but with the reluctance of a turtle leaving its shell. He knew the risks.

When the Americans captured André the next day, he was wearing civilian clothes. Had he been captured in his uniform, he would have been treated as a British officer and not as a spy. Arnold intentionally betrayed his country but unintentionally betrayed André.

*"Having avowed myself a British officer, I have nothing to reveal but what relates to myself, which is true on the honor of an officer and a gentleman,"* André wrote to Washington.

No matter how Knox and the other generals may have felt over the matter, they could not ignore the facts. André was arrested as a spy and not a British officer. The board *"condemned Major André to death as a spy, a sentence which the usages of war compelled them to pronounce, but which was especially distasteful to him [Knox] since that chance meeting on Lake George,"* Knox historian Francis Drake later explained.

Such were the obligations of war. Henry Knox and the other generals rose to the occasion. Their own sense of character and duty compelled them to vote their conscience in front of God and the army.[289]

> "Paul looked straight at the Sanhedrin and said, 'My brothers, I have fulfilled my duty to God in all good conscience to this day'" (ACTS 23:1).

**PRAYER**

*May I go to sleep tonight knowing I have fulfilled my duty to you in good conscience throughout the day.*

# 290. Honoring Providence

The task of communicating to the army the news of America's most disloyal general fell to George Washington's most loyal general, Nathanael Greene.

*"TREASON of the blackest dye was yesterday discovered,"* Greene began his proclamation to the army. *"General Arnold, who commanded at West Point, lost to every sense of honor, of private and public obligation, was about to deliver up that important post into the hands of the enemy."*

He immediately inserted the good news: Arnold had failed. *"Such an event must have given the American cause a dangerous, if not a fatal wound; but the treason has been timely discovered, to prevent the fatal misfortune,"* Greene informed the troops.

Greene knew the treason would send shock waves through the army like an earthquake. To prevent fissures of fear, he decided to uplift the army's spirits by pointing them skyward. He appealed to their view of heaven and God's role as commander-in-chief on earth. If God was the Author of liberty, he was also the Protector against forces opposing liberty.

*"The providential train of circumstances which led to it affords the most convincing proof that the liberties of America are the object of Divine protection. At the same time that the treason is to be regretted, the general [Washington] cannot help congratulating the army on the happy discovery."*

Greene then used the proclamation to warn the army against aftershocks by the enemy. He had no way of knowing at the time if Arnold was the only American general, officer, or soldier involved in the plot.

*"Our enemies, despairing of carrying their point by force, are practicing every base art to effect by bribery and corruption what they cannot accomplish in a manly way. Great honor is due to the American army that this is the first instance of treason of the kind, where many were to be expected from the nature of the dispute,"* Greene continued.

He went on to report that although Arnold had escaped, his accomplice had not. *"His Excellency the Commander-in-Chief, has arrived at West Point from Hartford, and is no doubt taking proper measures to unravel fully so hellish a plot,"* Greene concluded.

Once again God's protection had intervened in the Revolution. If Arnold's accomplice had escaped, Arnold might have succeeded in helping the British seize West Point. He also might have captured Washington. Had he been successful, Arnold would have received a royal title, such as duke. George Washington would have been hanged as a traitor. But because of Providence's protection, the seismic tremors created by Benedict Arnold's act of treason were not catastrophic.[290]

> "For the LORD your God is the one who goes with you to fight for you against your enemies to give you victory" (DEUTERONOMY 20:4).

**PRAYER**

*God, thank you for your marvelous ways, for fighting on behalf of justice and honesty.*

# 291. Why Treason?

Why did Benedict Arnold commit treason? Why did a wounded war hero suddenly switch sides? If he was merely unhappy with his treatment by the military, Arnold could have resigned and lived quietly with his wife. He chose treason instead.

Arnold issued an address to *"the inhabitants of America"* in October 1780 to explain his motives. His explanation, however, was severely lacking. *"When I quitted the Domestick happiness for the Perils of the Field, I conceived the rights of my Country in Danger and that Duty and Honor called me to her Defence,"* he began, claiming first that a redress of grievances, not independence, was his personal aim in 1776.

Arnold second claimed he had supported the war as long as it was a defensive one. But France's entry turned the conflict into a war of offense in his opinion. Arnold's hatred of France had not faded since the Indians had slaughtered his colleagues during the French and Indian War.

He also was angry that the colonies had failed to form a government. *"Nor to this very hour have they authorized its ratification—the Articles of Confederation remain unsigned,"* he pointed out to support his third treason reason.

Arnold "prayed" for his former colleagues in his address. *"I pray God to give them all the lights requisite to their Own Safety before it is too late,"* he wrote of those who served *"blindly but honestly"* in the American ranks.

What makes Arnold's public defense difficult to believe is its timing. He wrote his explanation while aboard a British ship, less than a month after his betrayal. Arnold's audience was not Americans but King George III and his generals. His address was no doubt as much a ruse as he was. He was trying to use the publication to assure the British of his loyalty.

So what caused him to change? Was it his explosive personality or the slights against him, from Fort Ticonderoga to his court-martial? Was it a question of honor, which had been challenged one too many times? Was it his wife's influence? Was it his hatred of France?

All these are plausible explanations. Because the Revolution was a change in the hearts and minds of the people as much as it was a war, Arnold's treason revealed his true loyalties. His devotion was as superficial as the skin on an apple. Arnold's core was a mind plagued by twisted thinking, self-centeredness, and a warped view of his circumstances. All these prohibited him from enjoying the future blessings of American liberty.

> "O Lord God Almighty, the God of Israel, rouse yourself to punish all the nations; show no mercy to wicked traitors" (PSALM 59:5).

Once a traitor always a traitor. Arnold may have embraced the British, but they never fully trusted him. After the war, Benedict Arnold and his wife lived their remaining years in England, invisibly branded with distrust, like a scarlet letter.[291]

**PRAYER**

*Examine my motives today for any trace of betrayal against you or others.*

# 292. Election Predictions

Not everyone was surprised by Benedict Arnold's treason.

*"You know, that I have long had my Suspicions of this Traitor, & therefore you will not wonder that I am not so much astonishd as if any other officer had been,"* Samuel Adams wrote his wife, Betsy, in October 1780.

The Puritan hoped Arnold's treason would remind the people of Massachusetts to use wisdom as they voted for the first governor of Massachusetts in the upcoming election. *"Attention to the Administration of Government, I fancy, will soon determine whether they have acted with Wisdom or not,"* the Puritan wrote.

But Arnold's treason also had an unexpected effect on Adams. The Massachusetts gubernatorial election left Adams bitter. Although elated by the thought of being able to cast a ballot for representatives in the new government, one of the candidates soured the process for Adams. A former friend wounded him.

*"I expect soon to see it announcd in the Papers, that Mr Hancock is elected Governor of the Common Wealth of Massachusetts,"* Adams concluded to his wife. Betsy, however, misunderstood her husband's prediction. She thought he possessed inside information about the election's outcome. *"We are not so well informd,"* Adams wrote her a week later. *"I had Reason to believe that Mr Hancock would be the Governor. I am disposd to think, that my Fellow Citizens had upright Views in giving him their Suffrages."* Adams knew his wife was surprised at his prediction. *"You may wonder at my saying so,"* he added.

Betsy knew what her husband knew. As often happens in politics, Hancock had distanced himself from the eccentric Adams. They were once as close as brothers, who had harmoniously led the Sons of Liberty. The seeds of mistrust were most likely planted when Adams supported Washington over Hancock for commander-in-chief in 1775. Their closeness tapered off as they took on different roles in the Revolution.

Adams gained more perspective on his friendship with Hancock after Benedict Arnold's betrayal. Hancock had not committed treason. He was still a brother. Adams realized the distance between himself and Hancock was only as far as Philadelphia is from Boston, not as wide as the ocean separating Boston and London.

"*I am far from being an Enemy to that Gentleman, tho' he has been prevaild upon to mark me as such. I have so much Friendship for him,*" he wrote of having forgiven Hancock. "*Can I say more? If, with the best Advice he is able to hold the Reins of Government with Dignity, I wish him a Continuance of the Honor. If he renders our Country secure in a flourishing Condition, I will never be so partial & unjust as to withhold my Tribute of Applause.*"

> "A longing fulfilled is sweet to the soul, but fools detest turning from evil"
> (PROVERBS 13:19).

John Hancock won the election for governor, and Samuel Adams applauded.[292]

**PRAYER**

*Reveal to me a person I need to forgive. Give me the courage to forgive and the sweetness that comes with forgiveness.*

# 293. A Glowing Greene Recommendation

"We must have a permanent force; not a force that is constantly fluctuating and sliding from under us as a pedestal of Ice would do from a Statue in a Summers day,*" George Washington wrote to George Mason of Virginia, one of the South's most prominent men, on October 22, 1780. Washington sent the same message to four other influential Virginians.

Washington was low on numbers, especially generals. Benjamin Lincoln had been living as a prisoner of war since May. Baron de Kalb had died at Camden in August. Benedict Arnold had committed treason in September. Horatio Gates was facing court-martial.

Regardless of the trial's outcome, Gates's moral authority had fallen faster than sand in an hourglass. He had become the butt of jokes. Alexander Hamilton, an aide to Washington, satirically praised the elder man's ability to ride two hundred miles in a panic as a remarkable feat for a man his age.

"*In consequence of a resolve of Congress directing an inquiry into the conduct of General Gates, and authorizing me to appoint some other officer in his place during this inquiry, I have made a choice of Major General*

*Greene, who will I suspect have the honor of presenting you with this letter,"* Washington explained to Mason.

The loss of these generals had given Washington an opportunity to do something he had long wanted to do: give Nathanael Greene a battle command. Greene knew when to conform to the pattern of propriety and when to crack the cast of conformity. As both a mold maker and mold breaker, Greene was a mini-Washington, closer than anyone else to the commander-in-chief's strategic thinking. Washington had so much faith in him, he had decided that if he died, he wanted Greene to take over as commander-in-chief.

*"I can venture to introduce this gentleman to you as a Man of Abilities, bravery and coolness. (He has a comprehensive knowledge of our affairs, and is a Man of Fortitude and resources),"* Washington continued.

Washington explained he had no doubt of Greene's capabilities. Greene's ability to adjust to changing circumstances made him the most likely man to succeed in the South. Washington's high recommendation came with a practical purpose. He needed Mason to provide Greene with money, men, and munitions. *"With this character I take the liberty of recommending him to your civilities and support,"* concluded Washington.

> "He must also have a good reputation with outsiders" (1 TIMOTHY 3:7).

Nathanael Greene's reputation had earned him favor with George Washington. And through his commander-in-chief's glowing recommendation, this Rhode Islander would also soon develop a good reputation with the patriots in the South.[293]

**PRAYER**

*God, thank you for the value you place on fostering a good reputation among leaders. May I cultivate a reputation that honors you whether I lead an army of one or of ten thousand.*

# 294. The Revolution Today: Treason's Opposite

What is the opposite of treason? Loyalty. And recipients of the President's Medal of Honor are some of the best examples of loyalty to one's country.

"He had a natural gift for leadership, and a compassion that led him to take others under his wing. The Marine Corps took the best of this young man, and made it better," President George W. Bush said as he spoke about Corporal Jason Dunham in a ceremony in the East Room of the White House on January 11, 2007.

"As a Marine, he was taught that honor, courage, and commitment are not just words. They're core values for a way of life that elevates service above self. As a Marine, Jason was taught that leaders put the needs of their men before their own. He was taught that while America's founding truths are self-evident, they also need to be defended by good men and women willing to stand up to determined enemies," Bush told those in attendance.

Dunham had grown up in upstate New York. He had played basketball, soccer, and baseball. This son of a dairy farm worker and a teacher applied his leadership skills in the military.

"As a leader of a rifle squad in Iraq, Corporal Dunham lived by the values he had been taught. He was a guy everybody looked up to. He was a Marine's Marine who led by example," Bush said, noting that Dunham often stopped and played soccer with Iraqi schoolchildren. Dunham also signed up for an extra two months in Iraq so he could remain with his squad to "make sure that everyone makes it home alive."

"Corporal Dunham took that promise seriously and would give his own life to make it good," Bush said.

Bush related that during an attack near Iraq's Syrian border in April 2004, an insurgent jumped out of a car that was about to be searched and assaulted Dunham.

"As Corporal Dunham wrestled the man to the ground, the insurgent rolled out a grenade he had been hiding. Corporal Dunham did not hesitate. He jumped on the grenade, using his helmet and body to absorb the blast. Although he survived the initial explosion, he did not survive his wounds. But by his selflessness, Corporal Dunham saved the lives of two of his men, and showed the world what it means to be a Marine," Bush eulogized.

After his remarks, the president presented Cpl. Jason Dunham's Presidential Medal of Honor to the corporal's parents. "The Medal of Honor is the highest award for valor a President can bestow. The Medal is given for gallantry in the face of an enemy attack that is above and beyond the call of duty," shared Bush solemnly.

> "Teach me to do your will, for you are my God; may your good Spirit lead me on level ground" (PSALM 143:10).

Had the Medal of Honor existed during the Revolution, Benedict Arnold would have deserved it for his valor at Saratoga. But he chose treason instead of accolades. Leadership depends on loyalty. You can't have the first without the second.[294]

**PRAYER**

*God, you are the most loyal of leaders. Lead me on level ground in the coming week.*

# 295. Sabbath Rest: Capable Leadership

Simeon Howard's election sermon on leadership was as firm as George Washington's decision to appoint Nathanael Greene commander in the South. The business of rulers *"is to promote and secure the happiness of the whole community,"* this pastor proclaimed simply.

Howard believed leaders were to be God's ministers for the good of the people. But his message grew stronger with each sentence. *"Hence, their power is said to be from God; that is, it is so while they employ it according to his will. But when they act against the good of society, they cannot be said to act by authority from God, any more than a servant can be said to act by his master's authority while he acts directly contrary to his will,"* he told his parishioners.

Howard then outlined qualifications for leadership described in Exodus, when Moses chose leaders recommended by the people.

First, Howard said, leaders must be capable of doing their jobs. *"Woe unto thee, O land, when thy king is a child,"* Howard said, quoting Solomon (Ecclesiastes 10:16 KJV).

Capability required maturity. If leaders lacked maturity, then they mirrored a child. Such leadership would result in misery among the people. Howard described capable leaders as *"men of clear heads, who have improved their minds by exercise, acquired a habit of reasoning, and furnished themselves with a good degree of knowledge,—men who have a just conception of the nature and end of government in general, of the natural rights of mankind, of the nature and importance of civil and religious liberty."*

He continued by saying a leader needs to understand human nature and to know the people he governs. *"The more he excels in these things, the more likely he will be to rule well,"* he said.

Selecting capable leaders was crucial to the survival of society. Capable leaders knew how to promote commerce, negotiate on behalf of the people, and ensure the education of society. Able leaders were also courageous, firm, and resolute. Capable leaders would not *"sink into despondency"* at the sight of difficulties or desert their duty at the approach of danger.

*"By 'able men' may be further intended men capable of enduring the burden and fatigue of government, —men that have not broken or debilitated their bodies or minds by the . . . pleasures of luxury, intemperance, or dissipation. The supreme government of a people is always a burden of great weight, though more difficult at sometimes than others. It cannot be managed well without great diligence and application,"* asserted Simeon Howard.

> "But select capable men from all the people" (EXODUS 18:21).

The need for capable leadership hasn't changed over the years. Time and time again, God's model of leadership has proven its merit.[295]

**PRAYER**

*Strengthen my capabilities. Fortify my weakness that I may fulfill your purpose in me, when I lead and when I follow.*

# 296. Victory and Defeat

Although his appointment as quartermaster had left him parched in 1778, Nathanael Greene's heart overflowed with joy when Congress approved his appointment as commander of the southern army in 1780. From Washington's painful rebuke to Arnold's treason, this iron foundry owner had passed through the furnace's fire. He had emerged as a man with proven character. Greene knew, however, if he lost hope, this new role could destroy him faster than hot coals could melt iron ore.

Defeat, indeed, tried to burn him before he began. On his journey south, Greene visited Virginia and Maryland's assemblies to ask for help. He also asked for support from the legislatures in Delaware and North Carolina. His coffers, however, remained empty.

*"All the way through the country, as I passed, I found the people engaged in matters of interest and in pursuit of pleasure, almost regardless of their danger. Public credit totally lost, and every man excusing himself from giving the least aid to Government,"* Greene wrote to his friend Joseph Reed in January 1781. *"This afforded but a dull prospect, nor has it mended since my arrival,"* he added.

The feeling of defeat only increased when he reached Charlotte, North Carolina, to take over the southern forces there. Greene found only eight hundred men fit for service. *"The appearance of the troops was wretched beyond description, and their distress, on account of provisions, was little less than their suffering for want of clothing and other necessaries.*

*General Gates had lost the confidence of the officers, and the troops all their discipline, and so addicted to plundering, that they were a terror to the inhabitants,"* detailed Greene.

Because he ranked sacrifice higher than his own ambition, Greene was not easily defeated. He immediately put his hands to the task of hammering organization. *"I am endeavouring to bring everything into order, and perfect our arrangements as much as possible, but it is all an up-hill business,"* he told Reed.

But there was one more problem this former quartermaster had to conquer. Greene realized the army had foraged North Carolina's food supplies *"like the locusts of Egypt."* If the army turned North Carolina's forests into a desert by taking all the available food, they would lose the support of the local patriots, and perhaps the war.

*"Indeed, unless this army is better supported than I see any prospect of, the Country is lost beyond redemption, for it is impossible for the people to struggle much longer under their present difficulties,"* Greene wrote despairingly.

Until he found a solution for the lack of provisions, Nathanael Greene would make do with what he had. He would not give up. *"This Camp I mean as a Camp of repose, for the purpose of repairing our wagons, recruiting our horses, and disciplining the troops,"* he concluded, defeating defeat with determination.[296]

> "Not only so, but we also rejoice in our sufferings, because we know that suffering produces perseverance" (ROMANS 5:3).

**PRAYER**

*Thank you, Lord, for the gift of perseverance, for the courage to press on through suffering.*

# 297. The Carolinas' Civil War

Just as Gen. George Washington had found New Jersey tangled in a terrible civil war in 1776, Gen. Nathanael Greene found a similar tragedy in the South in 1781. The Carolinas had become a place where neighbors attacked neighbors with less mercy than a hurricane striking its coast.

Greene longed to share his observations with his wife, Catherine. A recently released prisoner of war came through Greene's camp on his way northward and offered to deliver a letter for the general.

*"Nothing can exceed my anxiety to know your situation, not having heard the least syllable from you since I left Philadelphia,"* he wrote to

Catherine. *"You can have no idea of the distress and misery that prevails in this quarter. Hundreds of families that formerly lived in great opulence are now reduced to beggary and want."*

He then shared a story that reminded him of their own painful war separation. Of their seven years as husband and wife, they had only spent one full year together. *"A Gentleman from Georgia was this morning with me, to get assistance to move his wife and family out of the Enemies way. They have been separated for upwards of eight months, during all which time the wife never heard from her husband, nor the husband from his wife,"* he told Catherine, noting that the man's wife had to sell all her plates, linens, and clothes to maintain her children.

*"In this situation she was tantalised by the Tories, and insulted by the British. Human misery has become a subject for sport and ridicule,"* Greene wrote angrily.

However, recounting the couple's sad tale also made him reflect on his and his wife's relative good fortune. *"When I compare our situation with those miserable people in this quarter, disagreeable as it may be from our long and distant separation, I cannot help feeling thankful that your cup has not a mixture of bitterness like theirs,"* he continued thankfully.

Unfortunately, this was not the worst situation Greene had encountered. *"A Captain who is now with me and who has just got his family from near the Lines of the Enemy had his Sister murdered a few days since, and seven of her children wounded, the oldest not twelve years of age,"* he wrote, adding that suffering in the Carolinas was beyond description.

*"I will not pain your humanity by a further relation of, the distresses which rage in this quarter; nor would I have mentioned them at all, but to convince you that you are not the most unhappy of all creation,"* he assured Catherine.

Nathanael Greene closed this section of his letter with a look heavenward. *"God grant us a speedy and happy meeting, by giving to the Country peace, liberty and safety,"* he concluded prayerfully.[297]

> "Do not be anxious about anything, but in everything, by prayer and petition, with thanksgiving, present your requests to God"
> (PHILIPPIANS 4:6).

**PRAYER**

*Thank you, God, for listening to my prayers. I know that gratefulness is a great remedy for unhappiness and anxiety.*

# 298. Backcountry Backup

The back-country people are bold and daring in their make, but the people upon the sea-shore are sickly and but indifferent militia," Nathanael Greene wrote of North Carolinians in his letter to Joseph Reed in January 1781.

There was one man, a roughneck frontiersman, who quickly came to Greene's aid. He had the backbone of the backcountry. His name was Daniel Morgan, and he was a veteran of the French and Indian War. The scars on his face were his badges of honor, marks of his fearlessness. And just as Morgan and his marksmen had saved Saratoga from surefire defeat in 1777, they were just as determined to become Greene's salvation in the South.

"I have been obliged to take an entire new position with the army. General Morgan is upon Broad River with a little flying army," Greene briefed Reed.

To keep his army alive, Greene decided to divide them. He gave Morgan command of one division. He commanded the other. Greene headed southeast, and Morgan headed southwest into the backcountry.

Once again Greene knew when to break with tradition. His decision was reminiscent of a previous decision against convention. Twenty years earlier Greene had received the smallpox inoculation, which was against the wishes of his Quaker friends and the law of Rhode Island at the time. Yet his decision proved to be his survival against the disease. And in North Carolina, he found similar cover by breaking with convention. He chose to divide his army as insurance for their endurance.

"Nathanael Greene adopts what might be considered an unconventional approach to this war. He's going to break his force. He's going to break into something like flying columns," described West Point historian John Hall.

Greene had two reasons for splitting the army. By dividing them, he preserved as much of North Carolina's natural food supplies as possible. A smaller division would not ravage the food sources in the countryside as badly as a larger army would. A smaller army was also faster and easier to move.

Greene may have broken with convention, but he was able to torment his foe. British General Cornwallis soon picked up on Greene's trail, while the most brutal British colonel, Bannister Tarleton, detected Morgan's scent. Tarleton had developed a reputation as a savage merciless

> "Will you torment a windblown leaf? Will you chase after dry chaff?" (JOB 13:25).

avenger. Cornwallis chased Nathanael Greene while Tarleton pursued Daniel Morgan. Although the hounds began to chase their foxes, this would prove to be no ordinary hunt.[298]

**PRAYER**

*I seek your purpose for my life today. Lead me to pursue those things that are valuable to you and to avoid pursuits that are as dry as dust.*

# 299. Cowpens

Like foxes, Gen. Nathanael Greene and Gen. Daniel Morgan allowed General Cornwallis and Colonel Tarleton to chase them like hounds. The hunt would end in a cow pasture.

The triumph began after Tarleton learned Morgan was somewhere between the Broad and Catawba Rivers. He set out to cut him off. *"When Morgan heard of Tarleton's approach, he retired toward the Broad River, intending to cross it. Tarleton pursued with his usual rapidity. Morgan saw that he must be overtaken; he halted, refreshed his men, and prepared for the conflict. He chose his ground at a place known as 'The Cowpens' about thirty miles west of King's Mountain,"* historian William Jackman wrote of the pasture turned battlefield on January 17, 1781.

The armies were nearly equal in number. But Morgan had an advantage. More than half his men were Carolina militia. And unlike previous battles where the militia had failed, Morgan knew how to use them. He capitalized on their reputation of fight over flight.

*"Morgan disposed his men to the best advantage; the Continentals on a woody hill, and the militia in a line by themselves,"* recounted Jackman. When the British saw the militia on the front lines, they rushed in with their bayonets fixed. They shouted "Huzzah" like a bugler sounds his horn in a fox hunt.

*"The militia stood their ground, delivered their fire, but quailing before the bayonet, they broke and fled,"* Jackman wrote.

But their retreat was not unplanned, as they made it appear. Morgan had ordered the militia to fire a couple of rounds and then fall back.

*"This movement the British mistook for a retreat, and they commenced a vigorous pursuit,"* wrote Jackman, noting that Morgan's regular army then stepped forward. *"But when they [the British] approached within thirty yards, the Continentals suddenly wheeled, poured in a deadly volley, then charged with bayonet, completely routed them, and captured their colors and cannon. The fiery Tarleton, accompanied by a few fol-*

*lowers, barely escaped capture. Of his eleven hundred men he lost six hundred, while Morgan's loss was less than eighty."*

When Cornwallis learned of Tarleton's defeat, he pursued Morgan, hoping to catch him before he crossed the Catawba River. *"Morgan was too watchful to be thus caught. He knew Cornwallis would pursue him, and he left his wounded under a flag of truce, and hurried on to the Catawba, and crossed over,"* Jackman wrote.

> "He who works his land will have abundant food, but the one who chases fantasies will have his fill of poverty" (PROVERBS 28:19).

Nathanael Greene's divided army strategy was a success, at least for the moment. His work brought an abundant reward. It also allowed Daniel Morgan to retire as one of the war's great heroes.[299]

**PRAYER**

*Thank you for making my freedom a worthy pursuit, one that has resulted in rich abundance for America.*

# 300. Crossing the Dan

With Gen. Daniel Morgan's defeat of Col. Bannister Tarleton at Cowpens on January 17, 1781, only one hound remained to chase the foxes. If General Cornwallis could catch Gen. Nathanael Greene and his men before they crossed the Dan River into Virginia, he could snuff out the southern army and extinguish America's last hope for victory.

Greene was aware of the hounds nipping at his heels. And he knew he had two rivers to cross in order to escape Cornwallis. The first was the Yadkin River.

*"His [Greene's] encumbered army could move but slowly; just as his rear-guard was embarking on the river, the British van came up. A skirmish ensued, in which the Americans lost a few baggage wagons,"* historian William Jackman related, noting the effort ensured Greene's army's safety, at least for the night. Cornwallis rested his men with plans to cross the Yadkin the next morning.

*"The rain had poured in torrents, and in the morning the river was so much swollen, that his [Cornwallis's] army could not ford it, and Greene had secured all the boats on the other side."*

Greene chose to cast himself in Washington's mold at this river crossing. He had witnessed Washington's most successful strategy many times. Preserving his army became Greene's highest priority. He ordered his men to break down bridges after crossing them. He told them to kindle fires to make it appear they had stopped to camp. He pushed his army to travel thirty miles a day. He did everything he could to make sure his army did not fall prey to Cornwallis.

*"The half-clad Americans had toiled for nearly four weeks over roads partially frozen, through drenching rains, without tents at night,"* described Jackman. When they were within forty miles of the Dan River, Greene pushed his men even harder. They rapidly marched and crossed the river. Cornwallis's troops reached the Dan a few hours later, but like the Yadkin weeks earlier, this river was too swollen to cross.

*"After a chase of more than two hundred miles, the object of his [Cornwallis's] pursuit lay in sight, but the waters between could not be forded, nor could boats be obtained. As the two armies rested in sight of each other, how different were their emotions! The one overflowing with gratitude, the other chafed with disappointment,"* Jackman wrote.

Jackman saw Greene's twin river crossings as acts of God, examples of his advance hand and rear guard. *"Twice had the waters, through which they had safely passed, risen and become impassable to their pursuers, and again a river swollen by recent rains lay between them. Was it strange that those who were accustomed to notice the workings of Providence, believed that He who orders all things, had specially interposed His arm for the salvation of the patriots?"* Jackman asked rhetorically.[300]

> "But you will not leave in haste or go in flight; for the LORD will go before you, the God of Israel will be your rear guard" (ISAIAH 52:12).

**PRAYER**

*Thank you for your providence during the Revolution and for being my rear guard today.*

# 301. The Revolution Today: Sight

*I*n *your last letter, you wrote me that you had eight new Shirts and Stocks [scarves], and several pair of Stockings; which you intended to have brought to camp with you. As my stock is small, and the difficulty great in getting any here, I wish you to send me all you have,"* Nathanael Greene wrote to his wife, Catherine, in January 1781.

Greene knew it would be three months before he could receive a package from Catherine through the normal postal system. Instead he asked her to send them by *"persons who will undertake to have them safely delivered,"* and recommended someone he knew in Philadelphia.

"Snail mail" is still used to describe the postal service. As fast as other modes of communication have become, military mail from the States to locations abroad still takes a couple of weeks. If Nathanael Greene had served in the nation's modern military, he likely would have taken advantage of the latest technology to communicate with his family. Not only would he have written Catherine an email or called her on the phone, he just might have seen her.

During Operation Iraqi Freedom, the 1st Cavalry Division set up a video conferencing center at Camp Liberty, Iraq, to facilitate fast and visible communication between soldiers and their loved ones back home. "The guys love using the VTC [video teleconferencing] capabilities here, and we stay busy all the time," Army Staff Sgt. David Beach, who was in charge of the program, announced in a press account for the *Armed Forces Press Service.*

Videoconferencing gave the 1st Cavalry the ability to see their families. To use the VTC, a 1st Cavalry soldier could make the request through his or her chain of command. Then arrangements would be made with the family and a date set. In a room set up at headquarters, soldiers would usually have about fifteen minutes to speak with and see their loved ones.

"Last time I was deployed I didn't talk to my family for eight months," remembered Army Staff Sergeant Lorenzo Antley, a military intelligence analyst. "Being able to see my wife and children now keeps me motivated and ready to get back in the fight. They also get a chance to see me and know I am doing fine."

If Catherine Greene had been able to see her husband in 1781 through a video link, he probably wouldn't have asked her to send shirts and socks. She would have known of his need just by seeing him. He also wouldn't have had to ask her to be particular in *"giving an account"* of the children. He could have talked to them himself.

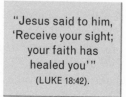

"Jesus said to him, 'Receive your sight; your faith has healed you'" (LUKE 18:42).

Vision is surely a blessing, whether we are watching someone through a video link or talking to them in person. Jesus knew how special this gift of God is, and that is one reason why he healed the blind. God uses sight to crystallize faith in those who seek his face.[301]

**PRAYER**

*God, thank you for the power of sight. Use my eyes to understand the needs of those around me this week.*

# 302. Sabbath Rest: Trustworthy Leaders

When Simeon Howard extolled the virtues of leadership to the venerable leaders of Massachusetts, he included as a qualification the ability to harness the power of respect. He believed capable leaders needed to fear God.

*"The fear of God, in the language of Scripture, does not intend a slavish, superstitious dread, as of an almighty, arbitrary, and cruel Being,"* defined Howard.

And just as the phrase *"fear of God"* seems quaint to modern-day ears, so it also needed fine-tuning for Howard's listeners. He stated that fearing God was a *"just reverence and awe of him which naturally arises from a belief and habitual consideration of his glorious perfections and providence."*

Fearing God also came from a belief in *"his being the moral governor of the world, a lover of holiness and a hater of vice, who sees every thought and design as well as every action of all his creatures, and will punish the impenitently vicious and reward the virtuous,"* Howard went on.

Fearing God led Howard to conclude that leaders must be truthful. A fear of God resulted in integrity. *"This means men free from deceit and hypocrisy, guile, and falsehood—men who will not, by flattery and cajoling, by falsehood and slandering a competitor, endeavor to get into authority,"* he said, noting that leaders needed to speak truthfully and make timely decisions.

No matter what issues the Revolution's leaders faced, integrity was important to governing a free people. Integrity brought respect from the governed and respect from other nations. Integrity resulted in *"happy"* subjects held together by the bonds of truth and justice. Integrity was a pillar of a strong government.

*"They will show the same integrity and fidelity in their conduct towards individuals. They will not promise to any one what they have*

*reason to think they cannot or do not intend to perform,"* Howard explained.

Howard also feared the danger of covetousness in public leadership. Covetousness did not have anything to do with integrity. Howard defined covetousness as a desire for inordinate riches for personal gain. *"Such a desire will make a man pursue them [riches] by unlawful means, and prevent his using them in a right manner."*

The preacher reminded his audience that oppression, fraud, and violence were rooted in covetousness. *"It hardens the heart, and makes it deaf to the cries of distress and the dictates of charity."*

> "But select . . . men who fear God, trustworthy men who hate dishonest gain" (EXODUS 18:21).

Covetousness would lead rulers to oppress and defraud their subjects to promote their private interest, Simeon Howard told the listening legislators. But rulers who hated covetousness would look out for the public interest, promote good laws, and discharge their duties for the good of their country.[302]

**PRAYER**

*Thank you for reminding me what it means to fear you. Erase all forms of covetousness from me. May I speak and act with integrity in all things.*

# 303. A Greene Need

"Lord Cornwallis has been at our heels from day to day," Gen. Nathanael Greene wrote to Gen. George Washington from the Dan River on February 15, 1781.

*"Our movements from thence to this place have been of the most critical kind, having a river in our front, and the enemy in our rear. But, happily, we have crossed without the loss of either men or stores,"* he reported.

Although Greene's army had safely crossed the Dan, he feared the British would soon be able to ford the formidable river. *"The enemy are on the other side of the river, and, as it is falling, I expect it will be fordable before night; and the fords are so numerous, and the enemy lie in such an advantageous situation for crossing, that it would be a folly to think of defending them, as it would reduce our force to small parties, which might prove our ruin,"* he explained to the commander-in-chief.

Crossing the river in wintertime mirrored another mighty moment, when the army forded the Delaware River and defeated the British at Trenton in 1776. Both crossings were sealed with the same symbol: red footprints in the snow, an image Greene knew Washington would remember.

*"The miserable situation of the troops, for want of clothing, has rendered the march the most painful imaginable, several hundreds of the soldiers tracking the ground with their bloody feet. Your feelings for the suffering soldier, had you been here, must have been pained upon the occasion,"* Greene reflected.

Another threat nipped at Greene's heels. Attrition was a fierce enemy. Greene's army needed fresh troops. *"The enemy's movements have been so rapid, and the country under such terror, that few or no militia have joined us, and the greater part we had have fallen off. Inclosed I send your Excellency the strength of the British army, which you will see is much stronger than I had calculated upon in my last,"* he wrote, adding that he didn't have even a shilling to obtain good intelligence.

*"Your Excellency knows that good intelligence is the soul of an army, and ought to govern all its movements. I have done every thing to call out the militia of the upper country . . . Nothing is yet done to give me effectual support,"* a dismayed Greene wrote.

> "There the LORD will be our Mighty One. It will be like a place of broad rivers and streams. No galley with oars will ride them, no mighty ship will sail them" (ISAIAH 33:21).

He once again needed the Lord's mighty hand, the same hand that had revealed Benedict Arnold's treason and had stopped Cornwallis at the river's edge. He longed for good fighting men to hold back the broad rivers and streams of troops that threatened to overtake his army.

*"I must repeat again what I have said in several letters, that I fear nothing can save the Southern States but a good regular army,"* pleaded Nathanael Greene.[303]

**PRAYER**

*God, thank you for your might, for your ability to prevent the rivers in life from overtaking me.*

# 304. Recrossing the Dan

Gen. Nathanael Greene's sigh of relief rippled down the Dan River. Instead of crossing the receding river in pursuit of Greene, General

Charles Cornwallis decided to return to North Carolina. God's mighty hand had preserved the American army once again.

No sooner had the redcoats retreated than Greene learned of Cornwallis's latest proclamation appealing to the locals. He used *"every art to induce the people to join him,"* as Greene explained to Washington. And like his commander, Greene knew he was fighting both a war of weapons and a battle for the hearts and minds of many Americans.

Greene made a decision. He cast a mold of boldness and once again broke with convention. Remembering the stories he had heard of the Tories' torture, he feared local loyalists would rise and again terrorize North Carolina patriots if his army did not return. Greene decided to re-cross the Dan and pursue Cornwallis. The fox now chased the hound.

*"Cornwallis, almost destitute of supplies, changed his position, and moved further South. Greene cautiously followed . . . As for himself, he was so watchful against surprise, that he never remained more than one day in the same place, and never communicated to anyone beforehand where he expected to encamp,"* described historian William Jackman of Greene's return to the Carolinas.

And just as green grass emerged with the arrival of March, so Greene's previous requests for support finally sprouted. Fresh troops from Virginia and Maryland arrived and strengthened his army to four thousand. The Greene fox was ready to attack his hound.

*"[Greene] approached the enemy to give them battle. It was in the vicinity of Guilford Court House,"* detailed Jackman.

Greene arranged his army in two lines. One of his colonels boldly charged the enemy with his cavalry, but the British artillery stopped them. The battle seesawed until Greene ordered a retreat. Like Washington, Greene knew when to cut his losses and run.

*"Though Greene retreated from the field, Cornwallis was unable to pursue. More than a thousand of the militia deserted and returned home, and Greene's army was soon as weak as ever. This has been thought one of the severest battles of the whole war,"* Jackman stated.

Although the battle at Guilford Courthouse was a blow to Greene, it was a larger loss for Cornwallis, more severe than Morgan's magic tricks against Colonel Tarleton.

> "Therefore, since we have such a hope, we are very bold" (2 CORINTHIANS 3:12).

*"Cornwallis's army was so broken by this battle, and weakened by desertions and sickness, that it numbered but about fourteen hundred men. He was compelled to abandon his position, and fall back to Wilmington, near the seaboard,"* Jackman wrote.

Charles Cornwallis abandoned his plan to conquer the Carolinas. The wily fox, Nathanael Greene, had eluded him with his mold of boldness and spirit of hope.[304]

**PRAYER**

*Thank you for boldness. I pray for strength to discern the times when I need to be bold and the moments when I need to be cautious.*

# 305. The Federal Arch Completed

Reading English requires scanning from left to right. Building a house starts at the bottom and finishes with the top. But constructing a bridge or an arch is often an outside to inside job. The last piece is not usually either end, but the middle. Such was the crowning moment when the figurative federal arch was completed in March 1781. Appropriately, it was a middle state, not a northern or southern state, that finally ratified the Articles of Confederation.

*"This day will be memorable in the annals of America to the last posterity, for the final ratification in Congress of the articles of confederation and perpetual union between the States,"* a newspaper, the *Pennsylvania Packet*, heralded after Maryland became the last state to ratify the Articles of Confederation.

While Maryland's militia fought for Nathanael Greene and George Washington that year, the residents of this mid-Atlantic state completed the job of ratifying the Articles of Confederation. The United States of America was just that, finally united under a confederation constitution. The completion of the arch of thirteen colonies under a single government was as critical to winning the war as any battle. Why? Giving America a constitution was the middle plank on the bridge to independence.

The newspaper predicted that this great event *"will confound our enemies, fortify us against their arts of seduction, and frustrate their plans of division."* The news sounded throughout the colonies, giving them a rallying cry similar to that after the signing of the Declaration of Independence almost five years earlier.

*"The bells were rung, and every manifestation of joy shown on this occasion. The Ariel frigate, commanded by the gallant Paul Jones, fired a feu de joie, and was beautifully decorated with a variety of streamers in the day, and ornamented with a brilliant appearance of lights in the night,"* the newspaper described, adding that the whole town of Philadelphia witnessed an *"elegant exhibition of fireworks."*

The news was as much a bane to Britain as it was a boost to America. *"But Britain's boasted wealth and grandeur are crumbling to pieces, never to be again united,"* the newspaper predicted.

The arch was completed. The middle piece was in place, the crown crowned.

*"Thus has the union, began by necessity, been indissolubly cemented. Thus America, (like a well-constructed arch, whose parts harmonizing and mutually supporting each other, are the more closely united the greater the pressure upon them,) is growing up in war into greatness and consequence among the nations,"* boasted the Packet.

> "Jacob set up a stone pillar at the place where God had talked with him, and he poured out a drink offering on it; he also poured oil on it" (GENESIS 35:14).

Just as building this federal arch was an altar to democracy, so life often calls for monumental moments of jubilation, celebration, and thanksgiving. Nothing is sweeter than giving thanks for those crowning moments, when God sets the middle stone in place and completes a bridge in life.[305]

**PRAYER**

*Father, I celebrate the blessings you have brought to me. May I build a monument of joy in my heart today.*

# 306. Not Working

As the present Constitution is so defective, why do not you great men call the people together and tell them so; that is, to have a convention of the States to form a better Constitution?" Henry Knox wrote in a letter to Gouverneur Morris, the man responsible for Congress's finances, in February 1781. His political prophecy came a month before Maryland became the final state to ratify the articles and years before a solid federal government emerged.

Knox believed the Articles of Confederation had failed the military. He saw firsthand how the Congress, operating under the Articles, had been unable to adequately fund and supply the army. His own pay had been threatened on many occasions.

*"This appears to us, who have a superficial view only, to be the more efficacious remedy. Let something be done before a peace takes place, or we shall be in a worse situation than we were at the commencement of the war,"* Knox continued.

The solution was crystal clear to Knox—the Articles of Confederation were a disaster. Knox feared that if something wasn't done, all of the blood shed for liberty would have been shed in vain. If a secure government did not emerge along with victory, then the Revolution would be futile.

*"It is a favorite toast in the army, 'A hoop to the barrel,' or 'Cement to the Union.' America will have fought and bled to little purpose if the powers of government shall be insufficient to preserve the peace,"* Knox wrote.

Except for writing letters and expressing his views, Knox knew there was little he could do about Congress. What he could do was ensure that veterans would not be forgotten after the war. Once again, Knox turned his knowledge and know-how into action. He founded the Society of Cincinnatus, the first veterans' group. With some lobbying of his fellow officers, Knox convinced them to donate one month's pay for a fund for veterans and their families. Washington served as president and Knox as secretary.

War unites hearts in ways not easily explained. Nothing compares to the sacrifice of risking life for a cause, for families, for the good of all. Henry Knox's views on the Articles of Confederation proved prophetic. He discovered what others would later conclude. A revolution does not end with the cessation of combat. For a revolution to be effective, it requires a successful government.[306]

> "When you march up to attack a city, make its people an offer of peace" (DEUTERONOMY 20:10).

**PRAYER**

*Whatever combat I may face this week, whether it's in my heart or watching those around me struggle, remind me that you desire to govern my heart in peace.*

# 307. Which York?

"There is no fighting here, unless you have a naval superiority, or an army mounted upon race-horses," the Marquis de Lafayette wrote to General Washington from his command in Richmond, Virginia, in May 1781.

When Washington sent him south with a regiment, Lafayette embraced the opportunity to command. But he had changed since first greeting South Carolina's shores and racing to Philadelphia in 1777. He had put aside his childlike zeal and led with a teacher's eye for detail. As a commander, Lafayette arranged for his troops to wear signature black feathers in their caps.

As Lafayette's friendship with America grew, so did his maturity. From the Conway Cabal to Arnold's treason, the war had tempered this twenty-something's idealism and had prepared him for realistic leadership. *"I find that Lord Cornwallis, who, I had been assured, had sailed for Charleston, is advancing towards Halifax,"* Lafayette reported with a journalist's skill. His job was to reinforce Greene's check of Cornwallis. *"We have no boats for militia, and less arms. I will try to do for the best, and hope to deserve your approbation. Nothing can abstract my sight from the supplies and reënforcements destined to General Greene's army."*

As the summer progressed, what surprised Lafayette more than a lack of supplies were the British movements. Lafayette had assumed Cornwallis would sail for New York. *"Instead of continuing his voyage up the Bay, my Lord [Cornwallis] entered York River, and landed at York and Gloucester,"* Lafayette informed Washington in early August.

Although Lafayette did not know it at the time, Cornwallis had reluctantly obeyed his superior, General Clinton, who had ordered his eight thousand men to York, Virginia, not to New York. Surrounded by a river with a narrow entrance on one side and a morass on the other, Yorktown was a strategic spot. Cornwallis had a commanding view of the area from a hill.

*"His Lordship plays so well, that no blunder can be hoped from him to recover a bad step of ours,"* Lafayette wrote of his David-like position to Cornwallis's Goliath-like one. *"His Lordship's remaining in the State keeps me with this army,"* Lafayette wrote, explaining his reasons for not joining Greene in North Carolina.

Lafayette knew Washington's resolution was to conquer New York, not Yorktown. But he didn't let that keep him from expressing his own opinion. *"Had not your attention been turned to New York, something, with a fleet, might be done in this quarter. But I see New York is the object, and consequently I attend to your instructions,"* the marquis wrote obediently. Through this letter, Lafayette showed he understood his role as a middle commander. He communicated the truth about his circumstances to Washington, but he also deferred to his master teacher's judgment on Yorktown. This French star, the Marquis de Lafayette, had nearly reached his peak.[307]

> "A student is not above his teacher, nor a servant above his master"
> (MATTHEW 10:24).

**PRAYER**

*Lord, whenever I find myself in the middle, remind me to respect those above me and guide with integrity those under my leadership.*

# 308. The Revolution Today: Chapel

*W*e came up with the baggage belonging to the Marquess, who has a days march the start of us," Josiah Atkins recorded in his diary on June 10, 1781.

Atkins was part of the Continental army that joined Lafayette in the summer of 1781. Virginia, however, was a remote wilderness to this Connecticut medic. *"This is a long and tedious road, thro' a wilderness, where no water is to allay ones parching thirst: But there is a greater drought with respect to hearing the word of the Lord, the everlasting gospel dispens'd,"* Atkins lamented. *"Is not this the holy Sabbath? Yet where am I? & what am I about? O Lord, forgive my sins. For tho' I am here, yet my heart is at home with thy worshipping people."*

The desire for worshipping in the wilderness of battle has not changed. One Navy Seabees petty officer felt the same need as Josiah Atkins during his tour in Iraq in 2006. He decided to give his fellow service members a little taste of heaven. Donald J. Hodory, builder with the Naval Mobile Construction Battalion 25, 9th Naval Construction Regiment, decided to make the newly built military chapel in Al Asad more like a stateside sanctuary by constructing stained-glass windows.

Chapels are an integral part of the military today. The cool, steely beamed architecture of the chapel at the Air Force Academy in Colorado Springs, Colorado, appropriately points visitors skyward. John Paul Jones is buried in the crypt of the chapel of the U.S. Naval Academy in Annapolis, Maryland.

"When I heard that the new chapel was being built, it just made perfect sense to fabricate stained-glass windows for it," Hodory explained.

Hodory, who owns an architectural stained-glass studio in Illinois, arranged for supply donations from a stained-glass manufacturing company. He found time to work on the project while continuing his regular duties. "The gratification I received is far greater than any other project I have worked on in my life," Hodory said. "There is no other place in the world where spiritual health is more important than in Iraq."

Although Hodory received a commendation medal for his efforts, his greatest satisfaction came in knowing he had made a more lasting contribution. "My inspiration for the stained-glass windows came from the desire to contribute my talents for something that will have tremendous longevity. It was an opportunity for the

> "Worship the LORD in the splendor of his holiness; tremble before him, all the earth"
> (PSALM 96:9).

422

Seabees to leave a unique legacy, along with all the other major accomplishments they have had in the history of this deployment. These windows will remain long after we have returned to our lives in the [United States]," Petty Officer Donald Hodory proudly stated.[308]

**PRAYER**

*You are holy and worthy of the splendor of more stained-glass windows than could ever be constructed.*

## 309. Sabbath Rest: Puffy Motives

Vengeance made the king puffy, according to the patriot who wrote "A Dialogue between the Devil, and George III, Tyrant of Britain." Although this is a work of fiction, the story illustrates the depth of man's depravity as clearly as any sermon of the day.

"*O now, my royal master, now, now! see how my arms triumph! Georgia taken! Charleston humbled to the dust! Tories increasing—rebellion dying—the rebel army starving—mutinying—huzza! I'll complete my glorious plan, and have the necks of five hundred rebel chiefs in my noose e'er the sun has measured nine months on the reel of time,*" the fictionalized George III boasted to the devil after the victories of 1780.

The story continues in 1781 with the king's brashness and the devil's taunting as the centerpiece of this pretend dialogue. "*Rebellion breaks out with new kindled rage in the southern provinces . . . bestir yourself, George, or perdition will catch you!*" the devil cajoled.

And although this conversation is as unreal as a fairy tale, it rings of truth by showing the folly of vengeance. The king hoped Generals Clinton and Cornwallis would bring him the heads of the rebels to restore his kingdom. "*The rebels have no forces to make any figure in the field this year: Lord Cornwallis will sweep all before him, and the southern provinces will fall like leaves in autumn,*" the king answered.

The anonymous author of this story decided that vengeance drove the king's heart above all other motives. "*And then for a trip and twitch at Old Massachusetts, that ancient seat of rebellion—I have fire and brimstone, and wrath and vengeance . . . My soul burns to be at 'em. Adamses and Hancocks will be sweet fuel for my furnace!*" the boastful monarch predicted.

"*You have a satanic heart; I wish your head was equal to it. I warn you again to look out for the French and rebels, or they'll give you an Irish hoist e're long,*" the devil responded.

"*As to the French fleet, my lions of the ocean will crack their bones: I expect this campaign will nearly swallow up rebellion,*" the king bragged.

"*What avail your puffs,*" the devil responded.

Vengeance "availed" the king's predictions and his boasting, according to the patriot who wrote this pretend piece. He or she used the kingdom of the devil to question the king of England and his motives. And the one who spreads evil was a logical choice to show the utter futility of vengeance. It not only destroys those to be avenged, but it also ruins the avenger.

> "You have seen the depth of their vengeance, all their plots against me"
> (LAMENTATIONS 3:60).

Motives matter as much today as they did during the Revolution.[309]

**PRAYER**

*Guard my motives and keep me from drowning in the depths of vengeance. May my plans not be plots but patterns of your purpose.*

# 310. Important Particulars

Important particulars. That is how George Washington disguised the best news he had received all year.

"*Sir: I have been honored with Your Excellency's several late favors and the Count de Rochambeau has been kind enough to communicate to me the very interesting and important particulars,*" George Washington confirmed to Comte de Barras, a French navy commander, in a letter dated August 16, 1781.

Washington's brief note to de Barras was purposefully vague. The stakes were too high to risk putting too much information in ink, lest the letter find its way into British hands. The "*important particulars*" were in fact very specific measures, a strategy of surprise involving three French naval "*musketeers.*"

After Benjamin Lincoln's loss of Charleston and Horatio Gates's defeat at Camden, the South seemed the most unlikely place to end the war. Washington knew Greene's army wasn't strong enough to defeat Cornwallis, but he believed Greene was wily enough to elude him. Thus, when 1781 began, Washington increased his efforts to develop a strategy for taking back New York.

The quest was part personal, part public. Perhaps, with the French navy's help, he could end the war by recapturing the state he had so miserably lost in 1776. Washington held a war council in May 1781 with Rochambeau, who held the rank of lieutenant general, and other officers. Washington convinced the reluctant Rochambeau to embrace a plan to battle the British in New York.

Then an unexpected gale reversed Washington's New York–bound plans. It was hurricane season in the Caribbean. The Count de Grasse decided the changing weather pattern was a good opportunity to leave the West Indies and visit the American east coast. He notified Rochambeau and de Barras of his plans to sail his twenty-nine-ship fleet and three thousand soldiers into the Chesapeake Bay near Yorktown, Virginia.

"*He [Rochambeau] has also informed you of our joint opinion upon the measures which seemed to us most expedient at the present moment,*" Washington added in his note to de Barras. This joint operation—these expedient measures—were now in motion. Washington and Rochambeau left for Yorktown, Virginia. There they would join Greene, de Grasse, and Lafayette in an effort to beat Cornwallis.

Washington's sudden change in strategy revealed his true character. He may have been exhausted by the war but he had not lost his nimbleness. Unlike Gates, Lincoln, and Arnold, George Washington did not let his own personal ambition blind him from seeing what was best for the cause. He also listened to the French naval commanders and his other officers. He wasn't afraid to humble himself and change his mind.[310]

> "For where you have envy and selfish ambition, there you find disorder and every evil practice" (JAMES 3:16).

**PRAYER**

*God, thank you for the important particulars of selflessness and sacrifice. Replace my selfishness with service.*

# 311. Following Orders

H*e [Count de Grasse] will either be there by the time this reaches you, or you look for him every moment,*" George Washington wrote to the Marquis de Lafayette on August 15, 1781. Something just might be "*done in that quarter*" with the arrival of a formidable French fleet in Yorktown.

"*You will immediately take such a position as will best enable you to prevent their [the British] sudden retreat thro' North Carolina, which I presume they will attempt the instant they perceive so formidable an Armament,*" Washington ordered.

As a shepherd herds his sheep, Washington also commanded Lafayette to be discreet, an unusual admonishment to such a loyal officer. But this instruction showed how much Washington's concern was for the mission's security. *"You will be particularly careful to conceal the expected arrival of the Count, because if the enemy are not apprised of it, they will stay on board their transports in the Bay, which will be the luckiest Circumstance in the World,"* instructed Washington. *"In the meantime I have only to recommend a continuation of that prudence and good conduct which you have manifested thro' the whole of your Campaign."*

Lafayette immediately informed the Virginia and North Carolina militias of a possible retreat by Cornwallis. But he also noticed that instead of preparing to leave Yorktown, Cornwallis appeared to increase his fortifications. Lafayette conveyed these details to Washington in hopes of luring the commander himself to Yorktown. *"In the present state of affairs, my dear General, I hope you will come yourself to Virginia, and that, if the French army moves this way, I shall have, at least, the satisfaction of beholding you myself at the head of the combined armies . . . The men we have here would not be equal to the task of a campaign upon so large a scale,"* Lafayette wrote.

Lafayette wasn't sure which was more thrilling: Washington's strategic change of focus from New York to Yorktown or the possibility that the French and Americans might finally come together in both heart and arms.

*"Lord Cornwallis must be attacked with a pretty great apparatus. But when a French fleet takes possession of the Bay and rivers, and we form a land force superior to his, that army must, soon or late, be forced to surrender, as we may get what reënforcements we please,"* Lafayette wrote. *"Adieu, my dear General. I heartily thank you for having ordered me to remain in Virginia."*

> "My sheep listen to my voice; I know them, and they follow me" (JOHN 10:27).

Because he trusted in his shepherd, Lafayette was eager to follow George Washington's orders. Success by the French in Yorktown would provide redemption for the Rhode Island rout. It might also allow this French star, the Marquis de Lafayette, whose maturity was glowing more brilliantly than ever before, to bid the war adieu.[311]

**PRAYER**

*You are the Great Shepherd, who knows when to herd and when to nurture the flock in your care. Thank you for loving me.*

# 312. Family, Firesides, and Friends

Desire to be reunited with family permeated the air in 1781. The long-suffering colonial warriors were hungry for success and cessation. They were ready to trade their campfires for the firesides of home.

*"I sincerely pray God that the war may be ended this campaign, that public and private society may be restored,"* Henry Knox wrote to his brother William in July.

Now that Knox's family had increased to two children, he longed to taste the sweetness of a normal life. Hope for domestic tranquility filled the heart of this man who had shown as much character and capability as any of the generals.

Knox wrote to Lucy, *"Yesterday was your birthday. I cannot attempt to show you how much I was affected by it. I remembered it, and humbly petitioned Heaven to grant us the happiness of continuing our union until we should have the felicity of seeing our children flourishing around us, and ourselves crowned with virtue, peace, and years, and that we both might take our flight together, secure of a happy immortality."*

Nathanael Greene also felt the stirring. Just as Washington arrived at Yorktown, Greene wrote Knox of his optimism for victory. *"My dear Friend,—Where you are I know not, but if you are where I wish you, it is with the General [Washington] in Virginia,"* Greene wrote from North Carolina. *"The prospect is so bright and the glory so great, that I want you to be there to share in them. I was in hopes you would have operated seriously against New York, which would have been still more important,"* Greene said, noting the odds favored a campaign in Virginia.

Greene had accepted that his purpose was not to catch the final prey but to prepare the snare. *"We have been beating the bush, and the General has come to catch the bird. Never was there a more inviting object to glory. The General is a most fortunate man, and may success and laurels attend him. We have fought frequently and bled freely, and little glory comes to our share,"* Greene continued sadly.

Greene also expressed his desire to sit by a fireside and enjoy a good conversation with his pal Knox. He longed to meet his godson, Knox's second child.

As hope for victory filled the air, domestic tranquility finally seemed a real possibility. The independence Nathanael Greene and Henry Knox had fought so long to secure seemed within

> "You will be secure, because there is hope; you will look about you and take your rest in safety" (JOB 11:18).

reach. Thoughts of family, firesides, and friendship gave them hope for the battle ahead.[312]

**PRAYER**

*Thank you for the gift of family, for the drive it gives me to live, love, and labor in life.*

# 313. Unwelcome Arrivals

There were two unwelcome arrivals in the early days of September 1781. One took Charles Cornwallis's Yorktown force by surprise, and the other astounded George Washington's northern division.

"*I have made several attempts to inform your Excellency, that the French West India Fleet under Mons. De Grasse entered the Cape the 29th [August] ult,*" British Gen. Charles Cornwallis wrote to his commander, Gen. Henry Clinton, on September 8, 1781.

With the loudest trumpet he could sound, Cornwallis once again tried to alert Clinton of the arrival of the French fleet in the Chesapeake Bay. False information was the source of Clinton's lack of interest. When Clinton intercepted a letter revealing plans by Washington and Rochambeau to attack New York, he became more concerned about his own post on New York's Gibraltar than Cornwallis's tiny hill in Yorktown.

The letter was pure propaganda. Part of Washington's new southern strategy was to convince Clinton that the Continentals were going to attack New York. "*To 'misguide and bewilder' Sir Henry, a space for a large encampment was marked out in New Jersey, near Staten Island; boats were collected; ovens were built as if preparing for the sustenance of a large army,*" described historian William Jackman. "*Pioneers were sent to clear the roads toward King's Bridge, and pains were taken to keep the American soldier ignorant of their own destination.*"

With these activities in Clinton's plain view, he must have been shocked to receive a letter from Cornwallis. Outnumbered, the British fleet had fled, leaving the French fleet to block Cornwallis by the sea. De Grasse cut off Cornwallis's escape route by water.

Washington's northern division also experienced an unwelcome arrival: their own. When Washington and Rochambeau arrived in Philadelphia with their army, many men were shocked to discover that New York was not their goal. They were even unhappier to learn that Yorktown was their ultimate destination. They feared another Monmouth heat wave and a Camden food shortage.

*"When the Northern soldiers arrived in the vicinity of Philadelphia, and found that they were really going against Cornwallis, they manifested some discontent in prospect of the long southern march in the month of August,"* Jackman explained.

*"At this critical moment, John Laurens, son of Henry Laurens, President of Congress, arrived from France, whither he had been sent to obtain aid; he brought with him a large supply of clothing, ammunition, and arms; and what was just then very much wanted, half a million of dollars . . . Their good humor was restored, and they cheerfully marched on,"* wrote Jackman.

> "The time has come, the day has arrived"
> (EZEKIEL 7:12).

The stage was set. George Washington would battle Charles Cornwallis at Yorktown.[313]

**PRAYER**

*Prepare me for the unexpected arrivals in life.*

# 314.  A Mortifying End

Mortification, not age, drew lines on General Cornwallis's face in October 1781. Six years had passed since he helped command the British victory on Long Island. However, it was a hamlet in Virginia that humbled one of Britain's most experienced generals.

*"I HAVE the mortification to inform your Excellency that I have been forced to give up the Posts of York and Gloucester, and to surrender the troops under my command,"* General Cornwallis wrote to General Clinton.

Cornwallis's loss at Yorktown was the worst military defeat of his life. For weeks he had chased fox Nathanael Greene and his flying force. But it was Cornwallis who found himself surrounded at Yorktown. He explained to Clinton that George Washington and his army arrived on September 30th. Instead of implementing a frontal assault, the Continentals and French began a Charleston-like siege.

*"I never saw this post in a very favorable light, but when I found I was to be attacked in it in so unprepared a state, by so powerful an army and artillery, nothing but the hopes of relief would have induced me to attempt its defense,"* Cornwallis reminded of his opposition to Clinton's decision to send him to Yorktown to build a camp.

Anguish and anger poured from his pen. The now humble Cornwallis blamed Clinton for not backing him up. *"I would either have endeav-*

ored to escape to New York by rapid marches from the Gloucester side, immediately on the arrival of General Washington's troops," Cornwallis explained of his reasons for not retreating, "or I would, notwithstanding the disparity of numbers, have attacked them in the open field, where it might have been just possible."

Cornwallis rejected these options because his military math resulted in a negative answer. He had too much honor to retreat, but too few troops to attack. What frustrated him more than this formula was Clinton's failure to send reinforcements in a timely manner, something Cornwallis had requested on a number of occasions.

"But being assured by your Excellency's letters that every possible means would be tried by the navy and army to relieve us, I could not think myself at liberty to venture upon either of those desperate attempts," wrote Cornwallis, defending his decision.

Cornwallis also praised "the labor and firmness of the soldiers" to defend the post. "Everything was to be expected from the spirit of the troops, but every disadvantage attended their labor," Cornwallis noted of their supply shortages.

> "He will rule from sea to sea and from the River to the ends of the earth" (PSALM 72:8).

Charles Cornwallis surrendered when the hourglass dropped its last grain of sand. He did not have the supplies or manpower to wait any longer for reinforcements. On October 17th he sent a young drummer boy onto the field to play a song of truce.[314]

**PRAYER**

God, I surrender my purposes and plans to you, knowing you are the ruler of the sand and sea.

# 315. The Revolution Today: Bands

Had we not seen the drummer in his red coat when he first mounted, he might have beat away till doomsday. The constant fighting was too much for the sound of a single drum; but when the firing ceased, I thought I never heard a drum equal to it—the most delightful music to us all," Ensign Ebenezer Denny of the Pennsylvania Continental Regiment wrote from his field position at the battle of Yorktown. Denny heard the simple drumming that signaled Cornwallis's surrender on October 17, 1781.

"In the morning, before relief came, [I] had the pleasure of seeing a drummer mount the enemy's parapet, and beat a parley, and immediately *an officer, holding up a white handkerchief, made his appearance outside their works; the drummer accompanied him, eating,"* Denny explained.

*"Our batteries ceased. An officer from our lines ran and met the other, and tied the handkerchief over his eyes. The drummer sent back, and the British officers conducted to a house in rear of our lines. Firing ceased totally,"* Denny wrote with jubilation.

The world turned upside down for the British at Yorktown. General Cornwallis signaled his decision to surrender through the simplicity of a drum. One soldier recorded that a British unit played bagpipes while they waited for the surrender terms to be completed. A French unit responded to the bagpipes by playing their own song.

Music performs an important role in life. It brings joy to the heart and relaxes the mind. It calms the soul.

"Play music, travel the world, and get a regular paycheck. This is the gig of a lifetime and it all starts with an audition," advertise the U.S. Army Bands on their Web site.

Today's military bands are far from the fifes, drums, and bugles of yesterday. They are a sophisticated blend of instruments: saxophones, trombones, clarinets, tubas, and oboes, to name a few. The men and women who play in these bands are trained members of the Armed Services, but with the responsibility of playing an instrument. Their music styles are as varied as their instruments: jazz, classical, and of course, marches.

These bands—from all branches of the military—do in fact travel the world. They travel to bases to cheer servicemen and servicewomen serving on the front lines. They perform at the White House. They play at funerals for presidents and for those who have died serving their nation. They play at concerts for the public. They do what music has done since the beginning of time. They sing. They soothe. They stir. They salute.

> "The LORD will save me, and we will sing with stringed instruments all the days of our lives in the temple of the LORD" (ISAIAH 38:20).

Whether in the Revolution or in today's world, music has a role to play. Instruments may change, but they remain part of God's long-term plan. Music will fill His heavenly concert halls.[315]

**PRAYER**

*Thank you for the gift of music. No matter how well or how poorly I sing or play, put a special song in my heart today for you.*

# 316. Sabbath Rest: Mortified Monarchy

The only person more mortified than General Cornwallis over the loss at Yorktown was the king. Even the devil's legions blamed his obstinacy for his fall, at least an anonymous patriot thought so when he made up this dialogue between the devil and the king:

*"Let me alone for obstinacy, I've an heart of adamant [an impenetrable stone], there's no turn to me; my will never was broke, nor ever can be, there's no break nor bend to it if once I say no—neither soothing nor praying, nor freezing nor burning, will ever move me; there's no move to me, I tell you, I'll be curst if there is,"* the king said to the devil in the fictional parody called "Dialogue between the Devil, and George III, Tyrant of Britain."

And although these words of the king were the imaginative musings of an anonymous author, King George III knew himself to be as stubborn as the Emperor Nero, more resistant to change than a mountain. He may have embraced stubbornness as his trademark. But it was the volcanic eruption of Yorktown that left him covered in ashes.

This anonymous author longed to be in the room when King George heard the news. In this pamphlet, the writer pretended the devil brought the king the news. *"There's a report that Cornwallis is a prisoner!"* the devil told the king.

*"It's nothing but one of the rebel curst lies; they're eternally blowing about the victories, which ever turn out a royal triumph. Cornwallis surrender to the rebel Washington, no!"* the king denied.

The news, however, probably did send the king to cursing after a flurry of denials. *"He'd [Cornwallis] fight through the stygian sea first, and then he wouldn't. Mars and Jupiter would sooner surrender to the moon, and bow to a foot ball. Curse . . . the rebels, to think my heroes will ever yield to them!"* the king replied to the devil's report.

This anonymous author had a lot of fun at King George's expense. The king couldn't even curse correctly after hearing the news, at least according to this pretend dialogue. The writer noted that the devil's profanity, not printed here, was fitting for, well, the devil. *"George, you swear poorly, not fit for company, you'll disgrace swearing; you haven't observ'd my rules, for learning the art,"* the devil said.

This *"sermon on stubbornness"* may have poked fun at the monarchy, but it also revealed the destructive power of resistance. To the patriots, King George III was about as divine as the devil. They knew he was as human as they were. This story showed the depravity of darkness, the hot burning lava of sin. A mountain is not easily ruined from outside forces, but it can self-destruct from within.[316]

> "So I gave them over to their stubborn hearts to follow their own devices"
> (PSALM 81:12).

**PRAYER**

*Create a revolution in my heart to prevent me from falling into my own self-destruction.*

# 317. Happiest Presage

After two days of surrender negotiations, more than seven thousand British soldiers became prisoners of the joint American and French armies on October 19, 1781. Five days later General Henry Clinton arrived in the bay with seven thousand reinforcements. When he learned Cornwallis had surrendered, he fled faster than a New York minute.

George Washington had waited seven years for this moment. *"I HAVE the honor to inform Congress that a reduction of the British army, under the command of Lord Cornwallis, is most happily effected,"* Washington wrote to the Continental Congress.

As thrilled as he was, Washington did not allow the victory to lure him into false predictions of the war's end. Such premature boasting could deceive him into false security. With manners and practicality Washington praised the allies' valor. *"The unremitted ardor, which actuated every officer and soldier in the combined army on this occasion, has principally led to this important event at an earlier period than my most sanguine hopes had induced me to expect,"* he informed the Congress.

Washington, however, now had no doubt that abandoning New York for Yorktown was the right strategy. Never before had he seen his army come together with such unity and fervor. He was grateful he listened to the advice of his officers and the French rather than following his own desire for revenge in New York.

*"The singular spirit of emulation, which animated the whole army from the first commencement of our operations, has filled my mind with the highest pleasure and satisfaction, and has given me the happiest presages of success,"* he wrote.

Washington enclosed the terms of surrender with his letter to Congress, but his humility prevented him from revealing the most interesting details of the surrender. Claiming illness, Cornwallis sent his deputy general to surrender for him. The deputy tried to surrender to Rochambeau and the French line. Declining, Rochambeau directed the man to surrender to Washington. Annoyed with Cornwallis's slight, Washington directed the British deputy to surrender to one of his deputies, Gen. Benjamin Lincoln. After being humiliated a year earlier at Charleston, Lincoln embraced Washington's kind gesture and accepted the official surrender.

Washington appropriately gave high praise to the French, but he was most proud of his own forces. Gone were the fear-stricken boys of Long Island. In their place were men of valor. *"Nothing could equal the zeal of our allies, but the emulating spirit of the American officers, whose ardor would not suffer their exertions to be exceeded,"* boasted George Washington.

Time would show whether this happy presage would lead to lasting peace or prolonged war.[317]

> "The horse is made ready for the day of battle, but victory rests with the LORD" (PROVERBS 21:31).

**PRAYER**

*God, you are a victorious warrior. Thank you for the triumphs you give, whether they are as small as a handshake or as great as the surrender of a mighty army.*

# 318. Fluency and Forgiveness

How did victory come to Yorktown? It resulted from many moments and movements, including the culmination of a mega-merger. Under the smile of Providence, the French and Americans had finally learned to work together. Friendship, fluency, and forgiveness were beams of sunlight illuminating their teamwork.

General Washington had cultivated relationships with the French by consulting them with enough frequency to garner friendship and trust. General Rochambeau and Comte de Barras became key players on his strategy team. And an unlikely American general, one who nearly lost his job to a Frenchman, helped bridge the bothersome language barrier.

*"If I recollect, the Comte Rochambeau doesn't speak a word of English,"* William Knox wrote to his brother Henry. *"I suppose, from necessity, you are obliged to speak much French, which you having long since learnt the theoretic part, I should imagine, from a little practice, would come easy to you."*

William knew his brother Henry had learned French the same way he had learned artillery: from books. Although Henry had earlier felt disdain for the French when one of them tried to take his job in 1777, he had developed a respect for them by 1781. Unlike Benedict Arnold, Knox did not hold a grudge against the French. He knew how to forgive and make friends. *"All is harmony and good fellowship between the two armies. I have no doubt, when opportunity offers, that the zeal of the French and the patriotism of the Americans will go hand in hand to glory,"* Henry predicted to William in August 1781.

Knox's ability to speak the language of forgiveness also removed barriers to cooperation between him and his French fellow-soldiers. One of the best compliments Knox received after Yorktown came from Chevalier de Chastellux, a general under Rochambeau. *"We cannot sufficiently admire the intelligence and activity with which he [Knox] collected from different places and transported to the batteries more than thirty pieces of cannon and mortars of large caliber, for the siege,"* Chastellux wrote of Knox's efforts at Yorktown.

From February to October 1781 Knox had worked tirelessly to fulfill Washington's request to procure the armaments necessary for a *"capital operation against New York, or against Charleston, Savannah . . . &c."*

Chastellux praised Knox for being flexible enough to quickly gather and transport the artillery once Washington decided that Yorktown was the objective and not New York. *"As to General Knox, but one-half has been said in commending his military genius. He is a man of talent, well instructed, of a buoyant disposition, ingenuous and true: it is impossible to know him without esteeming and loving him,"* Chastellux wrote of his American friend.

Henry Knox had learned to appreciate the French. When the Americans accepted the strangers in their midst, they eventually reaped a huge earthly reward. Acceptance of those God sends us to is a reflection of accepting God himself.[318]

> "I tell you the truth, whoever accepts anyone I send accepts me; and whoever accepts me accepts the one who sent me" (JOHN 13:20).

PRAYER

*Show me those you have sent into my life whom I have not accepted. Give me the courage to extend a hand in your name.*

# 319. Name Changes

One of the heroes of Yorktown was a slave.

William Armistead of New Kent County, Virginia, gave his slave, James Armistead, permission to offer his services to the Marquis de Lafayette. Lafayette decided not to employ the slave as a servant. Instead, he turned him into a spy.

*"Lafayette's attempts at infiltrating British headquarters were futile until the first week of July, when Cornwallis hired James Armistead to spy on the Americans,"* noted historian Robert Selig, who participated in Colonial Williamsburg's 1997 *Brothers in Arms* symposium on African American soldiers in America's wars.

It took time before Armistead discovered any worthwhile news. But he was probably the one who informed Lafayette that Cornwallis was expanding his Yorktown fortress. *"The written and oral reports of the unlikely double agent kept the allies apprised of British plans. On August 25th, Lafayette could report that Cornwallis had begun 'fortifying at York.'"*

Armistead returned to Lafayette's service before the siege of Yorktown began. *"When Cornwallis [as a prisoner of war] paid a courtesy call on the marquis, he was surprised to encounter a black man there he considered to be in his pay,"* Selig explained of the custom of opposing generals meeting each other after the battle.

Armistead was far from the only black man to serve the Continental cause at Yorktown. About fifteen hundred African American men, one-fourth of the army, fought at Yorktown for the patriots. Former African slaves also served in the English, French, and Hessian ranks.

Although it took several years, Armistead ultimately received freedom for his service. He had infiltrated the enemy camp at the peril of his life. Lafayette wrote him a certificate citing Armistead's *"Essential Service"* in collecting *"Intelligence from the Enemy's Camp"* and asserted he (Armistead) was therefore *"Entitled to Every Reward His Situation Can Admit of."* Armistead used the document to prove to the Virginia legislature that he qualified for emancipation under a law they had passed for slaves who had fought in the Revolution on behalf of their masters.

Because of the Revolution, Armistead underwent tremendous change. He went from a slave to a freeman to a landowner. He bought forty acres of land in New Kent County, Virginia, in 1816 and raised a family. Virginia gave him a regular pension of $40 a year.

But he also made another significant change because of the Revolution. Because he was no longer the slave of William Armistead, James Armistead changed his name to James Lafayette, in honor of the man who trusted him to spy on the enemy.

> "The watchman opens the gate for him, and the sheep listen to his voice. He calls his own sheep by name and leads them out"
>
> (JOHN 10:3).

A name change is occasionally a sign of a revolutionary change. Saul became the apostle Paul after his encounter with Christ on the road to Damascus. Abram became Abraham after receiving God's promise to build a nation through him. It is fitting that a name change sometimes follows life's most significant moments.[319]

**PRAYER**

*You know me by name, Lord. Thank you for valuing something as simple as someone's name.*

# 320. London Fog

U ndoubtedly *the House of Commons seem to be wild at present, and to be running on to ruin,"* King George III wrote Lord North on February 26, 1782.

The recently arrived news of Cornwallis's surrender at Yorktown covered St. James Palace in a dense fog that threatened to last a long, long time. *"I [will] do what I can to save the empire, and, if I do not succeed, I will at least have the self-approbation of having done my duty, and of not letting myself be a tool in the destruction of the honour of the country,"* the king wrote despondently. Nothing, not even the latest expansion project at Buckingham Palace, could distract his attention.

But as was his habit, the king chose moping over maturity. He selected sulking over a solution. The culmination of the war magnified the king's weaknesses: his obstinacy, temper, mediocrity, sullenness, and inability to face reality. *"It looks as if the House of Commons is going to lengths that could not have been expected. I am resolved not to throw myself into the hands of Opposition at all events, and shall certainly, if things go as they seem to lead, know what my conscience as well as honour dictates as the only way left for me,"* the king wrote on March 17, 1782, after learning Parliament's former majority for supporting the war had shrunk to fewer than ten members.

Lord North asked the king to meet with Parliament's growing minority. But the king declared that his *"sentiments of honor"* would not allow him to *"personally treat with them."* He was hurt that North even bothered to ask him to do something so beneath his dignity as listen to the opposition.

Within ten days, the fog lifted. Reality was clear and sharper than any sword in the armory at St. James Palace. *"At last the fatal day has come which the misfortunes of the times and the sudden change of sentiments of the House of Commons have drove me to of changing the Ministry,"* King George wrote of his decision to ask Lord North to resign. The Parliament had not suddenly changed its sentiments—the king had suddenly faced reality.

*"I have to the last fought for individuals, but the number I have saved, except my Bedchamber, is incredibly few,"* he wrote.

The king's *"effusion"* of sorrows, as he described them, continued. Parliament decided to enter into peace negotiations with America. Sir Guy Carleton, General Clinton's replacement, would no longer execute a war, but instead would oversee the exodus of the British army from Savannah, Charleston, and ultimately, New York. Lord North's departure opened Parliament's floodgates of peace. When the conflict affected King George III's inner circle, this English Pharaoh let his people go.[320]

> "During the night Pharaoh summoned Moses and Aaron and said, 'Up! Leave my people, you and the Israelites! Go, worship the LORD as you have requested'"
> (EXODUS 12:31).

**PRAYER**

*God, thank you for moving mountains and softening the hardest of hearts.*

# 321. A Complicated Peace

Peace is complicated. If peace were easy, wars would not be fought.

Four American commissioners conducted the negotiations: John Adams, Benjamin Franklin, John Jay, and Henry Laurens. They met with two British commissioners, who were authorized by the British government to meet with *"certain colonies."* But a quartet and a duet do not a symphony make. More than a year elapsed between General Cornwallis's surrender at Yorktown and the announcement of a preliminary agreement between the United States and Britain. The Americans insisted on recognition of the *"United States of America"* and they got it, along with many other details.

*"WE have the honor to congratulate congress on the signature of the preliminaries of a peace between the Crown of Great Britain and the United States of America,"* the delegates announced in a letter to the Continental Congress on December 14, 1782. *"A copy of the articles is here inclosed, and we cannot but flatter ourselves that they will appear to congress, as they do to all of us, to be consistent with the honor and interest of the United States."*

Several factors complicated the peace talks, often bringing the diplomats to a discordant lack of harmony. Their diplomatic score was filled with more rests and pauses than musical notes. The American commissioners, though as different in their personalities as horns and violins, worked to identify the priorities and positions of the British representatives.

The off-key issues were details concerning the boundaries of the United States, navigation rights on the Mississippi River, refugee rights, and money owed to British creditors prior to the war. The challenge of the Americans was to figure out which of these issues mattered most to Britain. They also had to discern how much leverage they had in negotiating in the best interests of their young country.

Peace was also complicated by the awkwardness of playing as a quartet. Although Congress ordered them to work with the French crown, the American diplomats conducted the score mostly without them. *"As we had reason to imagine that the articles respecting the boundaries, the refugees, and fisheries, did not correspond with the policy of this Court [France], we did not communicate the preliminaries to the minister [of France] until after they were signed,"* the commissioners' joint letter revealed.

*"We hope that these considerations will excuse our having so far deviated from the spirit of our instructions. The Count de Vergennes, on perusing the articles appeared surprised, (but not displeased), at their being so favorable to us."*

Although peace was complicated and not yet finalized, it was worth pursuing.[321]

> "Seek peace and pursue it" (PSALM 34:14).

**PRAYER**

*God, sometimes my life plays off-key, without harmony. I seek the peace you can provide, knowing it is a worthy pursuit. You are the Supreme Conductor.*

# 322. The Revolution Today: Reenactors

I just got chills," Rose Morin said. "I felt like I'd been there before."

That's how this registered nurse from Branford, Connecticut, described her visit to a Revolutionary War-era encampment when interviewed by Gerry Gilmore, a reporter for the Armed Forces Press Service. But the focus of Gilmore's article was not a camp, but a retracing.

The site of the tents and the way of life inspired Morin to become a reenactor. And in the fall of 2006 that is exactly what she and three others did. David T. Holloway, Michael S. Fitzgerald, David Fagerberg, and Morin retraced the route followed by France's Count de Rochambeau from Rhode Island to Yorktown, known as the Washington-Rochambeau route. The intent of the reenactors was to travel to Yorktown for the 225th anniversary of the battle. "We follow the original schedule, marching the same distance each day as the army did," Fitzgerald told Gilmore. "We try as much as possible to camp on the original campgrounds that the army camped on."

The reenactors marched an average of sixteen miles a day. Two of the men wore red, white, and blue wool uniforms reminiscent of the Continental army. The other wore a white wool uniform similar to a soldier in Rochambeau's army. Morin, who often drove the support vehicle, donned a straw hat and homespun dress similar to what a female camp follower would have worn.

This quartet may have retraced a revolutionary route but they wore sensible sneakers and hiking boots bolstered by duct tape. *"The buckle shoes would be very hard on the feet,"* Fagerberg explained. Morin, a nurse, tended to blisters.

Their reenactment journey began in June 2006 in Rhode Island and followed Rochambeau's route as closely as possible. Rochambeau and his six thousand five hundred troops first traveled from Rhode Island to New York, where they joined General Washington and his men. Then together they traveled to Yorktown, Virginia, for what is now known as the Revolution's final showdown.

On this reenactment journey for the anniversary celebration of Lord Cornwallis's surrender, the participants carried flags and reproductions of Brown Bess smoothbore flintlock muskets. But when they marched through Washington, DC, they kept the firearms in the support vehicle to comply with the district's laws against carrying weapons.

The opportunity to retrace an important event in history and celebrate their heritage was all the motivation they needed to keep going. "I knew it was the chance of a lifetime for me," Rose Morin told the reporter, who ended his article with these words: "Très magnifique!"

Modern-day reenactors do what humanity has sought to do since the beginning. They trace their human ancestry, wondering what life was like for their patriarchs and matriarchs. The ultimate reenactment path leads to the feet of Christ and to the God who is Lord over all of human history.[322]

> "Theirs are the patriarchs, and from them is traced the human ancestry of Christ, who is God over all, forever praised! Amen" (ROMANS 9:5).

**PRAYER**

*Father, trace my steps today, and keep me on the path that does not wander.*

# 323. Sabbath Rest: The Wonder of Peace

H*ow wonderful the revolutions, the events of Providence! We live in an age of wonders; we have lived an age in a few years; we have seen more wonders accomplished in eight years than are usually unfolded in a century,"* Rev. Ezra Stiles, the president of Yale University, proclaimed in his election sermon in May 1783.

Indeed, they had lived a century in less than a decade. With hopes of peace blowing fresh air throughout the states, Stiles took the occasion to chronicle the story of the war and to praise God for victory. *"God be thanked, we have lived to see peace restored to this bleeding land, at least a general cessation of hostilities among the belligerent powers. And on this occasion does it not become us to reflect how wonderful, how gracious, how glorious has been the good hand of our God upon us, in carrying us through so tremendous a warfare!"* he cried out joyfully.

Stiles had not yet retired his ecclesiastical robes. Although he had assumed the presidency of Yale and turned his mind to scholarship, he still knew how to preach a fiery sermon in front of a congregation.

*"And who does not see the indubitable interposition and energetic influence of Divine Providence in these great and illustrious events? Who but a Washington, inspired by Heaven, could have struck out the great movement and maneuver at Princeton?"* he asked.

Stiles called the detection of Benedict Arnold's conspiracy a *"providential miracle."* He believed that God illuminated the minds of Washington and Rochambeau in choosing Yorktown over New York for a final clash. *"Who but God could have ordained the critical arrival of the Gallic fleet, so as to prevent and defeat the British, and assist and cooperate with the combined armies in the siege and reduction of Yorktown?"* he rhetorically asked his listeners.

But the greatest miracle of all was the unity that emerged among the states. The tie of liberty had bound them together. God deserved credit for such a miracle. *"What but a miracle has preserved the union of the*

States, *the purity of Congress, and the unshaken patriotism of every General Assembly? It is God,"* stated Ezra Stiles.

And indeed, it *was* God. He who authored liberty had preserved liberty once again. *"It is for freedom that Christ has set us free"* (Galatians 5:1). The Americans had stood firm for that freedom, and had thrown off England's yoke of slavery.

And that liberty is as real today as it was then. And God's commitment to stand firm for liberty is as true today as it was then.[323]

> "He has declared that he will set you in praise, fame and honor high above all the nations he has made and that you will be a people holy to the LORD your God, as he promised"
> (DEUTERONOMY 26:19).

**PRAYER**

*Thank you, God, for preserving freedom and establishing this nation in liberty. What miracles your hand reveals!*

# 324. Mutiny as Peace Dawns

As the momentum moved toward peace, Washington followed his singular purpose: preserving the army until a treaty was complete. His men continued to suffer, most acutely in their pocketbooks. With the economy in shambles, Congress had no money to pay these war veterans. Hence, as peace dawned, so did mutiny.

It began in March 1783. While camped at Newburgh, New York, one of Washington's senior officers circulated an anonymous letter calling for a secret meeting to implement a military solution to their financial woes. He wanted to march to Philadelphia and take up arms against Congress. When Washington learned about the letter, he decided to employ his most effective strategy against his own officers: surprise. He showed up at the "secret" meeting.

*"By an anonymous summons, an attempt has been made to convene you together; how inconsistent with the rules of propriety, how unmilitary, and how subversive of all order and discipline,"* Washington angrily began his address. He reminded his officers that he had been among the first to embark *"in the cause of our common country"* and had never left their side. Washington was furious that some wanted to raise their arms against their country for money.

He then expressed his own opinion that Congress *"from a full conviction of its [the army's] merits and sufferings, will do it complete jus-*

*tice.*" Washington once again found himself playing commander-in-the-center. His go-between status required him to translate his men's needs to Congress and interpret Congress's intentions for his army.

"*That their [Congress's] endeavors to discover and establish funds for this purpose have been unwearied, and will not cease till they have succeeded, I have not a doubt. But, like all other large bodies, where there is a variety of different interests to reconcile, their deliberations are slow. Why, then, should we distrust them?*" asked Washington.

The officers, however, were as anchored to their position as John Paul Jones was to his ship. Washington then opened a letter from Congress. As he tried to read the letter aloud, his face squinted into a thousand lines. He stopped, retrieved a pair of reading glasses from his coat, and placed them in front of his eyes so he could read.

Most, even his closest of officers, had never seen Washington wear glasses. "*Gentlemen, you will permit me to put on my spectacles, for I have not only grown gray but almost blind in the service of my country,*" Washington said, reading the letter and leaving.

The spectacle of his spectacles shocked Washington's officers and humbled them. Where Washington's words had failed, his actions had prevailed. His officers cast a unanimous vote supporting Congress. Henry Knox described the change as "*one of the happiest circumstances of the war.*" The mutiny was over.[324]

> "To him belong strength and victory; both deceived and deceiver are his" (JOB 12:16).

**PRAYER**

*Do not let selfishness keep me from the plans you have for me. Place your glasses in front of my eyes that I may see your purpose for my life.*

# 325. Farewell to Arms

Victory against the British had turned a rebellion into a revolution. And it was time to say "farewell."

"*The disadvantageous circumstances on our part, under which the war was undertaken, can never be forgotten,*" George Washington began his farewell address to his army in November 1783.

Washington, issuing these last orders, was perhaps more awestruck than when he had removed his bullet-strewn coat during the French and Indian War. He had no idea when Providence preserved his life in 1755 that it was for the awesome purpose of liberating a nation.

*"The singular interpositions of Providence in our feeble condition were such, as could scarcely escape the attention of the most unobserving,"* he acknowledged. *"[W]hile the unparalleled perseverance of the armies of the United States, through almost every possible suffering and discouragement for the space of eight long years, was little short of a standing miracle."*

Over and over again Washington had witnessed Providence's preserving hand. One swipe could have wiped out the army and dissolved the dream of independence, yet miracles were sprinkled over them a thousand times. A fog covered the army in their Long Island escape. A mistake in British strategy prevented a permanent halt at Harlem. Thwarted were the schemes of officers Gates, Lee, and Conway. Uncovered was the treason of Arnold. Knox cracked the ice of the Delaware River. A man on the road to Trenton tipped them off to the house of the Hessians. A Quaker woman risked her life to warn of a surprise attack at White Marsh. Rain washed away Cornwallis's pursuit of Greene over the river Dan. And Clinton's reinforcements arrived at Yorktown five days too late.

How did the Revolution change Washington? It reinforced his recognition and respect for God's intervention in the affairs of men. Washington used his farewell address to encourage his soldiers to embrace the miracle of their own transformation from an army of mediocrity into a force of might. *"For who has before seen a disciplined army formed at once from such raw materials?"* he asked, noting that men of different habits and education had become *"one patriotic band of brothers."*

Washington then baptized his soldiers into citizens, wishing them well in their pursuits of commerce and domestic tranquility. *"Every one may rest assured that much, very much, of the future happiness of the officers and men, will depend upon the wise and manly conduct which shall be adopted by them when they are mingled with the great body of the community,"* the commander reminded his troops.

George Washington concluded by offering his prayers to the *"God of armies"* on their behalf: *"May ample justice be done them here, and may the choicest of Heaven's favors, both here and hereafter, attend those, who, under the Divine auspices, have secured innumerable blessings for others."*[325]

> "But thanks be to God! He gives us the victory through our Lord Jesus Christ"
> (1 CORINTHIANS 15:57).

**PRAYER**

*Thank you for your miracles and for the victory of eternal salvation through Jesus Christ.*

# 326. Handoff

They had done it. They had secured liberty's table. And now it was time to say good-bye. *"Washington entered the room where they [his officers] were all waiting,"* Henry Knox historian Francis Drake wrote of that December night in 1783 at a New York tavern. As the British troops evacuated New York, Washington had triumphantly marched into Manhattan. He was thrilled to visit the city he had been driven out of seven years earlier. *"And taking a glass of wine in his hand he said, 'With a heart full of love and gratitude I now take leave of you. I most devoutly wish that your latter days may be as prosperous and happy as your former ones have been glorious and honorable.'"*

The moment was more emotional than any could express. At Washington's request, the officers took their commander's hand, and, one by one, said good-bye. The war had certainly given Washington plenty of reasons to cry: Long Island and Brandywine, to name only two. But it was this moment of farewell that finally brought tears to his eyes.

Their new commander-in-chief, Henry Knox, had arranged for this farewell. After Benedict Arnold left West Point in shambles, Washington entrusted Knox to rebuild it. In true bookworm style, Knox laid the groundwork to turn West Point into the military academy it is today. But Washington intended his handoff to Knox to be briefer than a college semester. By January 1784, Knox himself was ready to say good-bye. He had successfully disbanded the army he had worked to build. He was among the first to join and the last to leave.

*"Having brought the affairs here nearly to a close, I shall soon depart for Boston, for which place Mrs. Knox and her little family set out from New York,"* Knox wrote to Washington in January 1784. Yorktown brought Knox his wish for more domestic tranquility. Lucy and their children had joined him at West Point before he returned to Boston.

Nine years after Lucy sewed his sword into her coat before they sneaked from Boston to Cambridge, Knox said good-bye to the army. Now, his capabilities and his character thoroughly tested, he emerged with more honor than any number of medals could give.

*"I should do violence to the dictates of my heart were I to suppress its sensations of affection and gratitude to you for the innumerable*

> "You prepare a table before me in the presence of my enemies. You anoint my head with oil; my cup overflows. Surely goodness and love will follow me all the days of my life, and I will dwell in the house of the LORD forever" (PSALM 23:5, 6).

*instances of your kindness and attention to me . . . And, although I can find no words equal to their warmth, I may venture to assure you that they will remain indelibly fixed."*

"I devoutly pray the Supreme Being to continue to afford you his especial protection," Knox added. Indeed, it was Henry Knox's faith that had assured him a place at George Washington's table throughout the war. Faith also prepared him for the feast to come whenever he said his earthly good-bye.[326]

**PRAYER**

*Thank you for promising to prepare a table for me and for dwelling in the hearts of those who gather in your name.*

# 327. Resignation

After saying "farewell" to his men and officers in New York, General Washington prepared for the final stop on his Continental victory lap.

The Reverend William Gordon, author of one of the earliest histories of the Revolution, recorded that Washington then *"hastened"* to Annapolis, Maryland, where the Continental Congress had gathered. He arrived on December 19, 1783.

*"The next day he informed congress of his arrival in that city, with the intention of asking leave to resign the commission he had the honor of holding in their service, and desired to know their pleasure in what manner it would be most proper to offer his resignation—whether in writing or at an audience,"* Gordon wrote.

Congress decided to hold a public event at noon on the following Tuesday. Washington's decision to resign took them by as much surprise as Ethan Allen's capture of Fort Ticonderoga in 1775.

*"The general had been so reserved with regard to the time of his intended resignation, that congress had not the least apprehension of its being either so soon or so sudden,"* recalled Gordon. The unexpected news signaled a change in direction. Where Allen's unauthorized mission had forced Congress to establish a military, Washington's resignation radically reduced the military.

*"When the day was arrived, and the hour approached for fixing the patriotic character of the AMERICAN CHIEF, the gallery was filled with a beautiful group of elegant ladies, and some graced the floor of congress. On this were likewise the governor, council and legislature of Maryland,*

*several general officers, the consul general of France, and the respectable citizens of Annapolis,"* Gordon noted.

Congress took their seats *"as representatives of the sovereignty of the Union."* Spectators stood and filled the gallery.

*"The general was introduced to a chair by the secretary, who, after a decent interval, ordered silence. A short pause ensued, when the honorable Thomas Mifflin, the president, informed the general, that 'the United States in congress assembled were prepared to receive his communications,' on which he rose with great dignity."*

As the commander-in-chief stood to address Congress and offer his resignation, he showed his boldness and his humility. Resigning was the act of a gentleman, the mark of someone who put others above himself. It was a decision that a less modest man, such as Horatio Gates or Charles Lee, would never have made. Washington was so popular at this moment that he could have asked Congress to anoint him king of America. But in giving up power, George Washington embraced the true spirit of liberty.[327]

> "It was not by their sword that they won the land, nor did their arm bring them victory; it was your right hand, your arm, and the light of your face, for you loved them" (PSALM 44:3).

**PRAYER**

*Thank you for shining the light of your face on America, and illuminating the path of democracy with humility and dignity.*

# 328. Common Citizen

George Washington embraced his resignation with uncommon contentment.

*"Mr. President, The great events on which my resignation depended having at length taken place,"* George Washington began his resignation address to Congress. The standing crowd assembled in Annapolis on December 23, 1783, gulped with tears as they drank in each word of the commander's good-bye.

*"Happy in the confirmation of our independence and sovereignty, and pleased with the opportunity afforded the United States, of becoming a respectable nation, I resign with satisfaction the appointment I accepted with diffidence,"* he continued.

Washington's farewell to Congress was filled with as much modesty as his speech of acceptance eight years earlier. He reflected that his lack of ability in 1775 was *"superseded by a confidence in the rectitude of our cause, the support of the supreme power of the union, and the patronage of Heaven."*

Since Cornwallis's surrender at Yorktown, Americans had witnessed a remarkable shift. While the occupying redcoat army incrementally evacuated, the emerging nation acquired recognition and rewards. The British first evacuated Savannah, then Charleston, and finally New York. Massachusetts abolished slavery. Virginia gave freedom to slaves who had fought with the Continental army. Spain, Sweden, Denmark, and Russia recognized the new nation.

*"And my gratitude for the interposition of Providence, and the assistance I have received from my countrymen, increases with every review of the momentous contest,"* he reflected. Washington also praised the men who had served in the army, particularly his officers, and also Congress.

Then he said solemnly, *"I consider it as an indispensable duty to close this last act of my official life by commending the interests of our dearest country to the protection of Almighty God, and those who have the superintendence of them to his holy keeping."*

With an old warrior's wisdom, Washington knew his work was done, his purpose fulfilled. It was time to return to civilian life. *"Having now finished the work assigned me, I retire from the great theatre of action, and bidding an affectionate farewell to this august body, under whose orders I have so long acted, I here offer my commission, and take my leave of all the employments of public life,"* he concluded humbly.

He handed the president of Congress a copy of his address. With an exchange of paper and a few public remarks, he was no longer a commander-in-chief. No need to rebut British generals, such as General Howe, who failed to address him as "your Excellency" and recognize him as the leader of a legitimate army. George Washington was now a common citizen, a title he embraced as comfortably as he wore a plain black suit coat.[328]

> "Consequently, you are no longer foreigners and aliens, but fellow citizens with God's people and members of God's household" (EPHESIANS 2:19).

**PRAYER**

*Thank you for the gift of citizenship and for your purpose of membership in your household.*

# 329. The Revolution Today: Citizenship

George Washington may have worn a plain suit after giving up his command and becoming a common citizen, but some U.S. soldiers have worn the uniform while taking the oath of citizenship.

Twenty-seven U.S. servicemen and servicewomen serving in Afghanistan celebrated the nation's 230th birthday in a unique way on July 4, 2006. These soldiers, who had been serving on America's front lines in the war on terrorism, became U.S. citizens.

"Today, these fine soldiers will be unified as Americans," Army Maj. Gen. Benjamin Freakley, the coalition Joint Task Force 76 commander, stated proudly during the ceremony.

After the terrorist attacks of September 11, 2001, the U.S. government streamlined the process for permanent residents serving as soldiers to become U.S. citizens. By 2005, the U.S. Department of Homeland Security's U.S. Citizenship and Immigration Services had conducted more than one hundred fifty Fourth of July ceremonies for more than eighteen thousand men, women, and children in the United States including military members overseas.

Becoming a citizen is unique. It is made even more special when the new citizen is part of the Armed Services.

"The soldiers here who are about to become citizens already understand they have a unique responsibility, and that is the defense of the nation," said Freakley. "The citizen who is a soldier has to do more for the nation than other citizens, because the citizens of America count on (them) to defend her and make sure that life, liberty and the pursuit of happiness are guaranteed for all Americans. Thousands of immigrant soldiers are making extraordinary sacrifices for America in the war on terror."

For one new citizen, the ceremony that day was a childhood dream and a homecoming of sorts. Army Specialist Ahmed John came to America with his family from Afghanistan when he was ten. Becoming an American citizen had been a long-time dream. His deployment to Afghanistan with the U.S. Army was the first time he had been in the country of his birth since his migration years earlier.

"I came back to Afghanistan to protect my native land and also to defend my homeland—the United States of America," John said. "The United States has offered me so many opportunities I would not have had anywhere else, so I would not hesitate to give my life for my new country. I love the United States."

"As a nation that gives to others, we also like our citizens to be part of that ethic of giving to others. Clearly you are already demonstrating that by serving your nation in uniform. I wish you prosperity, health and happiness as Americans, and I hope that you will contribute to the nation, as you are already, throughout your entire life," Maj. Gen. Benjamin Freakley told the new citizens.

> "But our citizenship is in heaven. And we eagerly await a Savior from there, the Lord Jesus Christ"
> (PHILIPPIANS 3:20).

Here on earth, citizenship in a country is important. But citizenship in heaven is eternal. It doesn't require paperwork or years of bureaucracy. It simply requires an oath from the heart to the Savior.[329]

**PRAYER**

*I raise my right hand to salute you, and to pledge my allegiance to you and my acceptance of your Son, Jesus Christ.*

# 330. Sabbath Rest:
# Birth of a Nation

It's no wonder that George Duffield delivered a memorable sermon on December 11, 1783. He had served as a chaplain to the Continental Congress. Many members of the Congress, including John Adams, had attended his Pine Street Church during their stay in Philadelphia. As a result, Duffield knew the Congress and their struggles. But he was no stranger to danger himself. His patriotic impulses led the British to put a bounty on his head. When the war was officially over, Duffield was supremely qualified to lead his congregation in a day of thanksgiving.

News of the peace treaty with Britain led Duffield to turn to the *"emphatic"* prophet Isaiah. *"Shall the earth be made to bring forth in one day? or shall a nation be born at once?"* he asked by quoting 66:8 (KJV). Duffield explained that most scholars attributed this to a date in the future when the Gentiles *"shall in a sudden and surprizing manner, be converted to the knowledge and obedience of Christ."* The time period also referred to the time when the *"Jews, so long rejected of God, shall by an admirable display of divine power and grace, be gathered home from their dispersion, as in one day; and being formed into a people in their own land."* Remarkably, America has lived to see the creation of Israel as a state.

Duffield, however, saw a parallel between this passage and America's independence. *"The importance of that event we celebrate today; and the remarkable interposition of the providence of God, so manifestly displayed therein, will I trust, sufficiently justify my applying the passage before us to the present occasion,"* he told his congregation.

Duffield was excited as he heralded his conclusion. *"Who since time began, hath seen such events take place so soon? The earth has indeed brought forth, as in a day. A nation has indeed been born, as at once,"* he proclaimed, paraphrasing Isaiah.

He noted that Israel wandered in the desert for forty years. Rome was a *"long continued scene of arduous, dubious struggle."* But America's revolutionary struggle against Britain was contained to a fraction of one generation. After interpreting Scripture and comparing America's place in the history of liberty, Duffield enthusiastically cheered the peace resolutions. *"That with great propriety, may we hail every friend of liberty, on this auspicious day, in the language nearly following our text,"* he hailed.

> "Who has ever heard of such a thing? Who has ever seen such things? Can a country be born in a day or a nation be brought forth in a moment? Yet no sooner is Zion in labor than she gives birth to her children" (ISAIAH 66:8).

George Duffield then inserted "America" for "Jerusalem" in the text: *"Rejoice ye with America, and be glad with her, all ye that love her: rejoice for joy with her, all ye that mourn for her . . . . For thus saith the Lord, Behold, I will extend peace to her like a river, and the glory . . . like a flowing stream"* (Isaiah 66:10, 12 KJV).

Even though the war lasted for more than seven years, in the grand scheme of history, America was born in a day.[330]

**PRAYER**

*Father, give me a long view of the purpose of my life.*

# 331. A Flame Expires

Just as peace dawned on the horizon, the man who fanned the first flame met an undesirable, but fitting, end.

James Otis's later years were far from the excitement of opposing the Writs of Assistance or standing against the crown's decision to close the courts. His family had been the source of some deep disappointments.

Otis's wife could not bring herself to support the patriots when fighting broke out. She was too loyal to the government of her youth. One of Otis's daughters followed her mother's sentiments and married a British officer, who was injured at Bunker Hill. Otis's son and namesake, however, embraced his father's politics. He joined America's startup navy but died soon after at the age of seventeen. All was not lost for Otis's legacy. Another daughter inherited her father's loyalties. She married Benjamin Lincoln Jr., the son of American Gen. Benjamin Lincoln.

Thus Otis retired to the countryside during the war without the comfort of a close-knit family. Sometimes he lived with his sister Mercy Warren. Other times he lived with friends in Andover, Massachusetts. Occasionally he attended a dinner party, but it often took him all evening to tell a single story. He was harmlessly insane, but insane nonetheless.

Insanity also described his wild proclamations about how he wanted to die. *"I hope when God Almighty in his Providence shall take me out of time into eternity, it will be by a flash of lightning!"* Otis proclaimed to Mercy in early 1783.

Otis shared his eccentric prediction with friends often enough to make them pause when the end finally arrived at his doorstep. The bolt came out of the blue. A thunderstorm struck New England on May 23, 1783. The light show passed over the Andover house where Otis was staying.

*"James Otis stood against the lintel of the door watching the commotion of the elements. There was a crash of thunder. The lightning, serpent-like, darted from heaven to earth and passed through the body of the patriot! Instantly he was dead,"* Otis historian John Ridpath described.

Seven others were in the house at the time, but Otis was the only one struck by the lightning. *"There was no mark upon him; no contortion left its snarling twist on the placid features of him who had contributed so much of genius and patriotic fire to the freedom and future greatness of his country—so much to the happiness of his countrymen,"* wrote Ridpath.

> "The LORD does whatever pleases him, in the heavens and on the earth, in the seas and all their depths. He makes clouds rise from the ends of the earth; he sends lightning with the rain and brings out the wind from his storehouses" (PSALM 135:6, 7).

James Otis was buried in Boston. The man whose passionate court defense sparked a revolution died in the same way he had lived his life, like a thunderbolt.

Why do some die in disease, others in their sleep, and still others at the hand of lightning? The answer is unknowable. It is as mysterious as the depths of the ocean and as elusive as the end of the galaxy.[331]

**PRAYER**

*God, you are the Great Rainmaker and although I don't understand your ways, I stand in awe of your power to both calm a storm and create a crescendo of lightning.*

# 332. In the Name of the Trinity, "Peace"

Unity started with the Trinity.

*"IN the name of the Most Holy and Undivided Trinity,"* the official peace treaty boldly began. After what seemed like a hundred years of

bloodshed, peace finally reconciled the United States of America and his Britannic Majesty. Three threads came together to create this final tapestry of peace. Humility under God's sovereignty was the first thread to bind the wounds of war. And Providence became personal by stitching the king's heart with humility.

*"It having pleased the Divine Providence to dispose the hearts—of the most serene and most potent Prince George the Third . . . and of the United States of America, to forget all past misunderstandings and differences that have unhappily interrupted the good correspondence and friendship which they mutually wish to restore,"* the treaty continued.

Even though the treaty established *"a beneficial and satisfactory intercourse between the two countries"* and secured *"perpetual peace and harmony,"* it required an essential binding thread: recognition of independence.

*"His Britannic Majesty acknowledges the said United States, viz. New Hampshire, Massachusetts Bay, Rhode Island, and Providence Plantations, Connecticut, New York, New Jersey, Pennsylvania, Delaware, Maryland, Virginia, North Carolina, South Carolina, and Georgia, to be free, sovereign and independent States,"* the treaty proclaimed, adding that the king and his successors relinquished all claims to those territories.

The treaty was so detailed that it defined the boundaries of the United States and provided for American fishing rights in Canadian waters. But strands of humility and independence were not enough to complete the peace. Visible forgiveness on both sides of the tapestry was just as important. The treaty called for fair treatment and restoration of British loyalists who lived in the United States. The document also called for recognition of debts contracted in England and America before the war.

*"There shall be a firm and perpetual peace between His Britannic Majesty and the said States, and between the subjects of the one and the citizens of the other, wherefore all hostilities, both by sea and land, shall from henceforth cease: All prisoners on both sides shall be set at liberty,"* the document declared.

Wrapped in these three cords, the peace document ended where it began.

*"Done at Paris, this third day of September, in the year of our Lord one thousand seven hundred and eighty-three,"* the treaty concluded, calling on the name of the Lord, the Prince of Peace.

By January 1784, Congress ratified this treaty of unity that started with the Trinity. They came together in God's name, and he was with them.[332]

"For where two or three come together in my name, there am I with them" (MATTHEW 18:20).

*Thank you for the strength you provide when two or more come together in your name. Thank you for promising your Trinity among the unity of believers.*

# 333. America the Busy

I *t is rather a general happy mediocrity that prevails,"* Benjamin Franklin wrote about his beloved—and newly freed—country.

But Franklin was not referring to a poor work ethic. This man who loved his old blue velvet suit as much as he loved his newly invented bifocals was exalting the virtues of American uniqueness and individuality.

After signing the peace treaty, Franklin received some interesting mail from Europeans who wanted to emigrate to America. By this time Franklin was as comfortable with European culture as he was his beaver cap, which ignited a fashion trend when he began to wear it in Paris. He feared some immigrants had a false impression of America, which was not a "mini-Europe." He knew their expectations could dump them into despair. Franklin decided to enlighten these prospective Americans. He wrote a pamphlet in 1784 on the "Characteristics of America."

*"There are few great Proprietors of the soil, and few Tenants; most people cultivate their own lands, or follow some handicraft or merchandise; very few [are] rich enough to live idly upon their rents or incomes; or to pay the high prices given in Europe, for Painting, Statues, Architecture, and the other works of Art that are more curious than useful,"* described Franklin.

This senior statesman warned European immigrants about relying on their social status for employment. Americans valued hard work more than birthrights.

*"[In America] people do not enquire concerning a stranger, What is he? but What can he do? If he has any useful art, he is welcome; and if he exercises it, and behaves well, he will be respected by all that know him,"* Franklin wrote, noting that strangers were welcome. *"Industry and constant employment are great preservatives of the morals and virtue of a Nation."*

Franklin also noticed a difference between Europe and America on the subject of religion. These discrepancies went beyond Catholicism and Protestantism. They were ones of sincerity and sentiment. *"To this may be truly added, that serious Religion, under its various denominations, is not only tolerated, but respected and practised. Atheism is unknown there,"* this Quaker observed.

*"And the Divine Being seems to have manifested his approbation of the mutual forbearance and kindness with which the different sects treat each other, by the remarkable prosperity with which he has been pleased to favour the whole country."*

> "Diligent hands will rule, but laziness ends in slave labor" (PROVERBS 12:24).

And so with his characteristic diligence, Benjamin Franklin recognized both God's hand in America's freedom and his blessings on her industriousness.[333]

**PRAYER**

*Thank you for the blessings that hard work and diligence bring. May I honor you with my hands and heart today as I enjoy the freedom you have given this country.*

# 334. From Traitor to Diplomat

It was time for a one-time traitor to meet his once-obstinate king.

*"When we arrived in the antechamber, the œil-de-bœuf of St. James's, the master of the ceremonies met me and attended me, while the secretary of state went to take the commands of the King,"* John Adams wrote to John Jay as he described his presentation to King George III on June 1, 1785.

Adams had prepared his remarks and compliments to the king with the sensitivity of a violinist tuning his instrument. But what made Adams most uncomfortable was the staccato of stares he faced when he walked into the waiting parlor. As the first American diplomat to stand in the king's diplomatic room, he was a magnet for backward glances. Lords, bishops, courtiers, and other foreign ministers took notice of him.

*"You may well suppose I was the focus of all eyes,"* he wrote. *"I was relieved, however, from the embarrassment of it by the Swedish and Dutch ministers, who came to me, and entertained me in a very agreeable conversation during the whole time."*

Adams waited until an escort took him through the adjacent levee room and into the king's closet, where he found the king. It was time for the minuet between the first American diplomat and the English king to begin.

*"I made the three reverences,—one at the door, another about half way, and a third before the presence,—according to the usage established*

*at this and all the northern Courts of Europe,"* Adams wrote of bowing before the man he once thought of as America's Pharaoh. Adams then relayed his speech to Jay in his letter.

*"I think myself more fortunate than all my fellow-citizens, in having the distinguished honor to be the first to stand in your Majesty's royal presence in a diplomatic character,"* Adams said to the king, after stressing that he hoped to cultivate the most friendly relationships with Britain.

He also wished the king and his family good health. *"And I shall esteem myself the happiest of men, if I can be instrumental in recommending my country more and more to your Majesty's royal benevolence, and of restoring an entire esteem, confidence, and affection, or, in better words, the old good nature and the old good humor between people,"* Adams told the king precisely.

The moment was a crescendo for Adams, confirmation of his role in the rhapsody of the Revolution. He had hitherto played the secondary part, an advocate for Washington as commander, a supporter for Jefferson's draft of the Declaration, and a second fiddle to Franklin in France. Now it was his turn to share the first dance.

As the first American to represent the independent United States of America to her former king, John Adams embraced his new diplomatic purpose with hope for the future.[334]

> "For I know the plans I have for you," declares the LORD, "plans to prosper you and not to harm you, plans to give you hope and a future" (JEREMIAH 29:11).

**PRAYER**

*Thank you for fulfilling your purpose for me, and for giving me hope for the future.*

# 335. Obstinate Tyrant No More

Had the American Revolution really changed His Royal Obstinacy?

*"The King listened to every word I said, with dignity, but with an apparent emotion,"* John Adams continued in his letter to John Jay about his minuet meeting with King George III. After dancing through the delicate moves of diplomacy, Adams listened to the king. His reply was more revealing and humble than Adams had ever expected.

*"SIR,—The circumstances of this audience are so extraordinary, the language you have now held is so extremely proper, and the feelings you have discovered so justly adapted to the occasion, that I must say that I*

*not only receive with pleasure the assurance of the friendly dispositions of the United States, but that I am very glad the choice has fallen upon you to be their minister,"* King George III told Adams, who accepted the formal compliment with grace.

*"I wish you, sir, to believe, and that it may be understood in America,"* continued the king, hesitating with long pauses, *"that I have done nothing in the late contest but what I thought myself indispensably bound to do, by the duty which I owed to my people."*

Then the king made a surprising confession. *"I will be very frank with you. I was the last to consent to the separation; but the separation having been made, and having become inevitable, I have always said, as I say now, that I would be the first to meet the friendship of the United States as an independent power,"* the king continued with an occasional quiver in his voice.

*"He was indeed much affected, and I confess I was not less so,"* Adams wrote to Jay.

Then the conversation suddenly became more casual and took an unexpected turn, an improvisation. *"The King then asked me whether I came last from France, and upon my answering in the affirmative, he put on an air of familiarity, and, smiling, or rather laughing, said, 'There is an opinion among some people that you are not the most attached of all your countrymen to the manners of France,'"* Adams recalled, embarrassed that the king knew about his dislike of France. However, he did not want the king to think he preferred England over France.

*"That opinion, sir, is not mistaken; I must avow to your Majesty, I have no attachment but to my own country,"* Adams replied lightheartedly.

*"The King replied, as quick as lightning, 'An honest man will never have any other,'"* Adams reported.

> "Listen to advice and accept instruction, and in the end you will be wise" (PROVERBS 19:20).

With their meeting concluded, the new ambassador honored the king by stepping backward and out the door. The man John Adams met that day seemed more humble than the one who once refused to read the Continental Congress's olive branch petition.

How had the Revolution changed King George III? It had softened his obstinacy and turned him into a better listener.[335]

**PRAYER**

*Give me a listening heart today, one that hears what others have to say.*

# 336. The Revolution Today: The Tour Guide

Does America have a Judeo-Christian heritage? Absolutely. And over the years Ralph Weitz has best answered this question by guiding, not merely telling.

Weitz has taken groups from his church, Immanuel Bible Church in Springfield, Virginia, on tours of Philadelphia and Valley Forge since 1999. The annual trekking began when a few church members decided they wanted to tour Valley Forge. They turned to Weitz, their pastor of stewardship, who grew up thirty miles from Philadelphia. After agreeing to become their tour guide, Weitz reacquainted himself with Pennsylvania's history.

"I started by sifting out folklore from fact," Weitz said. That sifting led to a revolution of sorts, igniting in Weitz a passion to share America's historical spiritual heritage. Weitz shows his groups the usual Philadelphia sites: the Liberty Bell, Independence Hall, Franklin Square, and Betsy Ross's house. "Betsy Ross was married three times and buried three times," he tells his groups with a grin.

But Weitz's tours take a different turn from most. Along the way he points out the pews. He shows them the Free Quaker Meeting House where Quakers supporting the war later met after splitting with other Quakers. At Christ Church Weitz points out George Washington's pew and the donated baptismal font of Pennsylvania founder William Penn, who was baptized in an Anglican church in England and later became a Quaker.

As they pass by a modern Jewish synagogue, Weitz explains Philadelphia's Jewish heritage. A Jewish settler lived in the city as early as 1703. Weitz notes that Penn's "y'all come" openness is an important part of America's religious heritage. Penn penned his philosophy by writing that no person would be *"compelled to frequent or maintain any religious Worship."*

"What I'm trying to give is not just an evangelic view but what the spiritual climate was in colonial times through the establishment of our country," Weitz explains.

Weitz ends his day-long tour of Philadelphia at Washington Square, the site of a mass grave of Revolutionary War soldiers and others. Weitz then describes one of the square's greatest moments. *"It is in this square that George Whitefield proclaimed the gospel. It was there without any amplification that he preached to 25,000,"* he tells of Whitefield's unparalleled gift for preaching and of his friendship with Benjamin Franklin.

"My purpose is to show people our Judeo-Christian heritage. That's not debatable," emphasizes Weitz. "When you see the pews where the founders worshipped, learn of the great evangelist George Whitefield, read the scripture on the Liberty Bell, and discover Penn's philosophy, that's part of our Judeo-Christian heritage. It's missed today."

For Weitz the most rewarding part is watching people as they catch the significance of faith in America's history. He says it's not his enthusiasm that enlightens his groups. "Actually the historical and spiritual sites have done their job, I'm just the guide," Ralph Weitz says humbly.[336]

> "Send forth your light and your truth, let them guide me; let them bring me to your holy mountain, to the place where you dwell"
> (PSALM 43:3).

**PRAYER**

*From people to places, thank you for the guides you have sent in my life to point me to you and your Son, Jesus Christ.*

# 337. Sabbath Rest: United States

Q*uick as the flash of lightning glares from pole to pole, so sudden did a military spirit pervade these then united colonies; but now, blessed be God, confederated, established states,"* George Duffield proclaimed in the sermon he gave celebrating the end of the war.

This former chaplain of the Continental Congress eloquently reflected on the people of America and their sacrifices. *"The peaceful husbandman forsook his farm; the merchant relinquished his trade; the learned in the law dismissed their clients; the compassionate physician forgot his daily round; the mariner laid aside his compass and quadrant; the mechanic resigned his implements of employment,"* he pointed out to his congregation.

The colonists had become patriots regardless of their professions. Bookseller Henry Knox, foundry owner Nathanael Greene, and lawyer John Adams were proof enough of such Continental diversity. *"All prepared for war, and eagerly flew to the field. The delicate female herself forgot her timidity; and glowing with patriot zeal prompted the tardy to arms,"* he continued. For the sake of liberty, both civil and religious, the American people became *"faithful watchmen"* who *"blew the trumpet on the walls of our Zion."*

*"He that put the spirit of Moses on the elders of Israel, raised up senators, and guided them in council, to conduct the affairs of his chosen American tribes,"* Duffield said, referring to the Continental Congress. *"These, posterity will admire and revere; and wish to have seen the day when those men lived on the earth."*

Duffield praised God as *"the protector of the rights of mankind"* for moving the monarch of France to America's cause. He reminded his congregation about Monmouth and Cowpens. But it was Yorktown where God delivered America.

*"And oft shall the traveller turn aside to survey the seat of Gloucester and York in Virginia, and view the spot, ever to be remembered, where the great decisive event took place; and read inscribed on the memorative marble, the important victory there obtained . . . For, according to this time shall it be said of these United States, what hath God wrought for*

*them? Great indeed, is the salvation he hath
shown! And great the obligations we are under
to praise!"* he proclaimed.

> "Hallelujah! Salvation and glory and power belong to our God" (REVELATION 19:1).

Duffield stressed that God heard America's
cry of distress. *"Here has our God erected a banner of civil and religious liberty: And prepared an
asylum for the poor and oppressed from every
part of the earth. Here, if wisdom guide our affairs, shall a happy equality reign; and joyous freedom bless the inhabitants wide and far, from age
to age,"* Duffield predicted.

George Duffield believed the banner of God had led the patriots to
raise their own flag of independence to victory.[337]

**PRAYER**

*Thank you for your glorious eternal salvation and for the civil and religious liberty you have given our country.*

# 338. Can't Go On in the Same Train Forever

*Your sentiments, that our affairs are drawing rapidly to a crisis, accord
with my own,"* George Washington wrote to his friend John Jay on
August 1, 1786.

When Washington retired in 1783, he had planned to spend his
remaining days at Mount Vernon. Washington, whose name means
farmer, was just that. He longed to cultivate crops and harvest grain. But
an economic depression soon ensued across America. With resources ravaged and money as scarce as snow in summer, the people were suffering.
Washington feared the crisis would soon reach disaster proportions.

*"What the event will be, is also beyond the reach of my foresight.
We have errors to correct; we have probably had too good an opinion
of human nature in forming our confederation,"* Washington wrote. He
had concluded that the main cause of this Continental chaos was the
new government. The Articles of Confederation were failing the fledgling states.

*"I do not conceive we can exist long as a nation without having
lodged some where a power, which will pervade the whole Union in as
energetic a manner, as the authority of the State Governments extends over
the several States,"* he wrote of his wish for a stronger federal government.

The Articles had failed to adequately manage commerce among the states, contributing to the depressed condition of the economy. Virginia and Maryland, who had agreed on navigating their common tributaries, wanted to make trade arrangements with Delaware and Pennsylvania. However, they needed Congress's consent. But Congress didn't have clear authority to regulate commerce between states. Trade was locked as tightly as a box missing its key. Washington believed the solution was to broaden Congress's authority.

*"To be fearful of investing Congress, constituted as that body is, with ample authorities for national purposes, appears to me the very climax of popular absurdity and madness. Could Congress exert them for the detriment of the public, without injuring themselves in an equal or greater proportion? Are not their interests inseparably connected with those of their constituents?"* questioned Washington vigorously.

Congress was not the only problem. The *"thirteen sovereign independent disunited States"* were in the habit of ignoring what little authority Congress had. The state of affairs had become so desperate some wanted to return to royalty.

*"What astonishing changes a few years are capable of producing. I am told that even respectable characters speak of a monarchical form of Government without horror,"* Washington wrote, fearing that just one catastrophic event could lead to another Revolution.

*"What then is to be done?"* asked George Washington. *"Things cannot go on in the same train forever."*

> "Also in Judah the hand of God was on the people to give them unity of mind to carry out what the king and his officials had ordered, following the word of the LORD" (2 CHRONICLES 30:12).

Americans had come together in war. To complete the Revolution, they needed to unite in one heart, mind, and government.[338]

**PRAYER**

*May I be a team player, united in heart and mind with those you have placed in my life as co-laborers for the work of my hands.*

# 339. Shays's Rebellion

*"The unhappy time is come in which we have been obliged to shed blood,"* General Shepard wrote to Governor Bowdoin about the incident of January 25, 1787. The crisis point George Washington had feared

in his letter to John Jay reached its climax and threatened to forever shake the United States from the mountain of independence.

War veteran Daniel Shays was one of hundreds who returned to his farm only to be crushed by debt. Shays responded the only way he knew how: force. He organized militias to close debtors' courts in western Massachusetts. Shays's solution was simple. If the courts weren't open, then the government could not arrest debtors or foreclose on farms.

The Articles of Confederation were so weak that Congress did not have the power to send a military force into Massachusetts to stop the rebellion. Massachusetts Governor James Bowdoin responded by marshalling several generals and thousands of militia. General Shepard's forces caught up with Shays in Springfield, where the federal government kept one of its few arsenals. Shays and his men had escalated their tactics. No longer were they just closing courts—now they were operating perilously close to war by seizing ammunition from a federal arsenal.

*"Shays, who was at the head of about twelve hundred men, marched yesterday afternoon about four o'clock, towards the public buildings in battle array. He marched his men in an open column by platoons,"* detailed Shepard. *"He still proceeded on his march until he approached within two hundred and fifty yards of the arsenal. He then made a halt."*

Shepard warned Shays not to march toward the arsenal. *"Shays immediately put his troops in motion, and marched on rapidly near one hundred yards. I then ordered Major Stephens, who commanded the artillery, to fire upon them. He accordingly did. The two first shots he endeavored to overshoot them, in hopes they would have taken warning without firing among them, but it had no effect on them,"* Shepard wrote.

Shepard was careful not to turn the rebellion into martyrdom. *"Had I been disposed to destroy them, I might have charged upon their rear and flanks with my infantry and the two field pieces, and could have killed the greater part of his whole army within twenty-five minutes,"* he wrote of his restraint. The action he did take put a halt to the attempted seizure of the arsenal. *"There was not a single musket fired on either side,"* wrote Shepard proudly.

> "But everyone who hears these words of mine and does not put them into practice is like a foolish man who built his house on sand. The rain came down, the streams rose, and the winds blew and beat against that house, and it fell with a great crash" (MATTHEW 7:26, 27).

A few days later another man, Gen. Benjamin Lincoln, completed Shepard's mission and routed Shays, ending the rebellion. But the carriage had crashed down the mountain of independence. The clunky new government had skidded off its wheels. Shays's Rebellion had proved that America had built its new government on a heap of sand and not on solid rock.[339]

**PRAYER**

*Show me where I walk in sand, O Lord. May I build my life on solid ground that can not shake or shift with the wind.*

# 340. New Carriage or New Wheels?

What often follows a crisis such as Shays's Rebellion is a determination for change. That is exactly what began in May 1787 in the minds and hearts of the Founders, as many returned to Philadelphia for a convention to discuss the Articles of Confederation. But the question was this: How much change was needed? Did the carriage carrying the Articles merely need new wheels? Or was it time for a whole new carriage?

"*It has given me much pleasure to be informed that General Washington and yourself have gone to the Convention. We may hope, from such efforts, that alterations beneficial will take place in our Federal Constitution,*" Richard Henry Lee wrote cautiously to his friend George Mason on May 15, 1787. More than anyone in America, Lee had a vested interest in the Articles of Confederation. After all, he had led the committee in 1776 that drafted them. And although Lee saw deficiencies in the government, he believed the solution to the problem simple: no overhaul, just a new steering mechanism.

"*This rule [on trade] is, unfortunately, very difficult of execution, and, therefore the recommendations of congress on this subject have not been made in federal mode,*" he wrote, acknowledging that the document's commerce clauses were not easy to understand. Failure to use simple and plain language had led to confusion and noncompliance. Lee's solution was to slightly clarify the words. In his mind, the Articles simply needed a wordsmith's pen.

"*If the third paragraph of the sixth article were altered . . . and the proviso stricken out of the first section in the ninth article, Congress would then have a complete and unlimited right of making treaties of all kinds,*" he pointed out.

But Lee feared the convention meeting in Philadelphia would do more than merely alter the articles. He knew some wanted a wholesale overhaul of the government. Such news threatened Lee's crowning contribution to the Revolution.

*"The human mind is too apt to rush from one extreme to another,"* he wrote to Mason in anguish. *"Whence this immense change of sentiment, in a few years? For now the cry is power, give Congress power."*

Lee could not alter what his lips had uttered. He was too invested in the Articles to see them change dramatically. The fifty-five-year-old Lee took comfort in knowing that his mature friends Mason, age sixty-two, and George Washington, age fifty-five, were representatives to the convention.

*"I am glad, however, to find, on this occasion, that so many gentlemen, of competent years, are sent to the Convention, for, certainly, 'youth is the season of credulity, and confidence a plant of slow growth in an aged bosom,'"* he wrote, quoting William Pitt.

And while Richard Henry Lee put his faith in the wisdom of age, a thirty-six-year-old Virginian would soon prove that even a radical youth can become a founding father.[340]

> "I will not violate my covenant or alter what my lips have uttered"
> (PSALM 89:34).

**PRAYER**

*Thank you for your steadfastness to show me when I need a wholesale overhaul in my actions or when I merely need a new set of tires.*

# 341. Radical Jimmy

The letter James Madison received from George Washington thrilled him. The fact Washington agreed with the thirty-six-year-old, bookish Madison was significant. As a delegate to the upcoming Philadelphia Convention, Washington had moved from the battlefield to the debate table. He was the convention's likeliest president. No one was more aware of Washington's power than Madison.

*"I have been honoured with your letter of the 31 of March, and find with much pleasure that your views of the reform which ought to be pursued by the Convention, give a sanction to those which I have entertained,"* Madison wrote Washington on April 15, 1787.

Madison believed the Articles of Confederation had failed. Merely altering the words or *"temporising applications"* would foment the *"malignity of the disease."* He wrote passionately about his desire for a new system: *"Radical attempts, although unsuccessful, will at least justify the authors of them."*

Madison had spent most of the Revolution armed with a pen and a philosophy book. A tutor under the great John Witherspoon, this Princeton University graduate returned to his Virginia homestead as the war began. His feeble physique made him unfit for soldiering. But his giant mind found a natural place in Virginia's state legislature and in the Continental Congress. The Revolution changed Madison by making him into a powerful observer. Identifying the Articles' failings led him to advocate a radical new government in a detailed plan he shared with Washington before the Philadelphia Convention began.

*"Having been lately led to revolve the subject which is to undergo the discussion of the Convention, and formed in my mind some outlines of a new system, I take the liberty of submitting them without apology, to your eye,"* Madison told Washington.

Madison explained that giving states individual independence had proved *"irreconcilable."* However, *"a consolidation of the whole into one simple republic"* was unattainable. Madison preferred a compromise. *"I have sought for some middle ground, which may at once support a due supremacy of the national authority, and not exclude the local authorities wherever they can be subordinately useful,"* he explained.

Madison was well aware that the current system, favored passionately by patriots such as Richard Henry Lee, had failed. Likewise he also believed the other extreme, creating a new monarchy as some wanted, would erase the Revolution.

Although his position was radical, he knew painting a middle ground could not be done with broad strokes. It would require a fine-point brush combining both complexity and simplicity. When James Madison wrote his letter in April 1787, this youth had no idea his pen would lead others into the sunshine of a new day.[341]

> "The youth may have come from prison to the kingship, or he may have been born in poverty within his kingdom. I saw that all who lived and walked under the sun followed the youth, the king's successor" (ECCLESIASTES 4:14, 15).

**PRAYER**

*Thank you, God, for using the enthusiasm of youth to fulfill your plans in life. I also praise you for the number of years you have given me.*

# 342. Constitutional Tree

I would propose as the ground-work that a change be made in the principle of representation," James Madison wrote to George Washington of his plan for a new U.S. Constitution. He shared his ideas in April 1787 in advance of a convention in Philadelphia to discuss the Articles of Confederation.

Representation was the dominant drawing in Madison's new system. Writing that *"an equality of suffrage, does not destroy the inequality of importance,"* Madison painted a word picture showing the need for equal votes, or suffrage, among the states.

Madison argued that some matters, such as trade regulation and naturalization, required uniformity among the thirteen former colonies. The federal government should regulate interstate commerce, tax imports, and tax exports for the good of all. Madison also believed the states needed a *"disinterested,"* or impartial, federal government to serve as an umpire when conflicts arose between them.

With a fine-point brush Madison painted a complex picture of a government divided among three branches of the same tree. To the executive branch, Madison assigned the responsibility of *"the general protection and defence"* of the nation, which included the power to activate militias. But he had not yet decided on how the executive *"ought to be cloathed."* He did not show whether the executive should wear a simple suit, a military uniform, or a prime minister's robe.

Madison's second branch was thornier, requiring more strokes of his pen to draw subbranches. *"A Government composed of such extensive powers should be well organized and balanced,"* he proposed. *"The Legislative department might be divided into two branches; one of them chosen every years by the people at large, or by the legislatures; the other to consist of fewer members, to hold their places for a longer term, and to go out in such a rotation as always to leave in office a large majority of old members."*

Madison also drew a branch he considered just as essential as the other two. The new national government needed a judiciary. Sawing it off would leave the constitutional tree lopsided. *"It seems at least necessary that the oaths of the Judges should include a fidelity to the general as well as local constitution,"* he surmised.

Madison believed that no matter what new system emerged from the Philadelphia Convention, the support of the citizenry was essential. To be truly effective, a new constitution needed a trunk deeply rooted in support from the people. Acceptance by the people would allow it to flower.

*"To give a new System its proper validity and energy, a ratification must be obtained from the people, and not merely from the ordinary authority of the Legislatures,"* James Madison wrote to George Washington.[342]

"Consider this: You do not support the root, but the root supports you" (ROMANS 11:18).

PRAYER

*Build roots in me that will grow strong and sturdy for the days to come.*

# 343. The Revolution Today: Liberty's Visibility

Is liberty as visible as a tree or is it as unseen as the wind?

"No one can see liberty, but people have used the Liberty Bell to represent this important idea," the National Park Service Web site explains as it heralds the history of the Liberty Bell. Located in a glass pavilion, with Philadelphia's Independence Hall towering in the background, the Liberty Bell is one of the nation's most visible symbols of freedom.

This two-thousand-pound bell was created for a golden anniversary. The speaker of the Pennsylvania Assembly ordered a new bell for the State House, now Independence Hall, in 1751. The year was significant because it was the fiftieth anniversary of William Penn's Charter of Privileges, a foundational document for Pennsylvania's colonial government. The speaker wanted the bell to ring in celebration of the anniversary while fulfilling the meaning of Leviticus 25:10 (KJV): "And ye shall hallow the fiftieth year, and proclaim liberty throughout all the land unto all the inhabitants thereof: it shall be a jubile[e] unto you; and ye shall return every man unto his possession, and you shall return every man unto his family."

Although the bell tolled for many years, a crack eventually silenced it. While ringing on Washington's Birthday in 1846, the bell cracked and hasn't rung since. Its crooked smile is part of the bell's charm and a symbol of the imperfection of freedom.

On one of his tours of Philadelphia, Pastor Ralph Weitz had an opportunity to watch a member of his tour group see liberty by touching it. Because he was blind, John Fenton used his senses of sound, smell, and touch to take in the historical and spiritual focus of Weitz's Philadelphia tour.

A highlight of this tour was the Liberty Bell. As he often does, Weitz went ahead of his group to let the park ranger guarding the Liberty Bell know his group was coming. He asked the ranger if it was possible to allow Fenton to go behind the stanchion ropes surrounding the bell.

"Of course," the ranger replied.

Weitz led Fenton to the bell. While the ranger explained the bell's history, Fenton's fingers felt the cold cast of copper and tin. "John went over the bell with his hands. He felt the rough jagged edges of the bottom rim," recalled Weitz.

John Fenton also felt the niches carved by the inscription, a shortened version of Leviticus 25:10 (KJV): "Proclaim LIBERTY throughout all the Land unto all the inhabitants thereof – Lev. XXV, v. x." The moment brought tears to Weitz's eyes. "He saw it with his hands," Ralph Weitz said.

Liberty may be as invisible as the wind, but it's something humanity longs to touch and feel.[343]

"He has sent me to bind up the broken-hearted, to proclaim freedom for the captives and release from darkness for the prisoners" (ISAIAH 61:1).

### PRAYER

*Father, thank you for the symbols of liberty and for your desire to proclaim it throughout the land to everyone.*

# 344. Sabbath Rest: Walls of Compact

Just as fifty-five delegates made their way to Philadelphia to discuss the Articles of Confederation in 1787, one of Connecticut's finest preachers stood before his state's governor and legislature. Elizur Goodrich had personally fought against the Stamp Act nearly twenty years earlier. His passion was so strong he believed the Revolution had been as much a religious duty as a political one. He believed the current crisis created by the Articles' weakness threatened to tear down the walls of security constructed by the war. Goodrich believed *"the honour and safety of the confederate republic"* was just as important to America *"as the peace and prosperity of Jerusalem, were to the several tribes of Israel."* Goodrich's solution was to build *"walls of compact,"* or pillars of unity, instead.

*"Jerusalem was a city, defended with strong walls, the metropolis of the kingdom of Israel, and the capital seat of the Hebrew empire,"* described Goodrich. Its inhabitants were *"not a loose, disconnected people, but most strictly united, not only among themselves, but with all the tribes of Israel, into a holy nation and commonwealth, under Jehovah their king and their God,"* he continued.

Compact, as it says in the Psalms, was important to Israel. Likewise unity, or a *"compact,"* was critical to the future of America. *"If the national union, by concentrating the wisdom and force of America, was the means of our salvation from conquest and slavery,"* he reasoned, then unity and agreement was just as important to America's sovereignty after the war.

*"If these things are true, which I leave, gentlemen, to your own consideration, certainly there are no objects of greater magnitude and importance, more loudly calling the attention of America, than the national union, the necessity of supporting the national honour, and to give the federal government energy at home, and respectability abroad,"* asserted Goodrich.

Goodrich believed it was absurd to think that each state *"can singly preserve and defend itself."* He compared the idea to building a grand structure. Failing to unite was like men who poured a *"costly foundation"* and erected *"the mighty frame of a most magnificent palace"* and then retired to their own rooms without finishing the walls.

*"I only add, gentlemen, on this subject, my most sincere prayer, that heaven would guide all your deliberations,"* he continued.

> "Jerusalem is built like a city that is closely compacted together"
> (PSALM 122:3).

Elizur Goodrich knew that walls of unity were essential supports for *"securing the peace, and prosperity of the whole, and the benefit of it reach to the most distant ages, and increase from generation to generation to the latest posterity."* Unity is the heart of a constitution.[344]

**PRAYER**

*Father, erect walls of unity in my life that I may enjoy the blessings of "compact" with my family, my coworkers, and those closest to me.*

# 345. Debate's Discretion

*he people will not readily subscribe to the National Constitution if it should subject them to be disfranchised,"* James Madison wrote of Oliver Ellsworth's opinion on suffrage in the summer of 1787. Although he kept a record of the debate at the Philadelphia Convention, Madison worked with the same discretion as a priest listening to a confession.

The critical issue before the fifty-five delegates that day was this: Who should be allowed to vote?

This and other questions burned as intently as the June sun. As the summer of 1787 slogged along, the most important temperature was not the heat outside, but the tempers of the delegates who met behind closed doors. Instead of amending the Articles of Confederation, the delegates decided it was time to write a new constitution. It was time to solve complicated problems, such as, "Should only landowners vote?"

*"MR. DICKINSON had a very different idea of the tendency of vesting the right of suffrage in the freeholders [landowners] of that country. He considered them as the best guardians of liberty,"* Madison wrote of the idea of granting voting rights only to landowners.

*"MR. ELLSWORTH: How shall the freehold be defined? Ought not every man who pays a tax, to vote for the representative who is to levy and dispose of his money?"* Madison recorded of Ellsworth's retort. *"Taxation and representation ought to go together."*

But Ellsworth's words produced beads of sweat on the brow of Gouverneur Morris, who would not be *"duped"* by the idea of *"taxation and representation"* for both the landowning and non-landowning classes.

*"MR. GOUVERNEUR MORRIS: Give the votes to people who have no property, and they will sell them to the rich who will be able to buy them,"* Madison summarized Morris's thoughts.

After listening to the debate's rat-a-tat-tat, Madison decided it was time to voice his own opinion. *"The right of suffrage is certainly one of the fundamental articles of republican government,"* Madison said.

He then recorded Benjamin Franklin's reply. *"It is of great consequence that we should not depress the virtue and public spirit of our common people; of which they displayed a great deal during the war, and which contributed principally to the favorable issue of it,"* Franklin pointed out.

The delegates agreed on one point. By keeping their deliberations a secret, they gave themselves a gift. They could speak freely without fear of seeing their opinions in the next day's newspaper. Although thirty-six-year-old James Madison kept copious notes, his records would not be released until after his death. By agreeing to keep their disagreements to themselves they were better able to hear each other's arguments and pleas. Discretion led them to the purest and freest form of debate.[345]

> "Hear now my argument; listen to the plea of my lips"
> (JOB 13:6).

**PRAYER**

*Give me the grace to listen to the pleas and opinions of others. Thank you for listening to me and may discretion guide my lips.*

# 346. Abating the Debate

As the Philadelphia Convention continued into the summer of 1787, the debate failed to abate with every passing day. To the fifty-five delegates, each new argument seemed more intense than the previous one. What started as give-and-take conversations turned into lengthy monologues.

Such was the case when Maryland's Luther Martin took the floor to speak one day. Martin opposed Madison's plan for a new constitution. The issue for Martin was representation based on population. If the number of delegates in the legislature was calculated on state populations, the larger states would have more delegates and more power. Their political *"inheritance"* would be greater.

*"Mr. L. Martin contended at great length and with great eagerness that the general government was meant merely to preserve the State governments, not to govern individuals,"* James Madison recorded in his journal. Martin was so fearful of larger states dominating smaller states under the new constitution that he turned to reliable sources for backup.

*"In order to prove that individuals in a state of nature are equally free and independent, he read passages from Locke, Vattel, Lord Somers, Priestley,"* Madison recorded of Martin's lengthy explanation.

Martin feared that if the larger states had more delegates, they could also control the executive branch. *"That, as Virginia, Massachusetts and Pennsylvania have forty-two ninetieths of the votes, they can do as they please without a miraculous union of the other ten,"* wrote Madison, recording Martin's words.

Martin's mathematical madness made Madison yawn and Martin too tired to maintain his pace. *"This was the substance of a speech which was continued more than three hours. He was too much exhausted, he said, to finish his remarks, and reminded the House that he should to-morrow resume them,"* recorded Madison.

After some refreshment, Martin continued his diatribe against representation based on population. He believed the new constitution was a formula for dissolving the union.

James Madison described Luther Martin's discourse as *"faint"* and delivered with *"considerable vehemence."* Regardless of Martin's lack of rhetorical skills, his long speech revealed the

> "To a larger group give a larger inheritance, and to a smaller group a smaller one; each is to receive its inheritance according to the number of those listed" (NUMBERS 26:54).

naked truth. It would take a miracle for the convention to produce a new formula for government. The simple math divided them. They needed to find a balanced equation for representation in the houses of the legislature.

The inheritance of the nation depended on them and their ability to find a fair solution.[346]

**PRAYER**

*God, multiply my strength. Instill fairness and justice in my heart as I make decisions today.*

# 347. Coalition or Contention

R*ivalships were much more frequent than coalitions,"* James Madison told the delegates at the Philadelphia Convention on June 25, 1787. His historical discourse was in response to Luther Martin's seemingly endless monologue. Unlike Martin, Madison believed smaller states gained strength by uniting with the larger ones.

*"Among independent nations . . . Carthage and Rome tore one another to pieces instead of uniting their forces to devour the weaker nations of the earth,"* Madison said. He noted that neighbors England and France had chosen enmity, not cooperation, over the years. He continued to show that it was contention, not coalition, that killed nations.

*"In a word, the two extremes before us are a perfect separation and a perfect incorporation of the thirteen States. In the first case, they would be independent nations, subject to no law but the law of nations. In the last, they would be mere counties of one entire republic, subject to one common law,"* Madison said.

One delegate realized the convention had deteriorated faster than a sandcastle in a storm. *"The small progress we have made after four or five weeks' close attendance and continual reasonings with each other,"* Benjamin Franklin began, *"our different sentiments on almost every question, several of the last producing as many noes as ayes, is—me thinks—a melancholy proof of the imperfection of the human understanding."*

With rancor filling the room like a skunk's perfume, Franklin knew the time had come to call for the motion most on his mind. *"We, indeed, seem to feel our own want of political wisdom since we have been running about in search of it. We have gone back to ancient history for models of government,"* Franklin said.

If history had a place in the debate, how much more should faith play a role?

*"In this situation of this assembly, groping as it were in the dark to find political truth, and scarce able to distinguish it when presented to us, how has it happened, sir, that we have not hitherto once thought of humbly applying to the Father of lights, to illuminate our understandings?"* implored Franklin.

The acrimony in the room was so sharp at that point, no one but Franklin could have stated the naked truth with such authority. The delegates watched in awe at his dedication as aides carried the ailing Benjamin Franklin into the room on a sedan chair each day. Not only was the eighty-one-year-old the oldest delegate, but his commitment to finding a coalition was also indisputable.

They knew his discernment about quarrels was as real as the peace treaty he had forged for his country. They knew his American pride was as genuine as his plain wardrobe and blue velvet suit.[347]

> "Don't have anything to do with foolish and stupid arguments, because you know they produce quarrels"
> (2 TIMOTHY 2:23).

**PRAYER**

*May I flee unnecessary conflicts in life and embrace the moments that matter most.*

# 348. Franklin's Call to Pray

The elder statesman called on his countrymen to pray.

*"In the beginning of the contest with Great Britain, when we were sensible of danger, we had daily prayer in this room for the divine protection. Our prayers, sir, were heard; and they were graciously answered,"* Benjamin Franklin reminded the delegates as he praised the Continental Congress's decision to pray and put aside their religious distinctions in 1774.

One delegate, Jonathan Dayton, later reported that Franklin's suggestion appealed to George Washington, president of the Philadelphia Convention. *"Here the countenance of Washington brightened, and a cheering ray seemed to break in upon the gloom which had recently covered our political horizon."*

By 1787, more than a decade had passed since the Continental Congress had first convened. Franklin had since seen Providence's hand govern the affairs of man in miraculous ways during the war. The result was Franklin's abiding respect.

*"All of us who were engaged in the struggle must have observed frequent instances of a superintending Providence in our favor. To that kind Providence we owe this happy opportunity of consulting in peace on the means of establishing our future national felicity,"* Franklin continued.

Franklin returned to the faith of his youth in that moment. He recalled the same beliefs that had led his father to teach him about the diligence of Solomon in Proverbs. Franklin exalted the Providence who had so miraculously brought an end to war.

*"And have we now forgotten that powerful Friend? Or do we imagine that we no longer need His assistance? I have lived, sir, a long time; and, the longer I live, the more convincing proofs I see of this truth,—that God governs in the affairs of men. And, if a sparrow cannot fall to the*

ground *without His notice, is it probable that an empire can rise without His aid?"* he asked rhetorically.

With the power of a preacher, Franklin called on simple Scriptures for instruction and insight. *"We have been assured, sir, in the sacred writings that 'except the* LORD *build the house, they labor in vain that build it.' I firmly believe this; and I also believe that without His concurring aid we shall succeed in this political building no better than the builders of Babel,"* predicted Franklin, referring to the account in Genesis 11.

Franklin had worked too hard for peace to let petty disputes dissolve the Declaration of Independence and prevent the passage of a united constitution. *"We shall be divided by our little partial local interests, our projects will be confounded, and we ourselves shall become a reproach and byword to future ages,"* he concluded.

Benjamin Franklin then moved that the delegates begin each day's deliberations with a prayer. The man who once wanted to die unlamented made a move of public faith.[348]

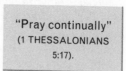

"Pray continually"
(1 THESSALONIANS 5:17).

**PRAYER**

*May my heart be filled with continual prayers and praises to you this day.*

# 349. **Senility or Spirituality?**

Benjamin Franklin's proposal for daily prayer was not enacted at the Philadelphia Convention. To some his gesture may have seemed as senile as misplacing a pair of his glasses. Several items prevented its implementation, including the cost of hiring a preacher.

*"However, the response to Franklin's motion should not be viewed as an atheistic or deistic expression from the delegates. In their view, prayer was an official ceremony requiring ordained clergy to 'officiate' (as Dr. Franklin noted), and the funds to pay them,"* historian David Barton, founder and president of Wallbuilders, wrote in an article for the national pro-family organization's Web site (www.wallbuilders.com).

Unlike today, public prayer was not a casual string of sentences lasting less than two minutes. During those days, public prayer was as formal as the robes adorning the preacher and sometimes as long as his sermon.

*"It was not as simple as asking 'Brother George' to ask God's blessings on their deliberations. This was not the general approach to religion during this time in history; orthodox formality was the preferable style and manner, at least in official settings,"* Barton pointed out.

*"For example, when Reverend Duché offered the first prayer in the Continental Congress, he appeared 'with his clerk and in his pontificals, and read several prayers in the established form' . . . Granted, he also unexpectedly 'struck out into an extemporary prayer,' but the point is made: religious formality was the order of the day,"* emphasized Barton.

The delegates, however, apparently responded to Franklin's call in another way. Led by George Washington, convention members attended a special Independence Day sermon at a Lutheran church in Philadelphia.

If the delegates did not implement his motion, then what is the significance of Franklin's call to prayer? *"Franklin, as well as all of the Framers of the Constitution, realized the value of religion in society. And they realized the value of prayer in the weightier matters of politics. As it turns out, Dr. Franklin was not senile at all; he was simply asking for divine assistance in what proved to be the formation of our American system. Perhaps there were no 'official' prayers during the Convention, but denying that the delegates wanted God's blessing and direction—now that would be senility,"* Barton wrote.

Nine days after the first Congress convened under the new U.S. Constitution in 1789, Franklin's recommendation took form. The House and Senate each appointed a chaplain, from different denominations, with a $500 salary.

*"This practice continues today, posing no threat to the First Amendment. How could it? The men who authorized the chaplains wrote the Amendment,"* Barton noted.

> "Brothers, pray for us" (1 THESSALO-NIANS 5:25).

What may have seemed like a moment of senility to some, has rained showers of spirituality on Congress for more than two hundred years. Asking brothers and sisters to pray is not delusional, but sensible.[349]

**PRAYER**

*I lift up to you the president and the leaders of Congress today, knowing you have called me to pray for my government.*

# 350. The Revolution Today: When Power Players Pray

Does Benjamin Franklin's call to pray for government continue today? Although it lives on through U.S. Senate and House chaplains, the legacy of prayer also comes to life every year in the form of a prayer breakfast.

"I think a breakfast such as this speaks to the true strength of the United States of America," President George W. Bush began his remarks at the Annual National Prayer Breakfast in 2007.

The Annual National Prayer Breakfast, which began in 1952, brings together nearly 4,000 leaders from the worlds of politics, government, and business. Journalists cover the event, but unlike many organized gatherings of the president, senators, congressmen, diplomats, cabinet members, and governors, this event is not geared for media madness. The organizers do not promote it on television news shows or host a Web site heralding its virtues. The Annual National Prayer Breakfast is an hour of power not because of who attends or how it's advertised. The prayer breakfast is an hour of power because it focuses on its purpose: prayer.

President Bush went on to note that America is a nation of prayer, with millions of citizens praying for themselves, their families, and the nation.

"In my travels, I often see hand-printed signs and personal messages from citizens that carry words of prayer. Sometimes it's a single little girl holding up a placard that reads: 'Mr. President, be encouraged, you are prayed for,'" shared Bush.

And just as people prayed for soldiers during the Revolutionary War, President Bush applauded those who pray for the military and their families. "During this time of war, we thank God that we are part of a nation that produces courageous men and women who volunteer to defend us," he added.

The president also told the story of a young American, Shannon Hickey. After her favorite priest, Father Mychal Judge, died in the terrorist attacks of September 11, 2001, Hickey started a nonprofit organization in his memory, dedicated to distributing items to the poor and homeless.

> "But those who hope in the LORD will renew their strength. They will soar on wings like eagles; they will run and not grow weary, they will walk and not be faint" (ISAIAH 40:31).

"With each gift to the needy, Shannon encloses a card with Father Mychal's personal prayer. It reads: 'Lord, take me where you want me to go, let me meet who you want me to meet, tell me what you want me to say, and keep me out of your way,'" quoted Bush.

"Father Mychal's humble prayer reminds us of an eternal truth: In the quiet of prayer, we leave behind our own cares and we take up the cares of the Almighty. And in answering His call to service we find that, in the words of Isaiah, 'We will gain new strength. We will run and not get tired. We will walk and not become weary,'" President George W. Bush said, paraphrasing Isaiah 40:31.[350]

## PRAYER

*Thank you for the strength and rest that prayer provides.*

# 351. Sabbath Rest: Prayer

Benjamin Franklin was not the only one who turned to prayer as a remedy for the state of the nation. Samuel Wales, a Connecticut minister, prescribed the same remedy as the good doctor from Philadelphia. He explained both the disease and its cure before the Connecticut Assembly in 1785, a year before the Philadelphia Convention convened. But it was commerce and wealth, not the constitution, that ailed the heart of this eloquent minister and Yale scholar.

*"The Lord hath done great things for us; whereof we are glad. He hath given us a very extensive country abounding with the richest gifts of nature,"* he noted of the many delicacies Americans enjoyed.

*"A proper view of all our various blessings will lead us to conclude that we are indeed the most highly favoured people under heaven. God hath not dealt so with any other nation,"* Wales reminded his listeners. He believed prosperity was not a replacement for the security of faith, something he feared his fellow Americans were quickly forgetting. *"But security in happiness is not the lot of humanity,"* he declared.

His was a bold statement in front of an audience of lawmakers. These were men who had fought for independence. They had lived through chaos. Wales, however, persisted in his message. *"When we are favoured with a profusion of earthly good, we are exceedingly prone to set our hearts upon it with an immoderate affection, neglecting our bountiful Creator from whom alone all good is derived. We bathe and bury ourselves in the streams, forgetting the fountain whence they flow. This is indeed a very disingenuous behaviour towards the Father of mercies,"* he warned.

Wales knew, however, that it was only human nature to take blessings for granted. *"When our wants are very pressing, we are willing, or pretend to be willing to apply to God for relief. But no sooner is the relief given than we set our hearts upon the gift, and neglect the giver; or rather make use of his own bounty in order to fight against him. The reason is, because we are more inclined to love the creature than the Creator, to be lovers of pleasure rather than lovers of God,"* Wales continued.

Wales outlined remedies to this common dilemma of humanity. He encouraged his audience to make every endeavor to promote the practice of religion and also to pray. *"[W]e ought especially in the use of all proper means, to pray fervently for the effusions of the divine Spirit,"* he noted. *"Without a divine and supernatural influence, true religion will never prevail."*

Samuel Wales understood the value of prayer to keep the excesses of life from overflowing into ingratitude and selfishness.[351]

> "And when your herds and flocks grow large and your silver and gold increase and all you have is multiplied, then your heart will become proud and you will forget the LORD your God, who brought you out of Egypt, out of the land of slavery"
> (DEUTERONOMY 8:13, 14).

**PRAYER**

*Thank you for your material blessings and the reminder to pray in humility. Please keep me from focusing on material wealth.*

# 352. Absentee Voters?

Two key patriots were surprisingly absent from the Philadelphia Convention. One who had the most experience of anyone in writing about constitutions. The other drafted the most significant declaration ever written. But diplomatic responsibilities kept John Adams and Thomas Jefferson from serving at the Philadelphia Convention. And while the convention could not benefit from their voices, both were there in patriotic spirit.

Adams spent the summer of 1787 in Europe, where he served as ambassador to England. Abigail, who had finally overcome her terror of the sea, joined him in London. She faced yet another fear while he took a trip to Holland: criticism over his book on American constitutions.

*"In various parts I thought I discoverd Satans cloven foot, but did not know that any individual was permitted to send in his comments upon a work,"* Abigail wrote to John about the shock she received when she read a monthly book review criticizing her husband's recently published book, *Defense of American Constitutions.*

In the book Adams had defended America's government and hailed the principle of balance. As the author of the Massachusetts Constitution, his qualifications were unquestionable. British reviewers, however, ripped Adams's book by calling it *"ostentatious."* The sting of such critics underscored the anguish of absenteeism for Adams, but he was not alone.

Thomas Jefferson was sharing the agony of absence from the Philadelphia Convention.

"*I am happy to find that the states have come so generally into the scheme of the Federal Convention, from which I am sure we shall see wise propositions,*" Jefferson wrote to a friend in August 1787 from his diplomatic post in France. Although he voiced optimism, Jefferson had his doubts about the proposed constitution. "*I confess I do not go as far in the reforms thought necessary as some of my correspondents in America; but if the Convention should adopt such propositions I shall suppose them necessary,*" he wrote.

Being absent from the convention was the worst kind of torture for the declaration-drafting Jefferson and the constitution-crafting Adams. "*My general plan would be to make the states one as to every thing connected with foreign nations, and several as to every thing purely domestic,*" Jefferson wrote, using his pen as his only therapy. "*But with all the imperfections of our present government, it is without comparison the best existing or that ever did exist.*"

So, although they could not serve as absentee voters, Thomas Jefferson and John Adams were with the convention in spirit. They, along with their fellow Americans, would soon read the immortal words, "*In order to form a more perfect union . . .*" The U.S. Constitution was about to emerge from the hallowed halls of Philadelphia.[352]

> "For though I am absent from you in body, I am present with you in spirit and delight to see how orderly you are and how firm your faith in Christ is" (COLOSSIANS 2:5).

**PRAYER**

*Father, thank you for the gift of absenteeism, for the opportunity it provides to sharpen my senses and to identify something important to me when I cannot see, touch, taste, or smell it.*

# 353. Franklin's Closing Confession

"I CONFESS *that I do not entirely approve of this Constitution at present; but, sir, I am not sure I shall never approve of it,*" Benjamin Franklin confessed to George Washington and the other delegates in his final speech at the Philadelphia Convention. He took the floor on September 17, 1787, to explain his decision to support the new constitution.

After watching the Constitutional Convention's painful deliberations, he was more convinced than ever that most people believed they possessed *"all truth."* Time may have tamed Franklin's intemperate tongue, but it had not dulled his keen sense of humor.

Franklin added satirically that many people considered their own opinions better than others, including *"a certain French lady, who, in a little dispute with her sister said: 'But I meet with nobody but myself that is always in the right.'"*

Franklin believed humility must be as much a hallmark of government as it is of righteousness. *"In these sentiments, sir, I agree to this Constitution with all its faults—if they are such—because I think a general government necessary for us, and there is no form of government but what may be a blessing to the people if well administered,"* he said.

Although Franklin could see imperfection in their efforts *"to form a more perfect Union,"* he knew it was the best possible document for unity among the states. Timeless perfection was as unrealistic as touching the sun.

*"I doubt, too, whether any other convention we can obtain may be able to make a better Constitution,"* he opined, noting that any assembly of men bring with them passions, errors of opinion, local interests, and selfish views. *"From such an assembly can a perfect production be expected?"* he asked the delegates. *"It therefore astonishes me, sir, to find this system approaching so near to perfection as it does; and I think it will astonish our enemies, who are waiting with confidence to hear that our counsels are confounded like those of the builders of Babel."*

Franklin elevated excellence over perfection. He knew the ability to amend the document would give future Americans the opportunity to fix its flaws. *"Thus I consent, sir, to this Constitution, because I expect no better, and because I am not sure that it is not the best,"* Franklin confessed. *"I hope, therefore, for our own sakes, as a part of the people, and for the sake of our posterity, that we shall act heartily and unanimously in recommending this Constitution wherever our influence may extend."*

> "But I did not want to do anything without your consent, so that any favor you do will be spontaneous and not forced" (PHILEMON 1:14).

An aging Benjamin Franklin hoped his acceptance of imperfection would lead the convention to unanimous consent in approving the new constitution. And with these words, the man who once wanted to die unlamented left a legacy of unity on America's greatest compact.[353]

**PRAYER**

*Father, teach me to voice my opinion to others in a respectful way.*

# 354. Winning Over a Friend

Unity is a miracle. James Madison may not have had four bullets sear his coat as George Washington did during the French and Indian War, but he emerged awestruck from the Constitutional battle in Philadelphia.

After thousands of seemingly century-long speeches, Madison saw wonderment in the majority that concluded the Philadelphia Convention, now known as the Constitutional Convention. Thirty-nine of the fifty-five delegates voted for the new Constitution. Before it could become law, however, nine states needed to approve it.

But there was one man who could influence the states' ratification process more than any other. Shortly after the convention's conclusion, Madison made one of the most politically smart decisions of his life. He sought to bring Thomas Jefferson into the miracle of the convention's constitutional unity by writing him a letter.

*"You will herewith receive the result of the Convention, which continued its session till the 17th of September,"* Madison wrote to Jefferson, serving as a diplomat in France, on October 24, 1787.

Madison knew how important it was to inform Jefferson about the details of the convention. After all, if the author of the Declaration of Independence opposed ratifying the U.S. Constitution, would any state vote to make it the law of the land? *"It appeared to be the sincere and unanimous wish of the Convention to cherish and preserve the Union of the States. No proposition was made, no suggestion was thrown out, in favor of a partition of the Empire into two or more Confederacies,"* Madison wrote encouragingly.

Madison first chose logical arguments to persuade Jefferson. He outlined the convention's objectives, such as uniting *"a proper energy in the Executive, and a proper stability in the Legislative departments."* Madison described the important job of defining the roles of the federal and state governments. He explained that the delegates sought to *"adjust the clashing pretensions of the large and small States."*

Noting that each objective was pregnant with difficulties, Madison explained how the delegates made conclusions and came to agreement. Madison's letter was so complete, Jefferson was sure to feel as if he had attended the convention himself. And as much as Madison relied on logic to persuade the politically influential Jefferson, his letter was also an act of friendship. Jefferson and Madison had been pals for years. Both Virginians, they had developed a mutual respect for each other's intellectual prowess. Madison knew Jefferson would have loved to serve as a delegate.

Hence he shared with his friend one of the most important outcomes of the convention.

*"It is impossible to consider the degree of concord which ultimately prevailed as less than a miracle,"* he told Jefferson.

> "And over all these virtues put on love, which binds them all together in perfect unity"
> (COLOSSIANS 3:14).

By characterizing the Constitutional Convention as a miracle, James Madison sealed his letter to Thomas Jefferson with the virtues of unity, friendship, and love.[354]

**PRAYER**

*Open my eyes to acts of love. Show me ways to reach out to my friends and encourage them in unity.*

# 355. Spicy Sentiments

The secrecy of the debate during the Philadelphia Convention resulted in an undesirable consequence. The new U.S. Constitution took many Americans by Boston-Tea-Party-like surprise. The delegates did not merely add seasoning or new ingredients to the American recipe for government known as the Articles of Confederation. The convention cooked a whole new dish, ripe with interesting textures and complex flavors. And although a majority of delegates supported the new document, it would have to become palatable to leaders and representatives throughout the states before it could become the permanent entrée of government. Americans began to learn about the new Constitution shortly after the delegates adopted it.

*"Weary from weeks of intense pressure but generally satisfied with their work, the delegates shared a farewell dinner at City Tavern. Two blocks away on Market Street, printers John Dunlap and David Claypoole worked into the night on the final imprint of the six-page Constitution, copies of which would leave Philadelphia on the morning stage,"* a National Archives and Records Administration historian recounted.

Whether or not to ratify the U.S. Constitution was the debate in the fall of 1787. The constitution could not become law unless nine states voted for its ratification. Proponents (Federalists) and opponents (Antifederalists) wrote hundreds of newspaper articles and pamphlets on whether to adopt the new constitution. Much of the discussion was spicy, to say the least.

*"I say the people . . . are now reversing the picture, are now lost to every noble principle, are about to sacrifice that inestimable jewel liberty,*

*to the genius of despotism,"* editorialist Samuel Bryan ranted against those who supported the constitution. His writings became a series known as the *Centinel.* Bryan called the constitution, *"A golden phantom held out to them, by the crafty and aspiring despots among themselves,"* and added that it was *"alluring them into the fangs of arbitrary power."*

This editorialist accused the delegates of *"gross deception and fatal delusion!"* Although he acknowledged that the new constitution strengthened Congress's commerce and treaty powers, he did not believe the result was sweet enough to overcome the sourness he tasted. *"Yet this benefit is accompanied in the new constitution with the scourge of despotic power . . . the gilded bait conceals corrosives that will eat up their whole substance,"* Bryan concluded.

By resorting to ranting and raving, Bryan sought to scare states into voting against the constitution. Although some Anti-federalists made reasonable arguments about a lack of a bill of rights, direct taxation, and the loss of state sovereignty, many attacks were like this one, full of labeling and fearmongering.

Probably Samuel Bryan's spicy sentiments merely reflected his fear. But the same Providence who brought unity to the majority of delegates in Philadelphia would thwart the craftiness of such name-calling partisans.[355]

> "He thwarts the plans of the crafty, so that their hands achieve no success" (JOB 5:12).

**PRAYER**

*God, you are the one who provides sweetness and seasoning in life. Thank you for spoiling the craftiness of others.*

# 356. Fear of Factions

Before the nation split into irreconcilable factions, James Madison used the very fear of factions to explain to the public the need for the new U.S. Constitution.

*"A republic, by which I mean a government in which the scheme of representation takes place, opens a different prospect, and promises the cure for which we are seeking,"* James Madison began in an article published in the *New York Packet* on November 23, 1787.

The most famous documents emerging from the ratification debate are the *Federalist Papers.* Alexander Hamilton and John Jay, with the help of James Madison, wrote eighty-five essays showing the weaknesses of the

Articles of the Confederation and arguing for a stronger national government through the new constitution. Madison's *Federalist Paper #10* emerged as one of the best tonics to soothe concerns and fears. Madison, perhaps reflecting on Daniel Shays's rebellion, diagnosed the dangers of factions, the kind that break the back of a nation.

*"There are again two methods of removing the causes of faction: the one, by destroying the liberty which is essential to its existence; the other, by giving to every citizen the same opinions, the same passions, and the same interests,"* Madison wrote. He acknowledged that liberty gave rise to factions, but abolishing liberty was not the answer to this ailment. He argued that a republican form of government, a union of states, had the greatest ability to prevent the destructive fires caused by factions.

*"The influence of factious leaders may kindle a flame within their particular States, but will be unable to spread a general conflagration through the other States,"* the doctor of the constitution reasoned. *"A religious sect may degenerate into a political faction in a part of the Confederacy; but the variety of sects dispersed over the entire face of it must secure the national councils against any danger from that source,"* he went on.

Madison argued that improper or *"wicked"* projects *"will be less apt to pervade the whole body of the Union than a particular member of it."* He assumed that such a malady, like a disease, is more likely to first taint a specific county than infect an entire state.

*"In the extent and proper structure of the Union, therefore, we behold a republican remedy for the diseases most incident to republican government,"* Madison wrote with the skill of a political surgeon.

Madison's prescription for preserving liberty against factions was simple: Americans needed to unite behind the new constitution. His arguments and appeal worked. The federalists organized a solid campaign that resulted in the final ratification of the U.S. Constitution by the states. For his efforts, James Madison became known as the Father of the Constitution.[356]

> "For I am afraid that when I come I may not find you as I want you to be, and you may not find me as you want me to be. I fear that there may be quarreling, jealousy, outbursts of anger, factions, slander, gossip, arrogance and disorder" (2 CORINTHIANS 12:20).

**PRAYER**

*Lord, guard my heart and hands against anything that will lead to dissension and factions in my life or the lives of others.*

# 357. The Revolution Today: A Scientist Prays

For one brief shining moment yesterday, bitter partisanship was replaced by prayer, and it couldn't have been more refreshing," *New York Times* best-selling author Joel Rosenberg wrote after attending the 55th Annual National Prayer Breakfast in Washington, DC, in February 2007.

Four thousand political, diplomatic, military, and business leaders and journalists from fifty states and one hundred and sixty different nations attended the breakfast. Although the sight of Republicans and Democrats breaking muffins together was a welcome break from Washington's usual morning jabs, it was a scientist, a Ben Franklin type, who stood out the most.

"The highlight of the morning, however, was the keynote address by Dr. Francis S. Collins, the director of the Human Genome Project and thus arguably the most important doctor and scientist on the planet today. He and his colleagues have mapped out the 3 billion letters of the human genetic code imprinted into each of our cells," Rosenberg reported.

Speaking at a prayer breakfast was far from Collins's childhood aspirations. This Virginia farm boy became fascinated with science and medicine. He eventually considered himself an atheist in a profession where only 40 percent of one's colleagues believe in God. But it was one of his cancer patients who made him question his beliefs. An elderly woman told him she had no fear of dying because she had a personal relationship with God through faith in Jesus Christ.

"She explained the good news that God loves us and has a wonderful plan for our lives, and offers us a way to eternal life through Jesus, and then she asked, 'Doctor, what do you believe?' Dr. Collins said he fled the room as fast as he could," quoted Rosenberg.

Touched by the woman's story, Collins didn't have an answer to her question. "He said it was as if all of a sudden 'the atheistic ice under my feet was cracking.'"

Collins then began to consider the evidence by studying Jesus' life and reading books by C. S. Lewis, who rejected atheism and embraced Christianity. "And along the way he said he found Jesus a man unlike any other—humble, caring, willing to love His enemies, ready to forgive sinners of any race, creed or color," wrote Rosenberg.

Deciding that the evidence demanded a verdict, Collins "bowed his head and prayed for God to forgive him and make him a fully devoted follower of Jesus, and it changed his life."

Francis Collins concluded his prayer breakfast remarks by playing his guitar and singing
"Praise the Source of Faith and Learning." And
just as inventor Benjamin Franklin called for a
time of prayer during the Constitutional Convention in 1787, so another scientist answered
the call of faith in front of national leaders who
had gathered to pray.[357]

> "Now faith is being
> sure of what we
> hope for and certain
> of what we do not
> see" (HEBREWS 11:1).

**PRAYER**

*Father, you are the God of all wonders and discoveries. I put my faith in
you.*

# 358. Sabbath Rest: Ratifying Wisdom

*I*f I am not mistaken, instead of the twelve tribes of Israel, we may sub-
*stitute the thirteen states of the American union,"* suggested Samuel
Langdon in his election sermon before the government leaders of New
Hampshire on June 5, 1788.

From Pharaoh's obstinacy to the miracle of crossing the Red Sea,
many ministers during the Revolutionary War had compared America to
Israel. It is no wonder Langdon turned to this parallel as the state of New
Hampshire considered whether to ratify the new U.S. Constitution.

*"The God of heaven hath not indeed visibly displayed the glory of his
majesty and power before our eyes, as he came down in the sight of Israel
on the burning mount; nor has he written with his own finger the laws of
our civil polity,"* admitted Langdon.

But just as the Lord had provided Moses with the Ten Commandments and designed the Israelite government around assemblies and
judges, so he had also given America a constitution, Langdon believed.
*"We cannot but acknowledge that God hath graciously patronized our
cause, and taken us under his special care, as he did his ancient covenant
people."*

The preacher recognized what George Washington and thousands of
others had concluded. The Revolution and the new constitution were nothing short of miracles. *"In giving us a Washington to be captain-general of
our armies, in carrying us through the various distressing scenes of war . . .
and finally giving us peace, with a large territory, and acknowledged independence; all these laid together fall little short of real miracles, and an
heavenly charter of liberty for these United-States,"* Langdon heralded.

Langdon was thrilled to preach this message in front of New Hampshire's governor and lawmakers. He also knew it was important to stress
the role of wisdom in continuing the work of government. *"Wisdom is
the gift of God, and social happiness depends on his providential government . . . we may with good reason affirm that God hath given us our
government,"* he asserted.

Langdon practiced what he preached. He believed wisdom was important in his upcoming role as a delegate to New Hampshire's state convention. The outcome of this meeting would not only determine the fate of the state but also the destiny of a nation. The U.S. Constitution would become law if nine of the thirteen states ratified it. If the delegates voted "yea," New Hampshire would become the ninth and final state needed to finish the job of ratification.

> "Observe them carefully, for this will show your wisdom and understanding to the nations, who will hear about all these decrees and say, 'Surely this great nation is a wise and understanding people'" (DEUTERONOMY 4:6).

*"Only one thing more remains to complete his favor toward us; which is, the establishment of a general government, as happily formed as our particular constitutions, for the perfect union of these states,"* proposed Samuel Langdon. *"Without this, all that we glory in is lost; but if this should be effected, we may say with the greatest joy, 'God hath done great things for us.'"*

God did do great things. Wisdom prevailed and New Hampshire made the U.S. Constitution the charter of the nation.[358]

**PRAYER**

*I pray for our nation, that you will unite us in wisdom and understanding.*

# 359. A Vulgar Puritan?

Samuel Adams's support for amending the new U.S. Constitution earned him an unusual new name: vulgar. This patriot known as the Puritan and Vindex faced more venom from those who disagreed with him than a barrel of snakes could ever produce. Although the name-calling bothered Adams, he knew the difference between truth and lies.

Adams may have returned to Boston after the war as a pauper, but his poverty was merely financial. He was rich in love for Massachusetts. Adams's view of the world and politics had always been Massachusetts-centric. He didn't want a strong federal government. He supported the Articles of Confederation because they created a confederation of independent states. He was too tired and impoverished to serve in the Constitutional Convention. His desire to spend hours in domestic happiness kept him from hearing the debate and understanding the details that led to the new U.S. Constitution.

After the states ratified the new document and the government commenced operations in 1789, Adams turned to Richard Henry Lee for comfort. Lee had chaired the committee to create the Articles of Confederation and shared his sentiments. They both believed that the liberty, independence, and happiness of the people were at stake unless the new constitution was amended.

*"I was particularly afraid that . . . such a Government would soon totally annihilate the Sovereignty of the several States so necessary to the Support of the confederated Commonwealth, and sink both in despotism,"* Adams wrote to Lee about his fears. *"I know these have been called vulgar opinions, and prejudices: be it so,"* he continued, fearlessly.

*"Should a strong Federalist as some call themselves see what has now dropt from my Pen, he would say that I am an Antifed, an Amendment Monger &c; those are truly vulgar terms,"* he wrote of his critics' choice of words.

Adams placed his hopes in proposed amendments to rectify the Constitution's sins of omission. *"I mean, my friend, to let you know how deeply, I am impressed with a sense of the Importance of Amendments; that the good People may clearly see the distinction, for there is a distinction, between the federal Powers vested in Congress, and the sovereign Authority belonging to the several States."*

Adams's desire to amend the Constitution was grounded in his view of natural rights and taxation without representation. His opinions may have differed from the federalists, but his intentions were hardly vulgar expressions of passion, as some claimed. They were real concerns for the continuation of liberty.

And with these words, Adams proved that having a different opinion is not vulgar. It's how you express it. This Puritan knew the difference between good and evil. As a result of the sentiments and efforts of Samuel Adams and others, Congress passed and the people approved ten amendments to the U.S. Constitution. Those amendments are known today as the Bill of Rights.[359]

> "Woe to those who call evil good and good evil, who put darkness for light and light for darkness, who put bitter for sweet and sweet for bitter"
> (ISAIAH 5:20).

**PRAYER**

*Father, give me the discernment today to separate good and evil. Remind me of your justice when I face dishonest name-calling.*

# 360. Inauguration

The Revolution changed George Washington in many ways, but perhaps the most obvious way is this: The Revolution changed him from a general into a president.

Washington displayed his executive skills when he served as president of the Constitutional Convention. And although the thrust of his role as commander-in-chief of the Continental army was a military focus, he emerged as a strong political leader. His role as a middleman between the Continental Congress and the army, along with what seemed like a million letters to local leaders requesting resources, sharpened his political skills. Thus, Washington emerged as the most logical and natural choice for the nation's first president.

*"No event could have filled me with greater anxieties,"* said Washington, describing the moment when he learned of his presidency. *"On the one hand, I was summoned by my country, whose voice I can never hear but with veneration and love,"* he told the first U.S. Congress in his inaugural address on April 30, 1789, in New York. *"On the other hand, the magnitude and difficulty of the trust to which the voice of my country called me . . . could not but overwhelm with despondence one who . . . ought to be peculiarly conscious of his own deficiencies."*

Calling his decision a *"conflict of emotions,"* he hoped he would not fail in this new and ominous task. The gravity of the task of building the executive branch of a new government was as weighty as leading a revolution against a king. No wonder he accepted the role with hesitation. No wonder he turned to the Great Author of life for direction in this new chapter in the young life of America.

*"It would be peculiarly improper to omit in this first official act my fervent supplications to that Almighty Being who rules over the universe, who presides in the councils of nations, and whose providential aids can supply every human defect,"* he said reverently, asking for *"His benediction"* over the liberty and happiness of the people.

With characteristic modesty and humility Washington recognized God's hand and purpose in the *"important revolution"* and the system of their new government. *"No people can be bound to acknowledge and adore the Invisible Hand which conducts the affairs of men more than those of the United States. Every step by which they have advanced to the character of an independent nation seems to have been distinguished by some token of providential agency,"* he reminded the lawmakers.

After expressing a few views on the Constitution, he pledged to work together with Congress. As he concluded his first inaugural address,

George Washington once more asked for *"His divine blessings"* on the government. After all he had witnessed, the president who had watched a monarchy melt and a people unite concluded his message with a recognition of God's hand and immovable, rocklike purpose.[360]

> "For the LORD Almighty has purposed, and who can thwart him? His hand is stretched out, and who can turn it back?"
> (ISAIAH 14:27).

**PRAYER**

*I praise you that your plans can not be thwarted and your purpose can not be reversed.*

# 361. Laughing at the Days to Come

M rs. Washington is one of those unassuming characters which create Love & Esteem. A most becoming pleasantness sits upon her countenance & an unaffected deportment which renders her the object of veneration and Respect,"* Abigail Adams gushed over her friend Martha.

Many historians believe Martha's mustard-seed-like faith multiplied over her lifetime. The key for her was learning that her circumstances could not bring her happiness.

By the time George Washington became president, Martha had survived threats of kidnapping and the trappings of travel during the war. She had braved the smallpox vaccination. Most difficult of all, she had outlived all four of her children, including Jack, who died of an illness contracted at Yorktown. She had every reason to be bitter, yet she was not. When she became the first lady, Martha wrote to her old friend, Mercy Otis Warren. She reflected on her life and the new role God had given her, one she did not want. Her words reflect her faith, strength, and dignity.

*"With respect to myself, I sometimes think the arrangement is not quite as it ought to have been, that I, who had much rather be at home should occupy a place with which a great many younger and gayer women would be prodigiously pleased,"* she wrote reflectively, adding that her grandchildren brought the *"felicity"* she sought.

Martha would have preferred the shade of Mount Vernon's oaks rather than the glare of government. But she accepted her new role with grace. *"I shall hardly be able to find any substitute that would indemnify me for the Loss of a part of such endearing society. I do not say this because I feel dissatisfied with my present station—no, God forbid:—for everybody and everything conspire to make me as contented as possible in it; yet I have too much of the vanity of human affairs to expect felicity from the splendid scenes of public life,"* she told her friend.

But just as she had embraced the role of the general's wife, so she also stepped into the slippers of the president's wife. She chose hospitality as her therapy, and laughter as her medicine.

*"I am still determined to be cheerful and to be happy in whatever situation I may be, for I have also learnt from experience that the greater part of our happiness or misery depends upon our dispositions, and not upon our circumstances; we carry the seeds of the one, or the other about with us, in our minds, wherever we go,"* the new first lady wrote optimistically.

Clothed in the strength and dignity of faith, Martha Washington's revolutionary journey of loyalty enabled her to laugh at the days to come.[361]

> "She is clothed with strength and dignity; she can laugh at the days to come"
> (PROVERBS 31:25).

**PRAYER**

*God, clothe me with strength and dignity. Bring an opportunity for me to laugh out loud today. Strengthen my faith so I can laugh at the days to come.*

# 362. Strong and Courageous

M*rs. Washington is excessive fond of the General and he of her. They are very happy in each other,"* Nathanael Greene once communicated to his wife about the perfume surrounding the Washingtons' love for each other.

An officer's wife made a similar observation. George Washington's *"Worthy Lady seems to be in perfect felicity while she is by the side of her Old Man as she calls him,"* the woman said.

And when Washington passed away on December 14, 1799, Martha no doubt reflected on their life together. Thoughts of their wedding, Mount Vernon, the war, and the presidency must have pervaded her mind thousands of times. She surely cherished her choice of 1775, when loyalty and love led her to Cambridge, Massachusetts, to begin a life with her husband on the road. In total Martha spent about fifty-two months, or half the war, with her husband in camp or at a nearby location.

As she replied to letters of condolences from friends, particularly friends from the revolutionary years, Martha revealed the tenets of her faith. *"When the mind is deeply affected by those irreparable losses which are incident to humanity the good Christian will submit Without Repining to the Dispensations of Divine Providence,"* she wrote to Jonathan Trumbull on January 15, 1800, *"and look for consolation to that Being who alone can pour balm into the bleeding Heart and who has promised to be the widow's God."*

The Trumbulls were among the Washingtons' many friends. Jonathan's father was the Connecticut governor who had encouraged Washington to be strong and courageous when he assumed command of the army. Jonathan's brother, John, was the young man who miraculously climbed the bullet-ridden hill at Newport to deliver messages in 1778. Today four of John's murals, including one of Washington at Yorktown, adorn the U.S. Capitol Rotunda. Martha replied to Jonathan's letter with sentiment.

*"I well knew the affectionate regard which my dear deceased husband always entertained for you and therefore conceive how afflicting his death must have been to you,"* Martha wrote, noting her appreciation for Trumbull's letter of condolence.

Her response also revealed her strength, courage, and faith. *"For myself I have only to bow with humble submission to the will of that God who giveth and who taketh away looking forward with faith and hope to the moment when I shall be again united with a Partner of my life,"* she concluded. *"But while I continue on Earth my prayers will be offered up for the welfare and Happiness of my Friends among whom you will always be numbered being."*

Martha Washington chose to praise God during the sunset of her life.[362]

> "From the rising of the sun to the place where it sets, the name of the LORD is to be praised"
> (PSALM 113:3).

**PRAYER**

*God, I praise your name. Your love, grace, and forgiveness transcend generations and are as real today as they were for Martha Washington after George's death.*

# 363. Thanksgiving

The death of a friend brought Samuel Adams's pen back to life once again.

*"IT having pleased the Supreme Being, since your last meeting, in His holy providence to remove from this transitory life, our late excellent Governour Hancock,"* Samuel Adams began, as he outlined for the legislature of Massachusetts his goals for the upcoming year.

His friend and fellow patriot John Hancock had died in October 1793 of an illness. Adams, who had become lieutenant governor by this time, assumed Hancock's responsibilities. Governor Adams looked to One he had always turned to during peace and war.

*"To Him I look for that wisdom which is profitable to direct. The Constitution must be my rule, and the true interest of my Constituents, whose agent I am, my invariable object,"* he continued.

Becoming governor of Massachusetts was the completion of a circle for Adams. The Revolution had finalized its orbit in the heart of this patriot. The man who once wrote a circular protesting taxation without representation by his governor was now the chief executive elected by the people. As his Puritan ancestors had done before him, Governor Adams took the opportunity to ask the people to turn their eyes to God, who had blessed them with liberty. He issued a proclamation calling for a day of public fasting, humiliation, and prayer.

Adams called on ministers to assemble their congregations for a day of penitence to the *"Supreme Governor, HE hath plainly directed us, we may with one heart and voice humbly implore His gracious and free pardon, thro' JESUS CHRIST, supplicating His Divine aid that we may become a reformed and happy people,"* Adams wrote in his proclamation.

An accomplished writer, Adams knew when to use flamboyance and when to employ humility in his words. He asked God for blessings on health, agriculture, and commerce by using phrases such as *"humbly beseeching HIM, mercifully to regard our lives and health"* and *"To favour our land with the alternate benefits of rain and warmth of the Sun."*

He asked the people to give thanks for their civil and religious liberties. He called for God's blessings to prosper their governments and schools. After expressing hopes for the revolution taking place in France, Adams called for the perpetuation of faith, the wellspring of liberty, in America.

*"And above all, to cause the Religion of JESUS CHRIST, in its true spirit, to spread far and wide, till the whole earth shall be filled with HIS glory,"* he wrote, adding a request that all *"unnecessary labor"* be suspended on the day of prayer and fasting.

> "Light is sweet, and it pleases the eyes to see the sun" (ECCLESIASTES 11:7).

The proclamation ended with these words: *"GOD save the Commonwealth of Massachusetts."*

Samuel Adams called on the Father of lights to shine on Massachusetts, the place where the war began. By doing so, he also reminded America to keep their eyes on the Son.

The Revolution in Adams was complete.[363]

**PRAYER**

*I look to you, and your Son Jesus Christ, for forgiveness and freedom. You are the Supreme Revolutionary, the One who forgives sins to save souls.*

# 364. The Revolution Today: Colorful Pride

W*hat is now their pride?"* a member of the British Parliament had asked Benjamin Franklin in 1766.

*"To wear their old clothes over again till they can make new ones,"* Franklin replied.

What is now our pride? The answer today could be as varied as the printed T-shirts hanging in Americans' closets. These cotton blends boast of sports teams, slogans, and schools. People take pride in their children, families, communities, churches, and businesses. There are as many sources of pride for Americans as there are stars in the sky. The most tangible example of national pride, however, is still found in a fabric, a cloth that would make Franklin proud. If one icon has united Americans since the Revolution, it's Old Glory. A 2002 poll confirmed it.

"Which of the following do you think of as the top three symbols of the United States—that stand for or represent America to you and the world?" a Harris poll asked Americans in May 2002. The flag topped the list at 81 percent, followed by the Statue of Liberty and the national anthem.

The Continental Congress could only imagine such statistics when they passed their resolution creating the flag on June 14, 1777. *"That the flag of the thirteen United States be thirteen stripes, alternate red and white: that the union be thirteen stars, white in a blue field, representing a new constellation,"* they proclaimed.

Third-grader Kaitlyn Kohler of Meridian, Mississippi, put her patriotism into simple words as she described her drawing of the American flag. "It means freedom," she said.

Pastor Ralph Weitz, who gives annual tours of Philadelphia, reminds his groups of the sacrifices that have led to this flag of freedom. "As much as you and I sit in a country of freedom, what we enjoy today is so easily taken for granted, back then it was so revolutionary and controversial," Weitz explained.

> "He who pursues righteousness and love finds life, prosperity and honor"
> (PROVERBS 21:21).

Weitz also tells his groups the story of attorney Francis Scott Key. After a tremendous battle against the British during the War of 1812, Key was surprised to see the American flag still flying at dawn. Key's resulting poem became the lyrics for the national anthem. In the atmosphere of the house of flag maker Betsy Ross, Weitz then shares the lyrics. Ralph Weitz puts a special emphasis on the anthem's last stanza.

> *"O thus be it ever when freemen shall stand;*
> *Between their loved home and the war's desolation!*
> *Blest with vict'ry and peace, may the Heaven-rescued land,*
> *Praise the Power that hath made and preserved us a nation.*
> *Then conquer we must when our cause it is just.*
> *And this be our motto: 'In God is our Trust.'*
> *And the Star-Spangled Banner in triumph shall wave,*
> *O'er the land of the free and the home of the brave!"*[364]

**PRAYER**

*Continue a revolution in my heart, one that seeks your righteousness and love, and finds life, prosperity, and honor.*

# 365. Epilogue: We the People

In fewer than five hundred words, a document created a pragmatic but principled federal government. By establishing executive, legislative, and judicial branches of government through the muscle of representation, the U.S. Constitution restored the health and dignity of a revolutionized people.

With the skill of political surgeons, the delegates to the Philadelphia Convention designed a plan, known as the Connecticut Compromise, to safeguard small states but also put power in population. Two representatives from each state composed the U.S. Senate. The number of members in the U.S. House of Representatives was to be based on a state's population. The U.S. Constitution is one of the greatest governmental remedies in history. Historian David Barton summarized the achievement this way: *"The doctrines of scholars would meet with the practical necessities of an emerging nation, resulting in a balanced blend of pragmatism and principle—the Constitution of the United States of America."*

The U.S. Constitution is the most tangible proof that the American Revolution was not merely a war. It was a change in the hearts and minds of the people. Gone was the sentiment of *"Long live the king."* Replacing it was a preamble of the public will: *"We the People of the United States."*

America had traded royalty for representation. Patriots had shed blood for the rights given them by their Creator. The recipe for victory required them to taste torture, terror, illness, death, financial ruin, fear, uncertainty, failure, and a thousand other bitter ingredients. What emerged was a government as practical as it was principled. Unity, not the singularity of monarchy, governed the people's will.

The preamble continues, *"in Order to form a more perfect Union."* Action followed this government of the people. The Stamp Act's disbandment of the courts and Thomas Paine's common sense quietly echo from the words *"establish Justice."* Lexington, Concord, Cowpens, Charleston, Newport, and Yorktown whisper *"insure domestic Tranquility."*

Footprints of giants such as Henry Knox, Nathanael Greene, the Marquis de Lafayette, and John Paul Jones—along with pathfinders Jonathan Trumbull, Alexander Scammell, and other lesser-known soldiers—carved the path to *"provide for the common defence."*

John Hancock, Samuel Adams, Benjamin Franklin, John Adams, Thomas Jefferson, and James Madison legislated and negotiated the way to *"promote the general Welfare."*

The leadership, modesty, manners, and nimbleness of George Washington, who understood the fate of *"unborn millions"* was at stake, served to *"secure the Blessings of Liberty to ourselves and our Posterity."*

> "When the righteous thrive, the people rejoice; when the wicked rule, the people groan" (PROVERBS 29:2).

All these worked together to turn patriots into a people who did *"ordain and establish this Constitution for the United States of America."*

*"This radical change in the principles, opinions, sentiments, and affections of the people was the real American Revolution,"* reflected John Adams.[365]

And indeed, a change of heart, mind, and spirit was the Revolution.

**PRAYER**

*Thank you for providing the U.S. Constitution. May righteousness thrive in the government and the people.*

# NOTES

1. "Revolution." Dictionary.com. Dictionary.com Unabridged (v 1.1). Random House, Inc. http://dictionary.reference.com/browse/revolution [accessed: May 17, 2007]; and John Adams, "Letter to H. Niles, Feb. 13, 1818." Printed from http://en.wikiquote.org/wiki/John_adams [accessed June 2006].

2. George Washington, "Letter to John Augustine Washington, July 18, 1755," in *The Writings of George Washington from the Original Manuscript Sources, 1745–1799*, ed. John C. Fitzpatrick. Library of Congress. Printed from http://memory.loc.gov/ [accessed June 2006].

3. George Washington, "Letter to His Mother," in *America*, Vol. 3, 51. Printed from http://www.originalsources.com [accessed June 2006].

4. James [2d] Earl Waldegrave, *Memoirs from 1754 to 1758*, ed. H. R. V. Fox (London, 1821), 8–10. Printed from http:www.originalsources.com [accessed June 2006].

5. Ibid.

6. E. H. Nolan, *The History of England, George III*, Vol. 3a (London: James S. Virtue, City Road and Ivy Land). Printed from http://www.gutenberg.org/files/19218/19218-h/smo3a.htm [accessed February 2007].

7. Ancient and Honorable Artillery Company of Boston, http://www.ahacsite.org [accessed May 2007]; and Benjamin Colman, "Christ Standing for an Ensign of the People, an Election Sermon, June 5, 1738." Printed from http://www.belcherfoundation.org/ensign.htm [accessed August 2006].

8. Jonathan Mayhew, "Unlimited Submission and Non-Resistance to the Higher Powers, Jan. 30, 1750," in *Pulpit of the Revolution*, ed. John Wingate Thornton, New York: Burt Franklin, Originally published 1860. Republished 1970, 39–104.

9. Benjamin Franklin, "The Countryman," *Poor Richard, 1744. An Almanack, etc.* Philadelphia. Printed from http://www.originalsources.com [accessed June 2006].

10. Benjamin Franklin, "A Man Diligent in His Calling, 1729–1732," in *American History Told by Contemporaries*, ed. Albert Bushnell Hart (New York: The Macmillan Company, 1902), Vol. 3, 229–35.

11. Benjamin Franklin, *Autobiography*, ed. John Bigelow, Philadelphia, 1868, 177–210. Printed from http://www.originalsources.com [accessed June 2006].

12. Benjamin Franklin, "Plan of Union" in *America*, Vol. 3, 38.

13. Franklin, *Poor Richard: An Almanac, 1744.*

14. Brad Randall, "Success, Aug. 11, 2006," The World of Wombat, Musings on Life, the Universe, Everything. http://theworldofwombat.blogspot.com/2006/08/success.html [accessed August 2006].

15. Samuel Davies, "The Mediatorial Kingdom and Glories of Jesus Christ, 1756," Foreword Ellis Sandoz, *Political Sermons of the American Founding Era 1730–1805."* Printed from http://oll.libertyfund.org/Texts/LFBooks/Sandoz0385/HTMLs/0018_Pt01_Foreword.html [accessed August 2006].

16. John Clark Ridpath and Charles K. Edmunds, "The Project Gutenberg Etext of James Otis," Project Gutenberg. Printed from http://www.gutenberg.org [accessed October 2006]; and "James Otis" http://en.wikipedia.org/wiki/James _Otis [accessed March 2006].

17. Ibid.

18. James Otis, "Argument on Writs of Assistance as Reported by John Adams," in Hart's *American History Contemporaries*, Vol. 3, 374–78; and Ridpath and Edmunds, "Project Gutenberg James Otis."

19. Ridpath and Edmunds, "Project Gutenberg James Otis."

20. Ibid.

21. James Otis, "Argument on Writs of Assistance as Reported by John Adams," in Hart's *American History Contemporaries*, Vol. 3, 374–78.

22. Samuel Dunbar, "The Presence of God with His People," in Ellis Sandoz's *Political Sermons.*

23. Martin Howard, "A Colonist's Defence of Taxation, 1765," in Hart's *American History Contemporaries*, 394–97.

24. John Burke, "History of Virginia 1765," in Snyder and Morris's *History First Person.*

25. Josiah Quincy, "From the Diary of Josiah Quincy, Jr., in Massachusetts Historical Society, Proceedings, 1858–60, Boston, 1860, 47–51," in Hart's *American History Contemporaries*, 397–400.

26. Quincy, "From the Diary of Josiah Quincy," 397–400.

27. "The Town Meeting of Cambridge, Oct. 14, 1765," in Hart's *American History Contemporaries*, 401–2.

28. Caryn D. Rivadeneira, "Good and Mad," *Marriage Partnership*, Spring 2000, Vol. 17, No. 1, 28.

29. Simeon Howard, "An Election Day Sermon, June 7, 1773." Printed from http://personal.pitnet.net/primarysources/howard.html [accessed June 2006].

30. "Stamp Act Congress, Oct. 19, 1765," in Hart's *American History Contemporaries*, 404.

31. Ridpath and Edmunds, "Project Gutenberg James Otis."

32. "Benjamin Franklin's Examination Before the House of Commons," first published in 1766 by J. Almon anonymously in London in *The World's Famous Orations*, Vol. 1, 37–52. Printed from http://www.originalsources.com [accessed June 2006].

33. Ibid.

34. William Pitt, "Pitt's Protest against the Stamp Act 1766," in *America*, Vol. 3, 77.

35. Dennis Cauchon, "Soaring Property Taxes Elicit Backlash among Homeowners," and "States Attack Property Taxes," *USA Today*, Aug. 24, 2006. Printed from http://www.usatoday.com/news/nation/2006-08-24-property-taxes-idaho_x.htm

and http://www.usatoday.com/news/nation/2006-08-24-states-property-taxes_x.htm [accessed August 2006].

36. Charles Chauncy, "A Discourse on 'The Good News from a Far Country, July 24, 1766," in Thornton's *Pulpit Revolution*, 105–46.

37. Charles Chauncy, "A Letter to a Friend, Containing Remarks on Certain Passages in a Sermon Preached by . . . John Lord Bishop of Landaff, Boston, 1767," 44–50 passim in Hart's *American History Contemporaries*, 418–20. And "Charles Chauncy," *Famous Americans*, http://www.famousamericans.net/charleschauncy/ [accessed July 2006].

38. Samuel Adams, *The Writings of Samuel Adams*, ed. Harry Alonzo Cushing, Vols. 1–3 (New York, London: G.P. Putnam's Sons, 1904). Printed from http://books.google.com/books [accessed August 2006].

39. Adams, Cushing's *Writings: Samuel Adams*.

40. Ibid.

41. John Dickinson, "The Pennsylvania Farmer's Remedy, 1768," in Hart's *American History Contemporaries*, 423–26.

42. Alicia Chang, "Online Merchants See Green in Pluto News," *USA Today*, Aug. 25, 2005. http://www.usatoday.com/tech/science/space/2006-08-25-pluto-memorabilia_x.htm [accessed August 2006].

43. Jonathan Mayhew, "The Snare Broken," in Sandoz's *Political Sermons*; and Brian Tubbs, "Called Unto Liberty," Jan. 29, 2002. http://www.suite101.com/print_article.cfm/us_founding_era/88715 [accessed August 2006].

44. Ridpath and Edmunds, "Project Gutenberg James Otis."

45. Thomas Hutchinson, "Private Letters" in Hart's *American History Contemporaries*, 420–23.

46. William Tudor, ed., "Deacon Tudor's Diary," in Hart's *American History Contemporaries*, 429–31; and Snyder and Morris's *History in the First Person*.

47. Ibid.

48. John Adams, "Diary, Mar. 5, 1773," *Adams Family Papers, An Electronic Archive*, Massachusetts Historical Society. Printed from http://www.masshist.org/digitaladams/aea/ [accessed August 2006].

49. William Tudor, ed., "Deacon Tudor's Diary," in Hart's *American History Contemporaries*, 429–31; and Snyder and Morris's *History in the First Person*.

50. Samuel Cooke, "Election Sermon, May 30, 1770," in Thornton's *Pulpit Revolution*, 47–86.

51. Joseph L. Andrews, Jr., ed. *Revolutionary Boston, Lexington and Concord*. Commonwealth Editions: Beverly, Massachusetts, 2002, 11–12; and Winthrop Sergeant, "Letters of John Andrews, Esq., of Boston, 1772–76," *Massachusetts Historical Society, Proceedings, 186-65*, Boston, 1866, 324–26, in Hart's *American History Contemporaries, 431–33*.

52. Joseph L. Andrews, Jr., ed. *Revolutionary Boston, Lexington and Concord*. Commonwealth Editions: Beverly, Massachusetts, 2002, 11–12; and Winthrop Sergeant, "Letters of John Andrews, Esq., of Boston, 1772–76," *Massachusetts Historical Society, Proceedings, 186-65*, Boston, 1866, 324–26, in Hart's *American History Contemporaries, 431–33*.

53. Thomas Hutchinson, "Letters," in *America*, Vol. 3, 96.

54. Daniel Boone, "Daniel Boone Migrates to Kentucky, 1769," *America*, Vol. 3, 89.

55. Ibid.

56. John Adams, *Diary, Nov. 14, 1760,* http://en.wikiquote.org/wiki/John _adams [accessed June 2006].

57. Samuel Langdon, "Election Sermon at Watertown, May 31, 1775," in *Pulpit of the Revolution,* edited by John Wingate Thornton (New York: Burt Franklin). Originally published 1860. Republished 1970), 227–66.

58. "Benjamin Franklin," *Falmouth Packet Archives,* http://www.falmouth .packet.archives.dial.pipex.com/id74.htm [accessed June 2006]; and Stacy Schiff, "Interview for History Channel," *The History Channel Presents: The American Revolution,* 2006, author transcription, 2006; and Benjamin Franklin, "Benjamin Franklin in His Own Words," online exhibit, Library of Congress. http://www .loc.gov/exhibits/treasures/franklin-break.html [accessed July 2006].

59. John Adams, "The First Continental Congress, 1774," in Hart's *American History Contemporaries,* 434–39.

60. "The First Prayer in Congress," Library of Congress Rare Book Collection, 11-10-30, printed from http://memory.loc.gov/cgi-bin/query/r?ammem/rbpebib:@ field(NUMBER+@band(rbpe+0140100a)): [accessed August 2006].

61. Adams, First Continental Congress.

62. Ibid.

63. "Americans and Canadians: Proud of Their Countries, but Not for the Same Things," University of Chicago Press Release, June 27, 2006. http:// www-news.uchicago.edu/releases/06/060627.pride.shtml [accessed August 2006]; and Megan Reichgott, "Americans Rank No. 1 in Patriotism Survey," Associated Press. Printed from http://www-news.uchicago.edu/citations/06/060627.pride-wp .html [accessed August 2006].

64. Benjamin Colman, "Government the Pillar of the Earth," in Sandoz's *Political Sermons.*

65. Samuel Johnson, "A Diatribe on the American Arguments, 1775," in Hart's *American History Contemporaries,* 445–48.

66. Governor the Earl of Dunmore, "Enforcement of the Association, 1774," in Hart's *American History Contemporaries,* 439–41.

67. Patrick Henry, "Give Me Liberty or Give Me Death, as told by William Wirt," *Great Epochs in American History,* Vol. 3, 103–9. Printed from http://www .originalsources.com [accessed June 2006].

68. Paul Revere, "The Life of Colonel Paul Revere," in *History in the First Person.* Printed from http://www.originalsources.com [accessed August 2006].

69. Ibid.

70. Association for Fund-raising Professionals, "Strong Growth for Walk, Run Events in 2005," Oct. 2, 2006. Printed from http://www.afpnet.org/ka/ka-3 .cfm?content_item_id=23782&folder_id=2545 [accessed February 2007]; and Associated Press, "Lance Gets Personal Tour de Crawford" and "Armstrong Pushed Bush for Cancer Research During Ride," Aug. 21, 2005, *USA Today.* Printed from http://www.usatoday.com/news/washington/2005-08-21-bush-

armstrong_x.htm and http://www.usatoday.com/news/washington/2005-08-21-armstrong-cash_x.htm [accessed February 2007].

71. David Jones, "Defensive War in a Just Cause Sinless, A Sermon Preached on the Day of the Continental Fast, Philadelphia, 1775," Gospel Plow. Printed from http://users.frii.com/gosplow/jones.html [accessed June 2006]; and "Baptist Church of the Great Valley During the American Revolution." Printed from http://www.bcgv.org/history/revolution.html [accessed August 2006].

72. "Conflicting Accounts of Lexington and Concord," in Hart's *American History Contemporaries*, 46–48.

73. Ethan Allen, "In the Name of the Great Jehovah and the Continental Congress," in *History in the First Person*.

74. Ibid.

75. William Sterne Randall, "Interview for History Channel," *The History Channel Presents: The American Revolution*, author transcription, 2006.

76. John Adams, "John Adams Autobiography, Part 1," in *Adams Family Papers*.

77. Mike Allen, "RNC Chief to Say It Was 'Wrong' to Exploit Racial Conflict for Votes," *Washington Post,* Thursday, July 14, 2005, A04. Printed from http://www.washingtonpost.com/wp-dyn/content/article/2005/07/13/AR2005071302342.html [accessed February 2007]; and "Strategy," Dictionary.com. Dictionary.com Unabridged (v 1.1), Random House, Inc. http://dictionary.reference.com/browse/strategy [accessed: February 02, 2007].

78. Jonathan Mayhew, "Unlimited Submission and Non-Resistance to the Higher Powers, Jan. 30, 1750," in Thornton's *Pulpit Revolution, 39–104.*

79. John Adams, "John Adams Autobiography, Part 1," in *Adams Family Papers*.

80. George Washington, "Acceptance Speech on Appointment as Commander-in-Chief, June 1775," in *America*, 3, 125.

81. George Washington, "Farewell to Mrs. Washington," in *America*, 3, 127.

82. Martha Washington, *Worthy Partner*, 166–67; and Mary Thompson, "As If I Had Been a Very Great Somebody."

83. Jonathan Trumbull, "Letter to George Washington, July 13, 1775," in Jared Sparks' *Correspondence of the American Revolution: Being Letters of Eminent Men to George Washington, from the Time of His Taking Command of the Army to the End of His Presidency* (Freeport, New York: Books for Libraries Press, 1853).

84. Jennifer Massengale, author interview, August 2006.

85. Howard, *Election Sermon, 1773.*

86. Drake, "Life and Correspondence of Henry Knox" (Boston: S. D. Drake, 1873), 15–17.

87. Abigail Adams, "A Woman at the Front," in Hart's *American History Contemporaries, 550–54*; and Andrews, *Revolutionary Boston, 11–12.*

88. Ibid.

89. Ridpath and Edmunds, "Project Gutenberg James Otis"; and James Warren, "To Mercy Warren, June 18, 1775."

90. George Washington, "Letter to John Hancock, July 3, 1775," in *America*, 3, 130–35.

91. John Anderson (name changed), author interview, August 2006.

92. Howard, *Election Sermon, 1773.*

93. Ibid.

94. Abigail Adams, "Letter from Abigail Adams to John Adams, 16 July 1775," in *Adams Family Papers*, Massachusetts Historical Society. Printed from http:www.masshist.org [accessed August 2006]; and "The Olive Branch Petition," Wikipedia http://en.wikipedia.org/wiki/Olive_Branch_Petition and http://en.wikisource.org/wiki/The_Olive_Branch_Petition [accessed August 2006].

95. "Dunmore Petition," *Black Loyalists Digital Collection*, http://collections.ic.gc.ca/blackloyalists/documents/official/dunmore.htm [accessed August 2006]; and Richard Smith, "Activities of the Continental Congress," in Hart's *American History Contemporaries*, 525–30; and James Horton, "Interview for History Channel," *The History Channel Presents: The American Revolution*, author transcription, 2006.

96. Samuel Curwen, "Journal and Letters (ed. George Atkinson Ward, New York, etc., 1842)" in Hart's *American History Contemporaries*, 477–80; and Abigail Adams, "A Woman at the Front," in Hart's *American History Contemporaries*, 550–54.

97. Thomas Paine, "Liberty Tree," in Hart's *American History Contemporaries*, 454–55.

98. American Translators Association, "Translation: Getting it Right," http://www.atanet.org/docs/Getting_it_right.pdf [accessed February 2007].

99. Nathaniel Niles, "Sermons, 1 Corinthians 7:21 and John 8:36, 1774," http://www.skidmore.edu/~tkuroda/gh322/Niles.htm [accessed June 2006].

100. King George III, "Declaration of Rebellion," in http://en.wikipedia.org/wiki/Olive_Branch_Petition and http://en.wikisource.org/wiki/Declaration_of_Rebellion [accessed August 2006].

101. Benedict Arnold, "To George Washington, Oct. 13, 1775," in Sparks' *Correspondence American Revolution*, Vol. I, 60–61.

102. William Gordon, "Thanksgiving Sermon, Dec. 15, 1774," in Thornton's *Pulpit Revolution*, 187–226.

103. Martha Washington, *Worthy Partner*, 164–65; and Mary Thompson, "As If I Had Been a Very Great Somebody."

104. Martha Washington, *Worthy Partner*, 164–65.

105. Sarah Hodgkins, "To Joseph Hodgkins, Feb. 20, 1776," in *Writings of the American Revolution*, ed. John Rhodehamel (New York: Penguin Putnam, 2001), 112; and Dan Sukman, "A Soldier's Diary," Aug. 12, 2006 and Biography, FOX News Channel. Printed from http://www.foxnews.com/story/0,2933,208078,00.html and "Meet Capt. Dan Sukman," Mar. 9, 2006. Printed from http://www.foxnews.com/story/0,2933,187267,00.html.

106. William Gordon, "Thanksgiving Sermon, Dec. 15, 1774," in Thornton's *Pulpit Revolution*, 187–226.

107. Benedict Arnold, "To George Washington, Jan. 14, 1776," in Sparks' *Correspondence American Revolution*, Vol. I, 116–18.

108. Thomas Paine, *Common Sense*, in *Revolution to Reconstruction*. Printed from http://odur.let.rug.nl/~usa/D/1776-1800/paine/CM/sense03.htm [accessed June 2006].

109. Ibid.

110. Ibid.

111. Thomas Paine, *Common Sense*; Gary Nash, *The History Channel Presents: The American Revolution*; and Abigail Adams, *A Woman at the Front*, 550–54.

112. Sarah Hodgkins, "To Joseph Hodgkins, Feb. 20, 1776," *Writings of the American Revolution*, ed. John Rhodehamel (New York: Penguin Putnam, 2001), 112; and Dan Sukman, "A Soldier's Diary," Aug. 12, 2006 and biography, FOX News Channel. Printed from http://www.foxnews.com/story/0,2933,208078,00.html and "Meet Capt. Dan Sukman," Mar. 9, 2006. Printed from http://www.foxnews.com/story/0,2933,187267,00.html.

113. Samuel Sherwood, "The Church's Flight into the Wilderness: An Address on the Times, Jan. 17, 1776," Gospel Plow. http://users.frii.com/gosplow/west.html [accessed June 2006].

114. Henry Knox, "Letters to George Washington, Dec. 5 and Dec. 17, 1775," in Jared Sparks, *Correspondence American Revolution*, Vol. I (Freeport, New York: Books for Libraries Press, 1853), 86–87, 95; and Joseph Andrews, Jr., *Revolutionary Boston*, 56–57.

115. Drake, *Life Correspondence Knox*, 23.

116. George Washington, in *America*, 3, 158–65; and Joseph L. Andrews, ed., *Revolutionary Boston, Lexington and Concord*, 55.

117. Ibid.

118. John Hancock, "To George Washington, Mar. 25, 1776," in Sparks' *Correspondence American Revolution*, Vol. I, 175–77.

119. Sarah Hodgkins, "To Joseph Hodgkins, Feb. 20, 1776," *Writings of the American Revolution*, ed. John Rhodehamel (New York: Penguin Putnam, 2001), 112; and Dan Sukman, "A Soldier's Diary," Aug. 12, 2006 and Biography, FOX News Channel. Printed from http://www.foxnews.com/story/0,2933,208078,00.html and "Meet Capt. Dan Sukman" Mar. 9, 2006. Printed from http://www.foxnews.com/story/0,2933,187267,00.html.

120. Samuel West, "On the Right to Rebel Against Governors: A Sermon Preached before the Honorable Council and the Honorable House of Representatives of the Colony of the Massachusetts Bay, May 29, 1776." Printed from http://users.frii.com/gosplow/west.html [accessed June 2006].

121. Nathanael Greene, "To George Washington, May 21, 1776," in Sparks' *Correspondence American Revolution*, Vol. 1, 206–7.

122. Ibid.

123. John Adams, "To Abigail, May 17, 1776," in *Adams Family Papers*.

124. Thomas Jefferson, *Writings*, in Hart's *American History Contemporaries*, 537–39; and Thomas Jefferson, "The Writing of the Declaration of Independence"; and John Adams, "Why Jefferson was Chosen to Write the Declaration of Independence," *America*, Vol. 3, 166–70, 180–83.

125. Thomas Jefferson, *Writings*, in Hart's *American History Contemporaries*, 537–39; and Thomas Jefferson, "The Writing of the Declaration of Independence"; and John Adams, "Why Jefferson was Chosen to Write the Declaration of Independence," *America*, Vol. 3, 166–70, 180–83.

126. John Peter Muhlenberg, *Penn in the 18th Century*. Printed from http://www.archives.upenn.edu [accessed February 2007]; Justin Grove, author interview, February 2007.

127. John Witherspoon, "The Dominion of Providence over the Passions of Men," in Sandoz's *Political Sermons*.

128. John Adams, "Letter, July 3, 1776, to Abigail Adams."

129. "The Declaration of Independence" in William MacDonald's *Documentary Source Book of American History, 1606–1913* (New York: The Macmillan Company, 1916), 191–94. Printed from http://www.originalsources.com [accessed August 2006].

130. Martha Washington, *Worthy Partner*, 166–67; and Mary Thompson, "'As If I had Been a Very Great Somebody.'"

131. Ibid.

132. Evan Thomas, "Interview with the History Channel," *The History Channel Presents: The American Revolution*, author transcription, 2006; and Samuel Adams, "Letter to James Warren, July 12, 1776," in "The Project Gutenberg Etext of The Writings of Samuel Adams," ed. Harry Alonzo Cushing, Vol. 3. Printed from http://www.guetenberg.org [accessed August 2006].

133. Samuel Adams, "Letter to James Warren, July 16, 1776," in "The Project Gutenberg Etext of The Writings of Samuel Adams," ed. Harry Alonzo Cushing, Vol. 3. Printed from http://www.guetenberg.org [accessed August 2006]; "Huzzah," printed from http://en.wikipedia.org/wiki/Huzzah [accessed August 2006]; and Rod Powers, "Origins of Hooah," printed from http://usmilitary.about.com/od/jointservices/a/hooah.htm [accessed August 2006].

134. John Witherspoon, "The Dominion of Providence over the Passions of Men," in Sandoz's *Political Sermons*.

135. Drake, *Life Correspondence Knox*, 28–29.

136. Marshall, *Life of Washington*.

137. Ibid.

138. Samuel Adams, "Letter to James Warren, July 16, 1776," in *The Project Gutenberg Etext of The Writings of Samuel Adams*, ed. Harry Alonzo Cushing, Vol. 3. Printed from http://www.guetenberg.org [accessed August 2006]; and John Marshall, *The Life of George Washington, Vol. 2 (of 5)*, 1926, *The Project Gutenberg EBook of The Life of George Washington*. Printed from http://www.gutenberg.org/files/18592/18592-h/18592-h.htm [accessed August 2006].

139. John Marshall, *The Life of George Washington, Vol. 2 (of 5)*, 1926, *The Project Gutenberg EBook of The Life of George Washington*. Printed from http://www.gutenberg.org/files/18592/18592-h/18592-h.htm [accessed August 2006].

140. Donna Miles, *Camp Pendleton Marines Make Final Preparations for Deployment*, American Forces Press Service. Printed from http://www.defenselink.mil/news/NewsArticle.aspx?ID=566 [accessed February 2007].

141. John Fletcher, "The Bible and the Sword," in Sandoz's *Political Sermons*.

142. Marshall, *Life of Washington*.

143. Ibid.

144. British Field Officer, "Battle of Long Island," in *America*, 3, 186–88.

145. British Field Officer, "Battle of Long Island," in *America,* 3, 186–88; and William J. Jackman, Jacob H. Patton, and Rossiter Johnson, *History of the American Nation,* 9 vols., Chicago: K. Gaynor, 1911, 609–31. Printed from http://www.originalsources.com [accessed September 2006].

146. Marshall, *Life of Washington.*

147. William J. Jackman, Jacob H. Patton, and Rossiter Johnson, *History of the American Nation,* 9 vols., Chicago: K. Gaynor, 1911, 609–31. Printed from http://www.originalsources.com [accessed September 2006]; and American Translators Association, "Translation: Getting it Right." Printed from http://www.atanet.org/docs/Getting_it_right.pdf [accessed February 2007].

148. Abraham Keteltas, "God Arising and Pleading His People's Cause," in Sandoz's *Political Sermons.*

149. Martha Washington, *Worthy Partner,* 170–71.

150. Marshall, *Life Washington.*

151. George Clinton, "Evacuation of New York," in *America,* 3, 189–92.

152. Drake, *Life Correspondence Knox,* 29.

153. George Bancroft, "The Progress of the Howes," in *History of the United States from the Discovery of the American Continent,* 6 vols. (New York: Harper & Bros, 1882), 39–52; and Jackman, Patton, and Johnson, *History American Nation,* 609–31; and "Nathan Hale." Printed from http://en.wikipedia.org/wiki/Nathan_Hale [accessed September 2006].

154. "Unwavering Spirit: Hope & Healing at Ground Zero," St. Paul's Chapel. Printed from http://www.saintpaulschapel.org/ [accessed September 2006].

155. Abraham Keteltas, "God Arising and Pleading His People's Cause," in Sandoz's *Political Sermons.*

156. Count De Mirabeau Honoré Gabriel Riquetti, "Appeal to the Hessians sold by their Princes, 1776," in Hart's *American History Contemporaries,* 500–4.

157. William Henry Heath, "White Plains," in *America,* 193–99; and Jackman, Patton, and Johnson, *History American Nation,* 609–31.

158. Drake, *Life Correspondence Knox,* 33–34.

159. Ibid.

160. George Washington, "Letter Nov. 21, 1776," in *Writings Washington Original, 1745–1799.* ed. John C. Fitzpatrick. Printed from http:www.loc.gov, [accessed September 1776].

161. "Unwavering Spirit: Hope & Healing at Ground Zero," St. Paul's Chapel. Printed from http://www.saintpaulschapel.org/ [accessed September 2006].

162. Abraham Keteltas, "God Arising and Pleading His People's Cause," in Sandoz's *Political Sermons.*

163. Drake, *Life Correspondence Knox,* 29–32.

164. Samuel Adams, "Letter to Elizabeth Adams, Nov. 29, 1776," in *The Project Gutenberg Etext of The Writings of Samuel Adams.*

165. John Hall, "Interview for the History Channel," *The History Channel Presents: The American Revolution,* author transcription, 2006; George Washington, "Letter to Congress," in *America,* Vol. 3, 206–10; and Jackman, Patton, and Johnson, *History American Nation.*

166. George Washington, "Letter to Augustine Washington, Dec. 18, 1776," in Hart's *American History Contemporaries*, 559–60; *History of the American Nation*, 609–31; and Bruce Chadwick, "Interview with the History Channel," *The History Channel Presents: The American Revolution*, author transcription, 2006.

167. Jackman, Patton, and Johnson, *History American Nation*.

168. "How to Conquer a Maze," The MAiZE, printed from http://www.cornfieldmaze.com/visit_howtoconquer.html [accessed October 2006].

169. "Religion and the American Revolution," Library of Congress. Printed from http://www.loc.gov/exhibits/religion/rel03.html [accessed January 2007].

170. George Washington, "Battles of Trenton and Princeton," in *America*, Vol. 3, 206–10.

171. Drake, *Life Correspondence Knox*, 37–38.

172. George Washington, "Battles of Trenton and Princeton," in *America*, Vol. 3, 206–10; and Jackman, Patton, and Johnson, *History American Nation*, 609–31.

173. Drake, *Life Correspondence Knox*, 37–38.

174. George Washington, "Battles of Trenton and Princeton," in *America*, Vol. 3, 206–10.

175. Donald Rumsfeld, "2005 Holiday Message From the Secretary of Defense." Printed from http://www.defenselink.mil/news/Dec2005/20051220_3711.html [accessed February 2007]; and Jonathan Jones, "Washington Crossing the Delaware." Printed from http://arts.guardian.co.uk/portrait/story/0,,909669,00.html [accessed February 2007].

176. George Whitefield, "Britain's Mercies, And Britain's Duties, 1746," in Sandoz's *Political Sermons*.

177. Drake, *Life Correspondence Knox*, 36–38.

178. George Washington, "Letter to Congress," in *America*, Vol. 3, 206–10; and Jackman, Patton, and Johnson, *History American Nation*, 609–31.

179. Ibid.

180. George Washington, *The Writings of Washington from the Original Manuscript Sources, 1745–1799*, ed. John C. Fitzpatrick. Printed from http://www.loc.gov [accessed September 2006].

181. Helen Bryan, *Martha Washington: First Lady of Liberty* (New York: John Wiley and Sons, 2002).

182. "The Flag," Betsy Ross House. Printed from http://www.betsyrosshouse.org/hist_flag/ [accessed February 2007].

183. Nathanael Emmons, "The Dignity of Man," in Sandoz's *Political Sermons*.

184. George Washington, "To Jonathan Trumbull, Feb. 1, 1777," in *The George Washington Papers at the Library of Congress, 1741–1799*. Printed from http://www.loc.gov [accessed February 2007].

185. Marshall, *Life Washington*.

186. Benedict Arnold, "To George Washington, Mar. 11, 1777," in Sparks' *Correspondence American Revolution*, Vol. I, 353–56.

187. Ibid.

188. Drake, *Life Correspondence Knox*, 41–43.

189. Abigail Adams, "To John Adams, Mar. 8, 1777," in *Adams Family Papers*; and Lynn Smith-Lovin, "Ties that Bind, Ties that Bridge, July 9, 2006," Duke University. Printed from http://www.dukenews.duke.edu/2006/07/smith _lovin.html [accessed July 2006]; and "Americans Have Fewer Friends Outside the Family, Duke Study Shows," June 23, 2006. Printed from http://www.dukenews .duke.edu/2006/06/socialisolation_print.htm [accessed July 2006].

190. Nathanael Emmons, "The Dignity of Man," http://www.founding.com/ library/lbody.cfm?id=486&parent=52 [accessed June 2006].

191. Drake, *Life Correspondence Knox*, 41–43; and Samuel Adams, "Letter to Samuel Cooper, Jan. 20, 1779," in *Gutenberg Writings Samuel Adams*.

192. Alexander Scammell, "A Soldier's Love Letter, June 8, 1777," in Hart's *American History Contemporaries*, 461–63.

193. Jackman, Patton, and Johnson, *History American Nation*, 609–31; and Horatio Gates, "To George Washington, Oct. 5, 1777," in Sparks' *Correspondence American Revolution*, 427–38.

194. John Hancock, "To Benedict Arnold, July 12, 1777," in *The Journals of the Continental Congress*. Printed from http://www.loc.gov [accessed October 2006]; and Benedict Arnold, "To Horatio Gates, Aug. 21, 1777," in Sparks' *Correspondence American Revolution*, Vol. 1, 518–19.

195. Marquis de Lafayette, "Lafayette Arrives in America," in *America*, 3, 217–21.

196. Candice Miller, "Short-Notice Deployment Puts Wedding on Fast Track." Printed from http://www.defenselink.mil/home/faceofdefense/fod/2007-01/ f20070130a.html [accessed February 2007]; and Marquis de Lafayette, "Lafayette in the American Revolution," in *America*, 3, 222–34.

197. Nathanael Emmons, "The Dignity of Man." Printed from http://www .founding.com/library/lbody.cfm?id=486&parent=52 [accessed June 2006].

198. Stanley J. Idzerda, *Lafayette in the Age of the American Revolution: Selected Letters and Papers, 1776–1790* (Ithaca and London: Cornell University Press, 1977).

199. Ibid.

200. Drake, *Life Correspondence Knox*, 54.

201. Horatio Gates, "Letter to George Washington, Oct. 7, 1777," in Sparks' *Correspondence American Revolution*, 437–38.

202. Jackman, Patton, and Johnson, *History American Nation*, 609–31; and John Hancock, "To Benedict Arnold, Nov. 29, 1777," in *Journals of the Continental Congress*, http://www.loc.gov [accessed October 2006].

203. John Adams, "To Abigail Adams, Apr. 13, 1777," *in Adams Family Papers*; and Lieutenant Colonel Oliver North, "Notes from a War Diary, Dec. 21, 2006." Printed from http://www.foxnews.com/printer_friendly_story/0,3566, 238058,00.html [accessed February 2007]; and "Tomb of the Unknown Soldier." Printed from http://www.ushistory.org/tour/tour_tomb.htm [accessed February 2007]; and "Tomb of the Unknown Revolutionary War Soldier." Printed from http://www.wikipedia.org [accessed February 2007].

204. Nathanael Emmons, "The Dignity of Man." Printed from http://www .founding.com/library/lbody.cfm?id=486&parent=52 [accessed June 2006].

205. Madame de Riedesel, "Letters and Memoirs Relating to the War of American Independence, etc., New York, 1827, 173–89 passim," in Hart's *American History Contemporaries*, 565–68.

206. Ibid.

207. Ibid.

208. Jackman, Patton, and Johnson, *History American Nation*, 609–31; John Hall, "Interview for the History Channel," *The History Channel Presents: The American Revolution*, author transcription, 2006.

209. "Lydia Darrah, Sometimes Spelled Darrach," adapted from the First Issue of the *American Quarterly Review*. Printed from http://www.americanrevolution.org/women15.html [accessed September 2006].

210. Timothy Dwight, "Columbia, Columbia to Glory Arise, 1777," in Hart's *American History Contemporaries*, 465–67; "Historical Columbia." Printed from http://en.wikipedia.org/wiki/Historical_Columbia [accessed February 2007]; and "Timothy Dwight." Printed from http://biographies.texasfasola.org/timothydwight.html [accessed February 2007].

211. John Wesley, "The Late Work of God in North America, 1778," (London: J. Fry and Co. in Queen-Street, Upper-Moorfields). Printed from http://www.ccel.org/ccel/wesley/sermons.viii.v.html [accessed January 2007].

212. "Lydia Darrah," *American Quarterly Review*.

213. George Washington, "Dec. 9, 1777," *The Writings of Washington Original, 1745–1799*, ed. John C. Fitzpatrick.

214. George Washington, "Headquarters, White Marsh, Nov. 30, 1777," *Writings Washington Original, 1745–1799*, ed. John C. Fitzpatrick; and Samuel Adams, "Resolution of the Continental Congress, Nov. 1, 1777," in *Gutenberg Writings Samuel Adams*.

215. Doctor Albigence Waldo, "Washington at Valley Forge—Conditions Described by Doctor Albigence Waldo," in *America*, Vol. 3, 235–43.

216. Ibid.; and Jackman, Patton, and Johnson, *History American Nation*, 609–31.

217. Eric Hayes, "Camp Lemonier Soldier Recalls Heart-warming Experience in Kenya," CJTF–HOA Civic Action Team. Printed from http://www.hoa.centcom.mil/Stories/Jan07/20070128-001.html [accessed February 2007].

218. Phillips Payson, "Election Sermon, May 27, 1778," in Thornton's *Pulpit Revolution*, 323–54.

219. George Washington, "Jan. 6, 1778," *Writings Washington Original, 1745–1799*, ed. John C. Fitzpatrick; and Caroline Cox, "Interview with the History Channel," *The History Channel Presents: The American Revolution*, author transcription, 2006.

220. George Washington, "Jan. 6, 1778, Feb. 8, 1778," *Writings Washington Original, 1745–1799*, ed. John C. Fitzpatrick.

221. Doctor Albigence Waldo, "Washington at Valley Forge—Conditions Described by Doctor Albigence Waldo," in *America*, Vol. 3, 235–43; Jackman, Patton, and Johnson, *History American Nation*, 609–31; and Drake, *Life Correspondence Knox*, 56.

222. Martha Washington, *Worthy Partner*, 170–71; and Mary Thompson, "'As If I Had Been a Very Great Somebody.'"

223. Doctor Albigence Waldo, "Washington at Valley Forge—Conditions Described by Doctor Albigence Waldo," in *America*, Vol. 3, 235–43.

224. Donna Miles, "Stryker Brigade Ceremony Focuses on Accomplishments, Sacrifices," American Forces Press Service. Printed from http://www.defenselink .mil/news/NewsArticle.aspx?ID=2402 [accessed February 2007].

225. Anonymous Author, "Dialogue Between the Devil, and George III, Tyrant of Britain, 1782," in Sandoz's *Political Sermons*.

226. King George III, "An Obstinate Gulph 1777–78," in Hart's *American History Contemporaries*, 451–53.

227. Ibid.

228. Benjamin Franklin, "A Treaty with France, Feb. 21, 1778," in Hart's *American History Contemporaries*, 574–75.

229. Samuel Adams, "Letter to Daniel Roberdeau, Feb. 9, 1778," and "Vote of Town of Boston, Jan. 21, 1778," in *Gutenberg Writings Samuel Adams*.

230. Marquis de Lafayette, "To Washington, March 1778," in *America*, Vol. 3, 245–50.

231. "Study: We All Tell Lies Over the Phone," ABC News, Feb. 24, 2004. Printed from http://abcnews.go.com/Technology/print?id=99576 [accessed February 2007}.

232. Cushing, *Divine Judgments*.

233. Marquis de Lafayette, "To Washington, March 1778," in *America*, Vol. 3, 245–50.

234. George Washington, "To Lafayette," in *America*, Vol. 3, 245–50.

235. Jackman, Patton, and Johnson, *History American Nation*, 609–31.

236. General Frederick William, Baron von Steuben, "A Foreign Officer well Received (1778–1779)," in Hart's *American History Contemporaries*, 582–85; and Jackman, Patton, and Johnson, *History American Nation*, 609–31.

237. Jackman, Patton, and Johnson, *History American Nation*, 609–31; and Bruce Chadwick, "Interview with the History Channel," *The History Channel Presents: The American Revolution*, author transcription, 2006.

238. Robert A Selig, "The Revolution's Black Soldiers." Printed from http://www.americanrevolution.org/blk.html [accessed February 2007]; and "Coca Cola Celebrates Black History Month," Feb. 4, 2007, author transcription. Printed from http://sports.aol.com/nfl/superbowlads [accessed February 2007].

239. Jacob Cushing, "Divine Judgments upon Tyrants: And Compassion to the Oppressed. A Sermon Preached at Lexington, Apr. 20, 1778," in Sandoz's *Political Sermons*.

240. Nathanael Greene, "To George Washington, July 21, 1778," in Sparks' *Correspondence American Revolution*, Vol. 2, 162–66.

241. Ibid.; and Jackman, Patton, and Johnson, *History American Nation*, 609–31.

242. Ibid.

243. John Trumbull, "A Dashing Young Officer in the Field, 1778," in Hart's *American History Contemporaries*, 575–78.

244. Ibid.

245. Bonnie Reid, author interview, July 2006.

246. "Religion and the American Revolution," Library of Congress. Printed from http://www.loc.gov/exhibits/religion/rel03.html [accessed January 2007].

247. Nathanael Greene, "To George Washington, Aug. 28, 1778," in Sparks' *Correspondence American Revolution*, Vol. 2, 194–98.

248. Marquis de Lafayette, "To George Washington, Aug. 25, 1778," in Sparks' *Correspondence American Revolution*, Vol. II, 181–88.

249. Ibid.

250. Greene, "To George Washington, Aug. 28, 1778, and Sept. 16, 1778," in Sparks' *Correspondence American Revolution*, Vol. 2, 194–98, 206–9.

251. Samuel Adams, "To Betsy, Oct. 28, 1778 from Philadelphia," and "To Samuel Phillips Savage, Aug. 11, 1778," in *Gutenberg Writings Samuel Adams*.

252. Bonnie Reid, author interview, July 2006.

253. Samuel Cooper, "A Sermon on the Day of the Commencement of the Constitution," http://www.founding.com/library/lbody.cfm?id=486&parent=52 [accessed June 2006].

254. Samuel Adams, "Manifesto of the Continental Congress, Oct. 30, 1778," in *Gutenberg Writings of Samuel Adams*.

255. Martha Washington, *Worthy Partner*, 180–81; and Mary Thompson, "'As If I Had Been a Very Great Somebody.'"

256. Benjamin Lincoln, "To George Washington, Jan. 5, 1779," in Sparks' *Correspondence American Revolution*, 244–47.

257. Richard Smith, "Activities of the Continental Congress, 1775," in Hart's *American History Contemporaries*, 525–30; and Benjamin Lincoln, "To George Washington, Jan. 5, 1779," in Sparks' *Correspondence American Revolution*, 244–47; and Jackman, Patton, and Johnson, *History American Nation*; and John Hall, "Interview with the History Channel," *The History Channel Presents: The American Revolution*, author transcription, 2006.

258. Benedict Arnold to George Washington, "Mar. 19, 1779," *Washington Papers Library Congress*.

259. Sukman, "A Soldier's Diary," Aug. 12, 2006, FOX News Channel; and Bonnie Reid, author interview, July 2006.

260. Elisha Williams, "The Essential Rights and Liberties of Protestants, 1744," in Sandoz's *Political Sermons*.

261. George Washington, "To Benedict Arnold, Feb. 24, Apr. 20, Apr. 26, Apr. 28, May 15, June 2, July 20, Dec. 4, 1779," and Benedict Arnold to George Washington, "Mar. 19, May 5, May 15, May 18, July 13, 1779," *Washington Papers Library Congress*.

262. Richard Dale, "I Have Not Yet Begun to Fight," in *History in the First Person*.

263. John Paul Jones, "A Desperate Sea-Fight, 1779," in Hart's *American History Contemporaries*, 587–90.

264. George Washington, "To Jonathan Trumbull, May 26, 1780," and "To Congress in mid May, 1780," *Washington Papers Library Congress*; and Bruce

Chadwick, "Interview with the History Channel," *The History Channel Presents: The American Revolution,* author transcription, 2006.

265. Benjamin Lincoln, "To George Washington, Jan. 23, 1780, Apr. 9, 1780," in Sparks' *Correspondence American Revolution,* 375–76. Printed from http://www.originalsources.com [accessed September 2006]; and John Hall, "Interview with the History Channel," *The History Channel Presents: The American Revolution,* author transcription, 2006.

266. Betty Rogers Bryant, author interview, February 9, 2007.

267. Samuel Cooper, "A Sermon on the Day of the Commencement of the Constitution," in Sandoz's *Political Sermons.*

268. Benjamin Lincoln, "To George Washington, Jan. 23, 1780, Apr. 9, 1780," in Sparks' *Correspondence American Revolution,*" 433–34.

269. George Washington, "To Jonathan Trumbull, May 26, 1780," in *Washington Papers Library Congress;* and Caroline Cox and John Hall, "Interview with the History Channel," *The History Channel Presents: The American Revolution,* author transcription, 2006.

270. King George III, "The Sudden Change in Sentiments," in Hart's *American History Contemporaries,* 619–20.

271. Samuel Adams, "*Boston Gazette,* June 12, 1780," in *Gutenberg Writings of Samuel Adams.*

272. Ibid.

273. Betty Rogers Bryant, author interview, Feb. 9, 2007.

274. Samuel Cooper, "A Sermon on the Day of the Commencement of the Constitution," in Sandoz's *Political Sermons.*

275. "The Sentiments of a Lady in New Jersey, *New Jersey Gazette,* July 12, 1780," *Writings of the American Revolution,* ed. John Rhodehamel (New York: Penguin Putnam, 2001), 575–77.

276. Ibid.

277. George Washington and Esther Reed, "Woman's Work for Soldiers, 1780," in Hart's *American History Contemporaries,* 467–69; and Mary Thompson, "'As If I Had Been a Very Great Somebody.'"

278. Ibid.

279. Isaac Senter, "Journal, Nov. 1 to Dec. 31, 1775," in Rhodehamel's *Writings American Revolution,* 96; and "Yankee Doodle," Library of Congress. Printed from http://memory.loc.gov/ammem/today/apr19.html#yankee [accessed February 2007].

280. "Laughter Helps Blood Vessels, Mar. 7, 2005," University of Maryland School of Medicine Study. Printed from http://www.umm.edu/news/releases/laughter2.htm [accessed February 2007]; and Abigail Adams, "To John Adams, Nov. 16, 1788," *Adams Family Papers, An Electronic Archive,* Massachusetts Historical Society. Printed from http://www.masshist.org/digitaladams/aea/ [accessed February 2007].

281. Henry Cummings, "A Sermon Preached at Lexington on the 19th of Apr.," in Sandoz's *Political Sermons.*

282. George Washington, "The Inconveniences of Militia, 1780," in Hart's *American History Contemporaries,* 490–92.

283. Jackman, Patton, and Johnson, *History American Nation*; and General Frederick William, Baron von Steuben, "A Foreign Officer Well Received, 1778–1779," in Hart's *American History Contemporaries, 582–85.*

284. Jackman, Patton, and Johnson, *History American Nation*; and John Hall, "Interview with the History Channel," *The History Channel Presents: The American Revolution,* author transcription, 2006.

285. George Washington, "To Benedict Arnold, Aug. 3, 1780," in *Washington Papers Library Congress*; and John Hall and Willard Stern Randall, "Interview with the History Channel," *The History Channel Presents: The American Revolution,* author transcription, 2006.

286. George Washington, "To Nathanial Wade, Sept. 25, 1780," and "To Congress, Sept. 26, 1780," in *Washington Papers Library Congress.*

287. Gerry J. Gilmore, "'Red Ball Express' Supplied Patton's Drive Toward Germany," Armed Forces Press Service. Printed from http://www.defenselink .mil/news/NewsArticle.aspx?ID=2900 [accessed February 2007].

288. Simeon Howard, "Election Sermon, May 31, 1780," in Thornton's *Pulpit Revolution,* 355–98.

289. Drake, *Life Correspondence Knox,* 62; and John André, "André, Facing Execution, Write to Washington," in *America,* Vol. 3, 286–90.

290. Nathanael Greene, "Address to Army after Arnold's Treason," in *America,* Vol. 3, 282–85.

291. Benedict Arnold, "To the Inhabitants of North America, Oct. 7, 1780," in Rhodehamel's *Writings American Revolution,* 592.

292. Samuel Adams, "To Betsy, Oct. 17, 1780 and Nov. 24, 1780," and "To James Warren, Oct. 24, 1780," in *Gutenberg Writings of Samuel Adams.*

293. George Washington, "Letter to George Mason, Oct. 22, 1780," in *Washington Papers Library Congress.*

294. George W. Bush, "President Bush Presents Medal of Honor to Corporal Jason Dunham, Jan. 11, 2007," The White House. Printed from http://www.whitehouse .gov/news/releases/2007/01/20070111-1.html [accessed February 2007].

295. Simeon Howard, "Election Sermon, May 31, 1780," in Thornton's *Pulpit Revolution,* 355–98.

296. Nathanial Greene, "Letter to Joseph Reed, Jan. 9, 1781," in Hart's *American History Contemporaries,* 609–12.

297. Nathanael Greene, "To Catherine Greene, Jan. 12, 1781," in Rhodehamel's *Writings American Revolution,* 724–25.

298. Nathanael Greene, "Letter to Joseph Reed, Jan. 9, 1781," in Hart's *American History Contemporaries,* 609–12; and John Hall, "Interview with the History Channel," *The History Channel Presents: The American Revolution,* author transcription, 2006.

299. Jackman, Patton, and Johnson, *History American Nation.*

300. Ibid.

301. Nathanael Greene, "To Catherine Greene, Jan. 12, 1781," in Rhodehamel's *Writings American Revolution,* 724–25; and Benjamin Gable, "Technology Helps Soldiers Stay Close to Loved Ones," Special to American Forces Press

Service. Printed from http://www.defenselink.mil/News/NewsArticle.aspx?id=3005 [accessed February 2007].

302. Simeon Howard, "Election Sermon, May 31, 1780," in Thornton's *Pulpit Revolution*, 355–98.

303. Nathanael Greene, "Letter to George Washington, Feb. 15, 1781," in Sparks' *Correspondence American Revolution*, Vol. 3, 233–36.

304. Jackman, Patton, and Johnson, *History American Nation*.

305. Pennsylvania Packet, "The Federal Arch Completed, Mar. 3, 1781," in Hart's *American History Contemporaries*, 604.

306. Drake, *Life Correspondence Knox*, 77–78.

307. Marquis de Lafayette, "To George Washington, May 8, 1781 and Aug. 6, 1781," in Sparks' *Correspondence American Revolution*, 306–7, 366–68.

308. Josiah Atkins, "Diary, June 5–July 7, 1781," in Rhodehamel's *Writings American Revolution*, 690; and Lance Corporal Brandon L. Roach and Lance Corporal James B. Hoke, "U.S. Navy Petty Officer 2nd Class Donald J. Hodory: Sailor Constructs Stained-Glass Windows at Al Asad Base Chapel, Sept. 5, 2006." Printed from http://www.defenselink.mil/home/faceofdefense/fod/2006-09/f20060905a.html [accessed February 2007].

309. Anonymous Author, "Dialogue Between the Devil, and George III, Tyrant of Britain, 1782," in Sandoz's *Political Sermons*.

310. George Washington, "To Jacques-Melchior Saint-Laurent, Comte de Barras, Aug. 16, 1781," in *Washington Papers Library Congress*.

311. George Washington, "To the Marquis de Lafayette, Aug. 15, 1781," in *Washington Papers Library Congress*; and the Marquis de Lafayette, "To George Washington, Aug. 21, 1781," Sparks' *Correspondence American Revolution*, 389–92.

312. Drake, *Life Correspondence Knox*, 66–69.

313. Charles Cornwallis, "To General Henry Clinton, Sept. 8, 1781," in *Washington Papers Library Congress*; and William J. Jackman, Jacob H. Patton, and Rossiter Johnson, *History of the American Nation*, 609–31.

314. Charles Cornwallis, "To Henry Clinton, October 1781," in *America*, Vol. 3, 301–6.

315. Ebenezer Denny, "Journal, September 1–Nov. 1, 1781," in Rhodehamel's *Writings American Revolution*, 724–25; and "Auditions," U.S. Army Bands. Printed from http://bands.army.mil/faq.asp [accessed February 2007].

316. Anonymous Author, "Dialogue Between the Devil, and George III, Tyrant of Britain, 1782," in Sandoz's *Political Sermons*.

317. George Washington, "To the Continental Congress, October 1781," in *America*, Vol. 3, 306–7.

318. Drake, *Life Correspondence Knox*, 67–70.

319. Robert A. Selig, "The Revolution's Black Soldiers." Printed from http://www.americanrevolution.org/blk.html [accessed February 2007].

320. King George III, "The Sudden Change in Sentiments," in Hart's *American History Contemporaries*, 619–20.

321. John Adams, "Explanation of the Peace, Dec. 14, 1782," in Hart's *American History Contemporaries*, 623–25.

322. Gerry J. Gilmore, "Revolutionary War Buffs Retrace Washington-Rochambeau Route," American Forces Press Service. Printed from http://www.defenselink.mil/news/NewsArticle.aspx?ID=1069 [accessed February 2007].

323. Ezra Stiles, "Election Sermon, May 8, 1783," in Thornton's *Pulpit Revolution*, 399–520.

324. "At the Close of the Revolutionary War," The History Place. Printed from http://www.historyplace.com/unitedstates/revolution/prevents.htm [accessed October 2006]; and Drake, *Life Correspondence Knox*, 66–69.

325. George Washington, "Farewell Address to the Army, November 1783," *America*, Vol. 3, 314–20.

326. Drake, *Life Correspondence Knox*, 82–83.

327. William Gordon, "The Closing Scene," in Hart's *American History Contemporaries*, 627.

328. Ibid.

329. Robert R. Ramon, "U.S. Soldiers Serving in Afghanistan Become American Citizens," American Forces Press Service. Printed from http://www.defenselink.mil/news/NewsArticle.aspx?ID=63 [accessed February 2007].

330. George Duffield, "A Sermon Preached on a Day of Thanksgiving." Printed from http://www.founding.com/library/lbody.cfm?id=486&parent=52 [accessed June 2006].

331. Ridpath and Edmunds, "Gutenberg James Otis."

332. The U.S. and British Governments, "Treaty of Peace," in *Harvard Classics*, Vol. 43, 185–91.

333. Benjamin Franklin, "Characteristics of America, 1784," in Hart's *American History Contemporaries*, 23–27.

334. John Adams, "To John Jay, June 2, 1785," *John Adams*, ed. Charles Francis Adams 8 (Boston, 1853), 255–59. Printed from http://www.originalsources.com [accessed December 2006].

335. Ibid.

336. Ralph Weitz, author interview, Feb. 6, 2007.

337. George Duffield, "A Sermon Preached on a Day of Thanksgiving," in Sandoz's *Political Sermons*.

338. George Washington, *Writings Washington Original*.

339. William Shepard, "Shays Leads the Veterans to Disaster," in *First Person: Eyewitnesses of Great Events: They Saw it Happen* (Harrisburg, PA: Stackpole Co., 1951).

340. Richard Henry Lee, "To George Mason, May 15, 1787," *The Papers of George Mason, 1725–1792*, ed. Robert A. Rutland. 3 vols. (Chapel Hill: University of North Carolina Press, 1970). Printed from http://press-pubs.uchicago.edu/founders/documents/v1ch5s11.html [accessed November 2006].

341. James Madison, "To George Washington, Apr. 17, 1787," *The Papers of James Madison*, ed. William T. Hutchinson et al. (Chicago and London: University of Chicago Press, 1962–77) (vols. 1–10) (Charlottesville: University Press of Virginia, 1977). Printed from http://press-pubs.uchicago.edu/founders/documents/v1ch8s6.html [accessed December 2006].

342. James Madison, "To George Washington, Apr. 16, 1787," *Papers of James Madison.*

343. Ralph Weitz, author interview, Feb. 6, 2007; and "Liberty Bell Center, National Parks Service." Printed from http://www.nps.gov/inde/liberty-bell-center.htm [accessed February 2007].

344. Elizur Goodrich, "The Principles of Civil Union and Happiness Considered and Recommended, 1787," in Sandoz's *Political Sermons.*

345. James Madison, "Democracy in the Balance at Philadelphia," in *History in the First Person.*

346. Ibid.

347. Ibid.

348. James Madison, "Framing the Constitution," in *America*, Vol. 4, 113–39.

349. David Barton, "Franklin's Appeal for Prayer at the Constitutional Convention," http://www.wallbuilders.com [accessed December 2006].

350. George W. Bush, "Remarks at National Prayer Breakfast, Feb. 1, 2007." Printed from http://www.whitehouse.gov/news/releases/2007/02/20070201.html [accessed February 2007].

351. Samuel Wales, "The Dangers of Our National Prosperity; And the Way to Avoid Them, 1785," in Sandoz's *Political Sermons.*

352. Abigail Adams, "To John Adams, June 7, 1787," *Adams Papers*; and Thomas Jefferson, "To Edward Carrington, Aug. 4, 1787," *The Papers of Thomas Jefferson*, ed. Julian P. Boyd et al. (Princeton: Princeton University Press, 1950–). Printed from http://presspubs.uchicago.edu/founders/documents/v1ch5s20.html [accessed November 2006].

353. Benjamin Franklin, "The World's Famous Orations," Vol. 1, 53–55.

354. James Madison, "Excerpted from letter to Thomas Jefferson, Oct. 24, 1787," *Papers Madison*, 343–57. Printed from http://www.jmu.edu/madison/gpos225-madison2/madexpcontojeff.htm [accessed November 2006].

355. Herbert J. Storing, ed., *The Complete Anti-Federalist.* 7 vols. (Chicago: University of Chicago Press, 1981). Printed from http://presspubs.uchicago.edu/founders/documents/v1ch5s24.html [accessed February 2007].

356. James Madison, "Federalist Paper #10." Printed from http://www.jmu.edu/madison [accessed November 2006].

357. Joel C. Rosenberg, "Breakfast with the President and Hillary," Feb. 2, 2007. Flash Traffic, E-mail Newsletter. http://www.joelrosenberg.com/.

358. Samuel Langdon, "The Republic of the Israelites: an Example to the American States, 1788," in Sandoz's *Political Sermons.*

359. Samuel Adams, "Letter to Richard Henry Lee, Aug. 24, 1789," in *Gutenberg Writings of Samuel Adams.*

360. George Washington, "First Inaugural Address, Apr. 30, 1789." Printed from http://www.originalsources.com [accessed February 2007].

361. Martha Washington, *Worthy Partner*, 223–24, 331.

362. Ibid.

363. Samuel Adams, "Day of Fasting Proclamation, Feb. 18, 1794," in *Gutenberg Writings of Samuel Adams.*

364. "Benjamin Franklin's Examination before the House of Commons," First published in 1766 by J. Almon anonymously in London in *The World's Famous Orations*, Vol. 1, 37–52. Printed from http://www.originalsources.com [accessed June 2006]; and Humphrey Taylor, "Pride in America," The Harris Poll #27, June 12, 2002. Printed from http://www.harrisinteractive.com/harris_poll/index.asp? PID=305 [accessed February 2007]; and Georgia E. Frye, "'Oh, Say Can You' Sing the National Anthem?" *Meridian Star*, September 15, 2006. http://www.meridianstar .com/local/local_story_258002607.html [accessed February 2007]; and Ralph Weitz, author interview."

365. William MacDonald, ed., "Constitution of the United States," *Documentary Source Book of American History, 1606–1913* (New York: The Macmillan Company, 1916), 217–32.

# BIBLIOGRAPHY

Adams, Charles Francis. *John Adams*. Boston, 3, 1853. Printed from http://www. originalsourcescom [accessed December 2006].

Adams, John. "Letter to H. Niles, Feb. 13, 1818," Wikiquote printed from http://en.wikiquote.org/wiki/John_adams [accessed June 2006].

———. *Adams Family Papers, an Electronic Archive*, The Massachusetts Historical Society. http://www.masshist.org/digitaladams/aea/ [accessed August 2006].

Allen, Mike. "RNC Chief to Say It Was 'Wrong' to Exploit Racial Conflict for Votes." *Washington Post,* Thursday, July 14, 2005; A04. Printed from http://www.washingtonpost.com/wp-dyn/content/article/2005/07/13/AR2005071302342.html [accessed February 2007].

American Translators Association. "Translation: Getting it Right." Printed from http://www.atanet.org/docs/Getting_it_right.pdf [accessed February 2007].

"Americans and Canadians: Proud of Their Countries, but Not for the Same Things." University of Chicago Press Release, June 27, 2006. Printed from http://www.news.uchicago.edu/releases/06/060627.pride.shtml [accessed August 2006].

"Americans Have Fewer Friends Outside the Family, Duke Study Shows." June 23, 2006. Printed from http://www.dukenews.duke.edu/2006/06/socialisolation_print.htm [accessed July 2006].

Americanization Department, Veterans of Foreign Wars of the United States, *America: Great Crises in Our History Told by Its Makers, A Library of Original Sources*, 12 Vols. (Chicago: Veterans of Foreign Wars of the United States, 1925).

Ancient and Honorable Artillery Company of Boston, http://www.ahacsite.org [accessed May 2007]

Andrews, Joseph L., Jr., ed. *Revolutionary Boston, Lexington and Concord* (Beverly, Massachusetts: Commonwealth Editions, 2002).

Associated Press. "Lance Gets Personal Tour de Crawford" and "Armstrong Pushed Bush for Cancer Research During Ride," Aug. 21, 2005. *USA Today.* Printed from http://www.usatoday.com/news/washington/2005-08-21-bush-armstrong_x.htm and http://www.usatoday.com/news/washington/2005-08-21-armstrong-cash_x.htm [accessed February 2007].

Association for Fundraising Professionals. "Strong Growth for Walk, Run Events in 2005." Oct. 2, 2006. Printed from http://www.afpnet.org/ka/ka-3.cfm?content_item _id=23782&folder_id=2545 [accessed February 2007].

"At the Close of the Revolutionary War." Printed from http://www.historyplace.com/unitedstates/revolution/prevents.htm [accessed October 2006].

"Auditions." U.S. Army Bands. Printed from http://bands.army.mil/faq.asp [accessed February 2007].

Bancroft, George. "The Progress of the Howes." *History of the United States from the Discovery of the American Continent,* 6 (New York: Harper & Bros, 1882).

"Baptist Church of the Great Valley during the American Revolution." Printed from http://www.bcgv.org/history/revolution.html [accessed August 2006].

Barton, David. "Franklin's Appeal for Prayer at the Constitutional Convention." Printed from http://www.wallbuilders.com [accessed December 2006].

"Benjamin Franklin." Printed from http://www.falmouth.packet.archives.dial.pipex.com/id74.htm [accessed June 2006].

Boyd, Julian P., et al. *The Papers of Thomas Jefferson.* (Princeton: Princeton University Press, 1950–.) Printed from http://presspubs.uchicago.edu/founders/documents/v1ch5s20.html [accessed November 2006].

Bryan, Helen. *Martha Washington: First Lady of Liberty,* New York: John Wiley and Sons, 2002.

Bryant, Betty Rogers. Author interview, February 2007.

Bush, George W. "President Bush Presents Medal of Honor to Corporal Jason Dunham, Jan. 11, 2007." The White House. Printed from http://www.whitehouse.gov/news/releases/2007/01/20070111-1.html [accessed February 2007].

_____. "Remarks at National Prayer Breakfast, Feb. 1, 2007." Printed from http://www.whitehouse.gov/news/releases/2007/02/20070201.html [accessed February 2007].

Chang, Alicia. "Online Merchants See Green in Pluto News." *USA Today,* Aug. 25, 2005. Printed from http://www.usatoday.com/tech/science/space/2006-08-25-pluto-memorabilia_x.htm [accessed August 2006].

"Charles Chauncy." Printed from http://www.famousamericans.net/charleschauncy/ [accessed July 2006].

"Coca Cola Celebrates Black History Month." Feb. 4, 2007. Author transcription from http://sports.aol.com/nfl/superbowlads [accessed February 2007].

Colman, Benjamin. "Christ Standing for an Ensign of the People, an Election Sermon June 5, 1738." Printed from http://www.belcherfoundation.org/ensign.htm [accessed August 2006].

Cushing, Harry Alonzo. *The Writings of Samuel Adams, 1–3, 1904* (New York, London: G. P. Putnam's Sons, 1907). Printed from http://books.google.com/books [accessed August 2006].

Cauchon, Dennis. "Soaring Property Taxes Elicit Backlash among Homeowners," and "States Attack Property Taxes." *USA Today,* Aug. 24, 2006.http://www.usatoday.com/news/nation/2006-08-24-property-taxes-idaho_x.htm and http://www.usatoday.com/news/nation/2006-08-24-states-property-taxes_x.htm [accessed August 2006].

Drake, Francis Samuel, ed. *Life and Correspondence of Henry Knox* (Boston: S.G. Drake, 1873).

"Dunmore Petition." Printed from http://collections.ic.gc.ca/blackloyalists/documents/official/dunmore.htm [accessed August 2006].

Eliot, Charles W. *Harvard Classics,* 43 (New York, 1909–10).

Emmons, Nathanael. "The Dignity of Man." Printed from http://www.founding.com/library/lbody.cfm?id=486&parent=52 [accessed June 2006].

Franklin, Benjamin. "Benjamin Franklin in His Own Words." Online Exhibit. Library of Congress. Printed from http://www.loc.gov/exhibits/treasures/franklin-break.html

[accessed July 2006].

————. *Autobiography*. (Edited from his manuscript by John Bigelow, Philadelphia, 1868). Printed from http://www.originalsources.com [accessed June 2006].

————. *Poor Richard, An Almanack, etc.* (Philadelphia, 1744). Printed from http://www. originalsources.com [accessed June 2006].

Frye, Georgia E. "'Oh, Say Can You' Sing the National Anthem?" *Meridian Star*, September 15, 2006. http://www.meridianstar.com/local/local_story_258002607.html [accessed February 2007].

Gable, Benjamin. "Technology Helps Soldiers Stay Close to Loved Ones." Special to American Forces Press Service. Printed from http://www.defenselink.mil/News/NewsArticle.aspx?id=3005 [accessed February 2007].

Gilmore, Gerry J. "'Red Ball Express' Supplied Patton's Drive Toward Germany." Printed from http://www.defenselink.mil/news/NewsArticle.aspx?ID=2900 [accessed February 2007].

————. "Revolutionary War Buffs Retrace Washington-Rochambeau Route." American Forces Press Service. Printed from http://www.defenselink.mil/news/NewsArticle. aspx?ID=1069 [accessed February 2007].

Grove, Justin. Author interview, Feb. 6, 2007.

*Great Epochs in American History*. 3, Printed from http://www.originalsources.com [accessed June 2006].

Hancock, John. "To Benedict Arnold, July 12, 1777." *Journals of the Continental Congress*, http://www.loc.gov [accessed October 2006].

Hart, Albert Bushnell, ed. *American History Told by Contemporaries*. New York: The Macmillan Company, 1902. Printed from http://www.originalsources.com [accessed June 2006].

Hayes, Eric. "Camp Lemonier Soldier Recalls Heart-warming Experience in Kenya." CJTF–HOA Civic Action Team. Printed from http://www.hoa.centcom.mil/Stories/Jan07/20070128-001.html [accessed February 2007].

"Historical Columbia." Printed from http://en.wikipedia.org/wiki/Historical_Columbia [accessed February 2007].

*History in the First Person*. Printed from http://www.originalsources.com [accessed August 2006].

Howard, Simeon. "An Election Day Sermon, June 7, 1773." Printed from http://personal.pitnet.net/primarysources/howard.html [accessed June 2006].

Hutchinson, William, et al. *The Papers of James Madison* (Chicago and London: University of Chicago Press, 1–10, 1962–77; and Charlottesville: University Press of Virginia, 11, 1977). Printed from http://press-pubs.uchicago.edu/founders/documents/v1ch8s6.html [accessed December 2006].

"Huzzah." Printed from http://en.wikipedia.org/wiki/Huzzah [accessed August 2006].

Idzerda, Stanley J. *Lafayette in the Age of the American Revolution: Selected Letters and Papers, 1776–1790* (Ithaca and London: Cornell University Press, 1977).

Jackman, William J., Jacob H. Patton, and Rossiter Johnson. *History of the American Nation*. 9 Vols. (Chicago: K. Gaynor, 1911). Printed from http://www.originalsources. com [accessed September 2006].

James [2d] Earl Waldegrave. *Memoirs from 1754 to 1758* (London, 1821). Printed from http:www.originalsources.com [accessed June 2006].

# BIBLIOGRAPHY

"John Peter Muhlenberg." *Penn in the 18th Century*. Printed from http://www.archives.upenn.edu [accessed February 2007].

Jones, David. "Defensive War in a just Cause SINLESS, A Sermon Preached On the Day of the Continental Fast, Philadelphia, 1775." Gospel Plow. Printed from http://users.frii.com/gosplow/jones.html [accessed June 2006].

Jones, Jonathan. "Washington Crossing the Delaware." Printed from http://arts.guardian.co.uk/portrait/story/0,,909669,00.html [accessed February 2007].

"Laughter Helps Blood Vessels, Mar. 7, 2005." University of Maryland School of Medicine Study. Printed from http://www.umm.edu/news/releases/laughter2.htm [accessed February 2007].

"Liberty Bell Center, National Parks Service." Printed from http://www.nPsalmgov/inde/liberty-bell-center.htm [accessed February 2007].

"Lydia Darrah, Sometimes Spelled Darrach." Adapted from the first issue of the *American Quarterly Review*. http://www.americanrevolution.org/women15.html [accessed September 2006].

MacDonald, William. *Documentary Source Book of American History, 1606–1913*. New York: The Macmillan Company, 1916. Printed from http://www.originalsources.com [accessed August 2006].

Madison, James. "Excerpted from letter to Thomas Jefferson, Oct. 24, 1787." *Madison Papers* 1. Printed from http://www.jmu.edu/madison/gpos225-madison2/madexpcontojeff.htm [accessed November 2006].

Marshall, John. *The Life of George Washington, Vol. 2 (of 5), 1926. The Project Gutenberg EBook of The Life of George Washington*. Printed from http://www.gutenberg.org/files/18592/18592-h/18592-h.htm [accessed August 2006].

Massengale, Jennifer. Author interview, August 2006.

"Meet Capt. Dan Sukman." Mar. 9, 2006. FOX News Channel. Printed from http://www.foxnews.com/story/0,2933,187267,00.html [accessed February 2007].

Miles, Donna. "Stryker Brigade Ceremony Focuses on Accomplishments, Sacrifices." American Forces Press Service. Printed from http://www.defenselink.mil/news/NewsArticle.aspx?ID=2402 [accessed February 2007].

_____. "Camp Pendleton Marines Make Final Preparations for Deployment." American Forces Press Service. Printed from http://www.defenselink.mil/news/NewsArticle.aspx?ID=566 [accessed February 2007].

Miller, Candice. "Short-Notice Deployment Puts Wedding on Fast Track." Printed from http://www.defenselink.mil/home/faceofdefense/fod/2007-01/f20070130a.html [accessed February 2007].

Niles, Nathaniel. "Sermons, 1 Corinthians 7:21 and John 8:36, 1774." http://www.skidmore.edu/~tkuroda/gh322/Niles.htm [accessed June 2006].

Nolan, E. H. *The History of England, George III*. Vol. 3a, (London: James S. Virtue, City Road and Ivy Land). Printed from http://www.gutenberg.org/files/19218/19218-h/smo3a.htm [accessed February 2007].

North, Lt. Col. Oliver. "Notes from a War Diary, Dec. 21, 2006." Printed from http://www.foxnews.com/printer_friendly_story/0,3566,238058,00.html [accessed February 2007].

Paine, Thomas. *Common Sense: Revolution to Reconstruction*. Printed from http://odur.let.rug.nl/~usa/D/1776-1800/paine/CM/sense03.htm [accessed June 2006].

Powers, Rod. "Origins of Hooah." Printed from http://usmilitary.about.com/od/jointservices/a/hooah.htm [accessed August 2006].

Ramon, Robert R. "U.S. Soldiers Serving in Afghanistan Become American Citizens." American Forces Press Service. Printed from http://www.defenselink.mil/news/NewsArticle.aspx?ID=63 [accessed February 2007].

Randall, Brad. "Success, Aug. 11, 2006." The World of Wombat, Musings on Life, the Universe, Everything. Printed from http://theworldofwombat.blogspot.com/2006/08/success.html [accessed August 2006].

Reichgott, Megan. "Americans Rank No. 1 in Patriotism Survey." Associated Press. Printed from http://www-news.uchicago.edu/citations/06/060627.pride-wp.html [accessed August 2006].

Reid, Bonnie. Author interview, July 2007.

"Religion and the American Revolution." Library of Congress. http://www.loc.gov/exhibits/religion/rel03.html [accessed January 2007].

"Revolution." Dictionary.com. Dictionary.com Unabridged (v 1.1). Random House, Inc. http://dictionary.reference.com/browse/revolution [accessed May 17, 2007].

Rhodehamel, John, ed. The American Revolution: Writings from the War of Independence (New York: Penguin Putnam, 2001).

Ridpath, John Clark and Charles K. Edmunds. "The Project Gutenberg Etext of James Otis." Printed from http://www.gutenberg.org [accessed October 2006].

Rivadeneira, Caryn D. "Good and Mad." Marriage Partnership, Spring 2000, 17:1.

Roach, Lance Cpl. Brandon L. and Lance Cpl. James B. Hoke. "U.S. Navy Petty Officer 2nd Class Donald J. Hodory: Sailor Constructs Stained-Glass Windows at Al Asad Base Chapel, Sept. 5, 2006." Printed from http://www.defenselink.mil/home/faceofdefense/fod/2006-09/f20060905a.html [accessed February 2007].

Rosenberg, Joel C. "Breakfast with the President and Hillary," Feb. 2, 2007. Flash Traffic, e-mail Newsletter. http://www.joelrosenberg.com/.

Rumsfeld, Donald. "2005 Holiday Message from the Secretary of Defense." http://www.defenselink.mil/news/Dec2005/20051220_3711.html [accessed February 2007].

Rutland, Robert A. The Papers of George Mason, 1725–1792. Vol. 3 (Chapel Hill: University of North Carolina Press, 1970). Printed from http://press-pubs.uchicago.edu/founders/documents/v1ch5s11.html [accessed November 2006].

Sandoz, Ellis. Foreword. Political Sermons of the American Founding Era 1730–1805, Indianapolis: Liberty Fund, 1998. Printed from http://oll.libertyfund.org/Texts/LFBooks/Sandoz0385/HTMLs/0018_Pt01_Foreword.html [accessed August 2006].

Selig, Robert A. "The Revolution's Black Soldiers." Printed from http://www.americanrevolution.org/blk.html [accessed February 2007].

Smith-Lovin, Lynn. "Ties that Bind, Ties that Bridge, July 9, 2006." Duke University. Printed from http://www.dukenews.duke.edu/2006/07/smith_lovin.html [accessed July 2006].

Snyder, Louis Leo and Richard B. Morris. History in the First Person: Eyewitnesses of Great Events: They Saw It Happen (Harrisburg, PA: Stackpole Co., 1951).

Sparks, Jared, ed. Correspondence of the American Revolution: Being Letters of Eminent Men to George Washington, from the Time of His Taking Command of the Army to the End of His Presidency 1 (Freeport, New York: Books for Libraries Press, 1853).

Storing, Herbert J., ed. The Complete Anti-Federalist 7 (Chicago: University of Chicago

Press, 1981). Printed from http://presspubs.uchicago.edu/founders/documents/v1ch5s24. htm [accessed December 2006].

"Strategy." Dictionary.com. Dictionary.com Unabridged (v 1.1). Random House, Inc. http://dictionary.reference.com/browse/strategy [accessed: February 2007].

"Study: We All Tell Lies over the Phone." ABC News, Feb. 24, 2004. Printed from http://abc-news.go.com/Technology/print?id=99576 [accessed February 2007].

Sukman, Dan. "A Soldier's Diary." FOX News Channel, Aug. 12, 2006. Printed from http://www.foxnews.com/story/0,2933,208078,00.html [accessed February 2007].

Taylor, Humphrey. "Pride in America." The Harris Poll #27, June 12, 2002. Printed from http://www.harrisinteractive.com/harris_poll/index.asp?PID=305 [accessed February 2007].

"The First Prayer in Congress." Library of Congress Rare Book Collection 11-10-30. http://memory.loc.gov/cgi-bin/query/r?ammem/rbpebib:@field(NUMBER +@band(rbpe+0140100a)): [accessed August 2006].

"The Flag." Printed from http://www.betsyrosshouse.org/hist_flag/ [accessed February 2007].

*The History Channel Presents: The American Revolution.* Interviews with Christopher Brown, Bruce Chadwick, Caroline Cox, John Hall, James Horton, Gary Nash, William Sterne Randall, Evan Thomas, Barney Schecter, Stacy Schiff. Author transcription, 2006.

*The World's Famous Orations* 1. Printed from http://www.originalsources.com [accessed June 2006].

Thompson, Mary. "'As If I Had Been a Very Great Somebody.' Martha Washington in the American Revolution: Becoming the New Nation's First Lady." A talk given at the annual George Washington Symposium, held at Mount Vernon, Virginia, Nov. 9, 2002.

Thornton, John Wingate. *Pulpit of the Revolution* (New York: Burt Franklin, 1860, 1970).

"Timothy Dwight." Printed from http://biographies.texasfasola.org/timothydwight. html [accessed February 2007].

"Tomb of the Unknown Soldier." Printed from http://www.ushistory.org/tour/tour_tomb.htm [accessed February 2007].

Tubbs, Brian. "Called Unto Liberty, Jan. 29, 2002." Printed from http://www.suite101. com/print_article.cfm/us_founding_era/88715 [accessed August 2006].

"Unwavering Spirit: Hope & Healing at Ground Zero." St. Paul's Chapel. http://www. saintpaulschapel.org/ [accessed September 2006].

Warren, James. "To Mercy Warren, June 18, 1775." The Massachusetts Historical Society. Printed from http://www.masshist.org/bh/accounts.html [accessed December 2006].

Washington, George. "Letter to John Augustine Washington July 18, 1755." In John C. Fitz-patrick's *The Writings of George Washington from the Original Manuscript Sources, 1745–1799.* Westport Connecticut: Greenwood Press, 1970. Library of Congress. Printed from http://memory.loc.gov/ [accessed June 2006].

———. *The George Washington Papers at the Library of Congress, 1741–1799.* Printed from http://www.loc.gov [accessed October 2006].

Weitz, Ralph. Author interview, Feb. 6, 2007.

Wesley, John. "The Late Work of God in North America, 1778" (London: J. Fry and Co. in Queen-Street, Upper-Moorfields). Printed from Christian Classics Ethereal Library, http://www.ccel.org/ccel/wesley/sermons.viii.v.html [accessed January 2007].

"Yankee Doodle." Library of Congress. Printed from http://memory.loc.gov/ammem/ today/apr19.html#yankee [accessed February 2007].